Politics
and the
International
System

THE LIPPINCOTT SERIES
IN INTERNATIONAL POLITICS
under the editorship of
STEVEN MULLER, *The Johns Hopkins University*

edited by
ROBERT L. PFALTZGRAFF, JR.
Fletcher School of Law and Diplomacy,
Tufts University

Politics and the International System

SECOND EDITION

J. B. LIPPINCOTT COMPANY
Philadelphia • New York • Toronto

Preface

M ANY CLASSICAL and contemporary writers have contributed to the development of international relations as a discipline. In the belief that access to a multiplicity of writings is essential to an appreciation of international relations as a field of study and an understanding of international phenomena, the editor has prepared this volume, which brings together selections from some of the most important writings on international relations and closely related fields.

Included are selections on the nature and scope of international relations major theory-building efforts from utopianism and realism to systems frameworks, and theories of integration at the international level. Moreover, the volume contains selections on nationalism in both its Western and non-Western settings, the nature of power and demand—response relationships, theories of conflict and contemporary military strategy, transnational images and national character, diplomacy, disarmament and arms control, balance of power and world government.

In preparing this second edition, the editor has surveyed the voluminous literature of international relations which has appeared since the completion of the first edition in 1968. Wherever appropriate, selections from the older literature of international relations have been included in this edition. Selections have been added on the nature of international studies in the 1970s, the levels of analysis in international relations, national self-determination and national disintegration, research on the causes of war, the nature of military potential, and the balance of terror. Because of the pervasive influence of technology on the political order, selections which assess the impact of technological change on the global system, and on the United States, in particular, have been added. New selections on foreign aid and statecraft, and economic sanctions as an instrument of foreign policy have been included. Because of the burgeoning literature on the multinational corporation as a major new "actor" in international politics, this edition contains a selection which examines the emergence of the multinational corporation and its relationships with the nation-state. New selections on alliances and alignment and the problems of strategic armaments limitation are included to acquaint the reader with the most recent manifestations of those areas which have been of increasing concern both to students and practitioners of international relations.

This second edition contains new sections which considerably broaden its framework and utility to the student of international relations. Selections examining the nature of domestic-international "linkages" have been added. Included are writings on the domestic sources of foreign policy and the major variables affecting foreign policy decision-making. Other new sections contain writings on the nature of international law and organization and their relationships both in the postwar period and in the emerging international system of the 1970s.

To take account of changes in the substance and organization of this second edition, the editor's introductions have been revised. As in the earlier edition, an effort has been made to relate major themes contained in readings, to show relationships between materials presented in separate sections, and to place the readings in an overall framework for the study of the international system.

An effort has been made to insure that selections are sufficiently concise to expose the reader to the principal themes of many authors, and long enough to give the student more than a cursory treatment of the ideas under consideration. Whenever possible, the editor has sought to include readings which contain divergent points of view. This volume can be used either as a companion to textual materials or as the principal source of assigned readings.

In the preparation of this edition, the editor is indebted to Karl Peter Sauvant and Miss Barbara Tornow, who helped in the collection of materials for this edition, and to Mrs. Barbara Sicherman, for secretarial assistance. The editor expresses gratitude to those authors whose writings are included for permission to reprint their selections in this volume.

Finally, he is indebted to students who have provided the opportunity for fruitful intellectual exchange and a classroom learning experience for which many selections in this volume have been selected, and from which others have emerged. To them this book is dedicated.

Robert L. Pfaltzgraff, Jr.

October 1971
Philadelphia, Pennsylvania

Contents

Part I

International Relations as a Discipline

WHY, IT MAY appropriately be asked, should international relations be studied as a separate field? It is, in fact, a relatively new discipline, for not until the period between the two world wars did American universities and colleges offer courses in international relations. Even today far greater emphasis is placed upon the study of international relations in the United States than elsewhere in the world.

To focus upon the study of international relations is to assume the existence of a distinctive series of relationships or processes. At the very least, international relations differ from other relations because they take place across the frontiers of the national political units into which the world is divided. According to Quincy Wright, international relations as a field of study designates the "relations between groups of major importance in the life of the world at any period of history, in particular those of territorially organized nation-states." According to Raymond Platig, international relations "studies the distribution of power on a global scale and the interplay between and among power centers." Although its primary focus is the actions and interactions of governments, the study of international relations also encompasses the multiplicity of factors influencing intergovernmental interaction. Platig asserts that such factors are of two kinds: (a) those related to the characteristics of the governments, including their relationships with the peoples they govern; and (b) those related to the context or international environment within which interaction among national governments occurs. To the extent that they affect interaction among govern-

1

ments, technological, economic, legal, social and cultural relationships are part of the study of international relations. International relations embraces not only the study of the contemporary international system, but also other international systems, past and future —multipolar or bipolar, conflictual or consensual. Broadly conceived, international relations includes all types of transactions between governments and between peoples, from the sending of letters to a recipient in another country to the exchange of gunfire between the military forces of two countries.

Thus defined, the study of international relations presents formidable problems for the would-be student. He would need first to have acquired extensive training in a variety of other disciplines, including political science, history, and economics, as well as psychology, anthropolgy, and sociology.

Although the term international relations remains in vogue, the focus of international studies is generally narrower than that advanced above. In fact, students of politics have usually bracketed for study only a part of this vast field, and have termed it international politics. Largely, but not exclusively, the focus of international politics is upon relations between the governments of the individual national units of the world. The student of international politics is primarily concerned with interaction between governments. He is interested in relations between peoples living in different countries only to the extent that they affect interaction between their governments. Moreover, he has as a central concern the study of demand-response or influence relationships. Nation-state "A" makes a demand upon nation-state "B," which in turn may respond with another demand, this time on nation-state "A." According to Wright, international politics is the "art of influencing, manipulating, or controlling major groups in the world so as to advance the purpose of some against the opposition of others." Demand-response or influence relationships may take many forms. They include the effort of a nation to mold the behavior of a long-term trusted ally. They include the attempts of one nation to prevent an opponent from taking undesirable action. In short, demand-response or influence relationships may exhibit conflict or collaboration.

In the aftermath of World War I, international relations emerged as a distinctive field of study in response to a perceived need to develop a greater understanding of the causes of conflict and to create institutions and norms to insure a more peaceful world. In this period, E. H. Carr suggests, international relations was "in that initial stage in which wishing prevails over thinking, generalization over observation, and in which little attempt is made at a critical analysis of existing facts or available means." Carr notes that students in the field then devoted themselves essentially to the development of schemes for world order and to the study of international law and organization, rather than to an analysis of the behavior of the actors of the international system.

Initially, the study of international relations was dominated by a school of thought called utopianism. According to utopian thought, man was improvable through education; enlightened peoples ruled by representative governments would choose peace rather than war. Utopianism contained the proposition that, with the growth of nationalism, the prospects for a more peaceful world might be enhanced. If peoples were given the right to national self-determination, they might cast off oppressive regimes in favor of representative governments. Erroneously, it was believed that nationalism would produce democracy. Utopianism established norms, or standards of conduct, to which political practice was expected to conform. Among students of international relations after World War II there was a feeling of great optimism about the potential for changing the behavior of man from conflict to collaboration at the international level.

Events of the 1930s contributed to the growth of dissatisfaction with the essentially normative utopian approach to the study of international relations. Contrary to earlier expectations, nationalism did not always lead to political systems in which both leaders and population had an abiding interest in peace. Certain powers had foreign policy objectives that were incompatible with, and took precedence over, the preservation of international peace. Men were slow to alter their behavior in conformity with the standards set forth in such documents as the Covenant of the League of Nations. General dissatisfaction with the utopian approach, together with the emigration to the United States of central European students of international relations, led to the emergence of realism as an approach to the field. In several ways, realism differed fundamentally from the utopianism. Realism emphasizd that man by nature was not only evil, but essentially unchanging and unchangeable. Therefore, international relations was characterized more by a clash, rather than a harmony, of interests among leading members of the international system. Nations strove to maximize national power and to achieve and preserve the national interest. Like Machiavelli, realist writers in international relations held that the statesman *qua* statesman has standards of conduct different from those of the private citizen. The statesman does what he must to preserve the national interest.

If man is essentially evil, unchanging, and unchangeable, it is impossible to expect world order to be derived from the establishment of standards of international conduct which do not conform to existing behavioral patterns. Through the study of history, the realist purportedly discovered the prevalent patterns of behavior of the international system. In contrast to utopianism, realists held that theory derived from political practice. The observation of political practice led the realist to believe that the prospects for a peaceful world based upon international organization were slim indeed. At best, nations could be restrained by balancing them with other nations. For the realist, the balance of power became the principal device for the management of power.

In the study of international relations the utopian-realist controversy has been superseded by what is called the traditionalist behavioralist controversy.

As the proponent of a more scientific approach, Morton A. Kaplan stresses the need for conceptual precision and the building of empirically based theories of international relations. Rather than emphasizing the accumulation of facts about seemingly unique events, the advocate of a more scientific study of politics is preoccupied with the development of generalizations derived from the comparative analysis of data about many events, such as wars, revolutions, alliances, and political integration. In general, the student supporting the scientific study of politics holds that much of the phenomena under observation can be quantified; furthermore, that there are discernible patterns of similarity in these phenomena; and conceivably that it is even possible to develop theories of political behavior with predictive power. The proponent of the scientific study of politics, as in the case of Kaplan, develops models consisting of hypotheses about relationship among variables. As Kaplan suggests, models provide criteria on the basis of which the student "can pick and choose from among the infinite reservoir of facts available to him. These initial hypotheses indicate the areas of facts which have the greatest importance for this type of investigation, presumably if the hypotheses are wrong, this will become reasonably evident in the course of attempting to use them." Thus models in international relations provide a guide to research.

Surveying not only his own work but also the writings of other advocates of a scientific study of international relations, Kaplan suggests that traditionalists, although they have sometimes accused "those using the scientific method of neglecting Aristotle's dictum to use those methods appropriate to the subject matter," have themselves been *insensitive* to such problems. For example, "traditional balance of power theory is asserted to apply regardless of the number and kinds of states, variations in motivations, and so forth." Moreover, traditionalist literature about international relations contains many implicit assumptions about *motivation* and the relationship among variables—important assumptions which have often been neither clearly stated nor subjected to rigorous examination. Although traditionalists have faulted the proponents of a scientific approach for their alleged neglect of history, traditionalist writers, Kaplan asserts, have largely confined themselves either to "problems of diplomatic history that are unrelated to their generalizations about international politics" or to "more specialized problems that are idiosyncratic." In short, they are said to have lacked either an articulated theoretical structure, or model, or the methodologies appropriate to finding answers to the questions of importance to international relations.

In contrast to Kaplan's sanguine view about the potential inherent in a scientific study of international relations, other writers believe that the behavioral approach has contributed little to international relations theory, and since it is encroaching upon and displacing the classical approach, it is harmful. They contend that the practitioners of a scientific approach are not likely to advance greatly the state of knowledge because of the nature of the data with which they deal. It is asserted that the emphasis upon quantification will exclude from study many important problems for which quantifiable data are either not available or irrelevant. In contrast to the supporters of a scientific approach, the traditionalist often argues that political events are unique; therefore, it is not possible, as the behavioralist would like, to find patterns of similarity between discrete events and situations.

Thus international relations has passed through three stages which may be characterized as utopian, realist, and behavioral or stated differently, normative, empirical-normative, and behavioral-quantitative. In the 1970s, the study of international relations appears to be entering a "postbehavioral" phase. As the concluding article of this section ("International Studies in the 1970s") suggests: "In this fourth stage an effort will be made to synthesize concepts and findings from existing literature and to develop theories and methodologies 'relevant' to major international issues facing mankind over the next decade; while at the same time pressing the quest for theories with greater explanatory and predictive capabilities."

SECTION ONE:

Origins and Scope

1. THE MEANING OF INTERNATIONAL RELATIONS

Quincy Wright

THE WORD *international* appears to have been first used by Jeremy Bentham in the latter part of the eighteenth century, although its Latin equivalent *intergentes* was used by Richard Zouche a century earlier. These men used the word to define the branch of law which had been called the law of nations or *jus gentium*, a term of Roman law referring to the principles applied by a Roman official—the *praetor peregrinus*—in cases involving aliens. The concept, therefore, was that of a universal law applicable to persons irrespective of nationality, discovered, however, by observing similarities of practice rather than by reasoning from generally accepted principles, as was the case with the *jus naturale* or natural law. As the concept of sovereignty developed in the sixteenth century and came to be applied to geographically defined societies known as nations in the seventeenth century, it was seen that the Roman law concept of *jus gentium* did not adequately express the devel-

From *The Study of International Relations* by Quincy Wright, pp. 3–8. Copyright 1955, by Appleton-Century-Crofts, Inc. Reprinted by permission of Appleton-Century-Crofts, Division of Meredith Corporation.

QUINCY WRIGHT (1890–1970) Formerly Professor of International Law, University of Virginia; Professor Emeritus of International Law, University of Chicago. Author of *The Study of War*, (Chicago: University of Chicago Press, 1965); *The Role of International Law in the Elimination of War* (New York: Oceana Publications, 1961); *Contemporary International Law: A Balance Sheet* (New York: Random House, 1961); *International Law and the United Nations* (New York: Asia Publishing House, 1960).

oping law between sovereign nations. Consequently, the term *international* served a genuine need in defining the official relations between sovereigns. Perhaps the word *interstate* would have been more accurate because in political science the state came to be the term applied to such societies.

There were relations between nations other than official, legal, and diplomatic relations. Trade and finance developed international economic relations sometimes official and sometimes unofficial. Activities of missionaries; travel of students, teachers, and tourists; migrations of peoples; and the development of the press, radio, and films developed international cultural relations mostly unofficial, but sometimes supervised or even conducted by governments. Private and public organizations representing groups within, or governments of, many nations were formed, especially since the mid-nineteenth century. Their activities in all aspects of human interest—communication, transportation, commerce, finance, agriculture, labor, health, sports, science, philosophy, education, arbitration, disarmament, peace—established innumerable international social relations and gave birth to the word *internationalism* to suggest both the fact of the increase of international relations of all kinds and the interest of many people in such an increase. The word *internationalism* has been preferred by modern writers because, without denying the existence and autonomy of nations, it recognizes them as parts of a larger whole. It excludes both the excessive standardization and integration of mankind implied by the words *imperialism* and *cosmopolitanism* and the militant insistence upon sovereignty implied by the words *nationalism* and *isolationism*.

The development of internationalism, however, gives rise to two questions: (1) Is it only the nations that are related? (2) Is there a universal community of which numerous groups or even individuals are members?

The words *nation, state, government,* and *people* are sometimes used interchangeably, but each has a distinct connotation. The word *nation* suggests a considerable group of people, united by common culture, values, standards, and political aspirations, usually occupying a definite territory, but not always, as witness the Jewish nation during the Diaspora, and usually enjoying legal sovereignty, but not always, as witness the Scotch nation within Great Britain or the Bohemian nation within the Habsburg Empire.

The word *state* has a legal flavor. It is a term of art in political science referring to political groups that enjoy legal sovereignty, but it is also commonly applied to nonsovereign political groups as the states of the United States or the states of India before independence. A state in the modern sense implies a population occupying a definite territory, subject to a government which other states recognize as having some legal status. The population may be a nation, but not necessarily so, as in the case of such multinational states as the Habsburg, British, and Russian Empires before World War I.

The word *government* refers to the organization which makes and enforces the law of the state, decides and carries out its policy, and conducts its official relations. In absolutisms, the government and the state merge in one man, but in democracies, the state is the entire people legally organized while the government is only that small portion of the people for the time being constituting and operating its organization.

The word *people* has biological and geographical implications with cultural and social overtones making it similar to the word *nation,* but without the element of self-consciousness. Anthropologists use the word *people* as a term of art to designate primitive groups that exhibit a considerable degree of biological, cultural, and often linguistic uniformity and occupy a defined territory even though not politically or socially organized as a group. Use of the word *people* suggests some type of similarity—racial, geographic, cultural, linguistic, political, or social—among the individuals who compose it, but without definite specification of a particular type of similarity. The United States Constitution was said to have been made by "we the people of the United States" while the United Nations Charter was said to have been made by "we the peoples of the United Nations," thus suggesting that it was easier to think of all the individuals of the United States as a "people" than to think of all the individuals of the world as a single "people." There was, however, a vigorous debate during the San Francisco Conference in which some urged that the word *people* be used in the singular in the Preamble of the Charter.

It is clear that international relations is intended to include not only relations between nations, but also relations between states, governments, and peoples. It does, however, ordinarily refer only to relations between nations, states, governments, and peoples which are *sovereign.* That term, however, presents new difficulties. The word is not static. There are entities like Massachusetts, Geneva, Bavaria, Hyderabad, the six nations of the Iroquois, Tunis, Algeria, and Scotland, which once were, but are no longer, entirely sovereign. And there are entities like Israel, Egypt, Ukraine, Iceland, Ireland, Pakistan, Jordan, Burma, Philippine Islands, Canada, Indochina, and Korea, which have recently become, or are in process of becoming, sovereign, or have certain aspects of sovereignty. Clearly international relations includes relations between many entities of uncertain sovereignty. As a subject of study it is not limited by the legal formalism which alone could at any moment precisely define what entities are sovereign and what are not.

It may be suggested that international relations, even if it abandoned the qualification of *sovereign* for the entities which it relates, must insist on the qualifications *political* and *territorial.* It is said to be concerned only with the relations among *political* communities occupying definite *territories*. The relations of Virginia and Pennsylvania may be international relations (certainly they were during the Battle of Gettysburg), but the relations of the United Mine Workers of America and coal mining companies seem not to be, even though both are large groups exercising considerable power imperfectly controlled by the laws of the United States to which both are nominally subject. But doubt arises whether even this limitation is always applicable. The United Nations makes agreements with the Specialized Agencies. The International Labor Organization has dealt with the World Federation of Trade Unions. UNESCO deals with numerous international, cultural, educational, and scientific organizations which are unofficial. Many *nongovernmental organizations* have a recognized status in relation to the United Nations. To the sociologist the difference between the co-operation, competition, bargaining, and fighting of industrial groups is in the same class as the co-operation, competition, bargaining, and fighting of states. Thus, for purposes of scientific treatment, it seems that international relations includes the relations of all groups exercising some degree of independent power or initiative. While it may be that the central interest in international relations today is the relation between sovereign nations, in the Middle Ages the central interest was in the relations of Pope and Emperor and in antiquity in the relations between cities.

Of the future one speaks with diffidence. Relations between great regions—the Atlantic community, the Soviet bloc, the Commonwealth—each composed of many nations, many states, many governments, and many peoples may be important. Perhaps the relations between universal parties—Communists, Democrats, Catholics, Moslems, Zionists—will be of increasing importance, or relations between universal organizations of labor, of agriculture, and of commerce. As once, in the United States, relations of North, South, and West were of major significance, so today relations of agriculture, labor, and capital are of equal or of greater importance. It has been said that the growth of national parties crossing sectional lines and the development of rivalries among them, superseding in importance sectional rivalries, accounts for the survival of the United States.

We must, therefore, answer our first question negatively. It is not only the nations which *international relations* seeks to relate. Varied types of groups—nations, states, governments, peoples, regions, alliances, confederations, international organizations, even industrial organizations, cultural organizations, religious organizations—must be dealt with in the study of international relations, if the treatment is to be realistic.

With this wide concept of the subject, we come to our second question. Should not our subject be renamed *world affairs*, or perhaps *cosmopolitanism*, with such divisions as *world economy*, *world politics*, *world culture*, *world organization,* and *world law?* Is not the subject matter of *international relations* really the history, organization, law, economy, culture, and processes of the world community? Should we not conceive of the human race as a community which, while divided into numerous geographic, functional, cultural, racial, political, economic, and other subgroups, is becoming integrated into a society with the progress of technology and the growth of population bringing the members of the subgroups into closer and closer contact with one another?

The adjective *world* certainly rivals the adjective *international* in textbooks and treatises on the subject. It suffers, however, from the objection that there are *international relations* which are not *world relations* as for instance Anglo-American relations, Latin American relations, relations among the Arab countries, and so forth. Until recently *international relations* generally concerned diplomatic or military relations between two states. The word *world* also fails to indicate the dominant problems dealt with in the subject, that is, the relations between the major groups. The phenomena of national, regional, functional, and political groups in rivalry with one another is likely to dominate the life of mankind even if the world shrinks much more than it has today, and even if the national sovereign state becomes less important. The divergencies of interest and policy inherent in climatic and geographical differences, varied resources, differences of culture and political tradition, assure that mankind will not in any foreseeable future be reduced to a uniform mass.

Cosmopolitanism, envisaged as an ideal by the Stoics of Rome and the Deists of the Enlightenment, failed to take adequate account of the factors making for a differentiation of mankind into groups with different objectives and often in opposition to one another. For this reason, as has been noted, modern writers like Jeremy Bentham, Nicholas Murray Butler, Sir Alfred Zimmern, and Inazo Nitobe have preferred the word *international.*

While recognizing that the term *international relations* is too narrow—perhaps *relations between powerful groups* would be technically better—it seems advisable to accept predominant usage. The term *international relations* will therefore be used as the subject of study, dividing it into such special studies as *international politics, international law, international organization, international economics, international education, international ethics,* and the *psychology and sociology of international relations.* The term will, however, also be used to include such studies as world history, political geography, political demography and technology which have a *world* rather than an *international* orientation. These studies are clearly fundamental to the understanding of *international relations.*

Before leaving the subject of terminology, reference should be made to the frequent use of the adjective *foreign* in preference to either *world* or *international* relations. Foreign relations, foreign affairs, foreign policy, foreign trade, are words of common discourse. Clearly the adjective *foreign* implies the point of view of one nation and thus is hardly suitable for use in a discipline or study designed to be of universal validity and understanding. The use of the word, however, raises the question whether a discipline of *international relations* is possible. It has been suggested that the conditions, material and ideological, of each nation are so peculiar that the *foreign relations* of each country must be studied as a unique discipline. As the American lawyer studies American law and can learn little useful to his professional activity from the study of French or Japanese law, so it is said that the American statesman or citizen should confine his study to *American foreign relations.* However, there are general disciplines of *jurisprudence, comparative law,* and *sociology of law,* useful to lawyers of all countries. The thesis is accepted in this book, as it has been in general practice, that general disciplines exist in the field of *international relations.* These disciplines have proved useful to statesmen and citizens of all countries and their synthesis is at least conceivable.

We will, therefore, accept the term *international relations* to designate the relations between groups of major importance in the life of the world at any period of history, and particularly relations among territorially organized nation states which today are of such importance. We will also use the term to designate the studies or disciplines describing, explaining, evaluating, or assisting in the conduct of those relations.

2. INTERNATIONAL RELATIONS AS A FIELD OF INQUIRY

E. Raymond Platig

SOME PRELIMINARIES

1. AS A FIELD of inquiry international relations studies the distribution of power on a global scale and the interplay between and among power centers.

   1.0 *Power:* Power is used here in a very broad sense to encompass the entire range of man's influence and control over his fellow man. It includes both his ability to exert and his actual exertion of influence and control over the minds and actions of other men.[1] It might be preferable to designate this "social power," but the simpler term will be retained with the understanding that power in this sense is distinguishable—if not always separable—from the physical, chemical, and biological power of the natural world.

From *International Relations Research: Problems of Evaluation and Advancement* by E. Raymond Platig. Copyright © 1967. Reprinted by permission of Clio Press. Footnotes have been renumbered to appear in consecutive order.

E. RAYMOND PLATIG (1924–   ) Director, Office of External Research, Department of State. Author of *The United States and the Soviet Challenge* (Forest River, Ill.: Laidlaw Brothers, 1963).

[1] The fact needs to be faced that the social sciences suffer from a lack of precision in the agreed meaning of key concepts. Whether this stems primarily from the nature of the subject matter with which the social sciences deal, from the nature of the minds that have applied themselves to the subject matter, or from the "youth" of the disciplines is a question on which it is easy to stimulate debate. How this lack of precision relates to the scientific claims, aspirations, and potentialities of the social sciences is also a matter of some dispute. The concept of power is a case in point. Some would prefer that the term encompass influence or control, but not both; some would prefer that it denote only an *ability* to influence (and/or control); while others that it denote only *actual* influence (and/or control). Many have offered operational definitions of the term. (For a brief but provocative commentary on the concept of power see Karl W. Deutsch, *The Nerves of Government: Models of Political Communication and Control* (New York, The Free Press of Glencoe, 1963), pp. 110–127. For a different and more extensive analysis see George Modelski, *A Theory of Foreign Policy* (New York, Frederick A. Praeger, 1962), pp. 21–64.) Neither these nor a host of other issues concerning the meaning of power have been settled in the vast literature on the subject and they cannot be settled here, though it is recognized that both empirical research and the substantive discussion of theoretical or policy issues in international relations often require a more refined definition of power than is offered here.

1.0–1 To the extent men can command the power of the natural world, they may be able to use it as an element of their social power. To the extent men do not command the power of the natural world, it may serve to alter their social power and relations.

1.0–2 The physical ability to influence and control the minds and actions of men is one fundamental aspect of social power. This is epitomized by the instruments of physical violence.

1.0–3 The other fundamental aspect of social power is perhaps best called the psychocultural aspect. This is epitomized by the instruments of rational and emotional persuasion.

1.0–4 All other forms of power are compounded from these two fundamental aspects. It would serve no useful purpose here to present a new or repeat an old typology of forms of power. The point to be made is simply that in all of its forms social power is compounded of these two fundamental aspects—physical and psychocultural.

1.1 *Distribution of power:* Each person in contact with others is possessed of some degree of ability—however trivial—to influence others. Power is thus broadly diffused on a global scale. However, the thorough study of interpersonal relations on this scale has not been undertaken, presumably because it is considered unmanageable or likely to be unrewarding or both.

1.1–1 In groups, men not only can combine—in an additive sense—some forms of the power each possesses but also can introduce a multiplier effect through organization and joint activity, thus creating new forms and orders of magnitude of social power. On a global scale, human groups are numerous, highly diverse in type, and often overlapping in membership and function. The thorough study of intergroup relations on this scale has not been undertaken, presumably because it, too, is considered essentially unmanageable.

1.1–2 In order to make manageable the unmanageable, it is necessary to select as a focus for study "those groups of greatest importance." If this phrase is not to mean everything and anything, it must refer, when we are speaking of international relations, to those groups which possess, in the global picture, major power.

1.1–3 Because man's command over the power of the natural world is one of the two fundamental aspects of social power, and because the power of the natural world is so closely associated with the physical characteristics of territory, it is not surprising that the extent and quality of territory under its control has traditionally been one of the significant indices of a group's power. Clearly the struggle for the exclusive or predominant control of territory has been one of the basic patterns of intergroup relations. Thus the territorially based goup (whether tribe, city-state, empire, nation-state, or principality) has been, and continues to be, one of the centers of major power.

1.1–4 Because a group's ability to organize and direct its activities in a given territory is in part a function of psychocultural factors (which form the second of the two fundamental aspects of social power), it is not surprising that the most stable territorially based groups are often those having a large measure of ideological or cultural unity.

1.1–5 It is, of course, true that the world has never been divided among territorially based groups all founded exclusively on the principle of one territory, one culture, one ideology, one organization. But the exceptions, no matter how numerous and how important, do not invalidate the proposition that organized, territorially based groups belong to a class all members of which are, compared with all other classes of groups and most other discrete groups, major centers of power. Such groups, therefore, have constituted and continue to constitute a class of power units or centers which are important foci for the study of the distribution of power on a global scale.

1.2 *Government:* A territorially based group in which an identifiable organization provides over-all management of the power of the group and monitors the power relations of subgroups is said to have a government and is properly called a state.

1.2–1 Historically there have been stateless territories, ones in which there were no governments. There have also been territories in which two or more governments operated simultaneously through either a hierarchical arrangement (e.g., federations, colonies, protectorates), or a horizontal arrangement (e.g., condominia), or a situation of conflict (e.g., civil war); in such cases the statehood of the territory has often been in doubt.

1.2–2 However, the most persistent and common arrangement throughout recorded history is that of the territorial state, an arrangement wherein it has been relatively easy to identify a dominant (sovereign) center of power (government) within the territory. This was true in the ancient Far East, ancient India, and the ancient Mediterranean world, as well as at times and places in medieval Europe and predominantly in the modern era of nation-states.

1.2–3 In brief, it is governments which, for the most part, exercise the powers in so-called sovereign states and among which, therefore, one might expect to find many of the main power centers that interact on a global scale.[2]

1.3 *Sovereignty:* The concept of sovereignty defies brief analysis and its full meaning defies brief and noncontroversial statement. Thus its utility as an analytical concept is limited. However, it is a useful word for designating that class of states in which can be found most of the major centers of power on the contemporary global scene. A few additional words about it are, therefore, required.

1.3–1 In a legal sense, sovereignty means that the government of a state does not recognize the legitimacy of any external human restraints upon its behavior unless it has consented to those restraints.

1.3–2 In a political sense, sovereignty might be equated with autonomy, the full exercise of which requires that the government of a state command sufficient power to be able to reject external restraints or reverse its acceptance of them.

1.3–3 It is obvious that not all states that enjoy sovereignty in the legal sense command sufficient power to enjoy autonomy.[3] It is equally obvious that not even the government

---

[2] All of the main power centers are not, of course, governments. See paragraph 2.2.

[3] Both the utility and the difficulty of distinguishing in practice the legal from the political meaning of sovereignty can be seen in the current phase of the Cyprus question. In a letter to *The New York Times* published on June 26, 1964, Ambassador Zenon Rossides pointed up the plight of a state that claims legal sovereignty but clearly does not enjoy autonomy. "Suffice it to say," wrote the Ambassador, "that a country that is deprived of the fundamental right to decide upon its own Constitution, or amend it even on matters of purely internal administration without the consent of three foreign powers, is obviously not an independent or sovereign country.

"It is an accepted principle of international law that a state cannot contract out of the substance of its internal independence and continue to be independent. Consequently either the treaties (the Zurich and London agreements of 1959–60) are valid and Cyprus is not independent but a territory under tutelage, or Cyprus is an independent country and the treaties, insofar as they negate or restrict that independence, are by that very fact rendered invalid. . . .

"Once having been admitted to the U. N., Cyprus enjoys equal rights of full independence and sovereignty of a member of the U. N., as prescribed by the Charter— including, of course, the right of self-determination.

"Aside from the legal aspect, the realities of life have shown that the conflict between the treaties and the provisions of the Charter has resulted in fighting and bloodshed in Cyprus.

of the most powerful of states is able to avoid having some of its actions, both external and internal, influenced by external forces, especially those that can be brought to bear by the governments of other sovereign states.

1.3–4 It is because the governments of legally sovereign states are centers of great power (even though the amount of power located in each center varies over a wide range) without, at the same time, being immune to the influence that can be brought to bear by their "sovereign equals," that the interplay between and among the governments of sovereign states is properly thought of as lying at the core of international relations.

THE CORE OF INTERNATIONAL RELATIONS

2. Thus it can be said that the substantive core of international relations is the interaction of governments of sovereign states.

2.0 *Forms:* The interactions of governments of sovereign states take many forms, all of which are of concern to international relations. Among the many forms of governmental interactions the most important are diplomatic, military, and economic.

2.0–1 Except in rare cases, the interactions of governments of sovereign states take place within a framework of constant concern for the relative power of the interacting states vis-à-vis one another and other states. Therefore all interactions—whatever their outward form—are either frankly and intensely political or subject to becoming so on short notice.

2.1 *Political Systems:* For these reasons, the interactions of the governments of two or more sovereign states can be said to take place within a multistate system which, for most purposes, is a multinational political system.

2.1–1 International relations is concerned with past, present, emerging, and hypothetical multinational political systems.

2.1–2 International relations is concerned with all sizes of multinational political systems, ranging from two-state systems to all-inclusive (in the contemporary world, "global")

"For a country cannot be independent and at the same time be subject to outside intervention, and be placed under an over-handing threat of invasion from another country on the preposterous claim that military intervention—in violation of the Charter—can be sanctioned as a lawful procedure under any treaty. Such logic would make nonsense of the Charter and of the main purpose for which the U. N. was established: the maintenance of peace in freedom."

international systems. In the contemporary world, local systems may usefully—but not exclusively—be thought of as subsystems of regional systems and the latter as subsystems of the international system.

2.1–3   International relations is concerned with all conditions of multinational political systems ranged along the continuum from violent conflict to peaceful integration.

2.1–4   International relations is concerned with all instrumentalities and forms of interaction among sovereign governments within multinational political systems: diplomatic, military, economic, psychological, legal, ethical, technical, and cultural.

2.2   *Actors:* The fact that governments of sovereign states are viewed as the most important actors in multinational political systems is not to be construed as meaning that they are the only important actors.

2.2–1   Governments have a virtual monopoly of the diplomatic and military forms of interaction.

2.2–1.0   International organizations play an increasingly important role in diplomatic relations not only by providing new settings for governmental interactions, but also as actors in their own right.

2.2–1.1   Multinational forces play an important role in military relations, as do rebel, guerrilla, volunteer, and mercenary forces.

2.2–2   In the economic, psychological, legal, ethical, technical, and cultural forms of interaction within a multinational political system, governments share participation with many other actors of various kinds.

2.2–2.0   No government of a sovereign state has total control over the people of the nation [4] it governs. To the extent a government's power is less than total, individuals and groups within the nation can and do enter into independent transnational relations and thus may become direct actors in multinational political systems.

2.2–2.1   In addition to nongovernmental actors based within the territory of a single sovereign state,

---

[4] In keeping with common and convenient usage, we here and elsewhere use the term "nation" interchangeably with the term "state," even though the principle "one nation (in the cultural sense), one state" is little reflected in the realities of the contemporary world.

there are also truly international groups that may play a direct role in a multinational political system. These may be organized religions (e.g., the Catholic Church), or organized political ideologies (e.g., communism) or international, intergovernmental organizations (e.g., the UN, the OAS, etc.) or international, nongovernmental organizations (e.g., international scientific unions, cartels, etc.).

2.3–3 From the point of view of a multinational political system, the importance of nongovernmental actors is a function of their power base, their independence from governmental power, and the ways in which their acts and goals are related to those of governments. To put it differently, the relevance of particular national subgroups and international groups to the core of international relations varies according to the extent to which their actions impinge upon the environment in which intergovernmental relations take place and upon the power and policies of governments of sovereign states.

2.2–4 In the contemporary world, governmental practices vary greatly as to when and to what degree they attempt to encourage, monitor, restrict, manage, or control these international transactions resulting from initiatives other than their own.

2.2–5 Thus the extent to which nongovernmental groups are direct and autonomous actors is a far-ranging but seldom an independent variable in contemporary multinational political systems.

THE SCOPE OF INTERNATIONAL RELATIONS

3. In its attention to the actions and interactions of governments within a multinational political system, international relations cannot ignore the factors that influence those actions. These factors serve to define the scope of international relations and are of two kinds: (a) the characteristics of the governments that act—especially their relationships to the social entities they govern; (b) the context within which the multinational political system exists.

3.0 *Intranational factors:* Not only does the power available to a government depend upon its ability to organize and direct the populace of its state, but individuals and groups within a nation can and do exert influence upon the government so that it will manage national power both internally and externally in ways that are supportive of the goals pursued by these individuals and groups.

Hence such individuals and groups may play important roles as indirect actors in multinational political systems.

3.0–1   International relations penetrates as deeply into the internal life of a nation as is necessary to understand the actions of the government and other nationally based actors in a multinational political system.

3.0–2   The depth of penetration cannot be established *a priori;* it varies from nation to nation, from interaction to interaction.

3.0–3   International relations does not encompass all national studies, but it overlaps them, draws upon them, and at times generates its own essentially national studies in order to elucidate the actions, potentialities, vulnerabilities, and policies of governments and other actors in multinational political systems.

3.1   *The international social system:* International relations recognizes that each multinational political system—even the all-inclusive, global international political system—exists within an environment that influences the system and the actors and interactions within it. For the international political system this environment is most usefully thought of as a general international social system.[5]

3.1–1   The international social system, like other social systems, may be thought of as a series of interdependent, functional subsystems; the international political system is the most important of these subsystems for the field of international relations. Among the other constituent functional subsystems of the international social system are an economic system, a legal system, an ethnic system, and a scientific system; at a different but overlapping level there can be found an exchange system, a postal system, a public health system, a natural resources system, etc.

3.1–2   These functional subsystems have varying degrees of autonomy and coherence; each differs in the extent and nature of its dependence upon the others, especially in its dependence upon the international political system. Not all subsystems are relevant to every interaction in the international political system.

3.1–3   International relations encompasses all general and specific analyses of the international social system and its

---

[5] Each multinational political system may be thought of as having a corresponding multinational social system. However, for the sake of brevity and clarity, the discussion to follow deals only with the general international social system.

various subsystems. However, it assigns higher priorities to those analyses that bear most directly upon the behavior of actors in the international political system.

3.2 *Core and scope:* In its full scope, therefore, international relations has occasion to draw upon or supplement the social sciences, history, the humanities, and the natural sciences at numerous levels of analysis. Though its reach is great, it limits its empirical and intellectual load by grasping only those items that most illuminate the core—the interactions of the main actors in multinational political systems.

SOME IMPLICATIONS: A DISCIPLINED MULTIDISCIPLINARY APPROACH [6]

4. Regardless of their origins, analytical methods and data processing techniques are characterized by a rapid rate of diffusion among the fields of social inquiry. Analytical methods are likely to remain more closely identified with specific fields of inquiry than are data processing techniques because the former employ the core concepts of a field; even so, diffusion of concepts and methods is more the rule than the exception. It is, therefore, as unrewarding to try to identify each and every field of social inquiry by its unique methodology or research techniques as it is to search for an exclusive and clearly delineated subject matter for each field.

4.0 Since the core concepts of international relations are political concepts, the central method of analysis is political. The scholar or analyst whose primary method of analysis is other than political is most likely to contribute to the field of international relations when he either relates his results (both his data and his style of thinking) to the core political concepts or so presents them that others can easily establish the relationship.

    4.0–1 International relations makes use of all data processing techniques appropriate to its historical, current, trend, and predictive interests.

    4.0–2 International relations draws heavily upon those aspects

---

[6] We disregard here the oft-debated question whether international relations is a discipline. An answer to the question is less a matter of intellectual necessity than a matter of academic structure and politics. Readers interested in the question may consult the basic treatments of it to be found in Wright, *The Study of International Relations*, pp. 16–61; C. A. Manning, *The University Teaching of Social Sciences: International Relations* (Paris, UNESCO, 1954); and Trygve Mathisen, *Methodology in the Study of International Relations* (New York, The Macmillan Company, 1959). For two recent perspectives see J. W. Burton, *The Year Book of World Affairs 1964*, pp. 213–229, and Ch. Boasson, *Approaches to the Study of International Relations* (Assen, the Netherlands, Van Gorcum & Comp. N. V., 1963).

of area studies that throw light upon local and regional multinational political systems; when necessary, it generates its own area studies.

4.0–3 International relations draws upon and stimulates those aspects of national studies that assist in the analysis of international political behavior; foreign policy, national security, and national economic studies are clearly the most relevant of these and are often undertaken directly as part of international relations inquiry.

4.0–4 International relations enriches its analysis of the conditions within multinational political systems by drawing upon the behavioral sciences for insights into the processes of conflict, cooperation, integration, transformation, pacification, negotiation, acculturation, communication, etc.

4.0–5 International relations draws upon and stimulates military, economic, and technological studies in order better to understand the material aspects of international political behavior; it draws upon psychological and cultural studies for the persuasive aspects; and ethical and legal studies for the normative aspects.

4.0–6 To enhance its understanding of the modes of interaction within multinational political systems, international relations draws upon and stimulates international organizational, administrative, small-group, and decision-making analyses.

4.0–7 International relations draws upon and stimulates non-political analyses of multinational systems where these are relevant to a more complete understanding of the operation of multinational political systems.

4.1 Ultimately, international relations scholars aspire to the same type of coherent analysis of the purposes, structures, and processes of the international social system as some social scientists [7] have recently been aspiring to for other social systems.[8]

---

[7] For a recent attempt to combine political science, sociology, and economics in a "tightly integrated approach" to society see Alfred Kuhn, *The Study of Society* (Homewood, Ill. Richard D. Irwin, Inc., and the Dorsey Press, Inc., 1963). See also, Peter M. Blau, *Exchange and Power in Social Life* (New York, John Wiley & Sons, Inc., 1964).

[8] Some may be concerned that analysts of the international social system, in their desire for a coherent analysis, may find in the system itself greater coherence than actually exists, but there is no inescapable reason why they should. Indeed, this type of analysis is capable of generating valuable comparisons of systems by means of which the peculiar characteristics of the international social system can be elucidated.

3. THE UTOPIAN BACKGROUND

E. H. Carr

THE FOUNDATIONS OF UTOPIANISM

THE MODERN SCHOOL of utopian political thought must be traced back to the break-up of the mediaeval system, which presupposed a universal ethic and a universal political system based on divine authority. The realists of the Renaissance made the first determined onslaught on the primacy of ethics and propounded a view of politics which made ethics an instrument of politics, the authority of the state being thus substituted for the authority of the church as the arbiter of morality. The answer of the utopian school to this challenge was not an easy one. An ethical standard was required which would be independent of any external authority, ecclesiastical or civil; and the solution was found in the doctrine of a secular "law of nature" whose ultimate source was the individual human reason. Natural law, as first propounded by the Greeks, had been an intuition of the human heart about what is morally right. "It is eternal," said Sophocles' Antigone, "and no man knows whence it came." The Stoics and the mediaeval schoolmen identified natural law with reason; and in the seventeenth and eighteenth centuries this identification was revived in a new and special form. In science, the laws of nature were deduced by a process of reasoning from observed facts about the nature of matter. By an easy analogy, the Newtonian principles were now applied to the ethical problems. The moral law of nature could be scientifically established; and rational deduction from the supposed facts of human nature took the place of revelation or intuition as the source of morality. Reason could determine what were the universally valid moral laws; and the assumption was made that, once these laws were determined, human beings would conform to them just as matter conformed to the physical laws of nature. Enlightenment was the royal road to the millennium.

By the eighteenth century, the main lines of modern utopian thought were firmly established. It was essentially individualist in that it made

From *The Twenty Years' Crisis 1919–1939* by E. H. Carr (New York: 1958) pp. 22–31; 36–38; 41–46; 51–53; 60–62. Reprinted by permission of St. Martin's Press, Inc., Macmillan & Company, Ltd., and the Macmillan Company of Canada, Ltd. Footnotes have been renumbered to appear in consecutive order.

EDWARD HALLET CARR (1892–   ) Fellow, Trinity College, Cambridge. Author of *International Relations Between the Wars, 1919–1939* (New York: St. Martin's Press, 1963); *What is History?* (New York: Alfred A. Knopf, 1962); *The Bolshevik Revolution, 1917–1923,* 3 vols. (London: Macmillan, 1950–1953).

the human conscience the final court of appeal in moral questions; in France it became associated with a secular, in England with an evangelical tradition. It was essentially rationalist in that it identified the human conscience with the voice of reason.[1] But it had still to undergo important developments; and it was Jeremy Bentham who, when the industrial revolution had transferred the leadership of thought from France to England, gave to nineteenth-century utopianism its characteristic shape. Starting from the postulate that the fundamental characteristic of human nature is to seek pleasure and avoid pain, Bentham deduced from this postulate a rational ethic which defined the good in the famous formula "the greatest happiness of the greatest number." As has often been pointed out, "the greatest happiness of the greatest number" performed the function, which natural law had performed for a previous generation, of an absolute ethical standard. Bentham firmly believed in this absolute standard, and rejected as "anarchical" the view that there are "as many standards of right and wrong as there are men." [2] In effect, "the greatest happiness of the greatest number" was the nineteenth-century definition of the content of natural law.

The importance of Bentham's contribution was twofold. In the first place, by identifying the good with happiness, he provided a plausible confirmation of the "scientific" assumption of the eighteenth-century rationalists that man would infallibly conform to the moral law of nature once its content had been rationally determined. Secondly, while preserving the rationalist and individualist aspect of the doctrine, he succeeded in giving it a broader basis. The doctrine of reason in its eighteenth-century guise was pre-eminently intellectual and aristocratic. Its political corollary was an enlightened despotism of philosophers, who alone could be expected to have the necessary reasoning power to discover the good. But now that happiness was the criterion, the one thing needful was that the individual should understand where his happiness lay. Not only was the good ascertainable—as the eighteenth century had held—by a rational process, but this process—added the nineteenth century—was not a matter of abstruse philosophical speculation, but of simple common sense. Bentham was the first thinker to elaborate the doctrine of salvation by public opinion. The members of the community "may, in their aggregate capacity, he considered as constituting a sort of judicatory or tribunal—

---

[1] While this is the form of utopianism which has been predominant for the past three centuries, and which still prevails (though perhaps with diminishing force) in English-speaking countries, it would be rash to assert that individualism and rationalism are necessary attributes to utopian thought. Fascism contained elements of a utopianism which was anti-individualist and irrational. These qualities were already latent in the utopian aspects of Leninism—and perhaps even of Marxism.

[2] Bentham, *Works,* ed. Bowring, i. p. 31.

call it . . . *The Public-Opinion Tribunal.*" [3] It was James Mill, Bentham's pupil, who produced the most complete argument yet framed for the infallibility of public opinion:

> Every man possessed of reason is accustomed to weigh evidence and to be guided and determined by its preponderance. When various conclusions are, with their evidence, presented with equal care and with equal skill, there is a moral certainty, though some few may be misguided, that the greatest number will judge right, and that the greatest force of evidence, whatever it is, will produce the greatest impression.[4]

This is not the only argument by which democracy as a political institution can be defended. But this argument was, in fact, explicitly or implicitly accepted by most nineteenth-century liberals. The belief that public opinion can be relied on to judge rightly on any question rationally presented to it, combined with the assumption that it will act in accordance with this right judgment, is an essential foundation of the liberal creed. In Great Britain, the later eighteenth and the nineteenth centuries were pre-eminently the age of popular preaching and of political oratory. By the voice of reason men could be persuaded both to save their own immoral souls and to move along the path of political enlightenment and progress. The optimism of the nineteenth century was based on the triple conviction that the pursuit of the good was a matter of right reasoning, that the spread of knowledge would soon make it possible for everyone to reason rightly on this important subject, and that anyone who reasoned rightly on it would necessarily act rightly.

The application of these principles to international affairs followed, in the main, the same pattern. The Abbé Saint-Pierre, who propounded one of the earliest schemes for a League of Nations, "was so confident in the reasonableness of his projects that he always believed that, if they were fairly considered, the ruling powers could not fail to adopt them." [5] Both Rousseau and Kant argued that, since wars were waged by princes in their own interest and not in that of their peoples, there would be no wars under a republican form of government. In this sense, they anticipated the view that *public opinion*, if allowed to make itself effective, would suffice to prevent war. In the nineteenth century, this view won widespread approval in Western Europe, and took on the specifically rationalist colour proper to the doctrine that the holding of the right moral beliefs and the performance of the right actions can be assured by process of reasoning. Never was there an age which so unreservedly pro-

---

[3] Bentham, *Works*, ed. Bowring, viii. p. 561.
[4] James Mill, *The Liberty of the Press*, pp. 22–3.
[5] J. S. Bury, *The Idea of Progress*, p. 131.

claimed the supremacy of the intellect. "It is intellectual evolution," averred Comte, "which essentially determines the main course of social phenomena." [6] Buckle, whose famous *History of Civilisation* was published between 1857 and 1861, boldly declared that dislike of war is "a cultivated taste peculiar to an intellectual people." He chose a cogent example, based on the assumption, natural to a British thinker, of the ingrained bellicosity of Great Britain's most recent enemy. "Russia is a warlike country," he wrote, "not because the inhabitants are immoral, but because they are unintellectual. The fault is in the head, not in the heart." [7] The view that the spread of education would lead to international peace was shared by many of Buckle's contemporaries and successors. Its last serious exponent was Sir Norman Angell, who sought, by *The Great Illusion* and other books, to convince the world that war never brought profit to anyone. If he could establish this point by irrefutable argument, thought Sir Norman, then war could not occur. War was simply a "failure of understanding." Once the head was purged of the illusion that war was profitable, the heart could look after itself. "The world of the Crusades and of heretic burning," ran the opening manifesto of a monthly journal called *War and Peace* which started publication in October 1913, ". . . was not a badly-meaning, but a badly-thinking world. . . . We emerged from it by correcting a defect in understanding; we shall emerge from the world of political warfare or armed peace in the same way." [8] Reason could demonstrate the absurdity of the international anarchy; and with increasing knowledge, enough people would be rationally convinced of its absurdity to put an end to it.

BENTHAMISM TRANSPLANTED

Before the end of the nineteenth century, serious doubts had been thrown from more than one quarter on the assumptions of Benthamite rationalism. The belief in the sufficiency of reason to promote right conduct was challenged by psychologists. The identification of virtue with enlightened self-interest began to shock philosophers. The belief in the infallibility of public opinion had been attractive on the hypothesis of the earlier utilitarians that public opinion was the opinion of the masses; and as early as 1859, in his essay *On Liberty*, J. S. Mill had been preoccupied with the dangers of "the tyranny of the majority." After 1900, it would have been difficult to find, either in Great Britain or in any other European country, any serious political thinker who accepted the Benthamite assumptions without qualification. Yet, by one of the ironies of history,

---

[6] Comte, *Cours de Philosophie Positive*, Lecture LXI.

[7] Buckle, *History of Civilisation* (World's Classics ed.), i. pp. 151–2.

[8] Quoted in Angell, *Foundations of International Policy*, p. 224. Internal evidence suggests that the passage was written by Sir Norman Angell himself.

these half-discarded nineteenth-century assumptions reappeared, in the second and third decades of the twentieth century, in the special field of international politics, and there became the foundation-stones of a new utopian edifice. The explanation may be in part that, after 1914, men's minds naturally fumbled their way back, in search of a new utopia, to those apparently firm foundations of nineteenth-century peace and security. But a more decisive factor was the influence of the United States, still in the heyday of Victorian prosperity and of Victorian belief in the comfortable Benthamite creed. Just as Bentham, a century earlier, had taken the eighteenth-century doctrine of reason and refashioned it to the needs of the coming age, so now Woodrow Wilson, the impassioned admirer of Bright and Gladstone, transplanted the nineteenth-century rationalist faith to the almost virgin soil of international politics, and, bringing it back with him to Europe, gave it a new lease of life. Nearly all popular theories of international politics between the two world wars were reflexions, seen in an American mirror, of nineteenth-century liberal thought.

In a limited number of countries, nineteenth-century liberal democracy had been a brilliant success. It was a success because its presuppositions coincided with the stage of development reached by the countries concerned. Out of the mass of current speculation, the leading spirits of the age took precisely that body of theory which corresponded to their needs, consciously and unconsciously fitting their practice to it, and it to their practice. Utilitarianism and *laissez-faire* served, and in turn directed, the course of industrial and commercial expansion. But the view that nineteenth-century liberal democracy was based, not on a balance of forces peculiar to the economic development of the period and the countries concerned, but on certain *a priori* rational principles which had only to be applied in other contexts to produce similar results, was essentially utopian; and it was this view which, under Wilson's inspiration, dominated the world after the first world war. When the theories of liberal democracy were transplanted, by a purely intellectual process, to a period and to countries whose stage of development and whose practical needs were utterly different from those of Western Europe in the nineteenth century, sterility and disillusionment were the inevitable sequel. Rationalism can create a utopia, but cannot make it real. The liberal democracies scattered throughout the world by the peace settlement of 1919 were the product of abstract theory, stuck no roots in the soil, and quickly shrivelled away.

RATIONALISM AND THE LEAGUE OF NATIONS

The most important of all the institutions affected by this one-sided intellectualism of international politics was the League of Nations, which was an attempt "to apply the principles of Lockeian liberalism to the building of a machinery of international order." [9] "The Covenant," observed General Smuts, ". . . simply carries into world affairs that outlook of a liberal democratic society which is one of the great achievements of our human advance." [10] But this transplantation of democratic rationalism from the national to the international sphere was full of unforeseen difficulties. The empiricist treats the concrete case on its individual merits. The rationalist refers it to an abstract general principle. Any social order implies a large measure of standardisation, and therefore of abstraction; there cannot be a different rule for every member of the community. Such standardisation is comparatively easy in a community of several million anonymous individuals conforming more or less closely to recognised types. But it presents infinite complications when applied to sixty known states differing widely in size, in power, and in political, economic and cultural development. The League of Nations, being the first large-scale attempt to standardise international political problems on a rational basis, was particularly liable to these embarrassments.

The founders of the League, some of whom were men of political experience and political understanding, had indeed recognised the dangers of abstract perfection. "Acceptance of the political facts of the present," remarked the official British Commentary on the Covenant issued in 1919, "has been one of the principles on which the Commission has worked" [11] and this attempt to take account of political realities distinguished the Covenant not only from previous paper schemes of world organisation, but also from such purely utopian projects as the International Police Force, the Briand-Kellogg Pact and the United States of Europe. The Covenant possessed the virtue of several theoretical imperfections. Purporting to treat all members as equal, it assured to the Great Powers a permanent majority on the Council of the League. [12] It did not

---

[9] R. H. S. Crossman in J. P. Mayer, *Political Thought*, p. 202.

[10] New Year's Eve broadcast from Radio-Nations, Geneva: *The Times*, January 1, 1938.

[11] *The Covenant of the League of Nations and a Commentary Thereon*, Cmd. 151 (1919), p. 12. "The great strength of the Covenant," said the British Government some years later, "lies in the measure of discretion which it allows to the Council and Assembly dealing with future contingencies which may have no parallel in history and which therefore cannot all of them be foreseen in advance" (*League of Nations: Official Journal*, May 1928, p. 703).

[12] The defection of the United States upset this balance, and left four major confronted with four minor Powers. Subsequent increases in membership, which have taken place at frequent intervals since 1923, gave a permanent preponderance to the minor Powers. The Council, in becoming more "representative," lost much of its effectiveness as a political instrument. Reality was sacrificed to an abstract principle. It should be added that the prudent Swiss delegate foresaw this result when the first increase was mooted in 1922 (*League of Nations: Third Assembly*, First Committee, pp. 37–8).

purport to prohibit war altogether, but only to limit the occasions on which it might legitimately be resorted to. The obligation imposed on members of the League to apply sanctions to the Covenant-breaker was not free from vagueness; and this vagueness had been discreetly enhanced by a set of "interpretative" resolutions passed by the Assembly of 1921. The starkness of the territorial guarantee provided by Article 10 of the Covenant was smoothed away in a resolution which secured an almost unanimous vote at the Assembly of 1923. It seemed for the moment as if the League might reach a working compromise between utopia and reality and become an effective instrument of international politics.

Unhappily, the most influential European politicians neglected the League during its critical formative years. Abstract rationalism gained the upper hand, and from about 1922 onwards the current at Geneva set strongly in the utopian direction.[13] It came to be believed, in the words of an acute critic, "that there can exist, either at Geneva or in foreign offices, a sort of carefully classified card-index of events or, better still, 'situation', and that, when the event happens or the situation presents itself, a member of the Council or Foreign Minister can easily recognise that event or situation and turn up the index to be directed to the files where the appropriate action is prescribed."[14] There were determined efforts to perfect the machinery, to standardise the procedure, to close the "gaps" in the Covenant by an absolute veto on all war, and to make the application of sanctions "automatic." The Draft Treaty of Mutual Assistance, the Geneva Protocol, the General Act, the plan to incorporate the Briand-Kellogg Pact in the Covenant and "the definition of the aggressor," were all milestones on the dangerous path of rationalisation. The fact that the utopian dishes prepared during these years at Geneva proved unpalatable to most of the principal governments concerned was a symptom of the growing divorce between theory and practice.

Even the language current in League circles betrayed the growing eagerness to avoid the concrete in favour of the abstract generalisations. When it was desired to arrange that the Draft Treaty of Mutual Assistance could be brought into force in Europe without waiting for the rest of the world, a stipulation was inserted that it might come into force "by continents"—a proviso with farcical implications for every continent except Europe. A conventional phraseology came into use, which

---

[13] By a curious irony, this development was strongly encouraged by a group of American intellectuals; and some European enthusiasts imagined that, by following this course, they would propitiate American opinion. The rift between the theory of the intellectuals and the practice of the government, which develop in Great Britain from 1932 onwards, began in the United States in 1919.

[14] J. Fischer-Williams, *Some Aspects of the Covenant of the League of Nations,* p. 238.

served as the current coin of delegates at Geneva and of League enthusiasts elsewhere and which, through constant repetition, soon lost all contact with reality. "I cannot recall any time," said Mr. Churchill in 1932, "when the gap between the kind of words which statesmen used and what was actually happening in many countries was so great as it is now." [15] The Franco-Soviet Pact, which was a defensive alliance against Germany, was so drafted as to make it appear an instrument of general application, and was described as a shining example of the principle of "collective security." A member of the House of Commons, when asked in the debate on sanctions in June 1936 whether he would run the risk of war with Italy, replied that he was prepared to face "all the consequences naturally flowing from the enforcement of the Covenant against an aggressor nation." [16] These linguistic contortions encouraged the frequent failure to distinguish between the world of abstract reason and the world of political reality. "Metaphysicians, like savages," remarks Mr. Bertrand Russell, "are apt to imagine a magical connexion between words and things." [17] The metaphysicians of Geneva found it difficult to believe that an accumulation of ingenious texts prohibiting war was not a barrier against war itself. "Our purpose," said M. Benes in introducing the Geneva Protocol to the 1924 Assembly, "was to make war impossible, to kill it, to annihilate it. To do this we had to create a system." [18] The Protocol was the "system." Such presumption could only provoke nemesis. Once it came to be believed in League circles that salvation could be found in a perfect card-index, and that the unruly flow of international politics could be canalised into a set of logically impregnable abstract formulae inspired by the doctrines of nineteenth-century liberal democracy, the end of the League as an effective political instrument was in sight.

.   .   .

THE NEMESIS OF UTOPIANISM

The nemesis of utopianism in international politics came rather suddenly. In September 1930, the President of Columbia University, Dr. Nicholas Murray Butler, ventured on the "reasonably safe prediction that the next generation will see a constantly increasing respect for Cobden's principles and point of view and a steadily growing endeavour more largely to give them practical effect in public policy." [19] On September 10, 1931, Lord Cecil told the Assembly of the League of Nations that

---

[15] Winston Churchill, *Arms and the Covenant*, p. 43.
[16] Quoted in Toynbee, *Survey of International Affairs, 1935*, ii. p. 448.
[17] B. Russell in *Atlantic Monthly*, clix. (February 1937), p. 155.
[18] *League of Nations: Fifth Assembly*, p. 497.
[19] N. M. Butler, *The Path to Peace*, p. xii.

"there has scarcely ever been a period in the world's history when war seems less likely than it does at present." [20] On September 18, 1931, Japan opened her campaign in Manchuria; and in the following month, the last important country which had continued to adhere to the principle of free trade took the first steps towards the introduction of a general tariff.

From this point onwards, a rapid succession of events forced upon all serious thinkers a reconsideration of premises which were becoming more and more flagrantly divorced from reality. The Manchurian crisis had demonstrated that the "condemnation of international public opinion," invoked by Taft and by so many after him, was a broken reed. In the United States, this conclusion was drawn with extreme reluctance. In 1932, an American Secretary of State still cautiously maintained that "the sanction of public opinion can be made one of the most potent sanctions of the world." [21] In September 1938, President Roosevelt based his intervention in the Czecho-Slovak crisis on the belief of the United States Government in "the moral force of public opinion;" [22] and in April 1939, Mr. Cordell Hull once again announced the conviction that "a public opinion, the most potent of all forces for peace, is more strongly developing throughout the world." [23] But in countries more directly menaced by international crisis, this consoling view no longer found many adherents; and the continued addition to it of American statesmen was regarded as an index of American unwillingness to resort to more potent weapons. Already in 1932, Mr. Churchill taunted the League of Nations Union with "long-suffering and inexhaustible gullibility" for continuing to preach this outworn creed.[24] Before long the group of intellectuals who had once stressed the relative unimportance of the "material" weapons of the League began to insist loudly on economic and military sanctions as the necessary cornerstones of an international order. When Germany annexed Austria, Lord Cecil indignantly enquired whether the Prime Minister "holds that the use of material force is impracticable and that the League should cease to attempt 'sanctions' and confine its efforts to moral force." [25] The answer might well have been that, if Neville Chamberlain did in fact hold this view, he could have learned it from Lord Cecil's own earlier utterances.

---

[20] *League of Nations: Twelfth Assembly,* p. 59.

[21] Mr. Stimson to the Council of Foreign Relations on August 8, 1932 (*New York Times,* August 9, 1932).

[22] "Believing, as this government does, in the moral force of public opinion . . ." (Sumner Welles in *State Department Press Releases,* October 8, 1938, p. 237).

[23] *The Times,* April 18, 1939.

[24] Winston Churchill, *Arms and the Covenant,* p. 36.

[25] *Daily Telegraph,* March 24, 1938.

Moreover, scepticism attacked not only the premise that public opinion is certain to prevail, but also the premise that public opinion is certain to be right. At the Peace Conference, it had been observed that statesmen were sometimes more reasonable and moderate in their demands than the public opinion which they were supposed to represent. Even Wilson himself once used—no doubt, in perfect sincerity—an argument which directly contradicted his customary thesis that reason can be made to prevail by appealing to "the plain people everywhere throughout the world." In the League of Nations Commission of the Conference, the Japanese had raised the issue of race equality. "How can you treat on its merits in this quiet room," enquired the President, "a question which will not be treated on its merits when it gets out of this room?" [26] Later history provided many examples of this phenomenon. It became a commonplace for statesmen at Geneva and elsewhere to explain that they themselves had every desire to be reasonable, but that public opinion in their countries was inexorable; and though this plea was sometimes a pretext or a tactical manœuvre, there was often a solid substratum of reality beneath it. The prestige of public opinion correspondingly declined. "It does not help the conciliator, the arbitrator, the policeman or the judge," wrote a well-known supporter of the League of Nations Union recently, "to be surrounded by a crowd emitting either angry or exulting cheers." [27] Woodrow Wilson's "plain men throughout the world," the spokesmen of "the common purpose of enlightened mankind," had somehow transformed themselves into a disorderly mob emitting incoherent and unhelpful noises. It seemed undeniable that, in international affairs, public opinion was almost as often wrong-headed as it was impotent. But where so many of the presuppositions of 1919 were crumbling, the intellectual leaders of the utopian school stuck to their guns; and in Great Britain and the United States—and to a lesser degree in France—the rift between theory and practice assumed alarming dimensions. Armchair students of international affairs were unanimous about the kind of policy which ought to be followed, both in the political and in the economic field. Governments of many countries acted in a sense precisely contrary to this advice, and received the endorsement of public opinion at the polls.

· · ·

THE UTOPIAN SYNTHESIS

No political society, national or international, can exist unless people submit to certain rules of conduct. The problem why people should sub-

---

[26] Miller, *The Drafting of the Covenant*, ii. p. 701.
[27] Lord Allen of Hurtwood, *The Times*, May 30, 1938.

mit to such rules is the fundamental problem of political philosophy. The problem presents itself just as insistently in a democracy as under other forms of government and in international as in national politics; for such a formula as "the greatest good of the greatest number" provides no answer to the question why the minority, whose greatest good is *ex hypothesi* not pursued, should submit to rules made in the interest of the greatest number. Broadly speaking, the answers given to the question fall into two categories, corresponding to the antithesis, discussed in a previous chapter, between those who regard politics as a function of ethics and those who regard ethics as a function of politics.

Those who assert the primacy of ethics over politics will hold that it is the duty of the individual to submit for the sake of the community as a whole, sacrificing his own interest to the interest of others who are more numerous, or in some other way more deserving. The "good" which consists in self-interest should be subordinated to the "good" which consists in loyalty and self-sacrifice for an end higher than self-interest. The obligation rests on some kind of intuition of what is right and cannot be demonstrated by rational argument. Those, on the other hand, who assert the primacy of politics over ethics, will argue that the ruler rules because he is the stronger, and the ruled submit because they are the weaker. This principle is just as easily applicable to democracy as to any other form of government. The majority rules because it is stronger, the minority submits because it is weaker. Democracy, it has often been said, substitutes the counting of heads for the breaking of heads. But the substitution is merely a convenience, and the principle of the two methods is the same. The realist, therefore, unlike the intuitionist, has a perfectly rational answer to the question why the individual should submit. He should submit because otherwise the stronger will compel him; and the results of compulsion are more disagreeable than those of voluntary submission. Obligation is thus derived from a sort of spurious ethic based on the reasonableness of recognising that might is right.

Both these answers are open to objection. Modern man, who has witnessed so many magnificent achievements of human reason, is reluctant to believe that reason and obligation sometimes conflict. On the other hand, men of all ages have failed to find satisfaction in the view that the rational basis of obligation is merely the right of the stronger. One of the strongest points of eighteenth- and nineteenth-century utopianism was its apparent success in meeting both these objections at once. The utopian, starting from the primacy of ethics, necessarily believes in an obligation which is ethical in character and independent of the right of the stronger. But he has also been able to convince himself, on grounds other than those of the realist, that the duty of the individual to submit to rules made in the interest of the community can be justified in terms of reason, and that the greatest good of the greatest number is a rational end even for those who are not included in the greatest number. He achieves this synthesis by maintaining that the highest interest of the individual and the highest interest of the community naturally coincide. In pursuing his own interest, the individual pursues that of the community, and in promoting the interest of the community he promotes his own. This is the famous doctrine of the harmony of interests. It is a necessary corollary of the postulate that moral laws can be established by right reasoning. The admission of any ultimate divergence of interests would be fatal to this postulate; and any apparent clash of interests must therefore be explained as the result of wrong calculation. Burke tacitly accepted the doctrine of identity when he defined expediency as "that which is good for the community and for every individual in it." [28] It was handed on from the eighteenth-century rationalists to Bentham, and from Bentham to the Victorian moralists. The utilitarian philosophers could justify morality by the argument that, in promoting the good of others, one automatically promotes one's own. Honesty is the best policy. If people or nations behave badly, it must be, as Buckle and Sir Norman Angell and Professor Zimmern think, because they are unintellectual and short-sighted and muddle-headed.

THE PARADISE OF LAISSEZ-FAIRE

It was the *laissez-faire* school of political economy created by Adam Smith which was in the main responsible for popularising the doctrine of the harmony of interests. The purpose of the school was to promote the removal of state control in economic matters; and in order to justify this policy, it set out to demonstrate that the individual could be relied on, without external control, to promote the interests of the community for the very reason that those interests were identical with his own. This proof was the burden of *The Wealth of Nations*. The community is divided into those who live by rent, those who live by wages and those who live by profit; and the interests of "those three great orders" are "strictly and inseparably connected with the general interest of the society." [29] The harmony is none the less real if those concerned are unconscious of it. The individual "neither intends to promote the public interest, nor knows how much he is promoting it. . . . He intends only his own gain, and he is in this, as in many other cases, led by an invisible hand to promote an end which was not part of his intention." [30] The invisible hand, which Adam Smith would perhaps have regarded as a metaphor, presented no difficulty to Victorian piety. "It is curious to observe," remarks a tract issued by the Society for the Propagation of

---

[28] Burke, *Works*, v. 407.
[29] Adam Smith, *The Wealth of Nations*, Book I. ch. xi. conclusion.
[30] *Ibid*. Book IV. ch. ii.

Christian Knowledge towards the middle of the nineteenth century, "how, through the wise and beneficent arrangement of Providence, men thus do the greatest service to the public when they are thinking of nothing but their own gain." [31] About the same time an English clergyman wrote a work entitled *The Temporal Benefits of Christianity Explained*. The harmony of interests provided a solid rational basis for morality. To love one's neighbour turned out to be a thoroughly enlightened way of loving oneself. "We now know," wrote Mr. Henry Ford as recently as 1930, "that anything which is economically right is also morally right. There can be no conflict between good economics and good morals." [32]

The assumption of a general and fundamental harmony of interests is *prima facie* so paradoxical that it requires careful scrutiny. In the form which Adam Smith gave to it, it had a definite application to the economic structure of the eighteenth century. It presupposed a society of small producers and merchants, interested in the maximisation of production and exchange, infinitely mobile and adaptable, and unconcerned with the problem of the distribution of wealth. Those conditions were substantially fulfilled in an age when production involved no high degree of specialisation and no sinking of capital in fixed equipment, and when the class which might be more interested in the equitable distribution of wealth than in its maximum production was insignificant and without influence. But by a curious coincidence, the year which saw the publication of *The Wealth of Nations* was also the year in which Watt invented his steam-engine. Thus, at the very moment when *laissez-faire* theory was receiving its classical exposition, its premises were undermined by an invention which was destined to call into being immobile, highly specialised, mammoth industries and a large and powerful proletariat more interested in distribution than in production. Once industrial capitalism and the class system had become the recognised structure of society, the doctrine of the harmony of interests acquired a new significance, and became, as we shall presently see, the ideology of a dominant group concerned to maintain its predominance by asserting the identity of its interests with those of the community as a whole.

But this transformation could not have been effected, and the doctrine could not have survived at all, but for one circumstance. The survival of the belief in a harmony of interests was rendered possible by the unparalleled expansion of production, population and prosperity, which marked the hundred years following the publication of *The Wealth of Nations* and the invention of the steam-engine. Expanding prosperity contributed to the popularity of the doctrine in three different ways. It attenuated

---

[31] Quoted in J. M. Keynes, *A Tract on Monetary Reform*, p. 7.

[32] Quoted in J. Truslow Adams, *The Epic of America*, p. 400. I have failed to trace the original.

competition for markets among producers, since fresh markets were constantly becoming available; it postponed the class issue, with its insistence on the primary importance of equitable distribution, by extending to members of the less prosperous classes some share in the general prosperity; and by creating a sense of confidence in present and future well-being, it encouraged men to believe that the world was ordered on so rational a plan as the natural harmony of interests. "It was the continual widening of the field of demand which, for half a century, made capitalism operate as if it were a liberal utopia." [33] The tacit presupposition of infinitely expanding markets was the foundation on which the supposed harmony of interests rested. As Dr. Mannheim points out, traffic control is unnecessary so long as the number of cars does not exceed the comfortable capacity of the road.[34] Until that moment arrives, it is easy to believe in a natural harmony of interests between road-users.

What was true of individuals was assumed to be also true of nations. Just as individuals, by pursuing their own good, unconsciously compass the good of the whole community, so nations in serving themselves serve humanity. Universal free trade was justified on the ground that the maximum economic interest of each nation was identified with the maximum economic interest of the whole world. Adam Smith, who was a practical reformer rather than a pure theorist, did indeed admit that governments might have to protect certain industries in the interests of national defence. But such derogations seemed to him and to his followers trivial exceptions to the rule. "*Laissez-faire*," as J. S. Mill puts it, ". . . should be the general rule: every departure from it, unless required by some great good, a certain evil." [35] Other thinkers gave the doctrine of the harmony of national interests a still wider application. "The true interests of a nation," observes a late eighteenth-century writer, "never yet stood in opposition to the general interest of mankind; and it can never happen that philanthropy and patriotism can impose on any man inconsistent duties." [36] T. H. Green, the English Hegelian who tempered the doctrines of his master with concessions to British nineteenth-century *liberalism*, held that "no action in its own interest of a state which fulfilled its idea could conflict with any true interest or right of general society." [37] though it is interesting to note that the question-begging epithet "true," which in the eighteenth-century quotation is attached to the interests of the nation, has been trans-

---

[33] *Nationalism: A Study by a Group of Members of the Royal Institute of International Affairs*, p. 229.

[34] K. Mannheim, *Mensch und Gesellschaft im Zeitalter des Umbaus*, p. 104.

[35] J. S. Mill, *Principles of Political Economy*, II. Book V. ch. xi.

[36] Romilly, *Thoughts on the Influence of the French Revolution*, p. 5.

[37] T. H. Green, *Principles of Political Obligation*, § 166.

ferred by the nineteenth century to the interest of the general society. Mazzini, who embodied the liberal nineteeth-century philosophy of nationalism, believed in a sort of division of labour between nations. Each nation had its own special task for which its special aptitudes fitted it, and the performance of this task was its contribution to the welfare of humanity. If all nations acted in this spirit, international harmony would prevail. The same condition of apparently infinite expansibility which encouraged belief in the economic harmony of interests made possible the belief in the political harmony of rival national movements. One reason why contemporaries of Mazzini thought nationalism a good thing was that there were few recognised nations, and plenty of room for them. In an age when Germans, Czechs, Poles, Ukrainians, Magyars and half a dozen more national groups were not yet visibly jostling one another over an area of a few hundred square miles, it was comparatively easy to believe that each nation, by developing its own nationalism, could make its own special contribution to the international harmony of interests. Most liberal writers continued to believe, right down to 1918, that nations, by developing their own nationalism, promoted the cause of internationalism; and Wilson and many other makers of the peace treaties saw in national self-determination the key to world peace. More recently still, responsible Anglo-Saxon statesmen have been from time to time content to echo, probably without much reflexion, the old Mazzinian formulae.[38]

. . .

THE COMMON INTEREST IN PEACE

Politically, the doctrine of the identity of interests has commonly taken the form of an assumption that every nation has an identical interest in peace, and that any nation which desires to disturb the peace is therefore both irrational and immoral. This view bears clear marks of its Anglo-Saxon origin. It was easy after 1918 to convince that part of mankind which lives in English-speaking countries that war profits nobody. The argument did not seem particularly convincing to Germans, who had profited largely from the wars of 1866 and 1870, and attributed their more recent sufferings, not to the war of 1914, but to the fact that they had lost it; or to Italians, who blamed not the war, but the treachery of allies who defrauded them in the peace settlement; or to Poles or Czecho-Slovaks who, far from deploring the war, owed their national existence to it; or to Frenchmen, who could not unreservedly regret a war which had restored Alsace-Lorraine to France; or to people of other

---

[38] Mr. Eden, for example, in 1938 advocated "a comity of nations in which each can develop and flourish and give to their uttermost their own special contribution to the diversity of life" (Anthony Eden, *Foreign Affairs*, p. 277).

nationalities who remembered profitable wars waged by Great Britain and the United States in the past. But these people had fortunately little influence over the formation of current theories of international relations, which emanated almost exclusively from the English-speaking countries. British and American writers continued to assume that the uselessness of war had been irrefutably demonstrated by the experience of 1914–18, and that an intellectual grasp of this fact was all that was necessary to induce the nations to keep the peace in the future; and they were sincerely puzzled as well as disappointed at the failure of other countries to share this view.

The confusion was increased by the ostentatious readiness of other countries to flatter the Anglo-Saxon world by repeating its slogans. In the fifteen years after the first world war, every Great Power (except, perhaps, Italy) repeatedly did lip-service to the doctrine by declaring peace to be one of the main objects of its policy.[39] But as Lenin observed long ago, peace in itself is a meaningless aim. "Absolutely everbody is in favour of peace in general," he wrote in 1915, "including Kitchener, Joffre, Hindenburg and Nicholas the Bloody, for everyone of them wishes to end the war." [40] The common interest in peace masks the fact that some nations desire to maintain the *status quo* without having to fight for it, and others to change the *status quo* without having to fight in order to do so.[41] The statement that it is in the interest of the world as a whole either that the *status quo* should be maintained, or that it should be changed, would be contrary to the facts. The statement that it is in the

---

[39] "Peace must prevail, must come before all" (Briand, *League of Nations: Ninth Assembly*, p. 83). "The maintenance of peace is the first objective of British foreign policy" (Eden, *League of Nations: Sixteenth Assembly*, p. 106). "Peace is our dearest treasure" (Hitler, in a speech in the German Reichstag on January 30, 1937, reported in *The Times*, February 1, 1937). "The principal aim of the international policy of the Soviet Union is the preservation of peace" (Chicherin in The Soviet Union and Peace (1929), p. 249). "The object of Japan, despite propaganda to the contrary, is peace" (Matsuoka, *League of Nations: Special Assembly 1932–33*, iii. p. 73). The paucity of Italian pronouncements in favour of peace was probably explained by the poor reputation of Italian troops as fighters: Mussolini feared that any emphatic expression of preference for peace would be construed as an admission that Italy had no stomach for war.

[40] Lenin, *Collected Works* (Engl. transl.), xviii. p. 264. Compare Spenser Wilkinson's dictum: "It is not peace but preponderance that is in each case the real object. The truth cannot be too often repeated that peace is never the object of policy: you cannot define peace except by reference to war, which is a means and never an end" (*Government and the War*, p. 121).

[41] "When a saint complains that people do not know the things belonging to their peace, what he really means is that they do not sufficiently care about the things belonging to his peace" (*The Note-Books of Samuel Butler*, ed. Festing-Jones, pp. 211–12). This would seem to be true of those latter-day saints, the satisfied Powers.

interest of the world as a whole that the conclusion eventually reached, whether maintenance or change, should be reached by peaceful means, would command general assent, but seems a rather meaningless platitude. The utopian assumption that there is a world interest in peace which is identifiable with the interest of each individual nation helped politicians and political writers everywhere to evade the unpalatable fact of a fundamental divergence of interest between nations desirous of maintaining the *status quo* and nations desirous of changing it.[42] A peculiar combination of platitude and falesness thus became endemic in the pronouncements of statesmen about international affairs. "In this whole Danubian area," said a Prime Minister of Czecho-Slovakia, "no one really wants conflicts and jealousies. The various countries want to maintain their independence, but otherwise they are ready for any co-operative measures. I am thinking specially of the Little Entente, Hungary and Bulgaria." [43] Literally the words may pass as true. Yet the conflicts and jealousies which nobody wanted were a notorious feature of Danubian politics after 1919, and the co-operation for which all were ready was unobtainable. The fact of divergent interests was disguised and falsified by the platitude of a general desire to avoid conflict.

THE HARMONY BROKEN

We must therefore reject as inadequate and misleading the attempt to base international morality on an alleged harmony of interests which identifies the interest of the whole community of nations with the interest of each individual member of it. In the nineteenth century, this attempt met with widespread success, thanks to the continuously expanding economy in which it was made. The period was one of progressive prosperity, punctuated only by minor set-backs. The international economic structure bore considerable resemblance to the domestic economic structure of the United States. Pressure could at once be relieved by expansion to hitherto unoccupied and unexploited territories; and there was a plentiful supply of cheap labour, and of backward countries, which had not yet reached the level of political consciousness. Enterprising individuals could solve the economic problem by migration, enterprising nations by colonisation. Expanding markets produced an expanding

---

[42] It is sometimes maintained not merely that all nations have an equal interest in preferring peace to war (which is, in a sense, true), but that war can never in any circumstances bring to the victor advantages comparable with its cost. The latter view does not appear to be true of the past, though it is possible to argue (as does Bertrand Russell, *Which Way Peace?*) that it is true of modern warfare. If accepted, this view leads, of course, to absolute pacifism; for there is no reason to suppose that it is any truer of "defensive" than of "offensive" war (assuming the distinction between them to be valid).

[43] *Daily Telegraph,* August 26, 1938.

population, and population in turn reacted on markets. Those who were left behind in the race could plausibly be regarded as the unfit. A harmony of interests among the fit, based on individual enterprise and free competition, was sufficiently near to reality to form a sound basis for the current theory. With some difficulty the illusion was kept alive till 1914. Even British prosperity, though its foundations were menaced by German and American competition, continued to expand. The year 1913 was a record year for British trade.

The transition from the apparent harmony to the transparent clash of interests may be placed about the turn of the century. Appropriately enough, it found its first expression in colonial policies. In the British mind, it was primarily associated with events in South Africa. Mr. Churchill dates the beginning of "these violent times" from the Jameson Raid.[44] In North Africa and the Far East, there was a hasty scramble by the European Powers to secure the few eligible sites which were still vacant. Emigration of individuals from Europe, the point of principal tension, to America assumed unparalleled dimensions. In Europe itself, anti-Semitism—the recurrent symptom of economic stress—reappeared after a long interval in Russia, Germany and France.[45] In Great Britain, agitation against unrestricted alien immigration began in the 1890's; and the first act controlling immigration was passed in 1905.

The first world war, which proceeded from this growing tension, aggravated it tenfold by intensifying its fundamental causes. In belligerent and neutral countries in Europe, Asia and America, industrial and agricultural production were everywhere artificially stimulated. After the war every country struggled to maintain its expanded production; and an enhanced and inflamed national consciousness was invoked to justify the struggle. One reason for the unprecedented vindictiveness of the peace treaties, and in particular of their economic clauses, was that practical men no longer believed—as they had done fifty or a hundred years earlier—in an underlying harmony of interests between victors and defeated. The object was now to eliminate a competitor, a revival of whose prosperity might menace your own. In Europe, the struggle was intensified by the creation of new states and new economic frontiers. In Asia, India and China built up large-scale manufactures to make themselves independent of imports from Europe. Japan became an exporter of textiles and other cheap goods which undercut European manufactures on the world market. Most important of all, there were no more open spaces anywhere awaiting cheap and profitable development and exploitation. The ample ave-

---

[44] Winston Churchill, *World Crisis*, p. 26.

[45] The same conditions encouraged the growth of Zionism; for Zionism, as the Palestine Royal Commission of 1937 remarked, "on its negative side is a creed of escape" Cmd. 5479, p. 13).

nues of migration which had relieved the economic pressures of the pre-war period were closed; and in place of the natural flow of migration came the problem of forcibly evicted refugees.[46] The complex phenomenon known as economic nationalism swept over the world. The fundamental character of this clash of interests became obvious to all except those confirmed utopians who dominated economic thought in the English-speaking countries. The hollowness of the glib nineteenth-century plati-tude that nobody can benefit from what harms another was revealed. The basic presupposition of utopianism had broken down.

What confronts us in international politics to-day is, therefore, nothing less than the complete bankruptcy of the conception of morality which has dominated political and economic thought for a century and a half. Internationally, it is no longer possible to deduce virtue from right rea-soning, because it is no longer seriously possible to believe that every state, by pursuing the greatest good of the whole world, is pursuing the greatest good of its own citizens, and *vice versa*. The synthesis of morality and reason, at any rate in the crude form in which it was achieved by nineteenth-century liberalism, is untenable. The inner mean-ing of the modern international crisis is the collapse of the whole struc-ture of utopianism based on the concept of the harmony of interests. The present generation will have to rebuild from the foundations. But before we can do this, before we can ascertain what can be salved from the ruins, we must examine the flaws in the structure which led to its collapse; and we can best do this by analysing the realist critique of the utopian as-sumptions.

---

[46] "The existence of refugees is a symptom of the disappearance of economic and political liberalism. Refugees are the by-product of an economic isolationism which has practically stopped free migration" (J. Hope Simpson, *Refugees: Preliminary Report of a Survey*, p. 193).

SECTION TWO:

Approaches to the Study of International Relations

4. SIX PRINCIPLES OF POLITICAL REALISM

Hans J. Morgenthau

1. POLITICAL REALISM believes that politics, like society in general, is governed by objective laws that have their roots in human nature. In order to improve society it is first necessary to understand the laws by which society lives. The operation of these laws being impervious of our preferences, men will challenge them only at the risk of failure.

Realism, believing as it does in the objectivity of the laws of politics, must also believe in the possibility of developing a rational theory that reflects, however imperfectly and one-sidedly, these objective laws. It believes also, then, in the possibility of distinguishing in politics between truth and opinion—between what is true objectively and rationally, supported by evidence and illuminated by reason, and what is only a subjec-

From *Politics Among Nations* by Hans J. Morgenthau (New York: 1967) pp. 4–14. Copyright 1948, 1954 by Alfred A. Knopf, Inc. Reprinted by permission. Footnotes have been renumbered to appear in consecutive order.

HANS J. MORGENTHAU (1904–   ) Alfred A. Michelson Distinguished Service Professor of Political Science and Modern History; Director of the Center for the Study of American Foreign Policy, University of Chicago. Author of *Truth and Power: Essays of a Decade, 1960–1970* (New York: Praeger Publishers, 1970); *New Foreign Policy for the United States* (New York: Praeger Publishers, 1969); *Politics in the Twentieth Century* (Chicago: University of Chicago Press, 1962); *Dilemmas of Politics* (Chicago: University of Chicago Press, 1958); *In Defense of the National Interest* (New York: Alfred A. Knopf, 1951).

tive judgment, divorced from the facts as they are and informed by prejudice and wishful thinking.

Human nature, in which the laws of politics have their roots, has not changed since the classical philosophies of China, India, and Greece endeavored to discover these laws. Hence, novelty is not necessarily a virtue in political theory, nor is old age a defect. The fact that a theory of politics, if there be such a theory, has never been heard of before tends to create a presumption against, rather than in favor of, its soundness. Conversely, the fact that a theory of politics was developed hundreds or even thousands of years ago—as was the theory of the balance of power —does not create a presumption that it must be outmoded and obsolete. A theory of politics must be subjected to the dual test of reason and experience. To dismiss such a theory because it had its flowering in centuries past is to present not a rational argument but a modernistic prejudice that takes for granted the superiority of the present over the past. To dispose of the revival of such a theory as a "fashion" or "fad" is tantamount to assuming that in matters political we can have opinions but no truths.

For realism, theory consists in ascertaining facts and giving them meaning through reason. It assumes that the character of a foreign policy can be ascertained only through the examination of the political acts performed and of the foreseeable consequences of these acts. Thus, we can find out what statesmen have actually done, and from the foreseeable consequences of their acts we can surmise what their objectives might have been.

Yet examination of the facts is not enough. To give meaning to the factual raw material of foreign policy, we must approach political reality with a kind of rational outline, a map that suggests to us the possible meanings of foreign policy. In other words, we put ourselves in the position of a statesman who must meet a certain problem of foreign policy under certain circumstances, and we ask ourselves what the rational alternatives are from which a statesman may choose who must meet this problem under these circumstances (presuming always that he acts in a rational manner), and which of these rational alternatives this particular statesman, acting under these circumstances, is likely to choose. It is the testing of this rational hypothesis against the actual facts and their consequences that gives meaning to the facts of international politics and makes a theory of politics possible.

2. The main signpost that helps political realism to find its way through the landscape of international politics is the concept of interest defined in terms of power. This concept provides the link between reason trying to understand international politics and the facts to be understood. It sets politics as an autonomous sphere of action and understanding apart from

other spheres, such as economics (understood in terms of interest defined as wealth), ethics, aesthetics, or religion. Without such a concept a theory of politics, international or domestic, would be altogether impossible, for without it we could not distinguish between political and nonpolitical facts, nor could we bring at least a measure of systematic order to the political sphere.

We assume that statesmen think and act in terms of interest defined as power, and the evidence of history bears that assumption out. That assumption allows us to retrace and anticipate, as it were, the steps a statesman—past, present, or future—has taken or will take on the political scene. We look over his shoulder when he writes his dispatches; we listen in on his conversation with other statesmen; we read and anticipate his very thoughts. Thinking in terms of interest defined as power, we think as he does, and as disinterested observers we understand his thoughts and actions perhaps better than he, the actor on the political scene, does himself.

The concept of interest defined as power imposes intellectual discipline upon the observer, infuses rational order into the subject matter of politics, and thus makes the theoretical understanding of politics possible. On the side of the actor, it provides for rational discipline in action and creates that astounding continuity in foreign policy which makes American, British, or Russian foreign policy appear as an intelligible, rational continuum, by and large consistent within itself, regardless of the different motives, preferences, and intellectual and moral qualities of successive statesmen. A realist theory of international politics, then, will guard against two popular fallacies: the concern with motives and the concern with ideological preferences.

To search for the clue to foreign policy exclusively in the motives of statesmen is both futile and deceptive. It is futile because motives are the most illusive of psychological data, distorted as they are, frequently beyond recognition, by the interests and emotions of actor and observer alike. Do we really know what our own motives are? And what do we know of the motives of others?

Yet even if we had access to the real motives of statesmen, that knowledge would help us little in understanding foreign policies, and might well lead us astray. It is true that the knowledge of the statesman's motives may give us one among many clues as to what the direction of his foreign policy might be. It cannot give us, however, the one clue by which to predict his foreign policies. History shows no exact and necessary correlation between the quality of motives and the quality of foreign policy. This is true in both moral and political terms.

We cannot conclude from the good intentions of a statesman that his foreign policies will be either morally praiseworthy or politically successful. Judging his motives, we can say that he will not intentionally pursue policies that are morally wrong, but we can say nothing about the probability of their success. If we want to know the moral and political qualities of his actions, we must know them, not his motives. How often have statesmen been motivated by the desire to improve the world, and ended by making it worse? And how often have they sought one goal, and ended by achieving something they neither expected nor desired?

Neville Chamberlain's policies of appeasement were, as far as we can judge, inspired by good motives; he was probably less motivated by considerations of personal power than were many other British prime ministers, and he sought to preserve peace and to assure the happiness of all concerned. Yet his policies helped to make the Second World War inevitable, and to bring untold miseries to millions of men. Sir Winston Churchill's motives, on the other hand, have been much less universal in scope and much more narrowly directed toward personal and national power, yet the foreign policies that sprang from these inferior motives were certainly superior in moral and political quality to those pursued by his predecessor. Judged by his motives, Robespierre was one of the most virtuous men who ever lived. Yet it was the utopian radicalism of that very virtue that made him kill those less virtuous than himself, brought him to the scaffold, and destroyed the revolution of which he was a leader.

Good motives give assurance against deliberately bad policies; they do not guarantee the moral goodness and political success of the policies they inspire. What it is important to know, if one wants to understand foreign policy, is not primarily the motives of a statesman, but his intellectual ability to comprehend the essentials for foreign policy, as well as his political ability to translate what he has comprehended into successful political action. It follows that while ethics in the abstract judges the moral qualities of motives, political theory must judge the political qualities of intellect, will, and action.

A realist theory of international politics will also avoid the other popular fallacy of equating the foreign policies of a statesman with his philosophic or political sympathies, and of deducing the former from the latter. Statesmen, especially under contemporary conditions, may well make a habit of presenting their foreign policies in terms of their philosophic and political sympathies in order to gain popular support for them. Yet they will distinguish with Lincoln between their *"official duty,"* which is to think and act in terms of the national interest, and their *"personal* wish," which is to see their own moral values and political principles realized throughout the world. Political realism does not require, nor does it condone, indifference to political ideals and moral principles, but it requires indeed a sharp distinction between the desirable and the possible—between what is desirable everywhere and at all times and what is possible under the concrete circumstances of time and place.

It stands to reason that not all foreign policies have always followed so rational, objective, and unemotional a course. The contingent elements of personality, prejudice, and subjective preference, and of all the weaknesses of intellect and will which flesh is heir to, are bound to deflect foreign policies from their rational course. Especially where foreign policy is conducted under the conditions of democratic control, the need to marshal popular emotions to the support of foreign policy cannot fail to impair the rationality of foreign policy itself. Yet a theory of foreign policy which aims at rationality must for the time being, as it were, abstract from these irrational elements and seek to paint a picture of foreign policy which presents the rational essence to be found in experience, without the contingent deviations from rationality which are also found in experience.

The difference between international politics as it actually is and a rational theory derived from it is like the difference between a photograph and a painted portrait. The photograph shows everything that can be seen by the naked eye; the painted portrait does not show everything that can be seen by the naked eye, but it shows, or at least seeks to show, one thing that the naked eye cannot see: the human essence of the person portrayed.

Political realism contains not only a theoretical but also a normative element. It knows that political reality is replete with contingencies and points to the typical influences they exert upon foreign policy. Yet it shares with all social theory the need, for the sake of theoretical understanding, to stress the rational elements of political reality; for it is these rational elements that make reality intelligible for theory. Political realism presents the theoretical construct of a rational foreign policy which experience can never completely achieve.

At the same time political realism considers a rational foreign policy to be good foreign policy; for only a rational foreign policy minimizes risks and maximizes benefits and, hence, complies both with the moral precept of prudence and the political requirement of success. Political realism wants the photographic picture of the political world to resemble as much as possible its painted portrait. Aware of the inevitable gap between good—that is, rational—foreign policy and foreign policy as it actually is, political realism maintains not only that theory must focus upon the rational elements of political reality, but also that foreign policy ought to be rational in view of its own moral and practical purposes.

Hence, it is no argument against the theory here presented that actual foreign policy does not or cannot live up to it. That argument misunderstands the intention of this book, which is to present not an indiscriminate description of political reality, but a rational theory of international politics. Far from being invalidated by the fact that, for instance, a perfect balance of power policy will scarcely be found in reality, it assumes that reality, being deficient in this respect, must be understood and evaluated as an approximation to an ideal system of balance of power.

3. Realism does not endow its key concept of interest defined as power with a meaning that is fixed once and for all. The idea of interest is indeed of the essence of politics and is unaffected by the circumstances of time and place. Thucydides' statement, born of the experiences of ancient Greece, that "identity of interest is the surest of bonds whether between states or individuals" was taken up in the nineteenth century by Lord Salisbury's remark that "the only bond of union that endures" among nations is "the absence of all clashing interests." It was erected into a general principle of government by George Washington:

> A small knowledge of human nature will convince us, that, with far the greatest part of mankind, interest is the governing principle; and that almost every man is more or less, under its influence. Motives of public virtue may for a time, or in particular instances, actuate men to the observance of a conduct purely disinterested; but they are not of themselves sufficient to produce a persevering conformity to the refined dictates and obligations of social duty. Few men are capable of making a continual sacrifice of all views of private interest, or advantage, to the common good. It is vain to exclaim against the depravity of human nature on this account; the fact is so, the experience of every age and nation has proved it and we must in a great measure, change the constitution of man, before we can make it otherwise. No institution, not built on the presumptive truth of these maxims can succeed.[1]

It was echoed and enlarged upon in our century by Max Weber's observation:

> Interests (material and ideal), not ideas, dominate directly the actions of men. Yet the "images of the world" created by these ideas have very often served as switches determining the tracks on which the dynamism of interests kept actions moving.[2]

Yet the kind of interest determining political action in a particular period of history depends upon the political and cultural context within which foreign policy is formulated. The goals that might be pursued by nations in their foreign policy can run the whole gamut of objectives any nation has ever pursued or might possibly pursue.

The same observations apply to the concept of power. Its content and the manner of its use are determined by the political and cultural environment. Power may comprise anything that establishes and maintains

---

[1] *The Writings of George Washington,* edited by John C. Fitzpatrick (Washington: United States Printing Office, 1931–44), Vol. X, p. 363.

[2] Marianne Weber, *Max Weber* (Tuebingen: J. C. B. Mohr, 1926), pp. 347–8.

the control of man over man. Thus power covers all social relationships which serve that end, from physical violence to the most subtle psychological ties by which one mind controls another. Power covers the domination of man by man, both when it is disciplined by moral ends and controlled by constitutional safeguards, as in Western democracies, and when it is that untamed and barbaric force which finds its laws in nothing but its own strength and its sole justification in its aggrandizement.

Political realism does not assume that the contemporary conditions under which foreign policy operates, with their extreme instability and the ever present threat of large-scale violence, cannot be changed. The balance of power, for instance, is indeed a perennial element of all pluralistic societies, as the authors of *The Federalist* papers well knew; yet it is capable of operating, as it does the United States, under the conditions of relative stability and peaceful conflict. If the factors that have given rise to these conditions can be duplicated on the international scene, similar conditions of stability and peace will then prevail there, as they have over long stretches of history among certain nations.

What is true of the general character of international relations is also true of the nation state as the ultimate point of reference of contemporary foreign policy. While the realist indeed believes that interest is the perennial standard by which political action must be judged and directed, the contemporary connection between interest and the national state is a product of history, and is therefore bound to disappear in the course of history. Nothing in the realist position militates against the assumption that the present division of the political world into nation states will be replaced by larger units of a quite different character, more in keeping with the technical potentialities and the moral requirements of the contemporary world.

The realist parts company with other schools of thought before the all-important question of how the contemporary world is to be transformed. The realist is persuaded that this transformation can be achieved only through the workmanlike manipulation of the perennial forces that have shaped the past as they will the future. The realist cannot be persuaded that we can bring about that transformation by confronting a political reality that has its own laws with an abstract ideal that refuses to take those laws into account.

4. Political realism is aware of the moral significance of political action. It is also aware of the ineluctable tension between the moral command and the requirements of successful political action. And it is unwilling to gloss over and obliterate that tension and thus to obfuscate both the moral and the political issue by making it appear as though the stark facts of politics were morally more satisfying than they actually are, and the moral law less exacting than it actually is.

Realism maintains that universal moral principles cannot be applied to the actions of states in their abstract universal formulation, but that they must be filtered through the concrete circumstances of time and place. The individual may say for himself: *"Fiat justitia, pereat mundus* (Let justice be done, even if the world perish),"* but the state has no right to say so in the name of those who are in its care. Both individual and state must judge political action by universal moral principles, such as that of liberty. Yet while the individual has a moral right to sacrifice himself in defense of such a moral principle, the state has no right to let its moral disapprobation of the infringement of liberty get in the way of successful political action, itself inspired by the moral principle of national survival. There can be no political morality without prudence; that is, without consideration of the political consequences of seemingly moral action. Realism, then, considers prudence—the weighing of the consequences of alternative political actions—to be the supreme virtue in politics. Ethics in the abstract judges action by its conformity with the moral law; political ethics judges action by its political consequences. Classical and medieval philosophy knew this, and so did Lincoln when he said:

> I do the very best I know how, the very best I can, and I mean to keep doing so until the end. If the end brings me out all right, what is said against me won't amount to anything. If the end brings me out wrong, ten angels swearing I was right would make no difference.

5. Political realism refuses to identify the moral aspirations of a particular nation with the moral laws that govern the universe. As it distinguishes between truth and opinion, so it distinguishes between truth and idolatry. All nations are tempted—and few have been able to resist the temptation for long—to clothe their own particular aspirations and actions in the moral purposes of the universe. To know the nations are subject to the moral law is one thing, while to pretend to know with certainty what is good and evil in the relations among nations is quite another. There is a world of difference between the belief that all nations stand under the judgment of God, inscrutable to the human mind, and the blasphemous conviction that God is always on one's side and that what one wills oneself cannot fail to be willed by God also.

The lighthearted equation between a particular nationalism and the counsels of Providence is morally indefensible, for it is that very sin of pride against which the Greek tragedians and the Biblical prophets have warned rulers and ruled. That equation is also politically pernicious, for it is liable to engender the distortion in judgment which, in the blindness of crusading frenzy, destroys nations and civilizatons—in the name of moral principle, ideal, or God himself.

On the other hand, it is exactly the concept of interest defined in terms of power that saves us from both that moral excess and that political folly. For if we look at all nations, our own included, as political entities pursuing their respective interests defined in terms of power, we are able to do justice to all of them. And we are able to do justice to all of them in a dual sense: We are able to judge other nations as we judge our own and, having judged them in this fashion, we are then capable of pursuing policies that respect the interests of other nations, while protecting and promoting those of our own. Moderation in policy cannot fail to reflect the moderation of moral judgment.

6. The difference, then, between political realism and other schools of thought is real and it is profound. However much the theory of political realism may have been misunderstood and misinterpreted, there is no gainsaying its distinctive intellectual and moral attitude to matters political.

Intellectually, the political realist maintains the autonomy of the political sphere, as the economist, the lawyer, the moralist maintain theirs. He thinks in terms of interest defined as power, as the economist thinks in terms of interest defined as wealth; the lawyer, of the conformity of action with legal rules; the moralist, of the conformity of action with moral principles. The economist asks: "How does this policy affect the wealth of society, or a segment of it?" The lawyer asks: "Is this policy in accord with the rules of law?" The moralist asks: "Is this policy in accord with moral principles?" And the political realist asks: "How does this policy affect the power of the nation?" (Or of the federal government, of Congress, of the party, of agriculture, as the case may be.)

The political realist is not unaware of the existence and relevance of standards of thought other than political ones. As political realist, he cannot but subordinate these other standards to those of politics. And he parts company with other schools when they impose standards of thought appropriate to other spheres upon the political shere. It is here that political realism takes issue with the "legalistic-moralistic approach" to international politics. That this issue is not, as has been contended, a mere figment of the imagination, but goes to the very core of the controversy, can be shown from many historical examples. Three will suffice to make the point.[3]

In 1939 the Soviet Union attacked Finland. This action confronted France and Great Britain with two issues, one legal, the other political. Did that action violate the Covenant of the League of Nations and, if it did, what countermeasures should France and Great Britain take? The

---

[3] See the other examples discussed in Hans J. Morgenthau, "Another 'Great Debate': The National Interest of the United States," *The American Political Science Review*, XLVI (December 1952), pp. 979 ff. See also Hans J. Morgenthau, *Dilemmas of Politics* (Chicago: University of Chicago Press, 1958), pp. 54 ff.

legal question could easily be answered in the affirmative, for obviously the Soviet Union had done what was prohibited by the Covenant. The answer to the political question depended, first, upon the manner in which the Russian action affected the interests of France and Great Britain; second, upon the existing distribution of power between France and Great Britain, on the one hand, and the Soviet Union and other potentially hostile nations, especially Germany, on the other; and, third, upon the influence that the countermeasures were likely to have upon the interests of France and Great Britain and the future distribution of power. France and Great Britain, as the leading members of the League of Nations, saw to it that the Soviet Union was expelled from the League, and they were prevented from joining Finland in the war against the Soviet Union only by Sweden's refusal to allow their troops to pass through Swedish territory on their way to Finland. If this refusal by Sweden had not saved them, France and Great Britain would shortly have found themselves at war with the Soviet Union and Germany at the same time.

The policy of France and Great Britain was a classic example of legalism in that they allowed the answer to the legal question, legitimate within its sphere, to determine their political actions. Instead of asking both questions, that of law and that of power, they asked only the question of law; and the answer they received could have no bearing on the issue that their very existence might have depended upon.

The second example illustrates the "moralistic approach" to international politics. It concerns the international status of the Communist government of China. The rise of that government confronted the Western world with two issues, one moral, the other political. Were the nature and policies of that government in accord with the moral principles of the Western world? Should the Western world deal with such a government? The answer to the first question could not fail to be in the negative. Yet it did not follow with necessity that the answer to the second question should also be in the negative. The standard of thought applied to the first—the moral—question was simply to test the nature and the policies of the Communist government of China by the principles of Western morality. On the other hand, the second—the political—question had to be subjected to the complicated test of the interests involved and the power available on either side, and of the bearing of one or the other course of action upon these interests and power. The application of this test could well have led to the conclusion that it would be wiser not to deal with the Communist government of China. To arrive at this conclusion by neglecting this test altogether and answering the political question in terms of the moral issue was indeed a classic example of the "moralistic approach" to international politics.

The third case illustrates strikingly the contrast between realism and the legalistic-moralistic approach to foreign policy. Great Britain, as one of the guarantors of the neutrality of Belgium, went to war with Germany in August 1914 because Germany had violated the neutrality of Belgium. The British action could be justified either in realistic or legalistic-moralistic terms. That is to say, one could argue realistically that for centuries it had been axiomatic for British foreign policy to prevent the control of the Low Countries by a hostile power. It was then not so much the violation of Belgium's neutrality per se as the hostile intentions of the violator which provided the rationale for British intervention. If the violator had been another nation but Germany, Great Britain might well have refrained from intervening. This is the position taken by Sir Edward Grey, British Foreign Secretary during that period. Under Secretary for Foreign Affairs Hardinge remarked to him in 1908: "If France violated Belgian neutrality in a war against Germany, it is doubtful whether England or Russia would move a finger to maintain Belgian neutrality, while if the neutrality of Belgium was violated by Germany, it is probable that the converse would be the case." Whereupon Sir Edward Grey replied: "This is to the point." Yet one could also take the legalistic and moralistic position that the violation of Belgium's neutrality per se, because of its legal and moral defects and regardless of the interests at stake and of the identity of the violator, justified British and, for that matter, American intervention. This was the position which Theodore Roosevelt took in his letter to Sir Edward Grey of January 22, 1915:

> To me the crux of the situation has been Belgium. If England or France had acted toward Belgium as Germany has acted I should have opposed them, exactly as I now oppose Germany. I have emphatically approved your action as a model for what should be done by those who believe that treaties should be observed in good faith and that there is such a thing as international morality. I take this position as an American who is no more an Englishman than he is a German, who endeavors loyally to serve the interests of his own country, but who also endeavors to do what he can for justice and decency as regards mankind at large, and who therefore feels obliged to judge all other nations by their conduct on any given occasion.

This realist defense of the autonomy of the political sphere against its subversion by other modes of thought does not imply disregard for the existence and importance of these other modes of thought. It rather implies that each should be assigned its proper sphere and function. Political realism is based upon a pluralistic conception of human nature. Real man is a composite of "economic man," "political man," "moral man," "religious man," etc. A man who was nothing but "political man" would be a beast, for he would be completely lacking in moral restraints. A man who was nothing but "moral man" would be a fool, for he would be completely lacking in prudence. A man who was nothing but "religious man" would be a saint, for he would be completely lacking in worldly desires.

Recognizing that these different facets of human nature exist, political realism also recognizes that in order to understand one of them one has to deal with it on its own terms. That is to say, if I want to understand "religious man," I must for the time being abstract from the other aspects of human nature and deal with its religious aspect as if it were the only one. Furthermore, I must apply to the religious sphere the standards of thought appropriate to it, always remaining aware of the existence of other standards and their actual influence upon the religious qualities of man. What is true of this facet of human nature is true of all the others. No modern economist, for instance, would conceive of his science and its relations to other sciences of man in any other way. It is exactly through such a process of emancipation from other standards of thought, and the development of one appropriate to its subject matter, that economics has developed as an autonomous theory of the economic activities of man. To contribute to a similar development in the field of politics is indeed the purpose of political realism.

5. THE GREAT DEBATE: TRADITIONALISM VERSUS SCIENCE IN INTERNATIONAL RELATIONS

Morton A. Kaplan

THE TRADITIONALIST asserts that those who aspire to a "science" of politics insist upon precision, rigor, quantification, and general theory. The traditionalist further claims that the complexity of international politics is such that these goals cannot be attained nor the important questions of international politics be investigated by these means. Whether the charge is correct cannot be answered in general. The appropriate degree of theory and of precision depends both on the state of the discipline and on the subject matter.[1] Since I am most familiar with my

---

From *World Politics,* XVIII, No. 9 (October 1966), 7–20. Reprinted by permission of the author and publisher. Footnotes have been renumbered to appear in consecutive order.

MORTON A. KAPLAN (1921–   ) Professor of Political Science and Chairman of the Committee on International Relations, The University of Chicago. Author of *On Historical and Political Knowledge: An Inquiry into Some Problems of Universal Law and Human Freedom* (Chicago: University of Chicago Press, 1971); *Macropolitics: Essays on the Philosophy and Science of Politics* (Chicago: Aldine Publishing Company, 1968); *The Revolution in World Politics* (New York: John Wiley and Sons, 1962); *System and Process in International Politics* (New York: John Wiley and Sons, 1957); *Dissent and the State in Peace and War* (New York: Dunellen, 1970). Co-author, *The Political Foundations of International Law* (New York: John Wiley and Sons, 1961). Editor, *Great Issues of International Politics* (Chicago: Aldine Publishing Company, 1970); *New Approaches to International Relations* (New York: St. Martin's Press, 1968).

[1] The assertion that my *System and Process in International Politics* (New York 1957) attempts a completely deductive theory has been made both by Hedley Bull and by Stanley Hoffmann. Hoffmann apparently quotes *System and Process* to this effect ("The Long Road to Theory," *World Politics,* XI [April 1959], 357). And Bull, apparently relying upon Hoffmann, then uses the admitted fact that not all assertions of the models are rigorously deduced as a disproof of the claims made for the models ("International Theory: The Case for a Classical Approach," *World Politics,* XVIII [April 1966], 366–67, 371–72). Yet the first page of the preface—the page from which Hoffmann takes his quotations—which contains the paragraph describing what an ideal deductive theory would look like, includes as the last line of that paragraph the following sentence: "If 'theory' is interpreted in this strict sense, this book does not contain a theory." It then goes on to say, "If some of the requirements for a theory are loosened; if systematic completeness is not required; if proof of logical consistency is not required; if unambiguous interpretation of terms and laboratory methods of confirmation are not required; then this book is, or at least contains, a theory. This theory may be viewed as an initial or introductory theory of international

own work, I should like to consider it first in some detail and then to examine a number of other scientific approaches criticized by traditionalists. I shall try to show that fundamentally different enterprises are involved and that blanket analyses obscure more than they clarify.

The conception that underlies *System and Process* is fairly simple. If the number, type, and behavior of nations differ over time, and if their military capabilities, their economic assets, and their information also vary over time, then there is some likely interconnection between these elements such that different structural and behavioral systems can be discerned to operate in different periods of history. This conception may turn out to be incorrect, but it does not seem an unreasonable basis for an investigation of the subject matter. To conduct such an investigation requires systematic hypotheses concerning the nature of the connections of the variables. Only after these are made can past history be examined in a way that illuminates the hypotheses. Otherwise the investigator has no criteria on the basis of which he can pick and choose from among the infinite reservoir of facts available to him. These initial hypotheses indicate the areas of facts which have the greatest importance for this type of investigation; presumably if the hypotheses are wrong, this will become reasonably evident in the course of attempting to use them.

The models of *System and Process* provide a theoretical framework within which seemingly unconnected kinds of events can be related. A few examples of these can be given. For instance, it is asserted in the traditional literature that the framework of European international law is the product of a common civilization, culture, set of values, and personal ties. Our hypotheses indicate that the "balance of power" type of system is likely to motivate and reinforce the kinds of norms that were observed during the modern European "balance of power" period. If the traditionalist hypothesis is correct, then one would expect that international law would have been strongest in the earliest part of the modern European "balance of power" period, when, as a consequence of a common Catholicism and interrelated dynasticism, the cultural factors making for uniformity of norms would have been strongest. If the systems model is correct, then one would instead expect the norms to develop

---

politics." This qualification is repeated in the conclusion (pp. 245–46): "A complete and systematic statement of these assumptions has not been offered. One reason for this gap lies in the belief of the author that international politics, and social science generally, is so poorly developed that the construction of a precise deductive system would be more constrictive and misleading than enlightening, that, at this stage of development, some ambiguity is a good thing." I did believe, however, that the ambiguity could be reduced and that more disciplined reasoning and scientific method could be introduced into the study of international politics. *That* was what *System and Process* tried to do.

over time as the actors learned how these norms reinforced their common interests. One would also expect on the basis of the systems model that a number of these norms would receive less reinforcement in a loose bipolar system. No systematic study of these hypotheses has yet been carried out. Peripheral results from comparative studies directed to other aspects of "balance of power" behavior, however, indicate the likelihood that the systems explanation will account for the historic evidence better than the traditionalist one. The early evidence indicates that the norms were weaker in the earlier phases of the period. Such results are not conclusive. We may find still other "balance of power" systems in which our initial expectations are falsified. This would then create a new problem for investigation. However, the systematic nature of the systems hypotheses would make this kind of comparative analysis easier by providing a framework within which questions could be generated and research carried on. It is perhaps no accident that the first set of comparative theories of international relations was developed within a systems framework and not within a traditionalistic framework.

An illustration of the way in which systems models may be used to connect or to explain seemingly discordant facts may also be offered. According to the systems model of the "balance of power" system, alliances will be short in duration, shifting as to membership, and wars will be limited in objectives. The reason offered for this is that the need to maintain the availability of potential alliance partners is greater than the need for the additional assets that would result from the destruction of the defeated foe. If one looks at Europe after 1870, however, one finds a set of relatively permanent alliances centered on France and Germany which produced a war that, according to the standards of the time, was relatively unlimited. The models, however, are closed in such a way that public opinion does not interfere with the rationality of external decision-making. The seizure of Alsace-Lorraine by Germany after the war of 1870, as Bismarck foresaw, produced in France a desire for revenge that, despite German attempts to buy France off, made it impossible for France and Germany to be alliance partners in any serious sense. For this reason, Germany considered a preventive war against France. That Germany and France became the hubs of opposing alliances therefore is consistent with the model if the parameter change is taken into account. Since neither France nor Germany viewed the other as a potential alliance partner, the motivation that served to limit war would not have been operative with respect to these two nations. Although this is surely not a complete—nor even a "proved"—explanation of the events leading to the First World War, it does establish a consistency between the predictions of the model suitably adjusted for a changed parameter and the actual course of events. Thus the systems model has some additional explanatory power even for some nonconforming events.[2] It may be possible to offer similar explanations for other parameter changes. One would not expect that this could be done with respect to problems of system change involving the transformation rules of the system. If this were possible, we should have a general theory of the system rather than a set of comparative theories. Although it cannot be demonstrated that a general theory is impossible, the reasons for its lack of likelihood have been stated by me elsewhere." [3]

In addition to empirical investigations, the systems theory of international politics calls for the use of models. The reason for this is quite simple. Even statesmen make statements about the relationship of states. From what assumptions are such statements derived? This is often unclear. Are they correctly derived? Only a much more systematic statement of the assumptions and of the conditions under which they are proposed to apply permits any kind of answer. Under what conditions do the generalizations apply, if at all? How much difference does it make to add one state or two states to a five-state system and under what conditions? Is Arthur Burns correct in asserting that five is the optimal number for security, with declining security both below and above that number,[4] or is Kaplan correct in believing that five is the minimal lower bound for security but that security increases as the number of states is increased up to some as-yet-undiscovered upper bound? How many deviant states can a system tolerate? What degree of deviance is tolerable? Can deviance be accommodated so that deviant states are forced to behave as if they were merely security-oriented? How will changes in weapons systems affect the problem of stability? What of geographic constraints? To what extent do internal decision-making organs, either by facilitating or impeding concentration on problems of external concern or by influencing the speed of reaction time, affect the stability of the system?

Some of these questions can be explored at a theoretical level in terms of the consistency and implications of the basic assumptions. Computer realizations are helpful to this end. The relevance of the questions for the real world can be explored by means of historical comparative studies. If the theoretical model is stable and the historical system is not, this is

---

[2] It was long known that certain poisons produced death. It was not known, however, how they did so. Eventually chemists learned that when certain poisons entered the blood stream, they combined with the oxygen in the blood and thereby deprived vital organs of the oxygen necessary for life. Although the end result of the poisoning was long known, the chemical explanation contributes to knowledge. Under some circumstances it has important utility. For instance, if one knows the mechanism involved, it may be easier to find the antidote.

[3] *System and Process*, xvii–xviii.

[4] Arthur Lee Burns, "From Balance to Deterrence: A Theoretical Analysis," *World Politics*, IX (July 1957), 494–529.

an indication that some factor not taken account of in the theory is operating. If both systems are stable, it is possible that this may be so for reasons other than those contained in the assumptions. Possible responses to this proposition may be obtained either through more thorough research into particular systems or by means of additional comparative studies that may permit discrimination of the cases. Elucidation of the constraining parameters would likely require a large series of comparative studies. The degree of confidence we place in our studies will never approach that which the physicist has in the study of mechanics (although other areas of physics may present problems as bad as those of politics); but without theoretical models we are unable even to make the discriminations open to us and to explore these questions to the same degree of depth.[5]

International systems theory is designed to investigate problems of macrosystem structure. It is not, for instance, easily adaptable to the investigation of microstructural problems of foreign policy. Techniques in this area would involve closer analogies with histology than with macrosystem analysis. This is an area in which extensive knowledge of a specific course of events, immense accumulations of detail, sensitivity and judgment in the selection of relevant factors, and intuitive ability of a high order are extremely important. We cannot easily use comparative evaluation, for the large number of variables involved in such events would not be even closely paralleled in other cases. In this sense, histology has an advantage over political science, for the histologist can at least examine generically similar material time and time again. Although elements of these problems can be subjected to scientific analysis, in many cases the use of intuitive judgment outweighs that of demonstrable knowledge. In these last cases, the conclusions can often be communicated, though usually in poorly articulated form, but the means by which they were reached can be only badly misrepresented.

International systems theory, however, is only one of the scientific approaches to the subject matter of international politics. I hesitate to speak of the research of other scholars because I have not examined their work with the care required of a serious critic. Yet even superficial analysis would seem to indicate that the scientific approaches discussed together by Hedley Bull, for instance, have little in common.[6] They address themselves to different questions and use different methods. I shall try to indicate what some of these differences are—and my own attitude

---

[5] The problem of confirmation of systems models is explored in greater depth in Kaplan, "Some Problems of International Systems Research," in *International Political Communities* (New York 1966), 497–502.

[6] Pp. 361–77.

toward these other approaches—with the understanding that I do not consider myself an entirely competent judge.

Hedley Bull discusses Kaplan, Deutsch, Russett, Schelling, and various others as if they represented a sufficiently common position that similar criticisms would apply to all of them. Whereas I begin with a macrosystem analysis, however, Karl Deutsch proceeds with an inductive analysis based upon the quantification of the parameters of systems.[7] Whereas I study general system behavior, Deutsch studies the growth of community. Hedley Bull criticizes Karl Deutsch for counting all communications as if they were equal in some respect. Yet surely that is a most economical initial hypothesis. Unless Deutsch makes that assumption or a similar one, he can not discover whether such an item count will provide him with meaningful indicators for the growth of community.

In any event, it is rather discouraging to find Deutsch attacked because he does not differentiate messages according to criteria of importance. Deutsch developed his indices on the basis of a sophisticated set of hypotheses and after elaborate historical studies. If the indices prove not to be exceptionally useful, this will likely be uncovered by further empirical work. If further categorizations prove necessary—as they have, for instance, in assessing group differences in intelligence—empirical scientific work will no doubt establish this fact. If Haas is right that elite activity that produces institutions is more important than an increased flow of communications in establishing a pluralistic security community, the empirical evidence will likely indicate this also.[8] If differentiation of flows according to the kinds of systems they develop within —a systems orientation—is likely to make for finer discrimination, it is again the empirical scientific evidence and not abstract literary considerations that will establish this point.[9]

Russett uses still a different technique.[10] I believe that his fitting curves to data by means of quadratic equations is not suited to the data he uses. This, however, is true, if true at all, not on the basis of some general philosophical principle, but on the basis of a specific evelution of the use of the technique in terms of the subject matter to which it is

---

[7] "Toward an Inventory of Basic Trends and Patterns in Comparative and International Politics," *American Political Science Review*, LIV (March 1960), 34–57. See also Deutsch and others, *Political Community and the North Atlantic Area* (Princeton 1957); Deutsch, *Nationalism and Social Communication* (New York 1953); and Deutsch, *Political Community at the International Level* (Garden City 1954).

[8] Ernst Haas, "The Challenge of Regionalism," *International Organization*, XII (Autumn 1958), 440–58.

[9] For a responsible discussion of Deutsch's categories and techniques, see Ralph H. Retzlaff, "The Use of Aggregate Data in Comparative Political Analysis," *Journal of Politics*, XXVII (November 1965), 797–817.

[10] Bruce M. Russett, *Trends in World Politics* (New York 1965).

applied. I am also, for instance, skeptical of the techniques employed by Zaninovich in his *Empirical Theory of State Response,* with respect to the Sino-Soviet case.[11] Although I find his conclusions unexceptional —for instance, the conclusion that when two states are involved in a critical relationship, each will misperceive the intentions of the other —I do not find them particularly useful in the form in which they are applied. The phenomenon of mistaken perception is well known. As a mere phenomenon, it does not require further documentation. Nor in this abstract form does it add much to our understanding of the political process. It is not very useful for policy-makers either. It does not tell them what the misperceptions will be or the particular kinds of responses they will produce. Moreover, since most of the analysis is based upon the coding of public statements and editorials in the party newspapers, there is the additional danger that the public stance of the state will be misperceived by the investigator as its private one. Whether my judgment of the procedure is right or wrong, however, depends not upon the crude general propositions enunciated by the traditionalists but upon a specific analysis of the application of the methodology to a specific subject matter.

One may desire to raise questions about some of the simulations of international politics that are being carried on. Whether small group simulations reveal more about small groups simulating international relations than about the more complex pattern of international politics is, at the minimum, an open question. If simulation is a quite useful tool for generating hypotheses, it is likely much less useful for confirming them. Here the reader must be warned: I am not here offering an analysis of whether this is the case or not, and may merely be asserting my own prejudice.

Much of the criticism of the work of Thomas Schelling seems misguided. It is generally agreed that there are many interesting insights in Schelling's work;[12] but the traditionalists, e.g., Hedley Bull, sometimes object that the insights are not derived from game-theoretic methods. This argument is misleading; Schelling rarely uses mathematical game-theoretic methods. Most of his analysis is sociological; that is the root of his assertion that he desires to reorient game theory. On the other hand, although his insights in the usual case are not rigorously derived from game theory, it must be admitted that insights of this kind did not seriously begin to enter the literature until the questions posed by game-theoretic analysis directed attention to them.

Schelling is so identified with game theory by the traditionalists that he is credited with contributions he has not claimed. According to Hoff-

---

[11] Martin George Zaninovich, *An Empirical Theory of State Response: The Sino-Soviet Case* (Stanford 1964), mimeographed.

[12] Thomas C. Schelling, *The Strategy of Conflict* (Cambridge, Mass., 1960).

mann, "Until now game theory has . . . weaknesses that Schelling reviews. The main flaw is that game theory has dealt *only* [italics added] with zero-sum games. . . ." [13] It is not entirely unexpected that a political scientist would commit a technical error in the area of game theory. It is surprising, however, that one who presumes to evaluate the utility of that theory would make this elementary mistake. The point is covered in every treatise on the subject (and by Schelling), and there is a large literature on the subject. The mixed-motive game is one of the basic classifications of mathematical game theory. However, Hoffmann does not rest there. He continues, "Therefore, game theory applies only to a marginal and paradoxical case: pure conflict with limited stakes, i.e., the characteristic conflicts of moderate, balance-of-power, international systems." [14] Unfortunately, the "balance of power" case is neither paradoxical nor zero-sum. Moreover, although there are many mixed-motive games for which there are appropriate game-theoretic models, the "balance of power" case is not one of them. Game theory has only limited applicability to most problems of international politics, but we are hardly likely to learn from the traditionalists what these limits are and why they exist.

Although traditionalists quite often have accused those using scientific method of neglecting Aristotle's dictum to use those methods appropriate to the subject matter, I would contend that it is the user of scientific method who has more often observed the dictum. This is illustrated by the fact that so intelligent a student of politics as Hedley Bull, who openly recognizes the danger that he might be talking about discordant things, nonetheless falls into what I would call the trap of traditionalism: the use of overparticularization and unrelated generalization. Thus Bull lists highly disparate methods and subjects with minimal discussion and inadequate or nonexistent classification and applies to them extremely general criticisms. Such broad and universal generalizations are extremely difficult, if not impossible, to falsify. Who would deny that the complexity of the subject matter places constraints on what can be said? But different subject matters and different degrees of complexity require different tools of analysis and different procedures. The traditionalist, however, as in the case of Bull, does not discuss how or why the complexity of a specific subject impedes what kind of generalization, or how and in what ways generalizations should be limited. The traditional literature in international relations, even when it is directly concerned with the subject matter, is of much the same order: a great mass of detail to which absurdly broad and often unfalsifiable

[13] Stanley Hoffmann, *The State of War* (New York 1965), 205.
[14] *Ibid.*, 206.

generalizations are applied. Thus traditional "balance of power" theory is asserted to apply regardless of the number and kinds of states, variations in motivation, kinds of weapons systems, and so forth. Remarkably the same generalizations are asserted to apply not merely to the macrostructure of international politics but to the individual decisions of foreign policy. The generalizations are applied indiscriminately over enormous stretches of time and space. They are sufficiently loosely stated so that almost no event can be inconsistent with them.

And the vaunted sensitivity to history that the traditionalists claim—and that they deny to the modern scientific approaches—is difficult to find. Those traditionalists who have done a significant amount of historical research—and they are the exceptions—confine themselves largely to problems of diplomatic history that are unrelated to their generalizations about international politics, as in the case of Martin Wight, or to more specialized problems that are idiosyncratic. This is not an accident but is a direct product of the lack of articulated theoretical structure in the traditionalist approach. It is ironic that the traditionalists are so sure that they alone are concerned with subject matter that they are unaware of the extent to which those applying the newer approaches are using history as a laboratory for their researches. This development is unprecedented in the discipline and is a direct product of the concern of those using scientific approaches for developing disciplined and articulated theories and propositions that can be investigated empirically.

If those writers of the newer persuasion sometimes seem to ignore the traditional literature, it may not be entirely without good reason. Yet ignoring it is a mistake. There are honorable exceptions among the traditionalists, such as Raymond Aron, whose remarkable writings are surely useful to political scientists and whose methodology may not be quite so far removed from the newer scientific approaches as some traditionalists like to believe. Hedley Bull, one of the more vociferous critics of the newer approaches, has himself contributed a solid study of arms control to the literature.

The traditionalist seems to feel that scientific models are inapt for a political world in which surprises may occur. He seems to feel that scientific theories must achieve generality and completeness or lack rigor. This seems more like a seventeenth-century view of science than like a modern view.

Physical science presents analogies to the surprises that stem from parameter changes in social or political systems. One of these is the phenomenon of superconductivity under conditions of extreme temperature and pressure. The phenomena associated with superconductivity had not been predicted by the then current physical theories. Only after experimentation with extreme temperatures and pressures were the phenomena noticed. And only then did it become necessary to explain them. Whether a highly general theory comprehending all novel phenomena, of which superconductivity is merely an example, can be developed by physical theory is still open to question. For reasons already evident, such a general theory would be even more questionable in the area of international politics. Were someone to suggest to a physicist that the discovery of *novel phenomena* such as superconductivity which had not been predicted by previous theory established either the lack of rigor of previous theory or the inappropriateness of the methodology employed, the argument would be dismissed.

Another major charge made by the traditionalist against the newer methods is that since they use models, their practitioners are likely to mistake the models for reality. If the causal connection were not insisted on, I would not lightly deny the charge. There is a human tendency to reification. Surely the psychologists, sociologists, and anthropologists—and even the physicists, who know very little about politics—have a tendency to apply very simplified assumptions to very complex events. If, however, the traditionalist were to examine the propositions of the psychologists, for instance, he would find them no different from empirical generalizations—a category he likes. When a psychologist talks of projection or of a mirror image he is not, in the usual case, deriving these generalizations from an integrated theory, but is simply asserting an empirical generalization explicitly. The trouble with a generalization of this kind, apart from its general inapplicability, is that no context for its application is specified. Thus, as in the case of traditionalist arguments, it can be applied safely, for, in the form offered, it can never really be falsified.

On the other hand, it is natural to expect sophistication with respect to models from one who explicitly uses them. Only someone who has worked with models and the methodology of models knows how sensitive at least some models are to parameter adjustments. Thus a builder of models does not think of them as generally applicable. They are applicable only within a specified context; and it is extremely important to determine whether that context in fact exists. Moreover, the person who has worked with models usually has gone through the difficult task of trying to associate the parameters of the model with the real world. No one who has attempted this is likely to take it lightly.

I would argue that it is rather the traditionalist, whose assumptions are implicit rather than explicit and whose statements are made usually without reference to context, who is more likely to mistake his model for reality. Of course, even traditionalists are not likely to be as incautious as the historian Webster, who asserted that Castlereagh inherited his phlegmatic disposition from his mother who died when he was one year old. Yet the traditional literature of diplomatic history and international politics is filled with implicit assumptions as to motivation, interrelationships between variables, and so forth, that are implicit rather than specified, and the limits of application of which are never asserted. Even so careful and intelligent a traditionalist as George Kennan has made assertions about the likely effectiveness of United States aid in encouraging diversity and pluralism within the Soviet bloc which hardly seem to be sustained by the evidence.[15] Kennan did not explicitly articulate his model. He no doubt assumed that the provision of American aid provided the Polish government with an alternative to Soviet pressure. I would argue that had Kennan explicitly articulated his model, he might more likely have considered variables not included in his implicit model. Had he done so, he might have considered the possibility that the Polish government could argue to the Polish citizens that if the United States gave aid to Poland it must be a sign that the Polish regime was an acceptable regime. Therefore it would be unwise for the Polish citizen to oppose that regime or to expect even psychological aid from the United States in opposition. He also might have considered the hypothesis that the Polish leaders, as good Communists, and as a consequence of accepting American aid, might find it important to reassert at least some elements of Communist doctrine more strongly either to reassure themselves or to assure elements within the Polish Communist party whose support they needed that the leadership was not becoming a stooge for United States imperialism.

The probability that traditionalists will mistake their models for reality is further exemplified by Hedley Bull's criticisms of the new scientific approaches. Bull is so confident, on the basis of his premises, that those following the scientific method will engage largely in methodology both in their research and in their teaching, graduate and undergraduate, that he ignores the abundant evidence to the contrary. He himself admits that the other traditionalist critics of the new methods do not have adequate knowledge of these methods; yet he somehow fails to draw the inference from his own evidence that these critics have mistaken their implicit models for reality.

The traditional techniques with their inarticulated suppositions, their lack of specification of boundaries, and their almost necessary shifting of premises create a much greater danger that their implicit assumptions will automatically be applied to reality and a much greater sense of complacency than do scientific methods. I have no desire to be invidious, but, just as the traditionalists find it legitimate to characterize what they believe to be the inadequacies of the newer approaches, so it is equally

---

[15] "Polycentrism and Western Policy," *Foreign Affairs*, XLII (January 1964), 178.

legitimate to relate the defects of traditionalism to their sources. Bull, for instance, points out that English political science, as contrasted with American political science, remains committed to traditionalism. It is surely no secret that English political science is somewhat less than distinguished.

The traditionalists talk as if the newer methods have excluded philosophy as a tool for the analysis of international politics. Unfortunately few of them—again Raymond Aron is a conspicuous exception—have demonstrated any disciplined knowledge of philosophy; and many of them use the word as if it were a synonym for undisciplined speculation. There are many profound questions that in some senses are genuinely philosophical; the systems approach, among others, is related to a number of philosophical assumptions. The relationship between these philosophical assumptions and the validity of empirical theories is more complicated. It is entirely possible for an erroneous philosophy to furnish the ideas from which a valid empirical theory is derived. And it is dubious that the relationship between philosophical position and empirical theory is so direct—in either traditional or scientific approaches—that the arguments between or within competing approaches or theories can be settled by philosophical argument. There are, moreover, some important mistakes that ought to be avoided. Political theory ought not to be called philosophy merely because it is formulated by a man who is otherwise a philosopher unless the ideas have a genuine philosophical grounding. If the ideas are merely empirical propositions, as in the case of most philosophical statements used by traditionalists, they stand on the same footing as other empirical propositions. There is hardly much point in quoting one of the philosophers unless one understands him and can apply him correctly. I remember listening to a lecture by a well-known scholar, one cited by Bull as a good example of the traditionalist approach, who attempted to disprove Hegel's philosophy of history by showing that there were accidents in history. He was obviously unaware that for Hegel history was the realm of accident, that a major element of the Hegelian system involves the working out of necessity (often contrary to the wills of the actors) in a realm characterized by accident, and that, in any event, the whole matter was irrelevant to the point he thought he was making. Even if some matters of concern to international politics are profoundly philosophical, not all are. It is essential, if I may use that philosophical term inappropriately, to address the proper methods to the proper questions and not to make global statements about international politics, as do the traditionalists, which assume the relevance of the same melange of methods regardless of the type of question.

I have no doubt that the early attempts at a scientific approach to international politics are guilty of crudities and errors. It would be amazing—and I do not expect to be amazed—if the earliest hypotheses and models designed as tools for the orderly and comparative investigation of the history of international politics survive in their original form in the face of sustained empirical and methodological investigations. The self-corrective techniques of science will, however, likely sustain orderly progress in the discipline. The traditionalists are unlikely to be helpful in this task.

Having read the criticisms of the traditionalists, I am convinced that they understand neither the simpler assertions nor the more sophisticated techniques employed by the advocates of the newer methods. They have not helped to clarify the important issues in methodology; they have confused them. The traditionalists have accused those writers who advocate modern scientific approaches of using deterministic models despite explicit statements by those writers to the contrary. The traditionalists mistake explicitly heuristic models for dogmatic assertions. They mistake assertions about deductions within the framework of a model for statements about the open world of history. They call for historical research and do not recognize either that they have not heeded their own call or that they are merely repeating the words of the advocates of the newer approaches.

The traditionalists are often quite intelligent and witty people. Why then do they make such gross mistakes? Surely there must be something seriously wrong with an approach that devotes so much effort to such ill-informed criticism. One suspects that this sorry product is the consequence of the traditionlist view of philosophy as elegant but undisciplined speculation—speculation devoid of serious substantive or methodological concerns. Thus traditionalists repeat the same refrain like a gramophone endlessly playing a single record; that refrain is beautifully orchestrated, wittily produced, and sensitive only to the wear of the needle in the groove.

6. INTERNATIONAL STUDIES IN THE 1970s

Robert L. Pfaltzgraff, Jr.

E. H. CARR has suggested that "when the human mind begins to exercise itself in some fresh field, an initial stage occurs in which the element of wish or purpose is overwhelmingly strong, and the inclination to analyze facts and means weak or nonexistent." [1] Whatever the validity of this statement in the development of other disciplines, it describes the growth of international relations, especially in its formative years, as a discipline between the two world wars. [2] Although the study of international relations has always had a normative element, and the study of causes and resolution of conflict has been of continuing concern to students of international relations, the focus both of teaching and research has shifted, especially since World War II. The study of international relations has passed through three stages which may be characterized as utopian, realist, and behavioral or, stated differently, normative, empirical-normative, and behavioral-quantitative. [3] On the threshold of the 1970s, the study of international relations appears to be entering a fourth phase, which may be called "postbehavioral." [4] In this fourth stage,

"International Studies in the 1970's," by Robert L. Pfaltzgraff, Jr., is reprinted from the *International Studies Quarterly,* Vol. 15, No. 15 (March, 1971), 104–126. By permission of the publisher, Sage Publications, Inc.

ROBERT L. PFALTZGRAFF, JR. (1934–) Associate Professor of International Politics, The Fletcher School of Law and Diplomacy, Tufts University; Visiting Lecturer, Foreign Service Institute, Department of State; Deputy Director of the Foreign Policy Research Institute. Author of *Britain Faces Europe, 1957–1967* (Philadelphia: University of Pennsylvania Press, 1969); *The Atlantic Community: A Complex Imbalance* (New York: Van Nostrand Reinhold, 1969). Coauthor of *Contending Theories of International Relations* (Philadelphia: J. B. Lippincott Company, 1971).

[1] E. H. Carr, *The Twenty-Years' Crisis, 1919–1939* (New York: Harper and Row [Torchbooks], 1964), p. 4.

[2] See Kenneth W. Thompson, *Political Realism and the Crisis of World Politics* (Princeton: Princeton University Press, 1960); William T. R. Fox, *The American Study of International Relations* (Columbia: University of South Carolina Press, 1968), pp. 1–35.

[3] This is not to suggest that the concerns of the students of international relations during each of these stages have been mutually exclusive. Examples of each can be found at every stage of the development of international relations.

[4] For an examination of current trends in political science, see David Easton, "The New Revolution in Political Science," *American Political Science Review,* LXIII (December, 1969), 1051–1061. Because the study of international relations has been closely linked with political science, the methodological, conceptual, and substantive trends of political science can be expected, as they have in the recent past, to influence the development of international relations.

an effort will be made to synthesize concepts and findings from existing literature and to develop theories and methodologies "relevant" to major international issues facing mankind over the next decade, while at the same time pressing the quest for theories with greater explanatory and predictive capabilities. The period which lies ahead is likely to be characterized by a continued search for concepts and methodologies from other disciplines, and by attempts to engage in comparative studies at many levels and units of analysis, but also by a greater effort to bridge the gaps between normative and behavioral-quantitative theories, and between theory and policy.

CRITIQUE OF INTERNATIONAL RELATIONS THEORY

If by the end of the decade of the 1940s, political realism had largely replaced a utopian, or normative, orientation in the study of international relations, and thus the field had moved from its first to its second stage of development, a rising generation of scholars was no more satisfied with prevailing modes of analysis than its predecessors. Over the past two decades, much of the proliferating literature of international relations has reflected dissatisfaction with the state of the field.[5] In this literature, in academic discussion, and thus in the behavioral-quantitative stage of the development of international relations, the following critical themes were present:

(1) Earlier approaches had only limited ability to enable the researcher to identify and analyze important problems, since the research tools available to the practitioner of traditional research were crude. Even when traditionally oriented scholars had identified the most important problems, they had not stated them in such a way as to enhance the prospects for their investigation.

(2) Traditional theory has been based upon international systems which differed fundamentally from the contemporary international system. Because it does not adequately describe the contemporary system, it does not provide adequate conceptualization or hypotheses for the building of theory.

(3) The explanatory and predictive capacity of theories is limited. Therefore, much of what passes for international relations theory has little relevance to the scholar or policymaker, either for understanding the present or for predicting the future. The scholar, and especially the policymaker, therefore, is cast back upon pragmatic solutions for specific problems.

(4) Existing literature is full of untested and implicit assumptions about human behavior and international conduct.

---

[5] See Andrew M. Scott, *The Functioning of the International System* (New York: Macmillan Company, 1967), pp. 2–6.

(5) Many of the most widely used terms in international relations, such as balance of power and collective security, are used in virtually incompatible ways by scholars—and even by the same scholar. Such usage contributes not only to theoretical fuzziness, but to the difficulty of communications within the discipline.[6]

(6) Because research efforts have not been based upon powerful and broadly based theoretical frameworks, they have not contributed adequately to a cumulative literature of international relations. Because scholars have not addressed themselves to similar hypotheses and have assumed instead the uniqueness of events, they have not contributed to the building of a body of generalizations about international phenomena.

(7) The availability of quantitative methodologies and conceptual frameworks borrowed or adapted from other disciplines provides the tools for major breakthroughs in the building of theory. The advent of the computer and advanced technologies of information storage, retrieval, and analysis enhance the prospects for testing theory. Given the research techniques now available, the present generation of scholars has an opportunity to make a major contribution to international relations theory. Since the conduct of research in international relations has been strongly influenced by younger scholars impatient with the conventional wisdom of the past, there emerged both a "credibility gap" and a "generation gap" in the study of international relations.

Although the assumptions of individual traditional writers were sometimes not explicitly stated, the "conventional wisdom" of international relations has contained a series of assumptions which scholars over the past generation have questioned and sought to subject to more systematic examination:

(1) It was assumed that nations were sovereign in their domestic affairs and that foreign powers could not exert major internal influence upon them. If such a model corresponded to the international system before the twentieth century, it does not fit the contemporary international system. In fact, there is a burgeoning literature whose authors seek to examine the "linkage" between national and international systems, and to examine what are called "penetrated" political systems whose domestic policies are influenced by developments beyond their frontiers.[7]

---

[6] See Inis L. Claude, Jr., *Power and International Relations* (New York: Random House, 1962), pp. 11–39; Ernst B. Haas, "Balance of Power: Prescription or Propaganda," *World Politics,* V (1953), 442–447.

[7] See, e.g., James N. Rosenau, ed., *Linkage Politics: Essays on the Convergence of National and International Systems* (New York: Free Press, 1969); "Compatibility, Consensus, and an Emerging Political Science of Adaptation," *American Political Science Review, LXI* (December, 1967), 983–988; and Wolfram F. Hanrieder,

(2) Decision-making units, it was assumed, were not subject to major internal strains and conflicts as to objectives, policies, and the nature of the national interest. Especially since World War II, however, literature on foreign policy has accorded a position of considerable prominence to the domestic factors which impinge upon foreign relations.[8]

(3) The traditional assumption was that only the nation-states could be the actors of international politics. The rise of international organization at the global and regional level, the increasing importance of the multinational corporation, the expansion of transnational contacts have given a new set of dimensions to international relations which has been reflected in the literature.

(4) Political behavior in an international context, it was once assumed, differs fundamentally from political behavior within the national unit. Therefore, there was justification for the separation of studies of international political behavior from the analysis of political behavior within the national unit. The distinction between domestic and international behavior stemmed principally from a model in which decision-making was centralized. Governments within the national units held a monopoly of the coercive capabilities of the units, in contrast with the decentralization of decision-making and the coercive capabilities within the international system. Increasingly, scholars have stressed the similarities rather than differences between the political process at the national and international levels. Scholarly interest in the political systems of less-developed areas, where tribal loyalties often compete with modernizing forces and effective political power remains decentralized, has contributed to a reassessment of older notions about the uniqueness of international political processes.

In short, much of the critique of international relations theory has been based both upon a questioning of the relevance of older assumptions and matters of technique and methodology. Such dissatisfaction has led to a proliferation of literature designed to remedy perceived deficiencies in the study of international relations.

"Compatibility and Consensus: A Proposal for the Conceptual Linkage of External and Internal Dimensions of Foreign Policy," *American Political Science Review,* LXI (December, 1967), 971–982.

[8] See, e.g., Gabriel Almond, *The American People and Foreign Policy* (New York: Harcourt, Brace and World, 1950). For a more recent example of such literature, see James N. Rosenau, ed., *Domestic Sources of Foreign Policy* (New York: Free Press, 1967).

TRENDS AND PROBLEMS

The basic trends which have characterized international relations in its behavioral-quantitative stage may be summarized as follows:

(1) the adaptation of theories, propositions, conceptual frameworks, methodologies, and ideas from other disciplines, including, in particular, sociology, social psychology, management-administrative science, psychology, anthropology, economics, and mathematics;

(2) an attempt to relate phenomena from other disciplines to allegedly similar phenomena at the international level, which takes the two mutually reinforcing forms of the examination of international phenomena by (a) the use of conceptual frameworks, theories, and propositions by which similar phenomena in other disciplines have been examined; and (b) the comparative analysis of phenomena such as conflict, integration, bargaining, negotiation, and deterrence in an international context and other fields;

(3) a focus upon problems of units of analysis, including attempts to distinguish conceptually and methodologically among such units as the individual decision-maker, the decisional unit, the state, international subsystems, and the international system itself;

(4) a concern about problems of level of analysis, including an effort to draw clear-cut distinctions between macro-theory or grand theory, and the so-called middle ranges of theorizing, with scholars attempting to focus explicitly upon one or the other level of theorizing;

(5) a greater effort to become comparative *within* the study of international relations, a tendency having essentially two dimensions: (a) greater comparative analysis of phenomena in a contemporary context, and (b) systematic attempts to compare various aspects of international relations in a historic context and to draw comparisons between contemporary and historic international phenomena;

(6) a focus upon problems of data collection, an attempt to exploit existing data more skillfully, to develop new resources, and to build archives or data banks equipped with facilities for the storage and retrieval of materials for scholarly use;

(7) an increase in the range of methodologies, but a lack of consensus as to those most appropriate for the study of international phenomena; and

(8) a more conscious effort to link research to theory-building, including the development of criteria of relevance for research, the statement of problems and their investigation in such a fashion as to make research replicable by other scholars; and an attempt to develop knowledge that is cumulative.

The problems of scope, methodology, the nature of theory, and the relevance of other disciplines to the study of international relations are by no means resolved. Critics of certain of the trends outlined above have expressed doubts about the extent to which events or other political phenomena can be treated as similar and the ability of the researcher to make hypotheses operational. Skepticism remains as to whether the most important problems of international relations can be made operational so that indicators of a quantitative nature can be developed.[9] Dogmatism, either "traditional" or "behavioral," does little to enhance the development of international relations. Such dogmatism, as well as the focus upon questions of method and scope, bespeaks the uncertainty of students of international relations about the appropriate techniques and focal points for analysis. The issue is not *whether* one methodology or another, one form of theorizing or another, one analytic focal point or another, is relevant. Far from being mutually exclusive, alternative methodologies and research interests have the potential of becoming mutually reinforcing and thus contributing to the advance of knowledge.[10] The question is less one of their appropriateness, than of the extent to which one methodology or approach to theory fulfills the specific research task set for it by the individual scholar.[11]

Several major focal points of research over the past generation are indicative of the interests of scholars in the behavioral-quantitative stage of international relations. General systems theory, theories of conflict, decision-making, and game theory are illustrative of borrowings from other disciplines. General systems theory, for example, has had a major impact upon theorizing efforts at a macro-level as well as upon the middle-range theories of decision-making, conflict, and integration. Writings in conflict and integration are illustrative of the growth of both a comparative and a quantitative focus, and of the rising interest in the

---

[9] For an examination of this debate, see Klaus Knorr and James N. Rosenau, "Tradition and Science in the Study of International Politics;" Hedley Bull, "International Theory: The Case for a Classical Approach;" Morton A. Kaplan, "The New Great Debate: Traditionalism vs. Science in International Relations;" J. David Singer, "The Incompleat Theorist: Insight without Evidence;" Marion J. Levy, Jr., " 'Does It Matter if He's Naked?' Bawled the Child?" in Klaus Knorr and James N. Rosenau, eds., *Contending Approaches to International Politics* (Princeton: Princeton University Press, 1969), pp. 3–110.

[10] See Johan Galtung, "The Social Sciences: An Essay on Polarization and Integration," in Knorr and Rosenau, eds., *op. cit.*, pp. 243–285.

[11] There is, of course, a need for criteria both for the establishment of research agendas and for the conduct of research itself. Given the differing conceptions of the nature of theory and the disparate research and methodological interests of students of international relations, prospects for reaching agreement upon such criteria are not great.

comparison of such phenomena in an international context with supposedly similar phenomena in other contexts. Writings in these fields, as well as those utilizing systems theory, show evidence of the growth of interest in broadening both the data base and the focus of concern, not only to comparative materials, but also to points of time in the recent and distant past. Studies utilizing general systems theory and decision-making theory, in particular, are indicative of the concern with the development of more explicitly defined units of analysis.

In both political science and international relations, theorizing efforts of the past generation have produced macro-theories, or grand theories, within which major categories of variables can be analyzed. In political science, both Almond's and Easton's formulations provide schema which include major categories of variables. In international relations, realist theory and general systems theory represent approximations to macro-theory.[12] Realism is a grand theorizing effort, because its proponents have generally sought to isolate one or a few variables capable of explaining and predicting a broad range of international behavior. In addition to its focus on power as a crucially important variable, realism provided frameworks for the analysis both of international politics and of foreign policy. At the level of the international system, realist writers made use of a framework based upon balance of power in many respects similar to the balance of power model subsequently developed more formally by Morton A. Kaplan. At the national level of analysis, realists were concerned with the elements of national power and for comparative purposes developed a classificatory scheme for the analysis of the respective capabilities of nations. The proponents of realism were not totally unaware of what J. David Singer has termed the "level of analysis problem" in international relations;[13] they concerned themselves with analysis both at the level of interaction between and among states, and with the behavior of individual states and their foreign policies.

More recently, students who have utilized general systems theory have sought not only to develop more clearly delineated levels of analysis, but to set forth a framework broadly enough based to encompass most, if not all, international behavior. If realism brought to bear materials and insights from history as well as other disciplines—including geography, strategic studies, economics, and political science—general systems theory

---

[12] The word "theory" itself has been used in several ways in the field of international relations, and there is disagreement among scholars about the nature of theory.

[13] See J. David Singer, "The Level-of-Analysis Problem in International Relations," Klaus Knorr and Sidney Verba, eds., *The International System: Theoretical Essays* (Princeton: Princeton University Press, 1961), pp. 77–92.

provides a framework for the utilization of data, concepts, and propositions from many disciplines. But realism and general systems theory differ in that the former seeks to achieve great explanatory and predictive capacity from power as a variable, while general systems theory provides a framework for the analysis of relationships among variables and seeks to develop explanatory and predictive constructs.

Other theorizing efforts represent "islands" of theory which may (or may not) be linked one day into a grand theory of international relations. How such linking will take place, whether by the enlargement of existing "islands" or new "islands" of theory, or by a major breakthrough toward a macro-theory within which middle-range theories can be linked, is an object of debate among social scientists. It is a debate which remains unresolved as the study of international relations enters its fourth stage.

Given the focus of interest over the past decade, it is possible to suggest several trends in international relations which will be operative in the fourth, or "postbehavioral" stage. Such trends are likely to reflect several major problems confronting international relations. They include

(1) not only the continuing effort to delineate the nature and scope of international relations, but also an attempt to establish international relations more firmly as an "autonomous" field of study;

(2) the kinds of efforts appropriate to the building of theories with greater explanatory and predictive capacity;

(3) the methodological tools appropriate for research, and especially the relationship between quantitative and qualitative research;

(4) the division of labor between "basic" and "applied" research and the question of the "relevance" of international relations research to the crucial international problems of the next decade; and

(5) efforts to develop more precise linkages between various levels of analysis (or "actors") along the continuum from the microcosmic (the individual person) to the macrocosmic (the international system).

The development and exploitation of new methodologies for research, as well as new research and substantive interests, have given new stature to international relations as a field of study. Students in other disciplines have also focused upon problems in international relations. Students in such disciplines as sociology or psychology who study conflict will continue to center their efforts at least in part upon conflict in an international context. Ideally, international relations provides the framework for an emerging discipline which integrates concepts, propositions, and methodologies from many disciplines and develops whatever concepts, propositions, and methodologies may be relevant specifically to the study of problems at the international level.[14] Ultimately, international relations may become a discipline which incorporates, builds upon, and synthesizes insights discovered by most, if not all, of the social sciences.[15] It is possible to envisage such a development in international relations in the stage which it is now entering.

Given the continuation and even the strengthening of international relations as a field of study, several substantive interests are likely to be dominant. Because of the *raison d'être* of international relations from its early years, the problems of war and peace can be expected to continue to attract principal attention. In particular, students of international relations are likely to retain an interest in the problem of conflict, which has been of central concern since its beginning as an organized field of study. In the years ahead, the study of conflict will differ from earlier approaches by the techniques, methodologies, conceptual frameworks, and data bases utilized to build theory. For example, the research of neurophysiologists on the midbrain and forebrain relating to how inputs such as injury, ablation, and electrical stimulation produce passivity and rage in animals may lead to advances in knowledge about conflict. In addition, the utilization of economic models to develop exchange or barter ratios for pairs of noneconomic goods, together with the utilization of insights from psychology about personality theory and the effects of organizational variables upon social and political behavior, may contribute to a greater understanding of several important problems of international relations, such as conflict, community-building, and decision-making.[16]

The study of integration, of concern to students of international relations ever since the work of David Mitrany in the period between the two world wars, is likely to attract the attention of not a few scholars. Over the past generation, the creation of international organizations at the global and regional levels not only contributed to the rise in interest

---

[14] E. R. Platig, *International Relations Research: Problems of Evaluation and Advancement* (Santa Barbara, Calif.: Clio Press, for the Carnegie Endowment for International Peace, 1967), pp. 26–44.

[15] One contemporary student of international relations, Johan Galtung has suggested: "One may say that the relationship between international relations and political science is the same as the relationship between sociology and psychology: it is the transition from the meticulous study of one unit at the time to the study of the interaction structure between the units that characterizes the relation between these pairs of sciences." Johan Galtung, "Small Group Theory and the Theory of International Relation," Morton A. Kaplan, ed., *New Approaches to International Relations* (New York: St. Martin's Press, 1968), p. 271.

[16] See Walter Isard, in association with Tony E. Smith, Peter Isard, Tze Hsiung Tung, and Michael Dacey, *General Theory: Social, Political, Economic and Regional* (Cambridge, Mass.: MIT Press, 1969).

in the study of integration, but also provided an important source of data for scholarly investigation. The growing importance of the international corporation adds yet another dimension to the study of integration, and can be expected to become the object of scholarly investigation by students of integration at the international level. Existing theories of political integration owe a considerable intellectual debt to earlier studies of nationalism, as well as to cybernetics and systems theory. The study of the normative conditions for political community, characteristic of the study of international relations in its first stage, has given way to specific case studies and comparative analyses of integration, at both the regional and global levels. Like conflict, the study of integration cuts across the traditional boundaries of political science, and serves as a link as well to the work of scholars in other disciplines.

In the integration literature, there is need for greater definitional and conceptual clarity. This is a task to which students of international relations can be expected to turn their attention in the next decade. Existing integration models will be decomposed and, where possible and feasible, made operational so that they may be tested. The achievement of greater agreement among writers about the nature of integration, its necessary components, and the stages and transformation rules by which it is achieved, would contribute to major breakthroughs in knowledge about the building and disintegration of political communities.

Students of integration at the international level, from Mitrany to Deutsch, have had as a major concern transnational forces. Although our knowledge about the precise effect of such forces upon national foreign policies is not great, few students would deny their importance to the policymaker, and hence the need for their inclusion in international studies. In the next decade, the number and importance of transnational actors, especially in the form of the multinational corporation, can be expected to grow. The fact that the majority of nation-states have annual GNPs which are less than the total assets of the leading multinational corporations is but one indicator of the emerging importance of this sector of international business. The multinational corporation as a catalyst for international integration or the reinforcement of residual nationalism, its implications for international monetary policy and for alignment patterns of nation-states, is an appropriate and likely focal point for scholarly investigation in the 1970s.[17]

---

[17] See, for example, Sidney E. Rolfe, *The International Corporation*, XXIInd Congress of the International Chamber of Commerce, Istanbul, May 31–June 7, 1969; Jack N. Behrman, *Some Patterns in the Rise of the Multinational Enterprise* (Chapel Hill: University of North Carolina Press, 1969); Werner J. Feld, *Transnational Business Collaboration among Common Market Countries: Its Implication for Political Integration* (New York: Praeger Publishers, 1970); C. F. Kindleberger, ed.,

THE FOCUS OF INTERNATIONAL RELATIONS STUDIES

If the thrust of scholarly literature and thought in the policy community has been the building of political units beyond the nation-state, there is evidence that scholars and policymakers alike have neglected one of the most important phenomena of the past decade, namely, the emergence of centrifugal forces within the existing national units. Neither the so-called developed nations nor the developing states have been immune to the rise of linguistic-ethnic nationalism. Even units such as Great Britain, France, and the United States, where the literature of political science long ago dismissed forces making for separateness in favor of assumptions about the homogeneity of population and the "melting pot," have faced disintegrative elements. Other countries, including, for example, Canada, Belgium, Nigeria, India, Pakistan, Vietnam, and Cyprus, have been beset with deep cleavages resulting in separatist movements. If the decade following World War II was characterized by a movement toward regional organization, we have now entered a period of dissatisfaction of peoples around the world with the political units in which they live. Although the causes of this ferment are complex, those who express dissatisfaction with the status quo seek (1) to gain a greater voice in the decision-making process of existing units; (2) to achieve greater decentralization of power; or (3) to replace existing units with wholly new structures. It is conceivable that we have entered a period of opposition to the bigness of units which reflect the impersonal forces of bureaucracy and technology. As the world approaches the year 2000, we face several conflicting forces, some giving impetus to larger political units, others contributing to the perpetuation of existing political units; and still others enhancing the prospects for the fragmentation of present units. The study of such forces, together with the creation of political forms which reconcile the need for bigness with the desire of peoples for greater freedom from centralized controls, is a task which will confront both scholars of international relations and policymakers over the decade ahead.

COMPARATIVE INTERNATIONAL STUDIES

The effort to examine linkages between foreign policy and domestic policy, as well as the importance attached to an understanding of both the domestic and international determinants of foreign policy, is illustra-

---

The International Corporation (Cambridge: The MIT Press, 1970); Endel J. Kolde, *International Business Enterprise* (Englewood Cliffs, N. J.: Prentice-Hall, 1968); Sidney Rolfe and Walter Damm, eds., *The Multinational Corporation in the World Economy* (New York: Praeger Publishers, 1970); Virgil Salera, *Multinational Business* (Boston: Houghton Mifflin Company, 1969).

tive of the growth of interest in comparative international studies. In the stage which international relations research is now entering, greater emphasis is likely to be placed, in particular, on the comparative study of foreign policy, although such interest is by no means new to international relations. The quest for theoretical frameworks for decision-making and notably the conceptualization and research nearly a generation ago of Richard C. Snyder [18] and his associates, as well as more recent efforts such as those of Wolfram F. Hanrieder and James N. Rosenau [19] are indicative of such interest. In the 1970s, the study of foreign policy can be expected to be subjected to conceptual and research tendencies similar to those which have characterized research elsewhere in the field.

Closely related to the comparative study of foreign policy is the need for a theory of strategic policy. Although the study of military strategy and the development of strategic theories has been a major concern of the scholarly community since World War II, and although the role of power in international behavior has been the focal point of much of international relations theorizing, there has been, with the notable exception of Kolodziej,[20] little effort to create frameworks for the comparative study of strategic policy or to employ such frameworks for systematic examination including several national units. Such a study could be conducted either as part of a larger model of international interaction, or as an important component of a decision-making framework. More reliable knowledge about the relationship between military force and other national capabilities, the development of strategic doctrine, and the propensity of nations to use specific types of power unilaterally or in collaboration with other nations would represent a significant contribution to international relations theory. If the study of foreign policy continues to become more comparative, we may expect similar trends in the study of national security policy.

Over the past decade, the tendency toward a more comparative focus in international relations research has been manifested in the growth of interest in cross-national analyses at the subnational level.[21] Such prob-

---

[18] See Richard C. Snyder, H. W. Bruck and Burton Sapin, eds., *Foreign Policy Decision-Making* (New York: Free Press of Glencoe, 1963).

[19] See Hanrieder, *op. cit.*, James N. Rosenau, "External Influences on the Internal Behavior of States," R. Barry Farrell, ed., *Approaches to Comparative and International Politics* (Evanston, Ill.: Northwestern University Press, 1966), pp. 27–92; James N. Rosenau, *Comparative Foreign Policy—Fad, Fantasy, or Field.* Paper prepared for presentation at the Conference-Seminar of the Committee on Comparative Politics, University of Michigan, 1967.

[20] For a notable exception, see Edward A. Kologziej, "Contemporary International Relations and Military Power: A Comparative Approach," mimeo. (University of Virginia, 1968).

lems include ecological change and its implications for the social and political order, urban studies, and the political values of elites. The growth of issue areas of common concern to postindustrial, industrial, or industrializing societies is likely to accelerate the tendency toward comparative studies of problems which until recently have not been considered central to the field of international studies.

As in the past, students of international relations will be faced both with too much and too little data for the validation of theories. On the one hand, vast amounts of data have always been available to the student of politics. On the other hand, the development of quantitative research techniques, together with elaborate theoretical frameworks, increases the need for large new amounts of data. Many of the most important kinds of data relevant, for example, to the study of comparative foreign policy (including health records of decision-makers) [22] are not easily gathered, and, in fact, may never be available to the scholar. This, in turn, will increase the need for indirect or "unobtrusive" measures of political behavior.[23]

Undoubtedly the development of new techniques for information storage and analysis will help to ease the problems of data availability. Data banks, linked by computer consoles, are making new data archives available to researchers in many parts of the world. Data generated for one project, contributed to a data bank, become available to other researchers. Technically advanced storage and retrieval systems now make it possible to desensitize data from governmental sources for the use of the scholarly community. The creation of a national archive consisting of data from government sources would contribute greatly to the conduct of research in international relations and the other social sciences. Such a project, funded by the U.S. government, deserves official consideration at the highest level. It has been estimated that, in the State Department alone, "original" items and distributed copies of "communications" were on the order of 64 million in one year.[24] Such archives, to the extent

---

21 See, for example, Robert T. Holt and John E. Turner, *The Methodology of Comparative Research* (New York: Free Press, 1970).

22 However, there are two volumes of potential use in a study of decision-making which take account of the medical histories of key participants. They include Hugh L'Etang, *The Pathology of Leadership* (London: William Heinemann Medical Books, Ltd., 1969); Lord Moran, *Churchill: Taken from the Diaries of Lord Moran, The Struggle for Survival, 1940–1965* (Boston: Houghton Mifflin Company, 1966).

23 See Eugene J. Webb, Donald T. Campbell, Richard D. Schwartz, and Lee Sechrest, *Unobtrusive Measures: Non-reactive Research in the Social Sciences* (Chicago: Rand McNally and Company, 1966).

24 Willard Fazan, "Federal Information Communities: the Systems Approach." Paper prepared for the annual meeting of the American Political Science Association

that they lessened the need for the collection of new data for research projects, would lower the cost of conducting research and bring a wider range of research problems within the capabilities of the individual scholar. One of the factors which undoubtedly contributed to quantitative research was the unprecedented availability of large-scale funds, without which such research would have been all but impossible. If the decade of the 1970s is a period of reduced foundation and government emphasis upon international affairs research funding, the need for data archives becomes even more vital if the cost of such research is to be reduced to fit slimmer research budgets and grants.

The existence of the computer has already enhanced man's ability to engage in the quantitative and qualitative analysis of political materials and the testing of theories containing causal and noncausal relationships among many variables. Although aggregate analysis has been utilized in the examination of relations among nations, there is scope for the application of such techniques and methodologies to phenomena such as violence, using data about units within nations which may be more readily available. In the 1970s, such research is likely to be conducted. At this stage, however, there is no widespread consensus within the academic community about the extent to which aggregate analysis will contribute significantly to the development of international relations theory.

It is not difficult to anticipate greater efforts to develop more refined indicators and to introduce a greater qualitative element to quantitative studies. The quest for a greater balance between quantitative and qualitative theory-building efforts can be expected to have important implications for the teaching of international relations. One example will suffice. In the postwar period, the so-called area programs took hold in political science and international relations programs in American universities. Such programs developed at a time increasing interest in both the official and the private sectors in international affairs. Because of their emphasis not only on governmental systems but also on the intellectual and political history, literature, language, and economic problems of specified regions, such programs attracted students preparing themselves for academic careers and persons in training for governmental and business careers abroad. In recent years, the orientation of international relations toward a more comparative and empirical focus has served to diminish interest in area programs, as the emphasis of academic training in international relations shifted toward the development of techniques and methods for the examination of political phenomena, such as conflict and

---

(September, 1966). Quoted in Davis B. Bobrow and Judah L. Schwartz," "Computers and International Relations," Bobrow and Schwartz, eds., *Computers and the Policy-Making Community: Applications to International Relations* (Englewood Cliffs, N. J.: Prentice-Hall, 1968), p. 9.

integration, on a comparative basis which cuts across older delineations both geographically and academically. (In addition, of course, area programs have been affected by reduced government funding.) Nevertheless, a regional focus is useful to the extent that data about problems under examination can be found only in one region.

Over the next decade, skepticism about the utility of area studies may be replaced by a growing awareness of their potential qualitative contribution to the quantitative study of political phenomena. For example, the area specialist is likely to have expertise needed both to propose hypotheses and to interpret the findings of persons engaged in bivariate or multivariate analysis. The area specialist may be able to give both meaning to the correlations presented by quantitatively oriented students of politics, and a qualitative dimension to the quantitative flows of information and transactions which are contained in certain of the literature on integration, conflict, and alignment.[25] Area specialists can bring an in-depth dimension to our knowledge of international processes, and make us properly cautious about drawing generalizations.

In the third stage of the development of international relations, the focus of research upon empirical-analytic theory has contributed to a reduction in interest among scholars and policymakers in each other's immediate problems, although much of the funding of social science research in the behavioral sciences has come from the U.S. government. To the policymaker charged with the formulation of immediate responses to pressing problems, the methodology-laden writings of international relations scholars sometimes appear to provide few, if any, solutions, even though much of the research in the field has been focused upon issues of war and peace which have relevance to the policymaker. For their part, many scholars are concerned with basic research and long-range problems rather than with offering solutions to the pressing problems which governments face from day to day. Both because of research techniques and problem orientation, much of international relations research may appear not only unintelligible but also irrelevant to the policymaker. Nevertheless, there is considerable evidence to suggest that the policy community has made some use of academic writings. In particular, the development in international relations of a subfield in strategic affairs, especially deterrence and defense, has furnished a body of literature upon which policymakers have called for insights.

---

[25] For a recent critique of such literature and an attempt to engage in qualitative analysis of transnational interaction and integration in Europe, see Carl J. Friedrich, *Europe: An Emergent Nation?* (Boston: Little, Brown and Company, 1969), pp. 24–25. See also Oran R. Young, *Systems of Political Science* (Englewood Cliffs, N. J.: Prentice-Hall, 1967), pp. 60–62.

THE FUTURE OF INTERNATIONAL RELATIONS THEORY

The longer-range outcome of basic research, including theory-building and testing, if the proponents of such research have their way, will be to produce a body of knowledge which will explain and perhaps even predict political phenomena. For example, it may eventually be possible to specify the conditions essential to political integration within a national or international context, or it may be possible to state with a greater degree of precision within carefully specified parameters, the conditions which give rise to particular forms of international conflict. If the study of international relations theory reaches this stage of development, we will have achieved an understanding of those international phenomena deemed most important to scholars. In addition, we will have developed a body of theories of considerable importance to the building of a new science of international relations. Although the quest for such an understanding of international phenomena is likely to be pressed in the 1970s, the research conducted thus far holds promise of only limited success in reaching such a goal in the foreseeable future.

If it were possible to develop and test theories, for example, about such phenomena as political integration or international conflict, it might be possible to set forth a series of "if-then" propositions relevant to the needs of both scholars and policymakers. For example, a greater understanding of the essential conditions for integration or conflict would make possible the prediction of alternative outcomes of various policy choices, since certain kinds of policy choices could be expected to produce certain kinds of outcomes. In short, with the development of a body of empirical-analytic theory, the problems of concern to scholars would have relevance to the interests of policymakers. A new linkage between international relations theory and policy formulation would have been forged.

The continued quest for "relevance" in international relations research can be expected to lead to a greater understanding of a fundamental relationship between basic and applied research devoted to matters of policy.

The literature of international relations, traditional and contemporary, qualitative and quantitative, contains assumptions and conclusions which have relevance to the policymaker. Policy decisions are affected by the underlying assumptions of the policymaker. For this reason there is need to engage in a systematic examination of the assumptions which guide policymakers. Therefore, the statements of policymakers and the memoirs of statesmen should be analyzed in order to develop a checklist of assumptions which guide their thought on policy. An effort should be made to match such assumptions, as well as policies, with assumptions and policies contained in theoretically oriented literature of international relations. A major systematic effort is needed to make international relations literature, especially the writings of the past generation, more relevant to the policymaker. An inventory and matching of major assumptions, theories, and findings about international phenomena from policy statements and the literature of international relations would enhance the relevance of academic research to the needs of the policymaker. Such an inventory would contribute to a greater understanding of the current status of international relations theory and provide an indication of those areas where concentrated new efforts are needed.

Of the highest importance to a study of international relations which purports to be "relevant" is the development of conceptual and methodological tools to anticipate change, for change must be anticipated if it is to be moderated for beneficial purposes. The speed of change as a result of technology has become a major concern of political leaders everywhere. Changes in the nature of the nation-state and the transformation of the international system make urgent the development of more systematic knowledge about the future. In the development of weapons systems, in the designing of policies, whether in foreign affairs or in the urban field, an understanding of future technological developments is of crucial importance.[26] Such knowledge is needed if governments are to develop means to influence change.

Although for centuries men have attempted to set forth their conceptions of the future, the need for more systematic forecasts has grown as the lead time for policy planning, the complexity of issues facing policymakers, and the urgency of problems have increased. The result has been the emergence of the "futurologist," who seeks to "invent the future" by engaging in technological forecasting. If technological forecasting can clarify the choices available to nations by reducing uncertainty about the future, it will contribute to innovative efficiency by making it possible to calculate more accurately the lead time and the resources needed for alternative policy choices. It may lead also to a more precise understanding of the outcomes of alternative policy choices. The urgency of problems facing political systems, advanced and less-developed, together with the quest for a more "relevant" field of inquiry, could combine over the next decade to give increasing impetus to the development within international relations of a subfield called "futurology."

This is not to suggest that it is even dimly foreseeable that theories of international relations will achieve a level of predictability which will make possible a high degree of specificity of alternative policy choices. To

---

[26] As a writer in the *New York Times* of February 19, 1970, has suggested: "Because of the lead-time in building new strategic systems, the decisions we make today substantially determine our military posture—and thus our security—five years from now. This places a premium on foresight and planning."

expect a high level of predictability in international relations theory, given the many variables which must be considered until and unless more parsimonious and reliable theories are developed, would be to anticipate from international relations theories a level of performance which exceeds even theories in the physical sciences. As Morton Kaplan has suggested:

> Modern theoretical physical science has reared its present lofty edifice by setting itself problems that it has the tools or techniques to solve. When necessary, it has limited ruthlessly the scope of its inquiry. It has not attempted to predict the path a flipped chair will take, the paths of the individual particles of an exploded grenade, or the paths of the individual molecules of gas in a chamber. In the last case, there are laws dealing with the behavior of gases under given conditions of temperature and pressure, but these deal with the aggregate behavior of gases and not the behaviors of individual particles. The physicist does not make predictions with respect to matter in general, but only with respect to the aspects of matter that physics deals with; and these, by definition, are the physical aspects of matter.[27]

In the fourth stage of its development, however, international relations may experience efforts to establish linkages between normative theory on the one hand, and empirical-analytic theory on the other. The question of a value-free science of politics is of long-standing interest to students of politics. Although normative assumptions may underlie empirical research, the quest for a value-free science of politics has diminished interest over the past generation in normative theory. If political scientists choose to emphasize empirical-analytic theory, to the relative neglect of normative theory, they will have removed themselves from a problem area which historically has been of great concern to them. They will have chosen to ignore the task of defining the meaning of "the good life," the designing of political structures and the establishment of normative standards for mankind in a future which is fraught with growing problems and even peril. The pressing problems created by the impact of technology upon political institutions, changes in the political environment brought about by changing techniques, nationalism and ideology, and the implications of increasing popular pressures and demands upon existing political structures, are likely to lead students of international relations to a greater interest in normative theory. Empirical-analytic theories will not necessarily provide answers to the question of the kinds of institutions and norms appropriate to the world of the future, although from the

---

[27] Morton A. Kaplan, "Problems of Theory Building and Theory Confirmation in International Politics," Klaus Knorr and Sidney Verba, eds., *The International System: Theoretical Essays* (Princeton: Princeton University Press, 1961), p. 7.

findings of such studies the student of policy and the policymaker may gain insights vital to the solution of pressing problems.

In almost dialectical reaction against the so-called behavioral revolution, those political scientists who have called for a greater "politicization" of their profession have had as a concern the question of values, goals, or preferences. The "new revolution" of postbehavioralism which, according to David Easton, is sweeping political science contains the following arguments:

(1) it is more important to be relevant to contemporary needs than to be methodologically sophisticated;
(2) behavioral science conceals an ideology based upon empirical conservatism;
(3) behavioral research, by its focus upon abstraction, loses touch with reality;
(4) the political scientist has the obligation to make his knowledge available for the general benefit of society.[28]

In the field of international relations there have always been groups of scholars whose principal interest was the development and analysis of public policy. In its utopian and realist phases, international relations study was strongly focused upon policy. Over the past generation, the efforts of scholars to give the field a more theoretical orientation and to emphasize the methodological basis of inquiry have represented more a supplement to than a replacement of a concern for policy problems.[29] Indeed, considerable emphasis has been placed on the development of more rigorous techniques for the analysis of public policy, especially in the forms of systems analysis.[30] The goal of such work has been to devise

---

[28] David Easton, "The New Revolution in Political Science," *American Political Science Review*, LXIII (December, 1969), 1052. Similarly, Easton was among the first to discern the behavioral revolution in political science. See David Easton, *The Political System: An Inquiry into the State of Political Science* (New York: Alfred A. Knopf, 1954), especially pp. 37–125; by the same author, *A Framework for Political Analysis* (Englewood Cliffs, N. J.: Prentice-Hall, 1965), pp. 6–9.

[29] For a collection of essays by scholars concerned with the relationship between social science and public policy in the post-World War II period, see Daniel Lerner and Harold D. Lasswell, eds., *The Policy Sciences* (Stanford, Calif.: Stanford University Press, 1951). For a more recent discussion, see Norman D. Palmer, ed., *A Design for International Relations Research: Scope, Theory, Methods, and Relevance*. Monograph 10, The American Academy of Political and Social Science (October, 1970), especially pp. 154–274.

[30] Charles J. Hitch and Ronald N. McKean, *The Economics of Defense in the Nuclear Age* (Cambridge: Harvard University Press, 1963); Ronald McKean, *Efficiency in Government through Systems Analysis* (New York: John Wiley and Sons, 1958); Raymond A. Bauer and Kenneth J. Gergen, eds., *The Study of Policy Formation* (New York: Free Press, 1968); Harold Lasswell, "Policy Sciences," in *Interna-*

criteria to aid in choosing and evaluating alternative policies or strategies, or mixes of policies or strategies, for the attainment of specified objectives. The effort has been to find "optimal" or preferable solutions among a series of alternatives based upon relative costs and benefits by the use of such techniques as mathematical models, human gaming, and the canvassing of expert opinion. Such cost-benefit studies represented a reaction against policy recommendations based upon unstated assumptions, untested hypotheses, and uncertainty as the implications of alternative choices and outcomes. The deficiencies of systems analysis in dealing with such irrational forces as charisma and ideology, and the propensity of actors to adopt high-risk or low-risk strategies, as well as the inadequacies of systems analysis in explicating value assumptions, all serve to point up the need for additional work in the decade ahead toward the development of a policy science field either within international relations or as a separate discipline or "interdiscipline." [31]

Given the likely increase in pressing political problems, it will be necessary to achieve a balance between empirical-analytic tested theory and normative theory, and between basic and applied research in the fourth stage of development which international relations is now entering. Indeed, despite the tendency over the past generation to place reduced emphasis on normative theory, it has been a major thesis of this paper that normative and empirical theory and basic and applied research are by no means incompatible with each other. Normative theory can suggest alternative goals and preferences as well as political institutions and can also provide propositions for testing. Empirical-analytic theory can furnish guidance as to the kinds of political behavior which are essential for the attainment of desired goals.

By focusing upon the building of theories of conflict, integration, and decision making, scholars have chosen problem areas of central concern not only to the study of political science, but also to the development of a policy science. The outcome of such research is of transcending importance both to scholars and policy makers.

Conceivably, just as the study of international relations has moved from the extreme of normative theory to preoccupation with empirical-analytic theory, the coming generation of scholars will seek to assure the relevance of international relations to the manifold problems facing international society, while at the same time pursuing the needed quest for

---

tional Encyclopedia of the Social Sciences (New York: Macmillan Company and the Free Press, 1968), XII, 181–189.

[31] See Yehezkel Dror, *Analytical Approaches and Applied Social Sciences* (Santa Monica, Calif.: The RAND Corporation, November, 1969), monograph.

broadly based theories which both explain and predict political behavior at the international level. Thus international relations will have achieved in its next stage of development a greater synthesis among those concerns that have been of principal importance in the stages through which the field has passed since its beginnings in the early years of this century.

Part II

The Nature of the International System

As suggested in Part I, scholars, in the past generation have focused on problems of scope and method in international relations. Answers have been sought to such questions as: What are the appropriate focal points for studying international relations? To what extent should the nation-state as the primary actor be the principal object of investigation? Should scholarly attention be focused only on the international system, which encompasses the dynamic interaction of national units, or nation-states?

Most scholars agree with J. David Singer that there is more than one level of analysis for the international relations student. In the first selection, Professor Singer assesses the theoretical implications, respectively, of two alternative levels of analysis: the international system and the nation-state, or to use his terminology, the national subsystem.

Because it is the most comprehensive of the levels available, the international system as a level of analysis enables the student to examine international relationships in their totality. This level of analysis stresses the development of generalizations about aggregate international behavior. Sweeping statements about similarities among all, or most, nations and about the operation of the international system are attempted, and correlations are made between various forms of behavior without, however, drawing causal inferences.

However, to understand more clearly the courses of certain forms of behavior, a shift in focus to another level of analysis, the nation-state, is necessary. In the national subsystem, as Singer points out, each of the nation-states can be examined in greater detail to determine similarities and differences in goals, motivation, decision-making structures, capabilities, and other factors that affect state action in international relations. The domestic inputs into foreign policy decision-making can be analyzed. Such domestic-international "linkages" are examined in readings contained in Part VII of this anthology. At this level, the comprehensive quality of generalizations possible at the international system level is lost, but a greater capacity for understanding the causes of a particular state's international behavior by detailed study of its foreign policy is gained.

Readings in this part deal with both of the levels of analysis outlined above. At the international system level, it is possible to delineate several distinct systems. The international system of the decade following 1945 differed in several fundamental respects from the international system of the decade before World War II. In the latter period two superpowers—the United States and the Soviet Union—played predominant roles, whereas in the earlier period, several great powers—Britain, France, Germany, Italy, and Japan—had major influence.

Historically, the international system has consisted of great powers and small powers. Great powers were those countries which were parties to a general settlement of international affairs; small powers had no claim to such participation, and more often than the great powers, were the object of revisions in the international status quo. Before 1914, the international system, which was essentially Europe-based, contained several great powers. In the post–World War II period, the term "superpower" became popular to describe the two vast continental countries that possessed nuclear weapons. In national capabilities, the disparity between the United States and the Soviet Union, on the one hand, and the remaining members of the international system, on the other, was far greater than had been the case in preceding periods.

Like the great powers of an earlier age, a superpower has worldwide interests. Therefore, a superpower either plays a major role in a political settlement anywhere in the world or, at the very least, wields such global influence that no political agreement is possible without its tacit approval.

It is possible to speak of several kinds of international systems in which there are regular patterns of interaction and interdependence. Some are composed of many great powers, others, of a few superpowers. One can envisage systems in which there are many nation-states, or one world government.

Writers on the international system have discussed in exhaustive detail the notion of the state. It is an abstraction. No one has ever seen a state, which is simply shorthand for designating a political unit containing a population, a government, a territory, and an economy. Historically, a state gains membership in the international system when many, or all, of the great powers have recognized it. In general, the act of recognition takes the form of a policy declaration or an announcement of the opening of diplomatic relations.

According to Charles McClelland, international relations consists of the study of "interactions between certain kinds of social entities, including the study of relevant circumstances surrounding the interactions." He views the student's task as the isolation, examination, and analysis of patterns of interaction among the national political units—the principal actors of the international system. McClelland suggests a systems framework for the study of international relations. Although there are many other possible frameworks, his suggestion is illustrative of contemporary efforts to gain a greater understanding of behavioral regularities among nation-states by analyzing data on a variety of forms of international interaction.

Many analysts have viewed the international system as bipolar or multipolar—as consisting of two major centers of power or several large national units each possessing formidable capabilities.

Oran Young describes the contemporary international system as one characterized by the growing interpenetration of global or system-wide forces, on the one hand, and several newly emerging but differing regional subsystems, on the other. Such forces as communism, nationalism, and economic development are system-wide in their impact, yet they have specific effects which may differ from one region to another. Patterns of conflict, power balances, and substantive interests of states differ among regional subsystems, even though the system-wide or global actors have much greater impact upon international politics today than they once did. Because of the rise of two superpowers and the emergence of several substantive issues of system-wide importance, Young concludes that "the contemporary system is not only more interdependent (in the general sense that what happens in any part of it is capable of exercising a very substantial influence on developments in any other part of it), but is also characterized by the existence of several discrete actors and issues of global significance which play very concrete and specific roles in the various regional subsystems."

In the twentieth century, several forces have transformed the international system from a Europe-centered to a global system. Despite the broad cultural, racial, economic, and political gaps between the developed and less-developed regions, there are unifying forces, represented by economic interdependence and regional and global international organizations.

The principal components of the contemporary international system are the nation-states, or national units, as they are sometimes called. The phenomenon of nationalism is a pervasive influence on their behavior. According to Hans Kohn, nationalism is a "will to nationhood" and the "integration of the masses into a common political form." With the advent of nationalism, larger numbers of people, and in many cases the entire population of a territory, feel themselves a part of a political system. In the age of nationalism the historic gap between the central government and the hinterland is narrowed.

In England, nationalism was linked to the extension of liberty and the increase in popular political representation. By the twentieth century, nationalism was often identified with the integration of the masses of the population into totalitarian political systems. Utopian thought about international relations, it will be recalled from the reading by E. H. Carr (Selection 3), contained the proposition that nationalism would lead to the emergence of peace-loving governments. Essentially, the nationalist "model" implicit in such thought was more akin to the nationalism of the twentieth century.

In Europe, nationalism was often based upon common language and culture, as well as a belief in common descent and a return to some imagined past. In the nonwestern world, John Kautsky suggests, nationalism was identified with the anticolonial movements. Initially, its supporters were western-educated elites as well as other persons who felt disadvantaged in the colonial system. Unlike Europe, there were few, if any, linguistic bonds. In the nationalisms of Africa and Asia, the process of the "integration of the masses into a common political form" is far from complete. In many cases, cultural, economic, and political gaps separate the leadership of new states from the masses. In such countries the process of nation-building is that of narrowing the psychological, political, and economic gap between the central government and population.

For several reasons the study of nationalism is vital to the study of the international system. As a process that integrates the masses into a common political form, nationalism has enhanced the capabilities of national units in the international system. Before the age of nationalism it was impossible to mobilize the masses of the population to sacrifice life and treasure in the attainment of a major foreign policy objective, and conversely, it was impossible for them to help shape foreign policy. In nonwestern areas, the coming of nationalism contributed to the demise of European empires and the emergence of many new national units in the international system. Those countries where the masses of the population have not yet been integrated into a common political form—where localistic, tribalistic loyalties still predominate—are susceptible to insurgency warfare, either by indigenous groups or forces infiltrated from abroad. Thus nationalism, where it has produced a common political system, has rendered such countries less vulnerable to insurgency activity from outside. Those countries not yet politically integrated are subject to pressures which may have a destabilizing effect upon the international system.

Among such pressures is the continued strength of the concept of self-determination. As Walker Connor stresses, there are many groups both in the old national units of the western world and in the newer states, which are only now attaining an awareness of national identity. Far from producing a sense of kinship with ever widening communities, one effect of increased communications is to kindle latent, separatist nationalism among groups within existing states. Within Canada, Britain, and Belgium, as well as India, Nigeria, and the Sudan—to mention just a few cases—there are groups claiming their own nationalism and calling for self-determination or at least for greater autonomy in the management of their own affairs. As Connor reminds us, nationalism has far from run its course, nor has it given way to the forces of supranational units. Instead, even existing states face formidable centrifugal tendencies that could affect the future shape of the principal components of the international system and provide a destabilizing input into international politics. The existence of groups demanding self-determination, engaging in activities which undermine several of the existing states furnishes the opportunity for states to disrupt international politics through support for "wars of national liberation."

Power is one of the most frequently used words in the study of international relations, and especially among realist writers it has become a focal point for study. According to K. J. Holsti, this concept contains several elements: influence and the use of influence; the capabilities—military and nonmilitary—available to a national unit. Holsti views power as a process in which one national unit attempts, by means of a variety of capabilities, to influence another national unit to behave in some desired fashion. Power may be studied as a demand-response relationship in which one member of the international system, in turn, responds in some way. Thus, using McClelland's model, and incorporating into it Holsti's conception of power, the international system may be viewed as consisting of national units in interaction, making demands upon each other and eliciting responses. In turn, these responses give rise to new demands and responses. Because there are fewer institutions for the resolution of conflict in the international system than in the domestic, the power element is more obvious.

SECTION ONE:

Levels of Analysis: The International System and the Nation-State

7. THE LEVEL-OF-ANALYSIS PROBLEM IN INTERNATIONAL RELATIONS

J. David Singer

IN ANY AREA of scholarly inquiry, there are always several ways in which the phenomena under study may be sorted and arranged for purposes of systemic analysis. Whether in the physical or social sciences, the observer may choose to focus upon the parts or upon the whole, upon the components or upon the system. He may, for example, choose between the flowers or the garden, the rocks or the quarry, the trees or the forest, the houses or the neighborhood, the cars or the traffic jam,

From *The International System: Theoretical Essays,* eds. Klaus Knorr and Sidney Verba (Copyright © 1961 by Princeton University Press; Princeton Paperback, 1967), pp. 77–92. Reprinted by permission of Princeton University Press.

J. DAVID SINGER (1925–   ) Professor of Political Science and Research Political Scientist, Mental Health Research Institute, University of Michigan. Author of *Deterrence, Arms Control and Disarmament: Toward a Synthesis in National Security Policy* (Columbus: Ohio State University Press, 1962); *Financing International Organization; The United Nations Budget Process* (The Hague: M. Nijhoff, 1961). Editor, *Quantitative International Politics: Contributions from the Socio-Psychological Sciences* (Chicago: Rand McNally and Company, 1965).

the delinquents or the gang, the legislators or the legislature, and so on.[1] Whether he selects the micro- or macro-level of analysis is ostensibly a mere matter of methodological or conceptual convenience. Yet the choice often turns out to be quite difficult, and may well become a central issue within the discipline concerned. The complexity and significance of these level-of-analysis decisions are readily suggested by the long-standing controveries between social psychology and sociology, personality oriented and culture-oriented anthropology, or micro- and macro-economics, to mention but a few. In the vernacular of general systems theory, the observer is always confronted with a system, its sub-systems, and their respective environments, and while he may choose as his system any cluster of phenomena from the most minute organism to the universe itself, such choice cannot be merely a function of whim or caprice, habit or familiarity.[2] The responsible scholar must be prepared to evaluate the relative utility—conceptual and methodological—of the various alternatives open to him, and to appraise the manifold implications of the level of analysis finally selected. So it is with international relations.

But whereas the pros and cons of the various possible levels of analysis have been debated exhaustively in many of the social sciences, the issue has scarcely been raised among students of our emerging discipline.[3] Such tranquility may be seen by some as a reassuring indication that the issue is not germane to our field, and by others as evidence that it has already been resolved, but this writer perceives the quietude with a measure of concern. He is quite persuaded of its relevance and certain that it has yet to be resolved. Rather, it is contended that the issue has been ignored by scholars still steeped in the intuitive and artistic tradition of the humanities or enmeshed in the web of "practical" policy. We have, in our texts and elsewhere, roamed up and down the ladder of organizational complexity with remarkable abandon, focusing upon the total system, inter-

---

[1] As Kurt Lewin observed in his classic contribution to the social sciences: "The first prerequisite of a successful observation in any science is a definite understanding about what size of unit one is going to observe at a given time." *Field Theory in Social Science,* New York, 1951, p. 157.

[2] For a useful introductory statement on the definitional and taxonomic problems in a general systems approach, see the papers by Ludwig von Bertalanffy, "General System Theory," and Kenneth Boulding, "General System Theory: The Skeleton of Science," in Society for the Advancement of General Systems Theory, *General Systems,* Ann Arbor, Mich., 1956, 1, part 1.

[3] An important pioneering attempt to deal with some of the implications of one's level of analysis, however, is Kenneth N. Waltz, *Man, the State, and War,* New York, 1959. But Waltz restricts himself to a consideration of these implications as they impinge on the question of the causes of war. See also this writer's review of Waltz, "International Conflict: Three Levels of Analysis," *World Politics,* xii (April 1960), pp. 453–61.

national organizations, regions, coalitions, extra-national associations, nations, domestic pressure groups, social classes, elites, and individuals as the needs of the moment required. And though most of us have tended to settle upon the nation as our most comfortable resting place, we have retained our propsensity for vertical drift, failing to appreciate the value of a stable point of focus.[4] Whether this lack of concern is a function of the relative infancy of the discipline or the nature of the intellectual traditions from whence it springs, it nevertheless remains a significant variable in the general sluggishness which characterizes the development of theory in the study of relations among nations. It is the purpose of this paper to raise the issue, articulate the alternatives, and examine the theoretical implications and consequences of two of the more widely employed levels of analysis: the international system and the national sub-systems.

I. THE REQUIREMENTS OF AN ANALYTICAL MODEL

Prior to an examination of the theoretical implications of the level of analysis or orientation employed in our model, it might be worthwhile to discuss the uses to which any such model might be put, and the requirements which such uses might expect of it.

Obviously, we would demand that it offer a highly accurate *description* of the phenomena under consideration. Therefore the scheme must present as complete and undistorted a picture of these phenomena as is possible; it must correlate with objective reality and coincide with our empirical referents to the highest possible degree. Yet we know that such accurate representation of a complex and wide-ranging body of phenomena is extremely difficult. Perhaps a useful illustration may be borrowed from cartography; the oblate spheroid which the planet earth most closely represents is not transferable to the two-dimensional surface of a map without *some* distortion. Thus, the Mercator projection exaggerates distance and distorts direction at an increasing rate as we move north or south *from* the equator, while the polar gnomonic projection suffers from these same debilities as we move *toward* the equator. Neither offers therefore a wholly accurate presentation, yet each is true enough to reality to be quite useful for certain specific purposes. The same sort of tolerance is necessary in evaluating any analytical model for the study of international relations; if we must sacrifice total representational accuracy, the problem is to decide where distortion is least dysfunctional and where such accuracy is absolutely essential.

---

[4] Even during the debate between "realism" and "idealism" the analytical implications of the various levels of analysis received only the scantiest attention; rather the emphasis seems to have been at the two extremes of pragmatic policy and speculative metaphysics.

These decisions are, in turn, a function of the second requirement of any such model—a capacity to *explain* the relationships among the phenomena under investigation. Here our concern is not so much with accuracy of description as with validity of explanation. Our model must have such analytical capabilities as to treat the causal relationships in a fashion which is not only valid and thorough, but parsimonious; this latter requirement is often overlooked, yet its implications for research strategy are not inconsequential.[5] It should be asserted here that the primary purpose of theory is to explain, and when descriptive and explanatory requirements are in conflict, the latter ought to be given priority, even at the cost of some representational inaccuracy.

Finally, we may legitimately demand that any analytical model offer the promise of reliable *prediction*. In mentioning this requirement last, there is no implication that it is the most demanding or difficult of the three. Despite the popular belief to the contrary, prediction demands less of one's model than does explanation or even description. For example, any informed layman can predict that pressure on the accelerator of a slowly moving car will increase its speed; that more or less of the moon will be visible tonight than last night; or that the normal human will flinch when confronted with an impending blow. These *predictions* do not require a particularly elegant or sophisticated model of the universe, but their *explanation* demands far more than most of us carry around in our minds. Likewise, we can predict with impressive reliability that any nation will respond to military attack in kind, but a description and understanding of the processes and factors leading to such a response are considerably more elusive, despite the gross simplicity of the acts themselves.

Having articulated rather briefly the requirements of an adequate analytical model, we might turn now to a consideration of the ways in which one's choice of analytical focus impinges upon such a model and affects its descriptive, explanatory, and predictive adequacy.

---

[5] For example, one critic of the decision-making model formulated by Richard C. Snyder, H. W. Bruck, and Burton Sapin, in *Decision-Making as an Approach to the Study of International Politics* (Princeton, N.J., 1954), points out that no single researcher could deal with all the variables in that model and expect to complete more than a very few comparative studies in his lifetime. See Herbert McClosky, "Concerning Strategies for a Science of International Politics," *World Politics*, VIII (January 1956), pp. 281–95. In defense, however, one might call attention to the relative ease with which many of Snyder's categories could be collapsed into more inclusive ones, as was apparently done in the subsequent case study (see note 11 below). Perhaps a more telling criticism of the monograph is McClosky's comment that "Until a greater measure of theory is introduced into the proposal and the relations among variables are specified more concretely, it is likely to remain little more than a setting-out of categories and, like any taxonomy, fairly limited in its utility" (p. 291).

II. THE INTERNATIONAL SYSTEM AS LEVEL OF ANALYSIS

Beginning with the systemic level of analysis, we find in the total international system a partially familiar and highly promising point of focus. First of all, it is the most comprehensive of the levels available, encompassing the totality of interactions which take place within the system and its environment. By focusing on the system, we are enabled to study the patterns of interaction which the system reveals, and to generalize about such phenomena as the creation and dissolution of coalitions, the frequency and duration of specific power configurations, modifications in its stability, its responsiveness to changes in formal political institutions, and the norms and folklore which it manifests as a societal system. In other words, the systemic level of analysis, and only this level, permits us to examine international relations in the whole, with a comprehensiveness that is of necessity lost when our focus is shifted to a lower, and more partial, level. For descriptive purposes, then, it offers both advantages and disadvantages; the former flow from its comprehensiveness, and the latter from the necessary dearth of detail.

As to explanatory capability, the system-oriented model poses some genuine difficulties. In the first place, it tends to lead the observer into a position which exaggerates the impact of the system upon the national actors and, conversely, discounts the impact of the actors on the system. This is, of course, by no means inevitable; one could conceivably look upon the system as a rather passive environment in which dynamic states act out their relationships rather than as a socio-political entity with a dynamic of its own. But there is a natural tendency to endow that upon which we focus our attention with somewhat greater potential than it might normally be expected to have. Thus, we tend to move, in a system-oriented model, away from notions implying much national autonomy and independence of choice and toward a more deterministic orientation.

Secondly, this particular level of analysis almost inevitably requires that we postulate a high degree of uniformity in the foreign policy operational codes of our national actors. By definition, we allow little room for divergence in the behavior of our parts when we focus upon the whole. It is no coincidence that our most prominent theoretician—and one of the very few text writers focusing upon the international system—should "assume that [all] statesmen think and act in terms of interest defined as power." [6] If this single-minded behavior be interpreted literally and narrowly, we have a simplistic image comparable to eco-

---

[6] Hans J. Morgenthau, *Politics Among Nations,* 3rd ed., New York, 1960, pp. 5–7. Obviously, his model does not preclude the use of power as a dimension for the differentiation of nations.

nomic man or a sexual man, and if it be defined broadly, we are no better off than the psychologist whose human model pursues "self-realization" or "maximization of gain"; all such gross models suffer from the same fatal weakness as the utilitarian's "pleasure-pain" principle. Just as individuals differ widely in what they deem to be pleasure and pain, or gain and loss, nations may differ widely in what they consider to be the national interest, and we end up having to break down and define the larger category. Moreover, Professor Morgenthau finds himself compelled to go still further and disavow the relevance of both motives and ideological preferences in national behavior, and these represent two of the more useful dimensions in differentiating among the several nations in our international system. By eschewing any empirical concern with the domestic and internal variations within the separate nations, the system-oriented approach tends to produce a sort of "black box" or "billiard ball" concept of the national actors.[7] By discounting—or denying—the differences among nations, or by positing the near-impossibility of observing many of these differences at work within them,[8] one concludes with a highly homogenized image of our nations in the international system. And though this may be an inadequate foundation upon which to base any *causal* statements, it offers a reasonably adequate basis for *correlative* statements. More specifically, it permits us to observe and measure correlations between certain forces or stimuli which seem to impinge upon the nation and the behavior patterns which are the apparent consequence of these stimuli. But one must stress the limitations implied in the word "apparent"; what is thought to be the consequence of a given stimulus may only be a coincidence or artifact, and until one investigates the major elements in the causal link—no matter how persuasive the deductive logic—one may speak only of correlation, not of consequence.

---

[7] The "black box" figure comes from some of the simpler versions of S-R psychology, in which the observer more or less ignores what goes on within the individual and concentrates upon the correlation between stimulus and response; these are viewed as empirically verifiable, whereas cognition, perception, and other mental processes have to be imputed to the individual with a heavy reliance on these assumed "intervening variables." The "billiard ball" figure seems to carry the same sort of connotation, and is best employed by Arnold Wolfers in "The Actors in International Politics" in William T. R. Fox, ed., *Theoretical Aspects of International Relations,* Notre Dame, Ind., 1959, pp. 83–106. See also, in this context, Richard C. Snyder, "International Relations Theory—Continued," *World Politics,* XIII (January 1961), pp. 300–12; and J. David Singer, "Theorizing About Theory in International Politics," *Journal of Conflict Resolution,* IV (December 1960), pp. 431–42. Both are review articles dealing with the Fox anthology.

[8] Morgenthau observes, for example, that it is "futile" to search for motives because they are "the most illusive of psychological data, distorted as they are, frequently beyond recognition, by the interests and emotions of actor and observer alike" (*op. cit.,* p. 6).

Moreover, by avoiding the multitudinous pitfalls of intra-nation observation, one emerges with a singularly manageable model, requiring as it does little of the methodological sophistication or onerous empiricism called for when one probes beneath the behavioral externalities of the actor. Finally, as has already been suggested in the introduction, the systemic orientation should prove to be reasonably satisfactory as a basis for prediction, even if such prediction is to extend beyond the characteristics of the system and attempt anticipatory statements regarding the actors themselves; this assumes, of course, that the actors are characterized and their behavior predicted in relatively gross and general terms.

These, then, are some of the more significant implications of a model which focuses upon the international system as a whole. Let us turn now to the more familiar of our two orientations, the national state itself.

III. THE NATIONAL STATE AS LEVEL OF ANALYSIS

The other level of analysis to be considered in this paper is the national state—our primary actor in international relations. This is clearly the traditional focus among Western students, and is the one which dominates almost all of the texts employed in English-speaking colleges and universities.

Its most obvious advantage is that it permits significant differentiation among our actors in the international system. Because it does not require the attribution of great similarity to the national actors, it encourages the observer to examine them in greater detail. The favorable results of such intensive analysis cannot be overlooked, as it is only when the actors are studied in some depth that we are able to make really valid generalizations of a comparative nature. And though the systemic model does not necessarily preclude comparison and contrast among the national sub-systems, it usually eventuates in rather gross comparisons based on relatively crude dimensions and characteristics. On the other hand, there is no assurance that the nation-oriented approach will produce a sophisticated model for the comparative study of foreign policy; with perhaps the exception of the Haas and Whiting study,[9] none of our major texts makes a serious and successful effort to describe and explain national behavior in terms of most of the significant variables by which such behavior might be comparatively analyzed. But this would seem to be a function, not of the level of analysis employed, but of our general unfamiliarity with the other social sciences (in which comparison is a major preoccupation) and of the retarded state of comparative government and politics, a field in

---

[9] Ernst B. Haas and Allen S. Whiting, *Dynamics of International Relations*, New York, 1956.

which most international relations specialists are likely to have had some experience.

But just as the nation-as-actor focus permits us to avoid the inaccurate homogenization which often flows from the systemic focus, it also may lead us into the opposite type of distortion—a marked exaggeration of the differences among our sub-systemic actors. While it is evident that neither of these extremes is conducive to the development of a sophisticated comparison of foreign policies, and such comparison requires a balanced preoccupation with both similarity and difference, the danger seems to be greatest when we succumb to the tendency to overdifferentiate; comparison and contrast can proceed only from observed uniformities.[10]

One of the additional liabilities which flow in turn from the pressure to overdifferentiate is that of Ptolemaic parochialism. Thus, in overemphasizing the differences among the many national states, the observer is prone to attribute many of what he conceives to be virtues to his own nation and the vices to others, especially the adversaries of the moment. That this ethnocentrism is by no means an idle fear is borne out by perusal of the major international relations texts published in the United States since 1945. Not only is the world often perceived through the prism of the American national interest, but an inordinate degree of attention (if not spleen) is directed toward the Soviet Union; it would hardly be amiss to observe that most of these might qualify equally well as studies in American foreign policy. The scientific inadequacies of this sort of "we-they" orientation hardly require elaboration, yet they remain a potent danger in any utilization of the national actor model.

Another significant implication of the sub-systemic orientation is that it is only within its particular framework that we can expect any useful application of the decision-making approach.[11] Not all of us, of course, will find its inapplicability a major loss; considering the criticism which has been leveled at the decision-making approach, and the failure of most of us to attempt its application, one might conclude that it is no

---

[10] A frequent by-product of this tendency to overdifferentiate is what Waltz calls the "second-image fallacy," in which one explains the peaceful or bellicose nature of a nation's foreign policy exclusively in terms of its domestic economic, political, or social characteristics (*op.cit.*, chs. 4 and 5).

[11] Its most well-known and successful statement is found in Snyder *et al.*, *op.cit.* Much of this model is utilized in the text which Snyder wrote with Edgar S. Furniss, Jr., *American Foreign Policy: Formulation, Principles, and Programs*, New York, 1954. A more specific application is found in Snyder and Glenn D. Paige, "The United States Decision to Resist Aggression in Korea: The Application of an Analytical Scheme," *Administrative Science Quarterly*, III (December 1958), pp. 341–78. For those interested in this approach, very useful is Paul Wasserman and Fred S. Silander, *Decision-Making: An Annotated Bibliography*, Ithaca, N.Y., 1958.

loss at all. But the important thing to note here is that a system-oriented model would not offer a hospitable framework for such a detailed and comparative approach to the study of international relations, no matter what our appraisal of the decision-making approach might be.

Another and perhaps more subtle implication of selecting the nation as our focus or level of analysis is that it raises the entire question of goals, motivation, and purpose in national policy.[12] Though it may well be a peculiarity of the Western philosophical tradition, we seem to exhibit, when confronted with the need to explain individual or collective behavior, a strong proclivity for a goal-seeking approach. The question of whether national behavior is purposive or not seems to require discussion in two distinct (but not always exclusive) dimensions.

Firstly, there is the more obvious issue of whether those who act on behalf of the nation in formulating and executing foreign policy consciously pursue rather concrete goals. And it would be difficult to deny, for example, that these role-fulfilling individuals envisage certain specific outcomes which they hope to realize by pursuing a particular strategy. In this sense, then, nations may be said to be goal-seeking organisms which exhibit purposive behavior.

However, purposiveness may be viewed in a somewhat different light, by asking whether it is not merely an intellectual construct that man imputes to himself by reason of his vain addiction to the free-will doctrine as he searches for characteristics which distinguish him from physical matter and the lower animals. And having attributed this conscious goal-pursuing behavior to himself as an individual, it may be argued that man then proceeds to project this attribute to the social organizations of which he is a member. The question would seem to distill down to whether man and his societies pursue goals of their own choosing or are moved toward those imposed upon them by forces which are primarily beyond their control.[13] Another way of stating the dilemma would be to ask whether we are concerned with the ends which men and nations strive for or the ends toward which they are impelled by the past and present characteristics of their social and physical milieu. Obviously, we are using the terms "ends," "goals," and "purpose" in two rather

---

[12] And if the decision-making version of this model is employed, the issue is unavoidable. See the discussion of motivation in Snyder, Bruck, and Sapin, *op.cit.*, pp. 92–117; note that 25 of the 49 pages on "The Major Determinants of Action" are devoted to motives.

[13] A highly suggestive, but more abstract treatment of this teleological question is in Talcott Parsons, *The Structure of Social Action*, 2nd ed., Glencoe, Ill., 1949, especially in his analysis of Durkheim and Weber. It is interesting to note that for Parsons an act implies, *inter alia*, "a future state of affairs toward which the process of action is oriented," and he therefore comments that "in this sense and this sense only, the schema of action is inherently teleological" (p. 44).

distinct ways; one refers to those which are consciously envisaged and more or less rationally pursued, and the other to those of which the actor has little knowledge but toward which he is nevertheless propelled.

Taking a middle ground in what is essentially a specific case of the free will vs. determinism debate, one can agree that nations move toward outcomes of which they have little knowledge and over which they have less control, but that they nevertheless do prefer, and therefore select, particular outcomes and *attempt* to realize them by conscious formulation of strategies.

Also involved in the goal-seeking problem when we employ the nation-oriented model is the question of how and why certain nations pursue specific sorts of goals. While the question may be ignored in the system-oriented model or resolved by attributing identical goals to all national actors, the nation-as-actor approach demands that we investigate the processes by which national goals are selected, the internal and external factors that impinge on those processes, and the institutional framework from which they emerge. It is worthy of note that despite the strong predilection for the nation-oriented model in most of our texts, empirical or even deductive analyses of these processes are conspicuously few.[14] Again, one might attribute these lacunae to the methodological and conceptual inadequacies of the graduate training which international relations specialists traditionally receive.[15] But in any event, goals and motivations are both dependent and independent variables, and if we intend to explain a nation's foreign policy, we cannot settle for the mere postulation of these goals; we are compelled to go back a step and inquire into their genesis and the process by which they become the crucial variables that they seem to be in the behavior of nations.

There is still another dilemma involved in our selection of the nation-as-actor model, and that concerns the phenomenological issue: do we examine our actor's behavior in terms of the objective factors which allegedly influence that behavior, or do we do so in terms of the actor's

---

[14] Among the exceptions are Haas and Whiting, *op.cit.*, chs. 2 and 3; and some of the chapters in Roy C. Macridis, ed., *Foreign Policy in World Politics*, Englewood Cliffs, N.J., 1958, especially that on West Germany by Karl Deutsch and Lewis Edinger.

[15] As early as 1934, Edith E. Ware noted that ". . . the study of international relations is no longer entirely a subject for political science or law, but that economics, history, sociology, geography—all the social sciences—are called upon to contribute towards the understanding . . . of the international system." See *The Study of International Relations in the United States*, New York, 1934, p. 172. For some contemporary suggestions, see Karl Deutsch, "The Place of Behavioral Sciences in Graduate Training in International Relations," *Behavioral Science*, III (July 1958), pp. 278–84; and J. David Singer, "The Relevance of the Behavioral Sciences to the Study of International Relations," *ibid.*, VI (October 1961), pp. 324–35.

perception of these "objective factors"? Though these two approaches are not completely exclusive of one another, they proceed from greatly different and often incompatible assumptions, and produce markedly divergent models of national behavior.[16]

The first of these assumptions concerns the broad question of social causation. One view holds that individuals and groups respond in a quasi-deterministic fashion to the realities of physical environment, the acts or power of other individuals or groups, and similar "objective" and "real" forces or stimuli. An opposite view holds that individuals and groups are not influenced in their behavior by such objective forces, but by the fashion in which these forces are perceived and evaluated, however distorted or incomplete such perceptions may be. For adherents of this position, the only reality is the phenomenal—that which is discerned by the human senses; forces that are not discerned do not exist for that actor, and those that do exist do so only in the fashion in which they are perceived. Though it is difficult to accept the position that an individual, a group, or a nation is affected by such forces as climate, distance, or a neighbor's physical power only insofar as they are recognized and appraised, one must concede that perceptions will certainly affect the manner in which such forces are responded to. As has often been pointed out, an individual will fall to the ground when he steps out of a tenth-story window regardless of his perception of gravitational forces, but on the other hand such perception is a major factor in whether or not he steps out of the window in the first place.[17] The point here is that if we embrace a phenomenological view of causation, we will tend to utilize a phenomenological model for explanatory purposes.

The second assumption which bears on one's predilection for the phenomenological approach is more restricted, and is primarily a methodological one. Thus, it may be argued that any description of national behavior in a given international situation would be highly incomplete were it to ignore the link between the external forces at work upon the nation and its general foreign policy behavior. Furthermore, if our concern extends beyond the mere description of "what happens" to the realm of explanation, it could be contended that such omission of the cognitive

---

[16] The father of phenomenological philosophy is generally acknowledged to be Edmund Husserl (1859–1938), author of *Ideas: General Introduction to Pure Phenomenology*, New York, 1931, trans. by W. R. Boyce Gibson; the original was published in 1913 under the title *Ideen zu einer reinen Phänomenologie und Phänomenologischen Philosophie.* Application of this approach to social psychology has come primarily through the work of Koffka and Lewin.

[17] This issue has been raised from time to time in all of the social sciences, but for an excellent discussion of it in terms of the present problem, see Harold and Margaret Sprout, *Man-Milieu Relationship Hypotheses in the Context of International Politics,* Princeton University, Center of International Studies, 1956, pp. 63–71.

and the perceptual linkage would be ontologically disastrous. How, it might be asked, can one speak of "causes" of a nation's policies when one has ignored the media by which external conditions and factors are translated into a policy decision? We may observe correlations between all sorts of forces in the international system and the behavior of nations, but their causal relationship must remain strictly deductive and hypothetical in the absence of empirical investigation into the causal chain which allegedly links the two. Therefore, even if we are satisfied with the less-than-complete descriptive capabilities of a non-phenomenological model, we are still drawn to it if we are to make any progress in explanation.

The contrary view would hold that the above argument proceeds from an erroneous comprehension of the nature of explanation in social science. One is by no means required to trace every perception, transmission, and receipt between stimulus and response or input and output in order to explain the behavior of the nation or any other human group. Furthermore, who is to say that empirical observation—subject as it is to a host of errors—is any better a basis of explanation than informed deduction, inference, or analogy? Isn't an explanation which flows logically from a coherent theoretical model just as reliable as one based upon a misleading and elusive body of data, most of which is susceptible to analysis only by techniques and concepts foreign to political science and history?

This leads, in turn, to the third of the premises relevant to one's stand on the phenomenological issue: are the dimensions and characteristics of the policy-makers' phenomenal field empirically discernible? Or, more accurately, even if we are convinced that their perceptions and beliefs constitute a crucial variable in the explanation of a nation's foreign policy, can they be observed in an accurate and systematic fashion? [18] Furthermore, are we not required by the phenomenological model to go beyond a classification and description of such variables, and be drawn into the tangled web of relationships out of which they emerge? If we believe that these phenomenal variables are systematically observable, are explainable, and can be fitted into our explanation of a nation's behavior in the international system, then there is a further tendency to embrace the phenomenological approach. If not, or if we are convinced that the gathering of such data is inefficient or uneconomical, we will tend to shy clear of it.

---

[18] This is another of the criticisms leveled at the decision-making approach which, almost by definition, seems compelled to adopt some form of the phenomenological model. For a comprehensive treatment of the elements involved in human perception, see Karl Zener et al., eds., "Inter-relationships Between Perception and Personality: A Symposium," *Journal of Personality*, xviii (1949), pp. 1–266.

The fourth issue in the phenomenological dispute concerns the very nature of the nation as an actor in international relations. Who or what is it that we study? Is it a distinct social entity with well-defined boundaries—a unity unto itself? Or is it an agglomeration of individuals, institutions, customs, and procedures? It should be quite evident that those who view the nation or the state as an integral social unit could not attach much utility to the phenomenological approach, particularly if they are prone to concretize or reify the abstraction. Such abstractions are incapable of perception, cognition, or anticipation (unless, of course, the reification goes so far as to anthropomorphize and assign to the abstraction such attributes as will, mind, or personality). On the other hand, if the nation or state is seen as a group of individuals operating within an institutional framework, then it makes perfect sense to focus on the phenomenal field of those individuals who participate in the policy-making process. In other words, *people* are capable of experiences, images, and expectations, while institutional abstractions are not, except in the metaphorical sense. Thus, if our actor cannot even have a phenomenal field, there is little point in employing a phenomenological approach.[19]

These, then, are some of the questions around which the phenomenological issue would seem to revolve. Those of us who think of social forces as operative regardless of the actor's awareness, who believe that explanation need not include all of the steps in a causal chain, who are dubious of the practicality of gathering phenomenal data, or who visualize the nation as a distinct entity apart from its individual members, will tend to reject the phenomenological approach.[20] Logically, only those who disagree with each of the above four assumptions would be *compelled* to adopt the approach. Disagreement with any one would be *sufficient* grounds for so doing.

The above represent some of the more significant implications and fascinating problems raised by the adoption of our second model. They seem to indicate that this sub-systemic orientation is likely to produce richer description and more satisfactory (from the empiricist's point of view) explanation of international relations, though its predictive power would appear no greater than the systemic orientation. But the descriptive and explanatory advantages are achieved only at the price of considerable methodological complexity.

---

[19] Many of these issues are raised in the ongoing debate over "methodological individualism," and are discussed cogently in Ernest Nagel, *The Structure of Science,* New York, 1961, pp. 535–46.

[20] Parenthetically, holders of these specific views should also be less inclined to adopt the national or sub-systemic model in the first place.

IV. CONCLUSION

Having discussed some of the descriptive, explanatory, and predictive capabilities of these two possible levels of analysis, it might now be useful to assess the relative utility of the two and attempt some general statement as to their prospective contributions to greater theoretical growth in the study of international relations.

In terms of description, we find that the systemic level produces a more comprehensive and total picture of international relations than does the national or sub-systemic level. On the other hand, the atomized and less coherent image produced by the lower level of analysis is somewhat balanced by its richer detail, greater depth, and more intensive portrayal.[21] As to explanation, there seems little doubt that the sub-systemic or actor orientation is considerably more fruitful, permitting as it does a more thorough investigation of the processes by which foreign policies are made. Here we are enabled to go beyond the limitations imposed by the systemic level and to replace mere correlation with the more significant causation. And in terms of prediction, both orientations seem to offer a similar degree of promise. Here the issue is a function of what we seek to predict. Thus the policy-maker will tend to prefer predictions about the way in which nation x or y will react to a contemplated move on his own nation's part, while the scholar will probably prefer either generalized predictions regarding the behavior of a given class of nations or those regarding the system itself.

Does this summary add up to an overriding case for one or another of the two models? It would seem not. For a staggering variety of reasons the scholar may be more interested in one-level than another at any given time and will undoubtedly shift his orientation according to his research needs. So the problem is really not one of deciding which level is most valuable to the discipline as a whole and then demanding that it be adhered to from now unto eternity.[22] Rather, it is one of realizing that

---

[21] In a review article dealing with two of the more recent and provocative efforts toward theory (Morton A. Kaplan, *System and Process in International Politics,* New York, 1957, and George Liska, *International Equilibrium,* Cambridge, Mass., 1957), Charles P. Kindleberger adds a further—if not altogether persuasive—argument in favor of the lower, sub-systemic level of analysis: "The total system is infinitely complex with everything interacting. One can discuss it intelligently, therefore, only bit by bit." "Scientific International Politics," *World Politics,* xi (October 1958), p. 86.

[22] It should also be kept in mind that one could conceivably develop a theoretical model which successfully embraces both of these levels of analysis without sacrificing conceptual clarity and internal consistency. In this writer's view, such has not been done to date, though Kaplan's *System and Process in International Politics* seems to come fairly close.

there *is* this preliminary conceptual issue and that it must be temporarily resolved prior to any given research undertaking. And it must also be stressed that we have dealt here only with two of the more common orientations, and that many others are available and perhaps even more fruitful potentially than either of those selected here. Moreover, the international system gives many indications of prospective change, and it may well be that existing institutional forms will take on new characteristics or that new ones will appeal to take their place. As a matter of fact, if incapacity to perform its functions leads to the transformation or decay of an institution, we may expect a steady deterioration and even ultimate disappearance of the national state as a significant actor in the world political system.

However, even if the case for one or another of the possible levels of analysis cannot be made with any certainty, one must nevertheless maintain a continuing awareness as to their use. We may utilize one level here and another there, but we cannot afford to shift our orientation in the midst of a study. And when we do in fact make an original selection or replace one with another at appropriate times, we must do so with a full awareness of the descriptive, explanatory, and predictive implications of such choice.

A final point remains to be discussed. Despite this lengthy exegesis, one might still be prone to inquire whether this is not merely a sterile exercise in verbal gymnastics. What, it might be asked, is the difference between the two levels of analysis if the empirical referents remain essentially the same? Or, to put it another way, is there any difference between international relations and comparative foreign policy? Perhaps a few illustrations will illuminate the subtle but important differences which emerge when one's level of analysis shifts. One might, for example, postulate that when the international system is characterized by political conflict between two of its most powerful actors, there is a strong tendency for the system to bipolarize. This is a systemic-oriented proposition. A sub-systemic proposition, dealing with the same general empirical referents, would state that when a powerful actor finds itself in political conflict with another of approximate parity, it will tend to exert pressure on its weaker neighbors to join its coalition. Each proposition, assuming it is true, is theoretically useful by itself, but each is verified by a different intellectual operation. Moreover—and this is the crucial thing for theoretical development—one could not add these two kinds of statements together to achieve a cumulative growth of empirical generalizations.

To illustrate further, one could, at the systemic level, postulate that when the distribution of power in the international system is highly diffused, it is more stable than when the discernible clustering of well-defined coalitions occurs. And at the sub-systemic or national level, the same empirical phenomena would produce this sort of proposition: when a nation's decision-makers find it difficult to categorize other nations readily as friend or foe, they tend to behave toward all in a more uniform and moderate fashion. Now, taking these two sets of propositions, how much cumulative usefulness would arise from attempting to merge and codify the systemic proposition from the first illustration with the sub-systemic proposition from the second, or vice versa? Representing different levels of analysis and couched in different frames of reference, they would defy theoretical integration; one may well be a corollary of the other, but they are not immediately combinable. A prior translation from one level to another must take place.

This, it is submitted, is quite crucial for the theoretical development of our discipline. With all of the current emphasis on the need for more empirical and data-gathering research as a prerequisite to theory-building, one finds little concern with the relationship among these separate and discrete data-gathering activities. Even if we were to declare a moratorium on deductive and speculative research for the next decade, and all of us were to labor diligently in the vineyards of historical and contemporary data, the state of international relations theory would probably be no more advanced at that time than it is now, unless such empirical activity becomes far more systematic. And "systematic" is used here to indicate the cumulative growth of inductive and deductive generalizations into an impressive array of statements conceptually related to one another and flowing from some common frame of reference. What that frame of reference should be, or will be, cannot be said with much certainty, but it does seem clear that it must exist. As long as we evade some of these crucial *a priori* decisions, our empiricism will amount to little more than an ever-growing potpourri of discrete, disparate, noncomparable, and isolated bits of information or extremely low-level generalizations. And, as such, they will make little contribution to the growth of a theory of international relations.

SECTION TWO:

The Contemporary International System

8. THEORY AND THE INTERNATIONAL SYSTEM

Charles A. McClelland

INTERNATIONAL RELATIONS is the study of interactions between certain kinds of social entities, including the study of relevant circumstances surrounding the interactions. In interaction between any two parties, the sources of the action are the parties. At any given instant, we should be required to admit that the only possible sources are within the involved parties or actors. Two complexities are involved, however, if interaction occurs over a period of time. Each actor may be influenced by the past experience of interacting, and on this basis it can be said that the interaction itself is a source of behavior. In the second place, from past experience with interaction, the actors may anticipate what will happen next and each may act according to the anticipation. Almost any example of human relations illustrates these matters concretely.

From *Theory and the International System* by Charles A. McClelland (New York: Macmillan Company, 1966), pp. 18–27; 99–106. Reprinted by permission of the author and the Macmillan Company. Footnotes have been renumbered to appear in consecutive order.

CHARLES A. McCLELLAND (1917–   ) Professor of Political Science, University of Michigan. Editor of *The United Nations: The Continuing Debate, Nuclear Weapons, Missiles and the Future of War* (San Francisco: Chandler Publishing Company, 1960).

On meeting Actor B, Actor A may make an insulting remark; if Actor A does, B may respond with an equally insulting remark; if B does, A may be irritated enough to strike B; if A does, B may retaliate in kind; however, A may anticipate that B will strike back and therefore A does not strike B. The point is clear: in this case only the two parties are interacting and they are the only real sources of behavior. Nevertheless, the character of the interaction—in the instance cited, insult returning insult—is a distinctive phenomenon. The interplay feeds back, so to speak, and affects the behavior of the involved actors, and it may be viewed as a source in itself. A block diagram (Fig. 1) symbolizes international relationships of whatever variety, once the relationships are broken down to their most elementary form:

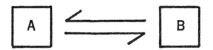

FIGURE 1 Basic pattern of interaction.

It follows that the facts of international relations can be selected and organized according to the references of actor and interaction. This is a basic statement of theory. It would be futile, however, to undertake to organize all possible information about all actors. Only some small portion of "all the facts" about given actors would be expected to be important in accounting for some particular interactions. To include more than the relevant facts would be inefficient, distracting, or even confusing in an explanation of how and why a sequence of interacting events has occurred. A conception of the nature of a given stream of interaction gains substance only to the extent that the idea matches *some* of the behavior of the involved parties.

When we are presented with such problems of explanation, we immediately go about the task of establishing relevance by putting facts in appropriate categories. Commonly, we build a map of the situation by asking a few questions: Who is involved? Where did the action occur? When did it happen and in what order? What happened? This is the historical method of investigation; everybody uses it; and it is, indeed, a powerful tool for ordering reports of events. Due to the complexity and multiplicity of the events of international relations, however, additional means of locating and ordering data are needed.

A conventional procedure is to superimpose a second category system on the first system of the *who, where, when,* and *what* variety. This is to separate and label groups of data under headings of political, economic, social, cultural, psychological, legal, military, and ideological factors (or aspects). These analytical categories are sometimes of help in organizing facts. For example, the assumption that the data falling in the political category are more significant than any other in explaining international relations—the *primacy of politics* idea mentioned earlier—leads to the subordination of the materials in the other categories to the class of *contributing influences.* This strategic conception is open to challenge, however. As we have already noted, a psychologist may argue that the political facts are not fundamental but reflect only partially a more deeply rooted set of psychological facts. There is no fixed hierarchy for arranging the analytical categories in the order of importance.

The analytical categories give some trouble in other ways. They sometimes are used as if they were qualities inhering in events—as if there were political acts, psychological acts, economic acts, and so forth, in Nature. On other occasions, the analytical categories appear to be regarded simply as different perspectives to be focused in turn on a body of facts. There is no consistency in the usage, and confusion arises from the lack of agreement among the special cultures of the social sciences on the matter.

In the theory of international relations, the recent tendency is to view the analytical categories as different perspectives (rather than as qualities inhering in events) and to call upon them for assistance in organizing data according to the particular intellectual needs and problems of international relations research. Thus it is said frequently that the field is interdisciplinary and that it borrows materials freely from political science, economics, sociology, history, psychology, and many other studies.

Although the historical and analytical category systems are indispensable for identifying, locating, and organizing data, the ordering idea of "the international system" appears increasingly to be a concept of great usefulness in giving the study of international relations the shape of a discipline.

The conception of *the international system* is an expanded version of the notion of two-actors-in-interaction. A view of a whole phenomenon is involved. The outermost boundaries of international relations are suggested if we imagine *all* of the exchanges, transactions, contacts, flows of information, and actions of every kind going on at this moment of time between and among the separately constituted societies of the world. To this picture in the mind we should add the effects created within societies from all such interflowing events in earlier times, both of the immediate and the more remote past. Finally, the stream of these actions and responses should be conceived as moving on to the future of tomorrow and beyond, accompanied by the expectations, plans, and proposals of all observers of the phenomena. This total picture is the reference intended in the term *the international system.*

The details of the transmitting and receiving of impulses through the international system cannot be made out from the lofty vantage point where the whole system is envisaged. From the knowledge of other complex systems, we can expect to find a number of characteristics in the structure and the operations of the international system.

COMPLEX SYSTEMS

A system of whatever kind is an ensemble of parts or subsystems capable of changing from one state to another state. It is the ability to change that is interesting to the observer and that allows the ensemble to be considered a system. Any system is a structure that is perceived by its observers to have elements in interaction or relationships and some identifiable boundaries that separate it from its environment. A complex system is one that is found to have much variety in the process of changing from one state to another. Usually, it is discovered that the parts of a complex system are not simple in *their* activities but have, instead, their own subparts capable of varying their combinations and otherwise carrying on changes of state. Thus, a part or subsystem is not always in the same condition as it operates over time in the ensemble of the whole system. As the observer shifts his gaze from the system to one of the constituting parts, he discovers that the part itself is internally a system. This progression of revealing the inner makeup of a complex system reminds one of the taking apart of a Chinese puzzle box. Inside each box is another that appears as soon as the preceding one is removed.

In considering the international system, we must be prepared for its complexity in the first place by realizing that it will show much variety in its change-of-state processes, and in the second place by recognizing immediately that its main operating parts have the Chinese box characteristic. For a rough approximation, reference is made to the largest and most external box as the national society or nation. The working together of all such entities in attaining one state of affairs and then another *is* the international system. It is to be held firmly in mind that the participation of each national society in the system will not be fixed and simple, but instead will be directed in part by what has been going on in the way of shift and change in the several smaller, more internal of its boxes. The nesting effect of interactions of subsystems, of subsystems of subsystems, and of sub sub-systems, all traced as far as significant pattern of change will carry, gives rise to complexity. It is the main task of empirical theory and research to identify, portray, measure, and relate the characteristics of the performances of the system down through the tiers or levels of the subsystems.

A vocabulary describing the parts, aspects, and operations of the international system has begun to develop. *The* international system is meant to take in and encompass all interactions, in full scope. An *international subsystem* is a portion of the whole international system. The international relations of Southeast Asia might well be described as one of the international subsystems. The United Nations might be taken to be another. The parts or components of the international system are *national systems*. The term national actor is also in common use as a description of a national system and it has been employed earlier in this discussion. *National* subsytems are components that contribute to the behavior of the national system in the latter's participation in the activity of the international system. Public opinion, for example, might be regarded as a national subsystem. So also, conceivably, would be the actions of a decision-making group, of a political party, of an organization, of a group, or of an individual person belonging in the structure of the national system.

An input is any discrete action that enters a system or subsystem and contributes thereby to a change of state within a system or subsystem. An output is the impulse emitted by a subsystem to a system, contributing to a change. Feedback is a kind of input; it is one that returns a report to the locus of the previous output and carries information about the resulting state of affairs in the system. A positive feedback is a report that causes a subsystem to continue or to increase its particular previous action sent into the system. A negative feedback is a report that causes a subsystem to change its previous line of action and to correct the behavior of that subsystem by changing its condition and its subsequent output. A system is said to be in a steady state when disturbances affecting the system and/or its subsystems are compensated for through feedbacks. The corrections prevent the changing of the basic arrangements of the structures and processes of the system. A steady state need not be an equilibrium struck among the components of a system and it is not a description of a *no change* situation. A complex system in a steady state will usually oscillate around a point with many variations in its conditions, often because of overcorrections and undercorrections by subsystems. A stable system is merely one in which the steady state is usually maintained and that has achieved a reputation among observers for doing so.

How, in general terms, do complex systems work? Generalizing statements for any complex system have been set forth in many different forms. Here are a few examples (they may or may not match the facts of the historical, existing international system):

(1) Complex systems tend to be self-organizing, due primarily to adjustments made to disturbing conditions according to negative feedback effects.

(2) Positive feedback effects lead to the filling in, over time, of a complex system with additional special purpose subsystems, to the extent of available space and energy resources.

(3) Leading characteristics in the performance of a complex system arise from the arrangement of its subsystems and of the relationships among these. Behavior depends on structure, in other words.

(4) Complex systems and their subsystems have normal operating ranges; the performance in these ranges usually is less than the maximum capacity for systems and subsystems.

(5) The loading or stressing of a system is the effect of extending a system and/or subsystem toward the maximum capacity. Several effects occur under stressing, including:

a. The tendency of the system to demand progressively larger contributions from subsystems with increases in stress.

b. The reorganization or the destruction of subsystems from overloading to preserve the system under extreme stress.

c. The tendency of the system to require increasing amounts of information with increasing stress.

d. The tendency under severe stress on the system for subsystems to underrespond at first and subsequently to overrespond.

e. The tendency under severe stress on subsystems for the overall system to underrespond at first and subsequently to overrespond.

(6) The larger the population of subsystems in a system, the greater is the tendency to organize specialized subsystems for the purposes of guidance, control, coordination, and information-processing.

(7) Subsystems establish boundaries of exchange with other subsystems and with the system; thus a given subsystem restricts some part of its activities to its own maintenance within its boundary. How much autonomy subsystems have in allocating their activities at the boundary—inwardly for self-maintenance and development and across the boundary in exchange with other systems and with the whole system —is an important element in the performance of the system.

(8) A complex system is not restricted in its performance to single relationship patterns among its subsystems. For example, a task that is frustrated by the blocking of a given network of subsystem functions may still be carried out by the utilization of different combinations of subsystem actions. The ability of a complex system to establish multiple, alternative routes for its operations constitutes a characteristic that is called equifinality.

(9) A basic change in either the structure or the processes of a system will tend to bring about changes in the structures, processes, and relationships of subsystems.

(10) A basic change in a subsystem may bring about changes in other subsystems and/or in the whole system.

To some readers, the preceding propositions may suggest interesting questions to be asked about the historical, existing international system, or they may lead to insights into how it works. To others, the propositions may be lacking entirely in such suggestions. Being extremely abstract, these ideas invite reformulations at lower levels of abstraction and generality.

The lowering of the level of abstraction is easily illustrated with the third proposition given above: that the structure of a complex system gives rise to its performance traits. Professor Morton A. Kaplan has produced models of six different types of international systems and has enunciated essential rules to describe the characteristic, maintaining behavior of each of the six types. The six are called the balance of power system, the loose bipolar system, the tight bipolar system, the universal system, the hierarchical system, and the unit veto system. The names refer to structural attributes of the systems. Only a few rules of behavior of two of the systems will be cited, since our objective is only to illustrate how the level of abstraction can be lowered.

The balance of power system contains, among others, two interesting behavioral traits:

(1) National actors will act in opposition to any actor or coalition of actors seen as rising to predominance in the international system.

(2) Defeated or subordinated national actors of the system will not be held to that status by the others; they will be allowed to resume a position roughly coordinate with other members of the system.

The unit veto system has not existed in history, but it is a model that, as Kaplan states, "exhibits features of genuine peculiarity." Kaplan notes also, however, that it might come into existence if all national actors in the system had "weapons of such a character that any actor is capable of destroying any other actor that attacks it even though it cannot prevent its own destruction." [1] Two of its rules are:

(1) Each national actor in the system will act to stand off every other member to preserve the existing steady state of the unit veto international system.

(2) The unit veto system can maintain a steady state only if its actors will, without exception, resist threats of destruction and be willing to retaliate if attacked. The unit veto system is, obviously, an unstable system, since it will be transformed into a system with a different structure if an actor starts a chain reaction by attacking or if blackmail by threats of destruction should prove to be too powerful to resist.

Kaplan's systems are at too general a level to assist greatly the ordering of facts, as theories are supposed to do. The shortcoming can be remedied, however, by reformulations until a level of reduced abstraction and generalization is reached where the ordering of time-place-topic identified facts will dovetail readily with the theory. No examples of step-by-step descent of the ladder of abstraction-generality will be given at this stage of the discussion. Instead, one other proposed device for bringing theory and facts together will be mentioned.

---

[1] Morton A. Kaplan, *System and Process in International Politics* (New York: John Wiley & Sons, Inc., 1957), p. 50.

The idea of treating some portions of the whole international system separately, according to geographical characteristics or other criteria, has been advanced by several scholars. One plan is to consider two groups of national actors and their interactions as an international subsystem. These two subsystems are viewed as interacting—or exchanging inputs and outputs. Theory and research are then to be addressed to the problems of how and why they interact. In one formulation, the East-West international subsystem, which has been operating since World War II in patterns called the Cold War, is conceived to be intersected by a North-South international subsystem. The latter is preoccupied by interests and problems of economic development, by disparities in wealth and power, and by a number of other considerations stimulating both conflict and cooperation. Another formulation for dividing the international system in two parts has already become popularized in the dichotomized concept of the Communist World and the Free World. More and more, the students of Soviet affairs have been turning to a theoretical outlook that portrays the Communist World as a dynamic, changing, interacting international system.[2] In the terminology used here, they are studying the structure and process of an international subsystem.

Yet another scheme for reducing complexity, generality, and abstraction is being championed by some students of international relations.[3] They suggest that the knowlege of international relations will advance through theory-directed research and a focusing of attention on partially self-contained international subsystems in geographical areas such as the Middle East, Southeast Asia, Latin America, and others. Their argument is that the problems of understanding the actors and the interactions in such international subsystems are not as great as in the study of the whole international system. The linking of subsystems to the whole can accompany the analysis of how and why the particular international subsystems are organized and oriented in their actions.

All the foregoing ideas and plans about international subsystems spring from the general conception of *the* international system. Eventually, it can be anticipated that interesting developments will appear from the leads to lower-level theory and research according to the international

---

[2] Jan F. Triska, "Stanford Studies of the Communist System: The Sino-Soviet Split," *Background,* 8 (November 1964), pp. 143–159.

[3] Leonard Binder, "The Middle East as a Subordinate International System," *World Politics,* 10 (April 1958), pp. 408–429; Michael Brecher, "International Relations and Asian Studies: The Subordinate State System of Southern Asia," *World Politics,* 15 (January 1963), pp. 214–215; George Modelski, "International Relations and Area Studies: The Case of Southeast Asia," *International Relations,* 2 (April 1961), pp. 143–155.

subsystem approach. There are a few more observations that should be made about the overall characteristics of the international system.

We should assume that the system is open and adaptive. That is to say, we shall not anticipate that its activities are running in foreordained cycles. Instead, it is better to assume that the total stream of interaction sometimes will flow in novel directions, according to influences brought to bear upon it from the environment. Because men operate it, we expect the international system to be somewhat changeable and to be adaptable to new conditions. Further, specialization of functions appears within the system and within its component parts. Societies will be observed to provide special organizations for coping with incoming and outgoing events. Again, because it is a human system, we should be surprised if it were not subjected to manipulation by its member-nations and therefore exposed to varied perturbations. Behind the disturbances and upheavals we expect to discover, however, much interacting that is of a highly regular and even routine character. Although it may not seem, at first, a helpful point to emphasize, we assume that the conditions and events produced in the international system will have but two possible sources— a source generated *within* nations and controlled by conditions, impulses, and decisions stemming from domestic national life, and a second source created by the interplay of activity *between* nations.

If every nation participating in the international system emitted a single stream of simple, slightly varying, and highly patterned behavior into the system, the problem of knowing how the system works would still be formidable. By making a false assumption of simple, single stream interaction, we can gain an idea of how much knowledge would need to be organized to understand the international system as a whole. Between two actors under this assumption there could be but a single stream of interaction. Among three actors there could be three streams. Among four and five actors, there could be, as the diagrams of Figure 2 show, respectively, six and ten streams. In the international system with about 130 recognizable national actors, there would be 8,385 streams to be taken into account for full knowledge of the flows of the system. It is hardly necessary to demonstrate how much more extensive and complicated the international system really is to discourage the hope of anyone to know all the relevant facts about the international system.

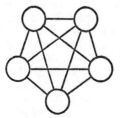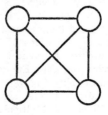

Figure 2   Interaction channels for 4- and 5-component systems.

9. POLITICAL DISCONTINUITIES IN THE INTERNATIONAL SYSTEM

Oran R. Young

THE INTERNATIONAL political system is currently undergoing changes that are both rapid and extensive. Especially since the early sixties, a number of trends have manifested themselves and become interrelated in such a way that, taken together, they are substantially altering the fundamental postwar patterns of international politics. These indications of change and flux have engendered a substantial debate concerning appropriate concepts for the analysis of the international system. Nevertheless, the resultant debate about the significance of these trends has evolved, for the most part, around the dichotomy between bipolar and multipolar models of the international system.[1] As a result, the debate has been cast in terms of a somewhat narrow conception of essentially structural problems. I submit, however, that the dichotomy between bipolar and multipolar models is clearly inadequate to deal with a number of the principal aspects and axes of change which are becoming increasingly important in international politics in the current period. Nor is the range of mixed types along a spectrum between the poles of bipolarity and multipolarity sufficient for a clear analysis of contemporary shifts.[2] While the notion of a vertically layered system combining elements of bipolarity and multipolarity at the same time, for example, is an interesting one, it too fails to capture much of the essence of the contemporary flux.[3]

From *World Politics*, Vol. xx, No. 3, pp. 369–392. Copyright © 1968 by Princeton University Press. Reprinted by permission of Princeton University Press.

ORAN R. YOUNG (1941–   ) Professor of Political Science, Princeton University. Author of *The Politics of Force: Bargaining During International Crises* (Princeton: Princeton University Press, 1968); *Systems of Political Science* (Englewood Cliffs, N.J.: Prentice-Hall, 1968); *The Intermediaries: Third Parties in International Crises* (Princeton: Princeton University Press, 1967).

[1] For a clear discussion of the bipolar model, see Kenneth Waltz, "The Stability of a Bipolar System," *Daedalus* (Summer 1964), 881–909. A somewhat parallel effort to develop the multipolar model is Karl W. Deutsch and J. David Singer, "Multipolar Power Systems and International Stability," *World Politics*, xvi (April 1964), 390–406.

[2] For various conceptions of the range of mixed types, see Arthur Lee Burns, "From Balance to Deterrence: A Theoretical Analysis," *World Politics*, ix (July 1957), 494–529; and Ciro Elliott Zoppo, "Nuclear Technology, Multipolarity, and International Stability," *World Politics*, xviii (July 1966), 579–606.

[3] This notion of a layered system has been developed by Richard Rosecrance in his article "Bipolarity, Multipolarity, and the Future," *Journal of Conflict Resolution*, x (September 1966), 314–27.

What are needed instead, therefore, are some new modes of conceptualizing the international political system. It is the thesis of this article that a constructive start in this direction can be made by emphasizing the growing interpenetration of the global or systemwide axes of international politics on the one hand and several newly emerging but widely divergent regional arenas or subsystems on the other hand.

THE DISCONTINUITIES MODEL

The alternative model I propose for the analysis of international politics in the present period is one that encompasses the concurrent influence of global and regional power processes in patterns that are strongly marked by elements of both congruence and discontinuity. In general, the concepts of congruence and discontinuity refer to the extent to which patterns of political interests and relationships of power are similar or dissimilar as between the global arena and various regional arenas and as between the different regional arenas themselves. There are, however, several more specific characteristics of this model of international politics that should be made explicit at the outset.

First, there are some actors and some substantive issues that are relevant throughout the whole international system, or at least throughout most of its subsystems. The superpowers, though their *effective* influence on many issues is declining, clearly fall into this category in the current international system. Similarly, substantive issues such as communism, nationalism, and economic development have systemwide as well as local aspects. Second, relevant actors, substantive interests, patterns of conflict, and specific power balances differ significantly from one subsystem to another. While global actors and issues are of some importance in each subsystem, the individual subsystems also contain a variety of unique features. Asian and African power balances, for example, are quite different from the more classical arrangements in Europe. And Asian communism is considerably more intertwined with the problems of active nationalism than is the case with communism in Europe. Third, the regional subsystems of the international system are therefore significantly discontinuous with one another in a number of respects. The degree of discontinuity between any two subsystems may of course vary, but for the moment it is the existence of discontinuities in general that needs to be stressed. Fourth, in all cases the subsystems are by no means totally discontinuous with one another since each is in fact an amalgam of global and local features. The existence of systemwide actors and issues is not the only source of congruence between the various subsystems. Several other types of links between subsystems are of some importance. To begin with, with regard to issues of reputation there is a spread effect that is important in shaping regional manifestations of systemwide issues. For example, the alliance behavior of a superpower in one subsystem can affect the posture of that power's allies in other subsystems. In addition, there are various demonstration effects that exercise a considerable influence on the atmosphere of international politics across subsystems. In other words, there are perceptual links between the subsystems as well as more substantive links. These perceptual links tend to be substantially spread and strengthened through the existence of various universal organizations, such as the United Nations, that serve as channels of communication. The fifth characteristic of the model is that the specific mixture between global and regional elements is apt to differ in a variety of ways from one subsystem to another. In short, levels and patterns of discontinuity are likely to be relatively volatile both horizontally across space and vertically over time.

It is important to clarify the essential differences between the discontinuities model outlined above and the other important models that have appeared in the contemporary discussion of international politics.[4] Bipolar models emphasize the importance of a single, dominant axis of conflict and the tendency for regional actors and issues to be conceptualized in relationship to the underlying bipolar axis of the system. The discontinuities model, on the other hand, stresses the importance of both systemwide and regional factors and emphasizes the complex patterns of their interpenetration, leaving room for shifting weights with regard to the question of which type of factor is dominant. For its part, the multipolar model tends to stress the existence of a multiplicity of axes of conflict and the phenomenon of crosscutting relationships among these axes.[5] The discontinuities model differs in several respects from the multipolar perspective: it deals primarily with subsystems rather than with individual actors; it stresses the differences between systemwide and regional axes of conflict; and it focuses on the complex interpenetrations between universal and regional issues rather than on the much less "lumpy" notion of a number of individual actors dealing with each other on a variety of issues in ways that produce numerous intersecting lines of conflict. Next, the distinctions between the discontinuities model and the model based on the notion of a small number of relatively distinct regional blocs are easily discernible.[6] Above all, the discontinuities model em-

---

[4] Perhaps the single most important statement of abstract models of the international system remains Morton A. Kaplan, *System and Process in International Politics* (New York 1957).

[5] In its intellectual origins, the multipolar model of the international system really stems from the conceptions of the American group theorists concerning domestic politics. For the original and in some ways clearest statement of these conceptions, see Arthur F. Bentley, *The Process of Government* (Chicago 1908).

[6] For conceptualizations of models along these lines, see Roger Masters, "A Multi-Bloc Model of the International System," *American Political Science Review*, LV

phasizes both the combination of global and regional factors within individual subsystems and the various interconnections between subsystems. Finally, there is a hypothetical model of the international system based on the notion of political fragmentation that would produce a situation somewhat similar to the old conception of atomistic liberalism within individual polities. In this case, the discontinuities model with its repeated stress on interactions and interpenetrations offers a conception of international politics that constitutes one form of direct opposition to the fragmentation model.[7]

One of the most interesting features of the discontinuities model of the international system is the extent to which it contains logical ambiguities that are very much analogous to some of the central problems of international politics in the current era. The sources of these ambiguities fall into several distinct categories. First, the tension between congruence and discontinuity among the various subsystems generates "limited adversary" relationships of a very peculiar nature, especially among the great powers.[8] In short, black-and-white distinctions are impossible in such a situation. The great powers, and especially the superpowers, are increasingly constrained to modify their conflicts in any given subsystem by the fact that they are apt to have important common interests in other subsystems which they do not want to jeopardize. At the same time, these powers are often hampered in the exploitation of common interests both within subsystems and on the global level by the fact that they find themselves engaged in sharp conflicts in other subsystems. There is little doubt, for example, that one important source of change in the postures of the United States and the Soviet Union in Europe is the development of incipient common interests between these powers in the Asian subsystem. Or to take another example, a major barrier to Soviet-American cooperation on the global issues of arms control arises from their conflicting interests in such concrete situations as Germany and Vietnam.

Second, there are important possibilities for manipulation across subsystems which tend to lend further ambiguities to the system, in addition to those emerging directly from the tension between congruence and discontinuity. These possibilities emerge, in essence, from the fact that, while the various subsystems are significantly discontinuous, there are nevertheless important interconnections between them. For this reason,

---

(December 1961), 780–98; and Wolfram Hanrieder, "The International System: Bipolar or Multibloc," *Journal of Conflict Resolution*, IX (September 1965), 299–308.

[7] Another form of direct opposition to fragmentation would be the development of genuine political integration among the units of the international system.

[8] The concept of "limited adversary" relationships is introduced and developed in Marshall D. Shulman, *Beyond the Cold War* (New Haven 1966).

it is sometimes possible to achieve advantages by utilizing political credit and reputation across subsystems. Victories won in a subsystem that is relatively easy to deal with may serve a country in pursuing its interests in other subsystems. Or again, it is sometimes possible to stir up trouble in one subsystem as a means of sowing confusion and of diverting attention from a country's prime area of interest.[9] There are also in a system of this kind some less tangible manipulatory possibilities arising out of perceptual problems. Especially in a dynamic and fast-changing world, it is sometimes possible to define and conceptualize emerging power balances in terms of perspectives and concepts developed originally for other arenas. Though this effort sometimes leads to dangerous misconceptions and rigidities (more on these problems below), the process can work to the advantage of an actor that can succeed in shaping perceptions about realities and relevant norms in a specific area in ways that work to its own advantage.

Third, the logical ambiguities that can arise from a discontinuities model increase considerably when we begin to move from a world of two important subsystems to one that contains a number of important subsystems. Both the specific issues and the mixture between regional and global concerns will vary from one subsystem to the next. From the point of view of the powers with systemwide interests, the complexities are increased on a straight numerical basis since there are a greater number of combinations of issues and of discontinuities to be dealt with in a situation of multiple subsystems. Moreover, the shift to multiple subsystems raises the possibility of new types of international problems that are not unique to any individual subsystem but that are still not universal problems since they do not arise in all of the subsystems of the overall system. And finally, the number of possibilities for manipulation, mentioned above, rises rapidly as the system shifts from two subsystems to multiple subsystems.

Given the complexities and ambiguities of the system summarized in the discontinuities model, it is hardly surprising that it tends to generate various intellectual problems and confusions that plague the work of analysts and decision-makers alike. In particular, the mixed and interpenetrated nature of the situation seems to go against the grain of very deep-seated psychological needs for clarity and relative simplicity in efforts to conceptualize reality. Perhaps because of these needs, there are two characteristic classes of simplifying devices that tend to crop up repeatedly in efforts to deal with a world of significant discontinuities. Though these classes of devices are, in a sense, opposites, both involve

---

[9] This particular possibility has always been a major source of American concern with regard to East-West problems in the postwar period.

substantial distortions of reality which are apt to generate very serious difficulties for sound analysis and decision-making.

The first class of simplifying devices falls under the heading of *segmentation* or *compartmentalization* and is based on a form of cognitive dissonance. The main thrust of these devices is an overemphasis on the uniqueness of individual, regional subsystems and a tendency to deny, at least tacitly, the extent of interpenetration and congruence between them. More specifically, segmentation is the characteristic failing of analysts who operate on the basis of area specialization and of decision-makers and bureaucrats who work through the country or regional-office system. This orientation not infrequently leads to an inability to assess the impact of systemwide actors and issues on regional power processes. Even more serious, however, is the extent to which segmentation of this kind tends to result in a failure to take account of interconnections between subsystems in such areas as reputation, demonstration effects, and the problems of manipulation across subsystems.

The second class of simplifying devices falls under the heading of *fusion* or *universalization* and stems from the search for a few underlying dimensions or concepts in terms of which it is possible to conceptualize all of international politics. This device is perhaps even more common than segmentation, especially among the lay public, because it satisfies the felt need for some sense of "understanding" concerning the basic meaning or significance of the whole of international politics. At the same time, fusion is apt to be even more distorting than segmentation, both because it requires simplification on an even more grandiose scale and because it leads to a polarized conception of the whole world rather than, as with segmentation, to a differentially inadequate conceptualization of particular regional subsystems. Even the most cursory consideration of such polarized conceptions as democracy versus communism, capitalism versus socialism, or the world city versus the countryside is ample to demonstrate the extent of distortion that the device of fusion is likely to produce.

THE EMERGENCE OF DISCONTINUITIES IN THE INTERNATIONAL SYSTEM

The problems arising from multiple power balances and political discontinuities are necessarily relatively modern developments in international politics. The fundamental precondition of reasonably extensive contacts between regional subsystems has been met, for the most part, only in the modern era. Within these limitations, however, there are some interesting historical examples of significant discontinuities between several regional subsystems. And some concrete examples of the ways in which such problems have manifested themselves in the past may lend perspective to our subsequent discussion of political discontinuities in the contemporary international system.

In the period between the Franco-Prussian War and the First World War several interesting discontinuities began to unfold more or less simultaneously in the international arena. From the 1880's onward, England and France were engaged in a variety of conflicts concerning the division of territories in Africa, a situation that created important rigidities when the common interests of the two countries on the European continent began to grow stronger, around the turn of the century, in the wake of various changes in Germany's posture. During the same period, England and Russia were in almost constant opposition to each other in the Middle East and in the Far East despite the existence of common interests between them in Europe and despite the growing Franco-Russian friendship on European issues. In fact, before the Anglo-Russian arrangement of 1907 concerning Persia, these two powers represented the principal axis of contention in the Middle East. Then, even during the First World War, England maintained a treaty relationship with Japan despite the fact that Russia and Japan were clear opponents in the Far East. Moreover, all of these divergent axes of contention were further complicated by the participation of all the major European powers except Austria-Hungary and Italy in the process of extracting concessions from China. Throughout this period, the lines of conflict in the Chinese arena, in which Japan and the United States also participated, tended to shift along different lines and at a different pace than the evolving pattern of conflict in Europe itself.

It is also possible to find important examples of discontinuities in international politics during the interwar years, though for the most part the complexities of this period seem somewhat less striking than those that characterized the system immediately prior to the First World War. England and France, in this period, developed sharply disparate views concerning the organization of security in Eastern Europe and, especially, concerning the appropriate role for the Soviet Union in this connection. More generally, the extensive and relatively acrimonious disputes between England and France in the Middle Eastern arena during the twenties and thirties clearly played a role in producing the uncertainty and unhappiness that marked Anglo-French efforts to coordinate in response to the resurgence of Germany in Europe. Even into the late thirties, for example, there were no formal alliance commitments or coordination procedures between the two countries. The United States in the interwar period allowed itself to become increasingly involved in the Far East, even while it continued to maintain an insistently isolationist posture with regard to developments in the European arena. Finally, the Second World War itself produced a striking example of political discontinuity in the efforts of the Soviet Union to remain on nonbelligerent terms with Japan long after the opening of the war in the Pacific and the entry of the United States into the European contest had polarized the war on a global basis. The sharpness of this discontinuity is particularly striking in the light of both the clear-cut interdependence of the allied powers in the European arena and the willingness of Britain to join the United States, at least formally, in the war in the Pacific.

Throughout most of the modern history of international politics, however, other types of relationships have tended to be considerably more salient and influential than the patterns of discontinuity under discussion in this article. To a very real extent, in fact, patterns of this kind have emerged on an extensive, worldwide scale and assumed a position of recognized importance only in the present international system. Several significant sets of causal factors underlie this present relevance of a discontinuities model of international politics.

To begin with, the impact of systemwide or global actors and issues is now much more strongly felt than has ever been the case before. The aftermath of the Second World War has seen a sharp acceleration in the rates of development of communications, transportation, and military technologies. As a result, the extent of interdependence of the various components of the overall international system, which has now become a full-fledged world system, has risen dramatically in the contemporary period.[10] Moreover, the period since World War II has witnessed the rise of two superpowers, in contrast to a larger number of great powers, as well as the emergence of several substantive issues that are relevant throughout the international system. Therefore, the contemporary system is not only more interdependent (in the general sense that what happens in any part of it is capable of exercising a very substantial influence on developments in any other part of it), but is also characterized by the existence of several discrete actors and issues of global significance which play very concrete and specific roles in the various regional subsystems.

These developments actually represent the acceleration of a fundamental trend that began in the second half of the nineteenth century. In themselves, however, they are not sufficient to produce an international system such as the one portrayed in the discontinuities model. In the period following World War II, for example, the dominance of the two superpowers became so clear-cut that some version of the bipolar model seemed to be the most accurate representation of reality. During these years, regional subsystems were nonexistent, effectively dominated by the superpowers, or sufficiently peripheral that the conditions of the discontinuities model other than its systemwide features were rarely met. In more recent years, however, a number of important developments in international politics have come together to reduce the salience of the

---

[10] Interdependence refers here to the extent to which actions in one part of the system affect the other parts of the system. It is therefore not a measure of common or overlapping interests. Interdependencies may be either positive or negative.

bipolar axis in international politics and to generate a variety of unique features in the power processes of the various subsystems of the international system.

First, a considerable period of time has passed without a large-scale international war to polarize and simplify the patterns of international politics. Because of this, the setting for political discontinuities has been growing increasingly favorable. Second, there has been a gradual diffusion of effective power in the system, despite the superpowers' great superiority in the physical elements of power. Third, the system has witnessed the rise or resurgence of a small number of new power centers that are of major significance even though they are still far less influential than the superpowers. Powers such as France, Germany, China, Japan, and India belong in this category. Fourth, the number of independent states in the system has grown rapidly since 1945, especially in the new regional subsystems of Asia and Africa. Here, the demise of colonialism represented the end of a major simplifying factor of earlier periods of international politics. Fifth, these shifts in the numbers and types of actors in the system have been accompanied by a general rise in levels of political consciousness and by the spread of active nationalism among the "new states." At the present time, even with such an avowedly international movement as communism, it is often difficult to tell whether its specific manifestations in particular states are based more on internationalism or on nationalism. Sixth, as effective influence diffuses in the system and as new lines of conflict emerge, the superpowers themselves are becoming more aware of their own common interests, even while they continue to prosecute a variety of conflicting interests in the various regional subsystems. The upshot of all these developments is that the major simplifying assumptions of the bipolar world of the fifties either are no longer valid or are increasingly hedged about by a variety of complicating relationships on a subsidiary level. The regional subsystems, therefore, are now coming more and more into their own as a complement to the global nature of the overall international system.

ASIA AND EUROPE

Let me continue this analysis of contemporary international politics by shifting to some more concrete remarks about the positions of the European and Asian subsystems in the overall international system. Increasingly, the relationships between these two subsystems offer illustrations of a number of the principal aspects of the general discontinuities model outlined above. At the same time, the emerging interconnections between Europe and Asia in contemporary international politics, which have become the subject of a number of ambiguities and misunderstandings, can be at least partially unraveled by applying the perspectives of the discontinuities model.

During most of the first half of the twentieth century, the Asian sub-system was essentially subordinate to rather than coordinate with the European subsystem. The degree of European dominance rose and fell in various patterns in the course of this period. Moreover, the various European powers were frequently at odds with one another over particular Asian issues during these years. The fact remains, nevertheless, that a great deal of the tone of Asian politics prior to World War II was set by the participation of various outside, and primarily European, powers in the Asian subsystem. In this perspective, the Second World War constitutes a sharp and decisive break with the previous pattern of relations between Europe and Asia that had, in any case, already begun to deteriorate during the thirties as the influence of Japan expanded.[11] For several reasons, however, the opening of the war did not lead immediately to the development of an independent or fully autonomous pattern of international politics in the Asian subsystem. First, Japan became the dominant political force in Asia during the war years, thereby effectively replacing the European powers in functional terms rather than exerting a significant pressure for the creation of a self-sustaining political system within Asia. Second, the outbreak of the war resulted in a thorough polarization of the patterns of conflict in the overall international system. For the duration of the war, the regional subsystems were effectively merged into a global pattern of dichotomous conflict.

The war itself destroyed the preconditions of the previous pattern of European dominance in Asia, but it did not, in the process, produce the makings of a new and autonomous Asian subsystem. In fact, in the years immediately following the war the Asian subsystem was almost entirely lacking in international relations of an indigenous variety. The individual units of the subsystem were often more deeply involved in bilateral relations with various external powers than in relations with one another. There were several important causes of this absence of local international relations in Asia. On the one hand, the situation was related to the activities of the outside powers. France, Britain, and Holland, for example, attempted to reestablish their former positions of dominance in Indochina, Malaya, and Indonesia, a posture that led to *inter*regional patterns of interaction as well as to a number of sharp conflicts. At the same time, its dominant role in the war in the Pacific and in the final defeat of Japan made the United States a prominent Asian power almost automatically. As a result, the aftermath of the war found the United States deeply involved in a number of Asian problems, a development

---

[11] It may be appropriate to take the Japanese invasion of Manchuria in 1931 as an important turning point. But the expansion of Japanese influence throughout the Asian subsystem continued on a fairly gradual basis until the actual beginning of the war.

that also tended to hinder the emergence of an autonomous Asian political system. On the other hand, this lack of genuine international relations within Asia after the war was also caused by a number of local, Asian factors. First, the most important Asian countries, including Japan and China, had been severely shattered by the war. The principal powers of the subsystem were therefore unable to function effectively as international actors. Second, a number of Asian countries were involved to a great degree with civil wars and a variety of other internal preoccupations during this period. China, Indonesia, Malaya, the Philippines, and various parts of Indochina all belong in this category. Third, many of the new states of Asia had not yet fully emerged from the ties of colonialism at this time. Much of the international effort of these states, therefore, was directed toward breaking the remaining bonds of colonial relationships, an interest that in fact complemented the concurrent attitudes of the European states in producing patterns of *inter*regional interactions. Among those states to which this set of problems was relevant were India, Pakistan, Indonesia, the Philippines, Korea, and the states of Indochina. In summary, then, the aftermath of the war witnessed a sharp break from the previous pattern of unequal relations between Asia and Europe, but it led, in the first instance, only to a peculiar ferment characterized by an absence of local international politics rather than to a new and independent format for international politics in Asia.

Starting from this rather chaotic base, the international politics of Asia have begun to change rapidly and extensively in recent years. The European powers ultimately lost their colonial conflicts. A number of new states appeared on the scene within the Asian subsystem. Though civil strife is still important in Asia, the most important civil war, in China, came to and end relatively early in the postwar period, thereby paving the way for the emergence of the People's Republic of China as an important force in Asian politics. At the same time, Japan reemerged very rapidly as a dynamic state and a key factor to be reckoned with in any current analysis of the Asian subsystem. In passing, even though these changes have also, to a very great degree, destroyed the physical bases of the tutelary position of the United States in Asia, American perceptions have often been quite slow in adapting to the consequences of this shift.

The unsettled quality of the Asian subsystem clearly remains in evidence today. But a number of fundamental issues have been either settled decisively or thrown into channels whose ultimate outcome is relatively clear. As a result, for the first time in the twentieth century a unique brand of Asian politics is beginning to take its place alongside the long-standing traditions of international politics within the European subsystem. In the contemporary world, of course, there is a great deal of interpenetration among all the regional subsystems in political relationships. And this interpenetration between the European and Asian sub-systems is very evident. To an increasing degree, however, the position of the Asian subsystem is becoming coordinate rather than subordinate.

The global features and components of this emerging Asian subsystem are not difficult to locate. Many specific issues in Asian politics still bear the imprint of the dominance of outside states in earlier years. The last vestiges of colonialism are only now disappearing. Many individual states in Asia are presently in the throes of various postcolonial shakedown processes. And the United States has not yet shown itself willing to draw back from its *de facto* emergence as a preeminent Asian power at the end of World War II. At the same time, Asian politics have been shaped in a number of ways by the global contours of the various ideological problems underlying the so-called cold war. Some form of communism has become a dominant, or at least powerful, force in a number of Asian countries.[12] The Asian states in general have become involved in the competition between the superpowers for the political favor of the non-aligned states of the world. And in Asia especially the ideologically tinged debate about which models of economic development are most appropriate has become virulent.[13] Finally, the global aspects of the Asian subsystem are further emphasized by the fact that the two superpowers have extensive power interests in the area. These interests have manifested themselves both in the extension of alliance systems to Asia and in the efforts of the United States to construct an Asian defense perimeter that is periodically probed and tested by Communist or Communist-influenced forces.[14] The existence of these interests in Asia on the part of both superpowers underlines the interconnection between the Asian subsystem and the overall international system, but it also tends to open up new possibilities for maneuver on the part of various second-order powers in Asia.

The global aspects of the Asian subsystem are therefore quite evident. More interesting perhaps are the unique features of the subsystem which are becoming increasingly evident and influential as Asian politics move away from their formerly subordinate role vis-à-vis the European arena. These unique features are particularly evident when defined in terms of

---

[12] At the present time, some form of communism is dominant in China, North Korea, and North Vietnam. There are, in addition, Communist movements of some significance in a number of the other Asian states.

[13] The models debated range from the pure forms of a free market economy to the pure forms of socialism. At the present time, many of the developing countries are becoming increasingly interested in various mixed forms.

[14] The most obvious cases of testing include (1) the attack on South Korea in 1950, (2) the probes in the Taiwan Strait in 1954–1955 and in 1958, (3) Laos, at least until the Geneva agreement of 1962, and (4) Vietnam from 1959 until the present.

discontinuities between the Asian and European subsystems. First, the Asian subsystem contains a large number of new states that are often lacking in the internal viability that characterizes most of the older and more established states of Europe. As a result, Asian politics are characterized by boundary problems, internal civil strife and shakedown processes, and the dangers of competitive external intervention in internal upheavals. Second, though the dividing lines are not always clear with regard to individual states, the two subsystems operate, for the most part, at very different levels of economic development. While the European states are increasingly interested in the politics of affluence, the states of Asia, by and large, are still struggling to reach the stage of sustained economic growth. Third, the brands of communism that have become prominent in Asia are quite different from the mainstream of European communism. In general, as was suggested earlier, Asian communism is more deeply colored by nationalism and agrarianism in the current period, a fact that has produced great variations in the Communist movements even within the Asian subsystem. Fourth, while European politics in the postwar period have been marked by a relatively clear demarcation between the Soviet and Western blocs, the Asian subsystem has always been rather amorphous with regard to these problems of political delineation. To some extent, this quality is related to geopolitical complexities and to the peculiar features of nonalignment and neutralism in Asia. More fundamentally, perhaps, the quality is also related to the fact that the basic East-West dichotomy essentially originated in Europe and spread only subsequently to the peculiar environment of the Asian subsystem. Fifth, though the superpowers are of critical importance in both subsystems, there are major differences between the second-order powers in the two subsystems. This point relates to such European states as Britain, France, and Germany and to such Asian powers as China, Japan, and India. Among other things, the second-order powers of the two subsystems differ on such matters as the nature of their political alignments, the extent and importance of sources of local conflict among the second order powers, and the degree of revisionism, directed toward the prevailing international system, manifested by these states.

While the European and Asian subsystems are related to one another in a number of important ways, therefore, they also exhibit a variety of very significant discontinuities. And it is essentially the mixed and complex quality of this relationship that accounts for a considerable amount of the confusion currently evident in efforts to understand the unfolding course of international politics. For this reason, let me now turn to an exploration of several sets of problems that emerge with some clarity from the application of the perspectives of the discontinuities model to the connections between the European and Asian subsystems in the current period.

First, despite the fact that the postwar patterns of international politics in Europe are now beginning to change, the Asian subsystem is characterized by a substantially greater fluidity of power relationships. In Europe we are now witnessing a gradual breaking down of the hard lines of conflict that emerged in the late forties and early fifties. Even with the appearance of a distinctive brand of international politics in Asia, on the other hand, no hard-and-fast lines of division and conflict have emerged. This fluidity in the Asian subsystem is ultimately related both to the peculiarities of communism in Asia and to the ambiguities created by the lack of internal viability in many of the individual states of the subsystem. Moreover, this political fluidity has manifested itself in a number of specific areas that generate problems for conceptions of international politics that stem primarily from the bipolar-multipolar spectrum.

Though the superpowers have attempted, from time to time, to extend their interbloc conflicts into Asia, this effort has met with increasing obstacles in recent years. On the Western side, the SEATO alliance has never become fully operational as a major factor in Asian politics.[15] And even from a very early stage in its history the Sino-Soviet alliance was more nearly a relationship of ideology, fraught with important ambiguities, than of complementary power positions.[16] As a result, there are no really solid alliance systems in Asia at the present time, a fact that produces considerably greater opportunities for shifts and alterations in power relationships than is presently the case in Europe. In addition, this picture has been further complicated in recent years by the growth of various common interests of a straightforward political nature which cut across the nominal lines of ideological alignments. Among the major powers, the current growth of common interests between the Soviet Union and Japan and between Japan and China is particularly significant. And the emerging pattern of crosscutting lines of conflict in Asia is further emphasized by the development of a number of very complex local conflicts involving, in the first instance, such states as Indonesia, Malaysia, India, and Pakistan. The consequences of this pronounced fluidity in the Asian subsystem are to create a political environment in which the

---

[15] Even at the outset in 1954, the SEATO alliance was notable for its failure to include many of the significant Asian states. In the intervening years, the alliance has occasionally been an instrument of American foreign policy, but has seldom functioned in any other way.

[16] Even in 1950 there were several aspects of the relationships between the Soviet Union and China that were obvious sources of potential disagreement. At the time, however, the weakness of China served to camouflage these problems. As a direct function of the emergence of China as a power of significance at least in the Asian sub-system, the basic political difficulties in the Sino-Soviet relationship have become increasingly prominent. In this sense, the relationship is essentially reverting to the patterns that predominated in the early years of the twentieth century.

simplifying assumptions of the European subsystem are often irrelevant, as well as to produce an expanding range of political opportunities and dangers in international relationships.

Second, we are now entering a period in which the coordinate relationships among the various second-order powers of the European and Asian subsystems are becoming increasingly interesting and important. This new type of interconnection between the subsystems is related to the gradual diffusion of effective influence in the overall international system as well as to the general development of coordinate rather than subordinate relations between Europe and Asia. As the overall international system begins to shift in these directions, a number of the second-order powers in the European and Asian subsystems are gradually coming to occupy positions in international politics which are somewhat analogous in structural terms. Under these circumstances, these states are becoming more and more interested in developing relationships with each other across the lines of the subsystems, not so much because they have strong common interests of a positive nature but because the analogous nature of their situations gives them common problems and, in some cases, common opponents in the form of the superpowers.

Although these developments are still at an early stage, these new forms of relationships across the subsystems are already manifesting themselves in a number of concrete areas. The French decision to recognize the People's Republic of China in 1964, for example, was the harbinger of a number of new trends in relations between France (and to some extent Germany) and China. At the present time, there are several sets of ideas emerging in France and Germany about the political value of relations with China for purposes of increasing European leverage in dealings with both the United States and the Soviet Union.[17] And the potential utility for China of developing ties with the major powers of Europe is evident. Moreover, these new interconnections between the subsystems are also emphasized by the increasing extent to which second-order powers in one subsystem are becoming independently active with regard to issues originating in the other. France, for example, has recently shown a growing interest in developing an independent and decidedly postcolonial position of influence with regard to the problems of Indochina. And the Japanese, as a result of their rapidly expanding economic power, have begun to participate extensively in several primarily Europe-based activities in the realm of international economics. This is true, for

---

[17] There are several alternative lines of thinking in this area at the present time. Some of these ideas have been discussed in a particularly interesting way by Richard Löwenthal. See his "China's Impact on the Evolution of the Alliances in Europe," in *Western and Eastern Europe: The Changing Relationship*, Institute for Strategic Studies, Adelphi Paper No. 33 (London, March 1967), 20–29.

example, of both the programs of the GATT and the growing efforts among the major powers to coordinate the means of regulating international monetary conditions.

Third, related to the general diffusion of effective influence in the international system and emphasized by developments such as the growth of relationships among the second-order powers in the system is the emerging trend toward the operationalization of common interests between the two superpowers. As is the case with the second-order powers, the superpowers are coming to occupy increasingly similar structural positions in the overall international system. Perhaps the most interesting feature of this trend in the context of this discussion, however, is the fact that the superpowers are finding it generally easier in the current period to activate their common interests in the Asian subsystem than in the European subsystem.[18] There are several reasons why this is so. As we have seen, the Asian subsystem has never been as rigidly structured as the European subsystem in the postwar period. International politics are more fluid in Asia than in Europe, a condition that provides more opportunities for significant change and therefore requires greater attention on a day-to-day basis. The Asian subsystem contains China, which is currently the most threatening of the emergent powers from the point of view of the power positions of the superpowers in the overall system. And finally, the Asian subsystem currently appears to be more actively dangerous than the European subsystem because of the challenges it generates for the stability of the overall international system. Under these circumstances, the superpowers have recently begun to show a noticeable interest in coordinating their activities in the Asian subsystem both generally, in order to maintain at least a minimally stable balance of power in the subsystem, and more specifically, in order to deal with the desires and the geopolitically critical position of China.

These growing interests of the superpowers in coordinating their activities in Asia have manifested themselves in a number of concrete situations.[19] The Indian subcontinent, for example, has in recent years been the focus of several issues that have served as catalysts for at least tacit coordination between the superpowers. Notable cases in point include the Sino-Indian conflict of the fall of 1962,[20] the problems of creating

---

[18] This point is especially interesting because of the fact that it is generally true despite the complexities and difficulties of the current struggle over Vietnam.

[19] These concrete efforts at coordination in the Asian subsystem are particularly interesting in contrast to the continuing strength of rigidities impeding the realization of common interests between the superpowers in the European subsystem.

[20] The temporal juxtaposition of this situation with the Cuban missile crisis makes the efforts at tacit coordination between the superpowers with regard to the Sino-Indian conflict even more significant.

favorable expectations about the future security of India in the wake of the Chinese nuclear test of October 1964,[21] and the various India-Pakistan clashes, which reached a high point in August and September 1965 and which shifted considerably in the wake of the Tashkent Declaration of January 1966.[22] In addition, the Soviet Union, as well as the United States, is currently beginning to show an interest in supporting the continued development of Japan, at least for the time being, to provide a balancing force that is likely to become increasingly important as a function of the emergence of China as an important actor in the Asian subsystem. Then, to take another example, the two superpowers have demonstrated considerable caution with regard to the disputes in the Maphilindo area in recent years and have tended to agree tacitly to avoid any possibility of being dragged into local disputes in this area. Thus, in 1962 the Soviet Union acquiesced in the American efforts to settle the West Irian issue, and in 1965 and 1966 the two superpowers were able to agree on an essentially "hands off" policy with regard to the internal upheavals in Indonesia. Finally, the current situation in Vietnam is extraordinarily peculiar in this perspective not only because the superpowers are in fact engaged on opposite sides of the principal conflict but also because this posture is at odds with some important common interests between the superpowers in the whole Indochina area. Underneath the current conflict and regardless of the future political status of South Vietnam, there is an important vein of common interests among the United States, the Soviet Union, and North Vietnam in the creation of viable political structures in Indochina capable of maintaining a stable balance in the area without succumbing to outside dominance.[23] And despite the current activities of the Soviet Union in aiding North Vietnam, it is undoubtedly a sense that the ongoing Vietnamese conflict is counterproductive of a stable balance in Indochina which lies behind both the half-hearted actions of the Soviet Union in this arena and the clear in-

---

[21] It was during this period that guarantees, and especially a tacit coordination of guarantees by both superpowers, began to become prominent in discussions of Indian security problems.

[22] In this connection, the *de facto*, though publicly denied, coordination of the superpowers in the United Nations Security Council was a prominent feature of the efforts to stop the overt hostilities between India and Pakistan during September 1965. During January 1966, the Soviet Union took the lead in playing the role of intermediary at Tashkent, but the United States operated in the background in a manner that indicated *de facto* approval and support of the Soviet iniative.

[23] The fundamental problem for the Soviet Union and the United States in this area is that there is every reason to suppose that the development of new patterns of outside dominance in Indochina would effectively mean Chinese dominance. The geo-political features of the area are such that it is much more plausible to foresee a situation in which a Chinese sphere of influence has reemerged than a situation characterized by the predominance of either superpower.

dications of Soviet unhappiness with the current course of events in Vietnam. For its part, the United States is not wholly oblivious to interests along these lines in Indochina. But the American perspectives on these issues at the present time are rather seriously confused by the influence of a set of doctrines which goes under the heading of containment and which raises a number of problems when applied to the politics of the Asian subsystem.

Fourth among the sets of problems under discussion, these American doctrines of containment, whose origins lie in the development of policies for Europe in the forties and fifties,[24] do not stand the strains of transfer to the Asian subsystem very well.[25] Although there has been in the contemporary period a considerable effort to accomplish this transfer, the effort has so far produced one fundamental ambiguity and a number of unanswered problems. The basic ambiguity stems from the fact that it has never become clear whether the focus of containment in the Asian context falls on the objective of containing China as an emerging great power or on the goal of restraining manifestations of communism in all forms throughout the Asian arena. This ambiguity is a crucial one because the two goals are not only not fully congruent in Asian politics, but also tend to require positions that are seriously incompatible on various specific issues. The fact is, as we have noted, that there are many brands of communism within Asia and that there are, in addition, important differences between most of the Asian brands of communism and the predominant European varieties. In containing China on the basis of power considerations, for example, the United States would have a strong positive interest in supporting the development of a strong and essentially nationalistic political system in the Democratic Republic of Vietnam, whereas this is clearly not the case if the objective is to restrain all forms of communism. Or again, Soviet-American common interests in Asia are increasingly evident from the perspective of the straightforward political interests of both countries in maintaining a minimally stable balance of power in the Asian subsystem. The growth of these common interests seems far less impressive, though, when filtered through the vestiges of the Communist versus non-Communist pattern of conflict in the global East-West arena.

In addition to this fundamental ambiguity, moreover, containment also runs into several more specific problems when applied to the Asian subsystem. To begin with, the political fluidity of the Asian arena and the absence of any clear geographical demarcations between Communist

---

[24] The classic formulation of this doctrine is the famous article by "X" (George Kennan), "The Sources of Soviet Conduct," *Foreign Affairs*, xxv (July 1947), 566–82.

[25] For some interesting additional points in this area see David Mozingo, "Containment in Asia Reconsidered," *World Politics*, xix (April 1967), 361–77.

and non-Communist areas make it almost impossible to develop meaningful blocs or systematic alignments based on the issue of communism in Asia. In addition, the frequent lack of political viability within individual states in the Asian subsystem makes it extraordinarily messy and costly to attempt to meet all manifestations of communism with forceful means. Whereas containment in Europe was largely a matter of constructing international coalitions and clarifying international boundaries, containment in Asia requires very extensive interventions in the internal politics of individual states. These interventions are generally ambiguously related to the basic goal of dealing with the sources of communism and are almost always politically costly in a variety of secondary effects.[26] It is primarily this lack of political viability in individual states, for example, that has led to a number of costly American interventions in Asian politics aimed at propping up dubious non-Communist regimes or at combating Communist-tinged insurgency movements. Finally, communism is only one of a number of important issues in Asian politics, and it has never acquired the overriding salience that it achieved in the European subsystem during the fifties. For this reason, any set of doctrines that ascribe a dominant role to the issue of communism is apt to produce both serious distortions and political contradictions when applied to the politics of the Asian subsystem.

These ambiguities of the concept of containment are also important in explaining the present American tendency to ascribe to the United States an especially critical balancing role in the Asian subsystem. Here again the key problem is one of conceptual confusion. Insofar as the principal goal is to contain all manifestations of communism in Asia, it is probably true that no country other than the United States will be both able *and* willing to shoulder major burdens in the Asian subsystem in the foreseeable future. This goal, however, is a highly ambiguous one in any case, both because communism in general is not considered as important an issue by most Asians as it is by many Americans and because there are so many varieties of communism in the Asian arena that it is exceedingly difficult to generalize about Asian communism, let alone worldwide communism. Insofar as the fundamental goal is to manage power successfully in the Asian subsystem in the face of the emergence of China, it is simply inaccurate to argue that the United States is the only important bulwark of stability. On the contrary, an interesting feature of the current Asian arena is the extent to which the emergence of China is serving as a catalyst in clarifying the common or overlapping interests of a num-

---

[26] These secondary effects range from the costs of a continuing commitment to support a shaky or unpopular regime to detrimental consequences for the reputation of the intervening state in the other subsystems of the overall international system.

ber of powers that have previously been separated by various ideological divergences.

Fifth, the development of a coordinate international subsystem in Asia has produced a number of new types of problems for the management of power in international politics, as well as some new ideas concerning specific regulatory mechanisms. Above all, it is difficult to conceive of any viable procedures for balancing the Asian subsystem in the absence of prominent participation on the part of both superpowers. This is so for a number of reasons including the political fluidity of the Asian arena, the lack of internal viability of many individual participants in the Asian subsystem, the sharpness of specific conflicts arising in this arena, and the extensiveness of the *ad hoc* political interests of both superpowers. From the point of view of managing power, this involvement of the superpowers in Asian politics is currently producing several consequences of interest. On the one hand, it opens up various possibilities for Asian powers to manipulate the interests and the commitments of the superpowers for local purposes. Both Chinas, for example, have successfully played this game in the various confrontations in the Taiwan Strait.[27] And increasingly, both Vietnams in the current struggle in Indochina are acting to lock the two superpowers into the conflict even though it means an actual or potential reduction in their own freedom of action on a number of issues.[28] While this process is sometimes of considerable importance in determining the specific outcomes of local conflicts, it carries with it some important dangers to overall international stability by involving the superpowers in situations of conflict that they are frequently unable to control very precisely.[29] On the other hand, however, this enforced coexistence of the superpowers in the Asian subsystem is increasingly leading to the growth of tacit agreements between these powers in the interests of developing rules for the maintenance of at least minimal stability in the Asian arena. Among other things, this limited and *de facto* coordination between the superpowers seems at present to be generating a new willingness to allow long-delayed processes of political shakedown to occur in a number of Asian states without

---

[27] During the 1958 crisis, activities along these lines were particularly evident in relationships between the People's Republic of China and the Soviet Union on the one hand and between the Nationalists and the United States on the other.

[28] For some interesting points concerning this problem in the Vietnam context, consult John T. McAlister, Jr., "The Possibilities for Diplomacy in Southeast Asia," *World Politics*, XIX (January 1967), 258–305.

[29] The possibilities of catalytic actions on the part of the local powers are particularly important. These dangers of catalytic actions do not refer, in the first instance, to nuclear exchanges, but rather to the possibilities of touching off escalatory sequences that are difficult to control.

attempting to exploit them very seriously for cold-war purposes.[30] In this sense, the current political environment in Asia may be considerably more conducive to a process of decisively throwing off the last vestiges of colonialism, in a genuine rather than a formal sense, than was the environment of the late forties and fifties, when the virulence of the cold war operated to freeze matters artificially in such a way that the necessary shakedowns were often prevented from being played out.

Perhaps the most characteristic problems of managing power in the contemporary Asian subsystem are those that arise from situations involving simultaneous and competitive interventions on the part of several outside parties in civil upheavals within individual states. The problem of competitive intervention is peculiarly characteristic of Asia, as compared with Europe, in the current period, and it is peculiarly dangerous in the existing international system, given the possibilities of escalation to superpower confrontations and the quality of military technologies available at the strategic level. Though this problem has not yet generated any clear-cut regulatory responses, it has produced some interesting movements in the direction of regulation. As mentioned above, the superpowers are now proceeding with considerable caution, for the most part, in the Asian arena, and they are showing increasing signs of a willingness to coordinate at least tacitly on procedures that will allow for political shakedowns in individual countries without disrupting the stabilty of the whole subsystem. More specifically, there is at the present time a growing interest in various arrangements of a more formal nature, such as neutralization agreements,[31] designed to allow the various outside parties with an interest in specific situations of internal upheaval to coordinate in setting up for the area a regime designed to prevent competitive intervention while still allowing the various internal forces to prosecute their conflicts in a manner that is as free of artificial impedi-

---

[30] Many of the Asian states emerged from colonialism with regimes that were highly successful in revolutionary activities but ill-suited to the requirements of creating viable political structures on a long-term basis. Adaptation problems of this kind are, in fact, relatively common in revolutionary situations. And they are an important cause of the continued political ferment that often follows the successful termination of a struggle for independence. In the Asian context, however, independence was gained by a number of states at a time when the bipolar conflict in the overall system placed artificial impediments in the way of this shakedown process. The current political ferment in several Asian states is actually a kind of delayed shakedown process that never occurred in the late forties and early fifties.

[31] For an exploration of the concepts of neutralization see "Neutralization in Southeast Asia: Problems and Prospects," A Study Prepared at the Request of the Committee on Foreign Relations, United States Senate, 89th Cong., 2nd Sess. (Washington 1966). This study was prepared by Cyril E. Black, Richard A. Falk, Klaus Knorr, and Oran Young.

ments as possible.[32] In the final analysis, however, the growth of thinking about the regulation of power along these lines in the Asian subsystem is not important so much for the merits of various specific formulations as for the fact that it constitutes evidence of the development of concepts in this area tailored especially for Asian problems rather than borrowed from prior experiences in the European subsystem.

CONCLUSION

The discontinuities model discussed in this article has no particular status as a set of answers concerning international politics. On the contrary, it is offered more as a set of concepts designed to generate fruitful insights concerning the changing state of the contemporary international system. And in this sense, it seems to me that the discontinuities model opens up a number of interesting lines of thought and problems for analysis which tend to be overlooked by the bipolar and multipolar models underlying most current debate in this area. It leads, for example, to ideas about a variety of types of complex interpenetration among subsystems each of which is sufficiently *sui generis* that it is impossible to assume direct correspondences among them. In this connection, the trade-offs and possibilities for manipulation across subsystems are particularly interesting in the contemporary world. In addition, the discontinuities model offers some useful perspectives on the problems of the actors with system-wide interests. Such perspectives are particularly useful in understanding current developments in international politics. Inconsistencies in Soviet and American behavior, for example, are far easier to explain when it is understood that both of these countries have patterns of interests that diverge substantially and are not infrequently incompatible with one another as between the various subsystems of the overall international system. The contrasts between the European and Asian subsystems, for example, offer illustrations of these problems.

The introduction of concrete material on the European and Asian subsystems also emphasizes some interesting triangular relationships. Here we have two important subsystems that are increasingly coordinate in their influence patterns, even though there are a number of very significant discontinuities between them. At the same time, the global pattern of relations between the superpowers intersects, at a number of points, with the patterns within each of the subsystems as well as with the interconnections between the two subsystems. As a result, an overall pattern of interaction is formed that contains two distinct classes of discontinu-

---

[32] Ideas of this kind have already been tried to a certain extent. Laos, for example, was formally neutralized by international agreement under the terms of the Geneva Convention of 1962. And Cambodia is presently a self-neutralized state whose act of neutralization has been received favorably by most of the relevant outside states.

ities. In addition to the discontinuities between the two subsystems, there are also discontinuities between the conceptually analogous patterns of international politics within the subsystems on the one hand and the global format of international politics focusing on the direct relationships between the superpowers on the other hand. Under these circumstances, it is hardly surprising that a substantive issue influenced simultaneously by several of these divergent patterns of international politics is virtually bound to become extremely complex and ambiguous. For example, a considerable degree of the opaqueness of the problems of Germany and of Southeast Asia at the present time is a result of this phenomenon of several distinct patterns of international politics focusing simultaneously on a given complex of substantive issues.

Finally, it is important to emphasize that the European and Asian problems discussed in this article are, in general terms, illustrative of a broader class of phenomena in contemporary international politics. In short, the relationships between various subsystems as well as between individual subsystems and the global patterns of international politics could be analyzed on a similar basis for such cases as Africa, Latin America, and the Middle East. While the particular substantive problems would vary from case to case, the general perspectives of the discontinuities model are equally relevant throughout the international system. Moreover, a shift from a focus on two subsystems to a consideration of a larger number of subsystems would raise additional questions that could be analyzed profitably. In general, a shift along these lines would open up possibilities for increasingly subtle analyses of the basic power processes of the contemporary international system.

SECTION THREE:

Nationalism and the Nation-State

10. NATIONALISM

Hans Kohn

NATIONALISM as we understand it is not older than the second half of the eighteenth century. Its first great manifestation was the French Revolution, which gave the new movement an increased dynamic force. Nationalism had become manifest, however, at the end of the eighteenth century almost simultaneously in a number of widely separated European countries. Its time in the evolution of mankind had arrived, and although the French Revolution was one of the most powerful factors in its intensi-

From *The Idea of Nationalism* by Hans Kohn (New York: Macmillan Company, 1960) pp. 3–7, 10–16. Reprinted by permission of The Macmillan Company. Copyright © 1944 by Hans Kohn.

HANS KOHN (1891–1971) Formerly Professor Emeritus of History, City College of New York; Visiting Professor, University of Texas, University of Pennsylvania, University of Berlin. Author of *Prologue to Nation-States: France and Germany, 1789–1815* (Princeton: D. Van Nostrand Company, 1967); *Political Ideologies of the Twentieth Century* (New York: Harper and Row, 1966); *Reflections on Modern History: The Historian and Human Responsibility* (Princeton: D. Van Nostrand Company, 1963); *The Age of Nationalism: The First Era of Global History* (New York: Harper Brothers, 1962); *The Mind of Germany: The Education of a Nation* (New York: Charles Scribner's Sons, 1960); *American Nationalism: An Interpretative Essay* (New York: Macmillan Company, 1957); *Pan Slavism: Its History and Ideology* (Notre Dame: University of Notre Dame Press, 1953); *Prophets and Peoples: Studies in Nineteenth Century Nationalism* (New York: Macmillan Company, 1953).

fication and spread, this did not mark the date of its birth. Like all historical movements, nationalism has its roots deep in the past. The conditions which made its emergence possible had matured for centuries before they converged at its formation. These political, economic, and intellectual developments took a long time for their growth, and proceeded at a different pace in the various countries. It is impossible to grade them according to their importance or to make one dependent upon another. All are closely interconnected, each reacting upon the others; and although their growth can be traced separately, their effects and consequences cannot be separated otherwise than in the analysis of the scholar; in life, they are indissolubly intertwined.

Nationalism is inconceivable without the ideas of popular sovereignty preceding—without a complete revision of the position of ruler and ruled, of classes and castes. The aspect of the universe and of society had to be secularized with the help of a new natural science and of natural law as understood by Grotius and Locke. The traditionalism of economic life had to be broken by the rise of the third estate, which was to turn the attention away from the royal courts and their civilization to the life, language, and arts of the people. This new class found itself less bound by tradition than the nobility or clergy; it represented a new force striving for new things; it was ready to break with the past, flouting tradition in its opinion even more than it did in reality. In its rise, it claimed to represent not only a new class and its interests, but the whole people. Where the third estate became powerful in the eighteenth century—as in Great Britain, in France, and in the United States—nationalism found its expression predominantly, but never exclusively, in political and economic changes. Where, on the other hand, the third estate was still weak and only in a budding stage at the beginning of the nineteenth century, as in Germany, Italy, and among the Slavonic peoples, nationalism found its expression predominantly in the cultural field. Among these peoples, at the beginning it was not so much the nation-state as the *Volksgeist* and its manifestations in literature and folklore, in the mother tongue, and in history, which became the center of the attention of nationalism. With the growing strength of the third estate, with the political and cultural awakening of the masses, in the course of the nineteenth century, this cultural nationalism soon turned into the desire for the formation of a nation-state.

The growth of nationalism is the process of integration of the masses of the people into a common political form. Nationalism therefore presupposes the existence, in fact or as an ideal, of a centralized form of government over a large and d stinct territory. This form was created by the absolute monarchs, who were the pacemakers of modern nationalism; the French Revolution inherited and continued the centralizing tendencies of the kings, but at the same time it filled the central organization with a new spirit and gave it a power of cohesion unknown before. Nationalism is unthinkable before the emergence of the modern state in the period from the sixteenth to the eighteenth century. Nationalism accepted this form, but changed it by animating it with a new feeling of life and with a new religious fervor.

For its composite texture, nationalism used in its growth some of the oldest and most primitive feelings of man, found throughout history as important factors in the formation of social groups. There is a natural tendency in man—and by "natural tendency" we mean a tendency which, having been produced by social circumstances from time practically immemorial, appears to us as natural—to love his birthplace or the place of his childhood sojourn, its surroundings, its climate, the contours of hills and valleys, of rivers and trees. We are all subject to the immense power of habitude, and even if in a later stage of development we are attracted by the unknown and by change, we delight to come back and to be at rest in the reassuring sight of the familiar. Man has an easily understandable preference for his own language as the only one which he thoroughly understands and in which he feels at home. He prefers native customs and native food to alien ones, which appear to him unintelligible and indigestible. Should he travel, he will return to his chair and his table with a feeling of relaxation and will be elated by the joy of finding himself again at home, away from the strain of a sojourn in foreign lands and contact with foreign peoples.

Small wonder that he will take pride in his native characteristics, and that he will easily believe in their superiority. As they are the only ones in which civilized people like himself can apparently feel at home, are they not the only ones fit for human beings? On the other hand, contact with alien men and alien customs, which appear to him strange, unfamiliar, and therefore threatening, will arouse in him a distrust of everything foreign. This feeling of strangeness will again develop in him sentiments of superiority, and sometimes even of open hostility. The more primitive men are, the stronger will be their distrust of strangers, and therefore the greater the intensity of their group feeling. Rudyard Kipling, in his poem "The Stranger," forcefully expressed this general feeling:

> The Stranger within my gate,
>   He may be true or kind,
> But he does not talk my talk—
>   I cannot feel his mind.
> I see the face and the eyes and the mouth,
>   But not the soul behind.
>
> The men of my own stock
>   They may do ill or well,
> But they tell the lies I am wonted to,
>   They are used to the lies I tell;

And we do not need interpreters
When we go to buy and sell.

The Stranger within my gates,
  He may be evil or good,
But I cannot tell what powers control—
  What reasons sway his mood;
Nor when the Gods of his far-off land
  May repossess his blood.

These feelings have always existed. They do not form nationalism; they correspond to certain facts—territory, language, common descent— which we also find in nationalism. But here they are entirely transformed, charged with new and different emotions, and embedded in a broader context. They are the natural elements out of which nationalism is formed; but nationalism is not a natural phenomenon, not a product of "eternal" or "natural" laws; it is a product of the growth of social and intellectual factors at a certain stage of history. Some feeling of nationality, it may be said, existed before the birth of modern nationalism—a feeling varying in strength and in frequency from time to time: at some epochs almost completely extinguished, at others more or less clearly discernible. But it was largely unconscious and inarticulate. It did not influence the thought and actions of men in a deep and all-pervading way. It found a clear expression only occasionally in individuals, and in groups only at times of stress or provocation. It did not determine their aims or actions permanently or in the long run. It was no purposeful will welding together all the individuals into a unity of emotions, thoughts, and actions.

Before the age of nationalism, the masses very rarely became conscious of the fact that the same language was spoken over a large territory. In fact, it was not the same language; several dialects existed side by side, sometimes incomprehensible to the man of a neighboring province. The spoken language was accepted as a natural fact. It was in no way regarded as a political or cultural factor, still less as an object of political or cultural struggle. During the Middle Ages, people deduced from the Bible that the diversity of languages was the result of the sinfulness of man, and God's punishment for the building of the Tower of Babel. Consciousness of language was aroused only at times of expeditions and travel or in frontier districts. There, the alien character of the group speaking the alien language was felt, and many national groups were first recognized as different and named by those of alien tongue. The Greek word *barbaros* (which meant "strange" or "foreign," and in consequence "rude" and "ignorant") probably had its source in the idea of stammering or inability to speak in a comprehensible way—a word akin to the Sanskrit expression *barbara*, which meant "stammering" or "non-Aryan." The Slavs called the Germans with whom they came into contact *niemci,* "the mutes," people who cannot make themselves understood. A man speaking an incomprehensible tongue seemed outside the pale of civilization. But language was accepted by the Slavs and by other peoples as a natural fact, not as a cultural inheritance. The language in which the treasures of civilization were inherited and transferred—in medieval Europe as well as in Islam, in India as well as in China—was generally not the language spoken by the people: it was a learned language accessible only to the educated class. Even if it was not a language of different origin, it was generally so archaic and so rich in many purely literary, classical associations that it was understood only by a small minority.

. . .

2

Nationalism is first and foremost a state of mind, an act of consciousness, which since the French Revolution has become more and more common to mankind. The mental life of man is as much dominated by an ego-consciousness as it is by a group-consciousness. Both are complex states of mind at which we arrive through experiences of differentiation and opposition, of the ego and the surrounding world, of the we-group and those outside the group. The collective or group consciousness can center around entirely different groups, of which some have a more permanent character—the family, the class, the clan, the caste, the village, the sect, the religion, etc.—whereas others are of a more or less passing character—schoolmates, a football team, or passengers on a ship. In each case, varying with its permanence, this group-consciousness will strive towards creating homogeneity within the group, a conformity and like-mindedness which will lead to and facilitate concerted common action. In that sense, we may speak of a group-mind and a group-action. We may speak of a Catholic mind and a Catholic action, of an English mind and an English action; but we may also speak of a rural mind or an urban mind, and of the action of rural or urban groups. All these groups develop their own character. The character of an occupational group, such as peasants, soldiers, civil servants, may be as clearly defined and stable as any character of a national group, or even more so. Each group creates its own symbols and social conventions, is dominated by social traditions, which find their expression in the public opinion of the group.

Group-consciousness is never exclusive. Men find themselves members of different groups at the same time. With the growth of the complexity of civilization, the number of groups of which men find themselves a part generally increases. These groups are not fixed. They have changing limits, and they are of changing importance. Within these pluralistic, and sometimes conflicting, kinds of group-consciousness there is generally one which is recognized by man as the supreme and most important, to which therefore, in the case of conflict of group-loyalties, he owes supreme loyalty. He identifies himself with the group and its existence, frequently not only for the span of his life, but for the continuity of his existence beyond this span. This feeling of solidarity between the individual and the group may go, at certain times, as far as complete submergence of the individual in the group. The whole education of the members of the group is directed to a common mental preparedness for common attitudes and common actions.

In different periods of history, and in different civilizations, we find different groups to which this supreme loyalty is given. The modern period of history, starting with the French Revolution, is characterized by the fact that in this period, and in this period alone, the nation demands the supreme loyalty of man, that all men, not only certain individuals or classes, are drawn into this common loyalty, and that all civilizations (which up to this modern period followed their own, and frequently widely different ways) are now dominated more and more by this one supreme group-consciousness, nationalism.

It is a fact often commented upon that this growth of nationalism and of national sectionalisms happened at the very time when international relations, trade, and communications were developing as never before; that local languages were raised to the dignity of literary and cultural languages just at the time when it seemed most desirable to efface all differences of language by the spread of world languages. This view overlooks the fact that that very growth of nationalism all over the earth, with its awakening of the masses to participation in political and cultural life, prepared the way for the closer cultural contacts of all the civilizations of mankind (now for the first time brought into a common denominator), at the same time separating and uniting them.

Nationalism as a group-consciousness is therefore a psychological and a sociological fact, but any psychological or sociological explanation is insufficient. An American psychologist defined a nation as "a group of individuals that feels itself one, is ready within limits to sacrifice the individual for the group advantage, that prospers as a whole, that has groups of emotions experienced as a whole, each of whom rejoices with the advancement and suffers with the losses of the group. . . . Nationality is a mental state or community in behavior." This definition is valid, as far as it goes, not only for the nation, but for any other supreme group to which man owes loyalty, and with which he identifies himself. It is therefore not sufficient to distinguish the national group from other groups of similar importance and permanence.

Nationalities are the product of the historical development of society. They are not identical with clans, tribes, or folk-groups—bodies of men united by actual or supposed common descent or by a common habitat.

Ethnographic groups like these existed throughout history, from earliest times on, yet they do not form nationalities; they are nothing but "ethnographic material," out of which under certain circumstances a nationality might arise. Even if a nationality arises, it may disappear again, absorbed into a larger or new nationality. Nationalities are products of the living forces of history, and therefore always fluctuating, never rigid. Nationalities are groups of very recent origin and therefore are of the utmost complexity. They defy exact definition. Nationality is an historical and a political concept, and the words "nation" and "nationality" have undergone many changes in meaning. It is only in recent history that man has begun to regard nationality as the center of his political and cultural activity and life. Nationality is therefore nothing absolute and it is a great mistake, responsible for most of the extremities of today to make it an absolute, an objective *a priori*, the source of all political and cultural life.

Nationality has been raised to an absolute by two fictitious concepts which have been accepted as having real substance. One holds that blood or race is the basis of nationality, and that it exists eternally and carries with it an unchangeable inheritance; the other sees the *Volksgeist* as an ever-welling source of nationality and all its manifestations. These theories offer no real explanation of the rise and the role of nationality: they refer us to mythical pre-historical pseudo-realities. Rather, they must be taken as characteristic elements of thought in the age of nationalism, and are subject themselves to analysis by the historian of nationalism.

3

Nationalities come into existence only when certain objective bonds delimit a social group. A nationality generally has several of these attributes; very few have all of them. The most usual of them are common descent, language, territory, political entity, customs and traditions, and religion. A short discussion will suffice to show that none of them is essential to the existence or definition of nationality.

Common descent seemed of great importance to primitive man, for whom birth was as great a mystery as death, and therefore was surrounded by legends and superstitions. Modern nationalities, however, are mixtures of different, and sometimes even very distant, races. The great migratory movements of history and the mobility of modern life have led everywhere to an intermingling, so that few if any nationalities can at present claim anything approaching common descent.

The importance of language for the formation and life of a nationality was stressed by Herder and Fichte. But there are many nationalities who have no language of their own—like the Swiss, who speak four different languages, or the Latin American nationalities, all of whom speak Spanish or Portuguese. The English-speaking nations (also the Spanish-speaking) are partly of similar descent; they speak the same language, and had until quite recently the same historical background, and also traditions and customs very much akin to each other; yet they represent different nationalities with frequently conflicting aspirations. Another example of the comparative irrelevance of objective criteria for the formation and continued existence of separate nationalities is to be found in Norway and Denmark, where the people are of common racial stock and speak almost the same language. Nevertheless, they consider themselves as two nationalities, and the Norwegians set up their own language only as the result of having become a nationality.

Customs and traditions were first stressed in their importance for nationality by Rousseau. Each nation undoubtedly has its customs, traditions, and institutions; but these often vary greatly from locality to locality, and, on the other hand, tend in our times to become standardized all over the world, or at least over large areas. Customs and manners nowadays often change with great rapidity.

Religion was the great dominating force before the rise of nationalism in modern times. This is true in Western as well as Eastern Christianity, in Islam and in India. The dividing lines were not drawn according to nationalities, but according to religious civilizations. Therefore the rise of nationalities and of nationalism was accompanied by transformations in the religious attitude of man, and in many ways the growth of nationalities has been helped or hindered by the influence of religion. Religious differences sometimes divided and weakened nationalities, and even helped to create new nationalities, as in the case of the Catholic Croats and the Orthodox Serbs. On the other hand, national churches have frequently been an important element in helping to arouse nationalism; and when conflicting nationalities were of different religions often played a large part in the defense mechanism of the weaker nationality, as Catholicism did in Ireland and in Prussian Poland.

The most important outward factor in the formation of nationalities is a common territory, or rather, the state. Political frontiers tend to establish nationalities. Many new nationalities, like the Canadian, developed entirely because they formed a political and geographic entity. Generally we may say, for reasons which will be considered later, that statehood or nationhood (in the sense of common citizenship under one territorial government) is a constitutive element in the life of a nationality. The condition of statehood need not be present when a nationality originates; but in such a case (as with the Czechs in the late eighteenth century) it is always the memory of a past state and the aspiration toward statehood that characterizes nationalities in the period of nationalism.

Although some of these objective factors are of great importance for the formation of nationalities, the most essential element is a living and active corporate will. Nationality is formed by the decision to form a nationality. Thus the French nationality was born of the enthusiastic manifestation of will in 1789. A French nation, the population of the French kingdom, existed before, as did some of the objective conditions necessary for the foundation of a nationality. But only the newly aroused consciousness and will made these elements active and effective, fused them into a source of immense centripetal power, and gave them a new importance and meaning. The English and the American nationalities were constituted by "covenants," by free acts of will, and the French Revolution evolved the plebiscite, as a result of which membership in a nationality was determined, not by objective characteristics, but by subjective declaration. The foundation of the Swiss nationality was dramatized by Friedrich Schiller in his *Wilhelm Tell* according to legendary tradition into the famous oath on the Rutli, "Wir wollen sein ein einig Volk von Brudern." This mythical declaration, "We wish to be one single nation of brothers," was uttered at the birth of every nationality, whether this birth happened, after a long pregnancy, in the enthusiasm of a revolutionary period, or whether the awakening of the masses required many years of ceaseless propaganda. Nationalities as "ethnographic material," as "pragmatic" and accidental factors in history, existed for a very long time; but only through the awakening of national consciousness have they become volitional and "absolute" factors in history. The extensive use of the word "nationality" must not blind us to the fact that the lack of this voluntaristic element makes what are sometimes called nationalities of the period before the rise of modern nationalism fundamentally different from nationalities of the present time. To base nationality upon "objective" factors like race implies a return to primitive tribalism. In modern times it has been the power of an idea, not the call of blood, that has constituted and molded nationalities.

11.   NATIONALISM IN UNDERDEVELOPED COUNTRIES

John H. Kautsky

THE CONCEPT of nationalism had taken its meaning from the "national" consciousness which began to grow in France with the Revolution and from the movements that completely changed the map of Central and Eastern Europe during the following century and a half. Nationalism may be defined from this European experience as an ideology and a movement striving to unite all people who speak a single language, and who share the various cultural characteristics transmitted by that language, in a single independent state and in loyalty to a single government conducted in the people's language. A looser and less meaningful connotation of the word nationalism has also been widespread, which would seem to define it merely as the loyalty and emotional attachment of a population, regardless of its language, to an existing government and state. In this sense, one can refer to Soviet, Swiss, Belgian, and American nationalism, though all of these countries include inhabitants of different language and cultural backgrounds and the languages spoken by at least some of them are also the languages of other countries.

When we now turn to a consideration of what is generally referred to as nationalism in the underdeveloped areas, it becomes clear immediately that we are confronted with a phenomenon quite different from European nationalism. While it might therefore have been preferable to avoid the use of the term with reference to underdeveloped countries altogether, this would be futile in view of its adoption on all sides. We can only hope that the use of a single term to designate the two phenomena will not obscure the differences between them, that an easy assumption that the "nationalism" of Europe will not obstruct recognition of the quite different forces producing it.

Neither of the two definitions of nationalism we derived from European experience can account for the nationalism of underdeveloped areas.

From *Political Change in Underdeveloped Countries: Nationalism and Communism*, by John H. Kautsky (New York: John Wiley and Sons, 1966) pp. 32–38; 45–49. Reprinted by permission of John Wiley and Sons, Inc. Footnotes have been renumbered to appear in consecutive order.

JOHN H. KAUTSKY (1922–   ) Professor of Political Science, Washington University. Author of *Communism and the Politics of Development* (New York: John Wiley and Sons, 1968); *Moscow and the Communist Political Change in Underdeveloped Countries,* (New York: John Wiley and Sons, 1962); *Moscow and the Communist Party of India: A Study in the Postwar Evolution of International Communist Strategy,* (Cambridge, Mass.: M.I.T. Press, 1956).

It seeks to create new independence states and governments where there were none before. This is clearly a nationalism different from one that may be defined as loyalty to an already existing state and government (although, once independent states do exist, this kind of nationalism may well emerge in underdeveloped countries, too). However, the nationalism that did create new states in Europe also proves to be irrelevant for the explanation of nationalism in underdeveloped countries, for in Europe the language or nationality factor was, as we saw, a key element in its growth. Only the American, Latin American, and Irish independence movements, for which the language factor was not responsible, may offer some fruitful parallels to present-day nationalism in underdeveloped countries. The independence movements in the Western Hemisphere, however, were directed against colonial powers that were then little more advanced industrially than their colonies. They differ, therefore, in significant respects from current anticolonial nationalism. Ireland, on the other hand, an agrarian country with a distinct culture, confronted highly industrialized Britain, and did, indeed, develop a nationalism akin to that of other underdeveloped countries, though it is located in Western Europe.

Being economically backward, the underdeveloped countries have not yet been subject (or were not until very recently) to the economic and political integration that created the pressure for the adoption of a single language in large areas of Europe. Nor, as we have seen, can there be in non-industrialized societies sufficiently widespread participation in politics to provide any large proportion of the population with the loyalty to "their" government that was essential to the growth of European nationalism. Typically, the more backward a country is economically, the more languages or dialects are spoken in a given area or by a given number of people. There are some striking exceptions to this generalization. Notable are the use of Arabic over a vast area, resulting from conquests which (like the earlier Roman ones) became sufficiently permanent to lead to gradual, voluntary adoption of the language of the conqueror by the conquered, the somewhat similar spread of Spanish and Portuguese in Latin America, and of Russian across northern Asia. Yet, even in these areas, many groups speak languages other than the major ones to this day, and the major ones themselves are frequently subdivided into various dialects.

In most underdeveloped countries, the existence of numerous languages inhibits communication among the population. Thus, the Chinese do not, in effect, speak a single Chinese language, but several mutually incomprehensible dialects.[1] Even more clearly, there is no such thing as a single

---

[1] The Chinese merely share a single system of writing which, being ideographic, is not bound to any particular language, and is, at any rate, not available to the

Indian or Indonesian language. Some ten or twelve major languages and hundreds of minor tongues and local dialects are spoken in India. Some thirty languages are spoken in the Republic of Indonesia, many of them totally unrelated to each other. In territories in which commerce and communications are not even so highly developed as in these three major Asian countries and which have not, like these countries, been united under a single government for centuries, many more languages may be in use. Thus, in Nigeria a population of approximately 34,000,000 speaks roughly 250 different languages, a situation that is not unusual in much of Africa and among the tribes in the interior of Southeast Asia and Latin America. In Australian-ruled Papua and New Guinea, perhaps the most backward area in the world, 1,750,000 natives speak 500 different languages and dialects, no one language being used by more than 50,000 and some by only 300.

In spite of the fact that most underdeveloped countries are inhabited by numerous "nationalities," i.e., language and culture groups, their nationalists have virtually nowhere sought to change the boundaries of their new states to conform to language lines. Apart from boundary changes due to the creation of Pakistan and of Israel, which were not chiefly motivated by language considerations, and the splitting of Korea and Vietnam into Communist—and non-Communist-governed halves, there have been only two significant boundary changes in the formerly colonial world: the somewhat tenuous linking of Egypt and Syria in the United Arab Republic and the unification of British and Italian Somaliland.[2] In each of these two cases, some, but not all, of the people speaking a single language were brought under a single government. Each of the unions, however, has been talked of as the nucleus of a future larger unification movement based on language. These exceptions apart, it is striking that existing boundaries have remained intact as colony after colony has become independent in recent years and already independent countries, too, have undergone nationalist revolutions. Countries including many language and culture groups, like most African and Asian ones, have not split up and those taking in only part of a single language group, like the Arab ones in the Near East and North Africa, have, with the two exceptions noted, not united. The colonial boundaries which have thus persisted beyond the attainment of political independence, like the

---

great bulk of the population. Their intellectuals can communicate in a single language, the Peking dialect of Mandarin Chinese, which serves roughly the same function as Latin in medieval Europe.

[2] As this essay goes to the printer (October 1961), an army coup in Syria is severing that country's ties with Egypt. On the domestic and international politics of the Somali area, see Leo Silberman, "Change and Conflict in the Horn of Africa," *Foreign Affairs*, XXXVII, No. 4 (July 1959), 649–659.

boundaries of older independent underdeveloped countries, were in virtually all cases drawn without any regard to language or cultural divisions among the natives. They chiefly reflected the political and economic requirements of the colonial powers, or of earlier conquerors, as in China, Turkey, and Latin America. Whatever it may be, then, nationalism in underdeveloped countries—if it does not aim at changing these boundaries—cannot be a movement seeking to unite all people speaking a particular language under a single independent government.[3]

Only after nationalism has been produced, chiefly by other factors, is an attempt sometimes made by Western-trained intellectuals to introduce the language and cultural element into it. The artificial resurrection of the Irish language may be a case in point. So is the pan-Arab movement insofar as it is not a mere tool of the nationalist movements of individual Arab states. The continuing failure of Arab unification would seem to indicate that these nationalist movements are in any case a good deal more powerful than pan-Arabism. More significant is the attempt of the Chinese Communist regime, itself a continuation of earlier Kuomintang policy, to impose a single language (that of the Peking region) and a simplified system of writing on all of China, a policy required, and facilitated, by the rapid economic and political integration of that area. Similar in nature, though not in the methods used to attain it, is the goal of the Indian government to spread the use of Hindi to all of India.

Though pursued with more awareness and greater speed, the Chinese and Indian policies (and similar ones in Indonesia) correspond roughly to those of the French kings, who integrated the population of their territory in terms of the language spoken at the seat of government. Just as French absolutism thereby laid the basis for the later language-based nationalism, so such a nationalism may arise in underdeveloped countries if and when most of their population speaks a single language.[4] However, in India there has arisen a counter-movement to the policy of language integration demanding that provincial boundaries be redrawn along linguistic lines to provide greater autonomy for the various major lan-

---

[3] On the relationship of nationalism to existing colonial boundaries, see Rupert Emerson, "Nationalism and Political Development," *The Journal of Politics,* XXII, No. 1 (February 1960), 3–28, an article offering many insights into the nature of nationalism in underdeveloped countries. See also William Bascom, "Obstacles to Self-Government," *The Annals of the American Academy of Political and Social Science,* vol. 306 (July 1956), 62–70; C. E. Carrington, "Frontiers in Africa," *International Affairs,* XXXVI, No. 4 (October 1960), 424–439; and E. R. Leach, "The Frontiers of 'Burma'," *Comparative Studies in Society and History,* III, No. 1 (October 1960), 49–67.

[4] Turkish nationalism under Kemal to some extent assumed this form when the Ottoman Empire was reduced to its Turkish-speaking provinces by its defeat in World War I.

guage groups. This may roughly correspond to the nationalism of some of the nationalities in the Austro-Hungarian and other multi-language empires of Europe. It remains to be seen whether the central government of India will, like the French kings, succeed in uniting its country around a single language or whether, as in Austria-Hungary, some of the other languages are too firmly established (at least among the literate and particularly the intellectuals) to be easily uprooted, leading India to disintegration.[5]

Even in India and China, as well as in Ireland and the Arab countries, the desire to make all people under one government speak one language (or to give a new autonomous government to those speaking one language) was not among the original motivations underlying the nationalist movement. In most underdeveloped countries no such desire has to this day appeared at all. If the origins of nationalism have nothing to do with nationality, i.e., with a common language and culture, nor with loyalty to an existing independent government, for there is none, then what is nationalism?

Nationalism in underdeveloped countries appears to have in common with European nationalism the desire of people to be rid of alien rulers and to have their own government, and it is probably for this reason that it has been labeled nationalism. In fact, the matter is not so simple, even if we leave aside the point made at greater length earlier, that in underdeveloped countries, until modernization progresses, most people have no desires with reference to the central government at all, and they do not play any active role in politics. Apart from that, the words "alien" and "own" as just used, however, assume what is yet to be proved, that there is a collectivity of people, somehow defined by a common element other than a language, who share "their" nationalism. Why does a community in the South of India regard a prime minister from the North more as their "own" ruler than a viceroy from Britain? Why does one tribe in the Congo think of a government dominated by another tribe as less "alien" than a government of Belgians? In terms of language differences, these questions cannot be answered.

In some underdeveloped countries, notably Moslem ones, a religion and other cultural characteristics shared by all the natives regardless of their language, but different from those of their colonial rulers, may have been a common element around which their nationalism could have grown. But in many underdeveloped countries there are caste, religious and cultural differences among the natives who nevertheless produced a single nation-

---

[5] On this problem, see Selig S. Harrison, "The Challenge to Indian Nationalism," *Foreign Affairs*, XXXIV, No. 4 (July 1956), 620–639, and the same author's *India: The Most Dangerous Decades* (Princeton, N.J.: Princeton University Press, 1960).

alist movement. And not infrequently, such movements are led by Christian natives who share their religion with their colonial rulers, whom they oppose, rather than with the great majority of the natives whom they claim to represent.

A more important element of unity setting the nationalists apart from their colonial rulers may be race, i.e., physical (as distinguished from cultural) characteristics. Some undeveloped countries are inhabited by people of more than one race, however, and yet, in the Sudan, a European remains more "alien" to an Arab than a Negro, in Bolivia a "North-American" is more alien to a white nationalist than an Indian, in Cuba the "Yanqui" is regarded by nationalists as the enemy of both whites and Negroes. Sometimes certain unity among the natives has been created by Europeans or Americans who set themselves apart by discriminatory practices directed against all natives or "colored" people regardless of their particular race. The racial factor, then, is undoubtedly an important element in an explanation of nationalist unity in some underdeveloped countries, particularly where all natives are of a single non-white race and where it appears as a reaction to racial discrimination by whites. But not everywhere is this the case. There is no clear racial distinction between the European and the native inhabitants of North Africa nor is there between the English and the Irish or between some Americans and some Mexicans or Cubans.

．　．　．

The key role of the intellectuals in the politics of underdeveloped countries is largely due to their paradoxical position of being a product of modernization before modernization has reached or become widespread in their own country.[6] In the universities, the intellectuals absorb the professional knowledge and skills needed by an industrial civilization; they became students of the humanities and social sciences qualified to teach in universities, and they became lawyers and doctors, administrators and journalists, and increasingly also scientists and engineers. When they return from the universities, whether abroad or not, the intellectuals find, all too often for their taste, that in their old societies their newly acquired skills and knowledge are out of place. Not only is there as yet little need—though it is often rapidly growing—for engineers and scientists where there is little industry, but professors will find few advanced stu-

---

[6] The leading role of the intellectuals is excellently stressed in Hugh Seton-Watson, "Twentieth Century Revolutions," *The Political Quarterly*, XXII, No. 3 (July-September 1951), 251–265, an article all the more valuable for relating, as we shall try to do, developments in Russia and Southern Europe to those in the present underdeveloped countries. See also Martin L. Kilson, Jr., "Nationalism and Social Classes in British West Africa," *The Journal of Politics*, XX, No. 2 (May 1958), 368–387.

dents and lawyers will find few clients in a society still operating largely through simple face-to-face contacts. Although there is plenty of sickness, most patients might prefer the traditional herb-doctor or medicine man to the trained physician and, in any case, could not pay him. Few administrators are needed where the sphere of government activity is still very limited and fewer still where all higher posts are occupied by representatives of a colonial power. Where the bulk of the population is illiterate journalists are confined to writing for their few fellow intellectuals. As a result, intellectuals in underdeveloped countries are frequently unemployed or underemployed, especially since, for all their "industrial" education, they are likely to have retained the aristocratic attitude that manual labor is demeaning and hence will refuse to do other than intellectual work.

During their studies, the intellectuals are likely to acquire more than new knowledge. They also absorb the values of an industrial civilization, above all the notion that continuing material improvement of the life of the mass of the population through continuing technological progress and popular participation in government is both possible and desirable, and they become admirers of the political systems and ideologies embodying these values, whether they be American liberalism, Western European democratic socialism or Soviet Communism. On their return, they discover that these values, too, are inappropriate to the old society. Continuous and cumulative technological progress, which is so typical of an industrial system, is absent from purely agrarian economies. Until industrialization (and changes in agricultural techniques resulting from industrialization) are introduced, a belief in any substantial improvement in the standard of living of the mass of the population is, in fact, unrealistic. At the same time, advocacy, based on such a belief, of ideals of democracy, equality, and social justice, which arose out of an industrial environment, is subversive to the existing order of government by the native aristocracy and the foreign colonial power and is therefore not likely to endear the intellectuals to these powerful forces.

To the extent, then, that a native intellectual has substituted for the values of his traditional society those of an industrial one—a process which need by no means be complete in each case—he becomes an alien, a displaced person, in his own society. What could be more natural for him than to want to change that society to accord with his new needs and values, in short, to industrialize and modernize it? A number of motivations intermingle to produce the intellectuals' drive for rapid modernization. Most obviously, there is their desire for gainful and satisfying employment for an opportunity to use the knowledge and to practice the skills they have acquired. But beyond this relatively narrow motive, there may be the more or less clear realization that only through industrialization can an eventual end be put to the poverty prevalent in underdeveloped countries, that only rapid industrialization can solve the problem posed by increasing populations, and that only industrialization can produce the "better" society at home which the intellectuals have come to admire abroad.

The peasant's typical response to overpopulation and his consequent hunger for land (if he is sufficiently politically conscious and organizable to respond effectively at all) is the demand for land reform. The intellectuals echo and support that demand, for one thing, because it is in accord with their new ideas of justice and equality. These ideas also make it desirable for them to become the leaders of a mass movement, of "the people." Since most of the people are peasants, they are inclined to seek peasant support, and advocacy of land reform is the most obvious way of mobilizing such support. Intellectuals may favor land reform also because a higher standard of living for the peasantry would create a better market for, and thus further the growth of, native industry. Finally, they press for land reform not because of anything it will do *for* the peasants, but because of what it will do *to* the aristocracy. The latter is the intellectuals' only powerful domestic enemy, and land reform strikes at the very root of its economic and social position.

However, where overpopulation is greatest, as in China, redistribution of land by itself is no longer an adequate solution to the problem, because there is simply not enough arable land to go around. Thus there is underemployment among the peasantry, which in turn tends to depress the wages of labor in the cities. Sooner or later only industrialization can satisfy the "rising expectations" in underdeveloped countries, which are, first and foremost, the expectations of the intellectuals, though they have spread them to the poorer strata accessible to them in the rural and especially in the urban areas. Only through industrialization can the intellectuals hope to realize their various dreams of democracy, equality, and social justice, of liberalism, socialism, or Communism in their own countries.

As the only ones in their societies who can even visualize a new, and, to them, a better order, the intellectuals naturally think of themselves as the leaders of the future society and of the transition to it. Thus a more narrowly political motivation is added to the others underlying their desire for modernization. Modernization serves to undermine and ultimately do away with the leadership of the old aristocratic ruling strata, and replace it with that of the intellectuals. Similarly, industrialization is the only road to the economic independence and military strength that can eventually provide freedom from colonial domination for their "country," that is, their government, which means more power for its new leaders, the intellectuals. Their anti-colonial nationalism thus makes the intellectuals desire industrialization.

It is equally true, however, that it is their desire to industrialize that makes the intellectuals nationalists. They see colonialism as opposed to industrialization, in part because the colonial power does not want industries in the colony to compete with its own industries for the colonial supply of raw materials or for the colonial market, and more generally because, as we have seen, modernization in the colony constitutes a threat to colonialism. Hence colonialism is regarded as an obstacle in the intellectuals' path to modernization as well as in their path to power. This helps explain the apparent paradox of intellectuals in underdeveloped countries who were trained in the West and came to admire it and yet turn against the West in their policies. They do so exactly because they admire it and at the same time see the West as denying them, through colonialism, the opportunity to make their own country more like the West.[7] To the intellectuals in underdeveloped countries nationalism and modernization have become inextricably intertwined as means and ends. Each has become an essential aspect of the other.

In Western Europe, during the process of industrialization, the intellectuals played an important role in developing the ideology of liberalism, but industrialization itself was accomplished by industrial capitalists. In underdeveloped countries, the intellectuals, in effect, play the roles of both groups. A native class of industrial capitalists is virtually or completely absent, and sufficient wealth for the development of industry is not available in private hands—or, if available in the hands of aristocrats, is (for reasons to be indicated later) not likely to be invested in industry. Under these circumstances, the government appears to be the only possible major domestic source of capital, and the intellectuals—if they want to industrialize their country—must wrest control of it from the native aristocracy and the colonial administrators who oppose industrialization. This need to control their government in order to industrialize provides another reason both for the intellectuals' anti-colonialist nationalism and for the appeal of various "socialist" ideas, whether Communist or not, to them. Thus, Nehru and U Nu, Nkrumah and Touré, Castro and many other nationalist intellectuals regard themselves as "socialists."

Through the dominance of the intellectuals in the nationalist movements, which we will have to analyze next, it is their peculiar form of

---

[7] The intellectuals' ambiguous attitudes are well discussed and documented in Mary Matossian, "Ideologies of Delayed Industrialization: Some Tensions and Ambiguities," . . . Her attempt to generalize about a large number of ideologies of nationalism in underdeveloped countries is most suggestive, though the inclusion of Shintoism, Fascism, and Nazism can, for reasons indicated later in this essay, be accepted only with some reservations. The ambivalence of the nationalist intellectuals toward the West is also noted by Rupert Emerson, "Paradoxes of Asian Nationalism," *The Far Eastern Quarterly*, XIII, No. 2 (February 1954), 131–142.

nationalism, which looks at steel mills both as symbols of anti-colonialism and as its instruments, that has become characteristic of nationalism in underdeveloped countries. To borrow some phrases from Marx's prophecies about capitalism, nowhere are the "internal contradictions" of colonialism, its dual nature as a modernizing and a conservative force in the underdeveloped countries,[8] clearer than in its relation to the intellectuals. It produces the intellectuals and yet by its very existence it frustrates them and hence arouses their opposition. In them, it has thus produced "its own gravediggers," it has sown "the seeds of its own destruction."

12. NATIONAL SELF-DETERMINATION AND NATIONAL DISINTEGRATION

Walker Connor

C AN TWO or more self-differentiating culture-groups coexist within a single political structure? The question may well seem clearly settled by the overwhelming factual evidence of contemporary international politics, for it is indeed a truism that political and ethnic borders seldom coincide. Thus, the very existence of a host of multinational states, including such a time-tested example as the Soviet Union, would appear to document an affirmative answer. On the other hand, a recent spate of political unrest within such geographically diverse and historically unrelated states as, *inter alia*, Canada, Guyana, India, Uganda, Belgium, the Sudan, Burma, Yugoslavia, Cyprus, Rwanda, the United Kingdom, and Iraq, focuses attention on the common root cause of intrastate yet

---

From Walker Connor, "Self-Determination: The New Phase," in *World Politics,* Vol. XX, No. 1, pp. 30–32, 35–53. Copyright © 1967 by Princeton University Press. Reprinted by permission of the publisher. Footnotes have been renumbered to appear in consecutive order.

WALKER CONNOR (1926–   ) Professor of Political Science, State University of New York, Brockport.

[8] On the effects on nationalism, both before and after the attainment of independence, of this dual character of colonialism, see S. N. Eisenstadt, "Sociological Aspects of Political Development in Underdeveloped Countries," *Economic Development and Cultural Change,* V, No. 4 (July 1957), 289–307.

international conflict and again brings into question the assumptions of the multinational state.

These assumptions were never seriously challenged until the rise of *popular* national consciousness, and the issue is therefore of relatively recent origin. As Sir Ernest Barker noted: "The self-consciousness of nations is a product of the nineteenth century. This is a matter of the first importance. Nations were already there; they had indeed been there for centuries. But it is not the things which are simply 'there' that matter in human life. What really and finally matters is the thing which is apprehended as an idea, and, as an idea, is vested with emotion until it becomes a cause and a spring of action. In the world of action apprehended ideas are alone electrical; and a nation must be an idea as well as a fact before it can become a dynamic force." [1] Barker here provides us with the means of avoiding the labyrinthine question, What constitutes a nation? In the final analysis, the coincidence of the customary tangible attributes of nationality, such as common language or religion, is not determinative. The prime requisite is subjective and consists of the self-identification of people with a group—its past, its present, and, most important, its destiny.

What lent political force to the growth of national consciousness was the ancillary doctrine that political self-expression was a necessary concomitant of cultural consciousness, a doctrine that seriously challenged, perhaps even totally denied, the legitimacy of the multistate structure. There is general agreement that the first indications of this concept of the right of nations to political self-expression can be detected in the fruits of the first Polish partition, and more evidently in the American and French revolutions. Denied by the Congress of Vienna and the Holy Alliance, national consciousness throve on adversity, spreading throughout Europe and Latin America during the nineteenth century.[2] Although the peace settlements that followed World War I honored the concept more in the breach than in application, the numerous wartime and postwar public espousals of the doctrine by leading statesmen of the Allied Powers accorded to it a recognition of validity that would thenceforth prove difficult to ignore or deny. The doctrine, by this time expressed in the phrase "self-determination of nations," was clearly never intended by Wilson and other contemporary advocates to have

---

[1] *National Character and the Factors in Its Formation* (London 1927), 173.

[2] Lord Acton believed that 1831 was the "watershed" year. He considered revolutionary movements prior to that date to be based upon either rival empirical claims or the refusal of people to be misgoverned by strangers. He noted that prior to 1831, Turks, Dutch, or Russians were resisted not as "usurpers" but as oppressors, "because they misgoverned, not because they were of a different race" (John E. E. Dalberg-Acton, *The History of Freedom and Other Essays* [London 1907], 284).

universal application. Rather, it was intended by them to apply solely to areas formerly under the sovereignty of defeated powers.[3] However, the principle had been consistently stated in the broadest of terms,[4] and it could therefore be cited with equal validity by any group desirous of repudiating foreign rule.[5] The doctrine thereafter became both a catalyst and a defense for independence movements throughout the world and was instrumental in the post-World War II recession of European power from Africa and Asia.

There was, however, a unique feature to the African and Asian independence movements. Although they had been conducted in the name of self-determination of nations, they were, in fact, demands for political independence not in accord with ethnic distributions, but along the essentially happenstance borders that delimited either the sovereignty or the administrative zones of the former colonial powers. This fact combined with the incredibly complex ethnic map of Africa and Asia to create, in the name of self-determination of nations, a host of multinational states.[6] Now in turn, these new political structures, along with some of the older European states, are the targets of growing demands that self-determination be carried a further step toward its natural conclusion. And the leaders of these new states, though recent espousers of national self-determination, are now perforce the defenders of multinationalism.

Consider Asia: Reports persist that the Chinese Communist government is turning the Turkic peoples of Sinkiang Province into a minority by promoting an intensive migration of Chinese into the province in order to ensure the region's allegiance to Peking. Moreover, earlier Tibetan resistance to Chinese rule has led to the continuous military occupation of that region since 1959. On Taiwan there are rumblings of dissatisfaction on the part of the indigenous population, who tend to look upon the ruling group of mainland expatriates as aliens. Despite Indonesia's recent preoccupation with the question of internal communism, it should not be forgotten that regionalism underlay the rebellion waged between 1958 and 1961 and that common awareness of cultural distinctions re-

---

[3] See Sarah Wambaugh, *Plebiscites Since the World War*, Vol. I (Washington 1933), 488.

[4] See, for example, Wilson's speech before the League to Enforce Peace on May 27, 1916: "We believe these fundamental things: First, that every people has a right to choose the sovereignty under which they shall live . . ." (quoted in Wambaugh, 4).

[5] Wilson was later to admit to the Senate Foreign Relations Committee his amazement and chagrin at the large number of requests for support of independence movements. Excerpts from his testimony are cited in Alfred Cobban, *National Self-Determination* (Chicago 1949), 21.

[6] Although Europe is similarly afflicted, its present political borders are not the result of fulfilled "self-determination" demands.

mains a source of resistance to rule from Djakarta.[7] In the case of Vietnam, the intra-Vietnamese (Annamese) struggles have tended to obscure an active "self-determination" movement on the part of tribal hill peoples who populate more than half of the country's territory. Popularly but mistakenly grouped under the single designation "Montagnards," they have made evident, by a number of open revolts against Vietnamese rule and by the creation of a liberation front, that the internal political problems of Vietnam would not terminate even with the highly unlikely creation of a government acceptable to all the ethnic Vietnamese.[8] In Laos, the confused and many-sided civil war has in no small part been due to the absence of transcultural identification with the Laotian state on the part of the diverse population.[9] In Thailand, the effectiveness of Bangkok's writ diminishes rapidly when one leaves the culturally compatible Chao Phraya Valley for the Lao-speaking northeast, for the Karen-populated hills of the west, or for the Malay- and Chinese-populated regions of the Malay Peninsula. In neighboring Malaysia, cohesion suffers from the antagonisms between the Malays and a strong Chinese minority, antagonisms that have already led to the expulsion of Singapore from the Federation.[10] In the case of Burma, it has been estimated that Rangoon controls only half of its territory; the remaining territory is populated by dissident, non-Burmese groups such as Shans, Kachins, Karens, Chins, and Mons.[11] Within East Pakistan, the inhabitants have long voiced strong dissatisfaction with their political ties to the peoples of West Pakistan from whom they are differentiable on practically every basis other than religion. In Ceylon, state unity has been frustrated by the intense rivalry between Sinhalese and Tamils which has periodically manifested itself in riots. Indian history has been even more often marred by eruptions of violence caused by the dissatisfaction of linguistic and cultural groups, and major governmental concessions concerning the delineating of provincial borders and the recognition of official languages have been the price of a return to order. In India's eastern areas, Naga and

---

[7] See, for example, George Kahin and others, *Major Governments of Asia*, 2nd ed. (Ithaca 1963), 674.

[8] The name of the liberation front is FULRO, a French acronym for the United Front for the Liberation of Oppressed Races. For references to two of the more important revolts of the tribesmen, see the *New York Times*, September 21, 1964, and December 20, 1965.

[9] For a description of the various ethnic strains and their relations, see Frank LeBar and others, *Laos* (New Haven 1960).

[10] For a report that Sarawak may also attempt to withdraw from the Federation because of ethnic considerations, see the *New York Times*, November 17, 1966.

[11] Robert McCabe, "When China Spits, We Swim," *New York Times Magazine* (February 27, 1966), 48.

Mizo tribesmen are in open rebellion against rule by New Delhi. Iraq is riven by the Kurdish movement for self-determination, a problem that cannot be dissociated from the continuation of Kurdish territory into neighboring Iran and Turkey. Perhaps the most publicized failure of multinationalism since World War II involves an Asian and a non-Asian people on Cyprus; the only noteworthy interlude to the communal warfare there between Greek and Turk coincided with the ill-fated attempt at transnational government in the period 1960-1963.

Sub-Sahara Africa's short history of broad-scale independence has also provided a number of challenges to the concept of the multiculture state. Indeed, there is very little evidence of the existence of supratribal allegiance to the new political entities that have been created south of the Sahara, and much contrary evidence, such as the entire anarchic history of the Congo. The rejection of transnation principles has been particularly pronounced in situations coinvolving "Europeans" and "Africans." Antagonisms between a white, ruling minority and a Negro majority within the southern tier of states and territories are one manifestation of the relative weakness of transracial sentiments; the pursuit of "Africanization" (the replacement of non-Negroes by Negroes in all endeavors as rapidly as possible) throughout much of the remaining area of sub-Sahara Africa is another. Nor has the presence of "Europeans" been a necessary prerequisite for racial tensions. Thus, the now rather lengthy insurrection waged by the Negro peoples of southern Sudan against the politically dominant Arabs of the northern sector, the overthrow and expulsion of the ruling Arab minority on Zanzibar in early 1964, the almost total elimination within Rwanda of the formerly dominant Watusi by the Bahutu between 1959 and 1963, sporadic genocidal conflicts between the same two peoples for political control of neighboring Burundi, the revolt during 1966 of the important Buganda tribe against the centralization of rule in Uganda, the Somali irredentist movements in Ethiopia and northeastern Kenya, and the general resentment of East Coast Negroes toward settlers of Asian ancestry are all cases in which consciousness of race (in the minimal sense of readily visible distinctions) has proved antithetical to the concept of the multination state. Although less apparent a source of intrastate dissension than either tribalism or race, a third cultural division that seriously affects a number of states is that between the coastal and riverine people, who were most influenced by European ways and institutions during the period of colonialism, and the more isolated people of the interior. This bifurcation helps to explain, for example, the demise of the Mali Federation brought about by the withdrawal of Senegal in 1960, as well as the animosity between the Hausas and Ibos which threatens the survival of Nigeria. Yet a fourth division of Africa, which cuts across state lines and which appears to be growing in political significance, is that between Islamic and non-Islamic cultures. This distinction is perhaps the most important factor in an Eritrean movement for independence from Christian Ethiopia, and it is also a contributing element in Somali irredentism within Ethiopia and Kenya, in attitudes toward political independence within French Somaliland, and in the internal strife of both Nigeria and the Sudan.

The most warranted conclusion to be drawn from a review of recent developments throughout Africa and Asia would therefore appear to be that the concept of self-determination has proved more powerful than could be appreciated from the vantage point of the 1940's. If the evidence were limited to these two continents, a demurrer could be made on the ground that analysis had been limited to societies in which political institutions are in an inchoate and therefore ephemeral and inconclusive stage; it could be contended that analysis of long-range trends should logically give greater weight to the time-tested, modern states of Europe and of regions politically dominated by people of European background. However, the recent history of multinationalism in such cases does not differ appreciably from the Afro-Asian experience. This becomes particularly evident when one examines the subsequent history of those states that were deemed successful examples of multinationalism by Mill, Acton, Barker, and Cobban. The purpose of such examination is not to sit in hindsight judgment of their observations, but to illustrate the acceleration of cultural-political consciousness, for cultural tensions have surfaced even where competent observers could not detect them at earlier points in history.

Events have already furnished conclusive answers to the fate of Acton's major examples, the Austro-Hungarian and the British empires. Of the former, Barker has noted: "Unfortunately they tried to unite a territory which, if one may use a geological term, was full of 'faults'; and they inevitably failed. A nation can only be made by a State if the population on which it works already possesses some homogeneity. The mixture of Magyar, German, and Slav was too rebellious to the potter's hand." [12] Barker's commentary would apply with equal validity to the British Empire, for—whether in a particular region the impetus for independence was indigenous or came from Britain, whether or not the new state opted for membership within the loose structure of the British Commonwealth—the basic cause of the disintegration of empire was the refusal of people to accept political rule by those deemed aliens.

But what of those "Western" multinational states that are still in existence? As previously noted, Alfred Cobban took exception to Barker's assertion that history indicated that democratic, multinational states could not survive. His empirical case on this point rested essentially upon

---

[12] P. 123.

the examples of Great Britain, South Africa, Canada, Belgium, and Switzerland.[13]

The inclusion of Britain as an example of multinationalism is puzzling; although Barker also acknowledged Britain to be an exception to his rule, it is an exception that cannot go unchallenged. Both Barker and Cobban had the transnationalism of the Scotch and Welsh in mind, but the view of most authorities holds that the self-identification of these people with London is the product of assimilation rather than of the continuing coexistence of prospering cultures. Indeed, authorities have customarily emphasized the remarkable homogeneity of Britain's major island.[14] Moreover, when this homogeneity was challenged by the postwar influx of immigrants from the West Indies and southern Asia, the result was racial friction and the passage of restrictive immigration legislation, antithetical to the concept of multinationalism. And in Northern Ireland, the attempts by the Catholic minority to express through the electoral process their long-standing discontent with political rule by a religiously and culturally distinct people, as well as the attempts of the moderate government to move toward equalization of opportunity for the minority, resulted in a series of violent reactions during 1966.[15]

As to the example of South Africa, it is assumed that this state would not have been included by Cobban could the subsequent governmental adherence to the policy of apartheid been prophesied. If, on the other hand, Cobban was referring solely to the relations between the two white minorities—Briton and Boer—it must be noted that fundamental differences of attitude persist, even though currently suffused by the overriding issue of black-white relations.[16] The political outcome of the cultural division between Englishmen and Boer therefore awaits a more normal environment.

The examples of Canada and Belgium are more instructive because of the elongated period during which two distinct cultures have survived within their borders on an apparently harmonious basis. Thus, Cobban

---

[13] P. 63.

[14] See, for example, Gwendolen Carter and others, *Major Foreign Powers,* 3rd ed. (New York 1957), 7, 8. The degree of assimilation is evidenced by the fact that only a minority of Welshmen and an insignificant number of Scotsmen are able to converse in their original languages, and all but a handful of these are fluent also in English. In both regions there have been recent nationalist movements whose goals range from minor alterations in administrative forms and school curricula to total independence. However, these movements are not considered to pose a serious challenge to "British nationalism," and, in any event, are a manifestation more of a resurgence of nationalist particularism than of cooperative multinationalism.

[15] J. H. Huizinga, "Captain O'Neil and the Anti-Papist," *The Reporter* (October 20, 1966), 43–44.

[16] Paul Fordham, *The Geography of African Affairs* (Baltimore 1965), 207.

wrote that French and British Canadians "have achieved a common political nationality without abandoning their characteristic cultural differences."[17] Tracing the unity of Canada back almost two hundred years to the French and Indian Wars, he credits its success to the wisdom of the British peace terms under which demands for compulsory anglicization were eschewed in favor of guarantees of cultural autonomy to the French community.[18] Similarly, with regard to Belgium, Mill, although the proponent of the nation-state, acknowledged more than a century ago the existence of a common national consciousness shared by the Flemish and Walloons; and Cobban, as late as 1944, could detect "no reason at all" for believing that cultural consciousness would lead to the disintegration of the state.[19] The contrast between these observations and recent events is striking. Contemporary relations between the two Belgian groups have been characterized more by street violence and demands for strict separation than by harmony. The breadth and fervor of the "Flanders for the Flemish" movement have been illustrated by broadly supported demands that French-speaking faculty members and students of Louvain University be forced to leave Flanders for Wallonia and by Flemish insistence on legislation that would preclude desirous Flemish parents from "denationalizing" their offspring by sending them to French schools.[20] Canada, meanwhile, has been troubled by (1) separatist movements, (2) the insistence of the culturally French province of Quebec for increased independence of the central government and a greater share of governmental revenues, (3) demands for a balancing of opportunities between French and non-French people, (4) resistance to a governmental requirement that civil servants be bilingual, and (5) even by a question of the degree to which the traditional flag (since replaced) did and should symbolize the hegemony of "Anglo" culture.

Cobban's final example, Switzerland, is the most commonly employed illustration of a multinational "going concern." Here again, mid-nineteenth- and mid-twentieth-century assessments are in accord, for Mill perceived a powerful sentiment of Swiss nationality which "went beyond different races, different languages, and different religions,"[21] and Acton, after noting the ethnological division of the population into French, Italian, and German components, concluded that "no nationality has the slightest claim upon them, except the purely political nationality of Switzerland."[22] It is tempting to pass over Switzerland as a rule-proving

---

[17] P. 60.
[18] Ibid., 79.
[19] Mill, 308; Cobban, 144.
[20] See, for example, the New York Times, October 9 and October 30, 1966.
[21] P. 308.
[22] Pp. 294–95.

exception attributable to the peculiarities of its size, location, topography, and special historical circumstances. And, admittedly, Swiss unity does not appear as seriously challenged by cultural cleavage as does that of Canada and Belgium. Nevertheless, the assertion that the subnationalities do not have the "slightest claim" upon the allegiance of the Swiss populace cannot be accepted as a valid characterization of the situation. It should be remembered that, as a result of Swiss neutrality, allegiance to Switzerland has not been severely tested against ethnic ties to Germany, France, or Italy. While the reasons for Swiss neutrality are multifold, there is reason to speculate upon the degree of adherence that the central government could have expected had it elected to enter the Franco-Prussian War or either of the World Wars. In each instance, even a policy of impartiality was threatened by considerable sympathy for France or Germany, particular preference following linguistic-cultural lines.[23] Vastly more significant, however, is the evidence that Switzerland has not been immune to the growing intrastate tensions that have recently plagued other multinational states. In Berne, the only canton with a substantial French-speaking minority (more than five percent, less than fifty percent), there has been an active secessionist movement in recent years, despite the fact that the boundaries of his canton were fixed more than 150 years ago.[24]

In addition to the foregoing states, Cobban also referred to the Soviet Union as an example of successful multinationalism. Although aware that Barker's analysis differentiated between "autocratic" and "democratic" states, Cobban felt the inclusion justified because the Soviet Union was, in his opinion, at least more democratic and yet more cohesive than had been the tsarist regimes. No matter where one places the Soviet Union on the democratic-authoritarian spectrum, however, it cannot be accepted as an exemplar of cultural cooperation. Authorities may disagree on the level of assimilation that has been attained within the Soviet Union, but it is generally held that the Soviet government has steadfastly followed a policy of russification. It is difficult to assess actual results because the government has purposefully tolerated the continued use of minority languages, while simultaneously eroding the wellsprings of the minority cultures, such as the Islamic religion. Thus, through a number of devices—some coercive, others seductive—the Soviet Union has moved toward assimilation while maintaining the most superficial

---

[23] George Codding, Jr., *The Federal Government of Switzerland* (Boston 1961), 154 and *passim*.

[24] *Ibid.*, 39. See also the article in the *New York Times* of March 19, 1966, which describes the sentencing of secessionists for terrorism, together with the judge's admission of a general climate of political tension.

guise of cultural autonomy.[25] Moreover, authorities anticipate an acceleration of the russification program which will include the denigration of non-Russian languages.[26] Such a move would be consonant both with Lenin's prerevolutionary plan that a short period of linguistic autonomy would be followed by the establishment of a single state language and with the statement in the new party program that "full-scale communist construction constitutes a new stage in the development of national relations in which the nations will draw still closer together until complete unity is achieved.[27] But a compelling reason for governmental acceleration of the assimilation process may well be the continuing discordant impact of culture-group orientation. Thus, a number of Latvian notables were accused in 1961 of fanning local nationalist sentiments. In a similar vein, the First Secretary of the Central Committee of the Uzbekistan Communist party was quoted in *Pravda* in early 1963: "There is no ground— either social or political or economic—for nationalism in our land. But we cannot forget that vestiges of it are still tenacious among a certain segment of politically immature people . . . [and are] always ready to break out to the surface. . . ."[28] The government also felt constrained to censure nationalist groups in the Ukraine during the spring of 1966.[29] Assuming that the Soviet Union would prefer to conceal such problems for both internal and external reasons, the few such official acknowledgements of the existence of nationalistic attitudes are probably indicative of what the government conceives to be a problem of serious magnitude. At the minimum, it can be said that Soviet policy-makers have not yet solved "the minority problem."

The elusiveness of a solution is illustrated by contrasting the experiences of two other nondemocratic European states, Yugoslavia and Spain. Following the Soviet example, the Yugoslavian government has

---

[25] For a historical account of this process as applied to the Turkic peoples of the USSR, see Michael Rywkin, "Central Asia and the Price of Sovietization," *Problems of Communism,* XIII (January-February 1964), 7–15. For a more general treatment of russification, see also the articles by Richard Pipes and Hugh Seton-Watson in the same issue.

[26] This was the consensus at a conference of specialists held at Brandeis University in the fall of 1965, as reported in the *New York Times,* October 31, 1965.

Confirmation of such a program was furnished at a meeting of the Ukrainian Writers Congress in early 1967. In response to complaints that heavy pressures to have Russian replace Ukrainian and other minority languages had been exerted during the early 1960's, a visiting secretary of the Russian Writers Union apologized for the haste with which the program of "merging the cultures" had been introduced (*New York Times,* January 29, 1967).

[27] Quoted by Richard Pipes, "The Forces of Nationalism," *Problems of Communism,* XIII (January-February 1964), 4.

[28] *Ibid.,* 5.

[29] *New York Times,* April 16 and April 20, 1966.

paid at least limited homage to the concept of cultural autonomy. Thus, the ostensible form of government is a federation of six ethnically delineated republics and two autonomous areas, and the use of diverse languages and alphabets is permitted. However, Yugoslavia has not been as successful as the Soviet Union in preventing the public airing of intercultural enmity. The prevalence of ethnic tensions became a major issue in the mid-1966 purge of Vice-President Rankovic and his followers. This group was accused of "Great Serbian chauvinism," thereby intensifying the hostility that Croatians, Slovenes, Albanians (Shiptars), Macedonians, and the other minority peoples felt toward the dominant Serbs. Even a year prior to these disclosures, the government had been forced to suppress a Croatian Liberation Movement, the average age of whose members, most of whom could not have remembered a pre-Tito regime, indicates that the movement represents a resurgence rather than a vestige of Croatian aspirations for independence. It is evident, then, that the Yugoslav policy of granting limited autonomy to culture groups has not furthered the cause of unity.

Franco's response to cultural division was enforced homogeneity. Although the Catalan and Basque minorities had enjoyed a short period of linguistic autonomy under the Spanish Republic, Franco ordered that only the Spanish language could be taught in the schools and used by the communications media. However, despite three decades of implementation, the policy continued to meet strong resistance and the government has recently retreated from its earlier position and become more permissive toward the use of minority tongues. Thus, the Spanish attempt at forceful eradication of minority cultures failed.

Additional evidence of European failure to accommodate multinationalism within a single state might include the often-expressed dissatisfaction of the German-speaking people of the Italian Tyrol, the strained relations between Rumanians and the Magyars of Rumanian Transylvania,[30] and the reappearance of the "Macedonian question," which involves minorities within Albania, Bulgaria, Greece, and Yugoslavia.[31] It is also pertinent to note that "European" Australia and New Zealand have determinedly resisted multinationalism. Although seriously underpopulated, both countries maintain barriers against the influx of non-Caucasoids while proffering a variety of allurements to the more readily assimilable people of northwestern Europe.

European experience, therefore, only tends to confirm a broad-scale trend toward political consciousness along lines of nationality. If the desires of nationalities were controlling, the second part of Ernest Barker's

---

[30] *Ibid.*, February 5, 1966.
[31] *Ibid.*, September 18, 1966.

prediction of a global political division "in which each nation is also a State, and each State is also a nation" would therefore rapidly be approaching realization. Yet, as indicated, seldom do political and ethnic borders coincide.

The principal reason for the wide gap between anticipation and realization in matters involving self-determination is the universal tendency of governments to render decisions upon the implicit assumption of the need to preserve the entire political unit. As against a claim of the right of self-determination, the government proclaims the right to stamp out rebellion and the duty to prevent secession. What is a self-evident truth to those desiring independence is treason to those in custody of the government. This polarization in the attitudes of the "ins" and the "outs" toward self-determination is most evident in the aboutface of those former proponents of self-determination who led successful independence movements. As earlier noted, the African and Asian leaders who once castigated European domination as violative of the right of self-determination are not now prepared to recognize such a right on the part of their own minorities.[32]

A survey of multinational states does not indicate that any particular form of government has solved this dichotomy between the need for unity and the fissiparous impact of ethnic consciousness. It will be remembered that Ernest Barker was willing to concede that nondemocratic governments might impede the rise of political consciousness among ethnic groups. Yet despite great variations in the form and effectiveness of their respective governments, most of the Afro-Asian states that are troubled by ethnic tensions are clearly not democratic. Nor, as we have noted, are nondemocratic states such as the Soviet Union, Rumania, Yugoslavia, and Spain free of such problems. The inability of authoritarian governments to cope successfully with multinationalism must therefore be considered still another testament to the increasing power of ethnic aspirations, for it indicates that the immunity believed to be enjoyed by authoritarian governments four decades ago is no longer effective.

The prevalence of ethnic dissonance within so many authoritarian systems must be considered significant because authoritarianism does enjoy real advantages in combating nationalist movements. Among the more formidable weapons at the disposal of such governments are a clandestine reporting apparatus and the ability to intern leaders for long periods without bringing formal charges. Control of communications is also important, for, if effective, it permits the government to cut the leadership off from possible domestic and foreign support. Such a govern-

---

[32] For a penetrating treatment of this phenomenon, see Rupert Emerson, *Self-Determination Revisited in the Era of Decolonization* (Cambridge, Mass., 1964), esp. 28.

ment, if it acknowledges at all the presence of a self-determination movement, will typically describe it as the activity of a few provocateurs or
malcontents. In such cases, evaluation of the actual situation is difficult,
perhaps impossible. The problem of assessing ethnic movements within the
Soviet Union has already been touched upon, but it should be noted that
a number of movements elsewhere were excluded from earlier consideration because of the unavailability of dependable data. How strong, for
example, is the Kashmiri desire for independence? How strong the movement within India for a Dravidistan? Tamilstan? Sikhistan? How much
support is there within West Pakistan or, for that matter, within Afghanistan for an independent Pushtunistan? In southwestern Iran for an
independent Arabistan? In eastern Turkey for an independent Armenian
state? In eastern Ethiopia for an independent Eritrea? In northwestern
Algeria for Berber independence? In each of these instances, and the list
could be greatly expanded, it is known that an ethnic movement does, in
fact, exist, but lack of information prevents a valid assessment of its
strength. However, it is safe to conclude that the political consciousness
of various ethnic groups is even much more prevalent than we can document.

This trend obviously conflicts with the widely held opinion that nationalism has proved too parochial for the modern age and that its zenith
is now well passed. This position has been lent credence by the postwar
proliferation of multistate organizations, which ranged, in their original
aims, from limited military or economic cooperation to complete unification. However, although the goals of a transstate organization may be
contrary to national aspirations, they need not be so. One factor will
be the degree of integration that is anticipated. There is nothing in
military or economic cooperation that is inconsistent with extreme national consciousness, when the results of such cooperation are viewed
as beneficial to the national interest. But the nearer one moves toward
the erection of a multinational state, the sharper becomes the conflict
between the organization and nationalism. For example, de Gaulle's nationalism does not blind him to the economic advantages that might flow
to the French from regional economic cooperation under the EEC, but
it explains his resistance to any proposed transfer of the decision-making
power away from the individual states. Similarly, he supports limited
military cooperation, but refuses to accept a position of national dependence concerning any aspect of military strategy. In short, there is
nothing intrinsically incompatible between the growth of national consciousness and organizations of such limited goals as the European or
Latin American Free Trade Associations. Significant, however, is the
fact that in the case of those organizations whose goals have most clearly
conflicted with nationalism, it is the organization that has been forced
into retreat. The EEC structure remains, but few are still optimistic

about its supranational objectives. Similarly, the amazingly short-lived "Sino-Soviet bloc" foundered on the incompatibility of Chinese and Soviet national aspirations. Subsequent attempts by the Soviet Union to perpetuate the monolithic nature of the geographically more limited Eastern European multinational structure (including the Council for Mutual Economic Assistance and the Warsaw Pact) have experienced a series of major setbacks due to the rising nationalism of the Poles, Rumanians, Czechs, Bulgars, and other East European peoples. In interstate relations, as within the typical multinational state, the centrifugal forces of national aspirations are proving more powerful than the centripetal forces of transnationalism.

There is, moreover, considerable reason to expect a further proliferation of self-determination movements. For most people, ethnic consciousness still lies in the future. National consciousness presupposes an awareness of other culture-groups, but, to a majority of the world's population, the meaningful world still ends with the village.[33] If the past and present are instructive, it can be expected that cultural and political consciousness will spread with increased communications and that the ethnic hodgepodges that are Asia and Africa will produce a host of new demands for the redrawing of political borders.

Should such demands for self-determination be met? The question can be viewed within two quite distinct contexts—the one, moral; the other, practical. If the question means whether each nationality, simply because it is a self-distinguishing culture-group, has a right to self-rule, then the question defies a provable conclusion. Axioms, such as "the right of self-determination," appear as moral imperatives until countered with opposing maxims. As earlier indicated, a "principle" of self-determination can be countered by other "principles," such as the right of states to preserve themselves, to protect their territorial integrity, to maintain internal order, to legislate against treasonable acts, and so forth. If, on the other hand, the question is intended to ask whether it is reasonable or even possible to grant statehood to each nation, it is doubtful that even those who are most sympathetic to the principle of self-determination would answer in the affirmative. Mill and Barker, for example, were both prepared to acknowledge the impracticality of self-determination in the case of two or more groups who were so geographically intermingled as to preclude a clear-cut geographic separation. Another possible objection to self-determination is that the people in question are not prepared for self-rule. Other critics have raised the issue of minimum standards, maintaining that self-determination should be denied when the group is too

---

[33] A 1962 UNESCO survey estimated that seventy percent of the world's population is essentially unaware of happenings beyond the village. See also Emerson, 36.

small, or the territory too limited, or the possibility of maintaining a viable economy too remote.

The interesting point is that such practical considerations have seldom had much influence upon ethnic aspirations. Even the absence of a clear geographic base has not necessarily prevented self-determination movements from arising. In the case of the Greeks and Turks on Cyprus and that of the Hindus and Moslems in British India, there was a high degree of geographic suffusion of the two cultures, but this intermingling did not prevent intergroup violence in the instance and actual partition in the second. So, too, the proposition that lack of readiness for self-rule is a legitimate bar to immediate independence: although accepted by Mill and later institutionalized in the mandate system of the League and the trusteeship system of the UN, this principle has been increasingly depicted as predicated upon bias and, consequently, is decreasingly heard in public debates concerning independence. With regard to criteria of size, it is again instructive to turn to Cobban in order to illustrate how self-determination has altered international affairs over the past two decades. In the course of emphasizing the impracticality of granting independence to each small nation, Cobban raised, as a *reductio ad absurdum*, the specter of granting independence to Malta and Iceland. The fact that these areas have been granted statehood and that they have been joined in this successful endeavor by such other tiny entities as Gambia, the Maldive Islands, Barbados, Trinidad-Tobago, and Western Samoa again illustrates that practical considerations are not apt to prove a match for the emotional power of self-determination in those cases in which the sentiments of the national group are decisive.

But are the sentiments of a national group apt to prove decisive? The last stages of the colonial era have produced a number of instances in which a realistic Britain and France took the initiative in ceding independence to overseas territories. Nevertheless, as Rupert Emerson has noted, history clearly establishes that governments are not apt to grant self-determination, and that cases in which it has been granted are rare indeed.[34] But history also clearly indicates that the refusal to grant self-determination hardly eradicates the problem. The peacemakers of 1920 may have thought that they could dictate the proper limits of self-determination in Eastern Europe, stopping short of balkanization, but ferment for a furtherance of the self-determination principle plagues the area a half-century later. The appeal and the power of self-determination are quite independent of considerations of what a government ought to do or what it is apt to do. It is granted that the governments of multination states will continue to resist their minorities' requests for inde-

---

[34] Pp. 63–64.

pendence, but, in such cases, it is also expected that the states' existence will be increasingly challenged by secessionist-minded groups.

A quite natural response to this challenge is assimilation. If the coexistence of differing cultures appears incompatible with continued unity and yet partition is deemed unthinkable, policies to further homogeneity would seem to be in prospect. Moreover, this negative, albeit compelling, reason for instituting a policy of assimilation may be joined by positive considerations, in that marked heterogeneity represents an impediment to the statewide social and economic integration demanded by the modern state. This is particularly evident when linguistic differences are present. Certainly the Soviet Union must find a multiplicity of languages an efficiency-sapping nuisance, requiring countless oral and written translations of orders, blueprints, directions for the use of machinery, and so forth. So, too, a tendency for people to identify themselves with a particular culture and territory must constitute a most serious impediment to the mobility of labor. Aside, then, from the need to combat the divisiveness that springs from ethnic factionalism, the demands of modernization also exert pressure upon the government to eradicate its multinational character.

It would be a mistake, however, to underestimate the resistance to assimilation which governments can be expected to encounter. A number of governments have discovered belatedly that the enmity of groups toward acculturation represented a more formidable adversary than had been contemplated. Thus, the Indian and Pakistani governments have both been forced to backtrack on their plans for a single, official language; and Franco, by discarding many features of his assimilation program, has confessed failure to overcome Basque and Catalan resistance. On the other hand, the example of the American "melting pot" is often employed to illustrate that the assimilation of diverse cultures can be accomplished within a relatively short time. But it is highly questionable whether the experience of the United States is germane elsewhere.[35] A number of important factors peculiar to United States history points up by their very presence some of the major hindrances to assimilation that are faced by other states. For example, the American policy of conquest eliminated the indigenous people as cultural competitors; the pattern of early settlement created a dominant, almost exclusive, Anglo-Saxon culture; upon this firmly entrenched cultural base, representatives of other cultures, on their own initiative,[36] were periodically added in relatively small numbers. As a result, ethnic problems in the United States have not been primarily

---

[35] Recent studies have even questioned the degree of melting that has occurred within the American pot. See, for example, Nathan Glazer and Daniel Moynihan, *Beyond the Melting Pot* (Cambridge, Mass., 1963).

[36] The major exception was the Negro slave.

characterized by minorities resisting assimilation, but rather by the unwillingness of the dominant group to permit assimilation at the tempo desired by the minorities. Dealing with a proportionately small number of people who have voluntarily left their homeland to enter an existent cultural-political structure within which acceptance of the mores and language is a *sine qua non* of success is one matter; treating the relations between two large and neighboring ethnic groups, each possessing impressive title to its respective territory, is something quite different. The second situation more closely characterizes Canada, Belgium, and, for that matter, most of the ethnic problems to which reference has been made.

The continuous spread of modern communication and transportation facilities, as well as statewide social institutions such as public school systems, can be expected to have a great influence upon programs of assimilation. But can the nature of that influence be predicted? It is a truism that centralized communications and increased contacts help to dissolve regional cultural distinctions within a state such as the United States. Yet, if one is dealing not with minor variations of the same culture, but with two quite distinct and self-differentiating cultures, are not increased contacts between the two apt to increase antagonisms? Improvements over the last two decades in what was an already effective transportation and communications network within Belgium have not been accompanied by improved relations between the Walloon and Flemish people. And in the less modern states, we have noted that cultural consciousness precedes political consciousness, and that cultural consciousness presupposes an awareness of other cultures. Is it not at least possible, then, that increased awareness of alien cultures on the part of the Baluchi people who inhabit either side of the Pakistani-Iranian border will result in Baluchistan's becoming a slogan rather than just the name of a geographic area?

The obvious point is that assimilation is even more of a natural foe of self-determination than is the multination state. The growing emotional power of ethnic consciousness, which threatens the multination state, also casts serious doubt upon the probable success of assimilation programs. Nonetheless, partly in resistance to the divisiveness of growing national consciousness and partly in response to the demands of modernization, an increased emphasis upon assimilation appears in prospect. As a consequence, the multination state faces a dual threat, consisting of demands for self-determination from below and governmental programs of assimilation from above.

Contemporary political forces, therefore, clearly move in the direction of that second part of Barker's prophecy that envisaged a world order in which "each State is also a nation." However, the first part of his prophecy, holding that "each nation is also a State," is clearly not upheld by the present political division of either the Arab world or the

Spanish-speaking region of Latin America. The conclusion appears to be that diversity of cultures tends to preclude political unity but that sameness of culture does not preclude political division.

On the other question that divided Mill, Acton, Barker, and Cobban—whether heterogeneity promotes authoritarianism or democracy—postwar developments indicate a link between multinationalism and pressure for nondemocratic actions. This is not to say that one can predict the form of government simply by the degree of cultural homogeneity within a state. Most of the governments of the multinational states merit, on balance, characterization as authoritarian. But so, too, did the prewar governments of highly homogeneous Germany and Japan, as well as the present governments of most of the Arab states. It is evident, then, that there are many factors that combine in a varying and unpredictable mixture to determine form of government. However, the aforementioned tendency of governments to stress their political and territorial integrity has not been conducive to democratic responses to the growing problem of cultural-political consciousness.

There is a logical relationship between the *self*-determination of nations and the democratic concept that popular opinion should determine political allegiance. It is therefore ironic that while so many governments pay lip service to self-determination, the instances in which a government has permitted a democratic process to decide a question of self-determination within its own territory are rare indeed.[37] The general position of African governments with respect to Rhodesia during 1965 and 1966 offers a striking illustration of this inconsistency. Motivated by the pragmatic desire to rid Africa of "white rule," they insisted that British cession of independence, prior to the instituting of popular government, would be a travesty of the self-determination principle. Yet, at the same time, these governments were not prepared to permit the popular will to determine the political allegiance of segments of their own territories.

The natural repugnance of governments toward democratic solutions to questions involving the political allegiance of minorities has been underlined by instances of the refusal to grant plebiscites despite prior promises. India, for example, has suffered years of international embarrassment rather than honor its promises concerning a vote for the Kashmiri. Similarly, there were those who suspected that Sukarno never intended to hold a plebiscite in West Irian (the former Netherlands New Guinea), even though his promise to this effect was a basic condition of

---

[37] The actions of France and the United Kingdom with respect to their overseas territories, after it became evident that the days of empire were numbered, are not considered true exceptions to this statement.

the UN's support for the Indonesian takeover in 1963. The subsequent abortive Communist coup brought into power a moderate group who were disposed to disagree with the major planks of Sukarno's domestic and foreign policies; but it was, nonetheless, under the authority of this group that the pledge for a plebiscite was in fact renounced during late 1966. It seems clear that governments believe that questions involving the political allegiance of groups residing within the sovereign territory are much too important to be left to popular opinion.

The methods by which governments have combated national movements have, in the main, been coercive. Where expedient, governments have shown little hesitancy in conducting military campaigns against such movements. Present or recent cases in point include Algeria (the Berbers), Burma, Burundi, mainland China (Tibet), the Congo, Cyprus, India (Mizos, Nagas), Indonesia, Iraq, Nigeria, Rwanda, South Vietnam (the "Montagnards"), and Uganda. Moreover, as indicated earlier, the leaders of self-determination movements have seldom been accorded the legal safeguards that would be deemed minimal to meet democratic requirements. Often their only choices have been to live in exile, as do the Dalai Lama and many of the leaders of the Formosan movement, or, like Khan Abdul Ghaffar Khan (an advocate of an independent state of Pushtunistan within present Pakistan), to be committed periodically to long terms of imprisonment without legal process. Viewing self-determination movements as threats to survival, governments have tended to react violently and to justify the cruelest of treatment accorded to implicated leaders by branding them as rebels or traitors and therefore something worse than criminals. Admirably suited to such attitudes are the emergency acts and detention acts authorizing, in the broadest and most ambiguous terms, the internment without due process of law of persons acting in a manner inimical to the interests of the state. Such laws are extremely common in multination states and, in some cases, are found even within countries whose political system is ostensibly democratic.[38] Whether

---

[38] Typical is a so-called Security Bill passed by the government of Guyana in late 1966 and obviously intended by the Negro-controlled government to restrict the activities of the East Indian segment of the population. Under its terms, the prime minister is empowered to intern without trial, for eighteen months, anyone he believes has acted or *will* act "in any manner prejudicial to public safety or public order or the defense of Guyana" (*New York Times,* December 9, 1966).

Within India, Kashmiri leaders have been periodically interned by the Indian government under an "emergency" measure. Moreover, in 1963, essentially in response to a Dravidistan movement, the Indian government passed the Sixteenth Amendment to the Constitution which sought to "prevent the fissiparous, secessionist tendency in the country engendered by regional and linguistic loyalties and to preserve the unity, sovereignty, and territorial integrity" of the Indian union (cited in Robert L. Hardgrove, Jr., "The DMK and the Politics of Tamil Nationalism," *Pacific Affairs,* XXXVII [Winter 1964–65], 397).

or not such responses are justified, either in general or in a particular
instance, is not at issue; the point is that multination states have tended
to become less democratic in response to the growing threat of nationalistic movements.

Political developments since World War II clearly establish that national consciousness is not on the wane as a political force, but is quite
definitely in the ascendancy. Its force is currently being felt throughout
sub-Sahara Africa and Asia, as ethnic consciousness demands political
recognition, in place of the present political division that reflects colonial
patterns. Moreover, the influence of nationalism is expected to increase
greatly throughout these continents as the multitude of ethnic groups,
many of whom are not yet cognizant of their identity, further acquire
national awareness. The multination states of Europe and of areas settled
by Europeans are also experiencing an increase in nationalistic orientations.

No multinational structure has been immune to this surge of nationalism. Authoritarian and democratic, Communist and non-Communist
societies have been similarly affected. Nor does the postwar proliferation
of transstate organizations and blocs repudiate the influence of nationalism; indeed, recent interstate developments further attest to the increasing tendency to think in nationalistic terms.

No government of a multination state has found the solution to the dilemma posed by the goal of state unity on the one hand and the centrifugal tendencies of growing national consciouness on the other. Motivated
both by the desire to prevent partition and by the demands of modernization, such governments can be expected to resist nationalistic movements,
with coercive methods if need be, while concurrently promoting assimilation.

The outcome of such programs is unpredictable, but the proven tenacity
and emotional power of nationalism make this abstraction a most formidable opponent. In any event, that pernicious and perhaps unrealistic
principle termed "self-determination of nations" is far from spent as a
significant force in international politics.

SECTION FOUR:

Power and the International System

13. THE CONCEPT OF POWER IN THE STUDY OF INTERNATIONAL RELATIONS

K. J. Holsti

H ANS MORGENTHAU [*Politics Among Nations,* New York: Alfred A. Knopf, 1967] is the foremost advocate of the concept of power as the theoretical core of international politics. In his view, all politics is a struggle for power. He derives this dictum from the assumption that the desire to dominate is "a constitutive element of all human associations." Thus, regardless of the goals and objectives of government, the immediate aim of all state action is to obtain and to increase power. Since by definition all states seek to maximize their power, international politics can be conceived of and analyzed as a struggle between independent units seeking to dominate others.

Professor Morgenthau unfortunately fails to submit the concept of power to further examination so that some ambiguity remains.[1] He im-

From *Background: Journal of the International Studies Association,* VII, No. 4, (February, 1964), 179–192. Reprinted by permission of the author and the publisher.

K. J. HOLSTI (1935–   ) Associate Professor of Political Science, University of British Columbia. Author of *International Politics: A Framework for Analysis,* (Englewood Cliffs, N.J.: Prentice-Hall, 1967). Coauthor of *Enemies in Politics.* (Chicago: Rand McNally and Company, 1967).

[1] Other noteworthy proponents of the "power" theory of international relations are Thorsten V. Kalijarvi [*Modern World Politics,* New York: Thomas Y. Crowell,

plies, for example, that power is also a major goal of policy or even a determining motive of any political action. Elsewhere, however, he suggests that power is a relationship and a means to an end. Because of this ambiguity, we do not know what the concept explains or fails to explain in international politics. Does the term "struggle for power" shed light on the many processes that go on within an international system? The word "struggle" certainly does not tell us much about the relations between Norway and Sweden or between Canada and the United States. Does the term "power," defined as the immediate goal of all governments, explain the major external objectives of Nicaragua or Chad or Switzerland?

In contrast to the "struggle for power" concept is the "anti-power theory" of international relations. The proponents of this theory (including Woodrow Wilson) claim that there is a distinction between "power politics" and some other kind of politics. Not pessimists regarding human nature, they assume that man is essentially tolerant and pacific and that the human community is united through many bonds. Statesmen, they claim, have a choice between practicing "power politics" and conducting foreign relations by some other means. Wilson and others made the further assumption that there is a correlation between a nation's social and political institutions and the way it conducts its foreign relations. To them, autocracies which did not consult "the people" usually engaged in deception, duplicity, and saber-rattling. Democracies, on the other hand, displayed tolerance, morality, and justice, and sought only peace and stability. In the new order which they envisaged for the post World War I period, negotiations would replace threats of war, and worldwide consensus on the desirability of peace would sustain democratic statesmen. In other words, power politics was synonymous with autocracy. But how democratic governments were supposed to achieve their objectives is left unexplained.[2] This view is also of limited use because it is mostly prescriptive: it enunciates how international processes *should* be carried on, but it fails to help us understand what actually occurs.

A third view of power is found in past and contemporary texts on international relations. Authors present the student with a brief and formal definition of power, often equating power with the physical assets a nation possesses. Most texts, in fact, concentrate on the analysis of these

---

1953] and Robert Strausz-Hupé and Stefan T. Possony [*International Relations,* New York: McGraw-Hill, 1954].

[2] There is room for disagreement on this characterization of the Wilsonian theory of power. Wilson was obviously aware of the role of power as military force and as public opinion. His concept of collective security, where all peaceful nations would band together to enforce the peace, implies that democracies no less than autocracies, should use force when necessary.

assets (often called the "elements of national power") without discussing the actual relations between governments and the techniques by which these assets are brought to bear on the pursuit of national objectives.

Should we not, however, define power in a way which best clarifies what we observe and what we wish to know? A definition should suggest areas of inquiry and reality, though no definition is likely to account for the totality of the subject. Thus, one definition of the concept may be useful for describing and analyzing social relations within a political party or within a family, but it may not be useful for studying international relations. Let us first describe an *act* which we conceive to be central to the process of international politics; that is, the act or acts that A commits toward B so that B pursues a course of behavior in accordance with A's wishes. The act can be illustrated as follows:

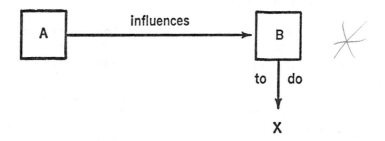

A seeks to influence B because it has established certain goals which cannot be achieved (it is perceived) unless B (and perhaps many other actors as well) does X. If this is an important act in international political processes, we can see that it contains several elements:

1. Influence (an aspect of power) is essentially a *means* to an end. Some governments or statesmen may seek influence for its own sake, but for most it is instrumental, just like money. They use it primarily for other goals, which may include prestige, territory, souls, raw materials, security, or alliances.

2. The act also implies a base of capabilities which the actor uses or mobilizes to use in his efforts to influence the behavior of B. A capability is any physical or mental object or quality available as an instrument of inducement. The concept of capability may be illustrated in the following example. Suppose an armed man walks into a bank and asks the clerk to give him all her money. The clerk observes clearly that the man has no weapons and refuses to comply with his order. The man has sought to influence the behavior of the clerk, but has failed. The next time, however, he walks in armed with a pistol and threatens to shoot if the clerk does not give him the money. This time, the clerk complies. In this instance the man has mobilized certain resources or capabilities (the gun)

and has succeeded in influencing the clerk to do as he wished. The gun, just like a nation's military forces, *is not synonymous with the act of influencing*, but it is the instrument that was used to induce the clerk to change her behavior to comply with the robber's objectives.

3. The act of influencing B obviously involves a *relationship* between A and B, though as we will see later, the relationship may not even involve communication. If the relationship covers any period of time, we can also say that it is a *process*.

4. If A can get B to do something, but B cannot get A to do a similar thing, then we can say that A has more power than B *vis à vis* that action. Power, therefore, is also a *quantity*. But as a quantity it is only meaningful when compared to the power of others. Power is therefore relative. To summarize, then, power may be viewed from several aspects: it is a means, it is based on capabilities, it is a relationship, and a process, and it can also be a quantity.

But for purposes of analyzing international politics, we can break down the concept of power into three separate elements: power is (1) the act (process, relationship) of influencing other factors; (2) it includes the capabilities used to make the wielding of influence successful; and (3) the responses to the act. The three elements must be kept distinct.[3] However, since this definition may seem too abstract, we can define the concept also in the more operational terms of policymakers. In formulating policy and the strategy to achieve certain goals, they would explicitly or implicitly ask the four following questions:

1. Given our goals, what do we wish B to do or not to do? (X)
2. How shall we get B to do or not to do X? (implies a relationship and process)
3. What capabilities are at our disposal so that we can induce B to do or not to do X?
4. What is B's probable response to our attempts to influence its behavior?

Before discussing the problem of capabilities and responses we have to fill out our model of the influence act to account for the many patterns of behavior that may be involved in an international relationship. First, as J. David Singer ["Inter-Nation Influence: A Formal Model," *American Political Science Review*, 57 (1963), 420–30.] points out, the exercise of influence implies more than merely A's ability to *change* the behavior of B. Influence may also be seen where A attempts to get B to *continue* a

---

[3] The recent texts of John Stoessinger [*The Might of Nations: World Politics in our Time*, New York: Random House, 1961.] and Charles Schleicher [*International Relations: Cooperation and Conflict*, Englewood Cliffs, New Jersey: Prentice-Hall, 1962.] distinguish between the act and the capabilities involved in the act.

course of action or policy which is useful to, or in the interests of, A. The exercise of influence does not always cease, therefore, after B does X. It is often a continuing process of reinforcing B's behavior. Nevertheless, power is "situational" to the extent that it is exercised within a framework of goals.[4]

Second, it is almost impossible to find a situation where B does not also have some influence over A. Our model has suggested that influence is exercised only in one direction, by A over B. In reality, however, influence is multilateral. State A, for example, would seldom seek a particular goal unless it had been influenced in a particular direction by the actions of other states in the system. At a minimum, there is the problem of feedback in any relationship: if B complies with A's wishes and does X, that behavior may subsequently prompt A to change its behavior, perhaps in the interest of B. Suppose, for example, that state A, after making threats, persuades B to lower its tariffs on the goods of state A. This would seem to be influence traveling only in one direction. But where state B does lower its tariffs, that action may prompt state A to reward state B in some manner. The phenomenon of feedback may be illustrated as follows:

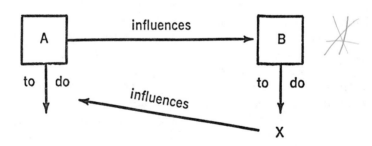

Third, the number of times a state becomes involved in acts of influence depends upon the general level of involvement of that particular actor in the system. The first requisite for attempting to wield influence is a perception that somehow state B (or any other) is related to the achievement of state A's goals and that there is, or will be, some kind of relationship of interdependence. If the relationship covers only inconsequential matters, few acts of influence may be necessary; but the greater the involvement of an actor in the system, the greater the necessity to wield influence over other actors. For example, except for limited trade relations, there is little perception of interdependence between Iceland

---

[4] State A might also wish state B to do w, y, and z, which may be incompatible with the achievement of X.

and Uganda, hence little need for the government of Iceland to attempt to influence the domestic or external policies of the African country.

Fourth, there is the type of relationship which includes what Herbert Simon ["Notes on the Observations and Measurement of Political Power," *The Journal of Politics,* 15 (1953), 500–517] has called "anticipated reaction." This is the situation, frequently found in international relations, where A might wish B to do X, but does not try to influence B for fear that B will do Y instead, which is an unfavorable response from A's point of view. In a hypothetical situation, the government of India might wish to obtain arms from the United States to build up its own defenses, but it does not request such arms because it fears that the United States would insist on certain conditions for the sale of arms which might compromise India's neutrality. This "anticipated reaction" may also be multilateral, where A wishes B to do X, but will not try to get B to do it because it fears that C, a third actor, will do Y, which is unfavorable to A's interests. India wants to purchase American arms, but does not seek to influence the United States to sell them for fear that Pakistan (C) will then build up its own armaments and thus start an arms race. In this situation, Pakistan (C) has influence over the actions of the Indian government even though it has not deliberately sought to influence India on this particular matter or even communicated its position in any way. The Indian government has simply perceived that there is a relatively high probability that if it seeks to influence the United States, Pakistan will react in a manner that is contrary to India's interests.

Fifth, power and influence may be measured quite objectively by scholars and statesmen, but what is important in international relations is the *perceptions* of influence and capabilities that are held by policy-makers. The reason that governments invest millions of dollars for the gathering of intelligence is to develop or have available a relatively accurate picture of other states' capabilities and intentions. Where there is a great discrepancy between perceptions and reality, the results to a country's foreign policy may be disastrous. To take our example of the bank robber again, suppose that the man held a harmless toy pistol and threatened the clerk. The clerk perceived the gun to be real and hence complied with his demand. In this case the robber's influence was far greater than the "objective" character of his capabilities, and the distorted perception by the clerk led her to act in a manner that was unfavorable to her and her employers.

Finally, as our original model suggests, A may try to influence B *not to do* X. Sometimes this is called "negative" power, where A acts in a manner to *prevent* a certain action it deems undesirable to its interests. This is a very typical relationship and process in international politics. By signing the Munich treaty, for example, the British and French governments hoped to prevent Germany from invading Czechoslovakia:

the Soviet government by using a variety of instruments of foreign policy, has sought to prevent West Germany from obtaining nuclear weapons; by organizing the Marshall Plan and NATO, the United States sought to prevent the growth of communism in western Europe and/or a Soviet military invasion of this area.

CAPABILITIES

The second element of the concept of power consists of those capabilities that are mobilized in support of the act of influencing. It is difficult to understand how much influence an actor is likely to wield unless we also have some knowledge of the capabilities that are involved.[5] Nevertheless, it should be acknowledged that social scientists do not understand all the reasons why some actors—whether people, groups, governments, or states —wield influence successfully, while others do not.

It is clear that in political relationships not everyone possesses equal influence. We frequently use the terms "great powers" and "small powers" as a shorthand way of suggesting that some actors make commitments abroad and have the capacity to meet them that others lack. The distinction between the "great powers" and the "small powers" is usually based on some rough estimation of tangible and intangible factors which we have called capabilities. In domestic politics it is possible to construct a lengthy list of those capabilities and attributes which seemingly permit some to wield influence over large numbers of people and over important public decisions. Robert A. Dahl [*Who Governs?* New Haven: Yale University Press, (1961)] lists such tangibles as money, wealth, information, time, political allies, official position, and control over jobs, and such intangibles as personality and leadership qualities. But not everyone who possesses these capabilities can command the obedience or influence the behavior of other people. What is crucial in relating capabilities to influence, according to Dahl, is that the person *mobilize these capabilities for his political purposes,* and that he possess skill in mobilizing them. A person who uses his wealth, time, information, friends, and personality for political purposes will likely be able to influence others on public issues. A person, on the other hand, who possesses the same capabilities but uses them to invent a new mousetrap is not likely to be important in politics.

The same propositions also hold true in international politics. Capabilities may also be tangible or intangible. We can predict that a country in possession of a high Gross National Product, a high level of industrial development, sophisticated weapons systems, and a large population will

---

[5] We might assess influence for historical situations solely on the basis of whether A got B to do X, without having knowledge of either A's or B's capabilities.

have more influence and prestige in the system than a state with a primitive economy, small population, and old-fashioned armaments. And yet, the intangibles are also important. In addition to the physical resources of a state, such factors as leadership and national morale have to be assessed. We could not, for example, arrive at an estimation of India's influence in world politics unless we regarded the prestige and stature of its leadership abroad.

Moreover, the amount of influence a state wields over others can be related, as in domestic politics, to the capabilities that are *mobilized* in support of foreign policy objectives. Or, to put this proposition in another way, we can argue that a capability does not itself determine the uses to which it will be put. Nuclear power can be used to provide electricity or depends less on their quality and quantity than on the external objectives to coerce and perhaps to destroy other nations. The use of capabilities depends less on their quality than on the external objectives that a government formulates for itself.

However, the *variety* of foreign policy instruments available to a nation for influencing others is partly a function of the quantity and quality of capabilities. What a government will seek to do, and how it attempts to do it will depend at least partially on the resources it finds available. A country such as Thailand which possesses relatively few and underdeveloped resources cannot, even if it desired, construct nuclear weapons with which to intimidate others, or establish a world-wide propaganda network, or dispense several billion dollars annually of foreign aid to try to influence other countries. And in other international systems, such as in the ancient Hindu interstate system, the level of technology limited the number of capabilities that could be used for external purposes. Kautilya suggested in the *Arthasastra* that only seven elements made up the capability of the state: the excellence (quality) of the king and the ministers, and the quality and quantity of the territory, fortresses, treasury, army, and allies [Narandra Nathaniel Law, *Interstate Relations in Ancient India*, London: Luzac, 1920; U. N. Ghoshal, "The System of Inter-State Relations and Foreign Policy in the Early Arthasastra Stage," *India Antiqua*, E. J. Brill, 1947]. In general, advanced industrial societies are able to mobilize a wide variety of capabilities in support of their external objectives. We can conclude, therefore, that how states *use* their capabilities depends on their external objectives, but the choice of objectives and the instruments to achieve those objectives are limited or influenced by the quality and quantity of available capabilities.

THE MEASUREMENT OF CAPABILITIES

For many years students of international politics have made meticulous comparisons of the mobilized and potential capabilities of various nations. Comparative data relating to the production of iron ore, coal, hydroelectricity, economic growth rates, educational levels, population growth rates, military resources, transportation systems, and sources of raw materials are presented as indicators of a nation's power. Unfortunately, few have acknowleged that in making these comparisons they are not measuring a state's power or influence, but only its base. Our previous discussion would suggest that such measurements and assessments are not particularly useful unless they are related to the foreign policy objectives of the various states. Capability is always the capability to do something; its assessment, therefore, is most meaningful when carried on within a framework of certain goals and foreign policy objectives.

The deduction of actual influence from the quantity and quality of potential and mobilized capabilities may, in some cases, give an approximation of reality, but historically there have been too many discrepancies between the basis of power and the amount of influence to warrant adopting this practice as a useful approach to international relations. One could have assumed, for example, on the basis of a comparative study of technological and educational level, and general standard of living in the 1920's and 1930's that the United States would have been one of the most influential actors in the international system. A careful comparison of certain resources, called by Frank H. Simonds and Brooks Emeny [*The Great Powers in World Politics*, New York: The American Book Company, (1939)] the "great essentials," revealed the United States to be in an enviable position. In the period 1925 to 1930, it was the only major country in the world that produced from its own resources adequate supplies of food, power, iron, machinery, chemicals, coal, iron ore, and petroleum. If actual influence had been deduced from the quantities of "great essentials" possessed by the major actors the following ranking of states would have resulted: (1) United States, (2) Germany, (3) Great Britain, (4) France, (5) Russia, (6) Italy, (7) Japan. However, the diplomatic history of the world from 1925 to 1930 would suggest that there was little correlation between the capabilities of these countries and their actual influence. If we measure influence by the impact these actors made on the system and by the responses they could invoke when they sought to change the behavior of other states, we would find for this period quite a different ranking, such as the following: (1) France, (2) Great Britain, (3) Italy, (4) Germany, (5) Russia, (6) Japan, (7) United States.

Other historical discrepancies can also be cited. How, for example, can we explain the ability of the French after their defeat in the Napoleonic wars to become, within a short period of time, one of the most influential members of the Concert of Europe? More recently, how could such figures as Dr. Castro, Colonel Nasser and Marshal Tito successfully defy the pressure of the great powers? The answer to these questions lies not solely in the physical capabilities of states, but partly in the personalities and diplomacy of political leaders, the reactions of the major powers, and other special circumstances. Hence, the ability of A to change the behavior of B is enhanced if it possesses physical capabilities which it can use in the influence act; but B is by no means defenseless because it fails to own a large army, raw materials, and money for foreign aid. Persuasiveness is often related to such intangibles as personality, perceptions, friendships, traditions, and customs, all of which are almost impossible to measure accurately.

The discrepancy between physical capabilities and actual influence can also be related to credibility. A nuclear capability, for example, is often thought to increase radically the diplomatic influence of those who develop it. Yet, the important aspect of a nuclear capability is not its possession, but the willingness to use it if necessary. Other actors must know that the capability is not of mere symbolic significance. Thus, a leader like Dr. Castro possesses a particular psychological advantage over the United States (hence, influence) because he knows that in almost all circumstances the American government would not use strategic nuclear weapons against his country. He has, therefore, effectively broken through the significance of the American nuclear capability as far as Cuban-American relations are concerned.

Finally, discrepancies between actors' physical capabilities and their actual influence can be traced to the habit of analyzing capabilities only in terms of a single state. The wielding of influence in modern international politics is, however, seldom a bilateral process. In a system where all states perceive some involvement and relationship with all other actors, governments seek to use the capabilities and diplomatic influence of other actors by forming diplomatic or military coalitions. Indeed, modern diplomacy is largely concerned with eliciting support of friends and neutrals, presumably because widespread diplomatic support for an actor's policies increases the legitimacy of those objections, thereby increasing the influence of the actor. "Small" states in particular can increase their influence if they can gain commitments of support from other members of the system.[6]

If effective influence cannot be deduced solely from the quantity and quality of physical capabilities and actual influence, how do we proceed to measure influence? Assessment of physical capabilities may be adequate for rough estimations of influence or war poten-

---

[6] This is one reason why international conflicts seldom remain confined to the original disputants. Recognizing the dangers of increasing the numbers of parties to a dispute, the United Nations has sought to "isolate" conflicts as much as possible.

tial and in some circumstances it may suffice to rely on reputations of power. But for precise knowledge, we have to refer to the actual processes of international politics and not to charts or indices of raw materials. We can best measure influence, according to Robert A. Dahl ["The Concept of Power," *Behavioral Science*, 2 (1957) 201–15], by studying the *responses* of those who are in the influence relationship. If A can get B to do X, but C cannot get B to do the same thing, then in reference to that particular action, A has more influence. Or, if B does X despite the protestations of A, then we can assume that A, in this circumstance, did not enjoy much influence over B. It is meaningless to argue that the Soviet Union is more powerful than the United States unless we cite how, for what purpose, and in relation to whom, the Soviet Union and the United States are exerting influence. We may conclude, then, that capabilities themselves do not always lead to the successful wielding of influence and that other variables have to be considered as well. In general, influence varies with (1) the type of goals an actor pursues, (2) the quality and quantity of capabilities (including allies and intangibles) at its disposal, (3) the skill in mobilizing these capabilities in support of the goals, and (4) the credibility of threats and rewards.

HOW INFLUENCE IS EXERCISED

Social scientists have noted several fundamental techniques that individuals and groups use to influence each other. In a political system which contains no one legitimate center of authority (such as a government, or a father in a family) that can command the members of the group or society, bargaining has to be used among the sovereign entities. A. F. K. Organski [*World Politics*, New York: Alfred Knopf, 1958], Charles Schleicher [*op. cit.*, (1962)], and Quincy Wright ["The Nature of Conflict," *The Western Political Quarterly*, 4 (1951), 193–209] suggest four typical bargaining techniques in international politics [7]: persuasion, offering rewards, threatening punishments, and the use of force. These categories are very useful for analyzing the wielding of influence in the system, but they can be expanded and refined to account for slightly different forms of behavior. Recalling that A seeks one of three courses of conduct from B (e.g., B to do X in the future, B not to do X in the future, and B to continue doing X) it may use six different tactics.

---

[7] Francois de Callieres, a renowned French diplomat of the eighteenth century, also suggested these techniques when he wrote: "Every Christian prince must take as his chief maxim not to employ arms to support or vindicate his rights until he has employed and exhausted the way of reason and persuasion. It is to his interest also, to add to reason and persuasion the influence of benefits conferred, which indeed is one of the surest ways to make his own power secure, and to increase it." *On the Manner of Negotiating with Princes,* trans. by A. F. Whyte, p. 7 (1919).

1. *Persuasion.* Persuasion may include threats, rewards and actual punishments, but we will mean here those situations in which an actor simply initiates or discusses a proposal or situation with another and elicits a favorable repsonse without explicitly holding out the possibility of rewards or punishments. We cannot assume that the exercise of influence is always *against* the wishes of others and that there are only two possible outcomes of the act, one favoring A, the other favoring B. For example, state A asks B to support it at a coming international conference on the control of narcotics. State B might not originally have any particular interest in the conference or its outcome, but decides, on the basis of A's initiative, that something positive might be gained not only by supporting A's proposals, but also by attending the conference. In this case there might also be the expectation of gaining some type of reward in the future, but not necessarily from A.

2. *The offer of rewards.* This is the situation where A promises to do something favorable to B if B complies with the wishes of A. Rewards may be of almost any type in international relations. To gain the diplomatic support of B at the narcotics conference, A may offer to increase foreign aid payments, to lower tariffs on goods imported from B, to support B at a later conference on communications facilities, or it may promise to remove a previous punishment. The latter tactic is used often by Soviet negotiators. After having created an unfavorable situation, they promise to remove it in return for some concessions by their opponents.

3. *The granting of rewards.* In some instances, the credibility of an actor is not very high and state B, before complying with A's wishes, may insist that A actually give the reward in advance. Frequently in armistice negotiations neither side will unilaterally take steps to demilitarize an area or to demobilize troops until the other shows evidence of complying with the agreements. One of the clichés of cold war diplomacy holds that deeds, not words, are required for the granting of rewards and concessions.

4. *The threat of punishment.* Threats of punishment may be further subdivided into two types:
   a) positive threats, where, for example, state A threatens to increase tariffs, to cut off diplomatic relations, to institute a boycott or embargo against trade with B, or to use force.
   b) threats of deprivation, where A threatens to withdraw foreign aid or in other ways to withhold rewards or other advantages that it already grants to B.

5. *The infliction of non-violent punishment.* In this situation, threats are carried out in the hope of altering B's behavior which, in most cases, could not be altered by other means. The problem with this tactic is

that it usually results in reciprocal measures by the other side, thus inflicting damage on both, though not necessarily bringing about a desired state of affairs. If, for example, A threatens to increase its military capabilities if B does X and then proceeds to implement the threat, it is not often that B will comply with A's wishes because it, too, can increase its military capabilities easily enough. In this type of a situation, then, both sides indulge in the application of punishments which may escalate into more serious form unless the conflict is resolved.

6. *Force.* In previous eras when governments did not possess the variety of foreign policy instruments that are available today, they had to rely frequently in the bargaining process upon the use of force. Force and violence were not only the most efficient tactics, but in many cases they were the only means possible for influencing. Today, the situation is different. As technological levels rise, other means of inducement become available and can serve as substitutes for force.[8]

PATTERNS OF INFLUENCE IN THE INTERNATIONAL SYSTEM

Most governments at one time or another use all of these techniques for influencing others, but probably over ninety per cent of all relations between states are based on simple persuasion and deal with relatively unimportant technical matters. Since such interactions seldom make the headlines, however, we often assume that more relations between states involve the making or carrying out of threats. But whether a government is communicating with another over an unimportant technical matter or over a subject of great consequence, it is likely to use a particular type of tactic in its attempts to influence, depending on the general climate of relations between those two governments. Allies, for example, seldom threaten each other with force or even make blatant threats of punishment. Similarly, governments which disagree over a wide range of policy objectives are more likely to resort to threats and to the imposition of punishments. We can suggest, therefore, that just as there are observable patterns of relations between states in terms of their foreign policy strategies (alliances, isolation, neutrality, etc.), there are also general patterns of relations between actors with reference to the methods used to influence each other. The methods of exerting influence between Great Britain and the United States are *typically* those of persuasion and rewards, while the methods of exerting influence between the Soviet Union

---

[8] Presumably, therefore, disarmament and arms control would become more feasible because other instruments of policy can be used in the influence act. In previous eras, to disarm would have led to the collapse of the most important—if not only—capability that could be mobilized for foreign policy purposes.

and the United States in the early post World War II era were typically those of threatening and inflicting punishments of various types. Since such typical patterns exist, we can then construct rough typologies of international relationships as identified by the typical techniques used in the act of influence.

1. *Relations of consensus.* Relations of consensus would be typical between actors that had few disagreements over foreign policy objectives, and/or had a very low level of interaction and involvement in each other's affairs. An example of the former would be Anglo-American relations, and of the latter, the relations between Thailand and Bolivia. In the relations of consensus, moreover, influence is exercised primarily by the technique of persuasion and through the subtle offering of rewards. Finally, since violence as a form of punishment is almost inconceivable between two countries, the military capabilities of neither actor are organized, mobilized, and "targeted" toward the other.

2. *Relations of overt manipulation.* Here, there may be some disagreement or conflict over foreign policy objectives, or state A might undertake some domestic policy which was disapproved by state B, such as a form of racial discrimination. Since there is some conflict, there will also be at least a modest degree of involvement between the two actors, or a perception that A and B are in some kind of a relationship of interdependence. The techniques used to influence will include, if normal persuasion fails, (a) offers of rewards, (b) the granting of rewards, (c) threats to withhold rewards (e.g., not to give foreign aid in the future), or (d) threats of non-violent punishment, including, for example, the raising of tariffs against B's products. Militarily, in relations of overt manipulation there is still no mobilization or targeting of military capabilities toward state B. Examples of overt manipulation would include the relations between China and the Soviet Union, 1960-1963, and the relations between France and the United States during this same period.

3. *Relations of coercion.* In relations of coercion, there are fundamental disagreements over foreign policy objectives. Almost all actions that A takes externally are perceived by B to be a threat to its own interests. Involvement is, therefore, high. A seeks to influence B's behavior typically by (a) threatening punishments, (b) by inflicting non-violent punishments and under extreme provocation, (c) by the selective and limited use of force as, for example in a peace-time blockade. Military capabilities, finally, are likely to be targeted towards each other. Examples would include the Soviet Union and the western coalition for most of the period since 1947, Cuba and the United States between 1960 and 1963, Nazi Germany and Czechoslovakia between 1937 and 1939 and Egypt and Israel since 1948.

4. *Relations of force.* Here there is almost total disagreement on foreign policy objectives and the areas of consensus are limited to a few necessities such as communications. The degree of involvement is obviously extremely high. The typical form of exercising influence is through the infliction of violent punishment, though in some instances rewards (e.g., peace offers) might be offered. National capabilities are mobilized primarily with a view to conducting the policy of punishment. However the quantity of military capabilities that is used will vary with the geographic and force-level boundaries which the disputants place on the conflict.

Though most relations between states could be placed in one of the previous categories, it should also be apparent that under changing circumstances, governments are required to resort to techniques of influence toward others that they would normally avoid. However, the cold war represents a curious phenomenon in the history of international politics because in the relations between east and west *all* of the techniques of influence are being used simultaneously. There are several areas of policy where consensus exists between the Soviet Union and the leaders of the west and where agreements—either in treaties or through "understandings"—can be reached without making threats or imposing punishments.[9] There are also areas of great controversy where the antagonists commit military capabilities and seek to influence each other's behavior most of the time by making threats and carrying out various forms of punishment.

---

[9] Areas of agreement between the Soviet Union and the west which have resulted either in treaties or "understandings" would include the cessation of nuclear tests, the demilitarization of the Antarctic and, possibly, outer space, the renouncing of nuclear war as an instrument of policy, and efforts to prevent the spread of nuclear weapons.

Part III

Conflict and Military Potential

S INCE ITS beginnings as a field of study, students of international relations, have been primarily concerned with the study of the causes of conflict. Most theories of conflict are reducible to formulations about motivations and the perceptions underlying such motivations.

I

Some theories of conflict are based upon economics as a determinant of international violence. Undoubtedly the most celebrated economic theory of conflict is found in Lenin's work on imperialism. According to Lenin, under capitalism, domestic markets become saturated, and capitalists engage in a life-and-death struggle to obtain control of overseas markets. Writing during World War I, he saw the war as the result of conflict among capitalist states for overseas colonies, with their raw materials, abundant labor supply, and markets for exports. Thus his theory of imperialism constitutes not only an important communist theory of conflict, but also a communist theory of international relations.

II

Many writers have criticized Lenin's theory of imperialism. Basic to such critiques is the contention that this view of imperialism focuses exclusively upon the economic factor and overlooks other important variables which cause conflict among nations. In addition, the history of the period about which Lenin was writing does not substantiate his argument. In the period before World War I, in some cases, European investment was greater in countries other than colonial possessions. Moreover, events since World War II have not dealt kindly with Lenin's theory of imperialism. In the postcolonial period, western Europe has experienced unprecedented levels of economic growth and prosperity. The greatest increases in trade have occurred among industralized nations themselves rather than between the advanced states and the developing countries.

III

Essential to an understanding of a state's military strength is an evaluation of its national capabilities, including population, administrative skills, level of technology, economic structure and capacity, geographic location, and leadership. Realist writers such as Morgenthau, relate the concept of military potential—the national resources available for producing and maintaining armed forces— to other national capabilities. These, in turn, have meaning only as they are linked to specific objectives, strategies and contingencies.

Especially since World War II, there has been a proliferation of writings on military strategy. Although for the most part these have been focused on nuclear strategy, there is a growing literature on limited and guerrilla warfare. This represents but the latest addition to writings on military strategy. Of great importance to the student of strategic affairs are the writings of Karl von Clausewitz. In the early nineteenth century, Clausewitz saw war as but one way of achieving political objectives, the "continuation of political intercourse, with a mixture of other means." Put in contemporary terms, war is but one of the many techniques available to national units in the demand-response relationships in which they are engaged in the international system.

As a result of the exponential increase in destructive capabilities from developments in military technology, the importance of Clausewitz's dictum about war has increased. In fact, implicit in writings on nuclear warfare is the notion that there are few political objectives for which nations would be prepared to use nuclear weapons. Hence at the nuclear level there is a form of international stability between the United States and the Soviet Union. If such stability exists, it is based upon the deterrent capabilities of each superpower. Each possesses sufficient nuclear forces to deter the other from attacking, since in the event of nuclear war both superpowers, their leaders are convinced, would be destroyed, or at least heavily devastated.

IV

The advent of nuclear weapons has had important implications for the conduct of international relations. Such weapons have given to those nations possessing them a destructive capacity of unprecedented dimensions. The result has been the creation of a "balance of terror" which, according to Glenn H. Snyder, exists when neither nuclear power can, by an attack against the adversary's weapons systems, reduce his retaliatory capacity to acceptable proportions. The balance of terror bears certain similarity to the traditional balance of power theory. (For a discussion of balance of power, see Part VIII.)

The balance of terror has "superimposed a new system of equilibrium upon the old system which was based on nonnuclear capabilities." The balance of terror is far more subjective in nature than was the balance of power. In the nuclear age, the existence of equilibrium is more a function of the opponents' perception than the product of a strict comparison of nuclear capabilities. Nevertheless, the numbers and quality of nuclear capabilities available to each power may influence its perception of a condition of equilibrium. Moreover, this perception depends on the opponents' ability to judge objectively the extent of their respective willingness to absorb a nuclear strike. A miscalculation on the part of either opponent, or both, may have disequilibrating effects on the balance of terror. Finally, the balance of terror is maintained by mutual deterrence to an extent unknown in the traditional balance of power. Deterrence, depending more on the credibility of the threat of serious nuclear punishment, is crucial to the balance. In contrast, the balance of power was based on the physical capacity of a state to seize and hold an opponent's territory.

The United States more than any other nation has attempted not only to develop theories of nuclear strategy , but to evolve official strategic doctrine reflective of prevailing technologies and U.S. security interests. An examination of the history of U.S. strategic doctrine since World War II reveals a changing emphasis upon nuclear as opposed to conventional forces in an effort to develop the appropriate mix of weapons systems. In Selection 17, William R. Kintner presents an account of tne evolution of U.S. doctrine and examines theories of massive retaliation, counterforce, and damage limiting strategies.

V

Students of strategic affairs have debated the issue of the appropriate level of nuclear capabilities needed to insure deterrence.

The possession of such a strategic capability would require major U.S. programs to insure the survival of its weapons systems and population centers from attack, as well as a vast nuclear capability for inflicting damage on an opponent *after* absorbing his first strike. In the early years of the Kennedy-Johnson administrations, the United States, as indicated by William R. Kintner opted for a counterforce strategy, but modified drastically both its strategic concepts and its goals as the Soviet Union developed vast new capabilities. By the early 1970s the United States and the Soviet Union had reached a rough "parity" in strategic weapons systems. In such a strategic context, a counterforce strategy becomes difficult, if not impossible, for the United States unless substantial increases are made in military related research and new weapons systems are deployed on a greater scale.

A nuclear war has never been fought, and after Hiroshima and Nagasaki, the world may even have entered the postnuclear age. However, there are not only historical, but also contemporary, examples of limited war. In the postwar period, Morton Halperin suggests, there have been several examples. In such war, there is general agreement among the participants over limitations on some or all of the following: targets, weapons systems, and political objectives. According to Halperin, with the advent of nuclear weapons, it is possible to envisage a "limited" conflict approximating in size World War II without its escalation to a general nuclear war. Thus the concept of limited war includes conflicts of varying intensity, whose common characteristic is agreement among the participants about limitations.

Historically there are many examples of guerrilla warfare. (The term guerrilla derives from the struggle of Spanish partisans against French forces occupying Spain during the Napoleonic wars.) Paradoxically, in an age of spectacular new military technologies, guerrilla warfare, with its emphasis upon relatively unsophisticated weapons systems, has gained new importance. Perhaps because of the effectiveness of nuclear deterrence, conflicts have been fought, and will continue to be fought, at the levels of limited and guerrilla warfare.

Much of the twentieth century has been a period of revolutionary upheaval, with new nation-states replacing colonial systems, and governments of existing nation-states being overthrown by revolutionary forces. In such circumstances, the strategy of guerrilla warfare has been peculiarly suited to the needs of those seeking to overthrow the existing order. In national units where the gap psychologically, politically, economically, and militarily between the central government and the hinterland is great, there is potential for guerrilla warfare. In addition, there are prospects for urban guerrilla warfare in many parts of the world. The existence of large groups of disaffected people offers opportunities which revolutionary elites have begun to exploit. Conceivably, urban areas, and the more developed countries, will face challenges from "national liberation wars" as serious as those in the less-developed states.

Mao Tse-tung, the greatest twentieth-century theorist and practitioner of guerrilla warfare, outlines its strategic framework. In much the same fashion of Clausewitz, Mao posits the existence of a close relationship between war, in this case, guerrilla operations, and political objectives. Mao explores this relationship in his analysis of the strategy of guerrilla warfare.

SECTION ONE:

The Cause of War

14. IMPERIALISM

V. I. Lenin

M ONOPOLIST capitalist combines—cartels, syndicates, trusts—divide among themselves first of all, the whole internal market of a country, and impose their control, more or less completely, upon the industry of that country. But under capitalism the home market is inevitably bound up with the foreign market. Capitalism long ago created a world market. As the export of capital increased, and as the foreign and colonial relations and the "spheres of influence" of the big monopolist combines expanded, things "naturally" gravitated towards an international agreement among these combines, and towards the formation of international cartels.

.   .   .

. . . International cartels show to what point capitalist monopolies have developed, and they *reveal the object* of the struggle between the various capitalist groups. This last circumstance is the most important; it alone shows us the historico-economic significance of events; for the

From *Imperialism: The Highest Stage of Capitalism* by V. I. Lenin (New York: 1939), pp. 68; 74–75; 81–82; 88–89; 118–119. Reprinted by permission of International Publishers Co., Inc. Copyright © 1939. Footnotes have been renumbered to appear in consecutive order.

VLADIMIR I. LENIN (1870–1924) Leader of Bolshevik group, Russian Communist Party, which seized power during the Russian Revolution. Chairman of the Council of People's Commission Union of Soviet Socialist Republics. Author of *The State and Revolution,* (New York: International Publishers, 1932); *What is to be Done?* (New York: International Publishers, 1929); *Collected Works,* (New York: International Publishers, 1927–1945).

forms of the struggle may and do constantly change in accordance with varying, relatively particular, and temporary causes, but the *essence* of the struggle, its class *content, cannot* change while classes exist.

.   .   .

Colonial policy and imperialism existed before the latest state of capitalism, and even before capitalism. Rome, founded on slavery, pursued a colonial policy and achieved imperialism. But "general" arguments about imperialism, which ignore, or put into the background the fundamental difference of social-economic systems, inevitably degenerate into absolutely empty banalities, or into grandiloquent comparisons like "Greater Rome and Greater Britain." [1] Even the colonial policy of capitalism in its *previous* stages is essentially different from the colonial policy of finance capital.

The principal feature of modern capitalism is the domination of monopolist combines of the big capitalists. These monopolies are most firmly established when *all* the sources of raw materials are controlled by the one group. And we have seen with what zeal the international capitalist combines exert every effort to make it impossible for their rivals to compete with them; for example, by buying up mineral lands, oil fields, etc. Colonial possession alone gives complete guarantee of success to the monopolies against all the risks of the struggle with competitors, including the risk that the latter will defend themselves by means of a law establishing a state monopoly. The more capitalism is developed, the more the need for raw materials is felt, the more bitter competition becomes, and the more feverishly the hunt for raw materials proceeds throughout the whole world, the more desperate becomes the struggle for the acquisition of colonies.

.   .   .

. . . Imperialism emerged as the development and direct continuation of the fundamental attributes of capitalism in general. But capitalism only became capitalist imperialism at a definite and very high stage of its development, when certain of its fundamental attributes began to be transformed into their opposites, when the features of a period of transition from capitalism to a higher social and economic system began to take shape and reveal themselves all along the line. Economically, the main thing in this process is the substitution of capitalist monopolies for capi-

---

[1] A reference to the book by C. P. Lucas, *Greater Rome and Greater Britain*, Oxford 1912, or the Earl of Cromer's *Ancient and Modern Imperialism*, London, 1910.

talist free competition. Free competition is the fundamental attribute of capitalism, and of commodity production generally. Monopoly is exactly the opposite of free competition; but we have seen the latter being transformed into monopoly before our very eyes, creating large-scale industry and eliminating small industry, replacing large-scale industry by still larger-scale industry, finally leading to such a concentration of production and capital that monopoly has been and is the result: cartels, syndicates and trusts, and merging with them, the capital of a dozen or so banks manipulating thousands of millions. At the same time monopoly, which has grown out of free competition, does not abolish the latter, but exists over it and alongside of it, and thereby gives rise to a number of very acute, intense antagonisms, friction and conflicts. Monopoly is the transition from capitalism to a higher system.

If it were necessary to give the briefest possible definition of imperialism we should have to say that imperialism is the monopoly stage of capitalism. Such a definition would include what is most important, for, on the one hand, finance capital is the bank capital of a few big monopolist banks, merged with the capital of the monopolist combines of manufacturers; and, on the other hand, the division of the world is the transition from a colonial policy which has extended without hinderance to territories unoccupied by any capitalist power, to a colonial policy of monopolistic possession of the territory of the world which has been completely divided up.

But very brief definitions, although convenient, for they sum up the main points, are nevertheless inadequate, because very important features of the phenomenon that has to be defined have to be especially deduced. And so, without forgetting the conditional and relative value of all definitions, which can never include all the concatenations of a phenomenon in its complete development, we must give a definition of imperialism that will embrace the following five essential features:

1) The concentration of production and capital developed to such a high stage that it created monopolies which play a decisive role in economic life.

2) The merging of bank capital with industrial capital, and the creation, on the basis of this "finance capital," of a "financial oligarchy."

3) The export of capital, which has become extremely important, as distinguished from the export of commodities.

4) The formation of international capitalist monopolies which share the world among themselves.

5) The territorial division of the whole world among the greatest capitalist powers is completed.

Imperialism is capitalism in that stage of development in which the dominance of monopolies and finance capital has established itself; in which the export of capital has acquired pronounced importance; in which the division of the world among the international trusts has begun; in which the division of all territories of the globe among the great capitalist powers has been completed.

.   .   .

. . . Let us consider India, Indo-China and China. It is known that these three colonial and semi-colonial countries, inhabited by six to seven hundred million human beings, are subjected to the exploitation of the finance capital of several imperialist states: Great Britain, France, Japan, the U.S.A., etc. We will assume that these imperialist countries form alliances against one another in order to protect and extend their possessions, their interests and their "spheres of influence" in these Asiatic states; these alliances will be "inter-imperialist," or "ultra-imperialist" alliances. We will assume that *all* the imperialist countries conclude an alliance for the "peaceful" division of these parts of Asia; this alliance would be an alliance of "internationally united finance capital." As a matter of fact, alliances of this kind have been made in the twentieth century, notably with regard to China. We ask, is it "conceivable," assuming that the capitalist system remains intact—and this is precisely the assumption that Kautsky does make—that such alliances would be more than temporary, that they would eliminate friction, conflicts and struggle in all and every possible form?

This question need only be stated clearly enough to make it impossible for any other reply to be given than that in the negative; for there can be *no* other conceivable basis under capitalism for the division of spheres of influence, of interests, of colonies, etc., than a calculation of the *strength* of the participants in the division, their general economic, financial, military strength, etc. And the strength of these participants in the division does not change to an equal degree, for under capitalism the development of different undertakings, trusts, branches of industry, or countries cannot be *even*. Half a century ago, Germany was a miserable, insignificant country, as far as its capitalist strength was concerned, compared with the strength of England at that time. Japan was similarly insignificant compared with Russia. Is it "conceivable" that in ten or twenty years' time the relative strength of the imperialist powers will have remained *un*changed? Absolutely inconceivable.

Therefore, in the realities of the capitalist system, and not in the banal philistine fantasies of English parsons, or of the German "Marxist," Kautsky, "inter-imperialist" or "ultra-imperialist" alliances, no matter what form they may assume, whether of one imperialist coalition against another, or of a general alliance embracing *all* the imperialist powers, are *inevitably* nothing more than a "truce" in periods between wars,

Peaceful alliances prepare the ground for wars, and in their turn grow out of wars; the one is the condition for the other, giving rise to alternating forms of peaceful and non-peaceful struggle out of *one and the same* basis of imperialist connections and the relations between world economics and world politics.

SECTION TWO:

The Nature
of War

15. WHAT IS WAR?

General Karl von Clausewitz

WAR IS NOTHING but a duel on an extensive scale. If we would conceive as a unit the countless number of duels which make up a War, we shall do so best by supposing to ourselves two wrestlers. Each strives by physical force to compel the other to submit to his will: each endeavours to throw his adversary, and thus render him incapable of further resistance.

War is therefore an act of violence intended to compel our opponents to fulfill our will.

Violence arms itself with the inventions of Art and Science in order to contend against violence. Self-imposed restrictions, almost imperceptible and hardly worth mentioning, termed usages of International Law, accompany it without essentially impairing its power. Violence, that is to say, physical force (for there is no moral force without the conception of States and Law), is therefore the *means*; the compulsory submission of the enemy to our will is the ultimate *object*. In order to attain this object fully, the enemy must be disarmed, and disarmament becomes therefore the immediate object of hostilities in theory. It takes the place of the final

---

From *On War* by General Karl von Clausewitz (London: 1911) Volume 1, pp. 1, 22–23; Volume 3, pp. 121–122. Reprinted by permission of Barnes and Noble, Inc., and Routledge and Kegan Paul, Ltd.

KARL VON CLAUSEWITZ (1780–1831) Prussian Chief of Staff and Director of the General War Academy, Berlin. Author *The Campaign of 1812 in Russia*, (London: J. Murray, 1843).

object, and puts it aside as something we can eliminate from our calculations.

. . .

The War of a community—of whole Nations, and particularly of civilised Nations—always starts from a political condition and is called forth by a political motive. It is, therefore, a political act. Now if it was a perfect, unrestrained, and absolute expression of force, as we had to deduce it from its mere conception, then the moment it is called forth by policy it would step into the place of policy, and as something quite independent of it would set it aside, and only follow its own laws, just as a mine at the moment of explosion cannot be guided into any other direction than that which has been given to it by preparatory arrangements. This is how the thing has really been viewed hitherto, whenever a want of harmony between policy and the conduct of a War has led to theoretical distinctions of the kind. But it is not so, and the idea is radically false. War in the real world, as we have already seen, is not an extreme thing which expends itself at one single discharge; it is the operation of powers which do not develop themselves completely in the same manner and in the same measure, but which at one time expand sufficiently to overcome the resistance opposed by inertia or friction, while at another they are too weak to produce an effect; it is therefore, in a certain measure, a pulsation of violent force more or less vehement, consequently making its discharges and exhausting its powers more or less quickly—in other words, conducting more or less quickly to the aim, but always lasting long enough to admit of influence being exerted on it in its course, so as to give it this or that direction, in short, to be subject to the will of a guiding intelligence. Now, if we reflect that War has its root in a political object, then naturally this original motive which called it into existence should also continue the first and highest consideration in its conduct. Still, the political object is no despotic lawgiver on that account; it must accommodate itself to the nature of the means, and though changes in these means may involve modification in the political objective, the latter always retains a prior right to consideration. Policy, therefore, is interwoven with the whole action of War, and must exercise a continuous influence upon it, as far as the nature of the forces liberated by it will permit.

. . .

WAR AS AN INSTRUMENT OF POLICY

. . .

We know, certainly, that War is only called forth through the political intercourse of Governments and Nations; but in general it is supposed that such intercourse is broken off by War, and that a totally different state of things ensues, subject to no laws but its own.

We maintain, on the contrary, that War is nothing but a continuation of political intercourse, with a mixture of other means. We say mixed with other means in order thereby to maintain at the same time that this political intercourse does not cease by the War itself, is not changed into something quite different, but that, in its essence, it continues to exist, whatever may be the form of the means which it uses, and that the chief lines on which the events of the War progress, and to which they are attached, are only the general features of policy which run all through the War until peace takes place. And how can we conceive it to be otherwise? Does the cessation of diplomatic notes stop the political relations between different Nations and Governments? Is not War merely another kind of writing and language for political thoughts? It has certainly a grammar of its own, but its logic is not peculiar to itself.

Accordingly, War can never be separated from political intercourse, and if, in the consideration of the matter, this is done in any way, all the threads of the different relations are, to a certain extent, broken, and we have before us a senseless thing without an object.

16. THE BALANCE OF TERROR

Glenn H. Snyder

I T IS now rather widely believed that the balance of power has been overtaken by technology; that nuclear weapons and missiles have brought the balancing process to a halt and substituted a new and quite different regulator—that of nuclear deterrence.* This article will challenge this view. The balance of power theory is still generally valid and

From Paul Seabury, ed., *The Balance of Power* (San Francisco: Chandler Publishing Company, 1965). Reprinted by permission of the publisher.

GLENN H. SNYDER (1924–   ) Professor of Political Science, State University of New York, Buffalo. Author of *Stockpiling Strategic Materials: Politics and National Defense* (San Francisco: Chandler Publishing Company, 1966); *Deterrence and Defense: Toward a Theory of National Security* (Princeton: Princeton University Press, 1961); *Deterrence by Denial and Punishment* (Princeton: Woodrow Wilson School of Public and International Affairs, 1958).

*For an early statement of this view, see Arthur Lee Burns, "From Balance to Deterrence," *World Politics*, Vol. IX (1957), pp. 494–529.

still a useful model of at least certain important aspects of contemporary world politics. The new military technology has not terminated but only modified the balance of power process. It has superimposed a new system of equilibrium (the phrase "balance of terror" will serve) upon the old system which was based on nonnuclear capabilities. The two systems operate according to different tendencies and principles and can be separated analytically, but in practice they are inextricably mixed in a new balance of power in which elements of the old coexist with the new. I will attempt to compare the two subprocesses at certain salient points and then describe the nature of their interaction in an integrated process.

THE BALANCE OF TERROR

There are naïve and sophisticated versions of the "balance of terror" or the nuclear strategic balance. The naïve view, the image held by relatively uninformed laymen, is simply that both sides are deterred from using nuclear weapons against the other by the fear of devastating retaliation. In this image, the targets of the nuclear strikes are cities. To initiate nuclear war would be to commit national suicide; hence a "balance" or "stalemate" exists.

The sophisticated version focuses on "counterforce" rather than "countervalue" (city) targeting. One or both sides could eliminate or drastically reduce the other side's retaliatory capacity by directing the first strike at the opponent's nuclear striking forces rather than at his cities. There are circumstances, theoretically at least, in which thermonuclear war initiated in this manner would be a rational act. According to this version, a "balance of terror" exists when neither side can, by executing a counterforce first-strike, reduce the opponent's retaliation to "acceptable" proportions. Or, to use the jargon of the trade, neither side has a "full first-strike capability," or (what amounts to virtually the same thing) both sides possess at least a "minimum strike-back capability"—i.e. a residual capacity which after suffering the attrition of the attacker's first blow, could still inflict intolerable damage on the attacker's cities, population and economic assets in a retaliatory blow.

But the "sophisticated" version, as here defined, is not sophisticated enough. What, for example, is the criterion for defining the degree of retaliation that is "acceptable"? What purpose does the victim serve by retaliation against the attacker's cities, other than revenge? What motivates the attacker to strike in the first place; what purpose of political goal is served by a counterforce first strike? Eliminating or reducing the victim's capacity to retaliate is not a purpose but a precaution. How is the war terminated after the initial strike and reprisal? What then determines the terms of settlement? What constitutes "victory" or "defeat"?

To make use of the sophisticated version for our purposes, it is necessary to return part way to the naïve image. I shall assert, somewhat heretically, that the *ultimate* function of nuclear weapons (especially the "strategic" variety) is either to destroy the enemy's cities and conventional war potential, or to support a threat to do so for purposes of blackmail or deterrence. To make this clear it is convenient to start with a model of the balance of terror in its "pure" form. Assume two states, A and B armed only with nuclear strategic missiles. Assume that both states are expansionist—i.e., that they both would like to subjugate all or part of the other if they could do so at acceptable cost.

In this model, the only means of subjugation is by nuclear blackmail. Blackmail, of course, cannot succeed as long as the opponent can make a "deterrent" counterthreat of devastating retaliation. But A, for example, may be able to blackmail B successfully if it can meet two requirements. First, it must be able to disarm B by a counterforce "first strike" or at least destroy enough of B's forces to restrict its retaliation to "acceptable" proportions. The criterion of "acceptability" is the amount of retaliatory damage to A which is just equivalent to the value which A places on B's capitulation to its demands. The demand may be for B's total capitulation or for some lesser concession. Secondly, A must maintain in reserve a force sufficient to blackmail B into conceding by the threat of "countervalue" or population destruction. Roughly, the necessary size of this force is measured by the value which A thinks B places on the things he is being asked to concede. If A fires all its forces in attempting to disarm B, it dissipates its blackmail or bargaining power and cannot achieve its political goal.

If (A or B, or both) can meet both of these requirements the balance of terror is in disequilibrium. If both sides fall short of one or both requirements, an attack by either side is either futile or too costly and the balance of terror is in a state of equilibrium.

Note that A's initial counterforce strike is merely preliminary, undertaken only to put itself in a position to blackmail B. Counterforce strikes do not contribute *directly* to "winning the war," as is suggested in some of the current literature; they contribute only indirectly by improving the attacker's relative bargaining power—i.e., his power to coerce the victim by the threat to strike cities. And they contribute to this end *with high confidence* only if they are sufficient to reduce the victim's retaliatory capacity to below A's "acceptable" level. If B is left with residual forces higher than this level, he may be able to resist A's postattack blackmail.

In the "real world," of course, A will have conventional forces; a combination of counterforce and countervalue strikes against B may so prostrate B as to make physical conquest possible and blackmail unnecessary. But such conquest would be the result of A's preponderance in the conventional balance after the nuclear exchange, and therefore falls under the heading of "interaction" between the two balances, which is discussed below.

DIFFERENCES BETWEEN THE CONVENTIONAL BALANCE AND THE NUCLEAR BALANCE

To compare and then integrate the two balancing systems, the first questions to be asked are: What is the nature of the "power" being balanced? What is the nature of "equilibrium" in each case? In traditional theory of (conventional) balance of power, the kind of power involved was the physical capability to take or hold territory. Equilibrium was said to obtain when military capabilities and war potential on each side were roughly equal, so that neither side had the capacity to defeat the other in war and by so doing to change the territorial status quo. The preceding discussion shows that this is not the case in the nuclear "balance of terror." Nuclear weapons cannot, when employed, in and of themselves, take or hold territory. Physical conquest during or after a nuclear exchange requires the intervention of conventional forces. In the "pure" balance of terror, the political status quo can be changed only by political coercion—that is, by a process of blackmail supported by the threat of severe punishment. The status quo is preserved by "deterrence" supported by a similar threat. Thus the power that is balanced in the balance of terror is essentially "political power" rather than physical capabilities; capabilities enter in only as the threatened sanction supporting the political demand; not as an instrument for the direct physical achievement of political goals as is usually the case in the traditional or conventional balance of power.

The balance of terror is more subjective in nature than the old balance of power. Whether "equilibrium" exists depends at least as much on factors "within the minds" of the opponents as upon an objective comparison of military capabilities. Subjectivity is obvious in the fact that equilibrium is defined in terms of "acceptability" of damage for both sides; what is acceptable depends on the values attached to the political stakes. Thus, in contrast to the old balance of power, in which the state of the equilibrium could be objectively—if roughly—determined by the uninvolved observer, such an observer can only intuitively guess at equilibrium in the balance of terror, since it depends principally on whether the gains to be made or losses to be avoided by striking first are less than the costs to be incurred—all as subjectively valued in the minds of the decision-makers.

The balance of terror is subjective in still another sense. The participants themselves, while presumably they can judge what is unacceptable damage for themselves, cannot be certain what is unacceptable for the opponent. Thus the determination of whether equilibrium exists is ultimately reduced to a guessing game about the opponent's values and intentions. There is therefore vast scope for disagreement or asymmetrical perceptions about the state of the balance and about the degree of political, military or technological change which would throw it "out of balance." For example, the balance may actually be in equilibrium, but one side may fear the other side *may* possess a full first-strike capability. Then the latter may achieve its political aims by bluff, whether these aims are of a deterrent or blackmail nature. In the obverse case—when the balance is in disequilibrium because one side can be provoked to strike first, but its opponent doesn't perceive this—the outcome could be war by "miscalculation."

Subjective considerations determine the "location" or "boundaries" of equilibrium within the spectrum of possible force ratios, but a comparison of relative capabilities is obviously still necessary for estimating whether equilibrium actually exists at any given time.

However, in sharp contrast to the traditional balance of power, the notion of quantitative equality between striking forces is totally irrelevant as a criterion for "balance." Equilibrium can exist when one side's offensive forces are far inferior to the other's, provided the inferior side's forces are relatively invulnerable to a counterforce strike and provided the forces surviving such a strike can penetrate the attacker's air defenses in sufficient numbers to inflict unacceptable damage. Or equilibrium might require having more striking forces than the opponent if one's own forces are highly vulnerable, and the enemy has a very good air defense and civil defense system. The essential criterion for equilibrium is a mutual capacity to inflict intolerable damage in retaliation, and this depends on a variety of technological factors in addition to numbers of delivery vehicles.

A corollary of this distinction is that, while a balance of conventional power can be said to exist only within a rather narrow range of relative capabilities on either side of strict equality, a balance of terror can exist within a wide range of force ratios. To illustrate: assuming relatively invulnerable offensive forces and rather impotent air-missile defense systems on both sides, side A, with 100 missiles, might be in a state of equilibrium against side B with 500 missiles; equilibrium might still obtain if side A were to increase its force to 1,000 missiles. In other words, even a ten-fold increase by one side might not overturn the balance. The "range of equilibrium" would be the difference between the forces which A needs for a "minimum strike-back capability" and the forces it needs for a "full first-strike capability." This consideration has important implications for the *stability* of the balance of terror, to be discussed below.

Another important contrast between the two systems lies in the relative weight given to the functions of *deterrence* and *defense*. Both were functions of the prenuclear balance (and still are in today's conventional balance of power); but deterrence was secondary in the sense that it was an incidental consequence of an obvious capacity to defend territory successfully. It was also secondary in the sense that the primary purpose of balancing techniques—armaments, alliances, etc.—was to be ready to frustrate an expansionist state rather than to influence the intentions of that state. If deterrence failed, defensive war was considered to be a normal technique of the balancing process, a continuation of the process by violent means.

By contrast, the balance of terror centers heavily on the function of deterrence. Deterrence is achieved by the threat of devastating punishment or damage, not as a simple by-product of a capacity to defend territory or otherwise to frustrate the aggressor's aims. If deterrence fails, the system will have broken down completely; nuclear war cannot be considered a normal "technique" for adjusting or restoring the balance. This does not mean that it is not useful or wise to take measures in advance of war to mitigate the dreadful consequences of nuclear war, or even to "win the war" in some sense. In particular, it may be desirable (as the United States has done) to develop a "surplus" of offensive striking forces far beyond the amount needed for a deterrent equilibrium, in order to be able to destroy a maximum amount of the attacker's post-attack residual forces, while holding in reserve a powerful force for bargaining purposes. Such additional forces do not essentially disturb the equilibrium, unless they create a degree of preponderance which begins to approach a full first-strike capability.

INTERACTIONS IN THE "MIXED" BALANCE OF POWER

Nuclear and conventional balancing processes do not operate independently; they impinge on each other in various ways. The contemporary balancing process, in an overall sense, is a mixture of the two. Generally speaking, the entire system is in overall "balance" when either of two conditions exist. One is when each of the two subprocesses is "out of balance" but in different directions—i.e., when one side preponderates in one component and the other side in the other. The other condition is when both conventional and nuclear balances are separately in equilibrium. If one is in balance and the other is not, the entire system is in a state of disequilibrium, at least with respect to any particular political issue. This is also the case when both processes are unbalanced in favor of one side.

To illuminate these somewhat cryptic remarks, let us turn away from our abstract model to the world of reality. We see a world of two nuclear powers (the Soviet Union, and the United States-Great Britain as a unit) which also have conventional forces; we also see two incipient nuclear powers and many nonnuclear powers. All possess conventional forces; some of them enjoy the protection of one or the other of the nuclear great powers.

That the latter enjoy the protection of the nuclear great powers means that the political function of nuclear weapons has been extended from strictly bilateral deterrence and blackmail between nuclear powers to that of deterring aggression against other (nonnuclear) countries. This function may require the nuclear protector to create an actual or apparent nuclear disequilibrium in his favor to make credible a determination to strike first if provoked by an attack on his allies. Short of this, or concurrent with it, he can threaten the *limited* use of nuclear weapons in either a "tactical" or "strategic" manner.

The best example of interaction is the balance of power in Europe. Here, the Soviets preponderate in the conventional balance (although not so greatly as we thought a few years ago); while the United States, as West Europe's protector, remains superior in nuclear forces. Yet it is doubtful whether the United States superiority, while quantitatively great, really constitutes a "full first-strike capability." If it did in its maximum sense—i.e., if we could completely eliminate the Soviet nuclear forces in a first strike—it would be possible, theoretically at least, to dispense with conventional forces in Western Europe. Total and obvious strategic nuclear disequilibrium would remove any need to even partially balance the Soviets at the conventional level. Conversely, if it were true that the United States obviously lacked a first-strike capability (meaning that we were clearly not willing to strike first in any circumstances), then this might reinstate the conventional balancing process in Europe in its full prenuclear dimensions—i.e., it might well stimulate a build-up of conventional forces sufficient to hold successfully against a Red Army invasion.

That this has not occurred, is due in part to the uncertainty of Soviet leadership as to whether equilibrium exists or whether the United States nuclear preponderance really amounts to disequilibrium. In other words, the Soviets may suspect that the United States has a full first-strike capability which could be activated if sufficiently provoked. Or they may believe that we are irrational enough to strike even when our force does not meet the objective requirements of such a capability. For in the case of deterrence (or blackmail) it is what the opponent thinks or fears that counts, and the United States nuclear superiority is great enough that the Soviet leadership no doubt fears some probability of a United States first strike in particularly tense or provocative circumstances. Considering the very great damage they would suffer if we did strike, a quite low probability in their calculations may be sufficient to deter.

Any remaining doubts which the Russians might have about our implicit threat of a strategic first strike are offset by the presence of tactical nuclear weapons in the hands of the NATO forces on the "central front" in West Germany. The American resolve in NATO to use these weapons if necessary to stop a Soviet invasion has been firmly declared and implemented by the rather thorough incorporation of their use into NATO's military plans and organization. It is no doubt highly credible to the Soviets that these weapons would be used if necessary and considering their own apparent belief that a tactical nuclear war in Europe could not remain limited, our tactical nuclear posture constitutes, in effect, a very credible threat of all-out nuclear war. Even if they were to assume that the *strategic* nuclear balance by itself was in a state of equilibrium, the tactical nuclear weapons would make it a rather unstable equilibrium. This instability is a potent deterrent of Soviet conventional provocations and reduces the need for balancing at the conventional level.

The function of the conventional NATO forces on the central front—apart from turning back small and medium-scale incursions—is further to enhance the credibility of nuclear deterrence by forcing the Soviets to undertake a major attack provocative enough to exceed the United States "threshold of nuclear response." Thus the overall balance of power in Western Europe is a function of three factors: the U. S. first-strike capability at the strategic level; the tactical nuclear threat; and the defense and deterrent effects of conventional forces. Each probably would be inadequate by itself, but the three together have created a mixed conventional-nuclear equilibrium which effectively deters Soviet aggression. The primary function of the tactical nuclear weapons is to form a "bridge" between a nonexistent conventional balance and a *possibly* extant strategic nuclear equilibrium. In other words, they assure the Soviets, in case they might otherwise have doubts, that a combined tactical-strategical nuclear imbalance in favor of the United States does exist.

We may turn the point around and note that during the period of the United States nuclear monopoly (strategic nuclear disequilibrium in our favor) we were deterred from capitalizing on this imbalance at least partly by the obvious Soviet superiority in the conventional balance which potentially enabled them to resist our nuclear pressure by credibly threatening to overrun Western Europe. An overall equilibrium obtained precisely because of a sharp disequilibrium in opposite directions in each of the two subcomponents.

Whereas in Europe conventional forces serve as auxiliary to the nuclear deterrent, in Asia the reverse is probably true. The obvious disequilibrium in the strategic nuclear balance between the United States and Communist China serves to deter the Chinese from openly committing their own conventional forces in internal wars (e.g. South Vietnam) and thus tends to create a conventional balance of power in Southeast Asia which might not otherwise exist. Alternatively, should the Chinese become involved with the United States in an overt conventional conflict, they probably would be deterred from committing enough forces to defeat the United States forces in fear of a United States nuclear response. Nuclear disequilibrium favoring the United States tends to limit our Communist opponents in Asia to a commitment of conventional forces which the U. S. and our allies can deal with successfully at the conventional level. In short, nuclear disequilibrium tends to promote conventional equilibrium or operational conventional preponderance for the United States.

When nuclear deterrence is extended to the protection of allies, the element of mutual assessment of *intentions* becomes critically important, much more so than in simple bilateral deterrence where the "credibility" of retaliation can more or less be taken for granted. In such "extended deterrence," the deterring side tries to create the impression that the balance of terror is out of balance in its favor or could be thrown into disequilibrium by sufficient provocation. He attempts to establish the "credibility" of his threat to strike first "all-out" or to initiate limited nuclear action. Estimates of relative capability are not irrelevant, but because of the essential subjectivity and hence uncertainty (in the opponent's mind) about what actually constitutes a "first-strike capability" for the deterrer, or about his willingness to run the risk of escalation, capability comparisons tend to be overshadowed by appraisals of the deterrer's apparent "resolve," "nerve," irrationality, gambling propensities and other subjective factors that bear upon his intentions. Paradoxically, it would seem that intent-perception has become more crucial in today's balance of power than in the prenuclear balance, even though (or perhaps, *because*) the physical capabilities have become many orders of magnitude more destructive.

Appraisals of intent not only are now more important, but important in a different way than in the old balance of power. In the latter, the relevant intentions were largely political in nature, centering on the question of *which* countries were likely to fight on either the offensive or the defensive side. It could reasonably be assumed that the countries which did participate in a war would do so to the full extent of their capabilities, but there was often considerable uncertainty about who would participate. With the emergence of bipolarity, the uncertainty about alliance partners drastically declined, but nuclear technology introduced a new form of intent-perception and a new form of uncertainty—that concerning what types of military capability the opponent was likely to use and what degree of violence he was willing to risk or accept.

One might say that this new kind of uncertainty has replaced the former uncertainty about alliance partners as a major source of stability in the balance of power. Or, to put it slightly differently, the implicit or explicit threat to "raise the ante" in order to avoid defeat has taken the place of the threat to recruit additional states to the defending alliance. Such a threat is more or less analagous to the practice of "holding the ring" in the old balance—when a state promised to be neutral if its ally were attacked by one country, but to come to its aid if it were attacked by two or more powers. In short, technology has to some extent provided a substitute for the political flexibility and stability which was lost to the balancing process when it shifted to a' bipolar structure after World War II.

STABILITY

A careful distinction should be made between "equilibrium" and "stability" in both the conventional balance of power and the nuclear balance. The two terms often are erroneously used interchangeably. Equilibria in both balances can have varying degrees of stability; and it is even possible to have disequilibrium with relatively high stability, if the dominant side is not aggressively inclined and this fact is recognized by other members of the system.

In the traditional balance of power theory, the idea of stability usually referred generally to a supposed perpetual tendency of the system to maintain itself at or near a state of equilibrium. Deviations from equilibrium generated "feedback" forces which moved the balance back in the direction of equilibrium. Within this general notion, stability had at least three subdimensions which, so far as I know, were never precisely delineated. These were: the tendency or lack of tendency toward an arms race, tendencies either to stimulate or inhibit war, and the tendency of the process to preserve the independence of the major actors. Theorists tended to emphasize the third dimension; in fact, armament and warfare often were treated not as types of instability but as *methods* for preserving stability in the third sense, along with alliances and other techniques.

By contrast, the dimension of stability which receives most attention in the balance of terror, and by extension, in the contemporary balancing process as a whole, is the propensity of the system to produce war, the obvious reason being the possibility of *nuclear* war, the horrifying nature of which seems to outweigh all other considerations. How stable is the contemporary balance of power in this sense?

The basic criterion of stability in the balance of terror is the "distance" which both sides are from possessing a full first-strike capability. If neither side has forces which even approach this capacity—i.e., if both have a very strong "strike-back" capability—the balance of terror is very stable. If one or both are very close to having a first-strike capability, or actually do have it, the balance can be very unstable. It might be only moderately unstable if only one side possessed such a capability if that side were benevolent; but if both sides had it, fears of a first strike by the other, and consequent incentives to preempt, would be strong, even despite intrinsic benevolence on both sides.

Stability can be defined alternatively as the degree of economic, technological, or politicomilitary "shock" which the system can sustain without creating for one side or the other a capability and willingness to strike first. Economic shock (or degree of instability) refers to the amount of resource expenditure required for one or the other to acquire the *quantity* of forces required for a successful first strike—assuming a given technology, if neither side has the economic resources to produce such a capability, the balance is stable in this sense. Technological instability refers to magnitude of the technological breakthrough (e.g., the degree of efficiency of an antimissile defense) which would create a sufficient first strike force for either side. Politicomilitary instability means the extent of "provocation" by either side which would touch off a first strike by the other. The word "provocation" includes a wide variety of contingencies: being "backed into a corner" in a confrontation of threats and counterthreats, becoming involved in a limited conventional war which one is in danger of losing, suffering a limited nuclear strike by the opponent, becoming involved in an escalating nuclear war, and many others. Any of these events may drastically increase the potential cost and risk of *not* striking first and thereby potentially create a state of disequilibrium in the strategic nuclear balance. As noted earlier, whether equilibrium exists depends on the context of events; the "acceptability" of damage is calculated not only against the gains to be made by striking first but also against the *losses to be avoided*, in any particular set of circumstances.

Although these three criteria of stability-instability interact, it is my judgment that the balance of terror is currently most stable in the "economic" or resource sense, somewhat less stable technologically, and least stable according to the "politicomilitary" criterion. The apparently firm United States commitment to use nuclear weapons in the defense of Western Europe, if necessary, indicates that there are types of Soviet provocation at the lower levels of violence which could touch off a United States strategic first strike, or more likely, a tactical nuclear response, from which the war could escalate. It is hoped, of course, that the Soviets' recognition of the U. S. commitment will deter the provocation; that instability in this dimension will preserve a stable equilibrium in the overall balance of power. However, the risks of Soviet miscalculation and subsequent escalation which this commitment creates should not be underestimated and probably are the most serious potential sources of instability in the contemporary balance.

The point is often made in the strategic literature that the greater the stability of the "strategic" balance of terror, the lower the stability of the overall balance at its lower levels of violence. The reasoning is that if neither side has a "full first-strike capability," and both know it, they will be less inhibited about initiating conventional war, and about the limited use of nuclear weapons, than if the strategic balance were unstable. Thus firm stability in the strategic nuclear balance tends to destabilize the conventional balance and also to activate the lesser nuclear "links" between the latter and the former. But one *could* argue precisely the opposite—that the greater likelihood of gradual escalation due to a stable strategic equilibrium tends to deter both conventional provocation and tactical nuclear strikes—thus stabilizing the overall balance. The first hypothesis probably is dominant, but it must be heavily qualified by the second, since nations probably fear the possibility of escalation "all the way" nearly as much as they fear the possibility of an "all-out" first strike.

There is another stability hypothesis which is just the reverse—although not contradictory to—the one just described: a stable conventional equilibrium tends to increase the stability of the nuclear component of the balance. When both sides can defend themselves successfully at the conventional level, conventional aggression is likely to be deterred, and if it is not, there is little pressure on the defender to resort to nuclear action. But this one also has its obverse: it is sometimes argued that when the *status quo* side attempts to create a conventional equilibrium, the credibility of its nuclear threats is undermined since it might thereby indicate an unwillingness to initiate nuclear war by seeking to create an alternative to it. The potential aggressor might be then more willing to attack when he believes (perhaps mistakenly) that he has achieved a margin of conventional superiority. The first hypothesis tends to stress the effect of conventional balance in reducing the probability of escalation if war occurs; the second stresses the increased chances of the outbreak of war due to the apparently lower risk incurred by starting it.

When a great nuclear power places smaller nonnuclear countries under its nuclear protection (as a substitute for creation of a conventional equilibrium), one effect may be to reduce the stability of the strategic nuclear balance in the sense of stimulating an arms race. Nuclear deterrence of attacks on "third parties" theoretically requires a strategic nuclear capability approaching first strike dimensions. Forces of this size may raise fears of an aggressive surprise first strike in the opponent's mind and therefore place psychological pressure on him to increase his nuclear force in order to strengthen his deterrence, perhaps to strengthen his chances of winning the war should his fears materialize, and, at the extreme, to develop a first-strike force himself to be in a position to preempt. This type of instability would be much weaker if the great nuclear powers were to limit themselves to bilateral mutual deterrence.

The nature of the "balance of power" process in a world of many nuclear powers is a challenging speculative problem which can only be touched upon here in connection with the question of stability. It is rather remarkable that the balance of terror is generally believed to be most stable when it is bipolar and least stable when it is multipolar, whereas the exact reverse was said to be true in the traditional theory of the balance of power. In the latter, bipolarity was said to be unstable because of the absence of a strong unattached power center (a "holder of the balance"), or several centers, which could be recruited to block one of the "poles" which had developed marginal preponderance of capabilities and apparently aggressive intentions. A multiplicity of power centers would provide such balancing material and create uncertainty for an incipient aggressor as to the amount of power which would oppose his designs. A bipolar balance of terror is said to be relatively stable because only two power centers have the capacity to initiate nuclear war and because they are likely to be cautious in conflict situations which involve the danger of nuclear war. The major powers in the contemporary bipolar balance are said to be relatively "responsible" powers.

Many specific arguments have been advanced in support of the hypothesis that nuclear diffusion would greatly increase instability, but two in particular are probably the most influential. One is the "statistical argument": the notion that the more countries that have nuclear weapons, the more likely it is that some of these weapons will be fired, accidentally or otherwise, and the firing of nuclear weapons anywhere in the world may trigger a global holocaust. The other is the "irresponsibility argument": the idea that some of the countries which may acquire nuclear power will lack the caution and restraint which seems to characterize the nuclear great powers; they may threaten or use their nuclear weapons recklessly, perhaps because of domestic instability or simply a lack of concern for, or lack of comprehension of, the broader consequences of their actions.

The point is raised merely to note the striking difference between the two sets of stability hypotheses, not to analyze either, which would be far beyond the scope of this paper.

IN LIEU OF CONCLUSION

International relations theory and military-strategic analysis have been ignoring each other for too long. This essay has attempted to introduce a measure of integration, focusing on an idea which is common to both fields—that of equilibrium. Balance of power theory cannot embrace all phenomena of international politics, not even all military phenomena. Yet it has enjoyed a rather high degree of historical validation, as political theories go, and deserves to be rehabilitated, refined and renovated.

Ancient ideas die hard; the notion that military preponderance means superior strength and that this means superior political power is so deeply ingrained that it continues to be believed and acted upon by both sides even though, in the strategic nuclear balance, it has little objective or logical basis. Further research would surely uncover many additional deviations which would serve to qualify and thus to enrich the logical analysis presented here.

17. THE NUCLEAR THRUST: FROM ALAMOGORDO TO CUBA

William R. Kintner

THE NUCLEAR AGE began on a Manhattan Project test stand at Alamogordo, New Mexico, in July, 1945, and the first two-sided contest was waged and won by the United States in the 1962 Cuban missile crisis. The thinking and the preparations leading to this bloodless [1] and novel but crucial confrontation comprise one of the shortest and most turbulent chapters of military history.

The advent of nuclear bombs threw an entirely new element into the military equation. Patterns of strategic thought were rendered obsolete almost overnight. Comprehending the significance of the nuclear weapon, the United States, and subsequently the Soviet Union, slowly began to formulate strategic concepts in keeping with the new era; but the task of the United States was made even more difficult by the Soviet Union's postwar challenge to U.S. power. The strategic revolution had been

---

From *Peace and the Strategy Conflict* by William R. Kintner (New York: 1967) pp. 22–26; 32–42; 45–47. Reprinted by permission of Frederick A. Praeger, Inc. Footnotes have been renumbered to appear in consecutive order.

WILLIAM R. KINTNER (1915–   ) Professor of Political Science, University of Pennsylvania; Director, Foreign Policy Research Institute, Philadelphia, Pennsylvania. Author of *Peace and the Strategy Conflict* (New York: Praeger Publishers, 1967). Co-author, *Building the Atlantic World* (New York: Harper Brothers, 1963); *The Haphazard Years: How America Has Gone to War* (Garden City, N.Y.: Doubleday and Company, 1960); *A Forward Strategy for America* (New York: Harper Brothers, 1961); *Protracted Conflict* (New York: Harper Brothers, 1959). Co-editor, *The Nuclear Revolution in Soviet Military Affairs* (Norman: University of Oklahoma Press, 1968).

[1] Major R. Anderson, Jr., who was shot down by Soviet missiles while flying a U-2 reconnaissance plane over Cuba, was the only casualty of this conflict.

spurred by the arrival of nuclear weapons, and strategic decisions had to be made for (and in spite of) a politically uncertain future.

THE TRUMAN YEARS

At the end of World War II, the United States demobilized its armed forces and acted as though the world was indeed at peace. But in late 1946 and early 1947, the United States began responding to the challenge of Soviet thrusts in Iran, Greece, Czechoslovakia, and Berlin.

At that time, the relatively small and poorly equipped Strategic Air Command (SAC) was the United States' prime instrument for containing Communist aggression. As long as the Soviet Union had neither strategic air power nor nuclear explosives, SAC's mission was clear and simple: to deter the Soviet Union from a land invasion of Europe by threatening a retaliatory nuclear strike against the Soviet Union itself.

The Soviet atomic explosion in the fall of 1949 ended U.S. atomic monopoly and foreshadowed a revision of U.S. strategic concepts.

In response to Communist aggression in South Korea, the United States increased its military outlay and helped to organize the defense efforts of its non-Communist allies. The defense budget rose from $15 billion in 1950 to $51 billion in 1952. In addition to increasing conventional forces, these funds allowed the Strategic Air Command to grow into a full-fledged fighting force.

In 1951, to convince the Soviets that the United States would fight if Western Europe were attacked, President Truman committed U.S. ground forces to the North Atlantic Treaty Organization, which had been formed by the allies in 1949 as a mutual defense alliance. Despite its atomic advantage, the United States began to plan for a conventional defense of Western Europe; and in Korea, combined units of the U.S. Army, Navy, and Air Force, armed with conventional weapons, were fighting a World War II type of war. Although superior U.S. strategic air power was never directly employed, its effect was to limit the Korean War and to keep the Soviets out of Western Europe.

THE U.S.S.R. ENTERS THE NUCLEAR AGE

Although by 1945, Soviet prestige as a world power had attained hitherto unknown heights, the Soviets were still militarily and economically weak in comparison with the United States. The Soviet Union ended World War II with essentially one basic force, the Red Army. During the war, the role of the Soviet Air Force remained subordinate to that of the Army, and the Soviet Navy was negligible. Soviet industry had been severely damaged, and probably 20 million Russian people had perished in World War II. The Soviet leaders knew that among the great powers, the United States alone not only survived unscathed but also possessed the weapons of the future—atomic bombs. Until the Soviets achieved equal capabilities,[2] they publicly disparaged the military value of atomic weapons.

In the history of the Soviet armed forces, an institutional bias for defense has been a persistent element. A prime task of Soviet forces since the Allied intervention in Russia in 1918 has been the preservation of Communism within the U.S.S.R. Thus, before the Soviet Union obtained a nuclear capability, it developed an air defense system designed to cope with nuclear attack by U.S. long-range bombers. Hundreds of captured German experts on early-warning radar were pressed into service by Stalin; and by 1950, the Soviets deployed a warning net from the Baltic to the Pacific. The development of jet interceptors kept pace with the Soviet warning system; by 1950, the Soviets had a 2,000-aircraft interceptor force. Billions of rubles were spent on surface-to-air missiles (SAM's), which replaced antiaircraft artillery and supplemented the interceptors.

Despite a traditional defense orientation (seen today in the emphasis on both active and passive defense), neither Russian military tradition nor Soviet military doctrine ever ignored the value of taking the offensive to achieve victory. Parallel with Soviet efforts for active and passive defense and before the Soviets possessed nuclear weapons, great strides were taken to obtain long-range delivery systems. Apparently, the Soviets were embarking on a broad and varied program of their own in the field of rockets and missiles. In April, 1944, a leading specialist in nuclear weapons and long-range missiles, Major General G. I. Pokrovski, published the first Soviet article on long-range missiles.[3] In 1946, A. A. Blagonravov, who was both a military officer and an academician, was named President of the Academy of Artillery Sciences, an institute that was to play an important role in developing ICBM's and space rockets.[4] As in the case of defensive weapons, the Soviets made use of captured German technicians for developing offensive weaponry. Meanwhile, Soviet interest in nuclear weapons and missile warfare amounted to almost an obsession.[5]

In 1947, our whole budget for research and development in the intercontinental field was eliminated for reasons of economy. In 1946

---

[2] See Marshall Shulman, *Stalin's Foreign Policy Reappraised* (Cambridge: Harvard University Press, 1963), Chapter 2, "Moscow in the Spring of 1949."

[3] *Science and Technology in Contemporary War,* trans. by Raymond L. Garthoff (New York: Praeger, 1959), pp. vi–vii.

[4] U.S. Congress, Senate Committee on Aeronautical and Space Sciences, *Soviet Space Programs: Organizations, Plans, Goals, and International Implications,* 87th Cong., 2nd Sess., 1962, p. 64.

[5] S. N. Koslov, M. V. Smirnov, I. S. Boz, and P. A. Sidorov, *O sovietskoi voennoi nauke* (*On Soviet Military Science*) (Moscow: Voenizdat, 1954), p. 249.

the Soviet budget for research and development in these categories
was trebled. It reconstituted its research bodies for jet engines, for
swept-wing aircraft design, for nuclear explosives, for rocket propulsion. The whole basis for a shift in the balance of power, as the
Soviet leaders saw it, was laid in the period at the end of the war;
and beginning immediately thereafter, the Soviets turned on an
intense concentration of resources in these categories in order to
shorten their period of vulnerabilty as much as possible. The Soviets' expectation was that when these things began to bear fruit,
a shift in the balance of power would result.[6]

Under Stalin, early Soviet moves toward obtaining the best that modern postwar technology had to offer were not, however, hand in hand
with a basic reformulation of Soviet military doctrine. A number of
retrospective Soviet accounts of the postwar development of Soviet military theory make clear that in the period before meaningful numbers of
modern weapons were acquired, Soviet thinking was directed toward
using new weaponry within the framework of past methods of warfare.[7]
Critical nuclear-age problems such as surprise attack and the decisive
initial period of a modern war bred new views that were confronting the
old outlook. The lag was not unnatural; for from the first Soviet atomic
test in the fall of 1949 until the Soviet acquisition of the hydrogen bomb
in 1953, quantities of nuclear weapons and numbers of long-range bombers were very small.

Stalin's insistence that Soviet military thinking focus on elaborating
the significance for warfare of his "permanently operating factors" was
another reason for discrepancy between technology and military doctrine
in his time. These "factors" dealt with stability of the rear, morale
of the army, quantity and quality of divisions, armament of the army,
and organizational ability of army commanders. Originally formulated
in 1942, these factors of warfare were, in part, an outgrowth of Soviet
experience in World War II. The subsequent emphasis given these principles represented an *ex post facto* rationalization for the kind of war
conducted by the U.S.S.R. under Stalin's guidance.

---

[6] Philip E. Mosely and Marshall Shulman, *The Changing Soviet Challenge*
(Racine, Wisc.: The Johnson Foundation, 1964).

[7] Colonel I. Korotkov, "The Development of Soviet Military Theory in the
Postwar Years," *Voennoi-istoricheskii zhurnal* (*Military-Historical Journal*), April,
1964, p. 43. This account is one of the most candid and critical treatments of the
subject to appear in Soviet literature to date.

THE MISSILE REVOLUTION

The so-called missile gap in the latter years of the Eisenhower Admin-istration had been sired by questionable information, inadequate analy-sis, and bad politics; and we now know that the Soviet missile force was not superior in either quantity or accuracy. The Soviets had built a large force of some 700 to 800 intermediate missiles that could strike Western Europe—a missile preponderance over NATO that still exists. They were ahead in some aspects of medium- and long-range-missile development, and in this sense, there was indeed a missile gap; but an intercontinental-missile gap never existed. The Soviets did not exploit their developmental advantage in booster thrust and did not procure large quantities of expensive, vulnerable, and inaccurate ICBM's. In view of the uncer-tainty of the strategic situation, President Eisenhower had placed part of SAC on airborne alert and energetically (though without fanfare) launched a crash missile-production program.

Regardless of the confusion surrounding the missile gap, Soviet devel-opment of the ICBM drastically and irrevocably altered the strategic balance—far more so than Soviet long-range bombers had. Under the pressure of growing Soviet strategic capabilities, the United States began to develop a command and control system that could survive a nuclear attack. If the command facilities of the Strategic Air Command could be destroyed by a few Soviet missiles, the President, as Commander in Chief, might not be able to communicate the "go" code to U.S. forces in case of war. Constitutionally, the decision of going to war or attacking the Soviet Union could not be left to subordinate commanders; and if the President's survival and his ability to communicate with American commanders could not be assured, there was a real possibility that under attack, the United States might never launch its retaliatory force (or what was left of it after the enemy's strike). During the later years of the Eisenhower Administration, measures were taken to provide suffi-ciently invulnerable command capabilities. Since then, the National Command and Control System has been further improved.

By 1960, U.S. military strategy was in a state of flux. Voices of dissent grew more strident both within and outside the Eisenhower Administra-tion, and from this opposition developed the strategic concepts that initially guided the military program of the Kennedy Administration.[8]

---

[8] See General Maxwell Taylor's criticism of the massive-retaliation strategy in his *The Uncertain Trumpet* (New York: Harper & Brothers, 1960), which had a profound effect on President Kennedy and, later, on President Johnson.

THE VOCABULARY OF NUCLEAR STRATEGY

Since the period when massive retaliation was in vogue, nuclear strategy has become subtler and more complex, and the vocabulary used to describe nuclear confrontation has become a language of its own.[9] To understand the issues and nuances of the Kennedy-McNamara strategic doctrine, one must first understand the semantics of nuclear war.

Terms describing various strategies are used to convey a general attitude toward nuclear conflict rather than to depict the complex reality of a given strategic posture or nuclear confrontation. The U.S. strategic posture has never fitted precisely into these or other descriptive molds, nor is it ever likely to for several reasons. Strategies have overlapping boundaries. Furthermore, there are always weapons around from an earlier strategic era that, for political and economic reasons are difficult to discard abruptly even though they do not fit the prevailing strategy. None of these strategies could be used in warfare with strict adherence to its presumed distinctions. The execution for example of a *finite-deterrence* (FD) strategy, which hypothetically includes only cities as targets, would also destroy military forces located in urban areas. Likewise, some damage to cities would result from a *counterforce* (CF) exchange, which, in theory, would be directed only toward enemy strategic forces. Shorthand terms, however, permit orderly distinctions between alternative force levels, targeting concepts, and even strategic intent.

Long before nuclear weapons, heavy bombers, and ballistic missiles were introduced, the Italian General, Giulio Douhet foresaw, almost prophetically, how total war could one day be waged by means of strategic bombing, with ground and naval forces playing a defensive, holding role. For many years, technology lagged behind Douhet's vision. With the development of the atomic bomb and then, and more importantly, the thermonuclear bomb, the defeat of an enemy without the need for round combat became possible.

In the early days of the Cold War—the period of U.S. monopoly of not only the atomic bomb but also strategic air power—most U.S. political leaders assumed that the complete solution to problems of national security had been found. As long as the United States constituted an invulnerable Western base from which an aggressor could be struck a devastating blow, it was unnecessary to build up ground forces for waging long-drawn-out wars like World Wars I and II. The enemy would

---

[9] One of the most articulate contributors to the Western glossary on nuclear warfare has been Herman Kahn. See Herman Kahn, *On Escalation: Scenarios and Metaphors* (New York: Praeger, 1965), Appendix, "Relevant Concepts and Language for the Discussion of Escalation," pp. 275–300.

instead be deterred from aggressive war by the very magnitude of the inevitable retribution.

When the Soviets developed atomic and nuclear weapons, as well as intercontinental aircraft and missile systems, Western strategists realized that it might become impossible to attack the enemy's forces so effectively as to annul his ability to retaliate. The array of opposing forces might be such that neither side could afford to initiate attack against the other without risking enormous damage to its own social and industrial structures.

As armies came to depend more and more on the full resources of the country, war progressively became more total. Industry became a target because troops depended on vast quantities of munitions and other implements of war. Before the airplane was developed, factories could not be directly attacked, so attempts were made to blockade the flow of raw materials or to seize areas that were producing war material. The airplane made it possible to reach over enemy defenses and attack the heartland of a nation. Thus, with the introduction of the airplane, three classes of targets emerged: enemy forces, industry, and population—the latter two comprising *value targets*. If, however, strategic bombing missions could destroy the enemy force in a matter of hours, why proceed to bomb his industries and his population? With its air force destroyed, a nation would lie helpless before an opponent. Yet, the strategists of the nuclear age only gradually perceived this theoretically simple point. Consequently, for some years, targets for nuclear war remained the same as the World War II targets. For example, the concept of bonus damage persisted for some time in strategic war planning: *bonus damage* or *collateral damage* is a result of bombing a military target so that nearby towns and industries are simultaneously destroyed. To an unprecedented degree, thermonuclear bombs made it possible to strike civilian targets in the proximity of the intended military objective; but the conditions of nuclear war made destruction of such targets both unnecessary and undesirable. For a long period of time, however, U.S. targeting doctrine remained tied to the concept of bonus damage.

Western military strategists now recognize that it is not necessary to maximize damage by extending it to nonmilitary targets. On the contrary, the more desirable objective may be to limit damage to hostile populations by a judicious combination of high-delivery accuracy and low-yield weapons. The logical use of nuclear weapons leads to a military strategy that pits armed force against armed force rather than against civilians. Yet, paradoxically, the civilian populations now play a key role as potential hostages, for in a nuclear war the fate of a civilian population is the final bargaining issue. Even though strategic military forces rather than people are the operational targets of nuclear war, the very life of a nation is still threatened. In "escalating" a limited conflict, not only military forces and supplies but also industrial and population centers could become targets.

ALTERNATIVES TO TOTAL WAR

As the strategic nuclear capability of the Soviet Union grew, the potential disaster of a general war came to be appreciated. Belatedly, the West, seeking alternatives to total war, sought a doctrine of war that would relate nuclear arms to the values they were supposed to defend.

When the Kennedy Administration assumed power, the two most commonly advocated strategies for U.S. strategic nuclear force were finite deterrence and counterforce.

By 1960, spasm war was no longer regarded as the only possible nuclear confrontation with an adversary. Moreover, an all-out disarming attack on the enemy's strategic forces was no longer considered feasible, since, as a practical matter, it was impossible to prevent some retaliatory attack. For this reason, an attempted *disarming strike*—a strike directed at all strategic weapons to compel *unconditional surrender*—was no longer a suitable strategy for the thermonuclear era.

Both finite deterrence and counterforce provide alternatives for dealing with the basic attribute of nuclear weapons—the ability to inflict almost unlimited damage. The counterforce concept is intended to lessen nuclear damage by inducing the enemy not to strike our cities because we would not strike his. The enemy would be assured that we would hit his cities if he attacked ours; that we could reduce his offensive striking power (and hence the damage he could do) by attacking his offensive forces that had not yet been launched; that we could defeat the attack that had been launched by means of active defense measures; and that we could minimize the destructiveness of his weapons that reached target by using our fallout shelters and blast shelters. In essence, this strategy focused on the destruction of enemy offensive forces rather than cities, so that ultimately the surviving populations would be the final bargaining issue.

Finite deterrence rejects the counterforce concept that nuclear wars can be fought in a controlled fashion, that a country's industry and population might be spared, and that damage can be held to acceptable limits. The goal of finite deterrence is to make nuclear war so catastrophic as to be unthinkable, and its purpose is to deter any nuclear attack on the United States by fact of a U.S. capability to destroy the enemy's cities in retaliation. In effect, this strategy would force each opposing state to offer the other its respective population and economy as hostage. The posture makes only limited provision for active air defense; it does not seek an antimissile system; it provides for only minimal civil defense. This strategy is also called *basic deterrence,* a felicitously descriptive name that conveys the key idea; it is a strategic posture that can deter attack on only this country and cannot offer protection to U.S. allies. In other words, by making the possibility of a first strike totally incredible, it repudiates the extension of U.S. deterrent capability, or "nuclear umbrella," to the NATO countries or other allies.

SECOND-STRIKE FORCES

As the Soviet Union gained the capability of launching a nuclear attack against the U.S. mainland, it became necessary for the United States to develop a *second-strike force*—a force capable of absorbing the enemy's blow and then striking back. Confusion then arose between first-strike *strategy* and first-strike *weapons*. First-strike weapons are delivery systems that could not survive an enemy attack and hence could be used only for a first strike, that is, for attacking the enemy before he is able to land his blow. When the Soviets acquired ICBM's, the United States faced a radically altered strategic situation, one in which the possibilities of a pre-emptive attack by either side became too great for comfort. At this point, the Soviet strategic force was as vulnerable as the U.S. force, both of which were comprised of bombers located on unprotected fields and vulnerable first-generation ICBM's. The danger of accidental war was considerably heightened by the instability of a tense international situation in which either side, anxiously aware of the vulnerability of its entire force, could launch a pre-emptive attack. The need for a second-strike force was clear.

Fundamentally, second-strike forces are to some degree invulnerable. *Invulnerability* can be acquired through a variety of means: (1) *dispersal of forces* from a few sites to many sites—for example, SAC bombers were dispersed from seventeen bases to sixty-one bases; (2) acquisition of *warning systems*—for example, the Ballistic Missile Early Warning System (BMEWS) was added to the already existing Distant Early Warning (DEW) line, which served to deter bomber attacks; (3) *mobility* and *concealment*—for example, the development of Polaris missile-firing submarines; and (4) *hardening*—for example, the placing of missiles in concrete silos for protection against the effects of nuclear warheads. Bombers, like missiles, were protected by a combination of warning and dispersal (permitting the bombers to take off before the enemy warheads exploded) and mobility.

Invulnerability, though, is never absolute. It depends not only on the measures taken to protect one's own forces but also on the kind and number of offensive weapons the enemy builds. A weapons system that is highly invulnerable today, such as Polaris, may become vulnerable if a break-through—for example, in antisubmarine warfare (ASW)—should occur.

No single hardened missile site is invulnerable, but the combination of the number of missiles and the hardening of the missile sites safeguards the whole force against destruction in an initial attack. Also, the degree of protection given to each missile site may compel the enemy to employ more than one missile in attacking it; on the other hand, improved accuracy and higher-yield warheads will reduce the number of missiles required to destroy a given target. For hardened missile sites, invulnerability may be lost by 1975.

An invulnerable, hardened, fixed-site command and control system may be difficult if not impossible, to build, man, and operate because of practical limitations. Since they are complex and costly, command sites cannot be dispersed by the hundreds as can missile sites. Thus the *exchange ratio*—the cost to the enemy of destroying a military command center in relation to the cost to the defender of adding an alternative command center—would be highly favorable to the enemy. For missile sites, the exchange ratio favors the defender as long as it is more than 1:1—that is, if it takes more than one attacking missile to destroy a single defending missile. If, for example, the missile exchange ratio is 5:1, an aggressor must build five missiles for every one that the defender adds to his force. In the case of command and control sites, however, a 5:1 ratio would be highly favorable to the attacker, since the cost of building five missiles is far less than the cost of adding another command site.

A second-strike force need not be inconsistent with a first-strike strategy. Invulnerable weapons systems, which constitute a second-strike force, could be launched in a first strike; however, the invulnerability of a second strike force may inhibit its use in a first strike. The key concept is *credibility*.[10] Any weapon can be used in a first strike, but the question is: How credible is a threat to do so? In the days when the Soviets did not have the capability to retaliate against the United States, the U.S. threat was entirely credible. Now a nuclear strike in response to Soviet aggression in Europe could lead to terrible damage to the United States. Hence the U.S. nuclear guarantee to Europe seems less credible.

Ironically, the U.S. first-strike threat remained credible as long as the United States had only a vulnerable force; for with such a vulnerability, the United States could not afford to sit out a Soviet attack on Europe. We would have had to attack to keep our own force from being destroyed on its home base. Similarly, the Soviets could not attack Europe without first attacking the United States for fear that the United States in turn would have to attack them. Mutually vulnerable systems, despite their advantages for deterrence, posed excessive dangers of war by accident or

---

[10] This question was reviewed in Herman Kahn's defense of a credible first-strike strategy. By adding the term "credible" to "first strike," Kahn attempted to deal with the problem of a U.S. first-strike strategy in reaction to a Soviet attack on Europe, in a situation in which the United States was vulnerable to a missile attack. See *On Thermonuclear War* (Princeton, N.J.: Princeton University Press, 1961), pp. 27–36.

miscalculation; whereas secure second-strike forces removed the necessity for a virtually automatic U.S. nuclear strike against the Soviet Union in the event of aggression against NATO. The United States, secure in its ability to ride out a Soviet attack, would be able to assess a threatening situation. Paradoxically, as the invulnerability of the U.S. force increased, the credibility of the U.S. nuclear guarantee to NATO declined.

A first-strike threat could, however, be made by a nation possessing a credible first-strike force—a force that possesses one of the merits of a second-strike force, namely, invulnerability. The primary purpose of a credible first-strike force is not to initiate war but to warn the adversary that he cannot attack Western Europe, for example, without running an unacceptable risk of U.S. retaliation. The expectation is that, faced with the necessity of attacking the United States, the Soviets would be deterred from major aggression in Europe.

The invulnerability of a second-strike force does not rule out the threat of an enemy's first strike against it; however, the term "second-strike force" can be, and often is, understood to rule out its credibility as a first-strike strategy. The force need not be—and this is the key to many strategic disputes—merely an invulnerable one, but logically it should be incapable of striking first. This would be the case if an invulnerable missile force had low accuracy and weapon yield—too low to strike first and successfully or even to issue a credible first-strike threat.[11]

PARITY, STABILITY, AND STALEMATE

A situation in which both sides have armed themselves only with vulnerable weapons, which are therefore suitable only for a first-strike strategy, is inherently unstable and accident-prone—like a Western gun duel in which the faster draw wins. Yet, when both sides possess invulnerable offensive forces and neither can rationally contemplate an attack given the retaliatory power of the other, a *stalemate* exists. According to many experts, the objective of U.S. second-strike forces should be the achievement of stalemate by such a margin of superiority that a potential enemy would realize that by attacking he would worsen his relative position rather than improve it.

In a strict sense, a condition of *parity* exists if two forces are approximately equal, although it is often asserted that parity exists even though the forces of the two great nuclear powers are quite unequal. In the latter sense, parity refers to a situation in which the party with the larger arsenal cannot afford to attack because the other side, though weaker, still is able to retaliate with a countervalue attack. Parity in the sense of equality of strategic forces is sometimes advocated as the U.S. goal in lieu of strategic superiority.

Opposing views on a strategic posture for the United States reflect a basic disagreement on the meaning of *nuclear stalemate*. According to one school of thought, nuclear stalemate renders nuclear weapons useless for any positive political purpose; consequently, their negative role—deterring nuclear attack—could just as well be played by *nuclear disarmament*. Since nuclear forces impose a burden on national economies and since nuclear war might be triggered by accident or miscalculation, nuclear disarmament is a more rational course of action. But since unresolved political issues bar the road to total nuclear disarmament for the near future, it is proposed that *arms control* measures either lead step by step toward disarmament or take the place of disarmament. Arms control can be accomplished by numerous methods, all of which have in common the objective of either reducing the risk of nuclear war or mitigating its effects.

THE KENNEDY PHASE

New strategic concepts for nuclear weapons began to be articulated during the late 1950's, and in the spring of 1961 President Kennedy called for new U.S. strategy and tactics to meet the continuing Soviet challenge. Early in his administration, President Kennedy announced the broad outlines of his military strategy:

> The primary purpose of our arms is peace, not war—to make certain that they will never have to be used—to deter all wars, general or limited, nuclear or conventional, large or small—to convince all aggressors that any attack would be futile—to provide backing for diplomatic settlement of disputes—to insure the adequacy of our bargaining power for an end to the arms race. . . . Our military policy must be sufficiently flexible and under control to be consistent with our efforts to explore all possibilities and to take every step to lessen tensions, to obtain peaceful solutions and to secure arms limitations.[12]

President Kennedy intended to achieve a wider range of strategic options primarily by increasing U.S. general-purpose forces and by increasing the invulnerability of our bombers and missiles. Doctrinally, Kennedy pioneered the concept of a deliberate, selective, flexible, controlled response to be prepared for any type of warfare at whatever level and to force on the adversary the onus of striking the first nuclear blow.

---

[12] U S. President, *Recommendations Relating to Our Defense Budget*, U.S. House Document No. 123 (Washington: Government Printing Office, 1961), p. 2. The concepts in this document were developed in the Pentagon under McNamara's aegis and were accepted *in toto* by President Kennedy.

A flexible response necessitated not only conventional forces capable of meeting limited aggression but also, and most crucially, second-strike nuclear forces capable of fighting a controlled nuclear war. The Eisenhower nuclear control system had tied virtually all the U.S. strategic forces together under "one button," leaving the President with the single option of pushing or not pushing. The Kennedy-McNamara combination was designed to give the President a series of options on his "nuclear console" as well as a range of nonnuclear options, thus avoiding an "all or nothing" dilemma.

An inherent part of the selective-response doctrine was a rapid build-up of conventional "below-the-threshold" forces, for without additional means to cope with limited conflicts, the new flexible strategy would be useless. A substantial increase in funds was consequently allotted for conventional armaments and forces. Concurrently, emphasis was placed on special forces for aiding nations subjected to Communist "wars of national liberation," and the number of personnel authorized for these activities was increased. Although conventional forces that are sufficient for meeting a range of contingencies are essential for Free World defense, these forces were never intended to be a substitute for a credible nuclear deterrent.

The policy developed by the Kennedy and Johnson administrations for strategic nuclear weaponry differed essentially from that of their predecessors. Rather than a missile gap, as had been touted during the 1960 Presidential campaign, the United States possessed nuclear superiority and a considerable lead in strategic delivery vehicles (primarily the manned bomber) on the day Secretary McNamara arrived in the Pentagon. Revised intelligence estimates, based on some new data, led to a changed assessment of the United States—Soviet strategic balance. Secretary McNamara nevertheless decided to increase the U.S. missile capability and to convert strategic retaliatory forces to second-strike forces, which entailed hardening the delivery systems and otherwise making the force invulnerable to an enemy first strike. To carry out these decisions, Secretary McNamara stepped up the production of first-generation Minuteman missiles and increased the number of nuclear bombers on fifteen-minute alert.

The Kennedy Administration took steps to assure civilian control over the military commanders of U.S. strategic forces. Constitutional provisions for civilian control of military forces have never been questioned; but in 1961, civilian control halted at the same point as did military control, namely, before the giving of the "go" orders. By his own authority, the SAC commander could put his force on alert and, if he concluded that an enemy attack was under way, could order his aircraft to fly to the positive control point. But without a direct order from the President (or a lawfully designated successor), he could not command his force to attack the enemy. When a Soviet surprise missile attack on the United States became a possibility, appropriate civilian authorities had to be endowed with means for surviving the initial attack and for commanding a controlled nuclear war; thus, a *national control system* became the capstone of the U.S. military posture.

·   ·   ·

THE SEARCH FOR OPTIONS

In 1961, Secretary of Defense McNamara, a major force in reorienting U.S. nuclear strategy in the years just before and after the Cuban missile crisis, began to seek new doctrine with which to govern U.S. strategic nuclear forces. Massive retaliation with its specter of spasm war was categorically rejected, but some consideration was given to the concept of finite deterrence, which was developed in the late 1950's. According to that strategy, anything beyond a capability to destroy a certain portion of enemy society would be considered "overkill" and would therefore be undesirable and unnecessary. Finite deterrence, which could not be used as a credible threat against the U.S.S.R., would provide minimal military support for U.S. allies and would have little usefulness in meeting crises. In the event of a Soviet attack, the United States, incapable of waging a controlled attack on the enemy's forces, would have no alternative except countervalue retaliation and thus would undoubtedly assure a similar retaliatory response from the enemy.

The United States sought an incentive for the Soviets to avoid targeting our cities in the event of nuclear war. A two-pronged concept of nuclear strategic war gradually emerged that would provide for: (1) retaliation against a large-scale Soviet attack, if American cities were avoided, using systems and command and control that would permit a deliberate, selective, and controlled option; and (2) a carefully controlled, discriminating response against a small-scale, ambiguous, or accidental attack. Furthermore, the use of conventional forces for NATO's initial defense was stressed repeatedly by U.S. authorities.

These innovations of the Kennedy and Johnson administrations signified a major reappraisal of the role of strategic weapons in supporting U.S. foreign policy—a role subsequently centering around two major alternative strategies. Counterforce reached its high point by mid-1962; the other strategy, *damage limiting*, gradually evolved after the Cuban missile crisis. The difference between these and other possible strategies is one of intent, degree, and emphasis. Counterforce hews to the classic military doctrine that the proper objective of military action is the destruction of the enemy's armed forces. It may be defined as the neutralization of hostile military actions against the United States through: (1) direct attack against enemy strategic bases and missiles sites; (2) in-flight destruction of launched hostile aircraft, missiles, and space vehicles; and (3) the blocking, interdiction, or destruction of hostile surface or undersea forces.

Secretary McNamara expressed the reasons for his initial attraction to the counterforce concept in a speech at Ann Arbor, Michigan, in June, 1962: [13]

> By building into our forces a flexible capability, we at least eliminate the prospect that we could strike back in only one way, namely, against the entire Soviet target system including their cities. Such a prospect would give the Soviet Union no incentive to withhold attack against our cities in a first strike.

He explicitly espoused the counterforce option:

> If, despite all our efforts, nuclear war should occur, our best hope lies in conducting a centrally controlled campaign against all of the enemy's vital nuclear capabilities, while retaining reserve forces, all centrally controlled.

Yet, McNamara gave two substantially different reasons for seeking a counterforce targeting strategy. On the one hand, he stated:

> The United States has come to the conclusion that to the extent feasible, basic military strategy in a possible nuclear war should be approached in much the same way that the more conventional military operations have been regarded in the past. That is to say, principal military objectives in the event of a nuclear war stemming from a major attack on the Alliance should be the destruction of the enemy's military forces, not of his civilian population.

On the other hand, he declared:

> [It is] possible for us to retain . . . reserve striking power to destroy an enemy society if driven to it. In other words, we are giving a possible opponent the strongest imaginable incentive to refrain from striking our own cities.

By introducing his thought, the Secretary suggested that the threat of a massive retaliatory attack could be used to deter an enemy's nuclear attack on U.S. cities—an objective quite different from the goal of a pure counterforce strategy: to disarm.

A U.S. counterforce posture also offered a powerful argument against proliferating national nuclear forces, particularly the French force. In returning to the more traditional view of warfare, in which battle is waged against enemy armed forces rather than population, McNamara

---

[13] Robert S. McNamara, commencement speech, University of Michigan, Ann Arbor, Michigan, June 16, 1962, cited in Department of Defense news release No. 980–62.

cited the fact that small national nuclear forces could not wage such a war against a major power like the Soviet Union. Moreover, the existence of small national nuclear forces within the Western Alliance would make it impossible for the United States to wage a controlled counterforce campaign in the event of Soviet aggression against Europe.

It subsequently became clear that strategy could take various forms either of counterforce or of the strategy known as damage limiting. Objections were quickly raised against the nascent counterforce doctrine. For one thing, a counterforce attack could not be easily distinguished from a countervalue attack if very high-yield warheads were used. This problem would be aggravated if some counterforce targets were located in urban complexes, as many Soviet targets were believed to be. At the time of the Cuban missile crisis, the United States fortuitously possessed superior nuclear delivery systems capable of both countervalue and counterforce targeting. Most of these forces were available because of the weapons decisions previously made by the Eisenhower Administration, and President Kennedy exploited these inherited capabilities to bring about the Soviet missile withdrawal.

18.   LIMITED WAR

Morton H. Halperin

WHEN THE UNITED STATES and the Soviet Union have clashed on local military battlefields, they have used far less than all of their military power. They have exercised what Bernard Brodie * has called "a

From *Limited War in the Nuclear Age* by Morton H. Halperin (New York: John Wiley and Sons, 1965) pp. 1–15. Reprinted by permission of the author and John Wiley and Sons, Inc.

MORTON H. HALPERIN (1938–   ) Senior Fellow, The Brookings Institution, Washington, D.C. Author of *Defense Strategies for the Seventies* (Boston: Little, Brown and Company, 1971); *Contemporary Military Strategy* (Boston: Little, Brown and Company, 1967); *China and Nuclear Proliferation* (Chicago: University of Chicago Center for Policy Study, 1966); *China and the Bomb* (New York: Praeger Publishers, 1965). Co-author, *Strategy and Arms Control* (New York: Twentieth Century Fund, 1961). Editor, *Sino-Soviet Relations and Arms Control* (Cambridge: M.I.T. Press, 1967).

* Bernard Brodie is a Senior Staff Member of the Rand Corporation and a lecturer at the University of California. His is the author of *Escalation and the Nuclear Options*, (Princeton, N.J.: Princeton University Press, 1966) and *A Guide to Naval Strategy*, 5th ed. (New York: Frederick A. Praeger, 1965). [Editor's Note.]

deliberate hobbling of a tremendous power that is already mobilized and that must in any case be maintained at a very high pitch of effectiveness for the sake only of inducing the enemy to hobble himself." On a number of occasions in the postwar period the United States and the Soviet Union have clashed directly or by proxy in local areas and have employed force or the threat of force. In Cuba in 1962, in Laos and Vietnam throughout the postwar period, in the Taiwan Straits in 1955 and 1958, in Korea in 1950–1953, in China in 1946–1949, in Lebanon in 1958, in Greece in 1946–1949, and in Berlin in 1948 and in 1958–1962, force or the threat of force has been used in local areas. Each of these was a "local war" (or potential local war), that is, a war in which the United States and the Soviet Union saw themselves on opposing sides but in which the homelands of the two major powers did not come under attack.

Not every war in the postwar period has been a "local war." The Arab-Israeli War of 1948 was one of the largest postwar incidents of violence in which the Soviet Union and the United States never lined up on opposite sides. In other cases Soviet-American opposition has played only a small role in the conflict. In the Suez crisis of 1956, for example, it was only when the Soviet Union made missile threats against Britain and France, and the United States made counterthreats against the Soviet Union, that the crisis became a potential local war. The Congo crisis of the early 1960's, on the whole, has not involved any East-West clash except for the short period when the United States was supporting Kasavubu and the Soviet Union was backing Lumumba. Similarly the Sino-Indian border dispute for a long time was not a "local war" but became one in November 1962 when the United States began to supply military aid to the Indians.

$\cdot \quad \cdot \quad \cdot$

Because the United States and the Soviet Union have a capability to destroy very large parts of each other's homelands, they share an interest in restraining their mutual destruction in the event of war. It is sometimes argued that this condition makes war obsolete in the sense that we will never have another major war. Demonstrating the necessity for a condition, however, does not demonstrate its possibility, not to say its probability. Even for a number of years prior to the atomic age, it has not been in the interest of a major power to go to war in most situations. Though the development of thermonuclear weapons and intercontinental missiles makes the disutility of warfare even clearer, it by no means eliminates the possibility of war. If war does come the major powers have shared and will continue to share an interest in trying to limit the use of force to something short of the all-out use of their military powers in an effort to destroy each other. The existence of thermonuclear weapons and the lack of any mechanism for guaranteeing the absence of war makes it necessary to take seriously the problem of how war, once it erupts, can be kept limited.

The Sino Soviet threat to the United States makes it even more imperative that the United States develop an understanding of and an ability to engage in limited war. The Sino-Soviet bloc has demonstrated an understanding of the techniques of various forms of local warfare (including guerrilla warfare) as well as a willingness to exploit the use and the threat of force to advance its international objectives. The experience of the postwar period suggests that the United States will continue to be faced with the local use of violence by the Soviet Union, China, and other Communist states and indigenous Communist forces.

Both major powers have shown a willingness to use force and the threat of force when they have felt it necessary to secure vital objectives. In engaging in the local use of force, either directly or by supporting indigenous groups, the major powers have been concerned with avoiding "explosion"—the sudden transformation of a local war into a central war by the unleashing of strategic nuclear forces. In fighting a local war the major powers have been and will be trying to prevent an explosion, but they will also be making a series of decisions about when and how to expand, contract, or conclude a local military encounter. During a local war both sides will be continually assessing the likelihood of an explosion and the question of whether or not they ought to unleash their strategic forces. They will also be assessing the likelihood and desirability of "expansion"—a gradual increase in the level of military force employed.

These two processes, "explosion" and "expansion," are frequently discussed together as "escalation." However it is important to keep the two processes separate. The considerations that go into the decision to begin a central war would be very different from the considerations that have gone and will go into decisions to expand a local war. These latter decisions will be influenced by a number of factors, including the foreign-policy objectives of the two sides, their estimate of the risk of central war, their images of the role of force, and their domestic political objectives. Each of these factors will be discussed to show how it influences the decisions of the major powers during a local war.

FOREIGN-POLICY OBJECTIVES

The United States and the Soviet Union will have three levels of foreign-policy objectives that will influence their conduct in a local war: basic foreign-policy objectives, political-effects objectives, and battlefield objectives. The desire to avoid central war, which may be viewed as an additional foreign-policy objective, is discussed in the following section.

The basic foreign-policy objectives of the two sides provide the framework in which decisions about the use of particular tools, including local violence, are made. One basic objective of the Soviet Union is to expand the area of Communist control and to reduce Western influence throughout the world. In the long run the Soviet leaders may envision the total Communization of the world. To what extent this long-run objective influences Soviet policy is a matter of much dispute, but there seems to be little doubt of the Soviet leaders' desire to increase Russian influence and decrease Western influence throughout the world. The United States, on the other hand, whatever hopes its leaders may have for an ultimate transformation of Communist society, is committed to seeking to stop the growth of the area under the control of Communist regimes. The Soviet Union has an incentive to use as much force as is necessary to accomplish this objective, and the United States has an incentive to use whatever amount of force is sufficient to hold the area being attacked. Other pressures, however, will lead the major powers to temper their military efforts to expand their area of influence or to prevent the expansion of the influence of the other major power by force. Within these constraints the leaders of the Soviet Union and the United States will be guided by the political effect they hope to gain by supporting the use of force.

POLITICAL-EFFECTS OBJECTIVES

When the major powers participate in a local war it is because of the expected political effects of doing so and not because of the direct pay-off from battlefield success. Neither the United States nor the Soviet Union, for example, has any interest in the small Quemoy and Matsu islands off the coast of China. Nor is the precise parallel that divides North Korea from South Korea something that in itself is worth fighting a war over. It is rather the political consequences of losing or gaining territory that are the major concern of the two sides in committing their forces, their matériel, or their prestige in a local war.

Perhaps the most important political-effects objective with which each side has been and will be concerned in a local war is the message which its conduct will give to its main enemies. The estimates which the leaders of the United States and the Soviet Union have about each other's willingness to use force or the threat of force to secure objectives will be influenced by the conduct of the major powers at any time at which they clash on a local battlefield. In deciding, for example, to prevent the Soviets from establishing a missile base in Cuba, the United States was at least partly motivated by the feeling that it was important to demonstrate to Soviet Premier Nikita Khrushchev that the United States was prepared to use force and risk a nuclear war in order to secure its objectives. The United States acted to convince Khrushchev that the Kennedy Administration was not too "liberal" to fight when it felt its rights were threatened.

Another major political-effects objective in a local war is to demonstrate, to other countries in the area, which way the tide is running. The manner in which the United States responds to Communist aggression in Indochina, for example, affects the orientation of Thailand, the Philippines, and other Asian nations. Our willingness to support the Chinese Nationalist Government in the Taiwan Straits has been seen by at least some of our Asian allies as a test of our willingness to support them under pressure. In the same sense the Korean War may be seen partly as a fight over the orientation of Japan.

Though the ramifications of the outcome of a local war are likely to be felt most keenly in the immediate geographic area of the battle, the implications may also be world-wide. If, for example, the Russians have been restraining the Chinese in the Taiwan Straits for fear of active American intervention, they are likely to be more ready to approve of a Chinese military move if the Western position has collapsed in Berlin. Alternatively, Chinese Communist success in the Taiwan Straits might well embolden the Russians in Central Europe. Soviet success in establishing a missile base in Cuba might have led America's NATO allies to believe that the United States would not defend Berlin.

Even when the battlefield itself may have some intrinsic value, as in the case of Berlin, the political-effects objectives of the two sides will still be more important. It has been clear to at least some Western leaders, since the renewed Soviet effort to change the status of Berlin dating from 1958, that the real Russian objective concerned Germany, the NATO alliance, and the consolidation of Soviet control in Eastern Europe. If the United States uses force over Berlin it will be clearly fighting to maintain the Western orientation of Germany and the cohesion of the NATO alliance as well as to defend the freedom of the West Berliners.

The United States is interested in defending an abstract principle of international conduct—that international boundaries cannot be changed by the use of force. This was a major consideration in dealing with the 1958 Chinese Communist attempt to seize Quemoy. Although the American government may at times have been willing to cede the offshore islands, it has not been prepared to give them up if this would weaken the principle of no change of boundaries by the use of force. In some situations even when there is no clear violation of international law the United States wants to demonstrate its willingness to commit military forces and matériel, to "act tough" when necessary to defend its allies. In some situations, as in the case of covert aggression in South Vietnam, for example, the United States has had to act to secure this objective in the face of less clear-cut violations of international law. From the Sino-Soviet point of view the aim is to convince nations that the West is not prepared to defend them against either overt or covert aggression and that the wave of the future is international Communism.

These political-effects objectives of the two sides produce pressures to intervene in local-war situations and to expand the level of military effort. However there are other political-effects objectives which tend to work in the other direction.

In contrast to a period of central war when attention will be focused almost exclusively on political and military implications of the "battle-field" encounter and its effects, during a local war the attention of policy makers on both sides will be divided between the particular local encounter and other aspects of the international political struggle. There will continue to be other points of contact and dispute between the two sides. Some of these may be other local wars or situations of potential local war, in which the political-effects objectives will be those tending toward expansion, but at other points of contact one or both sides may be trying to come to accommodation. Each side will be conscious of the possible impact of a local war on its efforts to reach accommodation in other geographic areas or on other problems. In 1954, for example, the Sino-Soviet bloc was about to launch a peace offensive which would have been embarrassed by the continuation or expansion of the war in Indochina. Similarly in 1958 when East and West were beginning to clash over Berlin, they were at the same time attempting to negotiate a treaty to ban nuclear tests. The successful conclusion of these negotiations would have been highly unlikely in the event of armed conflict on the European continent.

Another major restraint on the fighting of a local war will be the reluctance of the major powers to commit resources that may be required to deal with other areas of potential violence or to deter central war. In committing troops to Lebanon in 1958, for example, the United States was faced with the fact that it was thereby reducing its ability to deal with possible violence in the Taiwan Straits; and in 1962 American moves in Southeast Asia must have been restrained by the consciousness of the need to maintain an ability to deter or fight on the European continent. With both sides aware of the possibility of simultaneous or future clashes in other geographic areas, neither will be disposed to commit resources to one local conflict at the risk of dangerously exposing itself at other points. The degree to which this consideration restrains local war depends, of course, on the magnitude of the military action and on the size of the local-war forces of the two sides.

Although the desire to convince other allies that the United States is prepared to defend them produces pressures to use force sufficient to defend the local areas, this objective also generates pressures to use only that force which does not destroy the area being defended. For example, if the United States defended Taiwan by engaging in a nuclear duel with the Sino-Soviet bloc and if this led to the total destruction of Taiwan, it would hardly encourage other nations to seek American defense support. Similarly the initiation of local military action to defend Berlin might cause such devastation in Central Europe as to lead to the disintegration of the Atlantic alliance. To show an ability to restrain the use of violence may be as important as demonstrating a willingness to use violence.

For similar reasons the United States may find it necessary to try to maintain in power the government which was in control at the beginning of the crisis and which called for American support. If the outcome of a local-war situation in which American intervention is invited is always or frequently a change of government, a group in power may seek an accommodation with its enemies rather than accept American support.

The Sino-Soviet bloc on the other hand has an incentive to increase the destruction in a local war fought outside the Communist bloc, in order to demonstrate the lack of utility of American military aid. It also has an interest in a change in government, particularly if the change is from a strongly pro-Western to a neutral government. The Soviet leadership may also be seeking to demonstrate in dealing with a local-war situation that it is prepared to act vigorously to expand the area under Communist control and that it is not unduly afraid of Western counteraction. In its competition with the Chinese for the support of Communist revolutionary groups, the Soviet leadership may feel compelled to expand its intervention to prove to other Communist groups that Russia is prepared to support them when they are close to a seizure of power.

To some extent the policymakers themselves of the major powers will be conscious of the political effects of local war, but in addition both their allies and the neutral nations will continually bombard them with advice, suggestions, and other forms of pressure. Again these pressures may be to expand the war in particular ways or to contract it or to bring it to an end. For example, the United States has received conflicting advice from its SEATO allies as to its policy in dealing with military action in Vietnam and Laos. Beginning in 1954 the British, later joined by the French, have continually opposed proposals for the intervention of SEATO or American forces into the internal wars in Laos and Vietnam. On the other hand, the Thais, the Filipinos, and the Pakistanis have frequently urged a more active intervention by the United States into these situations. More extensive action by the United States in support of the Chinese Nationalists has been opposed by America's European allies.

The ability of allied countries to influence American policy in a local-war situation will in part depend on their general relationship with the United States. The British have exercised a major influence on American local-war policy during the entire postwar period beginning with their transfer to the United States of primary responsibility for aiding the suppression of the Greek Communist rebellion. On the other hand, the extent of the influence of any particular allied country will be affected by whether or not it is actively engaged in the combat. Allied pressure seems to have been most effective in the Korean War when a number of nations joined the United States by committing forces, albeit token ones, in the defense of South Korea. Allied pressure was least important in the 1962 Cuban crisis when the United States was prepared to act alone. The Soviet Union may find that the influence of its Chinese or even North Vietnamese allies increases as they make greater contributions to joint efforts. Though Chinese influence in the present period probably tends toward the use of force, this was not the case in 1956 when the Chinese seem to have counseled restraint on the Soviets in Poland.

TERRITORIAL OBJECTIVES

Since the battlefield itself is likely to be of little intrinsic importance, territorial objectives in a local war will be determined by the nature of the perceived political effects of different outcomes. Some battlefields such as Western Europe, however, will have significant intrinsic value, and in some cases the loss of a particular area will make it more difficult, for tactical military reasons, to defend nearby areas. A Communist takeover in Laos might, for example, make it harder for the United States to defend South Vietnam and Thailand.

As long as the United States and the Soviet Union confine a war to the territories of other countries, they cannot demand or expect the unconditional surrender of the other major power. However, their objectives may be very extreme, including the ceding of large amounts of territory and the unconditional surrender of the local government; or they may be extremely limited, involving a return to the *status quo ante* or even less. At least at some times, and perhaps at all times, during a local war, both sides will have at least implicitly formulated war-termination conditions, that is, battlefield conditions which if accepted by the other side will lead them to terminate the local conflict. However these war-termination conditions may fluctuate during the war through a range of possible territorial objectives. The territorial objectives, as they are determined by political-effects objectives and other pressures to be discussed hereafter, will be the most immediate determinant of the decision to expand a local war. A side with relatively limited territorial objectives is less likely to find it necessary to expand the scope of its military operations. As each side recognizes the relatively limited objectives of the other, the danger of *explosion* into central war will be substantially reduced. However, even minor objectives may produce pressures to *expand* the war if one or both sides find that their limited objectives cannot be obtained at the level at which the battle is being fought, or if the objectives of the two sides are incompatible.

In addition to the extent of territorial objectives of the two sides, another crucial factor will be whether or not the objectives are specific, concrete, and clearly stated. Although some commentators have suggested that specific objectives clearly stated are more likely to lead both sides to contract rather than to expand a local war, this is not necessarily the case. Certainly if the specific battlefield objectives of the two sides were clearly incompatible, there would be strong pressures toward the expansion of the war. The United States in particular might find it more difficult to compromise if it had clearly stated its territorial objectives than if it had not spelled out its objectives in advance, and if they were in fact flexible. Flexible and moderate battlefield objectives of the two sides are likely to be most conducive to the stabilization, contraction, and termination of a local war. On the other hand, extreme war-termination conditions which expand with success on the battlefield are likely to lead to the expansion of a local war.

The fluctuation of war-termination conditions in a local war will stem in part from the difficulty of assessing the relationship between political-effects objectives and territorial objectives. For example, the United States is not really sure what the impact of a withdrawal from the Chinese Nationalist-held offshore islands would be on its foreign-policy objectives. During the Korean War, the political effect of the stopping of the war at the thirty-eighth parallel clearly would have been different from what it was when it finally occurred if the United States had stopped of its own volition after routing the North Korean army. And no one can really be sure as to the difference in political effect of stopping at the thirty-eighth parallel as opposed to moving to the narrow neck, or seeking to capture all of North Korea. This difficulty of clearly correlating political-effects objectives with territorial objectives is likely in general to be a pressure to expand the local war. When in doubt as to their ability to secure their objectives with particular war-termination conditions, the leaders of a major power may play it safe by expanding their war-termination conditions. Territorial objectives will also fluctuate with military success or failure. The American decision to unite Korea by force stemmed directly from the defeat of the North Korean army. The importance given to defending Taiwan is the result of Communist control of the Chinese mainland. Military success and defeat, and changes in the loyalty of indigenous groups drastically alter the range of possible battlefield objectives.

The role of foreign-policy objectives in influencing the decision to expand or contract a local war, then, may be summarized as follows: unconditional surrender of the other major power is incompatible with local warfare. Neither of the major powers will be seeking in a single local war to implement all of its foreign-policy objectives. The major objectives of the two sides in a local war will be their political-effects objectives, particularly those centering around the legitimacy of the use of force and the need to convince enemies that they will be opposed and allies that they will be supported. Territorial objectives and the war-termination conditions will be shaped largely by the general political-effects objectives although the relationship between the two will not always be clear.

RISK OF CENTRAL WAR

The desire to avoid central war exercises a major influence on decision makers during a local war. Though this desire is one of the foreign-policy objectives of each side, it is sufficiently critical to require separate consideration. Almost all analysts agree that the fighting of a local war increases the possibility of central war, but it is impossible to determine precisely the extent to which any local war in fact increases the danger of central war. One can, however, envision several ways in which a local war might lead to central war. These include expansion which seems most likely to occur in an important region such as Europe and in a nuclear war. There is also the possibility of an explosion which may occur for one of two reasons. Central war which results from explosion may be an "inadvertent war" that occurs although neither side wants it. It may be the result of pressure to strike first in the event of war which become aggravated as the local war goes on. However central war might also be "deliberate war" resulting from the decision of the losing side in a local war to initiate a strategic strike rather than accept defeat on the local battlefield. If the losing side in a local war considers the area under contest to be of vital significance to it and if it feels that it can win a central war, it might unleash its strategic forces rather than accept local defeat.

It is impossible to make a general assessment in the abstract of the probability that a local war will cause a central war. Certainly there is a widespread belief shared by many decision makers that local wars are dangerous because of the likelihood that they will spark a nuclear holocaust. Whether this danger is as great as decision makers think is less important in this context than the recognition that decision makers will be motivated in the conduct of a local war by their perception of the danger of a central war taking place.

19.   WHAT IS GUERRILLA WARFARE?

Mao Tse-tung

I N A WAR of revolutionary character, guerrilla operations are a necessary part. This is particularly true in a war waged for the emancipation of a people who inhabit a vast nation. China is such a nation, a nation whose techniques are undeveloped and whose communications are poor. She finds herself confronted with a strong and victorious Japanese imperialism. Under these circumstances, the development of the type of guerrilla warfare characterized by the quality of mass is both necessary and natural. This warfare must be developed to an unprecedented degree and it must coordinate with the operations of our regular armies. If we fail to do this, we will find it difficult to defeat the enemy.

These guerrilla operations must not be considered as an independent form of warfare. They are but one step in the total war, one aspect of the revolutionary struggle. They are the inevitable result of the clash between oppressor and oppressed when the latter reach the limits of their endurance. In our case, these hostilities began at a time when the people were unable to endure any more from the Japanese imperialists. . . .*

Guerrilla warfare has qualities and objectives peculiar to itself. It is a weapon that a nation inferior in arms and military equipment may employ against a more powerful aggressor nation. When the invader pierces deep into the heart of the weaker country and occupies her territory in a cruel and oppressive manner, there is no doubt that conditions of terrain, climate, and society in general offer obstacles to his progress and may be used to advantage by those who oppose him. In guerrilla warfare, we turn these advantages to the purpose of resisting and defeating the enemy.

During the progress of hostilities, guerrillas gradually develop into orthodox forces that operate in conjunction with other units of the regular army. Thus the regularly organized troops, those guerrillas who

---

From *On Guerrilla Warfare* by Mao Tse-tung. Translated by Samuel T. Griffith (New York: Frederick A. Praeger, 1961), pp. 41–47; 51–56; 77–81; 82–87. Reprinted by permission of Frederick A. Praeger, Inc. and Cassell and Co., Ltd.

MAO TSE-TUNG (1893–   ) Chairman of the Politburo, Communist Party of China. Author of *Selected Military Writings,* (Peking: Foreign Language Press, 1966); *An Analysis of the Classes in Chinese Society,* (Peking: Foreign Language Press, 1955): *On Coalition Government,* (Peking: Foreign Language Press, 1955).

* Editor's Note: This statement on guerrilla warfare was written in 1937. China was at war with Japan, and Mao Tse-tung and his communist followers had been fighting the Nationalist government of President Chiang Kai-shek for many years.

have attained that status, and those who have not reached that level of development combine to form the military power of a national revolutionary war. There can be no doubt that the ultimate result of this will be victory.

Both in its development and in its method of application, guerrilla warfare has certain distinctive characteristics. We first discuss the relationship of guerrilla warfare to national policy. Because ours is the resistance of a semicolonial country against an imperialism, our hostilities must have a clearly defined political goal and firmly established political responsibilities. Our basic policy is the creation of a national united anti-Japanese front. This policy we pursue in order to gain our political goal, which is the complete emancipation of the Chinese people. There are certain fundamental steps necessary in the realization of this policy, to wit:

1. Arousing and organizing the people.
2. Achieving internal unification politically.
3. Establishing bases.
4. Equipping forces.
5. Recovering national strength.
6. Destroying enemy's national strength.
7. Regaining lost territories.

There is no reason to consider guerrilla warfare separately from national policy. On the contrary, it must be organized and conducted in complete accord with national anti-Japanese policy. It is only those who misinterpret guerrilla action who say, as does Jen Ch'i Shan, "The question of guerrilla hostilities is purely a military matter and not a political one." Those who maintain this simple point of view have lost sight of the political goal and the political effects of guerrilla action. Such a simple point of view will cause the people to lose confidence and will result in our defeat.

What is the relationship of guerrilla warfare to the people? Without a political goal, guerrilla warfare must fail, as it must if its political objectives do not coincide with the aspirations of the people and their sympathy, cooperation, and assistance cannot be gained. The essence of guerrilla warfare is thus revolutionary in character. On the other hand, in a war of counterrevolutionary nature, there is no place for guerrilla hostilities. Because guerrilla warfare basically derives from the masses and is supported by them, it can neither exist nor flourish if it separates itself from their sympathies and cooperation. There are those who do not comprehend guerrilla action, and who therefore do not understand the distinguishing qualities of a people's guerrilla war, who say: "Only regular troops can carry on guerrilla operations." There are others who, because they do not believe in the ultimate success of guerrilla action, mistakenly say: "Guerrilla warfare is an insignificant and highly specialized type of operation in which there is no place for the masses of the people" (Jen Ch'i Shan). Then there are those who ridicule the masses and undermine resistance by wildly asserting that the people have no understanding of the war of resistance (Yeh Ch'ing, for one). The moment that this war of resistance dissociates itself from the masses of the people is the precise moment that it dissociates itself from hope of ultimate victory over the Japanese.

What is the organization for guerrilla warfare? Though all guerrilla bands that spring from the masses of the people suffer from lack of organization at the time of their formation, they all have in common a basic quality that makes organization possible. All guerrilla units must have political and military leadership. This is true regardless of the source or size of such units. Such units may originate locally, in the masses of the people; they may be formed from an admixture of regular troops with groups of the people, or they may consist of regular army units intact. And mere quantity does not affect this matter. Such units may consist of a squad of a few men, a battalion of several hundred men, or a regiment of several thousand men.

All these must have leaders who are unyielding in their policies—resolute, loyal, sincere, and robust. These men must be well educated in revolutionary technique, self-confident, able to establish severe discipline, and able to cope with counterpropaganda. In short, these leaders must be models for the people. As the war progresses, such leaders will gradually overcome the lack of discipline, which at first prevails; they will establish discipline in their forces, strengthening them and increasing their combat efficiency. Thus eventual victory will be attained.

Unorganized guerrilla warfare cannot contribute to victory and those who attack the movement as a combination of banditry and anarchism do not understand the nature of guerrilla action. They say: "This movement is a haven for disappointed militarists, vagabonds and bandits" (Jen Ch'i Shan), hoping thus to bring the movement into disrepute. We do not deny that there are corrupt guerrillas, nor that there are people who under the guise of guerrillas indulge in unlawful activities. Neither do we deny that the movement has at the present time symptoms of a lack of organization, symptoms that might indeed be serious were we to judge guerrilla warfare solely by the corrupt and temporary phenomena we have mentioned. We should study the corrupt phenomena and attempt to eradicate them in order to encourage guerrilla warfare, and to increase its military efficiency. "This is hard work, there is no help for it, and the problem cannot be solved immediately. The whole people must try to reform themselves during the course of the war. We must educate them and reform them in the light of past experience. Evil does not exist in guerrilla warfare but only in the unorganized and undisciplined activities that are anarchism," said Lenin, in *On Guerrilla Warfare.*[1]

What is basic guerrilla strategy? Guerrilla strategy must be based primarily on alertness, mobility, and attack. It must be adjusted to the enemy situation, the terrain, the existing lines of communication, the relative strengths, the weather, and the situation of the people.

In guerrilla warfare, select the tactic of seeming to come from the east and attacking from the west; avoid the solid, attack the hollow; attack; withdraw; deliver a lightning blow, seek a lightning decision. When guerrillas engage a stronger enemy, they withdraw when he advances; harass him when he stops; strike him when he is weary; pursue him when he withdraws. In guerrilla strategy, the enemy's rear, flanks, and other vulnerable spots are his vital points, and there he must be harassed, attacked, dispersed, exhausted and annihilated. Only in this way can guerrillas carry out their mission of independent guerrilla action and coordination with the effort of the regular armies. But, in spite of the most complete preparation, there can be no victory if mistakes are made in the matter of command. Guerrilla warfare based on the principles we have mentioned and carried on over a vast extent of territory in which communications are inconvenient will contribute tremendously towards ultimate defeat of the Japanese and consequent emancipation of the Chinese people.

A careful distinction must be made between two types of guerrilla warfare. The fact that revolutionary guerrilla warfare is based on the masses of the people does not in itself mean that the organization of guerrilla units is impossible in a war of counterrevolutionary character. As examples of the former type we may cite Red guerrilla hostilities during the Russian Revolution; those of the Reds in China; of the Abyssinians against the Italians for the past three years; those of the last seven years in Manchuria, and the vast anti-Japanese guerrilla war that is carried on in China today. All these struggles have been carried on in the interests of the whole people or the greater part of them; all had a broad basis in the national manpower, and all have been in accord with the laws of historical development. They have existed and will continue to exist, flourish, and develop as long as they are not contrary to national policy.

The second type of guerrilla warfare directly contradicts the law of historical development. Of this type, we may cite the examples furnished by the White Russian guerrilla units organized by Denikin and Kolchak;

---

[1] Presumably, Mao refers here to the essay that has been translated into English under the title "Partisan Warfare." See *Orbis,* II (Summer, 1958), No. 2, 194–208.

those organized by the Japanese; those organized by the Italians in Abyssinia; those supported by the puppet governments in Manchuria and Mongolia, and those that will be organized here by Chinese traitors. All such have oppressed the masses and have been contrary to the true interests of the people. They must be firmly opposed. They are easy to destroy because they lack a broad foundation in the people.

.   .   .

The general features of orthodox hostilities, that is, the war of position and the war of movement, differ fundamentally from guerrilla warfare. There are other readily apparent differences such as those in organization, armament, equipment, supply, tactics, command; in conception of the terms "front" and "rear"; in the matter of military responsibilities.

When considered from the point of view of total numbers, guerrilla units are many; as individual combat units, they may vary in size from the smallest, of several score or several hundred men, to the battalion or the regiment, of several thousand. This is not the case in regularly organized units. A primary feature of guerrilla operations is their dependence upon the people themselves to organize battalions and other units. As a result of this, organization depends largely upon local circumstances. In the case of guerrilla groups, the standard of equipment is of a low order, and they must depend for their sustenance primarily upon what the locality affords.

The strategy of guerrilla warfare is manifestly unlike that employed in orthodox operations, as the basic tactic of the former is constant activity and movement. There is nothing comparable to the fixed, passive defense that characterizes orthodox war. In guerrilla warfare, the transformation of a moving situation into a positional defensive situation never arises. The general features of reconnaissance, partial deployment, general deployment, and development of the attack that are usual in mobile warfare are not common in guerrilla war.

There are differences also in the matter of leadership and command. In guerrilla warfare, small units acting independently play the principal role, and there must be no excessive interference with their activities. In orthodox warfare, particularly in a moving situation, a certain degree of initiative is accorded subordinates, but in principle, command is centralized. This is done because all units and all supporting arms in all districts must coordinate to the highest degree. In the case of guerrilla warfare, this is not only undesirable but impossible. Only adjacent guerrilla units can coordinate their activities to any degree. Strategically, their activities can be roughly correlated with those of the regular forces, and tactically, they must cooperate with adjacent units of the regular army. But there are no strictures on the extent of guerrilla activity nor is it primarily characterized by the quality of cooperation of many units.

When we discuss the terms "front" and "rear," it must be remembered, that while guerrillas do have bases, their primary field of activity is in the enemy's rear areas. They themselves have no rear. Because an orthodox army has rear installations (except in some special cases as during the 10,000-mile[2] march of the Red Army or as in the case of certain units operating in Shansi Province), it cannot operate as guerrillas can.

As to the matter of military responsibilities, those of the guerrillas are to exterminate small forces of the enemy; to harass and weaken large forces; to attack enemy lines of communication; to establish bases capable of supporting independent operations in the enemy's rear; to force the enemy to disperse his strength; and to coordinate all these activities with those of the regular armies on distant battle fronts.

.   .   .

While it is improper to confuse orthodox with guerrilla operations, it is equally improper to consider that there is a chasm between the two. While differences do exist, similarities appear under certain conditions, and this fact must be appreciated if we wish to establish clearly the relationship between the two. If we consider both types of warfare as a single subject, or if we confuse guerrilla warfare with the mobile operations of orthodox war, we fall into this error: We exaggerate the function of guerrillas and minimize that of the regular armies. If we agree with Chang Tso Hua, who says, "Guerrilla warfare is the primary war strategy of a people seeking to emancipate itself," or with Kao Kang, who believes that "Guerrilla strategy is the only strategy possible for an oppressed people," we are exaggerating the importance of guerrilla hostilities. What these zealous friends I have just quoted do not realize is this: If we do not fit guerrilla operations into their proper niche, we cannot promote them realistically. Then, not only would those who oppose us take advantage of our varying opinions to turn them to their own uses to undermine us, but guerrillas would be led to assume responsibilities they could not successfully discharge and that should properly be carried out by orthodox forces. In the meantime, the important guerrilla function of coordinating activities with the regular forces would be neglected.

Furthermore, if the theory that guerrilla warfare is our only strategy were actually applied, the regular forces would be weakened, we would be divided in purpose, and guerrilla hostilities would decline. If we say, "Let us transform the regular forces into guerrillas," and do not place our first reliance on a victory to be gained by the regular armies over the

---

[2] It has been estimated that the Reds actually marched about 6,000 miles.

enemy, we may certainly expect to see as a result the failure of the anti-Japanese war of resistance. The concept that guerrilla warfare is an end in itself and that guerrilla activities can be divorced from those of the regular forces is incorrect. If we assume that guerrilla warfare does not progress from beginning to end beyond its elementary forms, we have failed to recognize the fact that guerrilla hostilities can, under specific conditions, develop and assume orthodox characteristics. An opinion that admits the existence of guerrilla war, but isolates it, is one that does not properly estimate the potentialities of such war.

Equally dangerous is the concept that condemns guerrilla war on the ground that war has no other aspects than the purely orthodox. This opinion is often expressed by those who have seen the corrupt phenomena of some guerrilla regimes, observed their lack of discipline, and have seen them used as a screen behind which certain persons have indulged in bribery and other corrupt practices. These people will not admit the fundamental necessity for guerrilla bands that spring from the armed people. They say, "Only the regular forces are capable of conducting guerrilla operations." This theory is a mistaken one and would lead to the abolition of the people's guerrilla war.

A proper conception of the relationship that exists between guerrilla effort and that of the regular forces is essential. We believe it can be stated this way: "Guerrilla operations during the anti-Japanese war may for a certain time and temporarily become its paramount feature, particularly insofar as the enemy's rear is concerned. However, if we view the war as a whole, there can be no doubt that our regular forces are of primary importance, because it is they who are alone capable of producing the decision. Guerrilla warfare assists them in producing this favorable decision. Orthodox forces may under certain conditions operate as guerrillas, and the latter may, under certain conditions, develop to the status of the former. However, both guerrilla forces and regular forces have their own respective development and their proper combinations."

THE METHOD OF ORGANIZING GUERRILLA REGIMES

Many of those who decide to participate in guerrilla activities do not know the methods of organization. For such people, as well as for students who have no knowledge of military affairs, the matter of organization is a problem that requires solution. Even among those who have military knowledge, there are some who know nothing of guerrilla regimes because they are lacking in that particular type of experience. The subject of the organization of such regimes is not confined to the organization of specific units but includes all guerrilla activities within the area where the regime functions.

As an example of such organization, we may take a geographical area in the enemy's rear. This area may comprise many counties. It must be subdivided and individual companies or battalions formed to accord with the subdivisions. To this "military area," a military commander and political commissioners are appointed. Under these, the necessary officers, both military and political, are appointed. In the military headquarters, there will be the staff, the aides, the supply officers, and the medical personnel. These are controlled by the chief of staff, who acts in accordance with orders from the commander. In the political headquarters, there are bureaus of propaganda organization, people's mass movements, and miscellaneous affairs. Control of these is vested in the political chairmen.

The military areas are subdivided into smaller districts in accordance with local geography, the enemy situation locally, and the state of guerrilla development. Each of these smaller divisions within the area is a district, each of which may consist of from two to six countries. To each district, a military commander and several political commissioners are appointed. Under their direction, military and political headquarters are organized. Tasks are assigned in accordance with the number of guerrilla troops available. Although the names of the officers in the "district" correspond to those in the larger "area," the number of functionaries assigned in the former case should be reduced to the least possible. In order to unify control, to handle guerrilla troops that come from different sources, and to harmonize military operations and local political affairs, a committee of from seven to nine members should be organized in each area and district. This committee, the members of which are selected by the troops and the local political officers, should function as a forum for the discussion of both military and political matters.

All the people in an area should arm themselves and be organized into two groups. One of these groups is a combat group, the other a self-defense unit with but limited military quality. Regular combatant guerrillas are organized into one of three general types of unit. The first of these is the small unit, the platoon or company. In each county, three to six units may be organized. The second type is the battalion of from two to four companies. One such unit should be organized in each county. While the unit fundamentally belongs to the county in which it was organized, it may operate in other counties. While in areas other than its own, it must operate in conjunction with local units in order to take advantage of their manpower, their knowledge of local terrain and local customs, and their information of the enemy.

The third type is the guerrilla regiment, which consists of from two to four of the above-mentioned battalion units. If sufficient manpower is available, a guerrilla brigade of from two to four regiments may be formed.

Each of the units has its own peculiarities of organization. A squad, the smallest unit, has a strength of from nine to eleven men, including the leader and the assistant leader. Its arms may be from two to five Western-style rifles, with the remaining men armed with rifles of local manufacture, bird guns, spears, or big swords. Two to four such squads form a platoon. This, too, has a leader and an assistant leader, and when acting independently, it is assigned a political officer to carry on political propaganda work. The platoon may have about ten rifles, with the remainder of its weapons being bird guns, lances, and big swords. Two to four of such units form a company, which, like the platoon, has a leader, an assistant leader, and a political officer. All these units are under the direct supervision of the military commanders of the areas in which they operate.

The battalion unit must be more thoroughly organized and better equipped than the smaller units. Its discipline and its personnel should be superior. If a battalion is formed from company units, it should not deprive subordinate units entirely of their manpower and their arms. If, in a small area, there is a peace-preservation corps, a branch of the militia, or police regular guerrilla units should not be dispersed over it.

The guerrilla unit next in size to the battalion is the regiment. This must be under more severe discipline than the battalion. In an independent guerrilla regiment, there may be ten men per squad, three squads per platoon, three platoons per company, three companies per battalion, and three battalions to the regiment. Two of such regiments form a brigade. Each of these units has a commander, a vice-commander, and a political officer.

.   .   .

All these units from the lowest to the highest are combatant guerrilla units and receive their supplies from the central government. . . .

All the people of both sexes from the ages of sixteen to forty-five must be organized into anti-Japanese self-defense units, the basis of which is voluntary service. As a first step, they must procure arms, then they must be given both military and political training. Their responsibilities are: local sentry duties, securing information of the enemy, arresting traitors, and preventing the dissemination of enemy propaganda. When the enemy launches a guerrilla-suppression drive, these units, armed with what weapons there are, are assigned to certain areas to deceive, hinder, and harass him. Thus, the self-defense units assist the combatant guerrillas. They have other functions. They furnish stretcher-bearers to transport the wounded, carriers to take food to the troops, and comfort missions to provide the troops with tea and rice. If a locality can organize such a self-defense unit as we have described, the traitors cannot hide nor can bandits and robbers disturb the peace of the people. Thus the people will continue to assist the guerrillas and supply manpower to our regular armies. "The organization of self-defense units is a transitional step in the development of universal conscription. Such units are reservoirs of manpower for the orthodox forces."

.   .   .

Equipment of Guerrillas

In regard to the problem of guerrilla equipment, it must be understood that guerrillas are lightly armed attack groups, which require simple equipment. The standard of equipment is based upon the nature of duties assigned; the equipment of low-class guerrilla units is not as good as that of higher-class units. For example, those who are assigned the task of destroying railroads are better-equipped than those who do not have that task. The equipment of guerrillas cannot be based on what the guerrillas want, or even what they need, but must be based on what is available for their use. Equipment cannot be furnished immediately but must be acquired gradually. These are points to be kept in mind.

The question of equipment includes the collection, supply, distribution, and replacement of weapons, ammunition, blankets, communication materials, transport, and facilities for propaganda work. The supply of weapons and ammunition is most difficult, particularly at the time the unit is established, but this problem can always be solved eventually. Guerrilla bands that originate in the people are furnished with revolvers, pistols, bird guns, spears, big swords, and land mines and mortars of local manufacture. Other elementary weapons are added and as many new-type rifles as are available are distributed. After a period of resistance, it is possible to increase the supply of equipment by capturing it from the enemy. In this respect, the transport companies are the easiest to equip, for in any successful attack, we will capture the enemy's transport.

An armory should be established in each guerrilla district for the manufacture and repair of rifles and for the production of cartridges, hand grenades, and bayonets. Guerrillas must not depend too much on an armory. The enemy is the principal source of their supply.

For destruction of railway trackage, bridges, and stations in enemy-controlled territory, it is necessary to gather together demolition materials. Troops must be trained in the preparation and use of demolitions, and a demolition unit must be organized in each regiment.

As for minimum clothing requirements, these are that each man shall have at least two summer-weight uniforms, one suit of winter clothing, two hats, a pair of wrap puttees, and a blanket. Each man must have a haversack or a bag for food. In the north, each man must have an overcoat. In acquiring this clothing, we cannot depend on captures made from the enemy, for it is forbidden for captors to take clothing from their prisoners. In order to maintain high morale in guerrilla forces, all the clothing and equipment mentioned should be furnished by the representatives of the government stationed in each guerrilla district. These men may confiscate clothing from traitors or ask contributions from those best able to afford them. In subordinate groups, uniforms are unnecessary.

· · ·

In the guerrilla army in general, and at bases in particular, there must be a high standard of medical equipment. Besides the services of the doctors, medicines must be procured. Although guerrillas can depend on the enemy for some portion of their medical supplies, they must, in general, depend upon contributions. If Western medicines are not available, local medicines must be made to suffice.

The problem of transport is more vital in North China than in the south, for in the south all that are necessary are mules and horses. Small guerrilla units need no animals, but regiments and brigades will find them necessary. Commanders and staffs of units from companies up should be furnished a riding animal each. At times, two officers will have to share a horse. Officers whose duties are of minor nature do not have to be mounted.

Propaganda materials are very important. Every large guerrilla unit should have a printing press and a mimeograph stone. They must also have paper on which to print propaganda leaflets and notices. They must be supplied with chalk and large brushes. In guerrilla areas, there should be a printing press or a lead-type press.

For the purpose of printing training instructions, this material is of the greatest importance.

In addition to the equipment listed above, it is necessary to have field glasses, compasses, and military maps. An accomplished guerrilla group will acquire these things.

Because of the proved importance of guerrilla hostilities in the anti-Japanese war, the headquarters of the Nationalist Government and the commanding officers of the various war zones should do their best to supply the guerrillas with what they actually need and are unable to get for themselves. However, it must be repeated that guerrilla equipment will in the main depend on the effort of the guerrillas themselves. If they depend on higher officers too much, the psychological effect will be to weaken the guerrilla spirit of resistance.

ELEMENTS OF THE GUERRILLA ARMY

The term "element" as used in the title to this section refers to the personnel, both officers and men, of the guerrilla army. Since each guerrilla group fights in a protracted war, its officers must be brave and positive men whose entire loyalty is dedicated to the cause of emancipation of the people. An officer should have the following qualities: great powers of endurance so that in spite of any hardship he sets an example to his men and is a model for them; he must be able to mix easily with the people; his spirit and that of the men must be one in strengthening the policy of resistance to the Japanese. If he wishes to gain victories, he must study tactics. A guerrilla group with officers of this caliber would be unbeatable. I do not mean that every guerrilla group can have, at its inception, officers of such qualities. The officers must be men naturally endowed with good qualities which can be developed during the course of campaigning. The most important natural quality is that of complete loyalty to the idea of people's emancipation. If this is present, the others will develop; if it is not present, nothing can be done. When officers are first selected from a group, it is this quality that should receive particular attention. The officers in a group should be inhabitants of the locality in which the group is organized, as this will facilitate relations between them and the local civilians. In addition, officers so chosen would be familiar with conditions. If in any locality there are not enough men of sufficiently high qualifications to become officers, an effort must be made to train and educate the people so these qualities may be developed and the potential officer material increased. There can be no disagreements between officers native to one place and those from other localities.

A guerrilla group ought to operate on the principle that only volunteers are acceptable for service. It is a mistake to impress people into service. As long as a person is willing to fight, his social condition or position is no consideration, but only men who are courageous and determined can bear the hardships of guerrilla campaigning in a protracted war.

A soldier who habitually breaks regulations must be dismissed from the army. Vagabonds and vicious people must not be accepted for service. The opium habit must be forbidden, and a soldier who cannot break himself of the habit should be dismissed. Victory in guerrilla war is conditioned upon keeping the membership pure and clean.

It is a fact that during the war the enemy may take advantage of certain people who are lacking in conscience and patriotism and induce them to join the guerrillas for the purpose of betraying them. Officers must, therefore, continually educate the soldiers and inculcate patriotism in them. This will prevent the success of traitors. The traitors who are in the ranks must be discovered and expelled, and punishment and expulsion meted out to those who have been influenced by them. In all such cases, the officers should summon the soldiers and relate the facts to them, thus arousing their hatred and detestation for traitors. This procedure will serve as well as a warning to the other soldiers. If an officer is discovered to be a traitor, some prudence must be used in the punishment adjudged. However, the work of eliminating traitors in the army begins with their elimination from among the people.

Chinese soldiers who have served under puppet governments and bandits who have been converted should be welcomed as individuals or as groups. They should be well treated and repatriated. But care should be used during their reorientation to distinguish those whose idea is to fight the Japanese from those who may be present for other reasons.

Part IV

Technology and the
International System

TECHNOLOGY, or applied science, has had a major impact upon the international system and upon political relationships in general. Since the industrial revolution of the eighteenth century, technological changes have narrowed distances and vastly increased the coercive and destructive capabilities available to man. As a result of these advances, the volume of transactions—movements of persons, trade, and messages—has increased dramatically. With greater ease and speed than ever before, people, goods, and messages can move from one part of the globe to another. Depending upon the meaning attached to them, the effect of such greatly increased transactions is either to promote the prospects for a more peaceful world, or to contribute to a growth in international tensions.

Technology has made available to national units greater capabilities for affecting the behavior of other national units. In many cases technology has contributed to their cohesiveness, for modern communication has narrowed the distance which historically separated the central government from the population living in the hinterland. But technology has also outmoded many of the political units into which mankind is organized.

The resulting crisis for the national unit is most evident in western Europe. Over the past generation, the cost of research and development has risen astronomically, and the opportunities for exploiting science and technology have grown enormously. There the national units are inadequate to maximize the potential inherent in advanced science and technology.

261

Advanced technology has created new resources and assisted man in the exploitation of existing ones. While historically the location of raw materials and energy sources has influenced greatly the location of power centers, the great advances in, and reduced costs of, transportation and the mobility of raw materials have made the availability of superior technology the principal variable governing the location of new industrial centers. Thus, technology is more important than ever as a determinant of national power.

Examining technology's impact upon the political order, Victor Basiuk describes both the integrative effect of technology in society and the integrative process within technology. The integrative effect has been a "highly complex and multifaceted phenomenon" operating at cross currents on different levels. As a result of technological advances, there will be further progress in transportation and telecommunications over the next generation, the conversion of arid land into productive areas through water desalination and controlled-environment structures, exploitation of resources from the seabed, and greater use of computer technology for the processing of vast new amounts of data. But the integrative effect of technology, paradoxically, may not necessarily diminish conflict, since it will bring men into ever closer contact—one of the essential preconditions for conflict. In fact, technology will continue to furnish new capabilities for nations to project their influence on a global scale.

As in the past, technology may spread from its point of origin to peoples around the world. Other nations can duplicate existing technologies for less than the pioneering nation spends to develop them. Nevertheless, the cost of producing new technology may continue to increase, so that no nation, not even the United States or the Soviet Union, will have adequate resources for the full exploitation of the potentials inherent in science and technology.

These advances will contribute to the integration of technology itself, with technologies in seemingly discrete fields becoming mutually reinforcing. Victor Basiuk suggests, for example, that the computer, space satellites, atmospheric devices and oceanography, will contribute to weather prediction and climate modification. Breakthroughs in chemistry, electronics, and the biological sciences will revolutionize medicine, especially in the field of body organ transplants. Increased understanding of the relationship between technology in various fields will give impetus to technological innovation and ultimately, if Zbigniew Brzezinski is correct, to the emergence of a "technetronic" society.

During the next several decades, life in the developed countries will undergo a transformation, according to Brzezinski, as great as that experienced in the slow process of evolution from animal to human consciousness. Technological advances will prolong life, alter human values and career patterns, transform the character of education, raise living standards, and create problems related to the distribution of power between the individual and society.

America is the first society to have passed through the industrial revolution into the technetronic age. The United States is already grappling with issues which other advanced societies will face as they enter the technetronic phase of development. These issues revolve about the fundamental question: can the individual and science coexist, or will forces of technological change become the dominant societal factor? The rise of antitechnological sentiment in the United States and the growing concern about the effects of technology upon ecology are indicative of problems confronting the technetronic society. The challenge for the United States, in this new age, is to find a synthesis which harnesses the vast potential of technology while simultaneously enabling man to grow in intellectual depth, personal liberty, and philosophical meaning in appropriate ecological circumstances. In facing such perplexing issues, America is unique because it is the first society to experience the future.

If the authors in this section are correct, technology will continue for the remainder of this century to transform both the international system and its national units. There is, already, evidence of the implications of technological change for the military capabilities of nation-states. Technology has led to a balance of terror differing in many respects from the historic balance of power. (See Parts III and VIII.) It has altered the significance of alliance systems, for the destructive capabilities available to the leading nation-states complicate the problem of defending allies in at least two ways: (1) a power risks its own destruction to an unprecedented extent in defending an ally, and (2) the ally himself risks destruction. The exponential increase in technology has complicated greatly the problems of disarmament and arms control (See Part IV), since it becomes nearly impossible to guard against destabilizing technological breakthroughs or to inspect and verify for compliance with international agreements. Technology has affected the economic capabilities of nation-states and has altered the organization of corporations. The rise of the multinational corporation, discussed in Part V, represents a product of technological change, as well as an instrument for the transfer of technology from one country to another. Finally, technology creates formidable problems for international law and organization. The potential for the exploitation of resources on the seabed and the need for various forms of international organization, discussed in Part IX, can be traced directly to the impact of technology upon the international system.

20. THE IMPACT OF TECHNOLOGY IN THE NEXT DECADES *

Victor Basiuk

LOOKING AHEAD a quarter of a century, one can discern technological developments certain to affect the economies of every advanced industrial society: (1) Development of large-scale generation of power to meet expanded needs, accompanied by important reductions in the cost of energy. (2) Growth of telecommunications by means of global satellites ringing the earth. (3) Exploitation of the untapped marine resources of the world. (4) Refinement of weather prediction and expanded capability for weather and climate modification.

Significant in themselves, they loom even more important because of the way they will interact with and shape some dominant scientific and technological trends: e.g., the change of scale on which science and technology have to be conducted today and the impetus to integration— economic and perhaps political. For the essential fact is that the cost of developing these new technological areas is so great that only giant industrial nations, or combinations of nations, will be able to afford to do so. The unfolding of the new technology of the next twenty-five years and its enormous political ramifications are the subjects this article will explore.

From *ORBIS,* a quarterly journal of world affairs published by the Foreign Policy Research Institute, Philadelphia, Pennsylvania, Spring 1970, 17–32, 36–39. Reprinted by permission of the Trustees of the University of Pennsylvania.

VICTOR BASIUK (1932–   ) Advisor to the Chief of Naval Operations, Department of the Navy. Formerly Associate Professor of Political Science, Case Institute of Technology; Research Associate, Institute of War and Peace, Columbia University. Author of *Technology and World Power* (New York: Foreign Policy Association, 1970).

* This article is based in part on research sponsored by the U.S. Arms Control and Disarmament Agency under contract with the Institute of War and Peace Studies, Columbia University, and in part on research sponsored by the Institute for the Study of Science in Human Affairs, Columbia University. The judgments expressed are those of the author and do not necessarily reflect the views of the U.S. Arms Control and Disarmament Agency or any other agency of the U.S. government.

DECLINE IN THE DETERMINISTIC EFFECT OF RESOURCE LOCATION

Historically, technology has always played a major role in creating new resources or helping to exploit the traditional ones, but in most instances it tended to be tied down to its physical resource base. Major industrial centers were built around coal-iron ore complexes, such as those in the Durham-Cleveland, Great Lakes-Pennsylvania, Ruhr, and Krivoi Rog-Donbas regions. The development of railroads was fairly closely tied to the availability of resources—either mineral or agricultural —on the land the railroads crossed. Electricity made water power a significant source of energy, but hydroelectric stations and the economic activity stimulated by them were narrowly confined to rivers and their vicinity.

What is noteworthy today is the decline in importance of the location of raw materials and sources of energy as a determining factor in economic development and the rise of new power centers. No single invention was responsible for this decline, but the most significant technologies initially responsible were chemistry and transportation. By combining and recombining elements and thus converting them into more useful products, chemistry undertook to make "resources" out of the most ubiquitous materials, such as air, water and sand. Substitution of raw materials became relatively easy and prevalent; e.g., if natural rubber was not locally available, synthetic rubber could be produced from coal, oil or foodstuffs.

Technological advance in transportation, resulting in the reduction of costs, greatly increased the mobility of raw materials. Perhaps the most striking example in this respect is the post-World War II development of the steel industry in Japan, which by 1964 had become the third largest in the world (after the United States and the Soviet Union). In 1965, Japan imported 88 per cent of her iron ore and 64 per cent of her coking coal at an average distance of 5,500 miles. The magnitude of Japan's achievement (aided, besides transportation, by other technological improvements) was driven home in April 1969 when the merger of the two largest Japanese steel companies generated serious concern on the part of both American and European steel manufacturers about their ability to compete with the Japanese. It has been estimated that if the two companies, Yawata Iron and Steel and Fuji Iron and Steel, merge and continue to grow at their present rate, they will overtake United States Steel by the middle 1970's, thus becoming the largest steel company in the world.

In brief, the availability of superior technology—and not the location of raw materials or sources of energy—has become the principal factor in the emergence of new industrial centers and the economic viability of nations and regions. The extent of this trend is illustrated by the nuclear agro-industrial centers which have been proposed for the 1970's.[1] These centers, located on the coast of a water-deficient area, would combine desalinization of water for irrigation purposes with large-scale production of those chemicals, fertilizers and metals which require cheap and abundant electricity. Seawater and air would provide the raw material for such chemicals as hydrochloric and nitric acids and ammonia, while other raw materials (e.g., bauxite and phosphorus) would be imported. These centers would offer many millions of people new sources of food and employment.

The decline in the deterministic effect of resource location has a number of implications. The vistas for organized human will backed by advanced technology have broadened immensely. On the other hand, the historically built technological superstructure of advanced societies creates rigidity and a deterministic effect of its own. Thus, what will increasingly matter in producing differential benefits from science and technology among the advanced nations will be not so much the extent of the present advance, but rather farsightedness in planning, determination in the pursuit of selected goals, and willingness to reshape and restructure the existing social institutions and technological superstructure to meet the requirements of future technology.

THE INTEGRATIVE EFFECT OF TECHNOLOGY

With the freeing of technology from a resource base has come a different trend: the integrative effect of technology on society and the integrative process within technology itself. Many loose statements have been made in this connection: e.g., progress in transportation and telecommunications has "shrunk" the world; the peoples of the world or a given region have become interdependent. In fact, the integrative influence of technology is a highly complex and multifaceted phenomenon that has not been fully understood and probably will not be for some time. It operates on different levels, and its impact on society frequently runs at cross currents.

One level is the integration of human activity and spatial units into

---

[1] See Oak Ridge National Laboratory, *Nuclear Energy Centers—Industrial and Agro-Industrial Complexes; Summary Report* (Oak Ridge, Tenn., July 1968). The concept was developed at Oak Ridge and the feasibility study undertaken produced encouraging and economically attractive results. The Indian government was sufficiently interested to participate in the Oak Ridge study. At present, Oak Ridge National Laboratory is conducting a detailed study of uses for large energy centers in the Middle East, and a study has been undertaken for a large energy center for Puerto Rico. See also Edward A. Mason, "Nuclear Reactors: Transforming Economics as well as Energy," *Technology Review,* March 1969, pp. 32–33.

one global geo-technical system. The advanced industrial societies are highly interrelated, technologically and politically. The three remaining areas which have not been fully—or at all—integrated into the global system are the underdeveloped regions, the scarcely inhabited regions (the Amazon, the Arctic), and the ocean floor. Technological developments in the next decade or so will contribute significantly toward the integration of these areas.

Thanks largely to satellites, costs of telecommunications are rapidly decreasing; by 1980 it may be possible to telephone anywhere in the world for one dollar during off-business hours. The drop in telecommunications costs will be a major factor in the process of integrating the less developed countries internally and with the world system. A satellite-based television network for less developed nations as large as India could be developed, built, and made operational in about four years. To construct a comparable terrestrial network would take perhaps as long as two or three decades and the cost would be about twice as great.[2] Provided the government of the receiving state cooperates, such a network would make possible direct transmission of programs from an advanced nation into community receivers of the less developed countries. If the presently available receivers are appropriately augmented (at a cost of at least $40 each), a global television network, involving direct transmission through satellites into home receivers, could be operational by the late 1970's.[3] Without such augmentation, a highly advanced country could develop, at substantial cost, the capability for transmitting programs directly into home receivers of foreign nations by the early 1980's.

Preferences of the public in advanced countries for local programs, the time differential, and political considerations will probably hinder the establishment of a truly global television network in the next twenty-

---

[2] The cost of constructing and operating a satellite broadcast television system for India for ten years, with 500,000 ground community receivers, has been estimated at $87 million. A terrestrial system, including ten years of operation, would cost $150 million. Assumptions of the study included a 1971 technology base. For details on a satellite community TV network for India, see General Electric Company, Space Systems Organization, *Television Broadcast Satellite (TVBS) Study; TVBS Technical Report* (Prepared for the National Aeronautics and Space Administration, Contract No. NAS 3-9708, November 15, 1969), Vol. III, pp. 2–19, 7–81, 7–106, 7–108. An agreement has been concluded between the United States and India to establish a smaller experimental network of 5,000 ground satellite-broadcast community receivers, to be operational by 1973. India will transmit its own programs from a ground station, but use an American satellite for relay to community receivers. See "India/United States Experimental Satellite Project," UN Document A/AC.105/72, December 11, 1969.

[3] Cf. "Report of the Working Group on Direct Broadcast Satellites," UN Document A/AC.105/51, February 26, 1969, p. 3.

five years. It is likely that a greater interchangeability of programs among the advanced nations will take place in the near future; selected programs from abroad will be transmitted, with the aid of a satellite, through local television stations. Since the less developed countries have only limited resources for their own programs, they will rely to a greater extent on programs from abroad, beamed into community receivers or perhaps directly into home sets. New audio-visual techniques of instruction, combined with satellite-aided television, promise not only a much more rapid integration of the less developed societies with the rest of the world, but a social transformation whose effects are not entirely clear.

The nuclear agro-industrial complexes described above will contribute to the integration of arid and hitherto sparsely inhabited areas. Even now, conventional means of desalinization of water combined with controlled-environment greenhouses of air-inflated plastic are beginning to be used successfully to convert deserts into economically productive areas.[4] The techniques for controlling rainfall will improve significantly by 1980,[5] thus helping to increase geographic areas capable of sustaining agricultural productivity and possibly to expand the areas of human habitat in general. It appears that, by diverting the flow of ocean currents, large-scale changes in climate are economically feasible even at the present cost of energy.[6] As the cost of energy declines, projects designed

---

[4] See Carle O. Hodge, "The Blooming Desert," *Bulletin of the Atomic Scientists,* November 1969, pp. 32–33. This was a project developed by scientists at the University of Arizona which resulted in bumper yields of tomatoes, cucumbers and other crops harvested from a virtually rainless Mexican beach. Their achievement prompted the ruler of Abu Dhabi, a sheikdom on the Arabian Peninsula rich in oil, to offer to finance the inauguration by the Arizonans of a power-water-food center using engine-driven electric generators in his own country; he also agreed to support further research in this field in Arizona. The goal of the project is to produce perhaps two million pounds of high-quality vegetables a year at about twenty cents per pound, as compared with the presently air-freighted vegetables sold at $1.50 per pound. The principal advantages of air-inflated plastic greenhouses are their extreme conservation of water (moisture is trapped and evaporation is minimal) and their relative cheapness. The University of Arizona scientists expect that the Abu Dhabi installation will be a prototype that should be applicable to vast regions where almost nothing now grows.

[5] See Thomas F. Malone, "New Dimensions of International Cooperation in Weather Analysis and Prediction," *Bulletin of the American Meteorological Society,* December 1968, p. 1138.

[6] P. M. Borisov, "Can We Control the Arctic Climate?," *Bulletin of the Atomic Scientists,* March 1969, pp. 43–48. This is a translation of an article by a Soviet scientist which received currency in both the Soviet Union and Canada. The author points out that the Gulf Stream system, the most powerful warm current of the entire globe, pours into the depth of the Arctic basin. Since the water of the stream is more saline and heavier than the Arctic waters, it sinks and spreads under the

to implement such changes will become increasingly more attractive; eventually, they may lead to freeing huge areas of permafrost for agriculture and other economic activity and improve the means for converting present deserts into productive regions.

The use of the earth resource survey satellites, to be introduced in the early 1970's, is expected to facilitate the discovery of mineral resources, thus generating economic activity in geographic regions hitherto not considered to be economically attractive and perhaps not even habitable.[7]

Exploitation of oil and gas from the sea bed has advanced rapidly in recent years; the present gross annual revenue of the U.S. offshore oil industry exceeds $9 billion. Human underwater missions of long duration at a depth of 600 to 1,000 feet are expected to take place in the near future. It has been predicted that commercial capability for extensive and prolonged engineering operations on continental slopes as deep as 3,000 feet will take place by 1980, while commercial deployment of vehicles and machines at 6,000 feet and beyond is expected sometime in 1980–1990.

Computers, capable of processing vast amounts of data, provide a major instrument of in-depth integration. They greatly facilitate large-scale organization, control of both men and materials, and regional and national planning. Computations on a scale that would have taken months and years before—or could not have been made at all—are either possible now or will soon become possible within seconds and at very low cost. Sometime in the period between 1976 and 1981, computing is likely to become a public utility, with many thousands of remote terminals for the use of individuals and organizations to obtain the information

---

cold and less saline Arctic waters. Borisov calculated that if the Bering Strait is dammed and the water is pumped from the Arctic Ocean, the warm water of the Gulf Stream would not sink; instead, it would be diverted into the Bering Sea, thus ameliorating the climate of Northern Siberia, Alaska and Northern Canada. By increasing and decreasing the rate of pumping the water, climate could be controlled in much more remote areas: e.g., the climate of the Sahara could eventually be changed by increasing rainfall and thus stimulating vegetation.

[7] The first experimental Earth Resources Technology Satellite (ERTS) will be launched by NASA in 1971–1972; this will be followed by an operational system by the mid-1970's. The satellites are expected to provide multiple benefits, on the order of perhaps many billions of dollars. They will help to identify potential areas where mineral resources may be found. They will provide repetitive coverage of snow distribution and vegetation, thus assisting in the control of floods and in power and irrigation planning. They will help in prediction and prevention of crop diseases over wide areas and will also provide repetitive coverage of ocean currents, arctic ice and ocean temperature for scientific and economic purposes. For the potential of satellites with respect to earth resources, see National Research Council, Division of Engineering, *Useful Application of Earth-Oriented Satellites: Summaries of Panel Reports* (Washington: National Academy of Sciences, 1969).

they need. A concomitant development will be the replacement of money and checks by the computer-controlled credit card. The present trend in computer technology is great increase in memories and the speed of retrieval. The main memories of some two million characters and the auxiliary memories of half a billion characters are considered to be large in the present generation of computers. In the next computer generation, to become available in the late 1970's, the main memories will contain hundreds of millions of characters, while the auxiliary memories will have many billions of characters. The retrieval of information will be increased to about twenty to forty million characters per second between the auxiliary and the main memory, as compared with the one to three million per second now.

Last but not least, integration proceeds within science and technology itself. The combination of computers, satellites, atmospheric sciences and oceanography opens up broad vistas for weather prediction and modification. Transplantation of body organs and their increasing substitution by synthetic items—which is revolutionizing medicine—represents the meeting of medicine, mechanics and chemistry. The combination of electronics and chemistry, electronics and physics, biological sciences and chemistry are further examples of the growing trend. It appears that the synergistic effect resulting from the meeting and integrating of two or more sciences and technologies produces the most rapid progress.

What are the implications of this integrative trend? Instrumentally speaking, the capability to understand and control the integrative trend of technology is highly important and will be increasingly crucial in the future. There is a growing need for conceptual instruments on how to integrate various technologies to achieve particular social goals. Systems analysis is but one such instrument, and it has not yet been adequately developed. The ability to control the forms and phases of the integrative trend—particularly on the "horizontal" level—is an increasingly important leverage of international power and influence. A better understanding and the fostering of integration between the various sciences and technologies will accelerate technological innovation and progress.

The integrative trend of technology creates an appreciable measure of global, regional and local interdependence, but it does not necessarily create unity. Indeed, in a number of its forms this trend can create or exacerbate conflict. A growing settlement and integration of Northern China and Eastern Siberia may increase rather than diminish conflict between the USSR and China, and the better integrated instruments of military force are likely to intensify a clash. There is no conflict for the sea bed in the deep ocean areas at this time, but such a conflict looms as a definite possibility in the future as the ocean floor begins to be integrated into global economic activity.

These examples are not intended to confirm the somewhat simplistic statement that "technology unites, while humans divide." Technology itself, as an independent variable, may divide. Computers, by integrating human and material resources of educational institutions, make it possible to create a mega-university, but these same computers, by facilitating impersonality, may split asunder the mega-university and even the entire society. In terms of political division or unification or political impact in general, it is not always clear what the general integrative trend signifies for the future. The rise of multinational corporations [8] (of which the Intelsat is but one) and the technological integration of the ocean floor—which may involve companies of various nationalities working, and eventually multinational personnel living, side by side on the bottom of the sea—are truly major developments. They might modify, if not undermine, the present nation-state system in the next decades. But it will take some time before the exact nature of their political impact becomes clearly discernible.

GLOBAL PROJECTION OF INFLUENCE
THROUGH TECHNOLOGY

The integrative impetus of technology is accompanied by the increasingly versatile, global projection of national influence and power through technology. In the nineteenth century this phenomenon was manifested by Great Britain's global projection of power, first through the Royal Navy and later through telecommunications (cables and radio). In the post-World War II period, the United States eclipsed all other powers by a wide margin in the magnitude of its global projection and the multiplicity of its instruments. After the massive display of U.S. military power in both Europe and Asia during World War II, the United States made an effort to withdraw, but was compelled to stay. The forms of its military power grew in variety and size—from bombers to ICBM's and Polaris IRBM's trained on various targets in Eurasia. Global military operations have been improved—and are continuously improving—through nuclear propulsion in naval vessels, better communications systems, more effective logistics support, worldwide surveillance through satellites and other means, and long-range airlift.

On the nonmilitary level, the Voice of America provides another form

---

[8] An indication of the magnitude of this development is provided by figures of U.S. participation in multinational corporations. The value of output (sales) from U.S. subsidiaries abroad and from the U.S. share in foreign-owned companies has been estimated at over $200 billion in 1968. The value of U.S. exports, on the other hand, amounted to only $34 billion in 1968. The Department of State is currently considering the advisability of reorienting the focus of its economic activity toward multinational corporations and foreign investment, as distinguished from its traditional concern with foreign trade.

of projection of global influence. Physically, the recent lunar landings were aimed at the moon, but politically they were aimed at Earth. Foreign aid is, in part, a means of extending America's influence through more advanced technology into the less developed world. The multinational corporation—primarily a subsidiary of the technologically and managerially superior American companies—is a projection mainly into industrialized nations.

The Kremlin imitated the American global strategic nuclear projection, and now the Soviets are expanding their global capability in subnuclear military technology. The Soviet Union is roughly equal to the United States in global extension of its influence through outer space technology (but not communications satellites), broadcasting and oceanology. In other respects, its efforts at projecting Soviet power are less significant than those of the United States.[9]

In comparison with the United States and the Soviet Union, Western Europe has not scored conspicuously in the global projection of its power and influence. In the first place, Western Europe lacks the unified political will required for such an undertaking. The foreign aid programs of the largest West European states have grown recently from about a half to almost two-thirds of that of the United States,[10] but they are not effectively coordinated. Europe participates in Intelsat, the Europeans have an outer space program of their own, and Great Britain and France have a nuclear striking capability; but, on the whole, the present capability of Western Europe to project its power and influence globally is small when compared with U.S. and Soviet capabilities. Perhaps the only exception is the large West European merchant marine. In 1967, the gross tonnage of the merchant fleets of the EEC countries and the United Kingdom amounted to 44,194,000 tons, compared with 19,179,000 tons under U.S. registry and 8,562,000 tons flying the Soviet flag. Under peace-

---

[9] Soviet economic foreign aid, actually delivered (as distinguished from commitments), has amounted to about $300 million annually in recent years, while American foreign aid has been about ten times this amount. (For an analysis of Soviet foreign aid, see U.S. Department of State, Director of Intelligence and Research, *Communist Governments and the Developing Nations: Aid and Trade in 1967*, Research Memorandum RSE-120, August 14, 1968, especially pp. 1, 4–6.) Soviet air transport, welded into a single company, Aeroflot, has been estimated as being twice the size of the largest U.S. airline (United), but it carries only about 45 per cent of the traffic of all the major domestic airlines of the United States put together. "Top Airlines of 1967," *The Economist*, October 5, 1968, p. 100.

[10] In 1968, the total net official development assistance of the United Kingdom, France, Germany and Italy amounted to $2,002 million, as compared with $3,314 million for the United States. The increase in European foreign aid was more relative than absolute: American foreign aid began to decline in 1968. See OECD, Development Assistance Committee, *Development Assistance* (Paris, 1969), pp. 45, 48.

time conditions, however, a nation's merchant marine is not one of the most important instruments of power and influence. By shipping goods (rather than people) and having low visibility, the merchant marine has relatively limited impact on human psychology and values and is basically at the disposal of the customer, of whatever nationality he might be. One European power with formerly global interests, Great Britain, is in the process of retrenchment rather than augmentation of her projection capabilities.

Technological instruments for projecting one's power and influence globally will be significantly improved in the next decade or two, and entirely new instruments will appear. We noted above that global voice communications will become cheap and readily useable within the next ten years. In the 1970's, some highly advanced nations will have the technological capability for beaming television programs directly into the receivers of the less developed world, and this capability will probably be used. It is conceivable that in the 1980's the superpowers will increasingly project themselves through television broadcasts directly into the receivers of the more advanced countries, such as those of Western Europe. Computers, global communications and high-speed transportation make it possible to control a scattered international enterprise from a central point; further progress in all of these areas will enhance the role of foreign investment in extending a nation's influence. The era of global mass travel is just beginning and will witness rapid growth with the introduction of "air buses" and, later, supersonic aircraft.[11] Control of the means of telecommunications and of mass travel—through ownership of manufacturing facilities, the media themselves, or both—is an important lever of power. Quite apart from this leverage, proliferation of global mass travel and mass communications tends to favor those who are technologically more powerful, affluent and numerous: they have much more to project, and can afford to project more. The influence exerted may produce important modifications in the value systems of those who are the primary objects of the projection.

Major developments will likely occur in large-scale climate modification, perhaps as early as the late 1970's, and with a correspondingly greater certainty in subsequent years.[12] If unilaterally developed, climate

---

[11] Present projections of revenue passenger-miles by the Federal Aviation Administration for U.S. air carriers anticipate an almost fourfold increase between FY 1968 and FY 1980 (from 106.5 billion to 379.0 billion). Federal Aviation Administration, *Aviation Forecasts, Fiscal Years 1969–1980* (Washington, January 1969), p. 23. These projections are considered to be fairly conservative; projections by nongovernmental authorities are higher.

[12] See Thomas F. Malone, "Current Developments in the Atmospheric Sciences and Some of Their Implications for Foreign Policy," in *The Potential Impact of*

and weather modification provides a valuable instrument for projecting one's power externally. The cost of energy is likely to be dramatically reduced in the next ten to twenty-five years. According to present and admittedly conservative projections based on "surprise-free" developments in nuclear technology, the cost of power to U.S. industry will decline from about 8 mills/kw-hr. to 1.5 mills/kw-hr. (in 1968 dollars) by the year 2000.[13] However, technological breakthroughs might reduce the cost of energy to this level—and possibly below—much sooner than estimated. The nations that capitalize on technologies where major breakthroughs are likely to occur—which would include such areas as controlled thermonuclear reaction (CTR), superconductivity, and magnetohydrodynamics (MHD)—and possess the capability of utilizing them on a sufficiently large scale, will be in a position to control world markets through superior and cheaper products. Marine resources development represents still another important area. It will permit the projection of national substance into hitherto unoccupied and unexploited parts of the globe, and its geopolitical impact will grow in the next decades.

We live in a period when attributes of power and influence become increasingly diffuse; differing from attributes in the pre-World War II decades, they do not necessarily accrue narrowly to individual nations. In an integrating world, where regional differences are perhaps more important now than national, it would be an oversimplification to equate each manifestation of ability for global projection by a nation with the actual attainment of power and influence. The effect of some external projections of national substance will be neutralized by other developments, and still other projections are likely to be counterproductive in terms of power and influence. This, in particular, may pertain to the potential impact of global projections on the values and motivations of

---

Science and Technology on Future U.S. Foreign Policy (Papers Presented at a Special Joint Meeting of the Policy Planning Council, Department of State, and a Special Panel of the Committee on Science and Public Policy. National Academy of Sciences, June 16–17, 1968, Washington, D.C.), p. 91. Malone points out that interface processes between the atmosphere and the underlying surface appear to be important to large-scale modification of the climate; if these expectations are justified, "there is a high probability that the technology could go through explosive developments during the period 1975 to 1995."

[13] See James A. Lane, "Rationale for Low-Cost Nuclear Heat and Electricity," in *Abundant Nuclear Energy* (Oak Ridge, Tenn.: U.S. Atomic Energy Commission, 1969), pp. 3, 23. Eight mills/kw-hr. is an average generating cost for 1967. The low generating cost of 1.5 mills is expected to be achieved through the development of very large (5,000 megawatts) high-performance breeder reactors. In the case of industry, sales costs of power are about the same as the generating costs, although they are more than twice as high for residences and commercial customers (because of transmission and distribution costs).

those peoples who become their targets. However, we are still far from attaining a homogeneous world, and, on balance, the ability for global projection through technology will be an important attribute of power of nations, regions, and those international institutions capable of commanding the necessary resources for it.

THE GROWING SCALE AND COSTS OF TECHNOLOGY

To this list of basic consequences of the new technology one has to add its growing scale. Large economies of scale entail enormous costs and require enormous resources. Even in such "conventional" items as transformers for power networks, the minimum economic size of a plant needed to produce the huge transformers to take advantage of the economies of scale is pushing producers into cooperation or mergers. Most European companies are incapable of producing the huge transformers needed for the continuously increasing voltage in the networks. This development has forced even such giants as Siemens and Telefunken to join forces in the heavy electrical engineering field. In the United States, five producers supply the entire market, while in Europe there are as many as thirty.

The scale and cost of the present advanced technology—outer space, particle accelerators for advanced nuclear research, supersonic transport, and nuclear weapons development—are of gigantic proportions, and they are imposing a heavy burden even on a country of America's wealth and resources. Future technologies will become even more demanding in this respect. The benefits from the nuclear agro-industrial complexes are expected to be important, but the economic scale of operation requires an investment of between half a billion and a billion dollars for each complex. Economies of scale are important in advanced technology of power generation.

Recent progress in controlled thermonuclear reaction led to anticipation that operational prototype reactors would be ready in the United States perhaps as early as the late 1970's.[14] While these reactors are expected to be relatively small (2,000 megawatts), commercial fusion reactors may have a capacity as large as 10,000 megawatts, and reactors of 20,000 megawatts are conceivable and would be even more economical.

---

[14] In a letter to the author dated May 21, 1969, Dr. Amasa S. Bishop, Assistant Director (for Controlled Thermonuclear Research), Division of Research, U.S. Atomic Energy Commission, stated that, according to an "optimistic" schedule, the operation of a prototype fusion reactor in the United States could begin in 1978. However, since the Soviet Union has a considerable lead in this area, the Soviets may build a prototype fusion reactor ahead of the United States. For the Soviet breakthrough in CTR, see "British Verify Russians' Strides Towards Taming H-Bomb Power," *New York Times,* October 31, 1969, p. 1.

A reactor of this size would have a generating capacity more than twice as large as that of Poland in 1967. MHD power is particularly responsive to economies of scale. If the expected progress in the technology of MHD power materializes, the economies of scale might push the size of generating plants even higher than the above figures suggest; furthermore, huge MHD plants are likely to become operational before commercial CTR becomes a reality.[15]

There are other technologies on the horizon which will require major initial outlays. Current projections anticipate the availability of nuclear-propelled surface-effect ships, perhaps as large as an aircraft carrier, in 1985–1990. These vessels, moving at a speed of 100 knots, would have both land and sea mobility. Since there will be no need to construct roads and dock facilities and since they will be highly automated, they are expected to be attractive commercially after the initial R & D costs are met.[16] Various schemes for large-scale climate modifications will demand immense expenditures. The present exploitation of ocean resources is limited to relatively shallow depths. To move to greater depths and to widen the scope of exploitable resources, the necessary exploration and research and development will require billions of dollars.

In a somewhat different category—but nonetheless real—are the costs generated by undesirable by-products of technological progress. The present highly advanced nations have been developing and applying science and technology with little or no need to how this activity might affect the environment in the future. The result has been badly polluted rivers, lakes and the air; ecological imbalances that annihilated, or threaten to annihilate, certain species, vegetation and other substances important to man's livelihood, health and the beauty of his environment; and direct hazards to human health and life through such phenomena as excessive chemicals in food and unsafe means of transportation. These characteristics of technological advance in the highly developed nations are no longer tolerable. It will require vast expenditures to compensate

---

[15] It should be pointed out that huge size in generating plants is not peculiar only to such advanced technologies as CTR, MHD or fast breeder reactors. The study by the Office of Science and Technology, Executive Office of the President, on "Considerations Affecting Steam Power Plant Site Selection" shows that 147 thermal generating plants for the year 1990 will have capacities of from 2,000 to 10,000 megawatts. (Quoted in Dr. Bishop's letter to the author, May 21, 1969, *op. cit.*) By comparison, the largest thermal plants at present have a capacity of about 1,000 megawatts, while plants of 500 megawatts are still considered to be huge.

[16] Small vehicles carrying about fifteen people, moving on a variant of the surface-effect principle (aircushion) and having both land and sea mobility, are currently operational. They use a gas turbine engine and can clear obstacles up to five feet. Three such vehicles have been used in Viet Nam. See "Monsters that Float on the Air," *Army*, June 1968, pp. 80–81.

for many years of neglect and to effect the necessary planning and re-adjustment for the future.

The foregoing discussion suggests at least three points. First, rising costs are such that even the superpowers will not be able individually to take advantage of the full potential of future technology. This factor will increasingly generate pressure for international cooperation in technological developments among the middle-rank powers, between the superpowers and the middle-rank powers—and perhaps between the superpowers themselves. Second, huge scales of effort will be needed to utilize advanced technology. This will put pressure on the middle-rank powers and smaller nations to cooperate in its utilization—a step that would involve restructuring institutions and the existing "technological superstructure"—or to forgo the advantages of the technology altogether. Third, some forms of future technology—such as large-scale climate modification—will require international cooperation not so much because of the costs involved but because more than one geographic region will be affected and the participation of those concerned will be essential. All three considerations have significant implications for functionalism either as an independent variable affecting the future world order or as an instrument of national policy for the attainment of specific objectives in international affairs.

THE RAPIDITY OF TECHNOLOGICAL CHANGE

The continuously accelerating growth of technological innovation and change constitutes another major trend. Over half of the products manufactured by American industry today did not exist twenty years ago. Only ten years ago it used to take from five to seven years for a chemical product to advance from the laboratory to the production stage; the process has now been shortened to from one to three years. When the Communications Satellite Corporation was established, it was viewed as an investment in a technology several years away; its operational capability and earnings potential proved to be much faster and greater than originally anticipated. Only a year ago it was expected that commercial use of controlled thermonuclear reaction would be available sometime after the year 2000; now nuclear scientists are thinking in terms of an operational prototype reactor in the late 1970's, which would make CTR economical perhaps in the late 1980's or the early 1990's.

The total body of currently existing science and technology is so large and so versatile that a particular socially significant impact need not depend on progress in one area of technology. It may come from an advance or a breakthrough in one area or another, or it may come from all of them at about the same time, in which case the impact is likely to be truly revolutionary. This can be illustrated by the case of future progress in reducing the cost of energy. It can be achieved by technological advance in the application of superconductivity; indeed, major progress in that area is currently taking place.[17] Cheap energy can be obtained through controlled thermonuclear reaction. Progress in the technology of MHD power would also result in lower costs of energy.[18] But

---

[17] Application of superconductivity to the reduction of the cost of power involves the use of superconductors (pure unstrained lead, tin, mercury, or the "non-ideal" superconductors like niobium and vanadium) at very low temperatures (absolute zero); this results in a complete, or nearly complete, elimination of resistance in the transmission of electric current through the metal. The area where progress has been slower—but promising—is the application of superconductivity to the transmission of power. Here electric current can be transmitted over large distances with no, or virtually no, loss, but the cost of refrigerating the lines still remains too high for commerical use at this time. Major strides, however, have been made in the application of superconductivity to the generation of power and motors. International Research and Development Company, Ltd., is building a 3,250-hp motor for the British government; it will be one-tenth the size of the conventional d.c. motor, will need much less power to run, and will cost roughly the same to build (not counting research and development). The economies of scale are important in the application of superconductivity to generation of power. The IR&D believes that an 8,000-hp motor would be 40 per cent cheaper to build than a conventional d.c. motor. The market in the application of superconductivity to transmission and generation of electric power is expected to be big business in the late 1970's. For recent developments in superconductivity, see "Tapping a Cool Idea for Power," *Business Week*, September 7, 1968, pp. 53–54. For a more fundamental discussion of the subject, see Richard McFee, "Application of Superconductivity to the Generation and Distribution of Electric Power," *Electrical Engineering*, February 1962, pp. 122–129.

[18] MHD power requires a brief explanation. In a conventional fossil fuel power generating station, for each input of thermal energy one gets only about 40 per cent of its energy equivalent in electric power; this is due to the loss in the conversion from thermal energy to mechanical energy and then to electric energy. The MHD principle employs superheated gases (about 4000° F.) which, when passed through a magnetic field, produce electric energy. The exhaust gases are further used to produce steam for conventional generation of electric power. When electric power from both sources is used, the total efficiency in early large MHD generators is expected to be increased to about 50 per cent, and to 60 per cent in advanced generators. Even a 50 per cent efficiency is a major improvement, since it represents about 25 per cent more electric power from a given amount of thermal energy. It has been estimated that potential savings to the U.S. consumer which appear possible with MHD will amount to billions of dollars by the end of the century.

In the present state of the art, relatively small MHD generators have been developed as an economical source for stand-by power, to operate in spurts for an hour or two. The expectation is that MHD power should be economically attractive on a large scale in about ten to fifteen years.

For a recent state-of-the-art discussion of MHD and projections into the future, see William D. Jackson, *et al.*, "Critique of MHD Power Generation," a paper presented at the Winter Annual Meeting of the American Society of Mechanical Engineers, November 16–20, 1969 (ASME publication, 69-WA/Pwr-12).

if significant advance is achieved in all of these, the cost of energy would be drastically reduced, since the three technologies are complementary and can be applied in a single power station. Quite apart from any major technological innovation that may take place in a particular field, synergistic effects involving innovations from various fields which reinforce each other provide a major dynamic force in modern technological change. . . .

THE GROWING IMPORTANCE OF NONMILITARY TECHNOLOGY FOR NATIONAL SECURITY

Still another trend in the technological impact has been a changing relationship between military and nonmilitary technologies with regard to their effect on national security, especially that of the superpowers. Nonmilitary technology is gaining in importance as an area of direct relevance to national security, mainly because its role in changing the distribution of world and regional power is growing faster than the role of military technology.

Historically, national power has been changed through both military and nonmilitary technology. Through wars and conquest, qualitative or quantitative gains in weapons could change the distribution of power much more swiftly and more dramatically. Hence, it was the military sector on which the nations' concern for security was focused. In the long run, however, nonmilitary technology accounted for at least as much change in the distribution of world power as military technology. In more recent times, the rise of states has been principally determined by the technologies that made it possible for them to become great industrial centers.[19] Military power usually followed in the wake of industrial capability.

The acquisition of nuclear weapons by the United States at the end of World War II was a revolutionary development that gave the United States vast superiority in military power over the rest of the world in the immediate postwar years. Politically, however, nuclear weapons have proven to be a "power-unrewarding" area. Their great destructiveness and the unwillingness to use them came to mean that even an overwhelming nuclear superiority had but limited transferability into political

---

[19] To illustrate: The initial industrial lead of Great Britain was undermined by the invention of the Bessemer process of steel production (1856) which, by allowing for mass production, made the United States the leading steel producer by the end of the nineteenth century. The Thomas-Gilchrist process (1879) enabled Germany to utilize the phosphoric iron ores of Alsace-Lorraine, thus making Germany the greatest European steel producer by 1893. Railroads were a major factor in the rise of the United States and Russia as great powers. Exploitation of hydroelectric power, chemical resources, telecommunications and cheap water transportation were important in Japan's rise to power before World War II.

power. The picture was further complicated by the progress of the Soviet Union in the development of nuclear technology, which accounted in large measure for the rise of Soviet power in the last two decades. However, after a certain point in weapons technology and the accumulation of "hardware" had been reached, the technological achievements of the two superpowers merely tended to neutralize each other, without any serious prospect for changing the distribution of world power.[20]

The acquisition of nuclear weapons by third states will not radically change the picture. If developed by responsible industrial powers (e.g., Japan) and accompanied by advanced means of delivery, they will have prestige value and will enhance the nation's military power to a point. But they will soon be absorbed and largely neutralized in the overall nuclear umbrella. If acquired by smaller states (e.g., Israel, Argentina), the weapons will temporarily change the regional distribution of power, but will eventually result in rudimentary regional nuclear umbrellas also characterized by mutual neutralization of power.

There are signs that, for political, technological and military reasons, the stalemate dominating nuclear affairs is beginning to spread into the conventional military sector as well. Concerned that a local conflict may escalate and trigger a nuclear war, the superpowers appear to be eager to restrict or smother it in an early stage, thus forestalling the stronger party from significantly changing the local balance of power through the force of arms (e.g., in the Middle East). The growing global projection of Soviet military power tends to deter potential American military action at various points of the globe; for example, the Soviet naval presence in the Mediterranean would make the U.S. government think twice before undertaking another Lebanon. The stalemate over Viet Nam suggests that substitution of technology for political solutions in limited conflict does not necessarily provide a solution. Viet Nam also indicates that modern conventional military technology, pitted against itself, has a tendency to manifest symptoms of a deadlock: American technology has been fighting not only the Vietnamese but also the products of Soviet and Chinese factories. Our aircraft, though superior, were practically stalemated by the effectiveness of the Soviet-built surface-to-air missile sites, assisted by anti-aircraft batteries.[21]

---

[20] For a good summary of what has come to be called "the nuclear umbrella," see The Washington Center of Foreign Policy Research, Johns Hopkins University, "Developments in Military Technology and Their Impact on United States Strategy and Foreign Policy," in U.S. Senate, Committee on Foreign Relations, *United States Foreign Policy* (Washington: GPO, 1961), pp. 718–730.

[21] See Anthony Verrier, "Strategic Bombing—the Lessons of World War II and the American Experience in Vietnam," *The Royal United Service Institution Journal*, May 1967, pp. 157–158.

Future technology is likely to reinforce the growing stalemate. Nearly instantaneous satellite surveillance will help the United States and the Soviet Union to be well and swiftly informed about the location of each other's forces, particularly at sea. Improving air and sea mobility will afford both sides the possibility of blocking each other's moves. If, as predicted by some sources, lasers are developed into operational weapons,[22] resort to warfare on the subnuclear umbrella level will be further discouraged. However, unlike the case of the nuclear umbrella, the subnuclear umbrella military level can only be partially stalemated; for a number of reasons, changes in the distribution of power on this level are still likely to take place.[23]

While the military sector is thus kept in check, there is no sign of a stalemate—either now or in the future—in the ability of nonmilitary technology to effect a change in world power distribution. To mention but a few examples: Computers can provide a major impetus to the growth of nation by facilitating economic planning and the investment and marketing strategy of corporations, thus providing differential advantage to the countries and regions leading in this field. Technological capability for the development of marine resources opens up new vistas in three quarters of the globe that is virtually unexplored, unexploited and unsettled, with concomitant geopolitical implications. Nations that succeed in reducing the costs of energy sooner than others will be able to gain important advantages in the world markets, and strengthen their industrial capability and leverages of influence in the less developed world. The capability for controlling hurricanes, for covertly removing moisture from the atmosphere over a foreign nation, or for interfering with the layer of ozone surrounding the earth (and thus subjecting the ground underneath to severe burns by ultraviolet rays of the sun) [24]—for all of which the technologies could be developed by the late 1980's, if not sooner—would provide a more direct and dramatic means of changing the power distribution. The internal impact of technology on society and the resultant social discontinuities, which we have discussed previously, may also have implications of consequence for national power.

---

[22] Lt. Col. Martin Blumenson, "The Incredible Laser," *Army*, April 1968, p. 35 ff.; Herman Kahn and Anthony J. Wiener, *The Year 2000* (New York: Macmillan, 1967), p. 51.

[23] The superpowers may not choose to stalemate each other (e.g., the USSR may let the United States defeat Red China in a localized conflict); or they may not succeed in restraining each other because of certain characteristics of the particular situation.

[24] For potential developments in weather modification and how they relate to national power, see Gordon J. F. McDonald, "How to Wreck the Environment," in Nigel Calder, editor, *Unless Peace Comes* (New York: Viking, 1968), pp. 187-191.

21. THE EMERGING "TECHNETRONIC" AGE

Zbigniew Brzezinski

O URS IS NO LONGER the conventional revolutionary era; we are entering a novel metamorphic phase in human history. The world is on the eve of a transformation more dramatic in its historic and human consequences than that wrought either by the French or the Bolshevik revolutions. Viewed from a long perspective, these famous revolutions merely scratched the surface of the human condition. The changes they precipitated involved alterations in the distribution of power and property within society; they did not affect the essence of individual and social existence. Life—personal and organised—continued much as before, even though some of its external forms (primarily political) are substantially altered. Shocking though it may sound to their acolytes, by the year 2000 it will be accepted that Robespierre and Lenin were mild reformers.

Unlike the revolutions of the past, the developing metamorphosis will have no charismatic leaders with strident doctrines, but its impact will be far more profound. Most of the change that has so far taken place in human history has been gradual—with the great "revolutions" being mere punctuation marks to a slow, eludible process. In contrast, the approaching transformation will come more rapidly and will have deeper consequences for the way and even perhaps for the meaning of human life than anything experienced by the generations that preceded us.

America is already beginning to experience these changes and in the course of so doing it is becoming a "technetronic" society: a society that is shaped culturally, psychologically, socially and economically by the impact of technology and electronics, particulary computers and communications. The industrial process no longer is the principal determinant of social change, altering the mores, the social structure, and the values of society. This change is separating the United States from the rest of the world, prompting a further fragmentation among an increasingly, differ-

From "America in the Technetronic Age," by Zbigniew Brzezinski, in *Encounter*, Vol. XXX, No. 1 (January, 1968), 16–26.

ZBIGNIEW BRZEZINSKI (1928–   ) Professor of Public Law and Government, Columbia University; Director, Research Institute of Communist Affairs. Author of *Between Two Ages: America's Role in the Technetronic Age* (New York: Viking Press, 1970); *Dilemmas of Change in Soviet Politics* (New York: Columbia University Press, 1969); *The Soviet Bloc: Unity and Conflict* (Cambridge: Harvard University Press, 1967); *Alternative to Partition: For a Broader Conception of America's Role in Europe* (New York: McGraw-Hill Book Company, 1965); *Political Power: USA/USSR* (New York: Viking Press, 1964).

entiated mankind, and imposing upon Americans a special obligation to ease the pains of the resulting confrontation.

THE TECHNETRONIC SOCIETY

The far-reaching innovations we are about to experience will be the result primarily of the impact of science and technology on man and his society, especially in the developed world. Recent years have seen a proliferation of exciting and challenging literature on the future. Much of it is serious, and not mere science-fiction.[1] Moreover, both in the United States and, to a lesser degree, in Western Europe a number of systematic, scholarly efforts have been designed to project, predict, and possess what the future holds for us. Curiously, very little has been heard on this theme from the Communist World, even though Communist doctrinarians are the first to claim their 19th-century ideology holds a special pass-key to the 21st century.

The work in progress indicates that men living in the developed world will undergo during the next several decades a mutation potentially as basic as that experienced through the slow process of evolution from animal to human experience. The difference, however, is that the process will be telescoped in time—and hence the shock effect of the change may be quite profound. Human conduct will become less spontaneous and less mysterious—more predetermined and subject to deliberate "programming." Man will increasingly possess the capacity to determine the sex of his children, to affect through drugs the extent of their intelligence and to modify and control their personalities. The human brain will acquire expanded powers, with computers becoming as routine an extension of man's reasoning as automobiles have been of man's mobility. The human body will be improved and its durability extended: some estimate that during the next century the average life-span could reach approximately 120 years.

These developments will have major social impact. The prolongation of life will alter our values, our career patterns, and our social relationships. New forms of social control may be needed to limit the indiscriminate exercise by individuals of their new powers. The possibility of extensive chemical mind-control, the danger of loss of individuality inherent in extensive transplantation, and the feasibility of manipulation of the genetic structure will call for a social definition of common criteria

---

[1] Perhaps the most useful single source is to be found in the Summer 1967 issue of *Daedalus*, devoted entirely to *"Toward the Year 2000: Work in Progress."* The introduction by Professor Daniel Bell, chairman of the American Academy's Commission on the Year 2000 (of which the present writer is also a member) summarises some of the principal literature on the subject.

of restraint as well as of utilisation. Scientists predict with some confidence that by the end of this century, computers will reason as well as man, and will be able to engage in "creative" thought; wedded to robots or to "laboratory beings," they could act like humans. The makings of a most complex—and perhaps bitter—philosophical and political dialogue about the nature of man are self-evident in these developments.

Other discoveries and refinements will further alter society as we now know it. The information revolution, including extensive information storage, instant retrieval, and eventually pushbutton visual and sound availability of needed data in almost any private home, will transform the character of institutionalised collective education. The same techniques could serve to impose well-nigh total political surveillance on every citizen, putting into much sharper relief than is the case today the question of privacy. Cybernetics and automation will revolutionise working habits, with leisure becoming the practice and active work the exception—and a privilege reserved for the most talented. The achievement-oriented society might give way to the amusement-focused society, with essentially spectator spectacles (mass sports, TV) providing an opiate for increasingly purposeless masses.

But while for the masses life will grow longer and time will seem to expand, for the activist élite time will become a rare commodity. Indeed, even the élite's sense of time will alter. Already now speed dictates the pace of our lives—instead of the other way around. As the speed of transportation increases, largely by its own technological momentum, man discovers that he has no choice but to avail himself of that acceleration, either to keep up with others or because he thinks he can thus accomplish more. This will be especially true of the élite, for whom an expansion in leisure time does not seem to be in the cards. Thus as speed expands, time contracts—and the pressures on the élite increase.

By the end of this century the citizens of the more developed countries will live predominantly in cities—hence almost surrounded by man-made environment. Confronting nature could be to them what facing the elements was to our forefathers: meeting the unknown and not necessarily liking it. Enjoying a personal standard of living that (in some countries) may reach almost $10,000 per head, eating artificial food, speedily commuting from one corner of the country to work in another, in continual visual contact with their employer, government, or family, consulting their annual calendars to establish on which day it will rain or shine, our descendants will be shaped almost entirely by what they themselves create and control.

But even short of these far-reaching changes, the transformation that is now taking place is already creating a society increasingly unlike its industrial predecessor.[2] In the industrial society, technical knowledge was applied primarily to one specific end: the acceleration and improvement of production techniques. Social consequences were a later by-product of this paramount concern. In the technetronic society, scientific and technological knowledge, in addition to enhancing productive capabilities, quickly spills over to affect directly almost all aspects of life.

This is particularly evident in the case of the impact of communications and computers. Communications create an extraordinarily interwoven society, in continuous visual, audial, and increasingly close contact among almost all its members—electronically interacting, sharing instantly most intense social experiences, prompting far greater personal involvement, with their consciousnesses shaped in a sporadic manner fundamentally different (as McLuhan has noted) from the literate (or pamphleteering) mode of transmitting information, characteristic of the industrial age. The growing capacity for calculating instantly most complex interactions and the increasing availability of bio-chemical means of human control increase the potential scope of self-conscious direction, and thereby also the pressures to direct, to choose, and to change.

The consequence is a society that differs from the industrial one in a variety of economic, political and social aspects. The following examples may be briefly cited to summarise some of the contrasts:

1. In an industrial society, the mode of production shifts from agriculture to industry, with the use of muscle and animals supplanted by machine-operation. In the technetronic society, industrial employment yields to services, with automation and cybernetics replacing individual operation of machines.

2. Problems of employment and unemployment—not to speak of the earlier stage of the urban socialisation of the post-rural labour force —dominate the relationship between employers, labour, and the market in the industrial society; assuring minimum welfare to the new industrial masses is a source of major concern. In the emerging new society, questions relating to skill-obsolescence, security, vacations, leisure, and profit-sharing dominate the relationship; the matter of psychic well-being of millions of relatively secure but potentially aimless lower-middle class blue collar workers becomes a growing problem.

3. Breaking down traditional barriers to education, thus creating the basic point of departure for social advancement, is a major goal of social reformers in the industrial society. Education, available for limited and

---

[2] See Daniel Bell's pioneering "Notes on the Post-Industrial Society," *The Public Interest,* Nos. 6 and 7, 1967.

specific periods of time, is initially concerned with overcoming illiteracy, and subsequently with technical training, largely based on written, sequential reasonings. In the technetronic society, not only has education become universal but advanced training is available to almost all who have the basic talents. Quantity-training is reinforced by far greater emphasis on quality-selection. The basic problem is to discover the most effective techniques for the rational exploitation of social talent. Latest communication and calculating techniques are applied to that end. The educational process, relying much more on visual and audial devices, becomes extended in time, while the flow of new knowledge necessitates more and more frequent refresher studies.

4. In the industrial society social leadership shifts from the traditional rural-aristocratic to an urban "plutocratic" élite. Newly acquired wealth is its foundation, and intense competition the outlet—as well as the stimulus—for its energy. In the post-industrial technetronic society plutocratic pre-eminence comes under a sustained challenge from the political leadership which itself is increasingly permeated by individuals possessing special skills and intellectual talents. Knowledge becomes a tool of power, and the effective mobilisation of talent an important way for acquiring power.

5. The university in an industrial society—rather in contrast to the medieval times—is an aloof ivory-tower, the repository of irrelevant, even if respected wisdom, and, for only a brief time, the watering fountain for budding members of the established social élite. In the technetronic society, the university becomes an intensely involved *think-tank*, the source of much sustained political planning and social innovation.

6. The turmoil inherent in the shift from the rigidly traditional rural to urban existence engenders an inclination to seek total answers to social dilemmas, thus causing ideologies to thrive in the industrial society.[3] In the technetronic society, increasing ability to reduce social conflicts to quantifiable and measurable dimensions reinforces the trend towards a more pragmatic problem-solving approach to social issues.

7. The activisation of hitherto passive masses makes for intense political conflicts in the industrial society over such matters as disenfranchisement and the right to vote. The issue of political participation is a crucial one. In the technetronic age, the question increasingly is one of ensuring real participation in decisions that seem too complex and too far-removed from the average citizen. Political alienation becomes a problem. Similarly, the issue of political equality of the sexes gives way to a struggle

---

[3] The American exception to this rule was due to the absence of the feudal tradition, a point well developed by Louis Hartz in his work *The Liberal Tradition in America* (1955).

for the sexual equality of women. In the industrial society, woman—the operator of machines—ceases to be physically inferior to the male, a consideration of some importance in rural life, and she begins to demand her political rights. In the emerging society, automation discriminates equally against males and females; intellectual talent is computable; the pill encourages sexual equality.

8. The newly enfranchised masses are coordinated in the industrial society through trade unions and political parties, and integrated by relatively simple and somewhat ideological programmes. Moreover, political attitudes are influenced by appeals to nationalist sentiments, communicated through the massive growth of newspapers, relying, naturally, on native tongues. In the technetronic society, the trend would seem to be towards the aggregation of the individual support of millions of uncoordinated citizens, easily within the reach of magnetic and attractive personalities effectively exploiting the latest communication techniques to manipulate emotions and control reason. Reliance on TV—and hence the tendency to replace language with imagery, with the latter unlimited by national confines (and also including coverage for such matters as hunger in India or war scenes)—tends to create a somewhat more cosmopolitan, though highly impressionistic, involvement in global affairs.

9. Economic power in the industrial society tends to be personalised, either in the shape of great *entrepreneurs* like Henry Ford or bureaucratic industrialisers like Kaganovich in Russia, or Minc in Poland. The tendency towards de-personalisation of economic power is stimulated in the next stage by the appearance of a highly complex interdependence between governmental institutions (including the military), scientific establishments, and industrial organisations. As economic power becomes inseparably linked with political power, it becomes more invisible and the sense of individual futility increases.

10. Relaxation and escapism in the industrial society, in its more intense forms, is a carry-over from the rural drinking bout, in which intimate friends and family would join. Bars and saloons—or fraternities—strive to recreate the atmophere of intimacy. In the technetronic society social life tends to be so atomised, even though communications (especially TV) make for unprecedented immediacy of social experience, that group intimacy cannot be recreated through the artificial stimulation of externally convivial group behaviour. The new interest in drugs seeks to create intimacy through introspection, allegedly by expanding consciousness.

Eventually, these changes and many others, including the ones that affect much more directly the personality and quality of the human being itself, will make the technetronic society as different from the industrial as the industrial became from the agrarian.

THE AMERICAN TRANSITION

America is today in the midst of a transition. U.S. society is leaving the phase of spontaneity and is entering a more self-conscious stage; ceasing to be an industrial society, it is becoming the first technetronic one. This is at least in part the cause for much of the current tensions and violence.

Spontaneity made for an almost automatic optimism about the future, about the "American miracle," about justice and happiness for all. This myth prompted social blinders to the various aspects of American life that did not fit the optimistic mould, particularly the treatment of the Negro and the persistence of pockets of deprivation. Spontaneity involved a faith in the inherent goodness of the American socio-economic dynamic: as America developed, grew, became richer, problems that persisted or appeared would be solved.

This phase is ending. Today, American society is troubled and some parts of it are even tormented. The social blinders are being ripped off— and a sense of inadequacy is becoming more widespread. The spread of literacy, and particularly the access to college and universities of about 40% of the youth, has created a new stratum—one which reinforces the formerly isolated urban intellectuals—a stratum not willing to tolerate either social blinders nor sharing the complacent belief in the spontaneous goodness of American social change.

Yet it is easier to know what is wrong than to indicate what ought to be done. The difficulty is not only revealed by the inability of the new social rebels to develop a concrete and meaningful programme. It is magnified by the novelty of America's problem. Turning to 19th-century ideologies is not the answer—and it is symptomatic that the "New Left" has found it most difficult to apply the available, particularly Marxist, doctrines to the new reality. Indeed, its emphasis on human rights, the evils of depersonalisation, the dangers inherent in big government—so responsive to the felt psychological needs—contain strong parallels to more conservative notions about the place and sanctity of the individual in society.

In some ways, there is an analogy here between the "New Left" and the searching attitude of various disaffected groups in early 19th-century Europe, reacting to the first strains of the industrial age. Not fully comprehending its meaning, not quite certain where it was heading—yet sensitive to the miseries and opportunities it was bringing—many Europeans strove desperately to adapt earlier, 18th-century doctrines to the new reality. It was finally Marx who achieved what appeared to many millions a meaningful synthesis, combining utopian idealism about the future of the industrial age with a scorching critique of its present.

The search for meaning is characteristic of the present American scene. It could portend most divisive and bitter ideological conflicts—especially as intellectual disaffection becomes linked with the increasing bitterness of the deprived Negro masses. If carried to its extreme, this could bring to America a phase of violent, intolerant, and destructive civil strife, combining ideological and racial intolerance.

However, it seems unlikely that a unifying ideology of political action, capable of mobilising large-scale loyalty, can emerge in the manner that Marxism arose in response to the industrial era. Unlike even Western Europe or Japan—not to speak of Soviet Russia—where the consequences and the impact of the industrial process are still re-shaping political, social, and economic life, in America science and technology (particularly as socially applied through communications and increasing computarisation, both offsprings of the industrial age) are already more important in influencing the social behaviour of a society that has moved past its industrial phase. Science and technology are notoriously unsympathetic to simple, absolute formulas. In the technetronic society there may be room for pragmatic, even impatient, idealism, but hardly for doctrinal utopianism.

At the same time, it is already evident that a resolution of some of the unfinished business of the industrial era will be rendered more acute. For example, the Negro should have been integrated into U.S. society *during* the American industrial revolution. Yet that revolution came before America, even if not the Negro, was ready for full integration. If the Negro had been only an economic legacy of the pre-industrial age, perhaps he could have integrated more effectively. Today, the more advanced urban-industrial regions of America, precisely because they are moving into a new and more complex phase, requiring even more developed social skills, are finding it very difficult to integrate the Negro, both a racial minority and America's only "feudal legacy." Paradoxically, it can be argued that the American South today stands a better long-range chance of fully integrating the Negro: American consciousness is changing, the Negro has stirred, and the South is beginning to move into the industrial age. The odds are that it may take the Negro along with it.

Whatever the outcome, American society is the one in which the great questions of our time will be first tested through practice. Can the individual and science co-exist, or will the dynamic momentum of the latter fundamentally alter the former? Can man, living in the scientific age, grow in intellectual depth and philosophical meaning, and thus in his personal liberty too? Can the institutions of political democracy be adapted to the new conditions sufficiently quickly to meet the crises, yet without debasing their democratic character?

The challenge in its essence involves the twin-dangers of fragmentation and excessive control. A few examples. Symptoms of alienation and depersonalisation are already easy to find in American society. Many Americans feel "less free"; this feeling seems to be connected with their loss of "purpose"; freedom implies choice of action, and action requires an awareness of goals. If the present transition of America to the tech-netronic age achieves no personally satisfying fruits, the next phase may be one of sullen withdrawal from social and political involvement, a flight from social and political responsibility through "inner-emigration." Political frustration could increase the difficulty of absorbing and in-ternalising rapid environmental changes, thereby prompting increasing psychic instability.

At the same time, the capacity to assert social and political control over the individual will vastly increase. As I have already noted, it will soon be possible to assert almost continuous surveillance over every citizen and to maintain up-to-date, complete files, containing even most personal information about the health or personal behaviour of the citizen, in addition to more customary data. These files will be subject to instantaneous retrieval by the authorities.

Moreover, the rapid pace of change will put a premium on anticipating events and planning for them. Power will gravitate into the hands of those who control the information, and can correlate it most rapidly. Our existing *post*-crisis management institutions will probably be increas-ingly supplanted by *pre*-crisis management institutions, the task of which will be to identify in advance likely social crises and to develop pro-grammes to cope with them. This could encourage tendencies during the next several decades towards a technocratic dictatorship, leaving less and less room for political procedures as we now know them.

Finally, looking ahead to the end of this century, the possibility of bio-chemical mind-control and genetic tinkering with man, including eventually the creation of beings that will function like men—and reason like them as well—could give rise to the most difficult questions. Accord-ing to what criteria can such controls be applied? What is the distribution of power between the individual and society with regard to means that can altogether alter man? What is the social and political status of artificial beings, if they begin to approach man in their performance and creative capacities? (One dares not ask, what if they begin to "outstrip man"—something not beyond the pale of possibility during the next century?)

Yet it would be highly misleading to construct a one-sided picture, a new Orwellian piece of science-fiction. Many of the changes transforming

American society augur well for the future and allow at least some optimism about this society's capacity to adapt to the requirements of the metamorphic age.

Thus, in the political sphere, the increased flow of information and more efficient techniques of co-ordination need not necessarily prompt greater concentration of power within some ominous control agency located at the governmental apex. Paradoxically, these developments also make possible greater devolution of authority and responsibility to the lower levels of government and society. The division of power has traditionally posed the problems of inefficiency, co-ordination, and dispersal of authority; but today the new communications and computer techniques make possible both increased authority at the lower levels and almost instant national co-ordination. It is very likely that state and local government will be strengthened in the next ten years, and many functions currently the responsibility of the Federal government will be assumed by them.[4]

The devolution of financial responsibility to lower echelons may encourage both the flow of better talent and greater local participation in more important local decision-making. National co-ordination and local participation could thus be wedded by the new systems of co-ordination. This has already been tried successfully by some large businesses. This development would also have the desirable effect of undermining the appeal of any new integrating ideologies that may arise; for ideologies thrive only as long as there is an acute need for abstract responses to large and remote problems.

It is also a hopeful sign that improved governmental performance, and its increased sensitivity to social needs is being stimulated by the growing involvement in national affairs of what Kenneth Boulding has called the Educational and Scientific Establishment (EASE). The university at one time, during the Middle Ages, was a key social institution. Political leaders leaned heavily on it for literate confidants and privy counsellors, a rare commodity in those days. Later divorced from reality, academia in recent years has made a grand re-entry into the world of action.

Today, the university is the creative eye of the massive communications complex, the source of much strategic planning, domestic and international. Its engagement in the world is encouraging the appearance of a new breed of politicians-intellectuals, men who make it a point to mobilise and draw on the most expert, scientific and academic advice in

---

[4] It is noteworthy that the U.S. Army has so developed its control-systems that it is not uncommon for sergeants to call in and co-ordinate massive air-strikes and artillery fire—a responsibility of colonels during World War II.

the development of their political programmes. This, in turn, stimulates public awareness of the value of expertise—and, again in turn, greater political competition in exploiting it.

A profound change in the intellectual community itself is inherent in this development. The largely humanist-oriented, occasionally ideologically-minded intellectual-dissenter, who saw his role largely in terms of proffering social critiques, is rapidly being displaced either by experts and specialists, who become involved in special governmental undertakings, or by the generalists-integrators, who become in effect house-ideologues for those in power, providing overall intellectual integration for disparate actions. A community of organisation-oriented, application-minded intellectuals, relating itself more effectively to the political system than their predecessors, serves to introduce into the political system concerns broader than those likely to be generated by that system itself and perhaps more relevant than those articulated by outside critics.[5]

The expansion of knowledge, and the entry into socio-political life of the intellectual community, has the further effect of making education an almost continuous process. By 1980, not only will approximately two-thirds of U.S. urban dwellers be college-trained, but it is almost certain that systematic "élite-retraining" will be standard in the political system. It will be normal for every high official both to be engaged in almost continuous absorption of new techniques and knowledge, and to take periodic retraining. The adoption of compulsory elementary education was a revolution brought on by the industrial age. In the new technetronic society, it will be equally necessary to require everyone at a sufficiently responsible post to take, say, two years of retraining every ten years. (Perhaps there will even be a constitutional amendment, requiring a President-elect to spend at least a year getting himself educationally up-to-date.) Otherwise, it will not be possible either to keep up with, or absorb, the new knowledge.

Given diverse needs, it is likely that the educational system will undergo a fundamental change in structure. Television-computer consoles, capable of bringing most advanced education to the home, will permit extensive and continuous adult re-education. On the more advanced levels, it is likely that government agencies and corporations will develop

---

[5] However, there is a danger in all this that ought not to be neglected. Intense involvement in applied knowledge could gradually prompt a waning of the tradition of learning for the sake of learning. The intellectual community, including the university, could become another "industry," meeting social needs as the market dictates, with the intellectuals reaching for the highest material and political rewards. Concern with power, prestige, and the good life could mean an end to the aristocratic ideal of intellectual detachment and the disinterested search for truth.

—and some have already begun to do so—their own advanced educational systems, shaped to their special needs. As education becomes both a continuum, and even more application-oriented, its organisational framework will be re-designed to tie it directly to social and political action.

It is quite possible that a society increasingly geared to learning will be able to absorb more resiliently the expected changes in social and individual life. Mechanisation of labour and the introduction of robots will reduce the chores that keep millions busy doing things that they dislike doing. The increasing GNP (which could reach approximately $10,000 per capita per year), linked with educational advance, could prompt among those less involved in social management and less interested in scientific development a wave of interest in the cultural and humanistic aspects of life, in addition to purely hedonistic preoccupations. But even the latter would serve as a social valve, reducing tensions and political frustration. Greater control over external environment could make for easier, less uncertain existence.

But the key to successful adaptation to the new conditions is in the effective selection, distribution and utilisation of social talent. If the industrial society can be said to have developed through a struggle for survival of the fittest, the technetronic society—in order to prosper—requires the effective mobilisation of the ablest. Objective and systematic criteria for the selection of those with the greatest gifts will have to be developed, and the maximum opportunity for their training and advancement provided. The new society will require enormous talents—as well as a measure of philosophical wisdom—to manage and integrate effectively the expected changes. Otherwise, the dynamic of change could chaotically dictate the patterns of social change.

Fortunately, American society is becoming more conscious not only of the principle of equal opportunity for all but of special opportunity for the singularly talented few. Never truly an aristocratic state (except for some pockets such as the South and New England), never really subject to ideological or charismatic leadership, gradually ceasing to be a plutocratic-oligarchic society, the U.S.A. is becoming something which may be labelled the "meritocratic democracy." It combines continued respect for the popular will with an increasing role in the key decision-making institutions of individuals with special intellectual and scientific attainments. The educational and social systems are making it increasingly attractive and easy for those meritocratic few to develop to the fullest their special potential. The recruitment and advancement of social talent is yet to extend to the poorest and the most underprivileged, but that too is coming. No one can tell whether this will suffice to meet the unfolding challenge, but the increasingly cultivated and programmed American society, led by a meritocratic democracy, may stand a better chance.

THE TRAUMA OF CONFRONTATION

For the world at large, the appearance of the new technetronic society could have the paradoxical effect of creating more distinct worlds on a planet that is continuously shrinking because of the communications revolution. While the scientific-technological change will inevitably have some spill-over, not only will the gap between the developed and the underdeveloped worlds probably become wider—especially in the more measurable terms of economic indices—but a *new one* may be developing *within* the industrialised and urban world.

The fact is that America, having left the industrial phase, is today entering a distinct historical era: and one different from that of Western Europe and Japan. This is prompting subtle and still indefinable changes in the American psyche, providing the psycho-cultural bases for the more evident political disagreements between the two sides of the Atlantic. To be sure, there are pockets of innovation or retardation on both sides. Sweden shares with America the problems of leisure, psychic well-being, purposelessness; while Mississippi is experiencing the confrontation with the industrial age in a way not unlike some parts of South-Western Europe. But I believe the broad generalisation still holds true: Europe and America are no longer in the same historical era.

What makes America unique in our time is that it is the first society to experience the future. The confrontation with the new—which will soon include much of what I have outlined—is part of the daily American experience. For better or for worse, the rest of the world learns what is in store for it by observing what happens in the U.S.A.: in the latest scientific discoveries in space, in medicine, or the electric toothbrush in the bathroom; in pop art or LSD, air conditioning or air pollution, old-age problems or juvenile delinquency. The evidence is more elusive in such matters as music, style, values, social mores; but there, too, the term "Americanisation" obviously defines the source. Today, America is *the* creative society; the others, consciously and unconsciously, are emulative.

American scientific leadership is particularly strong in the so-called "frontier" industries, involving the most advanced fields of science. It has been estimated that approximately 80% of all scientific and technical discoveries made during the last few decades originated in the United States. About 75% of the world's computers operate in the United States; the American lead in lasers is even more marked; examples of American scientific lead are abundant.

There is reason to assume that this leadership will continue. America has four times as many scientists and research workers as the countries of the European Economic Community combined; three-and-a-half times as many as the Soviet Union. The brain-drain is almost entirely one-way. The United States is also spending more on research: seven times as much as the E.E.C. countries, three-and-a-half times as much as the Soviet Union. Given the fact that scientific development is a dynamic process, it is likely that the gap will widen.[6]

On the social level, American innovation is most strikingly seen in the manner in which the new meritocratic élite is taking over American life, utilising the universities, exploiting the latest techniques of communications, harnessing as rapidly as possible the most recent technological devices. Technetronics dominate American life, but so far nobody else's. This is bound to have social and political—and therefore also psychological—consequences, stimulating a psycho-cultural gap in the developed world.

At the same time, the backward regions of the world are becoming more, rather than less, poor in relation to the developed world. It can be roughly estimated that the per capita income of the underdeveloped world is approximately ten times lower than [that] of America and Europe (and twenty-five times of America itself). By the end of the century, the ratio may be about fifteen-to-one (or possibly thirty-to-one in the case of the U.S.), with the backward nations *at best* approaching the present standard of the very poor European nations but in many cases (*e.g.*, India) probably not even attaining that modest level.

The social élites of these regions, however, will quite naturally tend to assimilate and emulate, as much as their means and power permit, the life-styles of the most advanced world, with which they are, and increasingly will be, in close vicarious contact through global television, movies, travel, education, and international magazines. The international gap will thus have a domestic reflection, with the masses, given the availability even in most backward regions of transistorised radios (and soon television), becoming more and more intensely aware of their deprivation.

It is difficult to conceive how in that context democratic institutions (derived largely from Western experience—but typical only of the more stable and wealthy Western nations) will endure in a country like India, or develop elsewhere. The foreseeable future is more likely to see a turn towards personal dictatorships and some unifying doctrines, in the hope that the combination of the two may preserve the minimum stability

---

[6] In the Soviet case, rigid compartmentalisation between secret military research and industrial research has had a particularly sterile effect of inhibiting spill-over from weapons research into industrial application.

necessary for social-economic development. The problem, however, is that whereas in the past ideologies of change gravitated from the developed world to the less, in a way stimulating imitation of the developed world (as was the case with Communism), today the differences between the two worlds are so pronounced that it is difficult to conceive a new ideological wave originating from the developed. world, where the tradition of utopian thinking is generally declining.

With the widening gap dooming any hope of imitation, the more likely development is an ideology of rejection of the developed world. Racial hatred could provide the necessary emotional force, exploited by xenophobic and romantic leaders. The writings of Frantz Fanon—violent and racist—are a good example. Such ideologies of rejection, combining racialism with nationalism, would further reduce the chances of meaningful regional co-operation, so essential if technology and science are to be effectively applied. They would certainly widen the existing psychological and emotional gaps. Indeed, one might ask at that point: who is the truer repository of that indefinable quality we call human? The technologically dominant and conditioned technetron, increasingly trained to adjust to leisure, or the more "natural" and backward agrarian, more and more dominated by racial passions and continuously exhorted to work harder, even as his goal of the good life becomes more elusive?

The result could be a modern version on a global scale of the old rural-urban dichotomy. In the past, the strains produced by the shift from an essentially agricultural economy to a more urban one contributed much of the impetus for revolutionary violence.[7] Applied on a global scale, this division could give substance to Lin Piao's bold thesis that:

> Taking the entire globe, if North America and Western Europe can be called "the cities of the world," then Asia, Africa and Latin America constitute "the rural areas of the world." . . . In a sense, the contemporary world revolution also presents a picture of the encirclement of cities by the rural areas.

In any case, even without envisaging such a dichotomic confrontation, it is fair to say that the underdeveloped regions will be facing increasingly grave problems of political stability and social survival. Indeed (to use a capsule formula), in the developed world, the nature of man as man is threatened; in the underdeveloped, society is. The interaction of the two could produce chaos.

To be sure, the most advanced states will possess ever more deadly means of destruction, possibly even capable of nullifying the consequences

---

[7] See Barrington Moore's documentation of this in his pioneering study *Social Origins of Dictatorship and Democracy* (1967).

of the nuclear proliferation that appears increasingly inevitable. Chemical and biological weapons, death rays, neutron bombs, nerve gases, and a host of other devices, possessed in all their sophisticated variety (as seems likely) only by the two super-states, may impose on the world a measure of stability. Nonetheless, it seems unlikely, given the rivalry between the two principal powers, that a fool-proof system against international violence can be established. Some local wars between the weaker, nationalistically more aroused, poorer nations may occasionally erupt—resulting perhaps even in the total nuclear extinction of one or several smaller nations?—before greater international control is imposed in the wake of the universal moral shock thereby generated.

The underlying problem, however, will be to find a way of avoiding somehow the widening of the cultural and psycho-social gap inherent in the growing differentiation of the world. Even with gradual differentiation throughout human history, it was not until the industrial revolution that sharp differences between societies began to appear. Today, some nations still live in conditions not unlike pre-Christian times; many no different than in the medieval age. Yet soon a few will live in ways so new that it is now difficult to imagine their social and individual ramifications. If the developed world takes a leap—as seems inescapably the case—into a reality that is even more different from ours today than ours is from an Indian village, the gap and its accompanying strains will not narrow.

On the contrary, the instantaneous electronic intermeshing of mankind will make for an intense confrontation, straining social and international peace. In the past, differences were "livable" because of time and distance that separated them. Today, these differences are actually widening while technetronics are eliminating the two insulants of time and distance. The resulting trauma could create almost entirely different perspectives on life, with insecurity, envy, and hostility becoming the dominant emotions for increasingly large numbers of people. A three-way split into rural backward, urban-industrial, and technetronic ways of life can only further divide man, intensify the existing difficulties to global understanding, and give added vitality to latent or existing conflicts.

The pace of American development both widens the split within mankind and contains the seeds for a constructive response. However, neither military power nor material wealth, both of which America possesses in abundance, can be used directly in responding to the onrushing division in man's thinking, norms, and character. Power, at best, can assure only a relatively stable external environment: the tempering or containing of the potential global civil war; wealth can grease points of socio-economic friction, thereby facilitating development. But as man—especially in the most advanced societies—moves increasingly into the phase of controlling and even creating his environment, increasing attention will have to be given to giving man meaningful content—to improving the quality of life for man *as man*.

Man has never really tried to use science in the realm of his value systems. Ethical thinking is hard to change, but history demonstrates that it does change. . . . Man does, in limited ways, direct his very important and much more rapid psycho-social education. The evolution of such things as automobiles, airplanes, weapons, legal institutions, corporations, universities, and democratic governments are examples of progressive evolution in the course of time. We have, however, never really tried deliberately to create a better society for man *qua* man. . . .[8]

The urgent need to do just that may compel America to redefine its global posture. During the remainder of this century, given the perspective on the future I have outlined here, America is likely to become less concerned with "fighting communism" or creating "a world safe for diversity" than with helping to develop a common response with the rest of mankind to the implications of a truly new era. This will mean making the massive diffusion of scientific-technological knowledge a principal focus of American involvement in world affairs.

To some extent, the U.S. performs that role already—simply by being what it is. The impact of its reality and its global involvement prompts emulation. The emergence of vast international corporations, mostly originating in the United States, makes for easier transfer of skills, management techniques, marketing procedures, and scientific-technological innovations. The appearance of these corporations in the European market has done much to stimulate Europeans to consider more urgently the need to integrate their resources and to accelerate the pace of their own research and development.

Similarly, returning graduates from American universities have prompted an organisational and intellectual revolution in the academic life of their countries. Changes in the academic life of Britain, Germany, Japan, more recently France, and (to even a greater extent) in the less developed countries, can be traced to the influence of U.S. educational institutions. Indeed, the leading technological institute in Turkey conducts its lectures in "American" and is deliberately imitating, not only in approach but in student-professor relationships, U.S. patterns. Given developments in modern communications, is it not only a matter of time

---

[8] Hudson Hoagland, "Biology, Brains, and Insight," *Columbia University Forum*, Summer 1967.

before students at Columbia University and, say, the University of Teheran will be watching, *simultaneously*, the same lecturer?

The appearance of a universal intellectual élite, one that shares certain common values and aspirations, will somewhat compensate for the widening differentiation among men and societies. But it will not resolve the problem posed by that differentiation. In many backward nations tension between what is and what can be will be intensified. Moreover, as Kenneth Boulding observed:

> The network of electronic communication is inevitably producing a world super-culture, and the relations between this super-culture and the more traditional national and regional cultures of the past remains the great question mark of the next fifty years.[9]

That "super culture," strongly influenced by American life, with its own universal electronic-computer language, will find it difficult to relate itself to "the more traditional and regional cultures," especially if the basic gap continues to widen.

To cope with that gap, a gradual change in diplomatic style and emphasis may have to follow the redefined emphasis of America's involvement in world affairs. Professional diplomacy will have to yield to intellectual leadership. With government negotiating directly—or quickly dispatching the negotiators—there will be less need for ambassadors who are resident diplomats and more for ambassadors who are capable of serving as creative interpreters of the new age, willing to engage in a meaningful dialogue with the host intellectual community and concerned with promoting the widest possible dissemination of available knowledge. Theirs will be the task to stimulate and to develop scientific-technological programmes of co-operation.

International co-operation will be necessary in almost every facet of life: to reform and to develop more modern educational systems, to promote new sources of food supply, to accelerate economic development, to stimulate technological growth, to control climate, to disseminate new medical knowledge. However, because the new élites have a vested interest in their new nation-states and because of the growing xenophobia among the masses in the third world, the nation-state will remain for a long time the primary focus of loyalty, especially for newly liberated and economically backward peoples. To predict loudly its death, and to act often as if it were dead, could prompt (as it did partially in Europe) an adverse reaction from those whom one would wish to influence. Hence,

---

[9] Kenneth Boulding, "Expecting the Unexpected," *Prospective Changes in Society by 1980* (1960).

regionalism will have to be promoted with due deference to the symbolic meaning of national sovereignty—and preferably also by encouraging those concerned themselves to advocate regional approaches.

Even more important will be the stimulation, for the first time in history on a global scale, of the much needed dialogue on what it is about man's life that we wish to safeguard or to promote, and on the relevance of existing moral systems to an age that cannot be fitted into the narrow confines of fading doctrines. The search for new directions—going beyond the tangibles of economic development—could be an appropriate subject for a special world congress, devoted to the technetronic and philosophical problems of the coming age. To these issues no one society, however advanced, is in a position to provide an answer.

Part V

Economics and the International System

E CONOMIC FACTORS play a major role in international relations.
Trade and investment among nations, the negotiation of tariffs
and commercial arrangements, the creation of international liquid-
ity to insure adequate financial resources for trade, the balance of
payments problems of nations, the use of economic sanctions and
foreign aid as instruments of foreign policy represent some of these
economic factors. The perceived need to facilitate the international
movement of goods and services has contributed decisively to the
formation of economic unions, especially in Western Europe, over
the past generation. Economic factors have formed the basis for
theories of integration at the international level, drawing notably
on the experience of the European Coal and Steel Community and
the European Economic Community. Moreover, some writers have
considered economic factors a major determinant of international
conflict, while others have cautioned against an undue emphasis on
economics in the study of warlike behavior. Whatever the precise
link between economic factors and conflict, there can be little doubt
of the importance of economics to the study of international relations.

There is a close relationship between economic factors and the
technological revolution examined in Part IV. It is technology
which determines the level of economic capabilities available to a
nation. Economic capabilities, in turn, constitute major determinants of national power. (See Selections 20 and 21.)

Especially in the twentieth century, the development of advanced
technology has altered the significance of national economic capabilities. Only those national units with vast and advanced econ-

omies can provide the base needed to exploit fully the potential of science and technology for military and nonmilitary purposes.

Although practically all warfare is essentially economic in character, as it is designed to damage or destroy an opponent's economic base, it is necessary to define more clearly the idea of economic warfare. Economic warfare consists of nonviolent operations designed specifically to weaken an enemy's economic base and thus to undermine his political position, or to strengthen a friendly country's economic position. It is one of the forms which the demand-response relationships may assume. (See Part II, Selection 13.)

Robert Strausz-Hupé and Stefan T. Possony examine the major economic instruments available to national units. In their demand-response relationships, national units may use foreign investments for economic penetration and seek to exploit the dependence of another nation upon certain vital forms of trade. National units have made use of blockade, controls against certain types of trade with an opponent, preemptive buying, stockpiling, and subsidies designed to influence the international behavior of another government.

Of the many economic instruments in use since World War II, none has been more widely aclaimed or more widely criticized than foreign aid. Both the United States and the Soviet Union, as well as several European countries, and nations elsewhere in the world, have developed foreign aid programs. The U.S. program began during the postwar period, in the assistance provided to war-ravaged Europe. The rapid response of the shattered European economies to such programs as the Marshall Plan led the United States, with less satisfactory results, to inaugurate aid programs elsewhere in the world. After the death of Stalin, the Soviet Union developed a major foreign aid program. The U.S. and Soviet programs are based upon widely differing assumptions. In the case of the United States, it is felt that great social change can result from a relatively small aid program; that these changes will be beneficial both to the recipient country and the United States; and that populations in national units receiving aid will respond with a new emphasis upon economic modernization and self-improvement. In contrast, the Soviets assume the following about foreign aid: that social change is costly; that people resist change; that large-scale aid cannot induce immediate, or even long-range, transformation in the economic and social structure of recipient countries. Given such limitations, Soviet aid programs place greater emphasis upon the attainment of immediate political objectives than does American foreign assitance. Moreover, implicit in Soviet foreign aid is the assumption that Western political influence in recipient countries can be reduced by lessening the economic dependence of African, Asian, and Latin American countries upon the United States. an idea found also in Lenin's writings on imperialism (See Selection 14).

In recent years, both in the United States and the Soviet Union, there have been reductions in foreign aid programs. In the United States, according to Norman D. Palmer, there has been increased dissatisfaction with foreign aid based on the limited results of programs, impatience with certain policies followed by recipient nations, preoccupation with problems of higher priority such as the Vietnam War, the balance of payments, and the urban crisis. In fact, it is doubtful, despite the widespread need among impoverished nations around the world, that the developed countries—the United States, Canada, Japan and the major powers of Western Europe—will allocate substantially greater portions of their Gross National Product to economic aid.

As Palmer suggests, foreign aid may take many forms. It may be granted on a bilateral or multilateral basis, or in the form of grants, loans, or technical assistance in the form of experts from the donor country. It may include funds for the purchase of capital goods such as steel mills and power-generating facilities or foodstuffs needed to increase dietary levels of an underdeveloped country. Aid may be granted on a government-to-government basis, or through an international organization such as the United Nations, the European Economic Community, the Inter-American Development Bank, or the Asian Development Bank. As Palmer concludes: "Multilateral aid seems to be preferred by most recipient countries, since it reduces the dangers of political 'strings' and excessive dependence, whereas most donors, whatever their spokesmen may say about multilateralism, are reluctant to channel the greater part of their aid through multilateral agencies."

If foreign aid has as its primary goal the economic development of the recipient state, another economic instrument of statecraft, sanctions, is designed to have the opposite effect. Developing and applying a general theory of sanctions to Rhodesia, Johan Galtung examines both the goals of states employing sanctions and their impact upon states against which they are used. In Rhodesia, the imposition of sanctions led to such adaptive measures as smuggling, restructuring of the economy to absorb the impact of sanctions, and increased solidarity among the population as a result of common sacrifices. In addition, Galtung questions the commonly held belief that sanctions, to be effective, must be universal, i.e., all states must be prepared to enforce them against a country. Even under a totally effective blockade, it may be possible for a country to restructure its internal economy and to develop domestic social cohesion based upon a willingness to sacrifice in the face of sanctions by outside powers. Thus it cannot be inferred that, even in the unlikely event that sanctions are fully effective in halting commerce, such action will have the intended results.

Technology, it was suggested in Part IV, exerts a pervasive influence on international relations. Nowhere is this influence more keenly felt than in the emerging corporate structure of the international economy. The increase in the efficiency of transportation and communication has enabled corporations to develop, coordinate and execute business strategies in widely separated countries and regions. As Raymond Vernon concludes: "Today it begins to be feasible to think of great international networks of mines and plants, straddling national boundaries, that are interlocked by supply lines which implement a common strategy in production, marketing and control." Natural resources in one country, human skills in another, manufacturing capacity in a third state, and markets in all three, can be linked by means of the multinational corporation. Such a business unit can guide the development of a product such as petroleum from its extraction to its refining and marketing. In short, the multinational corporation organizes, and benefits from, the internationalization of production.

Of special concern to the international relations student are the implications of the multinational corporation for the nation-state and the international system. Clearly, the multinational corporation is a powerful unit. The assets of many multinational corporations exceed the GNP of a large number of the world's nation-states. Multinational corporations, by shifting the location of their production facilities from one country to another, can affect employment and income levels. In 1971, Ford Motor Company decided to locate a large new automobile factory in Germany rather than Britain because of the latter country's labor problems. To the extent that such decisions are made outside Britain or Germany, persons who may not be nationals of these countries may gain important leverage over their economies. In cases where the multinational corporation serves as a vehicle for the international transfer of technology, foreigners may acquire a major voice in decisions for or against providing technologies, perhaps of a defense-related nature, to another country. Multinational corporations, in their quest for international specialization, can draw capital and skilled personnel from one country to another. Thus the multinational corporation has the potential to encroach upon the historic jurisdiction of national governments. The unanswerable question at this time is: to what extent will the national governments permit multinational corporations to subordinate national interests to the requirements of international production? In an age of residual, and in some cases virulent, nationalism, it is difficult to conclude that national governments would acquiesce in the destruction of their prerogatives by multinational corporations.

22. ECONOMICS AND STATECRAFT

Robert Strausz-Hupé and Stefan T. Possony

NATIONAL SECURITY is the foremost obligation of any government..
Hence each government regulates its economic life in view of its defense requirements. The purpose of such regulatory policies is to strengthen a nation's own economy and to weaken the economy of prospective opponents. By strengthening is meant not only the securing of all raw materials which might become necessary in case of war, but also the acquisition of finished products, weapons, ammunition, technological know-how, financial support and the establishment of an international network of economic auxiliaries, while at the same time denying all these advantages to the opponent. The economic weapons also can be used for the acquisition of political friends and the development of alliances.

It is quite true that international trade, if unobstructed, flourishes spontaneously and that this spontaneous growth would strengthen the economic posture of all trading nations. Yet the play of the free market may make a nation rich in consumers' goods while depriving it of those items which are indispensable in wartime. A free-trade organization is the logical economic structure of a world at peace. In periods of conflict,

From *International Relations* by Robert Strausz-Hupé and Stefan T. Possony (New York: McGraw-Hill Book Company, 1954) pp. 509; 516–517; 519–520; 522–523; 526; 528; 530–532; 534. Copyright 1954 by McGraw-Hill, Inc. Used by permission of McGraw-Hill Book Company. Footnotes have been renumbered to appear in consecutive order.

ROBERT STRAUSZ-HUPÉ (1903–   ) United States Ambassador to Ceylon. Formerly Professor of Political Science, University of Pennsylvania, and formerly Director, Foreign Policy Research Institute, Philadelphia, Pennsylvania. Author of *Power and Community* (New York: Praeger Publishers, 1956); *The Zone of Indifference* (New York: G. P. Putnam's Sons, 1952); *The Balance of Tomorrow* (New York: G. P. Putnam's Sons, 1945); *Geopolitics: The Struggle for Space and Power* (New York: G. P. Putnam's Sons, 1942). Co-author, *Building the Atlantic World* (New York: Harper Brothers, 1963); *A Forward Strategy for America* (New York: Harper Brothers, 1961); *Protracted Conflict* (New York: Harper Brothers, 1959); *International Relations* (New York: Praeger Publishers, 1956). Coeditor, *The Idea of Colonialism* (New York: Praeger Publishers, 1958).

STEFAN T. POSSONY (1913–   ) Director of International Studies, the Hoover Institution on War, Revolution and Peace, Stanford University. Editor of *Lenin, A Reader,* (Chicago: Henry Regnery Company, 1966). Co-author of *The Geography of Intellect* (Chicago: Henry Regnery Company, 1963) *A Forward Strategy for America,* (New York: Harper and Brothers, 1961).

however, trade must be controlled, at least partially, in order to maximize a nation's military power.

Similarly, the sale of commodities in a peaceful world is highly advantageous for a nation's living standard. Yet when a prospective opponent wants to buy commodities in order to strengthen his war potential, economic logic must be displaced by military logic. For example, Japan bought in the United States large quantities of scrap iron. Normally the sale of scrap iron would have been highly advantageous to the United States. Yet Japan used American scrap iron to build up its war machine. Hence the United States ultimately was compelled to embargo the sale of scrap iron.

One of the most important means of economic warfare consists in attacks on the opponent's financial strength for the purpose of diminishing the exchange value of his currency. These attacks can take the form of withdrawals of credits, dumping of large amounts of currency in order to compel the target country to pay in gold, manipulation of international currency exchanges, and sometimes simply psychological means which undermine confidence in the victim's financial honesty or economic strength.

ECONOMIC PENETRATION

Nations may acquire economic interests in a given country and through economic pressure determine its policy. Such a policy can be most successfully applied against smaller and underdeveloped states. Foreign economic interest thus manipulated the politics of the Near East. But even in a large country foreign-owned firms can exert pressure on the government, as the history of Russia before 1914 and of Germany between 1919 and 1930 shows. For that matter, in the late 19th century British capital was influential in the United States, and prior to the First World War German capital played a minor, though by no means negligible, role in shaping the course of American foreign policy.

British capital in Argentina often oriented the country's policy toward British interests. The economic penetration of Austria, Czechoslovakia, and Hungary by German industrial firms and banks during the 1930's created powerful pro-German factions and prepared the eventual annexation of these countries. The technique is not a new one; the various "charter companies" organized by west European countries in the 17th and 18th centuries initiated the conquests of immense territories in the Orient—the trade preceded the flag.[1] Today, Soviet-controlled "joint

---

[1] The personnel of such charter companies was often trained by economists of the highest achievement. Malthus, for example, taught the cadets of the East India Company for more than thirty years; see James Bonar, "The Malthusiad: Fantasia

stock companies" are instruments of Soviet political domination of Hungary and Rumania.

Investments in foreign countries play a great role in the use of economics as a weapon. These investments serve subversive, political, financial, technological, and industrial purposes. Foreign investments can be made openly in the name of the true owner, whose nationality would be admitted, or ownership can be camouflaged. For example, a German firm may own openly a firm in the United States, or it may possess a large amount of stock in an American firm. If open ownership is not advisable, the German firm may set up a holding company which ostensibly is of Swiss nationality, as did the I.G. Farben when it founded the so-called I.G. Chemie Basel. This company took over all the foreign investments of the German I.G. Farben which, in turn, did *not* "own" even one share of I.G. Chemie Basel.[2] Control was maintained through private and personal commitments. Or again a German firm would send a few associates to the United States where they would found a company, in due time become American citizens, and thus end up with an "American" business enterprise. Or finally, a German firm would finance American friends to establish themselves in business without ever assuming legal title to the property.

Foreign investments can be exploited for subversive purposes and may serve the attainment of three objectives: (1) propaganda which would be paid for by the proceeds from the investment; (2) espionage which, among other methods, could be accomplished through the firms obtaining classified orders; and (3) economic sabotage which could take various forms, including slowdowns of output, stimulation of strikes, defective production, etc.[3]

. . .

CARTELS AND MONOPOLIES

Perhaps no topic of international economics is as important and as hotly debated by the experts as is the question of international cartels. Very little is known about their actual operations and in particular about their connections with individual governments. In most cases it is probably safe to say that cartels operate in order to maximize profits. Yet sometimes their activities appear to further deliberately the political

---

Economia," in *Economic Essays: Contributed in Honor of John Bates Clark*, edited by Jacob H. Hollander, New York, Macmillan, 1927, p. 237.

[2] Hearings before the Special Committee Investigating the Munitions Industry, U.S. Senate, 74th Cong., 2nd Sess., part 12, Government Printing Office, 1937, p. 2888.

[3] For examples, see Yuan-li Wu, *Economic Warfare*, New York, Prentice-Hall, 1952, pp. 166*f*.

objectives of governments. In other cases, governments take political advantage of the economic situation created by the cartels.

Statistically speaking, there were in 1939 somewhat less than 200 international cartels, with about one-third of international trade under some form of marketing control. About 75 per cent of these cartels provided for the division of international markets, while 44 per cent provided for licensing and mutual use of patents.[4]

There are two characteristics of cartels which are of great military and political consequence. First, firms which are members of an international cartel usually pool their patents and inform each other of technical procedures. Therefore firms participating in international cartels can procure intelligence about the economic, technological, and military preparations of foreign countries. For example, I.G. Farben supplied the German *Wehrmacht* with information about British chemical factories.[5]

Second, cartel agreements entail the reduction of output in various areas and sometimes lead to the discontinuance of production. A country which is the base of an interational cartel can thus acquire important patents and, at the same time, inhibit the production of military matériel in hostile countries. While such a procedure may be somewhat difficult to apply in democratic countries, it has been used effectively by countries operating under dictatorial controls. The Nazis succeeded in deriving great technical advantages from various German-controlled cartels; when it was their turn to live up to agreements entered into by these cartels with foreign firms, they hid behind the excuse of officially imposed restrictions and *ad hoc* legislation. In this fashion, they obtained foreign patents but refused to disclose their own by the simple device of classifying them as military secrets. They also insisted upon limitations of output, but themselves produced as much as they chose, sometimes by keeping the production secret, sometimes by paying the penalties prescribed in the cartel agreement. Generally speaking, the Germans were most successful in this tactic with respect to the production of aluminum, the ouput of which they were able to curtail in the Western countries.[6] Maximizing their own production, they gained a very considerable advantage in aircraft production. Similarly they gained a head start in the manufacture of medical drugs.

---

[4] *Ibid.*, p. 172. The number of national cartels is far greater. In Germany it rose from 385 in 1905 to about 2,500 in 1925.

[5] See *Trials of War Criminals before the Military Tribunals,* Government Printing Office, 1953, Vol. VII, "The Farben Case," pp. 676*ff.*

[6] A somewhat different view is taken by Louis Marlio, *The Aluminum Cartel,* Washington, Brookings, 1947, pp. 95*ff.*; see also Erwin Hexner, *International Cartels,* Chapel Hill, The University of North Carolina Press, 1946, pp. 133*ff.*; also Wendell Berge, *Cartels: Challenge to a Free World,* Washington, Public Affairs Press, 1944, p. 222.

Perhaps one of the most interesting episodes in the international competition for supremacy in the technological field prior to and during the First World War was the capture by Germany of the lead in the manufacture of dyes. The German chemical industry took advantage of the invention of the Englishman Perkin who showed how coal tars could be transformed into aniline dyes, and whose discoveries were not put to use by his countrymen. The German chemical industry had grown by leaps and bounds during the last third of the 19th century. Soon the world market for dye and derivative products was virtually under German control. The growth of competitive chemical industries abroad was deliberately stifled by patent manipulation, price cutting, cartel output agreements, buying up of installations, refusal of delivery of intermediate products, and similar practices.[7] While chemical factories were built in the United States, Britain, and France, the Germans either gained partial control or diverted them to the production of finished goods so that they were dependent on German imports for their requirements of so-called "intermediates" or semifinished products, sold to them at very high prices.

EXPLOITATION OF STRATEGIC ECONOMIC POSITION

Economic power based on the seller's or the buyer's monopoly (monopsony) wields great and, at times, decisive political influence. The War between the States deprived the world of most of its cotton supply, an event which both belligerents exploited to gain military and diplomatic advantages; if the North had not deprived the South of its export outlet, it might have lost the war. In 1905, the Austrians waged a "pig war" against Serbia.[8] Pigs were that little country's most important article of exportation, and Austria was practically its only customer. Since political relations between the two states were strained, the Austrian government hit upon the heroic device of stopping the importation of Serbian pigs. This measure was intended to create such economic dislocation in Serbia that the stricken country would be ultimately compelled to comply with Austrian demands. The Serbs, disappointing Austrian expectations, succeeded in reorienting their exports. Serbia, however, had suffered great economic damage, a circumstance which contributed to the radicalization of Serbian domestic politics and, indirectly, by aggravating Austro-Serbian antagonism, to the outbreak of the First World War.

Under modern conditions, rice-exporting countries like Burma and

---

[7] Victor Lefebure, *The Riddle of the Rhine: Chemical Strategy in Peace and War,* New York, Chemical Foundation, 1923, Preface and Introduction by Marshals Foch and Wilson, p. 146; see also Hearings . . . Munitions Industry, part 11, pp. 2560*ff.*

[8] See Sidney Bradshaw Fay, *The Origins of the World War,* 2d ed., New York, Macmillan, 1931, Vol. I, p. 359.

Thailand could exert considerable pressure on India or Japan, since both of the latter countries are heavily dependent on the importation of rice. Similarly, Russia has used her dominant position in manganese to obtain advantages from the United States. Improper use by Malaya of its tin resources could have vast repercussions on the preservation of food and thus affect practically the entire world.

. . .

ECONOMIC WARFARE

Economic warfare is an integral part of war. In one way or another, it has been waged at all times and in all climes. Many wars serve predominantly economic purposes. The nomads must conquer territory to live. In a society based on slave labor, the supply of the labor force must be maintained by war. The time-honored strategy of the attack upon the enemy's supplies and food reserves, destruction of crops, stealing or killing of cattle, plunder, and pillage—all these thrusts against the fabric of a people's wealth and economic warfare.

Economic motives are among the most potent causes of war. To give a lesser known but highly illustrative example, a memorandum written by an unknown French official in 1747 explains why British control of America would make Britain unconquerable, since America would furnish Britain gold and silver as well as trading outlets and thus the material resources required for the construction of a large navy. The memorandum concludes: "The balance of money in the hands of the British entails the balance of power. They would be the masters of the sea through their navy, and the masters of the land through their wealth. They would draw the means from America to dictate the law to Europe." Sainte-Croix, 18th-century historian of the British navy, explained the reason why the logic of the situation compelled France to support American independence: [9]

If she were to possess an immense and fertile country whose population doubles every twenty years, what high degree of power would England reach? What counterweight of force would be necessary to oppose against her? Was not the independence of the universe menaced? By taking the side of the Anglo-Americans, France helped general welfare as well as her own safety.

Blockade and Contraband

In modern times, the most telling weapon of economic warfare is naval blockade, *i.e.*, the halting of a country's maritime imports and exports of

---

[9] Quoted from Bertrand de Jouvenal, *Napoléon et l'économie dirigée: le blocus continental*, Brussels, Éditions de la Toison d'Or, 1942, pp. 22–23.

vital commodities. The purpose of naval blockade was defined as early as 1601 by Queen Elizabeth. Seizing upon Spain's dependence on overseas trade, she said: "The stopping, hindrance, and impeading of all commerce and traffick with him [Philip II] in his territories of Spain and Portugal will quickly in likelihood give an end to these bloodie unnatural warres which disturb the generall peace and quiet of all these parts of Christendome." [10]

.   .   .

MODERN NAVAL BLOCKADE

During the First World War the naval blockade of Britain against the Central Powers caused decisive shortages in oil and foodstuffs.[11] German strategy during the Second World War, adapted to the lessons of the first, was directed at defeating the naval blockade which Britain again, by automatic reflex as it were, imposed upon her adversary. The pursuit of that objective forced Germany to adopt an economy of substitutes and stockpiles, led to expansion into the Balkans and Scandinavia, and finally to German attack on Russia.

Naval blockade involves a highly complicated technique and a nice sense of discrimination between essentials and nonessentials. It is impractical to throw a line of ships around the blockaded country, seeking thereby to prevent the passage of every ship. Blockade runners will often break through the blockading patrols. Neutral states must be permitted a minimum of trade. A continental country always has access to supplies via land routes. None can be completely blockaded from the sea. Naval blockade must, therefore, be supplemented by measures designed to prohibit the reexport from neutral countries of sea-borne supplies, and to reduce the sales to the enemy of commodities originating in adjacent neutral states.

In the 19th century a distinction was evolved between absolute and conditional contraband. The distinction was not always clear, but in 1909 an international agreement on the meaning of the term was reached: absolute contraband consisted of every type of *war* material, while conditional contraband comprised goods needed for the civilian population but which, under certain conditions, could be used for military purposes; if there was evidence of such a use, they could be confiscated. During the subsequent wars, which were contests between the industrial capacities of the belligerents, this separation lost its validity, simply because virtually every important commodity must now be used for war produc-

---

[10] David L. Gordon and Royden Dangerfield, *The Hidden Weapon: The Story of Economic Warfare*, New York, Harper, 1947, p. 1.

[11] See M. W. W. P. Consett, *The Triumph of Unarmed Forces 1914–1918*, London, Williams & Norgate, 1923.

tion. The distinction was all but abandoned during the Second World War.

It made its reappearance during the Korean War when most trading nations, with Britain in front, sold to China commodities which allegedly were not of military significance. During the Cold War in Europe East-West trade in "civilian" goods also was continued without letup. These trading arrangements were criticized widely because, in modern times, there are barely any commodities which directly or indirectly cannot be put to military use or be used to enhance a nation's warmaking capacity. Undoubtedly, medicines and low-octane gasoline shipped to China were not unwelcome to the Chinese armies fighting in Korea against the very nations which traded with them.

. . .

PREEMPTION

Hand in hand with rationing went "preemption." [12] This euphemistic term means simply the purchase of a goods produced in a neutral country in order to forestall its delivery into hostile hands, lest it increase the enemy's war potential. Country A prevents country B from buying a product by buying itself that product regardless of price and regardless of whether it can be put to use or not. During the First World War the Germans bought several chemicals in the United States which the Allies were trying to secure for the production of explosives and gases. When preemption proved impossible, German agents resorted to sabotage as, for example, in the famous Black Tom case when they blew up ammunition ships lying in New York Harbor.

During the Second World War, the Iberian Peninsula was the principal theater of preemptive warfare; the bone of contention was the mineral wealth of Spain and Portugal. Copper and iron mines were largely in British possession, and therefore no great difficulty was encountered by the Allies in repelling German buyers of these metals—a good example of the military importance of capital holdings abroad. Yet the wolframite (tungsten) mines in Spain and Portugal were not owned by Allied nationals; some of them were actually in German hands. The flow of wolframite extracted from these mines to Germany was not altogether halted, though the control exercised through navicert reduced it. The Allies acquired some mines. Nevertheless, it became necessary to buy the output of the remaining mines. As the Allies bought the ores, prices rose disproportionately. The total cost of the operation ultimately reached fantastically high figures. Nevertheless, the Germans were deprived of great quantities of this vitally needed alloy and forced to reduce drasti-

---

[12] See Geoffrey Crowther, *Ways and Means of War*, New York, Oxford, 1940, p. 58. See also Wu, *op. cit.*, pp. 83*ff.*

cally the production of tungsten steel, thus lowering the quality of their ammunition. Similar operations were carried out with Turkish chromium and, at the beginning of the war, with Yugoslav copper and bauxite. In the case of Swedish ball bearings an entire yearly output of the principal factories was bought and purchases of future output guaranteed.

The method of preemption also can be employed effectively in the field of technology. For this purpose patent laws can be used. For example, the exploitation, though not the purchase, of a patent can be denied to foreign nationals. The Soviets for many years systematically acquired knowledge about patents issued in industrialized countries, but they denied similar information about their own patents to foreign nationals and, in fact, have failed to publish any information about Russian inventions.[13]

· · ·

STOCKPILING

To defend themselves against blockade and preemptive buying, nations often resort to the stockpiling of vital commodities. In previous times stockpiling extended mostly to raw materials, but under the threat of modern air war there is a tendency to stockpile machine tools and finished products, including weapons. Stockpiling must be undertaken in peacetime, or during the very first weeks of a war before blockade arrangements have been completed.

The difficulties of an adequate stockpiling program are very great. Most of the commodities needed are in short supply. This leads, first, to a considerable increase in the price of the commodity and therefore to economic dislocation affecting all nations habitually buying the particular commodity. Second, it leads to an overexpansion of production facilities. Once the stockpiling program has been completed, inevitable retrenchment must be paid for by unemployment and financial loss. Third, if the threat of

---

[13] On German methods in this area see *Trials of War Criminals before the Military Tribunals*, Vol. VII, "The Farben Case," pp. 1273–1295. See particularly Farben memorandum of January 25, 1940 (*i.e.*, after the outbreak of World War II), which reads: "There are agreements and arrangements between the German production companies (I.G. Farbenindustrie A.G. and Ruhrchemie) and the large oil companies such as Standard Oil, Shell, et cetera, with regard to mineral oil. Among other things, these agreements provide for the exchange of know-how with regard to mineral oil between the parties to the contract. This exchange of know-how, which is still being handled in the usual way by the neutral countries abroad even now and which is transmitted to us via Holland and Italy, first gives us an insight into the development work and production plans of the companies and/or their respective countries, and at the same time informs us about the progress of technical developments with regard to oil. . . . Up to now, we have carried out this exchange in such a way that from our side we have only sent reports . . . which contained only such technical data as concerned facts which are known or out of date according to the latest developments."

war has receded and the government decides to release its stockpiles, prices will fall. Necessary though stockpiling may be, it is a dislocating factor in world economy. This became obvious shortly after the outbreak of the Korean War, when the acceleration of the American stockpiling program produced repercussions all over Europe. One method to reduce the adverse effects of stockpiling is to fix prices by international agreements; another is to carry out the program over a long period of time, taking advantage of drops in prices and periods of overproduction as they occur in the economic cycle. But if large purchases have to be made rapidly, and if there is no time to arrive at intergovernmental agreements, grave disturbances are inevitable.

ECONOMIC SUBSIDIES

Economic warfare in wartime includes "supply programs." Unlike activities designed to *deny* supplies to certain countries, these programs serve to *support* neutrals which are to be influenced. At the beginning of the Second World War, the Allies maintained trade with Italy, a token demonstration of the profitability of neutrality. Vichy-controlled North Africa was supplied with sugar in order to keep the natives well disposed toward the Allies and facilitate continued control by the French. In addition, North Africa was supplied with all kinds of materials, including fuel, in order to increase French power of resistance against German pressure. Food was delivered to France and Greece to stave off famine among a friendly population. If Turkey could have been abundantly provisioned with military materials, she might have entered the war at a strategically opportune moment; as it was, Turkey was inadequately equipped for waging war against as formidable an enemy as Germany.

The Anglo-Saxon powers also helped to confirm Spain in her neutrality by providing her with foodstuffs and oil—positive economic warfare, as it were.[14] The German high command credited this policy with keeping Spain "nonbelligerent." Yet a similar policy against Japan failed; American scrap and oil shipped to Japan, in order to insure Japanese neutrality, actually made possible Japanese aggression. Russia's strategy to supply Germany with raw materials, foodstuffs, and oil failed and redounded to Russia's own detriment.[15]

During World War II lend-lease operations contributed greatly to Allied victory. The assertion has been rashly made that lend-lease was a historically unique operation. Economic subsidy is a time-honored means of war, employed whenever a rich state sought to induce poorer states to fight its battles or to replenish its effectives with troops from abroad. Subventions

---

[14] See Sir Samuel Hoare, *Complacent Dictator,* New York, Knopf, 1947, *passim.*
[15] See *Nazi-Soviet Relations,* pp. 85, 119, 196, 199, and 339.

always played an important role in coalition warfare. During the 17th and 18th centuries they were used on a large scale, chiefly by Britain, Holland, and France. Countries such as Prussia waxed powerful because they had been liberally subsidized; between 1674 and 1688, the Grand Elector received almost 900,000 thalers, while his successor Frederick I amassed 14 million. During the Seven Years' War, Frederick the Great received altogether 27 million thalers from Britain. While direct subventions fell into disrepute during the 19th century, credits were given by the Western powers to smaller European countries and Russia, and by the United States to England and France. Since some of these debts remained unpaid, they must be considered as subsidies in fact, though not in name.

23.   FOREIGN AID AND FOREIGN POLICY: THE "NEW STATECRAFT" REASSESSED

Norman D. Palmer

I

TODAY THE FOREIGN POLICIES of nations, and international relations generally, are encompassing new forms and new dimensions. Interlinkages between domestic and foreign policies, a proliferation of programs and agencies for carrying on the world's work, and countervailing tendencies toward conflict and cooperation are salient features of contemporary international life. The world is sharply divided by many kinds of walls, curtains, barriers and gulfs, even as transnational contacts are increasing in scope and significance. Nations and peoples are still failing to respond adequately to the challenges, crises and opportunities of the

---

From *ORBIS,* a quarterly journal of world affairs published by the Foreign Policy Research Institute, Philadelphia, Pennsylvania, Fall 1969, 763–679; 771–782. Footnotes have been renumbered to appear in consecutive order.

NORMAN D. PALMER (1909–   ) Professor of Political Science, University of Pennsylvania. Author of *The Indian Political System* (Boston: Houghton Mifflin Company, 1966); *South Asia and United States Policy* (Boston: Houghton Mifflin Company, 1966); *Sun Yat-Sen and Communism* (New York: Praeger Publishers, 1960). Coauthor of *International Relations: The World Community in Transition* (Boston: Houghton Mifflin Company, 1969).

twentieth century, while the greater challenges, crises and opportunities of the twenty-first century lie only a generation away.

For something less than a generation large-scale foreign aid has been one of the conspicuous features of the foreign policies of an increasing number of donor and recipient states, and of the operations of agencies for international cooperation and coordination. In the decade of the 1950's it assumed signal proportions on the part of certain states and international agencies, and in the 1960's it became an integral and, in spite of its *ad hoc* beginnings, apparently a continuing aspect of international relations. Although, as Hans Morgenthau stated, "The very assumption that foreign aid is an instrument of foreign policy is a subject of controversy,"[1] the political behavior of nations and the interpretations of scholars and other analysts clearly indicate that this assumption is gaining widespread acceptance and is fast becoming doctrine. "For more and more countries," Robert E. Asher has noted, "foreign aid has become an integral feature of foreign policy—a device designed to extend political influence, cement relations with other countries, provide an alternative to the offerings of rival powers, open trade channels, pave the way for private investment, and respond to myriads of other pressures."[2] It has assumed the status of "the new statecraft," to borrow George Liska's expressive terminology.[3]

The concept and practice of foreign aid, and the problems involved, are not new. They can be traced throughout recorded history, at least in embryonic form. Aristotle wrote, in poignantly timeless words, that "To give away money is an easy matter, but to decide to whom to give it, and how large a sum, and when, and for what purposes, and how, is neither in every man's power, nor an easy matter." And apparently giving away money—or goods or services—on an international scale is even more difficult than in personal relations. What is new is the scale of foreign aid, its integration into the foreign policies of many states, and its conspicuous role in international relations. In this sense, only in recent years has it really become "the new statecraft," of sufficient scope and importance to justify special consideration and analysis.

Large-scale foreign aid arose out of need and capability. It was extended by the United States to Britain, the Soviet Union and certain other countries during World War II, to many countries in the immediate

---

[1] Hans J. Morgenthau, "A Political Theory of Foreign Aid," *The American Political Science Review,* June 1962, p. 301.

[2] Robert E. Asher, "How to Succeed in Foreign Aid Without Really Trying," in John D. Montgomery and Arthur Smithies, editors, *Public Policy,* Volume 13 (Cambridge: Harvard University Press, 1964), p. 128.

[3] George Liska, *The New Statecraft: Foreign Aid in American Foreign Policy* (Chicago: University of Chicago Press, 1960).

postwar years for purposes of relief and rehabilitation, to the states of Western Europe under the Marshall Plan (the European Recovery Program), to nations associated with the United States in bilateral or multilateral security arrangements, to the countries of Latin America, especially under the Alliance for Progress, and to the new states of Asia and Africa to assist them in their uphill struggle for national and human survival, political integration and stability, and political, economic and social development. Many other capital-exporting countries of the Western world, and one non-Western state—Japan—have also been prominently and increasingly involved in the aid picture. Beginning in the mid-1950's the Soviet Union became a major contributor of external assistance, and the People's Republic of China and some of the communist states of Eastern Europe have provided foreign aid on a smaller and more selective scale. In short, over the past fifteen years or so foreign aid has been an important instrument of the foreign policy of both Western and communist states, as it has, in different ways, of the major recipient states. In addition, it has been a chief concern of the United Nations and many of its organs and agencies, of regional arrangements and associations, and of various other international organizations.[4]

The question of foreign aid is a delicate, controversial and sensitive one. It has already produced a vast literature, and a great deal of heated public and private debate. In recipient countries it ruffles sensitivities and stirs suspicions; in donor states it seems to have few friends and many critics. It has become, according to Felix Belair, "a catalytic agent that fuses all the occupational frustrations and resentments of average men into something approaching xenophobia."[5] Few subjects have been dealt with on such a high plane of unreality; few have been surrounded by more nonsense and more obfuscation. Supporters and critics alike have failed to document their case convincingly, or to win over those who are not already persuaded one way or the other.

Two of the many unfortunate consequences of "the new statecraft" deserve special emphasis. The first is that foreign aid distorts the entire relationship between major donors and major recipients, including private as well as official contacts and relations. The second is that it tends to create another and particularly undesirable division in the world, which affects thinking and approaches as well as national and international policies. John Kenneth Galbraith observed, "To divide the world as between the aiding and the aided is both wrong and psychologically

---

[4] See John D. Montgomery, *Foreign Aid in International Relations* (Englewood Cliffs, N.J.: Prentice-Hall, 1967).

[5] Felix Belair, "Opposition to Foreign Aid Mounts in Congress," *New York Times*, August 11, 1963.

damaging." [6] In a sense, this same kind of division is created by all references to the North-South problem, the "have" and "have-not" nations, and the developed and underdeveloped nations. Even UNCTAD, and the two main conferences it has held, in 1964 and 1968, can be criticized for sharpening and crystallizing the world's economic divisions, though it has served a useful purpose in providing an organization in which the interests and needs of the developing countries can find special emphasis and, hopefully, be better accommodated.

The amorphous term "foreign aid," embracing many different concepts, programs and approaches,[7] eludes precise definition, except in particular contexts. It might be better if it were eliminated from the vocabulary of international relations. With respect to economic development, at least, the practice of the Organization for Economic Cooperation and Development has much to commend it. OECD studies avoid the use of the word "aid" completely. "They compile from Government sources the total of funds of all kinds—not only grants and loans but export credits and private as well as public investment—everything except military expenditure, which contributes to the economic growth of the recipient countries." [8] But clearly, for a discussion of foreign aid this usage is at once too broad and too narrow. It covers funds not usually considered under the rubric of foreign aid and omits other sources of assistance usually regarded as its component parts. There is little rationale for including, for example, loans from the World Bank or from the U.S. Export-Import Bank under foreign aid, for these are "hard loans," on commercial terms; yet such loans are often listed in reports on foreign aid. Almost all donor countries are inclined to include items in their

---

[6] John Kenneth Galbraith, *Economic Development* (Cambridge: Harvard University Press, 1964), p. 52. "To see the countries of the world not as divided between the developed and the underdeveloped but as spread along a line representing various stages of development is essential if we are to have an accurate view of the problem of assistance. For when development is so regarded, we see that no group of countries is uniquely qualified to extend assistance and no other group is completely condemned to the role of recipient. . . . The provision of aid is seen, as it should be seen, as a cooperative endeavor in which all countries may participate." *Ibid.*, p. 51.

[7] "Under 'aid' or 'assistance' several countries include strictly commercial loans, often on short terms, along with grants and loans of the 'soft' variety; also, the distinction between economic and military assistance is often a very tenuous one. The published data refer sometimes to actual disbursements and sometimes to new commitments, and both disbursements and commitments may be figured on a net (that is, with interest and principal repayments deducted) or gross basis. For the most part, these various categories are not kept clearly separated in the statistical presentations." Gunnar Myrdal, *Asian Drama: An Inquiry into the Poverty of Nations* (New York: Pantheon Books, 1968), p. 634.

[8] Organization for Economic Cooperation and Development, ID 1446-1, May 1963.

reports which should probably not be included, such as reparation payments in the case of Japan and private investments in the case of West
Germany. Possibly the vast American food shipments are properly subsumed under foreign aid, but they constitute aid of a different type,
contributing to human survival more than to economic development
(although admittedly the two are not unrelated); they also represent a
means of disposing of food surpluses, which is no longer such a problem
for the United States.

II

The American foreign aid program is a hodgepodge. "It is a misnomer,"
Senator J. W. Fulbright, Chairman of the Senate Foreign Relations Committee, once remarked,

> to speak of *the* foreign aid program. It is not *a* program; it is a con-
> glomeration of programs—to support foreign armies; maintain Amer-
> ican military bases in foreign lands; build roads, dams, steel mills;
> pay foreigners' import bills; grow more food; rent communication
> stations; train foreign tax collectors; provide emergency relief from
> natural disasters; and support multifarious United Nations activities
> which themselves range from feeding children, to killing malarial
> mosquitoes, to irrigating Pakistan. . . . It is no wonder that Congress,
> the public, and perhaps the Administration has difficulty in under-
> standing the [assistance effort].[9]

The result is that other governments and peoples, including those in
recipient countries, are even more confused regarding the nature and
objectives of the vast American program and its implications for themselves. On the administrative side the program has often been a bureaucratic nightmare. During the period 1950-1963 there were seven major
structural changes in it, and at least eight major studies by Presidentially-
appointed commissions or groups. When David E. Bell became Administrator of the Agency for International Development in 1962, he was the
eleventh person to head the AID economic assistance program, a post
generally regarded as "the most thankless job in Washington."

In the postwar years the two principal types of American external
assistance have been military aid and economic aid. In many respects
military aid is even more closely and directly related to foreign policy
than is economic aid: it has been used to support security objectives, to
strengthen bilateral and multilateral alliance systems, and perhaps also
to influence the foreign policy orientation of various states. It is a large
and complex subject, which deserves careful examination, especially at

---

[9] Quoted in "Foreign Aid Is a Many-Splintered Thing," *Dialogue,* August 1968,
p. 2.

a time when the undesirable results of some large-scale programs are more apparent than they have been in the past, and when many observers judge that military aid as a weapon of foreign policy is becoming increasingly unproductive, in some cases even counterproductive. A strong argument can still be made for military aid, under special circumstances and hopefully on a temporary basis. In any event it is a phase of foreign aid in which many countries, including the United States, the Soviet Union, Communist China, India, Pakistan, the United Arab Republic, Nigeria, North and South Viet Nam, are deeply involved in various ways and for various reasons. This article will concentrate on economic assistance, but the importance of military aid, its special relevance for foreign policy, and the difficulty of distinguishing between military and economic aid in many instances, are both freely acknowledged and strongly underscored.

Foreign economic assistance assumes many forms. It may be examined in such broad categories as bilateral and multilateral assistance, or as grants and loans. Current U.S. AID reports analyze the American program under the broad headings of AID economic assistance and non-AID economic assistance.[10] The former is in turn subdivided into two main categories, namely grants and loans, with the largest appropriations now going for development loans, the Alliance for Progress, supporting assistance-Viet Nam, and technical assistance. The latter consists mainly of the Food-for-Peace Program, under Public Law 480, but "other non-AID programs" include or have included substantial sums for several countries, among them the United Kingdom, Germany, France and Italy in the days of the Marshall Plan, Japan during the period of occupation, and Brazil, Mexico, the Philippines and India.

Some foreign aid specialists have suggested that the best breakdown for current American economic aid programs would be Food-for-Peace, program assistance and project assistance. Others prefer more sophisticated categorizations. In this the economists have taken the lead, as they have in almost every other aspect of the foreign aid picture, and full credit must be given for their contributions. Nevertheless, to cite from Hans Morgenthau's now-famous article in *The American Political Science Review,* "As military policy is too important a matter to be left to the generals, so is foreign aid too important a matter to be left to the economists." [11] Morgenthau called attention to "the diversity of policies that go by the name, 'foreign aid,'" and pointed out that at least six different kinds of aid could, and should, be identified: humanitarian,

---

[10] See Agency for International Development, *Proposed Foreign Aid Program, FY 1968: Summary Presentation to the Congress* (Washington: GPO, 1967).

[11] Morgenthau, *op. cit.,* p. 307.

subsistence, military, prestige, bribery, and economic development.[12] This might be described as a motivation rather than a typology classification. It would be inappropriate for an economic analysis, but does provide a useful framework for analyzing the political aspects of foreign aid and for considering the place of aid in the broad context of foreign policy, especially from the viewpoint of the donor nations. It has less relevancy from the viewpoint of recipient countries or multilateral aid-giving agencies.

III

The objectives and motives of foreign aid are even more varied and nebulous than its types and forms. Obviously the basic approach of multilateral agencies is different from that of nations, of donors from that of recipients, of major aid-giving and aid-receiving states from that of states less directly involved in or affected by the aid-giving process, of communist states from that of non-communist states, and so on.

National boundaries are hard to leap and programs look different according to whether one views them from inside or outside the donor country. Add to the irrepressible suspicion of the motives of foreigners, the fact that no nation is monolithic. The objectives of one group of citizens or bureaucrats may be anathema to some other group. The public and ostensible aims of a country are not necessarily its real ones, and both sets of objectives are likely to change over time.[13]

Presumably for all states the objective of giving or receiving aid is to promote the national interest; but this too is a nebulous term, and may be interpreted in ways which will either hamper or further the basic interests of the nation or international cooperation. One well-known American student of the subject, writing in the Kennedy era, argued that U.S. aid and trade policies should be employed mainly as "strategic weapons in the Cold War" and that the United States should distribute aid "primarily on the basis of the recipient nations' attitudes toward our foreign policy objectives." He expressed regret that the Kennedy Administration had, in his judgment, not been conducting its programs in accordance with these objectives, and tried to console himself with this reflection: "Even if the primary goal of the assistance program is to promote economic development and social change in the assisted nations, it should be implicit in the program that we can look upon our own in-

---

[12] *Ibid.*, p. 301.
[13] Asher, *op. cit.*, pp. 110–111.

terest with a little tenderness, and that aid or trade may be curtailed if actions are taken which are provoking as well as provocative." [14]

. . .

IV

Soviet foreign aid outside the communist world, which began to assume significant proportions in the mid-1950's, has been concentrated on certain countries, notably India, Indonesia, the United Arab Republic, Afghanistan and Cuba, and on impact and showpiece projects, of which the Bhilai steel mill in India and the Aswan Dam in the UAR have been the most spectacular. Most of the aid has been in the form of low-interest loans, payable after a relatively short period, often either by barter or in local currencies.[15] From the beginning the political objectives and propaganda aspects of the Soviet program have been obvious. In recent months, however, the Soviet Union, like the United States, has been cutting back its aid commitments. One striking fact is that as of mid-1968 there was "a back-up in the Soviet aid pipeline of $3.9 billion in unused credits." [16]

Communist China has extended modest assistance to some twenty-five countries, mostly in Asia and Africa, and has sent many hundreds of technicians and laborers abroad. It has used aid efforts as part of its overall campaign to mobilize a common front against the United States and the Soviet Union. It has also rewarded Albania, its only real champion in Eastern Europe, with economic aid, and its various ties with Pakistan, stemming largely from a common desire to keep India on the defensive, have led to both economic and military aid.

While they differ greatly in size, emphasis and style, the foreign aid programs of the United Kingdom, France, Belgium and the Netherlands are similar in that they are channeled mainly to countries with which political ties have been long and close—meaning, for the most part, their former colonies. Portugal's program is directed almost exclusively to its overseas territories, chiefly Angola and Mozambique. Of the major donor states, only West Germany and Japan have been increasing rather than decreasing their aid programs. Both countries have tended to lag behind

---

[14] James R. Schlesinger, "Strategic Leverage for Aid and Trade," in David M. Abshire and Richard V. Allen, editors, *National Security* (New York: Praeger, 1963), pp. 688, 689, 693. See also Schlesinger's *The Political Economy of National Security* (New York: Praeger, 1960), pp. 227–232.

[15] See Marshall I. Goldman, "A Balance Sheet of Soviet Foreign Aid," *Foreign Affairs*, January 1965.

[16] Seymour Topping, "Aid to Developing Countries Shifting to Private Sector," *New York Times*, August 5, 1968.

in the aid field; both have used aid to promote exports and to improve their international image, influence and status. They have charged rather high interest rates, but they are now easing the terms of their aid and are broadening its scope and increasing its size.

Nationalist China and Israel have been both recipients and donors of aid. For understandable political reasons these two states, at opposite ends of Asia, faced with special problems of survival, have been carrying on limited aid activities, mostly in the form of technical assistance, in a surprisingly large number of Asian and African countries. The bulk of Canada's aid has gone to other Commonwealth members, and to a few countries in Latin America and French-speaking Africa—the latter an interesting concession to the French-Canadians and one of many illustrations of the influence of domestic politics on foreign policy.[17]

Among the major institutional sources of capital assistance to developing nations are the World Bank and its two affiliates, the International Development Association and the International Finance Corporation, the International Monetary Fund, the Inter-American Development Bank, and the Asian Development Bank. Of the various arrangements for coordinating aid programs the Colombo Plan and the international consortia organized for India, Pakistan and Indonesia by the World Bank, and for Greece and Turkey by the Organization for Economic Cooperation and Development, have been particularly effective and particularly acceptable to both donors and recipients.

The United Nations Conference on Trade and Development, now an established agency associated with the UN, represents the interests and needs of the developing countries, and also serves as a reminder that the developed nations can render far greater assistance to new states by following more liberal and better conceived trade policies than they can by any amounts of aid. Aid programs often seem to be used by developed states as an admittedly unsatisfactory substitute for more liberal trade policies. As Mrs. Gandhi observed in an address to the UN General Assembly on October 14, 1968, "Aid is only partial recompense for what the superior economic power of the advanced countries denies us through trade." This point was stressed again and again by representatives of the developing countries at the two major conferences of UNCTAD, in 1964 and 1968; but still the terms and conditions of international trade are weighted heavily against the less developed states.

---

[17] See Seymour J. Rubin, *The Conscience of the Rich Nations* (New York: Harper & Row, 1964), pp. 44–50. Rubin discusses the various aid programs of noncommunist nations and international agencies under the following heads: United States aid, programs stemming from colonial association, programs with no colonial association, programs of the European Economic Community, other programs, and multilateral programs.

Multilateral aid seems to be preferred by most recipient countries, since it reduces the dangers of political "strings" and excessive dependence, whereas most donors, whatever their spokesmen may say about multilateralism, are reluctant to channel the greater part of their aid through multilateral agencies. The relative merits of the two approaches have been debated *ad nauseam*. Although there has been some shift in the direction of multilateralism, the bulk of aid is still bilateral in nature, and any further shift in emphasis would probably reduce rather than increase the levels of aid-giving. "Whatever the instrumentality . . . multilateralization on any appreciable scale raises questions about the integration of foreign aid with total foreign policy and with considerations of national security." [18]

V

The problem of evaluating the impact of foreign aid programs is a particularly difficult one. Certainly there has been widespread criticism of almost all aid programs, and disappointment with their results, in both donor and recipient countries. There has also been widespread support for such programs. Even such an unlikely source as *Time* magazine has expressed the view that "for all its shortcomings, foreign aid has been a major instrument of U.S. foreign policy since World War II and, on the whole, spectacularly successful." [19] *Time* did not indicate what its criteria of success were. Criticisms range all the way from aversion to the very idea of foreign aid to failures in specific programs. Defense also ranges from humanitarian motives to those of the narrowest self-interest, from support of the overall aims and objectives to enthusiasm for specific aid efforts.

Foreign aid is in essence a long-range endeavor, which can be properly evaluated, if ever, only after many more years of massive effort. This point is lost sight of, however, because it is often regarded as a short-range and experimental program to deal with immediate crises of transition and development, and the funds to support it are made available reluctantly and mostly on a year-by-year basis.

In evaluating foreign aid programs provisionally, as policy-makers must do, special attention should be given to their impact on donor countries, recipient countries, relations among donor countries, relations among recipient countries, relations between donor and recipient countries, international and regional organizations and agencies, and international relations generally. Each type of impact merits careful study. Foreign

---

[18] "The Trouble with Foreign Aid," *The Morgan Guaranty Survey*, January 1964, p. 10.

[19] *Time*, February 16, 1968.

aid affects the balance of forces within as well as between nations, especially in recipient countries. In order to realize modernization goals most developing countries require substantial social change and substantial outside assistance. In both of these respects the modernization effort is lagging, as Gunnar Myrdal has demonstrated in his weighty three-volume *Asian Drama: An Inquiry into the Poverty of Nations.* This work may be criticized as an inquiry into "the poverty of notions," rather than "nations," as Romesh Thapar has insisted,[20] but no serious investigation of the situation in contemporary South and Southeast Asia can disregard the findings of Myrdal and his associates, based on a cooperative research effort lasting for some ten years.

In each recipient Asian country the foreign aid story has its own special features, its own priorities, successes and failures. The overall picture is not encouraging. In spite of massive military and economic assistance, none of the countries in noncommunist Asia, with the possible exception of developed Japan, and apparently none of the communist states, are in a healthy economic, political or social condition. It is impossible to say what the consequences would have been if outside assistance, of many types and from many sources, had not been forthcoming. While this assistance has shown no spectacular results, except perhaps in Japan and Taiwan, it is likely that without it the economic and security situation in noncommunist Asia would be far worse than it is today. Generalizations regarding the value and impact of aid should in any event be tested by a country-by-country analysis of the aid programs in their various dimensions, in actual operation.

Certainly disillusion about foreign aid is widespread. In the United States, the major contributor, increasing dissatisfaction with the results of aid programs, impatience with the reactions and policies of recipient nations, and preoccupation with problems that are bidding for higher priority, such as the balance of payments, the Viet Nam war, and urbanization and race relations inside the country, have led to a slackening of aid appropriations, perhaps on a long-term basis. Rebuffs from recipients —e.g., Nasser's invitation to "take a leap in the lake," and Sukarno's taunt, "To hell with your aid"—have not helped. Other capital-exporting countries have seemed all too content to let the United States bear the burden of appropriations and take criticisms, although several contribute a higher percentage of their gross national product to foreign aid than the United States does. Robert Asher described the situation in this tongue-in-cheek aside: ". . . the heavy involvement of the United States in aid to beleaguered nations has enabled other high-income countries to

---

[20] Romesh Thapar, "Poverty of Nations or Notions?," *Indian & Foreign Review,* August 1, 1968.

avoid some of the brickbats cast at the United States program and, in this sense, to succeed in foreign aid without really trying." [21] Like the United States, the Soviet Union seems to be curtailing its foreign aid efforts. "Today American and Soviet aid programs are regarded in some countries as complementary rather than competitive. Moscow and Washington have learned, sometimes painfully, that aid is not always an effective lever of influence." [22]

Given their sensitivities and weaknesses, their traditions and relative lack of external contacts and experience, it is only natural that the peoples and governments of many developing countries look upon foreign aid, especially from major powers, as a massive, unwelcome and dangerous involvement in their internal affairs. They recognize their need for aid, but are understandably apprehensive of some of the consequences. Since the motives of donors are by no means clear, even to their own people, it is little wonder that confusion about foreign aid is prevalent in the recipient states. As a Burmese scholar observed,

> Given the continued befogging of the issues, we cannot blame the people of the developing countries if they sometimes find it hard to distinguish the "crypto-philanthropists" who hide altruism behind the mask of national self-interest from the "neo-colonialists" whom they suspect of hiding national self-interest under the mask of altruism.[23]

The charge of "neo-colonialism" is frequently heard and widely accepted.

> In this charge reflected much of the bitterness of the developing countries about the fact that the speed of their development depends upon economic aid, that they still feel themselves the victims of a subtle imperialism, that they are important onlookers in the struggle for world power among the larger nations, and that they may become the victims of wars which they did nothing to provoke and much to prevent.[24]

In both donor and recipient countries attitudes toward foreign aid are unrealistic and paranoiac. Donors sometimes think of aid as a kind of undesirable but inescapable international charity, to be extended grudgingly and sparingly to unworthy and ungrateful mendicants. Recipients seem at times to look on it as an obligation of the rich toward the poor,

---

[21] Asher, *op. cit.*, p. 129.

[22] Topping, *op. cit.*, p. 3.

[23] H. Myint, *The Economies of the Developing Countries* (London: Hutchinson & Company, 1964), p. 183.

[24] Bert F. Hoselitz, *Economic Aid for Development* (New York: The Institute for International Order, 1960), p. 15.

or as an inadequate atonement for past exploitation. Even distinguished national leaders, who should know better, indulge in strange flights on the foreign aid theme. Two examples, out of many, may be cited. In December 1967 the late Senator Everett M. Dirksen wrote in a widely-syndicated newspaper column:

> India is 10,000 miles away. What has she ever done for us? Exactly nothing, although we have provided India with about $5 billion in economic aid, exclusive of military assistance. Don't you wonder, then, why we bleed the taxpayers of the United States to give aid to India? Just what can India do to us, just what can she do for us, to justify the sacrifices that Americans have been making for India? On a purely cold, material basis, a rather good case can be made against any aid whatsoever for India.[25]

Regardless of the merits of his arguments, Senator Dirksen was giving way to irresponsible hyperbole by suggesting that American aid to India, which at that time amounted to little more than one-twentieth of one per cent of the gross national product was bleeding the American taxpayers.

A few weeks later, the distinguished Deputy Prime Minister and Finance Minister of India, Morarji Desai, made this immortal contribution to the foreign aid debate: "For some time to come, I think it will be wise to take it if it comes. If it does not come we need not worry about it. . . . In fact, it might be a blessing in disguise if that happens. But if help comes we should not discard it saying we will go alone no matter how long we will take in our economic development." [26] To the extent that this statement reflected the commendable objective of gradual removal of the foreign aid crutch, and moving toward self-sustaining growth by greater national efforts, it makes a great deal of sense; but at a crucial stage of India's development effort, when the need for continued external assistance is indicated in almost every study by Indian and foreign experts and in every draft of a one-year or a five-year plan, such double talk seems almost ludicrous from a man who made periodic trips to Western countries and international aid-giving agencies to solicit continuing aid for his country. The absurdity of this trend of thought was expressed in a cartoon by Laxman in *The Times of India* for October 10, 1968, showing a Congress official looking at a large chart labeled "Project

---

[25] Everett M. Dirksen, "Why U.S. Taxpayers Are Bled for India," *Philadelphia Evening Bulletin*, December 31, 1967.

[26] Address at a meeting of the Subjects Committee of the Indian National Congress in Lal Bahadur Nagar (Hyderabad), January 9, 1968; quoted in *India News*, January 19, 1968, p. 4.

Progress" and remarking: "We can't give up at this stage! We will carry on without depending on external aid . . . or internal resources."

The need for continuing, and increasing, the levels of economic assistance to developing countries has been spelled out many times by key officials of national and international aid-giving or aid-coordinating agencies, such as Eugene Black, George Woods and Robert McNamara of the World Bank, by spokesmen of the developing countries at the two UNCTAD conferences, and by almost all serious students of the needs of development now and in years to come. It was underscored recently in the report of the Commission on International Development (the Pearson Commission), submitted to the World Bank on October 1, 1969. Unfortunately, considerations based on expert advice and national and international self-interest seem to be outweighed by the growing disillusionment with foreign aid generally, revelations of occasional administrative failures, bungling or even scandals in foreign aid programs, and apathy and indifference to the widening gap between the "have" and "have-not" nations.

VI

In 1961 the United Nations proclaimed the decade of the 1960's the Decade of Development, and called on all nations, developed and underdeveloped alike, to embark on a vast international effort to make the fruits of human progress and skills available on a more equitable basis to peoples everywhere. Foreign aid was envisioned as one of the major components of this effort—but by no means the most important one—and billions of dollars and vast human and material resources have been made available under foreign aid programs. But the net result of all these efforts has been disappointing. As the Decade of Development passed into history, a sense of frustration and pessimism hung over the world. The stark fact is that, as UN Secretary-General U Thant said in 1968, "We are not winning the war on want. The opportunity gap for many, if not most, of the nations and individuals of the world is growing wider, and inequality is increasing." [27] "The widening gap between the developed and developing countries," declared the Pearson Commission in the first sentence of its 230-page report, "has become a central issue of our time."

Obviously, efforts during the Development Decade, vast as they have been, have been inadequate to meet the growing needs, and any realistic look into the future indicates that even greater coordinated efforts will be required in the years ahead. Yet instead of gearing for this, many nations —developed and developing, communist and noncommunist—are growing

---

[27] Quoted in Topping, *op. cit.*, p. 3.

weary of the struggle and are slowing down the pace. This is noticeably true of foreign assistance programs. In August 1968, Seymour Topping, an astute reporter for the *New York Times*, wrote:

> Most of the major donor nations are leveling off or reducing their governmental economic and technical-assistance programs. In Western and Communist countries, popular support for foreign aid is diminishing because of competing domestic needs, international payment problems and doubts about the effectiveness of governmental programs. The developing countries are being advised by the United States and other Western countries to rely more on private business as a source of foreign credits and investments. Thus their planning must be revised at a time when expanding populations are widening the gap between what capital is needed and what is available.[28]

To use U Thant's phrase, a "climate of fatigue and disenchantment" has gradually been slowing down the support for and dimensions of foreign aid programs.

In a penetrating editorial on "International Finance," prompted by the joint annual meeting of the Governors of the World Bank and the International Monetary Fund in October 1968, *Dawn*, the leading newspaper of Pakistan, summed up many important aspects of the current dilemma of economic development:

> With a declining share of world trade, with poorer prospects for flows of official aid and with an increasing burden of interest and debt repayment, the newly developing countries have been finding it increasingly difficult to maintain the momentum of economic growth.
>
> N. M. Uqali [the Finance Minister of Pakistan] drew attention to the irony of the situation when he told the Governors' meeting that the international aid climate was becoming indifferent at a time when the developing countries . . . were just getting ready to enter upon a more ambitious phase of development.
>
> As the Commonwealth Finance Ministers noted recently, it is possible that, considering the heavy burden of interest and debt repayment, the net flow of external assistance may remain static or may even decline.
>
> The present aid climate in the industrially advanced countries coupled with the limitation through quota and tariff restrictions of trade opportunities available to the developing countries is bound to impinge adversely upon the economic growth of the latter.[29]

The implications of these trends should be clearly understood. After hardly two decades of large-scale experimentation, during which foreign

---

[28] *Ibid.*, p. 1.
[29] October 9, 1968.

aid became an important instrument of the foreign policies of many nations without developing an accepted body of theory or an adequate rationale or sustained public support, the "new statecraft" embodying it seems to be under increasing challenge. As Topping reported, "The world pattern of economic aid to the developing countries of Asia, Africa and Latin America is undergoing a fundamental change," [30] which will inevitably reduce its dimensions and its significance unless present trends can be reversed. If the decline of foreign aid leads to more realistic policies and greater efforts on the part of the developing countries and to more helpful policies in trade, investment and international cooperation on the part of the economically advanced states, this apparently premature drying up of aid funds may turn out to be a blessing in disguise. But if compensatory programs of equal or greater effectiveness do not replace those which are declining, the consequences for the developing countries could be well-nigh disastrous. In that case the developed countries might discover the painful wisdom of the warning of William S. Gaud, former Administrator of the U.S. Agency for International Development, that "To thwart the desire of the new nations for progress is to invite unrest and violence, to encourage hostility toward the developed half of the world and to jeopardize the possibilities for peace." [31]

All nations and peoples should consider the implications of the fact that the Decade of Development, so bravely proclaimed in the early 1960's, is likely to be judged one of frustration and disappointment, and that the situation in the 1970's will be even more grim unless heroic efforts are made by developed and developing countries alike. In his address to the UNCTAD Conference in New Delhi, on February 10, 1968, George Woods, retiring President of the World Bank, said that the most important change needed to correct the trend toward economic stagnation was a "realization on the part of the advanced nations that the development process demanded a more effective and constructive participation by them, and on a high-priority basis." Mrs. Indira Gandhi, in inaugurating that conference, observed: "We must all plead guilty to being tempted by the illusion that small efforts can yield big results. This is why we became disenchanted and international economic cooperation is the first casualty. Thus domestic pressures mount. Our affluent friends seek to curtail their contribution to development. In turn, recipients of aid retreat inward." And all the while, "the gap keeps growing." In her own country, Woods noted, "many millions of people have yet to experience more than the feeblest manifestations of progress," and India "is by no

---

[30] Topping, *op. cit.*, p. 1.

[31] Address at 34th American Assembly, Arden House, Harriman, N.Y., November 2, 1968.

means the only country where hope has dwindled toward despondency."

It is past time to reverse these trends. It is time for all of us, wherever we may live or whatever may be our personal situation, to get out of "the slough of despond" in which we seem to be mired, to elevate our sights and enlarge our horizons, and to accept in fact, as well as in profession, the truth that the world has become too small to wall ourselves in behind political frontiers and refuse to face international needs and realities. It is time to realize, as John F. Kennedy, then a United States Senator, declared over a decade ago, that international economic development calls for "a vast international effort, an enterprise of positive association." [32]

Foreign aid is only one of the instruments that have come into existence to attempt to deal with the immense problems of development, and it has never been a very satisfactory instrument, even on an *ad hoc* and emergency basis; but until the conditions of the developing countries and of the international economy have substantially changed and improved, it is hard to see how the curtailment of foreign aid, at a time of growing needs, can be anything but harmful to all concerned. Admittedly there is a great deal of confusion and disagreement on this point, but the burden of proof rests clearly on those who would throw new burdens on developing countries and impoverished peoples.

For better or worse, foreign aid of substantial dimensions will be a necessary feature of this "vast international effort" for some time to come. It will therefore continue to be a significant aspect of international endeavors and of the foreign policies of nations. We can agree with Seymour Rubin that there are limits to the effectiveness of aid in achieving economic development and in promoting social change," or, for that matter, in advancing any of the goals which aid is supposed to promote. There are also, to continue Rubin's analysis, "limits to the cooperation which can be expected between donors, between the developing countries themselves, and between the developed and the developing." [33] Certainly, however, there is need for greater cooperation on all of these fronts.

In particular, there is need for more candid and more cooperative relations between aid-giving and aid-receiving countries. In spite of an obvious mutuality of interests, the attitudes of both groups of countries toward foreign aid vary greatly, and aid has far different aspects and implications from different vantage points. The relationship between donors and recipients, as Rubin noted, "is fragile, subject to many strains. Resentment, on both sides, lies close beneath the surface." [34] This is a

---

[32] Address in the U.S. Senate, February 19, 1959.

[33] Rubin, *op. cit.*, p. 151.

[34] *Ibid.*, p. 152.

condition that should be recognized and faced, but it should not be allowed to obscure the more positive aspects of the relationship and the mutuality of interests involved, even when viewed from the point of narrowest self-interest. "Foreign aid is not politically neutral. Its effects are powerfully manifested in international relations and in the domestic politics of both the giver and the receiver. It represents a new international ethic, at least in that it compels nations to take a more sympathetic view of each other." [35]

VII

By and large, foreign aid, especially in its political aspects, remains more of an art than a science. It should be the subject of more extensive and more objective research. *Ad hoc*, temporary programs, varying greatly in size and objectives, have developed into major, and apparently long-term, instruments of international cooperation and national policy. Even aid-giving and aid-receiving agencies have given far too little attention to it as a subject for research and evaluation. In spite of extensive studies there is still much uncertainty about the whole foreign aid experience, including its essential rationale, its objectives, its relationship to economic growth, social change and political development, and its impact on national policies and international relations. Yet, to quote David Bell,

> the process of foreign assistance is inherently dependent on research. . . . If we understood our business better, it might well be that the whole process of foreign aid would be seen as a research process, aimed at learning how to move a particular society, with its special and unique characteristics of history and culture and physical geography, toward specified objectives. . . . there can be no doubt of the importance of incorporating far stronger programs of research and evaluation into our aid administration.[36]

Nor, as Bell added, can there be any doubt of the need to develop greater research facilities and competence in the developing countries themselves.

Research, and probably evaluation as well, should not be confined to agencies involved in the administration of aid or other official agencies; by far the greater part should be carried out by private scholars, at universities, research institutes and other centers for relatively disinterested investigation. It should be interdisciplinary in nature and approach, and

---

[35] John D. Montgomery, *The Politics of Foreign Aid: American Experience in Southeast Asia* (New York: Praeger, 1962), p. 278.

[36] David E. Bell, "The Quality of Aid," *Foreign Affairs*, July 1966, p. 606.

it should utilize all of the major techniques, theories and findings of modern social science research.[37]

24.   ECONOMIC SANCTIONS AND STATECRAFT

Johan Galtung

II. THE GENERAL THEORY OF ECONOMIC SANCTIONS

WE SHALL DEFINE SANCTIONS as actions initiated by one or more international actors (the "senders") against one or more others (the "receivers") with either or both of two purposes: to punish the receivers by depriving them of some value and/or to make the receivers comply with certain norms the senders deem important. This definition at once raises an interesting question. It is not obvious that the same action or sanction can serve both purposes; in fact, modern penology does not seem to warrant much belief in punishment as a *general* method for making people comply.[1] Punishment may have other effects, as when criminals are kept off the streets and isolated in prisons where their deviant actions are hidden from the general view and thus are less consequential to the outside world, but this is not the same as making them comply.

From Johan Galtung, "On the Effects of International Economic Sanctions: With Examples from the Case of Rhodesia," in *World Politics*, Vol. XIX, No. 3. Copyright © 1967 by Princeton University Press. Reprinted by permission of Princeton University Press.

Footnotes have been renumbered to appear in consecutive order.

JOHAN GALTUNG (1930–   ) Director of the Peace Research Institute, Oslo. Author of *Cooperation in Europe* (New York: Humanities Press, 1970); *Development in Three Villages in Sicily* (New York: Columbia University Press, 1970); *Theory and Methods of Social Research* (Oslo University: Universitetsforlaget, 1967).

[37] The subject of foreign aid and foreign policy, for example, can be profitably analyzed by using such concepts and approaches as formal and informal penetration and access, interlinkages between domestic politics and foreign policies, the spillover effect, the multiplier effect, the international demonstration effect, and political marginal analysis.

[1] For a general discussion of the problem of compliance, see Galtung, "On the Meaning of Nonviolence," *Journal of Peace Research*, No. 3 (1965), 228–57.

Thus, when sanctions are discussed it makes good sense to ask which purpose is dominant. Imagine, in the Rhodesian case, that another policy had been enacted: that of rewarding the Smith government for any positive step toward majority rule, instead of punishing it for any step interpreted as negative relative to the goal of majority rule. Expressed concretely, this would have meant a policy 'of increased trade, or increasingly favorable trade conditions, and more contact and more diplomatic cooperation as less discriminatory practices were introduced in Rhodesia, with a well-thought-out and well-communicated pattern of action: so much reward for so much compliance. Even a positive escalation process might be envisaged. Imagine that arguments in favor of such a policy as a method of bringing about compliance were in fact quite convincing. Nevertheless there would probably be counter-arguments to the effect that "This is selling out to the enemy," "This is rewarding sinfulness," "This means that any rascal can come around and do something nasty and then extort a reward for undoing the harm he has done—which is tantamount to blackmail," "There will be inflationary effects and we shall soon run out of rewards," and "Who will pay for all this, anyhow?"

Without belittling the significance of any one of these arguments, it makes good sense to ask a politician engaged in sanction policies, "If you cannot have both, which outcome would you prefer, punishment without compliance or compliance without punishment?" If he insists that punishment is a sufficient condition for compliance, then he is simply naive; if he insists that punishment is a necessary condition for compliance, then he is probably in addition highly punishment-oriented in the sense that punishment has become an automatic and probably also cherished goal in itself. This punishment-oriented attitude is probably fairly widespread, particularly as applied to the international system, and serves to maintain negative sanctions.[2] If compliance is not obtained, there is at least the gratification that derives from knowing (or believing) that the sinner gets his due, that the criminal has been punished. In this sense negative sanctions are safer than positive sanctions. And when hatred is strong, positive sanctions would probably be out of the question anyway.

In this article we shall disregard the punishment aspect and be interested in sanctions only as a way of making other international actors comply, and we shall concentrate on negative sanctions. As a reference for a more complete discussion, however, the following dimensions for classifying sanctions may be useful:

---

[2] The best treatment of this theme is probably found in Bjørn Christiansen, *Attitudes to Foreign Affairs as a Function of Personality* (Oslo 1959).

1. Are the sanctions *negative* (punishment for deviance) or *positive* (reward for compliance)?

2. Are the sanctions aimed at responsible *individuals* in a receiving nation, or are they *collective* (hitting the nation as a whole, including individuals and groups that are not particularly responsible)?

3. Are the sanctions *internal* (due to changes arising inside the receiving nation) or are they *external* (having to do with the interaction pattern with other nations)?

4. Are the sanctions *unilateral* (only one sending nation) or *multilateral* (several sending nations, with regional sanctions being a special case) or *universal* (with all or almost all other nations participating)?

5. Are the sanctions *general* or *selective* (involving all possible measures or only some special measures)?

6. Are the sanctions *total* or *partial* (involving all or only some measures of a special kind)?

7. Types of sanctions (types of values of which the receiving nation is deprived):

   a) diplomatic sanctions

   (1) nonrecognition
   (2) rupture of diplomatic relations
   (3) no direct contact with political leaders
   (4) no cooperation by international organizations

   b) communication sanctions

   (1) rupture of telecommunications
   (2) rupture of mail contact
   (3) rupture of transportation (ship, rail, road, air)
   (4) rupture of news communication (radio, newspapers, press agencies)
   (5) rupture of personal contacts (tourism, family visits)

   c) economic sanctions

   (1) internal destruction (economic sabotage, strikes)
   (2) rupture of trade relations (economic boycott)
       (a) hitting imports to receiving nation (import boycott)
       (b) hitting exports from receiving nation (export boycott)
       Economic boycott can comprise *goods, capital, services.* If passage of goods, capital, and/or services to or from the receiving country is reported, the boycott is *supervised;* if in addition passage is impeded, the boycott may be referred to as a *blockade.*

For simplicity we may disregard the cases of internal sanctions and sanctions directed at individuals: with the present structure of the international system, territorial integrity makes such actions—unilateral, multilateral, or universal—impossible unless they are combined with a military presence. In a future world, the supranational structure might include permanent enforcement machinery stationed in all nations—like local police stations in the nations of today—but this is for the future.[3] Thus, our discussion here is limited to *negative, collective,* and *external* sanctions, and like most other analysts we shall concentrate on the theory of *economic* sanctions.

The theory is simple. The input-output matrix of the economy of the receiving nation is inspected. The impact of partial or total boycott of selected imports or exports is calculated. As a matter of rational politics, maximum effect with minimum boycott is looked for; in the case of a receiving nation for which there are accessible data on the economic system, this is a problem that might be left to computers. The ideal case would be that of a system in which total boycott of one product alone would be sufficient, and oil is often held to be this product.[4]

If the goal is to damage the economic system of the receiving nation without similarly damaging the sending nation, this can obviously be attained if a number of conditions that we can refer to as "the ideal case for an economic boycott" are fulfilled. The ideal conditions would be more or less as follows:

1. that imports have a very high loading on important sectors of the economy of the receiving nation;
2. that there is no internal substitute for the imports;
3. that a high loading of the important imports comes from the sending nation(s);
4. that there is no external substitute for these imports, so that the receiving nation cannot threaten to change trade-partners;
5. that the imports make up a very small part of the exports of the sending nation(s), and/or that the products can be exported to other nations;
6. that the exports from the receiving nation are sent mainly to the sending nation(s), and that there are no easy substitutes for them, so that the receiving nation cannot obtain income easily;
7. that these exports from the receiving nation can easily be obtained

---

[3] For an excellent study, see Louis B. Sohn, "Responses to Violation: A General Survey," in Richard A. Falk and Richard J. Barnet, eds., *Security in Disarmament* (Princeton 1965), 178–203.

[4] The basic facts about the structure of the Rhodesian economy seen from this point of view can be found in the survey reported in a Supplement to the *Standard Bank Review* (November 19, 1965), according to which a boycott of the major product for export, tobacco, should affect Rhodesia more than the United Kingdom if the latter were to stop importing it from Rhodesia.

elsewhere by the sending nation(s) so that the sending nation(s) are not hurt economically and can threaten to change trade-partners, *or* that the exports cannot be obtained elsewhere by the sending nation(s) so that the sending nation(s) can demonstrate that they would rather suffer deprivation than touch products from the receiving nation; and

8. that trade relations are easily supervised and even controlled (as when the receiving nation is an island or is surrounded either by impenetrable terrain, such as swamps or deserts, or by nations that participate in the boycott).

It is easily seen that the case in which these conditions are met is that of a small economic satellite of a major economic power. In such a case, perhaps seventy-five percent, or perhaps even ninety percent, of both exports and imports of the small country may be with the big country, yet this trade volume may still be less than one percent of the big country's total trade. This trade structure occurs not infrequently in the present world, and it gives a major potential for control by the big nations of those small nations in their "sphere of interest," particularly since the power of any weapon lies more in its potential than in its actual use.

One could use this kind of situation as a point of departure for a complete theory of economic sanctions. The crucial concept here is *vulnerability*, which has an external and an internal component. The key to the understanding of vulnerability seems to be *concentration:* the more a country's economy depends on one product, and the more its exports consist of one product, and the more its exports and imports are concentrated on one trade-partner, the more vulnerable is the country. To launch economic sanctions without a careful examination of all these factors would be like launching a military campaign without military analysis.

Without going into a great many details, it is interesting to determine which countries rank highest in external vulnerability. As a first approximation, information about the percentage of the GNP comprising foreign trade (exports plus imports) is useful. Among the first ten ranks in the list given in the *World Handbook of Political and Social Indicators* [5] are four islands (Barbados, Mauritius, Cyprus, and Malta), and among the first ten ranks in a similar list in the UN's *Yearbook of National Accounts Statistics 1964* are three islands (Mauritius, Trinidad, Iceland) and Hong Kong, which for all practical purposes is an island. The two ranking lists are not identical, which reflects problems in connection with national accounts statistics more than changes between the

---

[5] Bruce M. Russett and others (New Haven 1964). The data are from Table 46.

periods of time the two lists cover. However, it is interesting to note that six of the first seven countries on the UN list are or have been under British rule. Also, the superpowers, the United States and the USSR, rank eightieth and eighty-first on the *World Handbook* list (with foreign-trade percentages of seven and five), which marks them as particularly invulnerable. The People's Republic of China ranks seventy-ninth, France ranks sixty-seventh, and the United Kingdom, fifty-first. Clearly, the big powers are very different from the smaller powers in external vulnerability. On the other hand, the rank order correlation between the foreign-trade variable and GNP per capita is less than .10, so vulnerability should be seen more as a property of the small power than as a property of the poor nation. Thus, the general picture is that economic sanctions as a source of power tend to preserve existing power structures.

This becomes even more evident when we examine the extent to which exports are limited to a few commodities and their markets to a few countries. The rank order correlation of .606 between Michael Michaely's indices of these two types of concentration suggests that these two aspects of external vulnerability tend to covary.[6] Most vulnerable on both counts (if we also take into consideration the percentage of the GNP comprising foreign trade) are Hong Kong, Trinidad, and Mauritius; least vulnerable are big countries such as the U.S., Brazil, Mexico, India, Argentina, and Colombia. Bigger countries of course have in general more diversity in raw materials and bigger domestic markets; hence they have more potential for diversified domestic industries, which can be converted to export industries. On the other hand, the rank order correlation between the *coefficient of commodity concentration* and the percentage of the GNP made up of trade is only .108, and the corresponding correlation for the *coefficient of geographic concentration* is only .098. Hence, even if there is concentration of exports in terms of commodities and trade-partners it does not follow that exports are very important for the GNP.

Let us then imagine that the three factors of concentration we have discussed (concentration in the economy, concentration in commodities, concentration in trade-partners) are of equal weight in determining external vulnerability. Of course, if sanctions were universal (and not unilateral) geographic concentration would not count; if sanctions were general (and not highly selective) commodity concentration would not count; and if sanctions were both universal and general (and total) then only the trade percentage of the GNP would count. But *a priori* it may be as difficult to make sanctions universal and general as it is to make them "bite." Hence, we have added the ranks for each country reported in Michaely's data on commodity concentration and geographic con-

---

[6] *Concentration in International Trade* (Amsterdam 1962), esp. chap. 2.

centration [7] to its rank for the trade percentage of the GNP. The distribution is interesting, but it should be noticed that the socialist countries are not included in Michaely's lists, which comprise only forty countries. A high score on this index means low vulnerability and a low score means high vulnerability.

The least vulnerable countries are the United States (109 of 120 possible points), France (108), Italy and Japan (104), the Federal Republic of Germany (100), and the United Kingdom (99)—as one would expect. Most vulnerable is Mauritius with 9 points (3 is the minimum); then follow Trinidad and Panama (20) and Rhodesia, which ranks high on both kinds of concentration (ninth and tenth) and on the trade percentage of its GNP (27 points, giving a rank of four on this composite vulnerability list; it ranks eighth on the list in the *World Handbook*). All countries with point scores lower than 50 are or have recently been colonies, which means that they are vulnerable relative to their former mother countries.

For our puropse it is significant that Rhodesia (here including Zambia and Malawi) ranks fourth on the score of external vulnerability, since what we say would apply *a fortiori* to less vulnerable countries. (This rank is based on combined data for the Federation of Rhodesia and Nyasaland for 1959, showing trade to be sixty-six percent of GNP, about half of that percentage comprising exports. Exports of Rhodesia alone, excluding Zambia and Malawi, constitute about forty-three percent of its GNP, according to the Supplement to the *Standard Bank Review*, indicating that Rhodesia's position on that variable is not lower than that of the former Federation, so that Rhodesia alone would not rank lower on the index of external vulnerability.) Most of the countries scored fall between Rhodesia and the United Kingdom, indicating that if they are vulnerable according to one of the variables, then they compensate for it on either or both of the remaining variables.

The determination of a nation's external vulnerability reflects only some of the ideal conditions for economic boycott described earlier. There are still the problems of how important the imports actually are, how easily internal or external substitutes can be found, and so on. Imagine then that all external conditions listed above (conditions 3-8) are obtained by extending the boycott from a unilateral through a regional to a universal action. Then the receiving nation is left with only three counterstrategies:

1. to train itself in sacrifice by doing without certain commodities, and preferably even liking it;

---

[7] *Ibid.,* 22.

2. to restructure the national economy so as to absorb the shock of the boycott, by producing locally the imported commodities denied it or by making some substitutes for them, by finding alternative employment for people made jobless, and so forth; and

3. to organize changes of trade *with* third parties, or *via* third parties,[8] or, if the boycott is truly universal, to engage in smuggling.

To what extent these counterstrategies are sufficient as defense will be discussed below; here it will be noted only that this repertory of defense measures is already quite limited. On the other hand, the world has yet to see a universal boycott.

The theory of the effects of economic warfare is now fairly similar to the theory of the effects of military warfare. Both kinds of warfare are means toward the same end: political disintegration of the enemy so that he gives up the pursuit of his goals. The method used is value-deprivation, which may or may not increase with time according to how the action proceeds and what countermeasures are enacted. Countermeasures may take the form of offensive measures (value-deprivation from the attacker) or defensive measures (reducing the value-deprivation inflicted upon oneself) of active or passive varieties.

We shall now distinguish between a naive and a revised theory of the effects of economic warfare. The *naive* theory of the relation between economic warfare (and also military warfare) and political disintegration sees some kind of roughly proportionate relation: the more value-deprivation, the more political disintegration.[9] The idea is that there is a limit to how much value-deprivation the system can stand and that once this limit is reached (resulting in a split in leadership or between leadership and people), then political disintegration will proceed very rapidly and will lead to surrender or willingness to negotiate.

However, this theory disregards the simple principle of *adaptation:* that which seems unacceptable at the beginning of the conflict becomes acceptable as one gets used to life under hardship. Thus, the "upper limit" of what can be tolerated recedes as the value-deprivation progresses, and political disintegration becomes less easily obtainable. However, there remains an upper limit of value-deprivation, short of total destruction, which presents difficulties for the attacker. Even if we exclude moral problems, the attacker must recognize that he may have to restore the

---

[8] An excellent account of how South Africa was able to get around the Indian boycott launched against it in July 1946 by means of trade via third parties is given in K. N. Raj, "Sanctions and the Indian Experience," in Segal, *Sanctions Against South Africa,* 197–203.

[9] This must, by and large, have been a major theory behind many efforts in recent history to bomb an adversary into submission.

attacked nation and have to coexist with its new leadership, not to mention its future and possibly revanchist generations. Thus, an important defense strategy is to indicate that one will hold out at least until the attacker's upper limit is reached.

But we refer to this theory as "naive" also because it does not take into account the possibility that value-deprivation may initially lead to political *integration* and only later—perhaps much later, or even never—to political disintegration. The basic point here is that value-deprivation creates the social conditions under which much more sacrifice is possible so that the limit for political disintegration will be reached much later.

The problem is now under which conditions the revised theory is the more valid and under which conditions the naive theory is less naive. A short list of such conditions includes these:

1. The attack from the outside is seen as an attack on the group as a whole, not on only a fraction of it;
2. There is very weak identification with the attacker, preferably even negative identification; and
3. There is belief in the value of one's own goals in the sense that no alternative is seen as better.

The interesting thing is that in economic warfare, often even more than in military warfare, the first condition is almost immediately and automatically satisfied. The collective nature of economic sanctions makes them hit the innocent along with the guilty. They are in practice, if not in theory, an application of the principle of collective guilt. However, if the other two conditions are not satisfied, then this *may* turn to the benefit of the attacker. Internal dissension in the receiving nation may result when the people feel harassed. The people may then bring pressure upon the leaders to change their policy—in other words, political disintegration.

Thus, the recipes for economic sanctions of various types are fairly obvious. Like a military operation, the logistics of sanctions can be worked out in great detail, and this can even have its bureaucratic appeal since there is an element of administrative challenge, as well a neatness, about the operation when modern, well-organized societies with good national bookkeeping are involved. At the same time it is obvious where the weaknesses of the theory of economic warfare lie. There are two weak points: (1) the idea that political disintegration is more or less proportionate to economic disintegration, and (2) the idea that economic disintegration cannot be counteracted. Of course, no politician of any standing would be so naive as to subscribe to the idea that economic sanctions —once they are effective, economically speaking—will automatically cause either partial or complete surrender. But the politician who is sophisticated at the verbal level may still be naive at the level of actions:

he may simply be at a loss as to what to do when faced with the complexities of the effects of economic sanctions—or of other sanctions, for that matter. We shall try to describe systematically some hypotheses about such effects that are negative from the point of view of the sending nation(s), but before we do that, let us look more closely at the kind of theory the sending nation(s) (in this case, the United Kingdom) may have as to how the sanctions will eventually work.

Prime Minister Wilson's methodology and theory of economic sanctions have been set forth in some detail in speeches given in Parliament on December 10, 1965, and January 25, 1966.[10] First of all, there has been a policy of graduated escalation along two dimensions: starting with the United Kingdom, measures have proceeded from selective and partial sanctions toward practically general and total economic sanctions; they have proceeded from relatively unilateral action by the United Kingdom toward the universal action envisaged and hoped for. Some of this gradualism has been deliberate (to permit the threat of worse measures to be invoked at any time, as well as to prevent too much damage to Rhodesia, which will have to function in the future) and some of it has been a virtue of necessity. On the day of UDI, a number of financial measures excluding Rhodesia from the sterling area and from the preference status enjoyed by Commonwealth members were introduced, together with a ban on Rhodesian tobacco imports to the United Kingdom and on weapons exports from the United Kingdom to Rhodesia. Then, in the three months that followed UDI, most moves toward complete boycott were made.

Incidentally, communications restrictions were remarkably underutilized, particularly considering how tempting it must have been to use them since white Rhodesians are heavily dependent on such communications for maintaining their identity as an outpost of British (if not Labour) civilization. The United Kingdom has, however, tried to control

---

[10] See the *Official Report* for these two days. For another and very similar example of a theory as to how sanctions might work, let us quote from the article "Can Smith be brought down?" *Peace News* (November 19, 1965), 1, 4. Six factors are mentioned: white supporters will desert Smith (1) "as the economic life of the country becomes more unmanageable"; (2) because of the staunch attitude of the governor and the symbolism of some people's indication of their support for him; (3) because of the blank spaces in the newspapers, indicating censorship; (4) because of "unrest among members of the civil service, police and army"; (5) because of "unrest among the African population"; and (6) because of "South Africa's refusal to deal in Rhodesian currency." This list shows a clear overestimation of the organizational power of the African population and an equally clear overestimation of the force and legitimacy of British symbols far from home. Moreover, there is always the question of how many people really worry about censorship, particularly when it is directed against opinions and writers they dislike themselves.

access to Rhodesia, probably partly to symbolize its sovereignty over the "runaway colony," partly to control the information flow.[11]

The Wilson theory as to exactly how political disintegration will take place within the very short time spans he announced in the first weeks and months after UDI contains such elements as increasing unrest among the whites due to unemployment and material deprivations resulting from reduced exports and imports. According to this theory, either development may be used by the existing opposition elements in Rhodesia or may lead to the formation of new centers of opposition; in either case the opposition may make an appeal to the governor, and a solution will be found through him. Thus, the governor may symbolize a return to "law and order," and the troops stationed in Zambia may be recalled at the governor's request. Exactly what may happen to Smith and his numerous followers in this context is not clear, but then Wilson is speaking as a politician, not as a social scientist.

Clearly, if political disintegration should take place it would happen through the dual effect of sanctions, which weakens the people in power and strengthens those in opposition. For this to happen, as Wallensteen points out, it is not sufficient that the sanctions are perceived as an evil; alternative courses of action must also be perceived as lesser evils.[12] Thus, it is Wilson's task not only to escalate into a sanction pattern as harsh as possible, but also to present alternatives as acceptable as possible. To achieve the latter aim, a vision of the near future that does not contain majority rule must be presented to the white Rhodesians—and the famous six points were designed to do this. What was held out to them was legal rule, not majority rule.[13]

---

[11] This control of access to Rhodesia dates from November 1965 when "Great Britain established a general requirement for visas for travel to Rhodesia, and stated, on this occasion, that the sole legal authorities outside Great Britain having the right to issue such visas are the British embassies and consulates." Later on, sanctions were added to this rule: "The British authorities . . . reserve the right to refuse entry into Great Britain to persons who have sought visas for entry into Rhodesia from the representatives of Ian Smith's regime" (quoted from Royal Norwegian Ministry of Foreign Affairs, Circular No. 27, March 11, 1966).

[12] *Aspekter*, 25–26.

[13] Wilson's thinking about how Rhodesia should be made to comply can be interestingly contrasted with the thinking of one Conservative M.P., Mr. G. Lloyd, who "suggested that Britain should look back and consider what might have been done and how much money could have been spent in the past to bring Rhodesia to a position today where it was felt independence could be granted. Britain could then get the Commonwealth together and raise, say, £200 million to bring Rhodesia to such a position by possibly 1980. Of this, possibly £50 million could be spent on education, £50 million on boosting the economy, £50 million on communications and £50 million on other projects" (the Salisbury correspondent in *The Star* [Johannesburg], January 12, 1966, 21). Although this suggestion reflects the paternalist posi-

Equally clear is Smith's counterstrategy: to reverse the order of utilities. For that purpose, sanctions must appear as manageable, even slightly ridiculous, and the alternatives must be defined not merely as a return to the pre-UDI situation but as alternatives that will of necessity have even more negative implications for the white Rhodesians. There are many ways of achieving this purpose. One of them is to maneuver Wilson into a position in which, because of the African Commonwealth members, he is unable to offer an alternative that does not contain majority rule. Another method is censorship, so that information about attractive alternatives (as well as information about serious effects of the sanctions) does not reach the Rhodesian reader. To the extent that that reader is in general agreement with Smith, this method will work, because there will be no demand for these two types of news; they will both cause severe cognitive dissonance. But the major counterstrategy will always be to channel the effects of the sanctions themselves in the best possible directions—and this is the topic to which we now turn.

III. THE DEFENSE AGAINST ECONOMIC SANCTIONS

Two principles for discussing counterstrategies against economic sanctions have here been presented. One of them follows from the logic of the attacker. There are three holes in this system, however, even when the sanctions are universal (adaptation to sacrifice, restructuring the economy to absorb the shock, and smuggling). The other principle follows from the logic behind what we have called the revised theory (that the collectivity is threatened, that there is no identification with the attacker, and that there is firm belief in one's own values).

The details about how the first three counterstrategies work out in the Rhodesian case are in a sense obvious aspects of the total situation. More important is the question the social scientist observing the situation will immediately ask: Are these strategies *self-reinforcing*, so that some immediate benefit or reward can be derived from engaging in them, and so that one does not have to rely on belief in ultimate victory or loyalty to the regime alone? The following accounts seem to indicate that this is the case for all three.

Q. How do you manage with so little petrol?
A. Oh, that is easy enough. You know, if a family has two cars and receives some petrol for both, to put one car in the garage is not very much of a sacrifice. Besides, some of us who live in the countryside and have offices in Salisbury join our rations and form a car

---

tion of "education for maturity," it also reflects the approach of the positive reward, provided there is a way of tying the transfer of £200 million to the steps toward majority rule.

pool and go in together. It is strange to see how much better friends one becomes with one's neighbors in such situations—we really did not know them before. And if even this should not work, this may be the great impetus that forces the city to develop adequate collective transportation, and if even that does not work, doctors are almost unanimous that walking is good for you.[14]

Thus, an important mechanism increasing group solidarity is revealed: the car pool seems to have some of the same functions as the bomb shelter during an air raid.[15] *Adaptive measures* have become goals in themselves.

Q. But what about all kinds of luxury goods, or household appliances?
A. You must remember that very many families here are quite well off. They have a refrigerator, maybe even two. They work. If refrigerators cannot be bought, well, some will be without and others will not have the latest models. But most will have refrigerators, and they will last—our technicians are not so bad that they cannot improvise some spare parts. And as to luxury goods—we have been without them during two world wars when we helped Britain, the same Britain that attacks us today, and we can do without them again. Besides, one family has some and another family will borrow from it. That was also the pattern during the war.

Again, there is the possibility of improvisation and of mutual aid, with the well-known social implications of both. Hence, there is immediate reward in the process, and this reward may be particularly attractive as more people are deprived of this kind of experience in their daily life. (Thus, in a more traditional and poorer society there would be only marginal reward to derive from this sort of experience, since it is not scarce.)

However, *sacrifice* also has its immediate, built-in reward. *Conspicuous sacrifice*, when indulged in by the leaders of a society, may have its obvious propaganda effect: the sanctions themselves may give the leaders pretexts to demonstrate their ability to share the plight of the people. Under normal conditions such occasions are denied them and such demonstrations would in fact make them appear ridiculous; under moderate hardship they can act out a carefully balanced amount of heroism and

---

[14] Thus, there were stories in the press about the Masais, who are able to keep fit and healthy because they walk to work (hunting) over long distances every day.

[15] A good account of the effects of air raids on Britain is found in R. M. Titmuss, "Argument of Strain," in Eric and Mary Josephson, eds., *Man Alone* (New York 1962), 505–15.

sacrifice. And this signal is communicated not only to their own believers and disbelievers, but also to the sending nation(s), conveying to them the message "We would rather suffer at your hands than give in." [16] Thus, the situation opens possibilities for the use of symbols out of which strong ideological sentiments can be made, and this is another self-reinforcing ingredient.[17] It should be noted in passing that this advantage does not apply equally to the case of military action, since there heroism may be too risky: the leaders may be captured or simply perish if they carry it too far.

Let us then turn to the possible consequences of *restructuring the economy*. People in key economic positions are also usually people with political influence. An economic boycott may reshuffle the relative importance of economic sectors so that new economic elites emerge. The question is, Will the new elites be more or less willing to comply with the norms of the sending nations? Since economic boycott in general implies a rapid decrease of import-export business and a change toward home-based production, the question is whether the cosmopolitan layer of the tertiary sector (engaged in trade), which stands to lose some of its significance, is more or less amenable to compliance than are the emerging leaders of home-based industry or agriculture (or other primary activities).

In the Rhodesian case, the farmers are seen as the group most solidly behind Smith.[18] In addition to the simple structural reasons that are conducive to making farmers nationalists in most nations,[19] and in favor of cheap labor, there is also the element of isolation from world trends and consequently a solid measure of conservatism, a kind of asynchrony relative to the second half of the twentieth century. For the cosmopolitan

---

[16] After UDI, shops in Salisbury displayed posters with drawings of Rhodesians in uniform, with rather determined faces, tightening their belts. The general idea was that of serving the country again, of "the men being called up," something of the prewar atmosphere described by Doris Lessing in her novel *A Proper Marriage*.

[17] Thus, the idea of the prime minister bicycling to his office might appeal to many. (Incidentally, the photograph of Smith on a bicycle that figured in many newspapers implied no permanent change in his means of transportation.) But just as important might be the idea of symbolizing "everything normal"; the receiving nation can make political gains on this as well as on conspicuous sacrifice.

[18] According to observers, the opposition in the white Rhodesian population amounts to around 20,000 and consists mainly of the press, the bankers, the industrialists, the lawyers, the teachers, and people in their primary circles. We know of no solid data to support this contention.

[19] One very simple reason is that ownership of farms is usually hereditary, which ties farmers to the territory for generations ahead. A professional's job is not hereditary; he can afford to be nonnationalist or even antinationalist since his position will not similarly affect his offspring.

businessmen nothing of this applies, or it applies much less. Businessmen are more likly to have connections abroad—or money. They depend for their personal needs less on development in Rhodesia, whereas the farmers have no or few alternatives. But for this same reason the farmers might also feel that the policies of the Smith government are rather hazardous, and one day the farmers could turn against him. In our view, however, this is unlikely precisely because of the way in which economy and sociology here seem to go hand in hand: changes in the economy put power more and more into the hands of the farmers; they increasingly become the symbol of national survival. Moreover, when an import-export firm has to close down there is little alternative use to which it can be put, whereas it makes a great deal of sense for the government to subsidize the conversion of tobacco land to grain fields or pasture.[20]

Thus, there is a built-in and ever more powerful mechanism of reinforcement here, and the same effect seems to apply to efforts to make substitute products. If such efforts fail, then Britain is to blame; if they succeed, then it is a proof of local ingenuity and justifies the claim to independence. To make automobile fuel out of sugarcane—or even out of coal, which is also a surplus product—would be the ideal.[21] To assume that the nation receiving sanctions will never be able to do such things because it never did them before is a little bit like trusting that children will never grow up when left alone. At any rate, the self-reinforcing power of such inventiveness will probably lead to a chain reaction both in inventiveness and in feelings of autonomy. Thus, it is almost certain that regardless of the political outcome, Rhodesian industry will come out of the crisis with a greater share of the home markets—and this possibility probably serves as an extra incentive.

In the pattern of employment, however, it is difficult to discover anything self-reinforcing. The governmental policy of letting imported labor from neighboring countries to be the first to absorb the shock so as to deflect the effects of sanctions and even turn them toward friends of the enemy (except for the case of Africans from Mozambique and South

---

[20] Of course, the list of people belonging to the opposition according to observers (footnote 18) is impressive, and these people could be most dangerous to the regime. However, they have lost much of their prestige simply from being less functional than the farmers, who will always have the important task of keeping the population alive during a period of crisis. Thus, our argument is in terms of transfer of legitimacy due to a dislocation of the center of gravity in being functional to the community at large. The result may be more legitimacy to sectors favoring more apartheid.

[21] Thus, in South Africa, the technology of extracting oil from coal is already quite advanced. According to the *Times Review of Industry* (December 1963), about ten percent of the country's needs are taken care of that way (the state-owned plant SASOL produces about forty million gallons of gasoline annually).

Africa) is probably clearer, but it is not internally stimulating. The next in line to absorb the shock would be, or could be, native Africans. A cleverer policy would be to distribute the impact more evenly and to display some cases of conspicuous sacrifice by the white community.

But very strong reinforcement, as far as we can judge, comes from the third strategy, that of *smuggling:*

Q. But haven't you all become so well adjusted to rather regular business patterns that it is difficult to do more irregular types of business?

A. As to the moral aspect, No—if we have to do something irregular, Britain is to blame, not we. And as to habits, I'll tell you how it is. Look at Salisbury; see how beautiful and perfect everything is. Look at the surroundings; see what a good life we have. My wife and I used to go to garden parties and give garden parties perhaps three times a week; there were shows and exhibitions; the weekend trip to Beira for a good swim, an occasional hunt—we had and still have everything except, I have to admit, life had a tendency to be somewhat boring. And then these blessed sanctions came into our existence and we had to get out of our smug practices and use all our talents again. I have never had so much fun since I came here— years ago! You have to figure out how products can be brought in by middlemen, how you can threaten that firms we used to import from will lose their markets here forever if they do not help us, how goods can eventually be smuggled into the country if that is necessary, how to get petrol more cheaply than from the Portuguese merchants who set up filling stations across the border from Umtali and charge exorbitant prices for the gallon. You really get a chance to show what you are worth.

At this point it must be added that the challenge of smuggling is not enough; one also has to be at least moderately successful in order to be rewarded in the process. Thus, if the sending nations are able to ensure that regardless of how much talent is invested in smuggling very few goods will in fact materialize, the rewards from this defense mechanism will dwindle away. But in Rhodesia, with its extensive borders adjoining friendly territories, even moderate talent should be able to bring about major success.

Thus, in general the thesis that economic sanctions, at least to start with, will have a tendency to create social and political integration rather than disintegration seems to be a relatively strong one. But this thesis is not unconditional. Thus, it will probably not hold in traditional societies based more on primary relationships, but then such societies are less likely to depend on trade for their continued existence. The theory also presupposes that there is strong support among the sectors that become dominant in a crisis economy, and it presupposes that smuggling is not entirely impossible. Under these conditions the short-term impact of economic sanctions will be negligible. . . .

The condition for sanctions to be effective that is most often referred to in more or less scholarly analyses is the problem of *universality*. The argument is that economic sanctions have failed because they were not universal; some countries did not participate, or some other way of circumventing the sanctions was found (smuggling, use of third parties, and so on). Only detailed analysis of individual cases can do justice to this argument. But even though the argument no doubt has some validity, there are also important reasons to believe that this validity is limited.

First of all, even under a totally effective blockade a country may continue to run on its internal resources, and these resources (economic, social, moral, political) may be strengthened rather than weakened by the sanctions. The question is whether these resources are sufficient to maintain a society and a political community—and this question cannot be answered in general and *a priori*.

Second, although the economic effect of sanctions by definition increases with the increasing participation of the senders, it is not obvious that the moral effect increases. On the contrary, to feel that the rest of the world is "ganging up" on one may serve as a very effective and hardening stimulus, supporting paranoid and psychopathic tendencies as well as more salutary forces.[22] However, we know very little about this.

But even if the direct and intended consequences of sanctions are unlikely to obtain, there may be other effects. When analyzing political actions in terms of their consequences, and particularly in terms of whether the actions serve the purposes intended for them, less rational purposes are often forgotten. If economic sanctions do not make a receiving nation comply, they may nevertheless serve functions that are useful in the eyes of the sending nation(s). There is, for example, the punishment aspect referred to earlier. There is the value of at least doing something, of having the illusion of being instrumental, of being busy in time of crisis. When military action is impossible for one reason or another, and when doing nothing is seen as tantamount to complicity, then *something has to be done to express morality*, something that at least serves as a clear signal to everyone that what the receiving nation has done is disapproved of. If the sanctions do not serve instrumental purposes they can at least have *expressive* functions. Thus, as a highly dramatic (and costly) way of reinforcing international morality, economic sanc-

---

[22] This is a major perspective in the well-known content analyses of German actions and reactions before the outbreak of World War I made by R. C. North and his colleagues.

tions may be useful, although it would be interesting to compare their effects with those of much cheaper means, such as declarations, resolutions, or demonstrations.

This judgment leads to the suspicion that economic sanctions may serve the purpose of expressing moral disapproval best when they are of a symbolic nature and value-deprivation is kept low. Moreover, we believe that this purpose is served still better if the senders deprive themselves of as much or even more value as the receivers are deprived of. Thus, a boycott of South African oranges may by itself be a meaningful demonstration of an attitude, an act of communication so to speak. But which case is more effective: when there is no other way for the boycotters to obtain oranges, whereas South Africa easily finds other markets, or when South Africa finds no substitute market, whereas the boycotters indulge in oranges from Israel, Cyprus, or Spain?—in other words, when only the senders are hurt, or when only the receivers are hurt? The dilemma may serve well as an illustration of the difference between nonviolent and violent reasoning, but where the resolution of the dilemma is concerned we simply do not know the answer.[23]

Let us now turn the argument around and imagine that experiences with economic sanctions in this century had been more positive. Let us imagine that economic sanctions as a coercive measure have become a permanent and frequent aspect of international interaction. What changes does this imply in the structure of the system? And, to what extent are these changes cherished results and to what extent lessapplauded consequences?

First of all, if economic sanctions have come to stay, it would be unwise of realistic and clever governments not to think about countermeasures. Some governments will even today define themselves as belonging to minority groups in the international system against whom such sanctions might be wielded; others are foresighted enough to appreciate that the world structure may change and that they may one day become the victims of such policies, however improbable that might seem today.[24]

The first and most obvious countermeasure would be to do what many nations do today as a part of their program of total defense: broaden their basis of production for exports so that their economy cannot be destroyed by actions pertaining to one or a few products only. One-crop

---

[23] See footnote 1.

[24] Thus, Norwegians would be most surprised and indignant if they heard that the Lapps had been influential enough to marshal nations into a boycott of Norway because of discriminatory practices. They would be less surprised, perhaps, but equally indignant if certain attitudes expressed at the UNCTAD conferences about Norwegian shipping policies crystallized into boycott actions.

countries are vulnerable because of the greater ease with which an economic boycott can be supervised.[25] This, then, leads to *diversification of the national economy.*

Second, nations will try to increase the number of recipients of their exports and suppliers of their imports in order to be less dependent on a single nation that might engage in unilateral boycott actions against them. This will also make boycott actions less easy to carry out since there will be fewer relationships like the one between Britain and Rhodesia. One may refer to this as the *defeudalization of international trade.*

Both of these strategies will be applauded by many today since they are compatible with general moves toward political and economic independence. This approval also applies partly, but only partly, to the third countermeasure: the tendency toward *economic self-sufficiency,* which has been a classical component of defense against military warfare and is an equally obvious component of defense against economic warfare. This tendency is also consistent with the almost universal need for economic structures that can save a nation from expenses in foreign currencies. But the consequence of self-sufficiency is decreased world interdependence; and to the extent that a high level of interdependence, economic and otherwise, between the nations of the world is seen as a way of strengthening the capacity of the international system to resist war, this is a rather negative consequence.

Thus, the countermeasures consequent to a declared policy in favor of the application of economic sanctions are consistent with economic policies pursued by many nations today, but are based on other reasons. This consistency will facilitate their implementation and, since there will then be less to fear, their implementation will probably also further the acceptance of economic sanctions. But these consequences do not appear to be consistent with a view of the interdependent international structure as more resistant against violent conflict than a structure very low in interdependence. Thus, one may run the risk of buying a (dubious) nonmilitary coercive measure at the expense of an even more dangerous international structure than that we already have. . . .

---

[25] Shipping is of course also a "crop," putting a nation like Norway in the same position as many developing, raw-material-exporting countries where vulnerability is concerned.

25. THE INTERNATIONALIZATION OF PRODUCTION AND THE MULTINATIONAL CORPORATION

Raymond Vernon

IT IS HARDLY a century since the corporation came to be the dominant mode for the conduct of modern business. It is an even shorter period since corporations became not only the principal buyers and sellers of goods, but the major borrowers and lenders of capital flowing between countries. And it is scarcely more than yesterday since groups of corporations, joined by a common parent but including diverse nationalities, began to play a major part in the national economic life of sovereign states.

To be sure, there are certain attributes of these corporate groups which suggest that the modern phenomenon is not wholly without precedent. The House of Rothschild and the Catholic Church, for instance, have maintained temporal interests on a large scale in many different states over long periods of time; and these interests, one presumes, have been managed to some extent in response to a common strategy.

But these cases do little to prepare us for the fact that nearly half of *Fortune*'s 500 largest U.S. companies today have extensive overseas investments in plants, mines, or oil fields, representing an aggregate stake that is on the order of $50 billion. A score or two of these large companies now have a third or more of their total assets abroad; even a greater number derive a third or more of their income from foreign sales through one channel or another.

As a result, transactions between members of corporate families now play a prominent part in the foreign trade and the foreign capital movements of the advanced countries. While it is impossible to measure such transactions completely, their influence must be considerable. For instance, the net capital outflows of U.S. parent companies to their foreign

From: "The Internationalization of Production and the Multinational Corporation" by Raymond Vernon. In "Multinational Corporations and National Sovereignty," *Harvard Business Review,* March–April 1967, pp. 156–172. © 1967 by the President and Fellows of Harvard College. All rights reserved.

RAYMOND VERNON (1913–   ) Professor, Harvard Business School. Author of *Manager in the International Economy* (Englewood Cliffs, N.J.: Prentice-Hall, 1968); *How Latin America Views the U.S. Investor* (New York: Praeger Publishers, 1966); *Myth and Reality of our Urban Problems* (Cambridge: Harvard University Press, 1966); *Metropolis 1985* (Cambridge: Harvard University Press, 1960); *Organizing for World Trade* (New York: Carnegie Endowment for International Peace, 1955).

subsidiaries have been running at $2 billion or $3 billion a year; royalties, fees, and dividends flowing annually to the U.S. parents from such subsidiaries are approaching $5 billion; yearly exports to foreign affiliates by U.S. parents now exceed $6 billion, while imports seem to be running at only a slightly lower rate.

These are not overwhelming sums in a world which counts its annual international transactions in hundreds of billions of dollars. But they are large enough to be noticed, and it would be astonishing if they did not grow very rapidly in the years just ahead. Besides, these family transactions tend to be looked on by nation-states in rather a different light from arm's-length transactions between independent actors. Corporate families, after all, are presumed to place their members in different national jurisdictions in order to pursue a common purpose—otherwise there would be little reason for their existence.

GLOBAL STRATEGIES

The common purpose may be a consequence of the fact that the corporate family shares a scarce resource, such as technology or capital funds or a communications network; or it may be the reflection of some basic strategy, such as the oil industry's maintenance of a vertical chain from crude oil to petrochemicals. Whatever the common purpose of an international corporate group, loose or tight, articulated or otherwise, it is seen by governments as a strategy which extends beyond the borders of any one nation.

The forces which have generated these multinational corporate groups are not simple. But by now some of them are fairly well understood. Two developments have provided the backdrop.

One has been the emergence of the corporate form itself, endowed with attributes that give it extraordinary advantages as a vehicle for doing business. The corporation can count on perpetual life; it can hope to attain unlimited size; it can bear children or create parents or generate siblings; and it can endow each of its newborn relations with such nationality as seems convenient.

The other has been the sharp increase in the efficiency of transportation and communication—with the resulting improvement in the capacity to develop and execute a strategy that embraces the activities of far-flung members of the group. It is platitudinous to comment on the speed with which goods and people can now be shuttled around the world's surface, as compared with 30 or 40 years ago. But it is far from platitudinous to speculate on the consequences of these past improvements—which have only just begun to work themselves out—and of the improvements that are yet to come.

One consequence, of course, is that the cost of acquiring knowledge about foreign environments is declining very fast. With each new advance, it becomes easier for corporate managements to (a) weigh remotely situated sites for their merits and drawbacks as producing and distributing points, (b) monitor the establishment of distant enterprises, and (c) nurse these enterprises through their teething troubles. Today it begins to be feasible to think of great international networks of mines and plants, straddling national boundaries, that are interlocked by supply lines which implement a common strategy in production, marketing, and control.

Thus one can picture the use of the cheap labor of Nigeria, the high skills of Israel, and the external economies of the United States in integrated industrial patterns which look on national boundaries as posing only a modest risk—a risk worth assuming for the advantages of least-cost locations and of specialized production facilities. The possibility can be viewed all the more easily, in fact, because a few cases of the sort already exist. Ford's facilities in Mexico which manufacture certain kinds of production equipment for use in the company's plants in the United States and Europe and IBM's facilities in Argentina for its world production of punchcard sorters are examples.

Possibilities of this sort, however, can only be extrapolated if nation-states can be expected to play the game. On the sovereign's part, the game demands a minimum of interference of the sort which would disturb the planning of the multinational group. But do sovereigns have any reason to play? Or can they rather be expected to try to constrain such global strategies on the grounds that the integrated operations of multinational groups constitute a clear and present danger to national sovereignty?

A LOPSIDED PHENOMENON

Before one can address the question seriously, there is a troublesome feature of existing multinational corporate groups that has to be weighed in the response. The overwhelming preponderance of these groups today are headed by a corporate parent of U.S. nationality, and the vast majority of the parent organizations are owned principally by stockholders who are residents of the United States. If one were to list every large U.S. corporation that owns and controls producing facilities in half a dozen or more countries abroad, the roster would contain about 200 names.

To be sure, a European list of the same sort would include the familiar, long-standing names of Unilever, Bowaters, Philips, Olivetti, Nestlé, Ciba, Royal Dutch-Shell, Pechiney, and a few others. But the European list would be considerably shorter, covering only 30 or so cases. And the overseas stakes of the companies on such a roster would not be as much as one fifth of the U.S. commitment.

There are those who assume that the lopsided character of this phenomenon is only transitory, due to the cumulative consequences of a destructive war, followed in Europe by a booming domestic market and a squeeze on available funds and manpower. This may be. But history suggests that the predominance of U.S. multinational corporate groups in manufacturing and in services is nothing new; actually, it began to manifest itself well before the beginning of the present century.

The Historical Pattern. In a study soon to be published, business historian Mira Wilkins reminds us that before the turn of the century U.S. producers of revolvers, sewing machines, printing and linotype machines, electrical machinery, agricultural machinery, and scores of other products had already set up branch producing units in Britain and on the European continent.

Moreover, throughout the first few decades of this century, eruptions over the ebullience and aggressiveness of U.S. business investors occurred sporadically in the public press of Canada, Britain, Germany, and other European countries, as well as in the newspapers and periodicals of Latin America. Accordingly, although it may be true that conditions following World War II were especially favorable to the development of U.S. corporate groups, history offers us a hint that some of these conditions existed for a long term earlier.

It is not yet altogether clear what all the necessary and sufficient conditions which spurred U.S. international investors on were. Perhaps the picture will be less murky when my colleagues and I have finished our research. But on the basis of what is already known, I feel reasonably secure about our understanding of some of the factors involved.

Elsewhere I have spelled out our tentative explanations in a set of explicit hypotheses.[1] It is a bit difficult to reproduce these hypotheses here very fully without an inordinate use of space; but at the risk of eliding some of the points in the argument, let me try to summarize their main features.

For a century or more, the U.S. economy has been distinguished from those of Europe and the rest of the world in a few basic respects. Relatively speaking, the United States has been a country in which per capita income has been high, wage rates for skilled and unskilled labor have been correspondingly elevated, and internal markets have been large. As a result, U.S. businessmen have been especially aware of certain kinds of market opportunities long before such favorable circumstances would have been apparent in a European setting. Notably, this awareness has provided the opportunity both to satisfy new consumer wants associated with high incomes and to replace scarce, high-cost labor with lower cost machines.

---

[1] See my article, "International Trade and International Investment in the Product Cycle," *Quarterly Journal of Economics*, May 1966, p. 190.

Fortunately, a stream of scientific advances which suggested provocative new ways to fill these needs were coming from Europe and the United States during the period. But because the needs these inventions might satisfy were acutely visible first in the United States, it was often the U.S. businessmen who were the first to risk their funds and energies in trying to fill those needs.

Once having developed a product, a process, or a service for the domestic market, U.S. entrepreneurs eventually found some demand in overseas markets. In time, as incomes and labor costs rose in those markets, demand also grew. At some point in the process, U.S. producers found it necessary or desirable to set up overseas producing facilities.

In some cases the sheer challenge of using their development lead to extend their business horizons was what seemed to move the U.S. entrepreneurs; at other times, the fear of being ousted from a newly established export market seemed to be a main motivating force; and on still other occasions, the instinct to follow the leader into new ventures—that is, to imitate a rival in order to maintain some kind of equilibrium in a carefully balanced competitive situation—appeared to dominate the investment decision.

Motives such as these seem steadily to have pushed U.S. producers into foreign markets—from the revolver and the sewing machine producers in the nineteenth century to the computer and frozen pea producers in the twentieth.

Future Possibilities. If this idealized and over simplified version comes anywhere near the mark in describing the main forces that have generated multinational corporate groups, then there is a real possibility that U.S. companies may continue to be the leaders in the proliferation of such groups for some time to come. The conclusion, however, has to be stated as a "real possibility," not as a foregone conclusion.

For one thing, Europe will certainly continue to innovate some products and processes in the future just as it has in the past. Europe, after all, has made some of the more spectacular modern contributions to the technology of glass, steel, and plastics production. Whether European companies will be disposed to use future innovations of this sort as a springboard for setting up producing facilities in the United States is another matter. But a few cases of this sort will certainly arise.

Even without innovations as the propelling factor, one must allow for the appearance in the future, as in the past, of a number of European-based companies with a built-in dynamism that leads them to tackle the challenge of producing in the U.S. market.

There is also a possibility that the appearance of the European Economic Community and the European Free Trade Association may help to shift the research and development balance. It may be that the larger markets offered by these communities will (a) lower the risks of investing in research and development, as those risks are perceived by European businessmen, and (b) lead to the generation of a bigger stream of products and processes from that part of the world. In that case, if my earlier hypothesis has any validity, the disposition of European business to invest in producing facilities abroad may very well increase.

Having paid due obeisance to these possibilities, however, one has to confess that there is little hard evidence to support any such expectations. While the initial response of European business to the widening of markets in postwar Europe did seem to suggest an increased disposition to seize new opportunities, the prevailing mood in recent years has been a shade more traditional and restrictive. There is more than a slight possibility of a reversion in Europe to some of the restrictive business practices of prewar years.

The nub of the argument is by now fairly evident. Transportation and communication improvements may continue to shrink the globe at a disconcerting rate. The responses to that fact may well be asymmetrical, at least for some years to come. Corporate groups headed by U.S. parents may exploit the opportunity (or respond to the threat) with investments in Europe and elsewhere on a much larger scale than the enterprises of other advanced countries are doing. And if that is the case, the problems posed by the growth of the multinational corporate groups may continue to be thought of as problems bearing a U.S. trademark, rather than as a global issue of national sovereignties confronting multinational enterprises.

HOST NATION REACTIONS

Perhaps a year or two from now, when my collaborators have finished their ambitious work, we may have a deeper understanding of the complex and ambivalent reactions of host governments to the investment overtures of multinational corporate groups. But since this is avowedly an interim view, intended to provoke discussion, let me state a few tentative conclusions.

As far as host governments are concerned, the superior ability of multinational corporate groups to mobilize capital and technology from outside the country and their ability to offer access to established export markets overseas are tempting attractions. If there are offsetting misgivings, as there usually are, these glittering prizes may be enough to overcome them. This is the sort of consideration which, in the end, obliged Charles de Gaulle grudgingly to accept the modified proposals of General Electric to absorb Machines Bull, and which also persuaded

Canada to permit U.S. automobile companies to solidify their position in the Canadian market.

Unease of Sovereigns. Nonetheless, the qualms of governments persist. And they are founded on many grounds.

One fear is that the multinational corporate group, far from bringing new capital and technology into the country, will simply use its magnetic presence to attract and absorb scarce domestic capital and skills, thereby depriving nationals of the use of those resources. And, indeed, the recent history of fund-raising activities by U.S. corporate groups in Europe and elsewhere suggests that this is not a wholly empty concern.

But the worries of host governments run deeper still. Every sovereign is aware that a multinational corporate group which is able to provide export markets for the product of the host country is also capable of withholding such markets and cutting off the jobs that depend on such exports. If Nigeria should eventually become a lower cost producer of widgets than Italy, the corporate group may shift the locus of its operations out of Italy into Nigeria.

Along similar lines, a multinational group that can provide foreign capital to the host government's economy is also thought capable of draining capital away for use elsewhere; hence, the perennial accusations of "decapitalization" with which foreign investors are confronted in Latin America. A group which is able to provide foreign technology and skills to the economy is seen as capable of drawing off skilled scientists and technicians to other lands.

It is therefore inevitable that most governments' reactions to the proposals of a multinational corporate group will usually contain elements compounded of hope and fear—hope that the group will mobilize resources on its behalf, and fear that the mobilization may in the end be reversed in direction.

The nation-state's reaction to the local subsidiary of a multinational corporate group is compounded of other elements. One of these is the nagging concern that such groups may be in a position to avoid the jurisdictional reach of the sovereign. There is a curious irony in this reaction. As a general rule, the subsidiaries of multinational corporate groups have a special sense of their "foreignness" and of their vulnerability to criticism and hostility on the part of the local community. Partly for that reason, the subsidiaries of such groups ordinarily appear to be among the better behaved members of any local business community. Usually, they seem both sensitive and responsive to the formal requirements of national law, to a degree which national enterprises seldom match.

Nonetheless, sovereigns characteristically have a sense of confronting an entity whose capacity for avoiding the impact of national law and policy seems very high. In the field of taxation, of course, problems of this sort are very common; transfer pricing practices, royalty fee payments, and headquarters cost allocations between members of the multinational corporate groups are constantly being scrutinized and criticized.

In other fields, such as monetary policy or employment policy, the problems are more subtle and the criticism is more muted. Still, a member of a group which can borrow informally from its parent, or through its parent's connections, is thought of as a more elusive subject for the regulatory net of the monetary authorities than the national borrower with more limited alternatives.

This unease on the part of national authorities comes close to being pathological when the suspicion exists that the multinational group is acting in partnership with some foreign sovereign. In the less developed world, for instance, there is always the fear that the subsidiaries of U.S. parents, even though they may be nominal nationals of the host country, may be able to call in the Marines to support a point, or—to draw on an illustration which is more timely—may be able to use the U.S. foreign aid program to influence the outcome of the dispute.

In Europe and Canada the concern is usually reversed. There the subsidiaries of U.S. parents are sometimes seen by their hosts as conduits, albeit less-than-joyous conduits, of misguided U.S. policies with regard to East-West trade, outlandish policies concerning restrictive business practices, and proscriptive policies with respect to military technology. Nor is it very difficult to document these fears with live cases from recent history.

Attitudes of Businessmen. The views of nation-states toward the members of multinational corporate groups within their borders are colored by still another factor, one which is probably more important than the weight it ordinarily receives. Local businessmen in many countries, like the sovereigns who rule over them, also have ambivalent reactions to the multinational entities in their economies. For some local businessmen, to be sure, the subsidiary of a multinational system is a prized customer, an esteemed creditor, an invaluable ally, or an easy mark. For other businessmen, however, the subsidiary of a multinational group may be seen as a rival competing for scarce customers or manpower, with limitless resources at its command to overwhelm its local opposition.

At times the first attitude dominates in the local business community; at other times, the second. And it is not easy to pinpoint all the factors which determine the prevailing state of mind. Presumably, it depends in part on the kind of activity in which the subsidiary is engaged and on the local community's current perception of its own capabilities for taking over the activity.

If the foreign subsidiary is engaged in some enterprise which the local community feels capable of preempting, it is an easy step from that state of mind to a sense of grievance. Such a feeling is based on the rationale that the business methods of the multinational group are "unfair" for many reasons, including: (a) the group's easy access to capital and technology; (b) its use of famous trade names; and (c) its eligibility to secure government guarantees against the hazards of currency inconvertibility, expropriation, and war. This general sense of grievance is an important element shaping the national policy of many countries toward multinational corporate groups.

Regional Groupings. The emergence of regional economic groupings of nation-states in various parts of the world, notably in Europe and Latin America, adds some new and difficult dimensions to the problems posed by multinational corporate groups. Four such regional markets have now achieved structures which are sufficiently secure to be regarded as part of the likely international landscape of the future. These, of course, are the European Economic Community, the European Free Trade Area, the Latin American Free Trade Area, and the Central American Common Market.

All four of these regional ventures have so far managed to achieve a considerable measure of their early promise. Trade among the countries within each system has grown considerably faster than trade with outside countries. In each case, businessmen have exhibited interest, sometimes followed by action, in regarding the area as an integrated unit for future exploitation.

In all these movements, the multinational corporate groups have played a prominent role. While research on the patterns of internal investment in these areas is not very complete, it is already apparent that there has been a marked disposition on the part of multinational corporate groups to take these regional groupings at their face value and to begin laying their plans on the assumption that the arrangements would survive.

The implications of that situation are just beginning to grow clear for the nation-states involved. When General Motors first decided to establish its new European plant in Antwerp, Belgium, instead of Strasbourg, France, it must have been apparent to de Gaulle that his asserted hostility to U.S. investment could have the result of saddling France with the worst of several possible worlds. Given France's commitment to keep her borders open to the products of the other five members of the EEC, France has to face the competition of Belgian-made General Motors products within her own country.

If that implication of membership in a regional grouping such as the EEC has not been evident to the French, it has certainly been evident to the Mexicans as regards their membership in the Latin American Free Trade Association. Concerns about the relatively relaxed foreign investment policies of their Brazilian, Colombian, Peruvian, and Venezuelan partners are obviously preoccupying the harder bargaining Mexicans as they confront their future in LAFTA.

Illustrating the complex reactions toward multinational corporate groups which these regional projects have unleashed is still another feature of these companies' operations. The "good Europeans" and the "good Latins" who originally provided much of the inspiration and the drive for their regional groupings had tended to think of them, naturally enough, as vehicles for joining their national economies in indissoluble ties, primarily for the benefit of the nationals in the member countries.

Yet the most spectacular illustrations of the development of business linkages in these regional communities are persistently provided by the foreign oriented groups. One finds IBM willing to make its plants in Chile and Argentina complementary rather than duplicative, Ford specializing its auto parts production in the different countries of LAFTA, and many other cases. It is the foreign enterprises that seem most disposed to use their internal network of intercorporate relations to begin welding the regional blocks into genuine unitary economies.

To be sure, in both Europe and Latin America, national enterprises do exhibit some disposition to plan on the assumption that the regional groupings will endure. But these enterprises seem to be finding it a great deal more difficult to stray far from their national points of origin and to make their locational and investment decisions without regard to the national boundaries that are contained within the region.

From time to time, one encounters an exception such as Philips, but the exceptions are usually drawn from a very brief and familiar list. For the most part, the reaction of the European and the Latin enterprises in their respective areas is to operate very close to home base or, if recent indications are any guide, to react to the existence of the regional community by trying to arrange an internal division of markets with their potential competitors from other member countries.

JURISDICTIONAL TENSIONS

In any projection of the future interplay between sovereign states and multinational corporate groups, it would be unwise to underestimate the force and the persistence of national hostilities toward the extranational intrusions epitomized by those groups. Yet it would be just as unwise to assume that such groups will inevitably be restricted and contained by national sovereigns.

The situation, as observed earlier, is one where the sovereign state may badly want something unique which it is in the power of the multinational group to provide. Unique technology and unique systems-organizing ability, in particular, are two ingredients which the advanced industrial state, anxious to remain in the competitive race, finds it constantly necessary to secure.

The Bargaining Game. Weakness is not always on the side of the sovereign, however. For instance, Mexico's hard bargaining tactics with foreign companies which want to set up new subsidiaries in the Mexican economy are a reflection of Mexico's view that her bargaining position, at least for the present, is strong. Mexico is bent on promoting her industrialization by a policy of import replacement—that is, by embargoing imports of industrial products while providing incentives for businessmen to set up local plants. A policy of this sort neither encourages nor requires the latest technologies.

Mexico's industry is buffered from foreign competition in her home markets and has no ambitions as yet to tackle foreign competition in other markets. Therefore, characteristically industry is devoted to the production of familiar products by familiar techniques. Mexico's output includes consumer hard goods, such as automobiles, refrigerators, and television sets; and standardized bulk chemicals, such as fertilizers and plastics; and so on.

These are areas of production in which no single multinational corporate group has anything especially unique to offer. When faced with proposals by such groups, Mexican officials feel that the foreigner who confronts them is not offering a unique resource; hence, Mexico has alternatives to which it can turn.

Mexico's relative invulnerability, as noted earlier, may be somewhat threatened as the Latin American Free Trade Area begins to take a less equivocal shape. But the member states of common markets such as EEC and LAFTA have obvious ways of avoiding some of their potential internecine competition for the subsidiaries of multinational corporate groups. They can, for instance, attempt to promote a uniform foreign investment policy among the member states. Ironically, de Gaulle's distaste for new initiatives within the EEC may well have delayed such a development in that area.

If the expansive qualities of foreign investment continue much longer to be thought of as principally a "U.S. problem," it seems highly likely that the common markets will feel tempted to generate common policies to contain "the problem."

The Question of Identity. The response of multinational corporate groups to the manifestations of hostility around them is unlikely to be wholly passive in the future, any more than it has been passive in the past. In some cases, for instance, in an effort to merge less obtrusively into the national scene, national partners will be invited to take an interest in the local subsidiary. But this device, experience suggests, is tolerable in only a minority of cases.

In many instances, joint ventures create problems which tend to undermine the concept of a concerted global strategy for the multinational group. The pricing of sales between affiliates in the group is no longer so readily responsive to the group's interests as a whole; the allocation of export markets among affiliates grows difficult, becoming tangled in the conflicting claims of irreconcilable interests; the dividend policy has to respond to a mixture of antagonistic values; the allocation of central office costs becomes a difficult and painful exercise. It is not at all surprising, therefore, that the joint-venture route has not been seized eagerly by many multinational corporate groups as the answer to their problems of identity.

Even if the joint-venture arrangement is avoided by most multinational corporate groups, however, every effort is still made to play the part of the good German in Germany, the good Frenchman in France, and so on. The practice of appointing non-Americans to the parent company's board of directors, already in evidence in a few cases, will no doubt spread. The practice of listing the parent's stock on foreign stock exchanges will continue to grow. The preference for Americans as the principal officers in foreign subsidiaries, already greatly diluted, will continue to decline. Executive personnel increasingly will acquire mobility through the multinational system, with a declining regard for national origins.

Such measures may or may not do very much to change the public "image" of the enterprises that adopt them; the issue is too complex and the evidence too tangled for any summary judgment. But there is less doubt that measures of this sort will have their eventual effect on the corporate psyche itself. Multinational groups which had once been crystal clear about their ultimate national identity may well find themselves becoming a trifle uncertain, a shade ambiguous, about that identity.

This development will not occur easily, however. Most modern men have been raised in a system of nation-states, conditioned to the idea that loyalty to a nation-state must be unclouded and unambiguous. Some aberrations from that ideal are tolerated, such as adherence to an international religious movement or to an international ethnic fraternity; but the exceptions are few and muted. Still the process of identity confusion could progress a little. And one might be tempted to conclude that if it did, it would begin to spell the beginning of the end of the tensions between multinational corporate groups and nation-states.

But such a judgment would run the risk of being sheer romanticism. If any conclusion is justified, it is that the increasing ambiguity of the identity of multinational corporate groups may change the quality of the tension, but not reduce it. Sovereigns will still have their national or their common market goals. They will still hope to enforce these national or common market policies in the monetary, fiscal, employment, trade, and national security fields. They are still likely to look on an integrated multinational group as being responsive to a common strategy stretching outside the national reach. And they are still likely to regard such a group as a source of unusual strength and flexibility, hence a power especially to be reckoned with in the pursuit of national policies.

The automatic assumption that most of these groups are "American" may conceivably be blurred somewhat, but the uncertainties of identity that take the place of that automatic association may be even more uncomfortable for nation-states to live with than the certainty that they are confronting Americans.

INTERNATIONAL HARMONIZATION

Eventually, perhaps, the nation-states may begin turning to questions of the control of multinational corporate groups by international agreement. It is not beyond present conception that multilateral treaties may yet be proposed, dealing with problems of jurisdictional conflict and jurisdictional avoidance in the fields of trade and investment. The right to assume and discard nationalities could conceivably be included in proposals for international regulation as well.

This is not a wholly novel approach in international relations, of course. Bilateral tax treaties, aimed at reconciling the conflicting and overlapping requirements of two national tax systems on taxpayers that are subject to both, already create the shadow of a precedent for action in the field. It would be unwise, however, to assume too readily that the problem will be disposed of by so rational a course.

For one thing, as long as the problem is thought of as primarily an "American" problem, the tendency of other governments to handle it on an ad hoc basis and by unilateral act may be fairly strong. Moreover, even if other nations were agreeable to an international approach to the problem, it is not at all clear that the U.S. government itself would favor the approach.

The United States, for instance, has shown no enthusiasm for accepting self-denying ordinances in the application of its antitrust laws or of its trading-with-the-enemy laws. While the United States sometimes restrains itself a little in the application of those statutes to foreign subsidiaries of U.S. parents, such instances are treated as very special exceptions.

More generally, the U.S. government would probably feel most uncomfortable with the idea that a system of enterprises controlled by a U.S. parent did not necessarily owe total and unambiguous loyalty to the United States.

Even if the U.S. government were prepared to accept the concept of negotiating on the problems of conflicting and overlapping jurisdictions, however, there is reason to doubt that the U.S. business community itself would willingly accept the idea. True, the business community has usually accepted the approach with respect to overlapping tax jurisdictions; but the tax problem may well be a special case, one in which the consequences of a failure to find some solution for the problem of overlap would be all too painfully apparent.

In other cases, such as those involving the harmonization of national trade policies or financial regulations, businessmen are likely to view the absence of an international coordinating mechanism as generating more benefits than pain. My guess is that this will be the prevailing conviction of U.S. business for a long time after the evidence points to the contrary.

The period of transition from jurisdictional conflict and overlap to jurisdictional coordination and harmonization, therefore, promises to be a long and stormy one. During that period, as suggested earlier, the businessman will not be idle. Ingenious, inventive, and adaptive, he will try to reduce the frictions by every means at his command. One such means, naturally enough, will be to insist that the frictions are not there; or, if there, that they are simply a passing phase.

The decision to fashion and support a system of international harmonization of national policies will, I am afraid, be imposed in the end by circumstances rather than by the thoughtful forward planning of those who stand to gain most from it.

Part VI

Man-Milieu Relationships

THE CONCERN DISPLAYED in recent years about environmental problems is only the latest manifestation of an age-old interest in man-milieu relationships. In all major approaches to the study of international relations, relationships between man and his environment are accorded a place of considerable importance. Utopian theorists, it was suggested in Part I, held that if man was corrupted by his environment, he could nevertheless be improved if new international norms and institutions could be developed; in short, if the international environment could be changed. The Realist approach posited the existence of an environment which was essentially unchangeable. Environmental factors, especially geography, conditioned international behavior. In behavioral approaches as well, scholarly activity is often directed to an examination of interaction between man and his environment. In fact, international relations is the study of interaction among political units occupying space, and in some cases, struggling for the control of strategically or economically important space. As suggested in Part II, the capacity of one state to achieve its international objectives is dependent vitally on its national power potential. This, in turn, is heavily influenced by such environmental factors as natural resource availability and geographical location, for example, near or distant from other hostile powers.

Some students of international relations have posited the existence of relationships between geography and political behavior. According to Harold and Margaret Sprout, environmental factors can affect human activities to the extent that they are perceived and taken into account by the actors in a given setting. It is in this way only that "environmental factors can be said to influence, condition, or otherwise affect human values and preferences, moods and attitudes, choices and decisions." Geography is said not only to influence political behavior, but to favor some national units more than others. In addition, environmental factors affect the outcome of decisions taken by the political leadership of a nation. If a leader decides on the basis of faulty perception, "environmental limitations on outcome or performance may be effective even though the limiting factors were not perceived and reacted to in the process of reaching a decision and initiating a cause of action." The Sprouts refer to the perception of U.S. commanders as to Japanese intentions on the eve of the attack on Pearl Harbor in December 1941. Thus the study of man-milieu relationships, as conceptualized by the Sprouts, is central to the study of politics and to much, if not all, of human behavior. The Sprouts propose a framework which relates perceptions of the environment to decision-making and brings to political analysis insights and theories from many other disciplines.

Geography, of course, constitutes one major environmental influence on political behavior. Many writers who have examined the political significance of geography have focused on the implications of the control of one territory for the extension of influence to other territories. For example, Nicholas J. Spykman, drawing upon the writings of earlier students of political geography, or geopolitics, such as Sir Halford Mackinder, maintained that the geopolitical significance of the Old and New Worlds is defined by the power potential and internal distribution of forces in each sphere. He saw the Eurasian continent as more self-sufficient than the American, and predicted future alignments which have since become realities. As a "realist," Spykman contended that international relations were characterized by a struggle for power. That nation which dominated the vast Eurasian land mass would possess the industrial, technological, natural, and human resources to achieve world rule. The objective of United States policy should be to prevent the domination of Eurasia by assuring the preservation of a balance of power there. Thus, Spykman, writing during the early stages of World War II, when there were demands for the unconditional surrender of enemy powers, argued for a policy designed to curb, but not to destroy Germany and Japan, both of which would prove important components of a postwar Eurasian balance of power.

In his analysis, Spykman drew upon a conception of the geopolitical significance of Eurasia analogous to that of Sir Eyre Crowe (See Selection 33). The maintenance of a balance of power in Eurasia was as important in the twentieth century to the United States as it had been historically to Britain. In fact, Spykman's model for U.S. security is essentially that of Crowe for Britain's security with the United States occupying the historic position of Britain.

In two world wars, the United States fought to prevent the domination of the Eurasian land mass by a nation, or combination of nations, hostile to the United States. In the postwar period, the U.S. commitment to the defense of Western Europe, as well as other regions on the Eurasian perimeter, has issued from similar considerations. In the 1970s, the goal of the United States, especially in a period of reduced commitments abroad, remains the creation of balanced forces in Europe and Asia, especially on the rimlands of the vast Eurasian land mass.

26.   GEOGRAPHY AND FOREIGN POLICY

Nicholas J. Spykman

THE TERRITORY of the United States is located on the northern land mass of the Western Hemisphere between Canada and Mexico. Our state is unique in that its base is of continental dimensions and fronts on two oceans. It represents an immense area in the temperate zone with large sections of fertile soil and a rich endowment of mineral resources. The national economy, in which a highly developed industrial structure supplements an extensive agriculture of great productivity, sustains a high standard of living for about 135 million people.* No other country in the Western Hemisphere has a war potential equal to our own. Our power position is one of unquestioned hegemony over a large part of the New World. We are far stronger than our neighbors to the north and south, we dominate completely the American Mediterranean, and we are able to exert effective pressure on the northern part of South America. The remoteness of the economic and political centers of the A.B.C. countries has given them a relative degree of independence and they represent the only region in the hemisphere where our strength could not be exerted with ease.

The Western Hemisphere is surrounded by the Old World across three ocean fronts, the Pacific, the Arctic, and the Atlantic, and, because the earth is a globe, the same applies in reverse, the New World also surrounds the Old. It is the power potential of these two worlds and the internal distribution of forces in each sphere that define the geo-political significance of this geographic fact. The Old World is $2\frac{1}{2}$ times as large as the New World and contains 7 times the population. It is true that, at present, industrial productivity is almost equally divided, but, in terms of relative self-sufficiency, the Eurasian Continent with the related continents of Africa and Australia is in a much stronger position. If the three land masses of the Old World can be brought under the control of a few

From *America's Strategy in World Politics* by Nicholas J. Spykman, pp. 447–450; 465–470. Copyright, 1942, by Harcourt, Brace & World, Inc. and reprinted with their permission.

NICHOLAS J. SPYKMAN (1893–1943) Formerly Chairman, Department of International Relations and Director, Institute of International Studies, Yale University. Author of *The Geography of the Peace*, (New York: Harcourt, Brace and Company, 1944); *The Social Theory of Georg Simmel*, (Chicago: University of Chicago Press, 1925).

* Editor's Note: As of February 1971 the population of the United States was 203,184,772.

states and so organized that large unbalanced forces are available for pressure across the ocean fronts, the Americas will be politically and strategically encircled. There is no war potential of any size in any of the southern continents and South America can, therefore, offer the United States no compensation for the loss of the balance of power in Europe and Asia.

It is true that the Western Hemisphere is separated from the Old World by large bodies of water, but oceans do not isolate. Since the Renaissance and the development of modern navigation, they have been not barriers but highways. The world has become a single field of forces. Because power is effective in inverse ratio to the distance from its source, widely separated regions can function as relatively autonomous power zones, but no area in the world can be completely independent of the others. Only if the available military forces within a zone balance each other out, will the area be inert and unable to influence other regions, but in that case the explanation lies in the power equilibrium, not in the geographic distance. If power is free, unbalanced, unabsorbed, it can be used in distant regions.

Originally, the center of military and political power was in Europe and it was the European balance that was reflected in other sections of the world. Later, relatively autonomous power zones emerged in the Western Hemisphere and in the Far East, but they have all continued to influence each other. The New World, notwithstanding its insular character, has not been an isolated sphere in which political forces found their natural balance without interference from outside. On the contrary, European power relations have influenced the political life of the people of this hemisphere from the beginning of their history. The growth and expansion of the United States has been challenged by every great power in Europe except Italy. We achieved our position of hegemony only because the states of that continent were never able to combine against us and because preoccupation with the balance of power at home prevented them from ever detaching more than a small part of their strength for action across the Atlantic.

Since the states of the Western Hemisphere have achieved their independence, there has never been a time in which the transatlantic and transpacific regions have been in the hands of a single state or a single coalition of states. Balanced power in Europe and Asia has been characteristic of most of the period of our growth. But four times in our history there has been a threat of encirclement and of destruction of the balance of power across the oceans. The first threat was the appeal of France to the Holy Alliance for co-operation in the reconquest of the Spanish colonies. Our reply was the Monroe Doctrine. The second threat came in 1917 when the defeat of Russia, the demoralization of the French army, and the success of the submarine campaign suggested that Germany might win the First World War. Japan was using the golden opportunity presented by European withdrawal from Asia to make herself the dominant power in the Far East. Our answer to the danger in Europe was full participation in the war. The completeness of the victory made the existing British-Japanese Alliance a minor danger to our security. In terms of geography, the agreement did mean encirclement and both partners had come out of the war with greatly increased naval strength, practically unbalanced in their respective spheres. We, therefore, made the termination of their alliance the condition of our participation in disarmament in 1921.

The fourth threat has emerged since 1940 and this time it is in a form more serious than ever before. The German-Japanese Alliance, signed in that year, provided for co-operation against the Western Hemisphere. By the fall of 1941, Germany had conquered most of Europe; Japan most of the coastal regions of the Far East. Only Great Britain and Russia in Europe and China and the Dutch East Indies in Asia stood between them and the complete conquest of the Old World. Victory would have meant for Germany the realization of her dream of a great Euro-African sphere controlled from Berlin. Victory would have meant for Japan the transformation of her island state into a unit of continental dimensions. For the New World, such a situation would have meant encirclement by two gigantic empires controlling huge war potentials.

HEMISPHERE DEFENSE?

In the face of this contingency, what was the correct policy for the United States to pursue? Public debate followed the traditional pattern of intervention versus isolation. Those interventionists who were impressed with the importance of power relations, contended that the first line of defense was of necessity the preservation of a balance of power in Europe and Asia. Those isolationists who were impressed with oceanic distances, felt convinced that we could disengage ourselves from the power struggles across the oceans and rely on hemisphere defense.

During the progress of the war, the interventionist position found wider and wider acceptance and the policy of the United States became one of increasing support to the Allies. The American people were spared the necessity of deciding on the last step, the transition from Lend-Lease Aid to full belligerency. The German-Japanese Alliance decided to strike before our war industries went into full production and large quantities of material became available for our allies. We are now full participants in the Second World War and our opponents have begun their attack on the outposts of the Western Hemisphere before their victory in the Old World is complete.

Isolation versus intervention is no longer a debate over war participation but the two geo-political theories which these attitudes represent will continue to influence our thinking about the principles of grand strategy that should guide us in the conduct of the war and in the formulation of the conditions of peace. There is still a danger that the erroneous ideas regarding the nature of the Western Hemisphere inherent in the isolationist position may tempt people to urge a defensive strategy in the belief that the New World could survive a German-Japanese victory abroad.

THE UNITED STATES AND EUROPE

The post-war policy of the United States will have to operate in a world of power politics under conditions very similar to those that prevailed before the outbreak of the conflict. It should be guided by a political strategy which demands the preservation of a balance of power in Europe and in Asia, and by the consideration that territorial security and peaceful change are more likely to be achieved if the individual states in the different power zones do not differ too widely in their relative strength.

. . .

The greatest difficulty will be that of balancing Germany and Russia. In case of Allied victory, the Soviet Union will come out of the war as one of the great industrial nations of the world with an enormous war potential. Germany, unless destroyed, will continue to represent an impressive military strength as demonstrated in the First and Second World Wars. The easiest solution would be to give them a common frontier. But if this should prove impossible, then the political unit between them should be a great eastern European federation from the Baltic to the Mediterranean, not a series of small buffer states. More troublesome is going to be the problem of Holland and Belgium, the old buffer states that have ceased to perform their protective function and that can neither shield Great Britain from bombing nor France from invasion under conditions of modern warfare. It is possible to conceive of several different combinations in addition to an eastern European federation, such as a British-Scandinavian group around the North Sea and the Baltic, and a Latin group around the Mediterranean. The Versailles settlement sacrificed economic and power considerations to the exclusive demands of the principle of self-determination with the result that the whole power structure came to rest on two weak crutches, a disarmed Germany and a non-fortified Rhineland. The new peace will not only have to correct the Balkanization of Europe, which was introduced after the First World War, but it will also have to achieve the integration of other states into a few large units.

. . .

THE UNITED STATES AND ASIA

The United States has been interested in the preservation of a balance of power in the Far East primarily for the protection of her position as an Asiatic power. But even if she were to withdraw from Asia and grant independence to the Philippines, she would still remain interested in the power relations of the transpacific zone. The Asiatic Mediterranean is perhaps the most important single source of strategic raw materials for the United States, and its control by a single power would endanger the basis of our military strength. The Far East was the last area to become an autonomous power zone and it is still inferior to both Europe and the United States as a source of political power. Advanced technology will however sooner or later translate the inherent power potential of the region into actual military strength, and, when that occurs, its relative importance compared to the two other zones will increase. The preservation of a balance will then be necessary not only because of our interest in strategic raw materials but also because of what unbalanced power in this region could do to the rest of the world.

The end of the Second World War will also find in existence in the Far East a number of independent units: Russia, China, and perhaps Japan; Great Britain, the Dutch East Indies, Australia, and New Zealand. The problem of building out of these units a balanced power structure in terms of states of approximately equal strength is going to be even more difficult than in Europe, and the main difficulty of the post-war period will be not Japan but China. The power potential of the former Celestial Kingdom is infinitely greater than that of the Land of the Cherry Blossom and once that power potential begins to express itself in actual military strength, the position of a defeated Japan as a small off-shore island near the Asiatic mainland is going to be very uncomfortable. When long-range bombing squadrons can operate from the tip of the Shan-tung peninsula as well as from Vladivostok, fire insurance rates in the Japanese paper cities will undoubtedly go up.

A modern, vitalized, and militarized China of 450 million people is going to be a threat not only to Japan, but also to the position of the Western Powers in the Asiatic Mediterranean. China will be a continental power of huge dimensions in control of a large section of the littoral of that middle sea. Her geographic position will be similar to that of the United States in regard to the American Mediterranean. When China becomes strong, her present economic penetration in that region will undoubtedly take on political overtones. It is quite possible to envisage the day when this body of water will be controlled not by British, American, or Japanese sea power but by Chinese air power.

It will be difficult to find public support in the United States for a Far Eastern policy based on these realities of power politics. It is true that intervention in Far Eastern affairs is traditionally much more acceptable than intervention in Europe, but this tradition is also tied up with a pro-Chinese and anti-Japanese orientation which the war itself will greatly intensify. Public opinion will probably continue to see Japan as the great danger, long after the balance has shifted in favor of China and it has become necessary to pursue in the Far East the same policy that we have pursued in regard to Europe. Twice in one generation we have come to the aid of Great Britain in order that the small off-shore island might not have to face a single gigantic military state in control of the opposite coast of the mainland. If the balance of power in the Far East is to be preserved in the future as well as in the present, the United States will have to adopt a similar protective policy toward Japan.

27. THE ECOLOGICAL PERSPECTIVE

Harold and Margaret Sprout

. . . So far as we can determine, environmental factors (both non-human and social) can affect human activities in *only two ways*. Such factors can be perceived, reacted to, and taken into account by the human individual or individuals under consideration. In this way, *and in this way only*, . . . environmental factors can be said to "influence," or to "condition," or otherwise to "affect" human values and preferences, moods and attitudes, choices and decisions. On the other hand, the relation of environmental factors to performance and accomplishment (that is, to the operational outcomes or results of decisions and undertakings)

From *The Ecological Perspective on Human Affairs* by Harold and Margaret Sprout, pp. 11–15. Copyright 1965 by the Princeton University Press, and reprinted with their permission. Footnotes have been renumbered to appear in consecutive order.

HAROLD SPROUT (1901–   ) Henry Grier Bryant Professor of Geography and International Relations, Princeton University. Co-author with Margaret Sprout of *An Ecological Paradigm for the Study of International Politics,* (Princeton: Center for International Studies, 1968); *The Ecological Perspective on Human Affairs with Special Reference to International Politics,* (Princeton: Princeton University Press, 1965); *Foundations of International Politics,* (Princeton: D. Van Nostrand Company, 1962); *Foundations of National Power,* (Princeton: D. Van Nostrand Company 1951).

may present an additional dimension. In the latter context, environmental factors may be conceived as a sort of matrix, or encompassing channel, metaphorically speaking, which limits the execution of undertakings. Such limitations on performance, accomplishment, outcome, or operational result may not—often do not—derive from or depend upon the environed individual's perception or other psychological behavior. In many instances, environmental limitations on outcome or performance may be effective even though the limiting factors were not perceived and reacted to in the process of reaching a decision and initiating a course of action.

The American debacle at Pearl Harbor is a historic example of this central thesis. The American commanders there made their defensive preparations for hostilities which they believed to be imminent. But they remained in ignorance of the approaching Japanese fleet. The environment as they perceived it contained no hostile fleet. Hence that fleet's presence was not reacted to in any way; that is to say, it had no effect whatever on the decisions of the American commanders prior to the moment of attack on that December morning in 1941. Yet the Japanese fleet was indubitably an ingredient of the environment in which the decisions of the American commanders were executed; and their ignorance of its presence did not prevent it from affecting decisively the operational outcome that occurred.

· · ·

While our discussion of ecological perspective, concepts, and theories is set specifically in the context of international politics, much of the illustrative material . . . is drawn from other fields, in particular from the field of human geography. This is appropriate for two reasons: (1) because geographic dimensions—identified by such terms as location, distance, space, distribution, and configuration—are nearly always significant in discussions of political undertakings and the operational results thereof; and (2) because geographers have given much attention to certain aspects of environmental relationships.

Perhaps we should insert here a few paragraphs that may seem to most geographers to be an elaboration of the obvious, but which may not be quite so obvious to many others. There is some tendency (probably diminishing, and discernible mainly among those relatively unfamiliar with modern geographic concepts) to think of geography as a subject that pertains chiefly to the physical earth. There can be no doubt that geographers are concerned with the physical conformation of the earth's surface: with the layout of lands and seas, the distribution of mineral rocks upon and beneath the surface, the patterns of vegetation and weather, the distribution of subhuman organisms that subsist upon the earth and on each other. All these phenomena exhibit geographic quality, in the sense that geographic science "is concerned with the arrangement of things on the face of the earth, and with the associations of things that give character to particular places." [1]

Applying this test, geographic quality also attaches to many kinds of phenomena besides the physical earth and subhuman organisms. People are geographic objects, in the sense that they are areally distributed in social groups of many kinds and sizes. The same holds for the physical structures—cultivated fields, planted forests, buildings, roads, and many other tangible structures—that human hands have superimposed upon the earth's surface, changing and often obliterating the primordial landscape. Geographic patterns are also observable in many kinds of human processes: for example, farming, manufacturing, commerce, recreation, governing; likewise, in many other intangibles of human behavior: values and norms, attitudes and preferences, customs and habits, as well as institutions and other more formal patterns. Geographic quality, in short attaches to any phenomena—human as well as nonhuman, intangible as well as tangible—that exhibit areal dimensions and variations upon or in relation to the earth's surface.

This concept of geographic quality is central to the ecological perspective and to any scheme for analysis of ecological relationships. This is so because systematic analysis confirms the common-sense observation that the distribution and arrangement of phenomena upon the earth's surface are always, or nearly always, related significantly to what people undertake and to what they accomplish. The ecological perspective and ecological theories bring the dimensions of location, distance, space, distribution, and configuration sharply into focus in many social contexts, not least in the context of politics in general and of international politics in particular.

Every political community (though not necessarily every political organization) rests upon a geographic base. Territory is universally recognized to be one of the essential attributes of statehood. Probably the geographic exhibits most familiar to the most people are the maps that delineate the boundaries and differentiate the territories of national and subnational political communities.

The territory of each political community differs from all the rest—in location, in size and shape, in distance from the others, in arable land and climate and other so-called natural resources. Each differs from the rest in numbers of people, in their level and variety of knowledge and skills, in their mechanical equipment and stage of economic development, in their form of government, and in many other respects. All these phe-

---

[1] P. E. James *et al., American Geography: Inventory and Prospect,* Syracuse University Press, 1954, p. 4.

nomena, nonhuman, and human, are unevenly distributed among the communities that comprise the society of nations. In most (if possibly not quite all) transactions among nations (and the same holds for relations among individuals and groups within national communities), at least some of the geographic dimensions noted above are certain to be significantly related to what is undertaken and also to what is accomplished.

This is conspicuously the case with transactions which exhibit some element of conflict of purpose or interest among the interacting persons, groups, or organized communities—transactions that exhibit political quality in the narrower sense of that term. Political demands and responses thereto are projected through space from one point to another upon the earth's surface. All the techniques of statecraft, domestic as well as international, involve expenditures of energy and consumption of other resources. This is obviously the case with respect to military operations and the administration of public order. But it is likewise the case in varying degrees with respect to nonsubversive public relations and propaganda, subversive conspiracy and internal war, economic and technical assistance, diplomacy and conference, and all the variants and combinations of these modes of operation. In any period of history, the results of international statecraft exhibit more or less clearly discernible patterns of coercion and submission, and influence and deference, patterns reflected in political terms with strong geographic connotations: such as balance of power, bipolarity, political orbit, satellite, bloc, coalition, alliance, the Monroe Doctrine, the Atlantic Community, the Near East, and many others.

Part VII

Domestic-International Linkages

THE DOMESTIC FACTORS which influence the formulation of foreign policy and the international forces which shape the domestic political systems of the nation-states are both of central importance to the study of international relations. Students of international politics have always been interested in such relationships. For example, utopian theory assumed that the creation of political systems based on representative government was an essential precondition for world peace (See Selection 3). Realist theorists held that the intrusion of uninformed publics into the complex process of foreign policy formulation represented a destabilizing input into international politics. Most international relations writers have attached considerable importance to such domestic factors as nationalism, popular attitudes toward the political system and its leaders, and the level of technological skills and economic organization as contributing to, or detracting from, the national capabilities of nation-states. Nevertheless, there has been a tendency to treat nation-states as units developing and pursuing a particular foreign policy, and having almost a personality of their own. How often has it been stated: "France (or any other country) has adopted a given policy"? Domestic policy is taken as given, and is somehow considered to be separate from foreign policy and international politics.

Especially in the past decade, there has been a growing concern among international relations writers with international-domestic "linkages," and primarily with studies designed to trace as explicitly as possible their role in the formulation of foreign policy. Such a realization stems from a greater appreciation for the multiplicity of factors influencing the foreign policy process. It relates also to the concern of international relations scholars with the various levels and units of analysis (described by J. David Singer in Selection 7). Each such unit and level affords the student and scholar the opportunity to gain valuable insights into the nature and practice of international relations. This section focuses upon several levels and units of analysis: the international system; the nation-state; the individual; and domestic subsystems, such as public opinion.

According to Henry A. Kissinger, there is a direct link between the domestic political structure of national units and the conduct of international affairs. When one or more states claims that its domestic structure provides a model having universal validity, the prospects for resolving substantive foreign policy differences, or for developing mutually acceptable international procedures for their resolution, grow dim. It is this condition which distinguishes much of twentieth-century international politics from that of preceding periods, in which there existed a greater compatibility of domestic structures and a more commonly held conception of consensus, or legitimacy, in the Europe-centered international system.

The bureaucratic structure itself introduces additional rigidities in the conduct of foreign policy. For example, the sheer bureaucratic complexity of decision-making, a characteristic of technologically advanced societies, makes difficult the development of a coherent foreign policy and renders nearly impossible changes in policy once developed. The internal requirements of bureaucracy, including the need for agreement among its disparate members, may overshadow the purposes for which it was created. Studying a problem may become a substitute for creative action designed to solve it. Moreover, differences in the characteristics of decision-makers may compound the problems of foreign policy formulation. Kissinger examines several types of decision-maker: the bureaucratic-pragmatic, the ideological, and the revolutionary-charismatic. He assesses the implications of each type for foreign policy.

Focusing upon the individual as a unit of analysis, some scholars contend that foreign policy decision-making represents an amalgam of structural constraints, derived from the organization of the national and international political systems; situational constraints, based on the specific context in which decision-makers interact with their counterparts and reach a decision; and the psychological factors of the decision-maker, including his expectations, images, and values. To neglect the personality factors influencing decision-making is as fatal to an understanding of the foreign policy process as the failure to recognize the importance of institutional or situational factors. Moreover, they argue for a greater recognition of the importance of official "personal interactions" at the international level.

People hold images both of themselves and other people. In the international system peoples hold images both of themselves as a nation and of other nations. Because such images may affect political behavior, and, thus foreign policy, many students of international relations have attempted to describe and analyze them. By devising methods for the study of such phenomena as national myths and traditions, patterns of morale and discipline, attitudes toward the allocation of resources, and commitments to certain goals, it might be possible to gain a more precise understanding of the phenomenon called national character, as well as the form which it takes in individual national units.

According to Gabriel A. Almond, the American national character conditions popular and elite attitudes toward foreign policy. Americans have a greater concern with "private," rather than with "collective" values. Since they tend to exhaust their energies in the pursuit of goals such as individual economic and social advancement based upon private values, their approach to problems of public policy in general, and foreign policy in particular, is one of indifference. Almond finds a tendency toward wide fluctuations of mood between withdrawal-intervention, optimism-pessimism, tolerance-intolerance, idealism-cynicism, and superiority-inferiority. Such moods affect not only the American outlook toward other peoples, but constrain U.S. foreign policy and affect the latitude available to decision-makers. "A foreign policy crisis, short of the immediate threat of war, may transform indifference to vague apprehension, to fatalism, to anger; but the reaction is still a mood, a superficial and fluctuating response."

Nearly all domestic political systems are "penetrated" by the international system. Largely as a result of the acceleration of communications and the transmission of vast amounts of information across frontiers, the boundaries between international systems and domestic political systems are obscured. Both the Soviet Union and the United States have influenced, in varying ways, the domestic political systems of other states. The effect of Soviet policy upon internal politics in eastern Europe, and the influence of the United

States in countries such as South Vietnam, and postwar Germany and Japan—although the U.S. and Soviet influences differ markedly —nevertheless emphasize the idea of penetrated political systems. Certain political systems, e.g., the German Federal Republic more than Saudi Arabia, are the object of influences from the international system. Such influences are perhaps most obvious in the case of Germany, whose political system was shaped by the postwar allied occupation. The granting of foreign aid with "strings attached," by one country to another, the conduct of insurgency operations supported directly or indirectly by an outside power, and the granting of large-scale military assistance by one government to another for combatting such an insurgency provide examples of the penetration of domestic political systems.

The Algerian conflict, (although constitutionally Algeria was a part of France) led to the fall of the Fourth Republic and the development of a fundamentally different French Constitution for the Fifth Republic. The Vietnam conflict has had a major effect upon the American political system, contributing to the polarization of domestic politics and efforts to limit the constitutional prerogatives open to the president in the conduct of foreign relations.

28. DOMESTIC SOURCES OF FOREIGN POLICY

Henry A. Kissinger

I. THE ROLE OF DOMESTIC STRUCTURE

I N THE TRADITIONAL CONCEPTION, international relations are conducted by political units treated almost as personalities. The domestic structure is taken as given; foreign policy begins where domestic policy ends.

But this approach is appropriate only to stable periods because then the various components of the international system generally have similar conceptions of the "rules of the game." If the domestic structures are based on commensurable notions of what is just, a consensus about permissible aims and methods of foreign policy develops. If domestic structures are reasonably stable, temptations to use an adventurous foreign policy to achieve domestic cohesion are at a minimum. In these conditions, leaders will generally apply the same criteria and hold similar views about what constitutes a "reasonable" demand. This does not guarantee agreement, but it provides the condition for a meaningful dialogue, that is, it sets the stage for traditional diplomacy.

When the domestic structures are based on fundamentally different conceptions of what is just, the conduct of international affairs grows more complex. Then it becomes difficult even to define the nature of disagreement because what seems most obvious to one side appears most problematic to the other. A policy dilemma arises because the pros and cons of a given course seem evenly balanced. The definition of what constitutes a problem and what criteria are relevant in "solving" it reflects to a considerable extent the domestic notions of what is just, the pressures produced by the decision-making process, and the experience which forms the leaders in their rise to eminence. When domestic structures—and the concept of legitimacy on which they are based—differ widely, statesmen can still meet, but their ability to persuade has been reduced for they no longer speak the same language.

Reprinted by permission from *DAEDALUS*, Journal of the American Academy of Arts and Sciences, Boston, Massachusetts, Volume 95, Number 2. (Spring 1966), 503–525.

HENRY A. KISSINGER (1923–   ) Assistant to the President for National Security Affairs. Formerly Professor of Government, Harvard University. Author of *The Troubled Partnership: A Reappraisal of the Atlantic Alliance* (New York: McGraw-Hill Book Company, 1965); *The Necessity for Choice: Prospects of American Foreign Policy* (New York: Harper Brothers, 1961); *Nuclear Weapons and Foreign Policy* (New York: Harper Brothers, 1958). Editor, *Problems of National Security* (New York: Praeger Publishers, 1965); *A World Restored* (New York: Grosset and Dunlap [Universal Library], 1964).

This can occur even when no universal claims are made. Incompatible domestic structures can passively generate a gulf, simply because of the difficulty of achieving a consensus about the nature of "reasonable" aims and methods. But when one or more states claim universal applicability for their particular structure, schisms grow deep indeed. In that event, the domestic structure becomes not only an obstacle to understanding but one of the principal issues in international affairs. Its requirements condition the conception of alternatives; survival seems involved in every dispute. The symbolic aspect of foreign policy begins to overshadow the substantive component. It becomes difficult to consider a dispute "on its merits" because the disagreement seems finally to turn not on a specific issue but on a set of values as expressed in domestic arrangements. The consequences of such a state of affairs were explained by Edmund Burke during the French Revolution:

> I never thought we could make peace with the system; because it was not for the sake of an object we pursued in rivalry with each other, but with the system itself that we were at war. As I understood the matter, we were at war not with its conduct but with its existence; convinced that its existence and its hostility were the same.[1]

Of course, the domestic structure is not irrelevant in any historical period. At a minimum, it determines the amount of the total social effort which can be devoted to foreign policy. The wars of the kings who governed by divine right were limited because feudal rulers, bound by customary law, could not levy income taxes or conscript their subjects. The French Revolution, which based its policy on a doctrine of popular will, mobilized resources on a truly national scale for the first time. This was one of the principal reasons for the startling successes of French arms against a hostile Europe which possessed greater over-all power. The ideological regimes of the twentieth century have utilized a still larger share of the national effort. This has enabled them to hold their own against an environment possessing far superior resources.

Aside from the allocation of resources, the domestic structure crucially affects the way the actions of other states are interpreted. To some extent, of course, every society finds itself in an environment not of its own making and has some of the main lines of its foreign policy imposed on it. Indeed, the pressure of the environment can grow so strong that it permits only one interpretation of its significance; Prussia in the eighteenth century and Israel in the contemporary period may have found themselves in this position.

But for the majority of states the margin of decision has been greater. The actual choice has been determined to a considerable degree by their interpretation of the environment and by their leaders' conception of alternatives. Napoleon rejected peace offers beyond the dreams of the kings who had ruled France by "divine right" because he was convinced that *any* settlement which demonstrated the limitations of his power was tantamount to his downfall. That Russia seeks to surround itself with a belt of friendly states in Eastern Europe is a product of geography and history. That it is attempting to do so by imposing a domestic structure based on a particular ideology is a result of conceptions supplied by its domestic structure.

The domestic structure is decisive finally in the elaboration of positive goals. The most difficult, indeed tragic, aspect of foreign policy is how to deal with the problem of conjecture. When the scope for action is greatest, knowledge on which to base such action is small or ambiguous. When knowledge becomes available, the ability to affect events is usually at a minimum. In 1936, no one could know whether Hitler was a misunderstood nationalist or a maniac. By the time certainty was achieved, it had to be paid for with millions of lives.

The conjectural element of foreign policy—the need to gear actions to an assessment that cannot be proved true when it is made—is never more crucial than in a revolutionary period. Then, the old order is obviously disintegrating while the shape of its replacement is highly uncertain. Everything depends, therefore, on some conception of the future. But varying domestic structures can easily produce different assessments of the significance of existing trends and, more importantly, clashing criteria for resolving these differences. This is the dilemma of our time.

Problems are novel; their scale is vast; their nature is often abstract and always psychological. In the past, international relations were confined to a limited geographic area. The various continents pursued their relations essentially in isolation from each other. Until the eighteenth century, other continents impinged on Europe only sporadically and for relatively brief periods. And when Europe extended its sway over much of the world, foreign policy became limited to the Western Powers with the single exception of Japan. The international system of the nineteenth century was to all practical purposes identical with the concert of Europe.

The period after World War II marks the first era of truly global foreign policy. Each major state is capable of producing consequences in every part of the globe by a direct application of its power or because ideas can be transmitted almost instantaneously or because ideological rivalry gives vast symbolic significance even to issues which are minor in geopolitical terms. The mere act of adjusting perspectives to so huge a scale would produce major dislocations. This problem is compounded by the emergence of so many new states. Since 1945, the number of participants in the international system has nearly doubled. In previous periods the addition of even one or two new states tended to lead to decades of instability until a new equilibrium was established and accepted. The emergence of scores of new states has magnified this difficulty many times over.

These upheavals would be challenge enough, but they are overshadowed by the risks posed by modern technology. Peace is maintained through the threat of mutual destruction based on weapons for which there has been no operational experience. Deterrence—the policy of preventing an action by confronting the opponent with risks he is unwilling to run—depends in the first instance on psychological criteria. What the potential aggressor believes is more crucial than what is objectively true. Deterrence occurs above all in the minds of men.

To achieve an international consensus on the significance of these developments would be a major task even if domestic structures were comparable. It becomes especially difficult when domestic structures differ widely and when universal claims are made on behalf of them. A systematic assessment of the impact of domestic structure on the conduct of international affairs would have to treat such factors as historical traditions, social values, and the economic system. But this would far transcend the scope of an article. For the purposes of this discussion we shall confine ourselves to sketching the impact of two factors only: administrative structure and the formative experience of leadership groups.

II. THE IMPACT OF THE ADMINISTRATIVE STRUCTURE

In the contemporary period, the very nature of the governmental structure introduces an element of rigidity which operates more or less independently of the convictions of statesmen or the ideology which they represent. Issues are too complex and relevant facts too manifold to be dealt with on the basis of personal intuition. An institutionalization of decision-making is an inevitable by-product of the risks of international affairs in the nuclear age. Moreover, almost every modern state is dedicated to some theory of "planning"—the attempt to structure the future by understanding and, if necessary, manipulating the environment. Planning involves a quest for predictability and, above all, for "objectivity." There is a deliberate effort to reduce the relevant elements of a problem to a standard of average performance. The vast bureaucratic mechanisms that emerge develop a momentum and a vested interest of their own. As they grow more complex, their internal standards of operation are not necessarily commensurable with those of other countries or even with other bureaucratic structures in the same country. There is a trend toward autarky. A paradoxical consequence may be that increased control over the domestic environment is purchased at the price of loss of flexibility in international affairs.

The purpose of bureaucracy is to devise a standard operating procedure which can cope effectively with most problems. A bureaucracy is efficient if the matters which it handles routinely are, in fact, the most frequent and if its procedures are relevant to their solution. If those criteria are met, the energies of the top leadership are freed to deal creatively with the unexpected occurrence or with the need for innovation. Bureaucracy becomes an obstacle when what it defines as routine does not address the most significant range of issues or when its prescribed mode of action proves irrelevant to the problem.

When this occurs, the bureaucracy absorbs the energies of top executives in reconciling what is expected with what happens; the analysis of where one is overwhelms the consideration of where one should be going. Serving the machine becomes a more absorbing occupation than defining its purpose. Success consists in moving the administrative machine to the point of decision, leaving relatively little energy for analyzing the merit of this decision. The quest for "objectivity"—while desirable theoretically —involves the danger that means and ends are confused, that an average standard of performance is exalted as the only valid one. Attention tends to be diverted from the act of choice—which is the ultimate test of statesmanship—to the accumulation of facts. Decisions can be avoided until a crisis brooks no further delay, until the events themselves have removed the element of ambiguity. But at that point the scope for constructive action is at a minimum. Certainty is purchased at the cost of creativity.

Something like this seems to be characteristic of modern bureaucratic states whatever their ideology. In societies with a pragmatic tradition, such as the United States, there develops a greater concern with an analysis of where one is than where one is going. What passes for planning is frequently the projection of the familiar into the future. In societies based on ideology, doctrine is institutionalized and exegesis takes the place of innovation. Creativity must make so many concessions to orthodoxy that it may exhaust itself in doctrinal adaptations. In short, the accumulation of knowledge of the bureaucracy and the impersonality of its method of arriving at decisions can be achieved at a high price. Decision-making can grow so complex that the process of producing a bureaucratic consensus may overshadow the purpose of the effort.

While all thoughtful administrators would grant in the abstract that these dangers exist, they find it difficult to act on their knowledge. Lip service is paid to planning; indeed planning staffs proliferate. However, they suffer from two debilities. The "operating" elements may not take the planning effort seriously. Plans become esoteric exercises which are accepted largely because they imply no practical consequence. They are a sop to administrative theory. At the same time, since planning staffs have a high incentive to try to be "useful," there is a bias against novel conceptions which are difficult to adapt to an administrative mold. It is one thing to assign an individual or a group the task of looking ahead; this is a far cry from providing an environment which encourages an understanding for deeper historical, sociological, and economic trends. The need to provide a memorandum may outweigh the imperatives of creative thought. The quest for objectivity creates a temptation to see in the future an updated version of the present. Yet true innovation is bound to run counter to prevailing standards. The dilemma of modern bureaucracy is that while every creative act is lonely, not every lonely act is creative. Formal criteria are little help in solving this problem because the unique cannot be expressed "objectively."

The rigidity in the policies of the technologically advanced societies is in no small part due to the complexity of decision-making. Crucial problems may—and frequently do—go unrecognized for a long time. But once the decision-making apparatus has disgorged a policy, it becomes very difficult to change it. The alternative to the *status quo* is the prospect of repeating the whole anguishing process of arriving at decisions. This explains to some extent the curious phenomenon that decisions taken with enormous doubt and perhaps with a close division become practically sacrosanct once adopted. The whole administrative machinery swings behind their implementation as if activity could still all doubts.

Moreover, the reputation, indeed the political survival, of most leaders depends on their ability to realize their goals, however these may have been arrived at. Whether these goals are desirable is relatively less crucial. The time span by which administrative success is measured is considerably shorter than that by which historical achievement is determined. In heavily bureaucratized societies all pressures emphasize the first of these accomplishments.

Then, too, the staffs on which modern executives come to depend develop a momentum of their own. What starts out as an aid to decision-makers often turns into a practically autonomous organization whose internal problems structure and sometimes compound the issues which it was originally designed to solve. The decision-maker will always be aware of the morale of his staff. Though he has the authority, he cannot overrule it too frequently without impairing its efficiency; and he may, in any event, lack the knowledge to do so. Placating the staff then becomes a major preoccupation of the executive. A form of administrative democracy results, in which a decision often reflects an attainable consensus rather than substantive conviction (or at least the two imperceptibly merge). The internal requirements of the bureaucracy may come to predominate over the purposes which it was intended to serve. This is probably even more true in highly institutionalized Communist states—such as the U.S.S.R.—than in the United States.

When the administrative machine grows very elaborate, the various levels of the decision-making process are separated by chasms which are obscured from the outside world by the complexity of the apparatus. Research often becomes a means to buy time and to assuage consciences.

Studying a problem can turn into an escape from coming to grips with it. In the process, the gap between the technical competence of research staffs and what hard-pressed political leaders are capable of absorbing widens constantly. This heightens the insecurity of the executive and may thus compound either rigidity or arbitrariness or both. In many fields—strategy being a prime example—decision-makers may find it difficult to give as many hours to a problem as the expert has had years to study it. The ultimate decision often depends less on knowledge than on the ability to brief the top administrator—to present the facts in such a way that they can be absorbed rapidly. The effectiveness of briefing, however, puts a premium on theatrical qualities. Not everything that sounds plausible is correct, and many things which are correct may not sound plausible when they are first presented; and a second hearing is rare. The stage aspect of briefing may leave the decision-maker with a gnawing feeling of having been taken—even, and perhaps especially, when he does not know quite how.

Sophistication may thus encourage paralysis or a crude popularization which defeats its own purpose. The excessively theoretical approach of many research staffs overlooks the problem of the strain of decision-making in times of crisis. What is relevant for policy depends not only on academic truth but also on what can be implemented under stress. The technical staffs are frequently operating in a framework of theoretical standards while in fact their usefulness depends on essentially psychological criteria. To be politically meaningful, their proposals must involve answers to the following types of questions: Does the executive understand the proposal? Does he believe in it? Does he accept it as a guide to action or as an excuse for doing nothing? But if these kinds of concerns are given too much weight, the requirements of salesmanship will defeat substance.

The pragmatism of executives thus clashes with the theoretical bent of research or planning staffs. Executives as a rule take cognizance of a problem only when it emerges as an administrative issue. They thus unwittingly encourage bureaucratic contests as the only means of generating decisions. Or the various elements of the bureaucracy make a series of nonaggression pacts with each other and thus reduce the decision-maker to a benevolent constitutional monarch. As the special role of the executive increasingly becomes to choose between proposals generated administratively, decision-makers turn into arbiters rather than leaders. Whether they wait until a problem emerges as an administrative issue or until a crisis has demonstrated the irrelevance of the standard operating procedure, the modern decision-makers often find themselves the prisoners of their advisers.

Faced with an administrative machine which is both elaborate and fragmented, the executive is forced into essentially lateral means of control. Many of his public pronouncements, though ostensibly directed to outsiders, perform a perhaps more important role in laying down guidelines for the bureaucracy. The chief significance of a foreign policy speech by the President may thus be that it settles an internal debate in Washington (a public statement is more useful for this purpose than an administrative memorandum because it is harder to reverse). At the same time, the bureaucracy's awareness of this method of control tempts it to shortcut its debates by using pronouncements by the decision-makers as charters for special purposes. The executive thus finds himself confronted by proposals for public declarations which may be innocuous in themselves—and whose bureaucratic significance may be anything but obvious—but which can be used by some agency or department to launch a study or program which will restrict his freedom of decision later on.

All of this drives the executive in the direction of extra-bureaucratic means of decision. The practice of relying on special emissaries or personal envoys is an example; their status outside the bureaucracy frees them from some of its restraints. International agreements are sometimes possible only by ignoring safeguards against capricious action. It is a paradoxical aspect of modern bureaucracies that their quest for objectivity and calculability often leads to impasses which can be overcome only by essentially arbitrary decisions.

Such a mode of operation would involve a great risk of stagnation even in "normal" times. It becomes especially dangerous in a revolutionary period. For then, the problems which are most obtrusive may be least relevant. The issues which are most significant may not be suitable for administrative formulation and even when formulated may not lend themselves to bureaucratic consensus. When the issue is how to transform the existing framework, routine can become an additional obstacle to both comprehension and action.

This problem, serious enough *within* each society, is magnified in the conduct of international affairs. While the formal machinery of decision-making in developed countries shows many similarities, the criteria which influence decisions vary enormously. With each administrative machine increasingly absorbed in its own internal problems, diplomacy loses its flexibility. Leaders are extremely aware of the problems of placating their own bureaucracy; they cannot depart too far from its prescriptions without raising serious morale problems. Decisions are reached so painfully that the very anguish of decision-making acts as a brake on the give-and-take of traditional diplomacy.

This is true even *within* alliances. Meaningful consultation with other nations becomes very difficult when the internal process of decision-making already has some of the characteristics of compacts between quasi-sovereign entities. There is an increasing reluctance to hazard a hard-won domestic consensus in an international forum.

What is true within alliances—that is, among nations which have at least some common objectives—becomes even more acute in relations between antagonistic states or blocs. The gap created when two large bureaucracies generate goals largely in isolation from each other and on the basis of not necessarily commensurable criteria is magnified considerably by an ideological schism. The degree of ideological fervor is not decisive; the problem would exist even if the original ideological commitment had declined on either or both sides. The criteria for bureaucratic decision-making may continue to be influenced by ideology even after its élan has dissipated. Bureaucratic structures generate their own momentum which may more than counterbalance the loss of earlier fanaticism. In the early stages of a revolutionary movement, ideology is crucial and the accident of personalities can be decisive. The Reign of Terror in France was ended by the elimination of a single man, Robespierre. The Bolshevik revolution could hardly have taken place had Lenin not been on the famous train which crossed Germany into Russia. But once a revolution becomes institutionalized, the administrative structures which it has spawned develop their own vested interests. Ideology may grow less significant in creating commitment; it becomes pervasive in supplying criteria of administrative choice. Ideologies prevail by being taken for granted. Orthodoxy substitutes for conviction and produces its own form of rigidity.

In such circumstances, a meaningful dialogue across ideological dividing lines becomes extraordinarily difficult. The more elaborate the administrative structure, the less relevant an individual's view becomes— indeed one of the purposes of bureaucracy is to liberate decision-making from the accident of personalities. Thus while personal convictions may be modified, it requires a really monumental effort to alter bureaucratic commitments. And if change occurs, the bureaucracy prefers to move at its own pace and not be excessively influenced by statements or pressures of foreigners. For all these reasons, diplomacy tends to become rigid or to turn into an abstract bargaining process based on largely formal criteria such as "splitting the difference." Either course is self-defeating: the former because it negates the very purpose of diplomacy; the latter because it subordinates purpose to technique and because it may encourage intransigence. Indeed, the incentive for intransigence increases if it is known that the difference will generally be split.

Ideological differences are compounded because major parts of the world are only in the first stages of administrative evolution. Where the technologically advanced countries suffer from the inertia of over-administration, the developing areas often lack even the rudiments of effective bureaucracy. Where the advanced countries may drown in "facts," the emerging nations are frequently without the most elementary knowledge needed for forming a meaningful judgment or for implementing it once it has been taken. Where large bureaucracies operate in alternating spurts of rigidity and catastrophic (in relation to the bureaucracy) upheaval, the new states tend to take decisions on the basis of almost random pressures. The excessive institutionalization of one and the inadequate structure of the other inhibit international stability.

III. THE NATURE OF LEADERSHIP

Whatever one's view about the degree to which choices in international affairs are "objectively" determined, the decisions are made by individuals who will be above all conscious of the seeming multiplicity of options. Their understanding of the nature of their choice depends on many factors, including their experience during the rise to eminence.

The mediating, conciliatory style of British policy in the nineteenth century reflected, in part, the qualities encouraged during careers in Parliament and the values of a cohesive leadership group connected by ties of family and common education. The hysterical cast of the policy of Imperial Germany was given impetus by a domestic structure in which political parties were deprived of responsibility while ministers were obliged to balance a monarch by divine right against a Parliament composed of representatives without any prospect of ever holding office. Consensus could be achieved most easily through fits of national passion which in turn disquieted all of Germany's neighbors. Germany's foreign policy grew unstable because its domestic structure did little to discourage capricious improvisations; it may even have put a premium on them.

The collapse of the essentially aristocratic conception of foreign policy of the nineteenth century has made the career experiences of leaders even more crucial. An aristocracy—if it lives up to its values—will reject the arbitrariness of absolutist rule; and it will base itself on a notion of quality which discourages the temptations of demagoguery inherent in plebiscitarian democracy. Where position is felt to be a birthright, generosity is possible (though not guaranteed); flexibility is not inhibited by a commitment to perpetual success. Where a leader's estimate of himself is not completely dependent on his standing in an administrative structure, measures can be judged in terms of a conception of the future rather than of an almost compulsive desire to avoid even a temporary setback. When statesmen belonged to a community transcending national boundaries, there tended to be consensus on the criteria of what constituted a reasonable proposal. This did not prevent conflicts, but it did define their nature and encourage dialogue. The bane of aristocratic foreign policy was the risk of frivolousness, of a self-confidence unrelated to knowledge, and of too much emphasis on intuition.

In any event, ours is the age of the expert or the charismatic leader.

The expert has his constituency—those who have a vested interest in commonly held opinions; elaborating and defining its consensus at a high level has, after all, made him an expert. Since the expert is often the product of the administrative dilemmas described earlier, he is usually in a poor position to transcend them. The charismatic leader, on the other hand, needs a perpetual revolution to maintain his position. Neither the expert nor the charismatic leader operates in an environment which puts a premium on long-range conceptions or on generosity or on subordinating the leader's ego to purposes which transcend his own career.

Leadership groups are formed by at least three factors: their experiences during their rise to eminence; the structure in which they must operate; the values of their society. Three contemporary types will be discussed here: (a) the bureaucratic-pragmatic type, (b) the ideological type, and (c) the revolutionary-charismatic type.

Bureaucratic-pragmatic leadership. The main example of this type of leadership is the American élite—though the leadership groups of other Western countries increasingly approximate the American pattern. Shaped by a society without fundamental social schisms (at least until the race problem became visible) and the product of an environment in which most recognized problems have proved soluble, its approach to policy is *ad hoc*, pragmatic, and somewhat mechanical.

Because pragmatism is based on the conviction that the context of events produces a solution, there is a tendency to await developments. The belief is prevalent that every problem will yield if attacked with sufficient energy. It is inconceivable, therefore, that delay might result in irretrievable disaster; at worst it is thought to require a redoubled effort later on. Problems are segmented into constituent elements, each of which is dealt with by experts in the special difficulty it involves. There is little emphasis or concern for their interrelationship. Technical issues enjoy more careful attention, and receive more sophisticated treatment, than political ones. Though the importance of intangibles is affirmed in theory, it is difficult to obtain a consensus on which factors are significant and even harder to find a meaningful mode for dealing with them. Things are done because one knows how to do them and not because one ought to do them. The criteria for dealing with trends which are conjectural are less well developed than those for immediate crises. Pragmatism, at least in its generally accepted form, is more concerned with method than with judgment; or rather it seeks to reduce judgment to methodology and value to knowledge.

This is reinforced by the special qualities of the professions—law and business—which furnish the core of the leadership groups in America. Lawyers—at least in the Anglo-Saxon tradition—prefer to deal with actual rather than hypothetical cases; they have little confidence in the possibility of stating a future issue abstractly. But planning by its very nature is hypothetical. Its success depends precisely on the ability to transcend the existing framework. Lawyers may be prepared to undertake this task; but they will do well in it only to the extent that they are able to overcome the special qualities encouraged by their profession. What comes naturally to lawyers in the Anglo-Saxon tradition is the sophisticated analysis of a series of *ad hoc* issues which emerge as problems through adversary proceedings. In so far as lawyers draw on the experience which forms them, they have a bias toward awaiting developments and toward operating within the definition of the problem as formulated by its chief spokesmen.

This has several consequences. It compounds the already powerful tendencies within American society to identify foreign policy with the solution of immediate issues. It produces great refinement of issues as they arise, but it also encourages the administrative dilemmas described earlier. Issues are dealt with only as the pressure of events imposes the need for resolving them. Then, each of the contending factions within the bureaucracy has a maximum incentive to state its case in its most extreme form because the ultimate outcome depends, to a considerable extent, on a bargaining process. The premium placed on advocacy turns decision-making into a series of adjustments among special interests—a process more suited to domestic than to foreign policy. This procedure neglects the long-range because the future has no administrative constituency and is, therefore, without representation in the adversary proceedings. Problems tend to be slighted until some agency or department is made responsible for them. When this occurs—usually when a difficulty has already grown acute—the relevant department becomes an all-out spokesman for its particular area of responsibility. The outcome usually depends more on the pressures or the persuasivenes of the contending advocates than on a concept of over-all purpose. While these tendencies exist to some extent in all bureaucracies they are particularly pronounced in the American system of government.

This explains in part the peculiar alternation of rigidity and spasms of flexibility in American diplomacy. On a given issue—be it the Berlin crisis or disarmament or the war in Viet-Nam—there generally exists a great reluctance to develop a negotiating position or a statement of objectives except in the most general terms. This stems from a desire not to prejudge the process of negotiations and above all to retain flexibility in the face of unforeseeable events. But when an approaching conference or some other pressures make the development of a position imperative and some office or individual is assigned the specific task, a sudden change occurs. Both personal and bureaucratic success are then identified with bringing the particular assignment to a conclusion. Where so much stock is placed in negotiating skill, a failure of a conference may be viewed as a reflection on the ability of the negotiator rather than on the objective difficulty of the subject. Confidence in the bargaining process causes American negotiators to be extremely sensitive to the tactical requirements of the conference table—sometimes at the expense of longer-term considerations. In internal discussions, American negotiators—generally irrespective of their previous commitments—often become advocates for the maximum range of concessions; their legal background tempts them to act as mediators between Washington and the country with which they are negotiating.

The attitudes of the business élite reinforce the convictions of the legal profession. The American business executive rises through a process of selection which rewards the ability to manipulate the known—in itself a conciliatory procedure. The special skill of the executive is thought to consist in coordinating well-defined functions rather than in challenging them. The procedure is relatively effective in the business world, where the executive can often substitute decisiveness, long experience, and a wide range of personal acquaintance for reflectiveness. In international affairs, however—especially in a revolutionary situation—the strong will which is one of our business executives' notable traits may produce essentially arbitrary choices. Or unfamiliarity with the subject matter may have the opposite effect of turning the executive into a spokesman of his technical staffs. In either case, the business executive is even more dependent than the lawyer on the bureaucracy's formulation of the issue. The business élite is even less able or willing than the lawyer to recognize that the formulation of an issue, not the technical remedy, is usually the central problem.

All this gives American policy its particular cast. Problems are dealt with as they arise. Agreement on what constitutes a problem generally depends on an emerging crisis which settles the previously inconclusive disputes about priorities. When a problem is recognized, it is dealt with by a mobilization of all resources to overcome the immediate symptoms. This often involves the risk of slighting longer-term issues which may not yet have assumed crisis proportions and of overwhelming, perhaps even undermining, the structure of the area concerned by a flood of American technical experts proposing remedies on an American scale. Administrative decisions emerge from a compromise of conflicting pressures in which accidents of personality or persuasiveness play a crucial role. The compromise often reflects the maxim that "if two parties disagree the truth is usually somewhere in between." But the pedantic application of such truisms causes the various contenders to exaggerate their positions for bargaining purposes or to construct fictitious extremes to make their position appear moderate. In either case, internal bargaining predominates over substance.

The *ad hoc* tendency of our decision-makers and the reliance on adversary proceeding cause issues to be stated in black and white terms.

This suppresses a feeling for nuance and makes it difficult to recognize the relationship between seemingly discrete events. Even with the perspective of a decade there is little consensus about the relationship between the actions culminating in the Suez fiasco and the French decision to enter the nuclear field; or about the inconsistency between the neutralization of Laos and the step-up of the military effort in Viet-Nam.

The same quality also produces a relatively low valuation of historical factors. Nations are treated as similar phenomena, and those states presenting similar immediate problems are treated similarly. Since many of our policy-makers first address themselves to an issue when it emerges as their area of responsibility, their approach to it is often highly anecdotal. Great weight is given to what people say and relatively little to the significance of these affirmations in terms of domestic structure or historical background. Agreement may be taken at face value and seen as reflecting more consensus than actually exists. Opposition tends to produce moral outrage which often assumes the form of personal animosity—the attitude of some American policy-makers toward President de Gaulle is a good example.

The legal background of our policy-makers produces a bias in favor of constitutional solutions. The issue of supra-nationalism or confederalism in Europe has been discussed largely in terms of the right of countries to make independent decisions. Much less weight has been given to the realities which would limit the application of a majority vote against a major country whatever the legal arrangements. (The fight over the application of Article 19 of the United Nations Charter was based on the same attitude.) Similarly, legal terms such as "integration" and "assignment" sometimes become ends in themselves and thus obscure the operational reality to which they refer. In short, the American leadership groups show high competence in dealing with technical issues, and much less virtuosity in mastering a historical process. And the policies of other Western countries exhibit variations of the American pattern. A lesser pragmatism in continental Europe is counter-balanced by a smaller ability to play a world-role.

The ideological type of leadership. As has been discussed above, the impact of ideology can persist long after its initial fervor has been spent. Whatever the ideological commitment of individual leaders, a lifetime spent in the Communist hierarchy must influence their basic categories of thought—especially since Communist ideology continues to perform important functions. It still furnishes the standard of truth and the guarantee of ultimate success. It provides a means for maintaining cohesion among the various Communist parties of the world. It supplies criteria for the settlement of disputes both within the bureaucracy of individual Communist countries and among the various Communist states. However attenuated, Communist ideology is, in part, responsible for international tensions. This is less because of specific Marxist tactical prescriptions—with respect to which Communists have shown a high degree of flexibility—than because of the basic Marxist-Leninist categories for interpreting reality. Communist leaders never tire of affirming that Marxism-Leninism is the key element of their self-proclaimed superiority over the outside world; as Marxist-Leninists they are convinced that they understand the historical process better than the non-Communist world does.

The essence of Marxism-Leninism—and the reason that normal diplomacy with Communist states is so difficult—is the view that "objective" factors such as the social structure, the economic process, and, above all, the class struggle are more important than the personal convictions of statesmen. Belief in the predominance of objective factors explains the Soviet approach to the problem of security. If personal convictions are "subjective," Soviet security cannot be allowed to rest on the good will of other statesmen, especially those of a different social system. This produces a quest for what may be described as absolute security—the attempt to be so strong as to be independent of the decisions of other countries. But absolute security for one country means absolute insecurity for all others; it can be achieved only by reducing other states to impotence. Thus an essentially defensive foreign policy can grow indistinguishable from traditional aggression.

The belief in the predominance of objective factors explains why, in the past, periods of détente have proved so precarious. When there is a choice between Western good will or a physical gain, the pressures to choose the latter have been overwhelming. The wartime friendship with the West was sacrificed to the possibility of establishing Communist-controlled governments in Eastern Europe. The spirit of Geneva did not survive the temptations offered by the prospect of undermining the Western position in the Middle East. The many overtures of the Kennedy administration were rebuffed until the Cuban missile crisis demonstrated that the balance of forces was not in fact favorable for a test of strength.

The reliance on objective factors has complicated negotiations between the West and the Communist countries. Communist negotiators find it difficult to admit that they could be swayed by the arguments of men who have, by definition, an inferior grasp of the laws of historical development. No matter what is said, they think that they understand their Western counterpart better than he understands himself. Concessions are possible, but they are made to "reality," not to individuals or to a bargaining process. Diplomacy becomes difficult when one of the parties considers the key element to negotiation—the give-and-take of the process of bargaining—as but a superstructure for factors not part of the negotiation itself.

Finally, whatever the decline in ideological fervor, orthodoxy requires the maintenance of a posture of ideological hostility to the non-Communist world even during a period of coexistence. Thus, in a reply to a Chinese challenge, the Communist Party of the U.S.S.R. declared: "We fully support the destruction of capitalism. We not only believe in the inevitable death of capitalism but we are doing everything possible for it to be accomplished through class struggle as quickly as possible."[2]

The wariness toward the outside world is reinforced by the personal experiences which Communist leaders have had on the road to eminence. In a system where there is no legitimate succession, a great deal of energy is absorbed in internal maneuvering. Leaders rise to the top by eliminating—sometimes physically, always bureaucratically—all possible opponents. Stalin had all individuals who helped him into power executed. Khrushchev disgraced Kaganovich, whose protegé he had been, and turned on Marshal Zhukov six months after being saved by him from a conspiracy of his other colleagues. Brezhnev and Kosygin owed their careers to Khrushchev; they nevertheless overthrew him and started a campaign of calumny against him within twenty-four hours of his dismissal.

Anyone succeeding in Communist leadership struggles must be single-minded, unemotional, dedicated, and, above all, motivated by an enormous desire for power. Nothing in the personal experience of Soviet leaders would lead them to accept protestations of good will at face value. Suspiciousness is inherent in their domestic position. It is unlikely that their attitude toward the outside world is more benign than toward their own colleagues or that they would expect more consideration from it.

The combination of personal qualities and ideological structure also affects relations *among* Communist states. Since national rivalries are thought to be the result of class conflict, they are expected to disappear wherever Socialism has triumphed. When disagreements occur they are dealt with by analogy to internal Communist disputes: by attempting to ostracize and then to destroy the opponent. The tendency to treat different opinions as manifestations of heresy causes disagreements to harden into bitter schisms. The debate between Communist China and the U.S.S.R. is in many respects more acrimonious than that between the U.S.S.R. and the non-Communist world.

Even though the basic conceptual categories of Communist leadership groups are similar, the impact of the domestic structure of the individual Communist states on international relations varies greatly. It makes a considerable difference whether an ideology has become institutionalized, as in the Soviet Union, or whether it is still impelled by its early revolutionary fervor, as in Communist China. Where ideology has become institutionalized a special form of pragmatism may develop. It may be just as empirical as that of the United States but it will operate in a different realm of "reality." A different philosophical basis leads to the emergence of another set of categories for the settlement of disputes, and these in turn generate another range of problems.

A Communist bureaucratic structure, however pragmatic, will have different priorities from ours; it will give greater weight to doctrinal considerations and conceptual problems. It is more than ritual when speeches of senior Soviet leaders begin with hour-long recitals of Communist ideology. Even if it were ritual, it must affect the definition of what is considered reasonable in internal arguments. Bureaucratization and pragmatism may lead to a loss of élan; they do not guarantee convergence of Western and Soviet thinking.

The more revolutionary manifestations of Communism, such as Communist China, still possess more ideological fervor, but, paradoxically, their structure may permit a wider latitude for new departures. Tactical intransigence and ideological vitality should not be confused with structural rigidity. Because the leadership bases its rule on a prestige which transcends bureaucratic authority, it has not yet given so many hostages to the administrative structure. If the leadership should change—or if its attitudes are modified—policy could probably be altered much more dramatically in Communist China than in the more institutionalized Communist countries.

The charismatic-revolutionary type of leadership. The contemporary international order is heavily influenced by yet another leadership type: the charismatic-revolutionary leader. For many of the leaders of the new nations the bureaucratic-pragmatic approach of the West is irrelevant because they are more interested in the future which they wish to construct than in the manipulation of the environment which dominates the thinking of the pragmatists. And ideology is not satisfactory because doctrine supplies rigid categories which overshadow the personal experiences which have provided the impetus for so many of the leaders of the new nations.

The type of individual who leads a struggle for independence has been sustained in the risks and suffering of such a course primarily by a commitment to a vision which enabled him to override conditions which had seemed overwhelmingly hostile. Revolutionaries are rarely motivated primarily by material considerations—though the illusion that they are persists in the West. Material incentives do not cause a man to risk his existence and to launch himself into the uncertainties of a revolutionary struggle. If Castro or Sukarno had been principally interested in economics, their talents would have guaranteed them a brilliant career in the societies they overthrew. What made their sacrifices worthwhile to them was a vision of the future—or a quest for political power. To revolutionaries the significant reality is the world which they are striving to bring about, not the world they are fighting to overcome.

This difference in perspective accounts for the inconclusiveness of much of the dialogue between the West and many of the leaders of the new countries. The West has a tendency to believe that the tensions in the emerging nations are caused by a low level of economic activity. To the apostles of economic development, raising the gross national product seems the key to political stability. They believe that it should receive the highest priority from the political leaders of new countries and supply their chief motivation.

But to the charismatic heads of many of the new nations, economic progress, while not unwelcome, offers too limited a scope for their ambitions. It can be achieved only by slow, painful, highly technical measures which contrast with the heroic exertions of the struggle for independence. Results are long-delayed; credit for them cannot be clearly established. If Castro were to act on the advice of theorists of economic development, the best he could hope for would be that after some decades he would lead a small progressive country—perhaps a Switzerland of the Caribbean. Compared to the prospect of leading a revolution throughout Latin America, this goal would appear trivial, boring, perhaps even unreal to him.

Moreover, to the extent that economic progress is achieved, it may magnify domestic political instability, at least in its early phases. Economic advance disrupts the traditional political structure. It thus places constant pressures on the incumbent leaders to re-establish the legitimacy of their rule. For this purpose a dramatic foreign policy is particularly apt. Many leaders of the new countries seem convinced that an adventurous foreign policy will not harm prospects for economic development and may even foster it. The competition of the superpowers makes it likely that economic assistance will be forthcoming regardless of the actions of the recipient. Indeed the more obstrusive their foreign policy the greater is their prospect of being wooed by the chief contenders.

The tendency toward a reckless policy is magnified by the uncertain sense of identity of many of the new nations. National boundaries often correspond to the administrative subdivisions established by the former colonial rulers. States thus have few of the attributes of nineteenth-century European nationalism: common language, common culture, or even common history. In many cases, the only common experience is a century or so of imperial rule. As a result, there is a great pressure toward authoritarian rule, and a high incentive to use foreign policy as a means of bringing about domestic cohesion.

Western-style democracy presupposes that society transcends the political realm; in that case opposition challenges a particular method of achieving common aims but not the existence of the state itself. In many of the new countries, by contrast, the state represents the primary, sometimes the sole, manifestation of social cohesion. Opposition can therefore easily appear as treason—apart from the fact that leaders who have spent several decades running the risks of revolutionary struggle or who have achieved power by a coup d'état are not likely to favor a system of government which makes them dispensable. Indeed the attraction of Communism for many of these leaders is not Marxist-Leninist economic theory but the legitimacy for authoritarian rule which it provides.

No matter what the system of government, many of the leaders of the new nations use foreign policy as a means to escape intractable internal difficulties and as a device to achieve domestic cohesion. The international arena provides an opportunity for the dramatic measures which are impossible at home. These are often cast in an anti-Western mold because this is the easiest way to recreate the struggle against imperial rule which is the principal unifying element for many new nations. The incentive is particularly strong because the rivalry of the nuclear powers eliminates many of the risks which previously were associated with an adventurous foreign policy—especially if that foreign policy is directed against the West which lacks any effective sanctions.

Traditional military pressure is largely precluded by the nuclear stalemate and respect for world opinion. But the West is neither prepared nor able to use the sanction which weighs most heavily on the new countries: the deliberate exploitation of their weak domestic structure. In many areas the ability to foment domestic unrest is a more potent weapon than traditional arms. Many of the leaders of the new countries will be prepared to ignore the classical panoply of power; but they will be very sensitive to the threat of domestic upheaval. States with a high capacity for exploiting domestic instability can use it as a tool of foreign policy. China, though lacking almost all forms of classical long-range military strength, is a growing factor in Africa. Weak states may be more concerned with a country's capacity to organize domestic unrest in their territory than with its capacity for physical destruction.

Conclusion. Contemporary domestic structures thus present an unprecedented challenge to the emergence of a stable international order. The bureaucratic-pragmatic societies concentrate on the manipulation of an empirical reality which they treat as given; the ideological societies are split between an essentially bureaucratic approach (though in a different realm of reality than the bureaucratic-pragmatic structures) and a group using ideology mainly for revolutionary ends. The new nations, in so far as they are active in international affairs, have a high incentive to seek in foreign policy the perpetuation of charismatic leadership.

These differences are a major obstacle to a consensus on what constitutes a "reasonable" proposal. A common diagnosis of the existing situation is hard to achieve, and it is even more difficult to concert measures for a solution. The situation is complicated by the one feature all types of leadership have in common: the premium put on short-term goals and the domestic need to succeed at all times. In the bureaucratic societies policy emerges from a compromise which often produces the least common denominator, and it is implemented by individuals whose reputation is made by administering the *status quo*. The leadership of the institutionalized ideological state may be even more the prisoner of essentially corporate bodies. Neither leadership can afford radical changes of course for they result in profound repercussions in its administrative structure. And the charismatic leaders of the new nations are like tight-rope artists—one false step and they will plunge from their perch.

29. AMERICAN CHARACTER AND FOREIGN POLICY

Gabriel A. Almond

IT IS POSSIBLE to distinguish those "traits" which are referred to frequently in the literature over a period of many decades. The fact that successive generations of observers tend to reach similar conclusions suggests a greater credibility. In addition, some propositions seem to have an inherent plausibility, as tending to agree with informal observation, while others convey the impression of gifted, if untrustworthy, fantasy or theoretical presuppositions which have focused attention on particular phenomena regardless of their connection or representativeness. In the systematic inventory which follows we have made an effort to include only those observations which have continually recurred and those which seem to have an inherent plausibility, recognizing that the criterion of "plausibility" is a purely subjective one.

From *The American People and Foreign Policy* by Gabriel A. Almond, pp. 47–65; 137–148; 226–244. Copyright, 1950, by Harcourt, Brace and World, Inc. and reprinted with their permission.

GABRIEL A. ALMOND (1911–   ) Professor of Political Science, Stanford University. Author of *Political Development: Essays in Heuristic Theory* (Boston: Little, Brown and Company, 1970); *Comparative Politics: A Developmental Approach*, (Boston: Little, Brown and Company, 1966). Co-author, *The Civic Culture* (Princeton: Princeton University Press, 1963); *The Politics of the Developing Areas* (Princeton: Princeton University Press, 1960).

GENERAL VALUE ORIENTATION

The characteristic American value orientation would appear to consist of the following interrelated traits.

a. The degree of atomization in the United States is perhaps greater than in any other culture. The American is primarily concerned with "private" values, as distinguished from social-group, political, or religious-moral values. His concern with private, worldly success is his most absorbing aim. In this regard it may be suggested by way of hypothesis that in other cultures there is a greater stress on corporate loyalties and values and a greater personal involvement with political issues or with other-worldly religious values.

b. The "attachment" of the American to his private values is characterized by an extreme degree of competitiveness. He views himself and his family as in a state of competition with other individuals and families for success and achievement. American culture tends to be atomistic rather than corporate, and the pressure of movement "upward," toward achievement, is intense. Here again a hypothesis might be proposed that in other cultures individual competition for success tends to be more localized within specific classes or regions, tends to be subordinated to, or assimilated in, political competition, and tends to be muted by religious conceptions of life.

c. The American views himself and his family as in a state of competition with other individuals and families for values which are largely "material" in character. What he appears to want are the material evidences of success—money, position, and the consumer-goods of the moment. While the stress is toward money, or what money can buy, the important thing is not the money itself, but the sense of accomplishment or fulfillment which it gives. This sense of accomplishment rests on matching and exceeding the material standard of community and social class; it requires external approval and conformity. Because of the stress in the American value system on having what others want, and because of the great emphasis on the elaboration of material culture, the American tends to be caught up in an endless race for constantly changing goals—the "newest" in housing, the "latest" in locomotion, the most "fashionable" in dress and appearance. This love of innovation, improvement, and change tends to be confined to the material culture. Attitudes toward human and social relations tend to be more conservative. By way of hypothetical comparison it may be said that in other cultures the criteria of accomplishment are more stable. Religious salvation and political resentment provide greater consolation for the poor and the failures. The material culture tends to be hemmed in by tradition. The criteria of achievement have a more stable subjective basis in the sense

of craftsmanship, esthetic and intellectual subtlety, and the fulfillment
of social and religious routines.

d. There are certain derivative elements of this general value orientation which call for comment. First, intense individualistic competitiveness,
in which the primary aim is to get more of what other people want,
produces diffuse hostile tension and general apprehension and anxiety,
which pervades every aspect of the culture including the competing unit
itself, the family. The fear of failure and the apprehension over the
hostility which is involved in one's relations with other persons produce
on the one hand an extraordinary need for affection and reassurance, and
on the other, an extraordinary tendency to resort to physiological and
spiritual narcosis. In other words, as a consequence of being impelled by
cultural pressure toward relationships in which one is aggressively pitted
against others, the resulting unease and apprehension is characteristically
mitigated by demands for external response, attention, and warmth, or by
resort to escapism. Thus an excessive concern with sexuality, an excessive
resort to alcohol, and, what is a uniquely American form of narcosis of
the soul—the widespread addiction to highly stimulating mass entertain-
ment, the radio, movies, comics, and the like—provide culturally legitimate modes of discharging hostility and allaying anxiety.

Thus, by way of summary, the value orientation of the American tends
to be atomistic rather than corporate, worldly rather than unworldly,
highly mobile rather than traditional, compulsive rather than relaxed,
and externally directed rather than autonomous. Needless to say, these
are presented as hypothetical tendencies, which are supported only by an
inadequate and quite heterogenous body of evidence.

VALUE EXPECTATIONS

The American is an optimist as to ends and an improviser as to means.
The riches of his heritage and the mobility of his social order have produced a generally euphoric tendency, that is, the expectation that one can
by effort and good will achieve or approximate one's goals. This overt
optimism is so compulsive an element in the American culture that
factors which threaten it, such as failure, old age, and death, are pressed
from the focus of attention and handled in perfunctory ways.[1] This belief
that "things can be done" is coupled with a faith in common sense and
"know-how" with regard to means. The American has a double approach
to complex reasoning and theory. He has great respect for systematic

---

[1] See the comment on this point by Wolfenstein and Leites in C. and F. Kluck-
hohn, "American Culture: Generalized Orientation and Class Patterns" in *Conflicts
of Power in Modern Culture*, Seventh Symposium of Conference on Science, Philosophy and Religion, Harper, 1947, p. 109.

thinking and planning in relation to technological and organizational problems. But even this type of intellectualism is brought down to earth by referring to it as "know-how." Know-how implies both the possession of formal technical knowledge and the capacity to improvise and overcome obstacles on the basis of a "feel" for the problem or the situation. In complicated questions of social and public policy there is a genuine distrust of complex and subtle reasoning and a preference for an earthy "common sense." Thus, in these important areas his compulsive optimism, his anti-intellectualism, and his simple rationalism leave the American vulnerable to deflation and pessimism when his expectations are thwarted and when threats and dangers are not effectively warded off by improvisations. This vulnerability is, to be sure, balanced by a certain flexibility and experimentalism, a willingness to try new approaches. If Americans typically avoid the rigidity of dogma in dealing with new problems, they also typically fail to reap the advantages of thoughtful policy-planning. What is involved here is not so much a net loss, but rather the failure to realize the net gain that would result from a greater intellectual discipline.

ATTITUDES TOWARD AUTHORITY AND MORALITY

The American tends to "cut authority down to his own size." He has a respect for achievement and a toleration of order-enforcing agencies, but a distrust of arbitrary or traditional authority. This attitude toward authority also carries over into the field of tradition and custom. Certainly the urban American, and many of the rural ones as well, are not seriously limited by traditional methods of doing things. They are iconoclasts with respect to earlier aspects of culture, and conformists in relation to the most recent value changes. They reject what was done in the past, and they conform to the new things that are being done *now*. But again this iconoclasm is especially noticeable in the sphere of material culture. A greater conservatism obtains in relation to social and political matters. This social and political conservatism is not unique to Americans. What seems to be unique is this combination of mobility of material values and fundamentalism with regard to social and political values.

Similar trends are observable in American attitudes toward moral norms. The norms of Christianity still constitute an important theme in contemporary American culture. Since these moral standards are in obvious and continual rivalry with the competitive ethic, Americans tend to suffer from ambivalence and conflicts in determining what is "proper." Under normal circumstances this conflict does not appear to have a seriously laming effect. It tends to be disposed of by adding a moral coloration to actions which are really motivated by expediency, and an expediential coloration to actions which are motivated by moral and humanitarian values. These tendencies are related to a rather widespread naïve belief in the compatibility of morality and expediency.[2] While this ambivalence is a factor which generally affects American behavior, there is also a characteristic pendulum movement between the two ethics. Thus, if generous actions, motivated by moral and humanitarian considerations, are accepted without gratitude, are misinterpreted, or are unrequited, a "cynical" rejection of humanitarianism may follow, resulting from the humiliation at having been "played for a sucker." To yield to humanitarian impulses in the "market place" or to moderate one's own demands in the light of "Christian" considerations, to give without the expectation of receiving, to suffer injury without retaliation—these are impulses which have a partial validity; but it is dangerous to give way to them since they dull the edge of competitiveness, confuse and retard the forward course of action.

MOOD VERSUS POLICY

Since Americans tend to exhaust their emotional and intellectual energies in private pursuits, the typical approach to problems of public policy is perfunctory. Where public policy impinges directly on their interest, as in questions of local improvements, taxation, or social security policy, they are more likely to develop views and opinions resting on some kind of intellectual structure. But on questions of a more remote nature, such as foreign policy, they tend to react in more undifferentiated ways, with formless and plastic moods which undergo frequent alteration in response to change in events. The characteristic response to questions of foreign policy is one of indifference. A foreign policy crisis, short of the immediate threat of war, may transform indifference to vague apprehension, to fatalism, to anger; but the reaction is still a mood, a superficial and fluctuating response. To some extent American political apathy is a consequence of the compulsive absorption of energy in private competitiveness. To inform oneself on public issues, to form policies on the basis of careful thought-taking, is hardly a task that is beyond the intellectual competence of a large proportion of the population. The intellectual demands of business life are in some respects as complicated as those of foreign policy. But the American has a powerful cultural incentive to develop policies and strategies relating to his business and professional career, and little incentive, if any, to develop strategies for foreign policy.

The orientation of most Americans toward foreign policy is one of mood, and mood is essentially an unstable phenomenon. But this instability is not arbitrary and unpredictable. American moods are affected by two variables: (1) changes in the domestic and foreign political-

---

[2] *Ibid.*, p. 111.

economic situation involving the presence or absence of threat in varying degrees, (2) the characterological predispositions of the population. Our knowledge of American character tendencies, meager as it may be, makes it possible to suggest potential movements of opinion and mood which may have significant effects on foreign policy.

WITHDRAWAL-INTERVENTION

Given the intense involvement of most Americans with private interests and pursuits, the normal attitude toward a relatively stable world political situation is one of comparative indifference and withdrawal. This was the case throughout the greater part of the nineteenth century, in the period between World Wars I and II, and as we shall show in a later chapter, in the period immediately following World War II. The existence of this cyclical withdrawal-intervention problem suggests at least two serious dangers for foreign policy decision-making: (1) possible over-reactions to threat; (2) possible overreactions to temporary equilibria in world politics. Under ordinary circumstances American emotion and action are directed with considerable pressure in the normal orbits of private competition. However, when threats from abroad become grave and immediate, Americans tend to break out of their private orbits, and tremendous energies become available for foreign policy. Thus, we see the explosions of American energy in World Wars I and II when, after periods of indifference and withdrawal, exceptional feats of swift mobilization were achieved. There is some evidence to suggest that the Russian threat may, if carelessly handled, produce dangerous overreactions. Thus the press conference of Secretary of State Marshall in the spring of 1947, in which he urged the American people to "keep calm," produced what amounted to a war scare. The volatility and potential explosiveness of American opinion must be constantly kept in mind if panic reactions to threat are to be avoided.

The danger of overreaction to threat is only one aspect of this withdrawal-intervention tendency of American opinion. Equally serious is the prospect of overreaction to temporary stabilizations in the world crisis. Because of the superficial character of American attitudes toward world politics, American opinion tends to react to the external aspects of situations. A temporary Russian tactical withdrawal may produce strong tendencies toward demobilization and the reassertion of the primacy of private and domestic values. The pull of "privatism" in America creates a strong inclination to self-deception. And while this is less characteristic of the informed and policy-making levels, it undoubtedly plays an important role here as well. The great American demobilization of 1945, both in the military establishment and in the civilian bureaucracy, and the hasty dismantling of war agencies and controls reflected the overwhelming eagerness to withdraw to private values and normal conditions. This movement was not based on a sober evaluation of the foreign situation and what this might require in military and political terms, but was a response to the overwhelming urge to have done with alarms and external interruptions and get back to the essential and important values.

MOOD-SIMPLIFICATION

Closely connected with the withdrawal-intervention pattern is a tendency which has to do with characteristic changes in the internal structure of American foreign policy moods. It has already been pointed out that under conditions of political equilibrium American attitudes toward world politics tend to be formless and lacking in intellectual structure. We define policy, as distinguished from mood, as consisting of a relatively stable intellectual structure including (1) explicit assumptions as to the values involved in domestic or international political conflict, (2) explicit evaluations of the relative costs and efficiency of alternative means of maximizing the value position of one's own country or political group. From the point of view of this criterion, American attitudes tend to range from unstructured moods in periods of equilibrium to simplification in periods of crisis. So long as there is no immediate, sharply defined threat, the attitude is vague and indefinite—e.g., apathetic, mildly apprehensive, euphoric, skeptical. When the crisis becomes sharpened American responses become more specific. Here American distrust of intellectualism and subtlety, the faith in "common sense," and the belief in simple answers lead to oversimplications of the threat and the methods of coping with it.

While these tendencies are more characteristic of the "uninformed" general run of the population, they affect policymakers as well. Thus during World War II, the Roosevelt shift from "Dr. New Deal" to "Dr. Win-the-War" reflected this need at the very highest level of policy-making to reduce the issues to simplified proportion. The "unconditional surrender" policy was a similarly oversimplified resolution of the moral and political problems of the war.[3] The journalists and writers who directed American propaganda efforts in World War II solved their complex policy problems by the slogan of "the strategy of truth," which left to the lower-level, competitive policy-making process practically all of the important decisions of propaganda policy during the war. The policy of "non-fraternization" with Germans which was imposed on the American

---

[3] See among others Wallace Carroll's book on American propaganda policy during the war, *Persuade or Perish*, Houghton Mifflin, 1948. Apparently Roosevelt had in mind Grant's rather benevolent treatment of Lee at the time of the Southern surrender. But Roosevelt apparently never got around to explaining this to top advisers and administrators. Robert Sherwood in *Roosevelt and Hopkins* (Harper, 1948, pp. 696 ff.) makes the same point in detail.

army of occupation similarly was understandable as a gratification of a need for moral simplism, but it bore only a slight relation to the complex and uncomfortable realities on which it was imposed. The entire sequence of American policies toward Germany had this character of mixed moral-expediential improvisations. At first these improvisations were motivated primarily by anti-German reactions; more recently the tendency is toward more pro-German improvisations. At the present time this tendency to over-simplify seems to be taking the form of reducing all the problems of world politics to a simple "East-West" conflict. There is considerable pressure to take as an ally any country or movement which is anti-Communist and anti-Russian.

It would, of course, be an exaggeration to attribute the same degree of "simplism" to policy-makers as might be expected of the "man in the street." But there can be little doubt that the process of foreign policy-making is strongly influenced by this common-sense, improvisation tendency. Faith in policy-planning (which means in simple terms, taking the "long view," acquiring sufficient reliable information on which sound policy can be based, weighing and balancing the potential value of military, political, diplomatic, and psychological means in relation to proposed course of action) has hardly taken root in the American policy-making process.

OPTIMISM-PESSIMISM

The problem of shifts in mood from euphoric to dysphoric expectations is clearly related to those aspects of American opinion already described. The involvement in private concerns, coupled with an optimistic faith in good will, common sense, and simple answers, renders the American public vulnerable to failure. This reaction tends to result from the frustration of successive improvisations, none of which have been adapted to the complex character of the problem. Under these circumstances there are two possible dangers: (1) withdrawal reactions; (2) hasty measures motivated by irritation and impatience. The development of American attitudes toward Russia since the end of the war is an excellent illustration of this problem. During the war and in the period immediately following its termination there was a widely shared belief among Americans and among American policy-makers that the Russian problem could be readily solved by good will and the "man-to-man" approach. The continued thwarting of American overtures and concessions to the Russians now seems to have produced an attitude of hopeless pessimism. Pessimism certainly seems to be justifiable on the basis of the facts, but the negativism which has resulted may possibly constitute a danger if negotiation and bargaining with the Russians in principle is interdicted. The objective problem would seem to be one of choosing the time, the occasion, and the conditions when negotiation might lead to advantage. There is a similar danger of excessive pessimism in relation to potential allies. Perhaps there is a tendency toward a premature "writing off" of peoples whose social and political structures are unstable, countries which don't react with "American speed" to American proposals or which are not ready to commit themselves to the American "side" in as wholehearted a fashion as we might desire.

TOLERANCE-INTOLERANCE

The point has already been made that the American attitude toward authority, toward moral and ideological norms, contains conflicting elements. On the one hand, the American is not hemmed in by the mores and morals of "the horse and buggy days," and at the same time he is a conformist, a value-imitator. He is ready to try new things and new methods, but not if they make him look "different" or "peculiar." The truth of the matter would seem to be that, while he has loosened himself from the bonds of earlier moral standards and beliefs, he has not replaced these guides for conduct with any other set of principles. The autonomous conscience of Puritanism has been replaced by the "radar-directed" conduct of the "marketer." [4] He tends to take his judgments as to what is right and wrong, proper and improper, from the changing culture as it impinges on him through the various social institutions and media of communication. This makes for a certain flexibility in attitudes toward other cultures and ideologies. But the flexibility is negative rather than positive. That is, the American has moved away from older moral and traditional norms without acquiring new bases of judgment. His toleration of difference therefore is unstable, and there is a substratum of ideological fundamentalism which frequently breaks through the surface and has an important impact on foreign policy. Thus in our efforts to stabilize the weakened and chaotic areas of Western Europe we have been prepared to go a long way in aiding "Socialist Great Britain" and the left-inclined powers of Western Europe. But there is a continual sabotage of this tolerance, frequent efforts at ideological imperialism, even occasional interferences at the administrative level, which are motivated by ideological fundamentalism.

In general, this intolerance of difference is more clearly expressed in periods of normalcy. Thus, even though the possibility appears to be remote, the prospect of a recrudescence of isolationism cannot be excluded. A tactical cessation of Russian pressure might produce just this kind of demobilization and withdrawal reaction and the reassertion of older principles of conduct. This is not to say that such a reaction would be

---

[4] D. Riesman and N. Glazer, "Character Types and Political Apathy," *Research Project in Mass Communications,* Yale University, May 26, 1948, p. 9.

decisive so far as policy is concerned; but it is a prospect which sound policy-planning should anticipate.

IDEALISM-CYNICISM

In still another respect American moral predispositions may have consequences for foreign policy. The annoyance and irritation of the peoples of foreign countries over American self-righteousness is, on the whole, a relatively minor source of difficulty. Americans would appear to be happiest when they can cloak an action motivated by self-interest with an aura of New Testament selflessness, when an action which is "good business," or "good security" can be made to "look good" too. Similarly there is resistance among Americans over the straightforward expression of conscience-motivated behavior. What is "good" has to be represented as satisfying the criteria of self-interest. They are happiest when they can ally the Christian conscience at the same time that they satisfy self-interested criteria. In this regard the peoples of foreign countries are well protected, perhaps overprotected, by their own cynicism.

But there are a number of respects in which this moral dualism may produce more serious problems for the policy-maker. There would appear to be a certain cyclical trend in American moral attitudes. The great wave of idealism in the first world war gave way to the cynicism about foreign countries of the 1920's. The friendliness for our British and French allies of World War I gave way to bitterness over their defaults on their indebtedness. A little more than a decade ago the little country of Finland had a place at the very center of the American heart because she had kept up her payments on her war debts, while the European powers which had defaulted, and on the fate of which our security rested, were prevented from borrowing money in the American capital market. The chiliastic faith in the reasonableness of the Russians has now been supplanted by deep resentment over their base ingratitude.

American generosity and humanitarianism is a tentative phenomenon. Along with impulses toward good will and generosity, there is a deep-seated suspicion that smart people don't act that way, that "only suckers are a soft touch." In this connection a recent study which appeared in a popular magazine is of considerable interest.[5] This investigation, claiming to have been based on "reliable sampling procedures," reflected a degree of religious piety among Americans considerably greater than had previously been estimated. Of greatest interest was its description of American attitudes toward ethics. It would appear that almost half of the sample was sharply aware of the conflict between what was "right" and the

---

[5] Lincoln Barnett, "God and the American People." *Ladies' Home Journal,* November, 1948, pp. 37 ff.

demands of secular life. A somewhat smaller proportion considered that religion influenced their activities in business, political and social life. Considerably more than half felt that their conduct toward neighbors was governed by the golden rule; but more than 80 per cent felt that their neighbors fell considerably short of the golden rule in their conduct toward their fellow men.

Quite aside from the question of the full reliability of a study asking such "loaded" and personal questions, there seems to be confirmation here for the proposition regarding the moral dualism in the American character. The aspiration to conform to Christian ethical ideals is clearly present among most members of the culture, but there would appear to be a strong apprehension that such standards of conduct are inapplicable because the outside world does not behave that way. Hence any impulse toward ethically motivated generosity is impaired not only by the feeling that it will go unrequited, but that one's neighbors will ridicule it or attribute it to some concealed, self-interested motive.

It would appear to be a reasonable speculation from the foregoing findings that any action involving the giving or loaning of American wealth to foreign peoples, even though it be motivated by calculations of self-interest, activates this fear that "only a sucker is a soft touch." Under conditions of threat, such as those of the present, these doubts and suspicions about "giving things away" have been kept within manageable proportions. But in a period of temporary stabilization when the superficial aspect of the foreign situation encourages withdrawal reactions, these feelings may play a role of some significance.

SUPERIORITY-INFERIORITY

In a sense America is a nation of parvenus. A historically unique rate of immigration, social, and geographic mobility has produced a people which has not had an opportunity to "set," to acquire the security and stability which come from familiar ties, associations, rights, and obligations. It is perhaps not accidental that in the vulgarization of psychoanalytic hypotheses in America in the last decades one of the first to acquire popular currency was the "superiority-inferiority" complex. In more stably stratified societies the individual tends to have a greater sense of "location," a broader and deeper identification with his social surroundings. He has not *made* his own identity, while in America a large proportion of each generation is *self-made*. Being self-made produces a certain buoyancy, a sense of mastery, but it leaves the individual somewhat doubtful as to his social legitimacy. This sense of insecurity and uncertainty may add a strident note to American claims for recognition. This may explain the stereotype of the American abroad, confronted with complex and ancient cultures, taking alcoholic refuge in assertions of American moral, political, and technical virtue. It may also account for a feeling in the United States that American diplomats are no match for the wiliness and cunning of Old World negotiators. In other words, Americans typically overreact in their self-evaluations. They over- and under-estimate their skills and virtues, just as they over- and under-estimate the skills and virtues of other cultures and nations.

It is perhaps this quality among Americans—and among the American elites—which strongly militates against a balanced and empathic appreciation of cultural and national differences so essential to the development of an effective diplomacy. One may entertain the hypothesis that Americans tend to judge other nations and cultures according to a strictly American scoreboard, on the basis of which America is bound to win. It is difficult for Americans to accept a humane conception of cultural and national differences. Somehow, other cultural values must be transmuted into an American currency so that it becomes possible in a competition of national cultures to rate the United States as the "best all-round culture of the year."

There is a noticeable sensitivity among Americans on the score of cultural and intellectual inferiority. Only recently the American press cited the throngs of visitors to art museums exhibiting the Habsburg collection of paintings as effectively refuting European claims of American cultural inferiority. Feelings of crudeness and inferiority are not only expressed in the form of direct refutation by citing such evidence as the above; they also are frequently expressed in the tendency to equate esthetic and intellectual subtlety with lack of manliness—artists and intellectuals are "queers."

This superiority-inferiority ambivalence may manifest itself in policy-making in a number of ways. It may take the direct and perhaps more typical form of cultural arrogance—assertions of the superiority of the American way in politics, in economics, in social relations, in morality, or in the physical amenities of life. In this case the psychological mechanism involved is a reaction-formation; unconscious feelings of inferiority lead to the assertion of superiority. Or it may take the form of an admission of inferiority and an attribution of superiority to other cultures or elite groups. In either case there is an alienation from the real character and potentialities of the self. One either becomes an ideal and non-existent American—a *persona* American— or one rejects one's Americanism entirely and attempts to "pass," for example, into English or French culture. These formulations, of course, state the problem in the extreme for purposes of clarity.

These reactions have a selective appeal among the various elite groups. Thus American artists, writers, and intellectuals have historically tended to manifest inferiority feelings in the form of imitativeness, or in expatriation. It has been asserted that members of the American foreign service have tended to assimilate themselves too readily to foreign cultures and aristocratic "sets," perhaps at the expense of their American perspective. The tendency for American families of wealth and prestige to ape the English and Continental aristocracies is too well known to call for detailed comment. All of these groups have in common the quality of having differentiated themselves from the American pattern through extraordinary wealth, through artistic or intellectual deviation, or through long residence abroad. The more "representative" American—the Congressman for example—tends to manifest the simpler form of cultural arrogance.

Either inferiority or superiority feelings in relation to other cultures may have a negative effect on the national interest. Cultural arrogance may alienate other peoples, impair confidence in the United States among actual and potential allies, or aid in some measure in the mobilization of hostile sentiment among neutrals and potential enemies. Cultural subservience, particularly if manifested by American diplomats and negotiators, may result in real and unnecessary sacrifices of the national interest.

The hypothesis may also be advanced that there is a certain periodicity of national moods of confidence and lack of confidence. These have perhaps been associated in the United States with the fluctuations of the business cycle. One may speculate that not least among the catastrophic foreign policy consequences of a serious depression in the United States would be an impairment of national self-confidence, a sudden welling to the surface of underlying doubt, which might result in a weakening of foreign policy resolution, a feeling of being overextended, a need for contraction, for consolidation, for withdrawal.

Part VIII

The Management of Power

IF STUDENTS OF international relations have devoted considerable attention to the phenomenon of power, they have also produced an abundance of literature on the management of power in the international system. The techniques for its management include: (1) institutions such as international organization and world government, (2) the development of procedures for resolving problems among nations, and (3) the conclusion of agreements, formal or tacit, for the balance of power, a reduction of levels of armaments, and the formation of alliances.

Diplomacy provides the oldest procedure for resolving problems among nations. When discussing diplomacy, a distinction is often drawn between the "old" and the "new" diplomacy. The old diplomacy was characterized by secrecy and was largely divorced from public opinion. Although the diplomat was a reporter of events, he was often a policymaker, since he could not communicate instantaneously with his home government. In several ways, diplomacy was considered important to the operation of the international system. It provided a method for adjusting international differences. Moreover, according to many writers, the diplomat as reporter was crucial to the functioning of another technique for the management of power—the balance of power. By reporting changes in the capabilities of the national unit to which he was assigned, the diplomat supposedly contributed to an ongoing effort to preserve a balance of power among the principal participants of the international system.

Harold Nicolson describes the decline of the "old" diplomacy and its replacement by the "new" diplomacy. Secret diplomacy was considered a principal cause for the outbreak of World War I. The rise in importance of public opinion led to an unwillingness to tolerate secrecy in diplomacy. At least in the West, international relations became democratized to an unprecedented extent. The increased speed of communications reduced the function of the diplomat as a policymaker and contributed to the rise of the policymaker as diplomat. Contrasting the diplomat's role before and after World War I, Nicolson concludes: "Before the war, the continental Powers allowed their foreign policy to be framed, as well as conducted, by professional diplomatists. After the war, Great Britain, and other countries, allowed their foreign policy to be conducted, as well as framed, by professional politicians."

Realists in the study of international relations have proposed a return to a form of diplomacy embodying at least some of the features of the "old" diplomacy. In particular, summit diplomacy illustrates the problems of the "new" diplomacy. In summit conferences, the chief policymaker, i.e., the president, becomes a diplomat, and thus performs a function for which by training and temperament he is likely to be unsuited. They occur in an atmosphere of intense publicity, and the expectation of major results can lead to frustration if the results of the summit conference are less than the expectations of the participants. Hence, to many writers, the summit conference exemplifies the "new" diplomacy at its worst.

Although the role of the diplomat today differs from the function he performed before World War I, diplomacy remains crucial to the management of power in the international system. To be sure, the growth of communications has diminished the diplomat's role as policymaker. Yet his tasks have increased in complexity because of the need to maintain contact with a variety of groups which historically were unimportant to the political process. Although communciations have accelerated, the information to be reported and analyzed has grown enormously. By his selection of such information, the diplomat becomes in effect a policymaker, for the formulation of foreign policy is related to the data available. Today, the ambassador presides formally over a diplomatic establishment far more complex than ever before in history. Thus to understand the operation of the international system one must visualize a continuing stream of diplomatic interaction, with messages passing from one government to another through accredited representatives. In fact, much of the interaction taking place within the international system relates to diplomacy.

According to Schelling, there is a process of bargaining which continues even after diplomacy has failed to prevent national units from resorting to armed conflict. War itself is a bargaining process about such issues as the rules for conducting conflict, including the treatment of civilian population, the exclusion of certain regions from the list of targets, the kinds of weapons systems to be employed. There is a bargaining process about reductions in the level of conflict, or even its termination. Often by their actions rather than as a result of formal agreement, participants may "signal" their intentions to each other. Thus they are engaged in an interactive process.

In the second category of techniques for the management of power are agreements, usually formally worked out among national units, for balance of power, alliances, or arms control. However, such arrangements may result from tacit understandings among the major participants.

Balance of power is considered one of the oldest and most enduring of these techniques. Particularly in the decade after World War I, however, balance of power was in disrepute, especially in utopian thought on international relations. Secret agreements for establishing opposing alliance systems, and hence balances of power, were assumed to have contributed to the outbreak of war. Among realists, the balance of power regained a measure of its lost stature. Realist emphasis upon balance of power accorded with the realist thought about the nature of man. If man was evil and power-seeking it was appropriate to devise techniques for the management of power in which one man, or group of men, whether within the national unit or the international system, would be balanced against another.

According to Sir Eyre Crowe, the balance of power represented one of the most enduring, and most important, principles of British foreign policy. In the most succinct and celebrated statement of this position, Crowe maintained that Britain sought to prevent the domination of Europe by any one power by joining the side of the weaker coalition to oppose the stronger. Nicholas Spykman, it will be recalled, suggested in Part VII that for geopolitical reasons, that national unit which dominated the Eurasian land mass would place itself in the position of potential ruler of the world. The concept of balance of power, contained in his memorandum, Crowe suggests, has guided British foreign policy.

Although balance of power is one of the most widely used techniques for the management of power in international relations, it is fraught with semantic ambiguity. A review of the extensive literature on this subject reveals the use of balance of power to describe such widely differing phenomena as an equilibrium between national units, a predonderance of power in the hands of one national unit, or simply a prevailing distribution of power among members of the international system. According to Ernst Haas, the absence of conceptual clarity has limited the utility of the term balance of power. Given its ambiguities, the student must attempt to ascertain the meaning, or meanings, of the term as used by different authors, or even the same author.

Historically, alliance systems and the balance of power have been closely related. Often the international system consisted of opposing alliances of nation-states in what was called a balance of power. Alternatively, weaker national units formed alliances to oppose a more powerful national unit. Within the international system, nations shift from one alliance to another in response to perceived national interest. As Robert E. Osgood suggests, alliances associate like-minded actors in the hope of overcoming a rival either by defeat or deterrence. For example, erstwhile allies may conclude a separate peace with the country against which they were once allied. Since alliances usually develop in an environment of actual or potential conflict, with the termination of conflict, or the decline in perception of threat, the system loses its *raison d'être* and begins to disintegrate.

Historically, alliances constituted the principal means by which nations could enhance their military position since in an age of few technological breakthroughs, national capabilities remained fairly constant. Since World War II, however, the role of alliances has changed markedly. In an age in which several nations possess nuclear weapons and delivery systems, the potential risks of alliance membership have increased dramatically. By using, or threatening to use its weapons in support of an ally, a state may risk its own destruction. Under such circumstances, the question arises as to whether a state would adhere to its alliance commitment except when its own national survival was at stake. Therefore, the effect of technological breakthroughs since 1945 has been several-fold: (1) alliance members join alliances less for aggressive purposes, as sometimes occurred before World War II, than for defensive purposes, or specifically for *deterrence* against an opposing state;

(2) even the deterrent utility of alliances, however, diminishes as the risks of national destruction to members increase; (3) the effect of a balance of terror (See Part III) or a form of strategic nuclear parity between the two leading superpowers is to decouple the defense of allies from the defense of the superpower. This, in turn, increases the need for allies to develop their own defense capabilities in order to reduce their exclusive reliance upon the superpowers. Osgood concludes that: "Their primarily deterrent function, the increased importance of peacetime military forces, the sensitivity of governments to public sentiment and ideological positions, the persistence of a dominant international conflict and structure of power that have been essentially bipolar—all these developments have tended to restrict the number of alliances and the frequency of shifts of alliance among major states."

At most times in the history of the international system, there have been states which were not allied with other states. With the emergence of a large number of newly independent states after World War II, mostly in Asia and Africa, there developed a grouping of the so-called nonaligned states. Such states eschewed military alliances with either of the superpowers, or with their former European colonial masters, although their leaders sought, and received, substantial amounts of aid from the West and the Soviet Union. According to Leo Mates, nonalignment flourished during the period in which bipolarity between the Soviet Union and the United States characterized the international system. Under conditions of bipolarity, a large group of newly independent states chose nonalignment to gain for themselves as great a freedom of maneuver as possible and to safeguard their independence. Bipolarity allows the nonaligned the opportunity to receive assistance from both superpowers and conceivably, on occasion, to play a mediatory role between them. However, by the end of the 1960s, with the emergence of China as a great power and Soviet competition for influence within the nonaligned world, the international ssytem had become tripolar. In addition to the increased intensity of the Sino-Soviet conflict, the United States and the Soviet Union have begun negotiations in certain issue areas such as arms control. The Chinese invasion of India in 1962, the Vietnam War, and the Six-Day War of June 1967 in the Middle East have also demonstrated the weakness of the nonaligned. The coups in Ghana and Indonesia resulted in the removal of two of the most distinguished leaders of nonalignment, Nkrumah and Sukarno. The death of Nehru, the defeat of Nasser's Egypt at the hands of Israel in June 1967, and the Egyptian president's death in 1970, removed the remaining first generation leaders of nonalignment in the Afro-Asian world.

If Mates is correct, the development of additional major power centers—the emergence of a multipolar world, including China—reduces the cohesiveness of the nonaligned states, and makes coordination on major international problems more difficult than in a bipolar system. China was considered a potential ally by some of the nonaligned, while others viewed Peking as a hostile influence. It is more difficult for the nonaligned to play the role of mediator than in a bipolar system, for they possess few of the diplomatic skills essential for such a part. Thus Mates raises a series of important questions about the nature of nonalignment and about its prospects in an international system moving from an essentially bipolar to a multipolar configuration. The nonaligned will be further circumscribed in their international role if additional centers of power such as a uniting Europe and Japan emerge during the next decade.

Especially in the twentieth century, disarmament and arms control have come to occupy an important place in the list of techniques for the management of power in the international system. According to Hedley Bull, disarmament may be defined as the reduction or abolition of armaments. Disarmament may be undertaken by one nation, or by many nations at a given time. It may be localized, that is, confined to a specific geographic region or weapons system; it may be comprehensive or partial; it may be controlled or uncontrolled. According to Bull's definition, arms control, in contrast, may be defined as the exercise of restraint by a national unit upon armaments policy. If a nation limits the levels of armaments, their character, deployment, or use, it is engaged in one form or another of arms control. In Bull's definition, a decision by the United States or the Soviet Union to reduce the numbers of intercontinental ballistic missiles in its arsenal, or to make cuts in military manpower would constitute disarmament. A decision by the United States or the Soviet Union not to develop some new weapons system, or not to deploy an existing weapons system, would represent a form of arms control.

The relationship between armed conflict and arms races has long preoccupied students of international relations. Do arms races produce conflict, or do they stem from, and reflect, underlying political disputes? Bull supports the latter position, and further contends that arms races subside with the resolution of these basic differences. Although disarmament and arms control agreements may help to ease tensions between nations desiring improved relations, they are often expensive, especially if they rely upon elaborate systems of inspection to detect violations. Bull contends that the objective of disarmament and arms control should be to promote international security. From this premise he argues that reductions in the quantities of forces or weapons, or restrictions in military expenditures, do not necessarily contribute to international stability, and may even lead to instability. Instead, he states a preference for controls that would contribute to international equilibrium.

Over the past decade the United States and the Soviet Union have concluded a series of limited arms control agreements: the Test Ban Treaty of 1962 banning the testing of nuclear weapons in outerspace, in the atmosphere, and under the seas; the Antarctica Treaty of 1959 in which both powers agreed not to place nuclear armaments in that region of the globe; the Nonproliferation Treaty of 1969, in which Britain, the United States and the Soviet Union— but not China or France—agreed not to assist non-nuclear states to build atomic capabilities for military purposes; and the Seabed Treaty of 1971, in which the superpowers agreed not to locate weapons systems on the seabed.

Since the autumn of 1969, the United States and the Soviet Union have engaged in Strategic Arms Limitations Talks (SALT) which have been held alternately in Helsinki and Vienna. Such talks, like those mentioned above contrast sharply with the elaborate plans for general and complete disarmament proposed at the beginning of the 1960s by the Soviet Union and the United States. As James E. Dougherty suggests: "It took only a few years of analysis and negotiation to demonstrate that the chasm between the rhetoric and the reality was so wide and deep, and the nature of the arms problem so complex, that the superpowers had no choice but to shift the diplomatic effort away from rapid total disarmament toward a series of limited arms control measures designed to improve the safety of the international environment."

The SALT come at a time of rough strategic nuclear parity between the United States and the Soviet Union. Both sides are uncertain about the other's future weapons prospects. For the

United States, the question arises as to whether the Soviet Union, in the coming years, will be content with crude parity, or will strive to achieve a wide margin of superiority. Such a development would have a psychologically and politically destablizing effect on the balance of terror (See Selection 38). From the Soviet perspective the question arises as to whether the United States will retain a more effective capability for rapidly improving the quality of strategic weapons through such devices as MIRV (Multiple Independent Reentry Vehicles). As Dougherty points out, such uncertainties create suspicion that one side may use the negotiations to gain a military superiority over its opponent. In addition, the prospects for major breakthroughs which advanced technology affords may render obsolete or irrelevant any agreements reached in SALT. Such problems are not unique to the SALT; they have confronted earlier arms control negotiations. But their significance is heightened by the crucial importance to each of the superpowers of the weapons systems under discussion.

The outcome of SALT will influence relationships between each of the superpowers, respectively, and its allies. It will affect also the prospects for the proliferation of nuclear weapons. To the extent that SALT diminishes the credibility of nuclear guarantees by superpowers to allies, it will increase the likelihood of nuclear proliferation and lessen the reliability of alliances to smaller powers. Thus SALT will affect alliance relationships and one of the products of earlier arms control negotiations, namely, the Nonproliferation Treaty.

SECTION ONE:
Diplomacy

30. THE "OLD" AND THE "NEW" DIPLOMACY

Harold Nicolson

DEFINITION

(a) The best definitions of diplomacy have been furnished by Martens, Cussy, and Sir Ernest Satow. Martens defined it as 'The science of the external relations, or foreign affairs, of States, and, in a more limited sense, the science, or art, of negotiation'. Cussy defined it as 'The sum of the knowledge and the principles necessary for the good conduct of public affairs between States'. Satow defined it as 'The application of intelligence and tact to the conduct of official relations between the Governments of independent States'.

(b) These definitions, although fully descriptive of monarchic and oligarchic diplomacy, do not provide democratic diplomacy with that sharp differentiation which it needs between 'foreign policy' and 'the methods by which that policy is executed'.

Such a differentiation is essential if democratic diplomacy is to benefit by, and not merely to break with, the experience of the past. Policy and negotiation should henceforward be regarded as two wholly separate things.

(c) This differentiation was blurred, not only in pre-war, but also in post-war, diplomacy.

From *Curzon: The Last Phase* by Harold Nicolson (New York: Harcourt, Brace and Company, 1934), pp. 385–387; 391–404. Reprinted by permission of Harcourt, Brace and World, Inc. and Curtis Brown Ltd.

SIR HAROLD NICOLSON (1886–1968) Member of Parliament, 1935–1945; Member of British Diplomatic Service, 1909–1929. Author of *Kings, Courts, and Monarchy* (New York: Simon and Schuster, 1962); *Evolution of Diplomatic Method* (New York: Macmillan Company, 1962); *Evolution of Diplomatic Method* (New York: Macmillan Company, 1954); *The Congress of Vienna* (London: Constable Ltd., 1946).

Before the war, the continental Powers allowed their foreign policy to be framed, as well as conducted, by professional diplomatists. After the war, Great Britain, and other countries, allowed their foreign policy to be conducted, as well as framed, by professional politicians.

Each of these methods is equally dangerous. Diplomatists should seldom be allowed to frame policy. Politicians should seldom be allowed to conduct negotiation. Policy should be subjected to democratic control: the execution of that policy should be left to trained experts.

(d) The necessity of defining what we mean by this term 'diplomacy' is therefore a primary necessity.

If the electorate are ever to rise to the standard of their sovereign responsibility in foreign affairs, they should be taught, before they discuss diplomacy, to ask themselves two questions, namely: 'Are we discussing foreign policy? or are we discussing negotiation?'

(e) Much value, in my opinion, will result from this habit of definition.

Once public opinion acquires the practice of differentiating between 'policy' and 'negotiation' it will be less inclined to use the word 'diplomacy' to express both.

Policy should never be, and need never be, secret. No system should ever again be tolerated which can commit men and women, without their knowledge or consent, to obligations which will entail upon them, either a breach of national good-faith, or the sacrifice of their property and lives. It should be established that no international obligation need ever be regarded as valid, unless it has been communicated to, discussed and approved by, the sovereign democracy. In other words, no treaty need ever be operative until it has been ratified by the parliament representing the will of the democracies whose interests are pledged by that treaty.

Once this principle is firmly embedded in the practice and conscience of mankind, there will be less hesitation in entrusting to trained experts the confidential conduct of negotiation. This hesitation derives, almost wholly, from the absence of any axiomatic differentiation between 'foreign policy' and 'the means or methods by which that policy is executed'.

* * *

DANGERS OF DEMOCRATIC POLICY

The essential defect of democratic policy can be defined in one word, namely *'irresponsibility'*. Under a monarchic or oligarchic system the 'sovereign' who enters into a contract with some foreign State feels himself personally 'responsible' for the execution of that contract. For a monarch or a governing class to repudiate a formal treaty was regarded as a dishonourable thing to do, and would have aroused much criticism both at home and abroad. Now, however, that the people are 'sovereign', this sense of individual or corporate responsibility no longer exists. The people are in no sense aware of their own sovereignty in foreign affairs and have therefore no sense of responsibility in regard to treaties or conventions entered into with other Powers, even when they have themselves, through their elected representatives, approved of those treaties. They are honestly under the impression that their own word has not been pledged and that they are therefore fully entitled to repudiate engagements which they may subsequently feel to be onerous or inconvenient. A state of mind is thus created which (to take an obvious instance) allows a popular newspaper publicly to preach the repudiation of the Locarno Treaties, not on the ground that these treaties were unconstitutionally concluded, but on the ground that their application at the present moment would prove inconvenient and unpopular.

Clearly, if such a state of mind is permitted to continue uncriticised and unchecked, there can be no hope for the future of democratic foreign policy. The foundations of policy, as of diplomacy, are reliability, and under a system of popular repudiation of all national engagements which may eventually prove to be onerous, not even the elements of reliability can exist. Compared with this basic defect in democratic foreign policy, all other dangers are insignificant. Not until the people and the press realise their own sovereignty will they be ready to assume their own responsibility. The period which must inevitably elapse between the fact of popular sovereignty in foreign affairs, and the realisation of that fact by the people themselves; in other words the zone of uncertainty which will have to be traversed before we leave the present quicksands of unconscious public irresponsibility and reach the firm ground of conscious public responsibility, constitute the period or zone of greatest danger. Until that zone has successfully been traversed, no sense of international security can possibly be fostered. The essence of the whole problem is how the danger period is to pass without either disturbance or disintegration. The statesmen of the post-war period have endeavoured to create an artificial sense of security by multiplying security pacts. Yet until the world is convinced that these pacts are regarded by the sovereign democracies as involving their own responsibility they merely serve to inflate the currency of international contract and thereby to diminish certainty rather than to increase confidence.

It will take one, or perhaps two, generations of wise education to create in the several democracies a responsible state of mind. Once that state of mind has been created, we may indeed hope for peace on earth. For the moment all we can hope to do is to guard against those secondary or subsidiary dangers which will menace democratic foreign policy and democratic diplomacy during the transition period.

I should define these dangers as follows:

(1) *The failure to differentiate* between 'policy' and 'negotiation' and the use of the term 'diplomacy' as applying to both. This danger has already been examined.

(2) *The tendency to identify* with 'the old diplomacy' the more realistic traditions of British foreign policy and the consequent underestimation, in such matters, of the continuity of public instinct and tradition.

(3) *Subjectivity,* manifesting itself either in dumb inertia or in patriotic excitement. A tendency to excuse these emotional extremes by attributing public lethargy or neurosis to the machinations, ignorance, malignity, class-privilege, or stupidity of those responsible for foreign policy and its execution. In extreme forms this subjectivity leads either to (*a*) jingoism or (*b*) defeatism. Each of these democratic sensations is equally dangerous.

(∢) *The time-lag* between informed opinion and popular feeling. This requires to be dealt with in greater detail.

Although the essential instincts of our democracy in regard to foreign affairs are continuous, stable and shared by a large majority, yet their momentary feelings on the subject are intermittent, variable and diverse. It is possible, I feel, to estimate with approximate certainty what policy the majority of the electorate will in the end desire; yet it is often impossible to elicit this majority approval at the moment when it is most needed.

An unfortunate factor in all representative systems is that the temporary emotions of certain sections of the electorate or the press are apt to manifest themselves in the shape of 'opinions' on the part of certain sections of the House of Commons. These 'opinions' obstruct and impede national policy at times when that policy ought to be formulated in the most categorical and immediate form.

Sir Edward Grey, for instance, ought to have been able in July 1914 to state the 'peace' and 'Balance of Power' doctrines in such drastic terms as would have discouraged Russia from mobilization and Germany from attacking France or Belgium.

In 1919, again, Mr. Lloyd George should have been able to expound the same doctrines in such a manner as to make it clear to France that Great Britain would not permit her to reduce Germany to ruin.

In both these cases, public opinion would in the end have approved such categorical statements; at the moment, however, public opinion would not have been prepared to accord approval. On each occasion, and with disastrous consequences, the opportunity was missed.

(5) *Imprecision.* The essence of a good foreign policy is certitude. An uncertain policy is always bad.

On the other hand, parliamentary and press opposition is less likely to concentrate against an elastic foreign policy than against one which is precise. It is thus a grave temptation for a Foreign Minister under the democratic system to prefer an idealistic formula, which raises only intellectual criticism, to a concrete formula which is open to popular attack. This temptation is one which should be resisted. Not merely does it promote in Foreign Secretaries a habit of complacent, unctuous and empty rectitude, but it diminishes the credit of international contract.

The Kellogg Pact, for instance, either meant a new heaven and a new earth, or it meant very little. Few people, apart from Mr. Kellogg himself, regarded it as a new revelation; its main effect was to discredit previous instruments, such as the Covenant, which had also endeavoured, though with greater precision, to provide for the pacific settlement of international disputes.

(6) *Hypocrisy.* Democratic foreign policy indulges in the (at present) sentimental fiction that relations between states can be conducted upon the same moral basis as those between individuals. As an ideal, this is a theory which I thoroughly endorse. Yet as a description of existing relations I can regard it only as a false description. Relations between individuals are ultimately governed by law. Relations between States are not governed by law. There can be no real analogy between the ethical values of an organised, and those of an anarchical, society.

Democratic diplomacy endeavours to conceal this awkward fact, and to hide the realities of force under the appearance of consent. For the downright lies of the fifteenth century system it has substituted a technique of self-righteous half-truths. It thus destroys confidence, and confidence, after certitude, is the most important element of good foreign policy.

(7) *Unreality.* Democratic foreign policy—proceeding again from a fallacious identification between states and individuals—pays lip-service to the doctrine of equality among nations.

This exposes it to that miasma of unreality which clouds all its actions. Nicaragua is not the equal of the United States, nor is San Domingo the equal of France. To advance the theory of such equality is to advance something which is senseless and unreal.

By this also are certitude and confidence diminished.

It is not, however, general certainty only which is embarrassed by this egalitarian fallacy, it is also the constructive authority of the British Empire which is damaged by this wholly unproductive fiction. Our physical power may be an unknown quantity: it may, at any given crisis, be either tiny or immense: our moral influence, on the other hand, should become a known and continuous factor in international affairs. In all essential issues, the British Dominions and even the United States *think* the same; although they *feel* in shapes of disconcerting difference. Our potential influence is immeasurable; our actual influence is intermittent; the proportions of power represented by the English-speaking world are overwhelming; the identity of theory shared in that world is, to all who have become accustomed to European psychology, very striking. I should like to see British democracy think more of democracy and less of policy. It is in our democratic consanguinity with our Dominions, as also with the United States, and not in any sentimental belief in egalitarianism, that we shall find our authority. I believe in authority, even as I believe in power. And I should wish to see democratic authority exercised with moderation, and without either arrogance or fear. It is the timidity of democratic policy which verges so frequently upon the selfish and the inert.

DANGERS OF DEMOCRATIC DIPLOMACY

In spite of the dangers noted above, democratic foreign policy is unquestionably less dangerous than any other form of foreign policy. Democratic diplomacy, on the other hand, is, owing to its disturbing inefficiency, very dangerous indeed.

By 'democratic diplomacy' I mean the execution of foreign policy, either by politicians themselves, or through the medium of untrained negotiators whom they have selected from among their own supporters or personal friends.

The failure to differentiate between 'policy' and 'negotiation' has led to the fallacy that all important negotiation should be carried out, not by persons possessing experience and detachment, but by persons possessing a mandate from the people. In its extreme form this fallacy has led to 'Diplomacy by Conference'—perhaps the most unfortunate diplomatic method ever conceived.

(1) *Diplomacy by Conference.* Obviously there are occasions when international agreement can only be achieved by oral discussion between plenipotentiaries. There are occasions, also, when the issues are so vital and immediate that 'policy' as well as 'negotiation' is involved. On such occasions the negotiators must be identical with the framers of policy, and the resultant congresses and conferences must be attended by the Prime Ministers or Foreign Secretaries of the several Powers.

It should be established, however, that such occasions are exceptional and dangerous. Such conferences should be entered into only after careful preparation, on the basis of a programme elaborated and accepted in advance, against a background of acute public criticism and with full realisation that many months of discussion will be required. The subjects for debate should moreover be rigidly curtailed to those requiring a decision of policy, and all secondary issues, entailing negotiation only, should be left in expert hands.

In the four years immediately following the war these principles were discarded. Innumerable conferences were held without adequate preparation, with no precise programme and within a time limit of three or four days. The subjects discussed were diverse, intricate and suitable only for expert negotiation. The meetings took place in an atmosphere of extreme publicity and uncritical popular expectation. The resultant conclusions, inevitably, were inconclusive, intangible, specious, superficial, and unreal. Compare the expert handling of such conferences as those of Washington,

Lausanne and Brussels with the hurried histrionics of Genoa or Cannes.*

'Diplomacy by Conference' is to-day so discredited that it may be thought that there is no danger of its revival as a method of international negotiation. The frame of mind which allowed of that method is still, however, a very general frame of mind. It is caused by uncertainty regarding the frontier between democratic control of policy and expert conduct of negotiation. That frontier can only be properly delimited if we have a clear conception of the dangers of amateurishness on the one hand, and of professionalism on the other.

(2) *The politician as negotiator.* It has already been stated that on exceptional occasions, or in dealing with vital issues of policy, the politician must himself negotiate. I should wish, however, to summarise some of the dangers to which, on such occasions, he is exposed.

(a) *Public opinion.* A politician suffers from the essential disadvantage of being a politician. In other words his position and his future career are dependent upon popular approval. He is acutely sensitive to transitory 'opinions' in the House of Commons, his party, or the press. He is apt to reject what he knows to be reasonable because he also knows that it will be difficult to explain; conversely, he is tempted (as Orlando was tempted in the Fiume controversy) to fabricate by propaganda an artificial popular approval in order to strengthen his diplomatic position.

The professional, on the other hand, places ultimate national interest above immediate popular applause.

(b) *Ignorance.* By this I do not mean an ignorance of foreign facts, but an ignorance of foreign psychology. It mattered nothing at all that Mr. Lloyd George should never have heard of Teschen; it mattered very much indeed that he should treat the French or the Germans as he would

---

* Editor's Note: The Washington Naval Conference of November 1921–February 1922, which resulted in one of the more successful arms control agreements of the twentieth century, established tonnage ratios between the capital ships (battleships and heavy cruisers) of the United States, Britain, France, Japan, and Italy. The Treaty of Lausanne of July 1923 represented the birth of modern Turkey, the successor state of the old Ottoman Empire, and the settlement of outstanding issues between Turkey, on the one hand, and Britain, France and Greece, on the other. In 1920, a general international conference on problems of post-World War I reconstruction was held in Brussels. In January 1922, French Premier Briand and British Prime Minister Lloyd George met at Cannes and failed to reach agreement on German reparations. In April and May 1922, an economic conference of European powers held in Genoa, had no greater success than had Briand and Lloyd George at Cannes in reaching agreement on German reparations. During the Genoa Conference, the foreign ministers of Germany and the Soviet Union signed a treaty of friendship at a nearby resort town of Rapallo. The Rapallo Agreement provided the basis for Soviet-German cooperation from 1923 until the rise of Hitler to power in 1933.

treat an English trades-union delegation. Those schoolboy levities which might put a Lancashire Labour leader at his ease were regarded by M. Briand as disconcerting; those rhetorical questions, those revivalist dithyrambs which, to the Mayor of Llanberis would appear as usual forms of human speech, were interpreted by Dr. Rathenau or M. Gounaris as signifying either invective or encouragement. Frequent and serious were the misunderstandings which therefrom resulted.

(c) *Vanity.* A British politician, unaccustomed to negotiation with foreign statesmen, is prone to disturbances of vanity. The fact that his general culture, as his knowledge of foreign languages, is generally below the level of that possessed by those with whom he is negotiating gives him a sense of inferiority to which he reacts in unfortunate ways. Either he will air his schoolboy French to the distress of his audience and the confusion of business, or else he will be truculently insular. Upon weaker minds the mere fact of being, although abroad, a centre of public interest, the lavish hospitality of foreign Governments, the actual salutes of people dressed in foreign uniforms, have a most disintegrating effect. Affability, gratitude and general silliness result.

Such subjective forms of vanity are perhaps less dangerous than its more objective manifestations. A Prime Minister, for instance, who is conscious of a firm majority at home, is apt to acquire an autocratic habit of mind. Not only is he irritated by the fact that he cannot compel foreign statesmen to obey his behests, but he resents, and thus endeavours to ignore, those circumstances which he is unable to influence as well as those areas of knowledge which he can never hope to possess. A tendency develops in him to deny the existence of those circumstances and that knowledge and to soar above them on the light wings of obscurantism and improvisation. Sir Charles Mallet in his *Lloyd George: a Study* (page 156) has well described the effect of this particular manifestation of human vanity. 'Unvarying self-assurance', he writes, 'tempered by an ever-varying opportunism is perhaps the most dangerous equipment that statesmanship can have.'

Democratic diplomacy is very apt to acquire this equipment.

(d) *Controversy.* A mind trained in parliamentary or forensic debate is apt to assume that a conference is a form of controversy. Such people start from the assumption that the interests of foreign countries are necessarily opposed. They tend to envisage negotiation in the form of a debate rather than in the form of a consultation. They thus endeavour to 'score points'. At many a Conference I have seen a whole hour wasted in purely artificial dialectics. The politician is always conscious of an audience; the trained negotiator is conscious only of the negotiation in hand. The reason why lawyers have always made the worst diplomatists is that their argumentative faculties are too much on the alert. Negotiation should never degenerate into an argument; it should be kept always on the level of a discussion.

(e) *Overwork.* The politician, again, is always pressed for time. It thus results that negotiation is seldom pursued to a precise conclusion, but is suspended halfway upon the first landing offered for compromise. This time-pressure, again, leads to impatience. The politician as negotiator is unwilling to listen to information which may tempt him to alter his own opinion and thus necessitate further discussion. Similarly he is prone to reject all suggestions, however admirable, which might entail further study or delay. Time-pressure, in every case, is accompanied by over-work: the results are expedients, half-solutions, evasion of essentials, improvisations, and imprecision.

Such are the major disabilities from which even the noblest politician, when he becomes a diplomatist, is apt to suffer.

DANGERS OF PROFESSIONAL DIPLOMACY

The virtues of professional diplomacy are implicit in the above catalogue of the vices of its opposite. The professional diplomatist is indifferent to public applause, has devoted some thirty years to the study of foreign psychology, is unaffected by vanity, dislikes controversy, eschews all forms of publicity, and is not subject to acute time-pressure or overwork. In addition, as a trained expert in a common science working with other experts, he is intent upon producing a piece of work which will satisfy his own professional standards. All that he cares for is the approbation of those whose judgment is worth having. He is completely indifferent to the opinion of those whose judgment is not worth having. This specialised vanity impels him to prefer competent to incompetent work, real achievement to achievements which have only the appearance of reality.

Yet he, also, has his dangers.

(a) *Professionalism.* A man who has spent some thirty years in the diplomatic service acquires, inevitably, an international frame of mind. More specifically he comes to have a masonic feeling for other diplomatists. On occasions he may lack a proper degree of reverence for politicians, or even Press magnates, and an unwarranted contempt for, and suspicion of, their ways and means. In extreme cases he may feel, even, that public and parliamentary opinion is foolish and ill-informed.

Upon himself the effect of these prejudices is seldom serious. Being a civil servant he has been trained to loyalty and obedience, nor would he (I am discussing only British diplomatists) dream of acting contrary to the wishes of the Government in power, and therefore of his democratic sovereign. His prejudices are of negative rather than of positive disadvantage. His experience of democracy in so many lands and in such different forms may induce in him a mood of scepticism. This absence of belief will be interpreted by those politicians with whom he comes into contact as an attitude of superiority. Suspicion and misprisal will result.

(b) *Lethargy*. The professional diplomatist is apt to lack initiative. Important problems, in his opinion, settle themselves; unimportant problems are unimportant. He has seen so much damage done by well-meaning officiousness; he has seen so little damage done by letting well alone. His whole training has tended to convince him that good diplomacy is a slow and cautious business, and he looks with exaggerated suspicion upon all dynamic innovations. For him reality is relative and never absolute: he believes in gradations, in grey zones; he is always impatient of those who think enthusiastically in terms of black or white. Lethargy of judgment descends upon him, a slightly contemptuous disbelief in all forms of human certainty. He is thus more prone to analysis than to synthesis, more ready to indicate doubts than to produce dynamic assurances, more inclined to deny than to affirm. This propensity proves very irritating to the politician anxious to score a rapid popular success.

(c) *Narrowness*. The professional diplomatist suffers also from certain limitations of outlook. He observes widely, but he does not observe deeply. He is inclined to attach to superficial events greater importance than he attaches to underlying causes. He is more interested in overt political symptoms than in obscure social or economic diseases. He is well aware that his judgment, if it is to be of any real value to his Government, must be 'sound': he tends therefore to allow the more imaginative and original sections of his brain to atrophy. True it is that a brilliant diplomatist is a grave public menace; the consciousness of this fact is apt to induce our professional diplomatists to attach exclusive importance to not being brilliant. This, certainly, is a fault on the right side. Our diplomatic service is without question (and no foreigner would deny it) the best in the world. Yet upon the casual observer it may produce a false impression of conservatism and mental rigidity.

(d) *Timidity*. This quality should, perhaps, have been cited in the category of virtues and not in the category of defects. The British diplomatist is in fact as frightened of 'causing trouble' as the British naval officer is frightened of sinking his ship. Inevitably, the Foreign Office prefer diplomatists who say soothing and optimistic things to diplomatists who tell home truths in defiant language. Smugness, rather than outspoken realism, is apt to colour many diplomatic reports. A certain narcotic quality thus pervades the information which they supply.

Yet this is but a venial sin.

31.   ON NEGOTIATIONS

Henry A. Kissinger

THE INTRACTABILITY OF DIPLOMACY

As ARMAMENTS have multiplied and the risks of conflict have become increasingly catastrophic, the demands for a "new approach" to end tensions have grown ever more insistent. No country, it is said, has any alternative except to seek to attain its aims by negotiations. The Cold War must be ended in order to spare mankind the horrors of a hot war: "The stark and inescapable fact is that today we cannot defend our society by war since total war is total destruction and if war is used as an instrument of policy eventually we will have total war," wrote Lester Pearson. "We prepare for war like precocious giants and for peace like retarded pigmies." [1]

There is no doubt that the avoidance of war must be a primary goal of all responsible statesmen. The desirability of maintaining peace cannot be the subject of either intellectual or partisan political controversy in the free world. The only reasonable issue is how best to achieve this objective.

And here there is reason for serious concern. A welter of slogans fills the air. "Relaxation of tensions," "flexibility," "new approaches," "negotiable proposals," are variously put forth as remedies to the impasse of the Cold War. But the programs to give these phrases meaning have proved much more difficult to define. The impression has been created that the missing ingredient has been a "willingness to negotiate." While this criticism is correct for some periods, particularly John Foster Dulles' incumbency as Secretary of State, it is not a just comment when applied to the entire post-war era. Hardly a year has passed without at least some negotiation with the Communist countries. There have been six Foreign Ministers' Conferences and three summit meetings. Periods of intransigence have alternated with spasmodic efforts to settle all problems at one fell swoop. The abortive summit meeting of 1960 proved that tensions have some-

---

From *The Necessity for Choice* by Henry A. Kissinger (New York: Harper and Brothers, 1961) pp. 169–175; 181–182; 185–189; 191. Copyright © 1960, 1961 by Henry A. Kissinger. Reprinted by permission of Harper and Row, Publishers, and Chatto and Windus, Ltd. Footnotes have been renumbered to appear in consecutive order.

HENRY A. KISSINGER See earlier Biographical Note.

[1] Lester Pearson, Speech at Oslo, Dec. 11, 1957, quoted in the *New York Times*, Dec. 12, 1957.

times been increased as much by the manner in which diplomacy has been
conducted as by the refusal to negotiate. The Cold War has been per-
petuated not only by the abdication of diplomacy but also by its emptiness
and sterility.

What, then, has made the conduct of diplomacy so difficult? Why have
tensions continued whether we negotiated or failed to negotiate? There
are four basic causes: (1) the destructiveness of modern weapons, (2) the
polarization of power in the contemporary period, (3) the nature of the
conflict, (4) national attitudes peculiar to the West and particularly to
the United States.

It is not an accident that the diplomatic stalemate has become more
intractable as weapons have grown more destructive. Rather than facilitating settlement, the increasing horror of war has made the process of
negotiation more difficult. Historically, negotiators have rarely relied
exclusively on the persuasiveness of the argument. A country's bargaining
position has traditionally depended not only on the logic of its proposals
but also on the penalties it could exact for the other side's failure to
agree. An abortive conference rarely returned matters to the starting
point. Rather, diplomacy having failed, other pressures were brought into
play. Even at the Congress of Vienna, long considered the model diplomatic conference, the settlement which maintained the peace of Europe
for a century was not achieved without the threat of war.

As the risks of war have become more cataclysmic, the result has not
been a universal reconciliation but a perpetuation of all disputes. Much
as we may deplore it, most major historical changes have been brought
about to a greater or lesser degree by the threat or the use of force. Our
age faces the paradoxical problem that because the violence of war has
grown out of all proportion to the objectives to be achieved, no issue has
been resolved. We cannot have war. But we have had to learn painfully
that peace is something more than the absence of war. Solving the problem of peaceful change is essential; but we must be careful not to deny its
complexity.

The intractability of diplomacy has been magnified by the polarization
of power in the post-war period. As long as the international system was
composed of many states of approximately equal strength, subtlety of
maneuver could to some extent substitute for physical strength. As long
as no nation was strong enough to eliminate all the others, shifting coalitions could be used for exerting pressure or marshaling support. They
served in a sense as substitutes for physical conflict. In the classical
periods of cabinet diplomacy in the eighteenth and nineteenth centuries, a
country's diplomatic flexibility and bargaining position depended on its
availability as a partner to as many other countries as possible. As a
result, no relationship was considered permanent and no conflict was
pushed to its ultimate conclusion. Disputes were limited by the tacit

agreement that the maintenance of the existing system was more important than any particular disagreement. Wars occurred, but they did not involve risking the national survival and were settled in relation to specific, limited issues.

Whenever the number of sovereign states was reduced, diplomacy became more rigid. When a unified Germany and Italy emerged in the nineteenth century, they replaced a host of smaller principalities. This reflected the dominant currents of nationalism. But from the point of view of diplomatic flexibility, some of the "play" was taken out of the conduct of foreign policy. To the extent that the available diplomatic options diminished, the temptation to achieve security by mobilizing a country's physical strength increased. The armaments race prior to World War I was as much the result as the cause of the inflexibility of diplomacy. France and Germany were in fundamental conflict. And neither state could organize an overwhelming coalition. As a result, power had to substitute for diplomatic dexterity and the period prior to World War I witnessed a continuous increase of the standing armies.

World War I accelerated the polarization of power. By the end of World War II only two major countries remained—major in the sense of having some prospect of assuring their security by their own resources. But a two-power world is inherently unstable. Any relative weakening of one side is tantamount to an absolute strengthening of the other. Every issue seems to involve life and death. Diplomacy turns rigid, for no state can negotiate about what it considers to be the requirements of its survival. In a two-power world these requirements are likely to appear mutually incompatible. The area where diplomacy is most necessary will then appear most "unnegotiable."

The inherent tensions of a two-power world are compounded by the clash of opposing ideologies. For over a generation now the Communist leaders have proclaimed their devotion to the overthrow of the capitalist world. They have insisted that the economic system of their opponents was based on exploitation and war. They have never wavered from asserting the inevitability or the crucial importance of their triumph. To be sure, periods of peaceful coexistence have alternated with belligerence, particularly since the advent of Mr. Khrushchev. But one of the principal Communist justifications for a *détente* can hardly prove very reassuring to the free world; peace is advocated not for its own sake but because the West is said to have grown so weak that it will go to perdition without a last convulsive upheaval. At the height of the spirit of Camp David, Khrushchev said: "The capitalist world is shaking under the blows of the Socialist camp. What shakes it even more than the rockets is the attitude of our workers towards their work. . . . We have the will to win." [2]

---

[2] *New York Times*, Dec. 3, 1959.

Negotiations with Communist leaders are complicated by one of the key aspects of Leninist theory: the belief in the predominance of "objective" factors. One of the proudest claims of the Communist leaders is that in Marxist-Leninist theory they possess a tool enabling them to distinguish appearance from reality. "True" reality consists not of what statesmen say but of the productive processes—the social and economic structure—of their country. Statesmen, particularly capitalist statesmen, are powerless to alter the main outlines of the policy their system imposes on them. Since everything depends on a correct understanding of these "objective factors" and the relation of forces they imply, "good will" and "good faith" are meaningless abstractions. One of the chief functions of traditional diplomacy—to persuade the opposite party of one's view point—becomes extremely difficult when verbal declarations are discounted from the outset. Khrushchev said in 1959: "History teaches us that conferences reflect in their decisions an established balance of forces resulting from victory or capitulation in war or similar circumstances." [3]

Much of the diplomatic stalemate has therefore little to do with lack of good will or ingenuity on the part of the statesmen. Without an agreement on general principles, negotiations become extremely difficult. What will seem most obvious to one party will appear most elusive to the other. When there is no penalty for failing to agree and when at the same time the balance of power is so tenuous, it is no accident that the existing dividing lines are so rigidly maintained. For the *status quo* has at least the advantage of familiarity while any change involves the possibility of catastrophe. At the same time, since these dividing lines are contested, protracted tension is nearly inevitable.

This impasse has led either to long periods in which diplomacy has for all practical purposes abdicated its role; or else it has produced a form of negotiations which has almost seemed to revel in *not* coming to grips with the issues dividing the world. The reference which is often made to the coexistence achieved by Mohammedanism and Christianity or by Protestantism and Catholicism is not fully relevant to the contemporary problem. In both cases, coexistence was the result of protracted, often ruinous, warfare—the very contingency diplomacy is now asked to prevent. We must be aware that the factors that intensify the desire to resolve the impasse of the Cold War may also make a creative response more difficult.

These obstacles to serious negotiations are magnified by Western, and in particular American, attitudes towards negotiating with the Communists. A *status quo* power always has difficulty in coming to grips with a revolutionary period. Since everything it considers "normal" is tied up

---

[3] Speech at Leipzig, March 7, 1959, quoted in *Foreign Radio Broadcasts: Daily Report*, No. 62, 1959, BB 16.

with the existing order, it usually recognizes too late that another state means to overthrow the international system. This is a problem especially if a revolutionary state presents each demand as a specific, limited objective which in itself may seem quite reasonable. If it alternates pressure with campaigns for peaceful coexistence, it may give rise to the belief that only one more concession stands in the way of the era of good feeling which is so passionately desired. All the instincts of a *status quo* power tempt it to gear its policy to the expectation of a fundamental change of heart of its opponent—in the direction of what seems obviously "natural" to it.

Were it not for this difficulty of understanding, no revolution would ever have succeeded. A revolutionary movement always starts from a position of inferior strength. It owes its survival to the reluctance of its declared victims to accept its professions at face value. It owes its success to the psychological advantage which single-minded purpose confers over opponents who refuse to believe that some states or groups may prefer victory to peace. The ambiguity of the Soviet challenge results in part from the skill of the Soviet leadership. But it is magnified by the tendency of the free world to choose the interpretation of Soviet motivations which best fits its own preconceptions. Neither Lenin's writings, nor Stalin's utterances, nor Mao's published works, nor Khrushchev's declarations has availed against the conviction of the West that a basic change in Communist society and aims was imminent and that a problem deferred was a problem solved.

It is only to posterity that revolutionary movements appear unambiguous. However weak it may be at the beginning, a revolutionary state is often able to substitute psychological strength for physical power. It can use the very enormity of its goals to defeat an opponent who cannot come to grips with a policy of unlimited objectives.

The United States has had particular difficulty in this respect. From the moment in our national history when we focused our attention primarily on domestic development, we met very few obstacles that were really insuperable. We were almost uniquely blessed with the kind of environment in which the problems that were presented—those at least that we really wanted to solve—were difficult but manageable. Almost from our colonial infancy we have been trained to measure a man, a government, or an era by the degree of energy with which contemporary problems have been attacked—and hence by the success in finding a final, definite solution. If problems were not solved, this was because not enough energy or enough resolution had been applied. The leadership or the government was clearly at fault. A better government or a better man would have mastered the situation. Better men and a better government, when we provide them, *will* solve all issues *in our time*.

As a result, we are not comfortable with seemingly insoluble problems.

There must be *some* way to achieve peace if only the correct method is utilized. Many of the erratic tendencies in American policy are traceable to our impatience. The lack of persistence, the oscillation between rigid adherence to the *status quo* and desire for novelty for its own sake show our discomfort when faced with protracted deadlock. We grow restless when good will goes unrewarded and when proposals have to be maintained over a long period of time.

When reality clashes with its anticipated form, frustration is the inevitable consequence. We have, therefore, been torn between adopting a pose of indignation and seeking to solve all problems at one fell swoop. We have been at times reluctant, indeed seemingly afraid, to negotiate. We have also acted as if all our difficulties could be removed by personal rapport among the statesmen. Periods of overconcern with military security have alternated with periods when we saw in a changed Soviet tone an approach to an end of tensions.

The quest for good will in the abstract has been as demoralizing and as fruitless as the insistence that negotiations are inherently useless. The abortive summit meeting in Paris is as certain a symptom of the perils of a purely formal conciliatoriness as Secretary Dulles' rigidity was a symptom of a largely mechanical intransigence. It is, therefore, necessary to examine Western, and particularly American, attitudes towards negotiations in more detail.

·   ·   ·

THE RELIANCE ON PERSONALITIES:
THE PROBLEM OF SUMMIT MEETINGS

The temptation to conduct personal diplomacy derives from the notion of peace prevalent in both the United States and Great Britain. If peace is the "normal" relation among states, it follows that tensions must be caused by shortsightedness or misunderstanding and that they can be removed by a change of heart of the leading statesmen. President Eisenhower, before embarking on an unprecedented round of visits to foreign capitals, was at pains to insist that his purpose was to "clear" the atmosphere rather than to negotiate. If peace ultimately depends on personalities, abstract good will may well seem more important than a concrete program. Indeed, the attempt to achieve specific settlements can appear as an obstacle rather than as an aid to peace. "Our many post-war conferences," said President Eisenhower in 1955, prior to the Geneva summit conference, "have been characterized too much by attention to detail, by an effort apparently to work on specific problems rather than to establish the spirit and the attitude in which we shall approach them." [4]

---

[4] *New York Times*, July 16, 1955.

Within two years of assuming office, President Eisenhower, whose party had charged its opponents with being soft towards Communism, found himself engaged in a summit meeting which called forth a flood of self-congratulatory comment, both in America and abroad. After a decade of Soviet intransigence, the press was almost unanimous in its assertion that Soviet policy had been mellowed by the personal charm of one man. "No one would want to underestimate the change in the Russian attitude," said the *New York Herald Tribune.* "Without that, nothing would have been possible. . . . But it remains President Eisenhower's achievement that he comprehended the change, that he seized the opening and turned it to the advantage of world peace." [5] "Mr. Eisenhower had done even better than defeat an enemy in battle as had been his assignment a decade ago," read an editorial in the *New York Times.* "He had done something to prevent battles from happening. . . . The occasion was, in fact, made for Mr. Eisenhower. Other men might have played strength against strength. It was Mr. Eisenhower's gift to draw others into the circle of his good will and to modify the attitudes if not the policies of the little band of visitors from the other side of the Elbe." [6]

The conviction was widespread on both sides of the Atlantic that the Cold War had been due largely to personal distrust. Since this had been removed at Geneva, an era of peace was beginning: "It is indeed an intense sense of relief which unites President Eisenhower with President [sic] Bulganin. Neither ever conceived that his own country would launch war. But each giant was quite convinced that the other giant was capable of doing so. It was this conviction which created the climate of cold war and precipitated the rearmament race. *The cold war was suddenly called off at Geneva because both sides recognized that these suspicions were entirely unfounded."* [7] [Emphasis added.]

· · ·

When the summit conference of 1960 collapsed before it had even started, a shudder of apprehension went through the world. A chance for peace seemed to have been lost. But what really imperiled peace was our self-righteousness and evasion of responsibility. After all, the prelude to the Paris summit conference had given little cause for the hopes attached to it. At first, we found ourselves maneuvered into the position of seeming to fear meeting the Soviet leaders face-to-face. By insisting on "progress" at a lower level before he would agree to a conference of heads of state,

[5] *New York Herald Tribune,* Editorial, July 21, 1955.

[6] *New York Times,* Editorial, July 25, 1955.

[7] "Problems of the Garden-Party Peace," *New Statesman and Nation,* Aug. 13, 1955.

President Eisenhower only brought about the preposterous situation where he finally claimed that Mr. Khrushchev's ambiguous postponement of an unprovoked threat and his willingness to go to the summit were in themselves an indication of progress. These vacillations were hardly calculated to motivate the Soviet leaders to approach the summit conference with responsibility.

Moreover, many of the arguments advanced on behalf of summit diplomacy were fatuous in the extreme. It was urged that only the heads of state could settle the really intractable disputes. No subordinate, it was said, would dare to abandon the rigid positions of the Cold War. In the Soviet Union, in particular, only Mr. Khrushchev was in a position to make really fundamental decisions. And the mere fact that a summit meeting was in prospect was thought to place constraints on Soviet intransigence. A series of summit meetings, according to this line of argument, could not fail to relieve tensions.

Many of these contentions were open to serious doubt even before the collapse of the Paris Conference. It is trivial to pretend that problems of the complexity of those which have rent the world for a decade and a half can be solved in a few days by harassed men meeting in the full light of publicity. It cannot be in the interest of the democracies to adopt a style of diplomacy which places such a premium on the authority of a few leaders. Mr. Khrushchev may be the supreme ruler in the Soviet Union and the only one with sufficient power to make binding agreements. It does not follow that the democracies can coexist with a dictatorship only by imitating its method of operation.

The notion that a series of summit meetings might induce Mr. Khrushchev to forget his demands on Berlin did not do justice to the intelligence of the Soviet dictator. Surely it bordered on the frivolous to suggest that Mr. Khrushchev could be induced to table his demands without noticing it, as it were. This view, moreover, took no account of Mr. Khrushchev's domestic position. Even assuming that he is the most "conciliatory" Soviet leader, he could hardly be expected to tell his colleagues in the Kremlin that the privilege of meeting Western leaders periodically seemed to him more important than specific gains. Indeed, personal diplomacy of the type preceding the Paris summit meeting may force a Soviet leader either to press for some tangible gain or into outbursts of intransigence to prove his ideological toughness to his colleagues. Far from being the most moderate policy, it is the most risky one.

In any case, it soon became apparent that whatever the benefits of high-level meetings for the Soviet Union, these could be realized without any concrete concessions and indeed without a summit conference. The "preparatory" meeting between Mr. Khrushchev and the Western heads of state individually still further reduced the already slight chances of the summit meeting. They gave Mr. Khrushchev all the symbolic gains he might have expected from a summit conference and without the need of confronting the Western alliance as a unit. They ensured that nothing of consequence could possibly happen at the summit. If concessions were to be forthcoming, it was certain that Mr. Khrushchev would prefer to make them to the Allies individually than at a summit conference—where they might appear as a response to Western unity.

At the same time, one crucial function of high-level meetings—to inform the heads of state of each other's point of view—had already been accomplished in individual conferences and with a greatly heightened possibility of misunderstanding. It has been argued that Mr. Khrushchev interpreted President Eisenhower's behavior at Camp David as indicating a readiness to make major concessions on Berlin and that part of his rage during the abortive summit conference was due to disappointment in this respect. Whether or not this was in fact the case, the diplomacy leading up to the summit was made to order for this kind of misapprehension. Moreover, since each side had staked a great deal on a presumed expertise in assessing the domestic situation of the other, they were forced into repeated public declarations designed to reassure their own public opinion and—in Khrushchev's case—their own die-hards. This in turn guaranteed that statements of extreme intransigence would alternate with intimations of normality through a year and a half of ambulatory diplomacy which was unable to settle any of the issues or even define them.

Finally, the idea that the imminence of a summit meeting places a constraint upon intransigence is not borne out by the record. In the period preceding the summit, both sides restated their positions in the sharpest possible forms. Mr. Khrushchev in particular delivered a series of extremely menacing speeches. The West, if it wanted to proceed with the summit, thus found itself in the humiliating position of having to explain that no threat had been uttered. These maneuvers were inherent in the nature of personal diplomacy. When heads of state are the principal negotiators, their most effective bargaining device—in some circumstances the only available one—is to stake their prestige in a manner which makes any concession appear as an intolerable loss of face.

The evasion of concreteness, the reliance on personalities, the implication that all problems can be settled with one grand gesture, all these tempt the Soviet leaders to use negotiations to demoralize the West. It is in the Soviet interest to turn all disputes into clashes of personalities. The peoples of the free world cannot be expected to run risks or to make exertions because of a personal dispute. If the only obstacle to peace is the absence of personal rapport among leading statemen, then all tensions and exertions of a decade and a half have been a frivolous imposition. Whenever the Soviet leaders succeed in giving the impression that all tensions are due to an unfortunate misunderstanding or else to the evil machinations of individuals, they make it that much more difficult for the

West to raise later the need for concrete settlements. This is why whenever the Communist leaders have pressed for a relaxation of tensions they have tied the success of it to personalities. Then, whenever the underlying causes of the tension reassert themselves—as they inevitably must if not resolved—the charge can be made that the breakdown is due to the operation of the capitalist system or to the predominant influence of hostile personalities—as is shown by Mr. Khrushchev's vicious attacks on President Eisenhower after the abortive summit conference at Paris. By contrast, it should be the responsibility of our statesmen to make clear that, while we are always ready to negotiate, the negotiation must be serious, detailed and specific.

This is not to say that summit conferences are always to be avoided. It does suggest that we must learn to distinguish form and substance. In assessing the utility of summit meetings, it is essential to weigh the pros and cons without sentimentality.

The advantage of a summit meeting is that the participants possess the authority to settle disputes. The disadvantage is that they cannot be disavowed. A summit conference can make binding decisions more rapidly than any other diplomatic forum. By the same token, the disagreements are liable to be more intractable and the decisions more irrevocable. The possibility of using summit conferences to mark a new departure in the relations of states should not be underestimated. At the same time, it would be foolish to deny the perils of having as principal negotiators the men who make the final decision about the use of hydrogen bombs. Frustration or humiliation may cause them to embark on an irrevocable course. A summit conference may contribute to clarification of the opposing points of view. But this is helpful only if the original tension was caused by misunderstanding. Otherwise, clarifying the opposing points of view may only deepen the schism. In short, the same factors which make for speed of decision also increase the risks of disagreement.

Moreover, when heads of state become the principal negotiators, they may soon find themselves so preoccupied with the process of bargaining that they have little time or energy available for formulating policy.[8] In the ambulatory diplomacy preceding the Paris summit conference, it was an oddity when all heads of state were at home simultaneously. During his last two years in office President Eisenhower was at conferences, preparing for or recuperating from good will visits almost constantly. Such a diplomacy may suit a dictatorship or a state which wishes to demoralize its opponents by confusing all issues. It is not conducive to developing

---

[8] For a brilliant discussion of the problem posed by summit diplomacy for the American presidency see Dean Rusk, "The President," *Foreign Affairs*, April, 1960, pp. 353–369.

constructive long-range policies. It is a useful device to buy time, though at a price which makes it unlikely that the time will be well used.

. . .

When the primary purpose of summit meetings is thought to be the fostering of abstract good will, they become not a forum for negotiations but a substitute for them; not an expression of a policy but a means of obscuring its absence. The constant international travels of heads of government without a clear program or purpose may be less an expression of statesmanship than a symptom of panic.

The real indictment of the diplomacy culminating in the fiasco at Paris, then, is the attitude of trying to get something for nothing, the effort to negotiate without goal or conception. This is what must be remedied. The problem is not to save summit diplomacy by leavening it with the presence of heads of state from the uncommitted areas—as has been suggested.[9] Rather, it is to clarify our program for whatever negotiations may take place at any level. We can negotiate with confidence if we know what we consider a just arrangement. If we lack a sense of direction, diplomacy at any level will be doomed.

32. NEGOTIATION IN WARFARE

Thomas C. Schelling

To THINK OF WAR as a bargaining process is uncongenial to some of us. Bargaining with violence smacks of extortion, vicious politics, callous diplomacy, and everything indecent, illegal, or uncivilized. It is bad enough to kill and to maim, but to do it for gain and not for some transcendent purpose seems even worse. Bargaining also smacks of appeasement, of politics and diplomacy, of accommodation or collaboration

From *Arms and Influence* by Thomas C. Schelling (New Haven: Yale University Press, 1966) pp. 215–220. Reprinted by permission of the Yale University Press.

THOMAS C. SCHELLING (1921–   ) Professor of Economics, Harvard University. Author of *The Strategy of Conflict*, (Cambridge: Harvard University Press, 1960), co-author, *Strategy and Arms Control*, (New York: Twentieth Century Fund, 1961), *International Economics* (Boston: Allyn and Bacon, 1958).

9 Denis Healey, "The View from London," *New Leader,* June 13, 1960.

with the enemy, of selling out and compromising, of everything weak and irresolute. But to fight a purely destructive war is neither clean nor heroic; it is just purposeless. No one who hates war can eliminate its ugliness by shutting his eyes to the need for responsible direction; coercion is the business of war. And someone who hates mixing politics with war usually wants to glorify an action by ignoring or disguising its purpose. Both points of view deserve sympathy, and in some wars they could be indulged; neither should determine the conduct of a thermonuclear war.

What is the bargaining about? First there is bargaining about the conduct of the war itself. In more narrowly limited wars—the Korean War, or the war in Vietnam, or a hypothetical war confined to Europe or the Middle East—the bargaining about the way the war is to be fought is conspicuous and continual: what weapons are used, what nationalities are involved, what targets are sanctuaries and what are legitimate, what forms participation can take without being counted as "combat," what codes of reprisal or hot pursuit and what treatment of prisoners are to be recognized. The same should be true in the largest war: the treatment of population centers, the deliberate creation or avoidance of fallout, the inclusion or exclusion of particular countries as combatants and targets, the destruction or preservation of each other's government or command centers, demonstrations of strength and resolve, and the treatment of the communications facilities on which explicit bargaining depends, should be within the cognizance of those who command the operations. Part of this bargaining might be explicit, in verbal messages and replies; much of it would be tacit, in the patterns of behavior and reactions to enemy behavior. The tacit bargaining would involve targets conspicuously hit and conspicuously avoided, the character and timing of specific reprisals, demonstrations of strength and resolve and of the accuracy of target intelligence, and anything else that conveys intent to the enemy or structures his expectations about the kind of war it is going to be.

Second, there would be bargaining about the cease-fire, truce, armistice, surrender, disarmament, or whatever it is that brings the war to a close—about the way to halt the war and the military requirements for stopping it. The terms could involve weapons—their number, readiness, location, preservation, or destruction—and the disposition of weapons and actions beyond recall or out of control or unaccounted for, or whose status was in dispute between the two sides. It would involve surveillance and inspection, either to monitor compliance with the armistice or just to establish the facts, to demonstrate strength or weakness, to assign fault or innocence in case of untoward events, and to keep track of third parties' military forces. It could involve understandings about the reassembling or reconstituting of military forces, refueling, readying of missiles on launching pads, repair and maintenance, and all the other steps that would prepare a country either to meet a renewed attack or to launch one. It could involve argument or bargaining about the degree of destruction to people and property on both sides, the equity or justice of what had been done and the need to inflict punishment or to exact submissiveness. It could involve the dismantling or preservation of warning systems, military communications, or air defenses. And it very likely would involve the status of sheltered or unsheltered population in view of their significance as "hostages" against resumption of warfare.

A third subject of bargaining could be the regime within the enemy country itself. At a minimum there might have to be a decision about *whom* to recognize as authority in the enemy country or with whom one would willingly deal. There might be a choice between negotiating with military or civilian authorities; and if the war is as disruptive as can easily be imagined, there may be a problem of "succession" to resolve. There could even be competing regimes in the enemy country—alternative commanders to recognize as the inheritors of control, or alternative political leaders whose acquisition of control depended on whether they could monopolize communications or get themselves recognized as authoritative negotiators. To some extent, either side can determine the regime on the other side by the process of recognition and negotiation itself. This would especially be the case in the decision to negotiate about allied countries—China, or France and Germany—or alternatively to refuse to deal with the primary enemy about allied and satellite affairs and to insist upon dealing separately with the governments of those countries.

A fourth subject for bargaining would be the disposition of any theater in which local or regional war was taking place. This could involve the evacuation or occupation of territory, local surrender of forces, coordinated withdrawals, treatment of the population, use of troops to police the areas, prisoner exchanges, return or transfer of authority to local governments, inspection and surveillance, introduction of occupation authorities, or anything else pertinent to the local termination of warfare.

The tempo and urgency of the big war and its armistice might require ignoring theater affairs in the interest of reaching some armistice. If so, there might be an understanding, implicit or explicit, that the theater war is to be stopped by unilateral actions or by immediately subsequent negotiation. There might conceivably be the expectation that the theater war goes on, risking renewed outbreak of the larger war; and possibly the outcome of the major war would have made the theater war inconsequential or its local outcome a foregone conclusion. A theater war would in any case pose acute problems of synchronization: its tempo would be so slow compared with that of the bigger war that the terms of the theater armistice simply could not be met within the time schedule on which the larger war had to be brought to a close.

Fifth would be the longer term disarmament and inspection arrangements. These might be comprised in the same package with the armistice itself; but stopping a war safely and reliably is different from maintaining safe and reliable military relations thereafter. The first involves conditions to be met at once, before the war is ended or before planes return to base, before relaxation has occurred and before populations have been brought from their shelters. The second involves conditions to be met afterward.

For that reason the armistice might, as in the days of Julius Caesar, involve the surrender of hostages as a pledge for future compliance. What form these might take is hard to foretell; but selective occupation of communication centers, preplaced demolition charges, destruction of particular facilities to make a country dependent on outside aid, or even personal hostages might appear reasonable. The purpose of any of these types of hostages—hostages not taken by force but acquired by negotiation—is to maintain bargaining power that would otherwise too quickly disappear. It is to provide a pledge against future compliance, when one's capacity for sanctions is too short-lived. The principle is important, because there is no necessary correspondence between the duration of one's power to coerce and the time span of the compliance that needs to be enforced.

A sixth subject for negotiation might be the political status of various countries or territories—dissolution of alliances or blocs, dismemberment of countries, and all the other things that wars are usually "about," possibly including economic arrangements and particularly reparations and prohibitions. Some of these might automatically be covered in disposing of a theater war; some would already be covered in deciding on the regime to negotiate with. Some might be settled by default: the war itself would have been so disruptive as to leave certain problems no longer in need of solution, certain issues irrelevant, certain countries unimportant.

Of these six topics for bargaining, the first—conduct of the war—is inherent in the war itself if the war is responsibly conducted. The second—terms of armistice or surrender—is inherent in the process of getting it stopped, even though by default most of the terms might be established through an unnegotiated pause. The third—the regime—is at least somewhat implicit in the process of negotiation; the decision to negotiate involves some choice and recognition. The fourth—disposition of local or regional warfare—might be deferred until after the urgent business of armistice had been settled; but the armistice may remain tentative and precarious until the rest of the fighting is actually stopped. The same is probably true of the longer-term disarmament arrangements, and of political and economic arrangements.

We are dealing with a process that is inherently frantic, noisy, and disruptive, in an environment of acute uncertainty, conducted by human beings who have never experienced such a crisis before and on an extraordinarily demanding time schedule. We have to suppose that the negotiations would be truncated, incomplete, improvised, and disorderly, with threats, offers, and demands issued disjointedly and inconsistently, subject to misunderstanding about facts as well as intent, and with uncertainty about who has the authority to negotiate and to command. These six topics are therefore not an agenda for negotiation but a series of headings for sorting out the issues that might receive attention. They are an agenda only for thinking in advance about the termination of war, not for negotiation itself.

How soon should the terminal negotiations begin? Preferably, before the war starts. The crisis that precedes the war would be an opportune time to get certain understandings across. Once war became an imminent possibility, governments might take seriously a "strategic dialogue" that could powerfully influence the war itself. In ordinary peacetime the Soviet leaders have tended to disdain the idea of restraint in warfare. Why not? It permits them to ridicule American strategy, to pose the deterrent threat of massive retaliation, and still perhaps to change their minds if they ever have to take war seriously. On the brink of war they would. It may be just before the outbreak that an intense dialogue would occur, shaping expectations about bringing the war to a close, avoiding a contest in city destruction, and keeping communications open.

It is sometimes wondered whether communications could be established mid-course in a major war. The proper question is whether communications should be cut off. There would have been intense communication before the war, and the problem is to maintain it, not to invent it.

SECTION TWO:

Balance of Power

33. ENGLAND'S FOREIGN POLICY

Sir Eyre Crowe

THE GENERAL CHARACTER of England's foreign policy is determined by the immutable conditions of her geographical situation on the ocean flank of Europe as an island State with vast oversea colonies and dependencies, whose existence and survival as an independent community are inseparably bound up with the possession of preponderant sea power. The tremendous influence of such preponderance has been described in the classical pages of Captain Mahan. No one now disputes it. Sea power is more potent than land power, because it is as pervading as the element in which it moves and has its being. Its formidable character makes itself felt the more directly that a maritime State is, in the literal sense of the word, the neighbour of every country accessible by sea. It would, therefore, be but natural that the power of a State supreme at sea should inspire universal jealousy and fear, and be ever exposed to the danger of being overthrown by a general combination of the world. Against such a combination no single nation could in the long run stand, least of all a small island kingdom not possessed of the military strength of a people trained to arms, and dependent for its food supply on oversea commerce. The danger can in practice only be averted—and history shows that it has been so averted—on condition that the national policy of the insular

---

From *British Documents on the Origins of the War, 1898–1914,* Vol. III, "The Testing of the Entente, 1904–06," edited by G. P. Gooch and Harold Temperley (London: HMSO 1929) pp. 402–403. Reprinted by permission of His Majesty's Stationery Office.

SIR EYRE CROWE (1864–1925) Formerly permanent Under-Secretary of State for Foreign Affairs, Foreign Office, Great Britain.

and naval State is so directed as to harmonize with the general desires and ideals common to all mankind, and more particularly that it is closely identified with the primary and vital interests of a majority, or as many as possible, of the other nations. Now, the first interest of all countries is the preservation of national independence. It follows that England, more than any other non-insular Power, has a direct and positive interest in the maintenance of the independence of nations, and therefore must be the natural enemy of any country threatening the independence of others, and the natural protector of the weaker communities.

Second only to the ideal of independence, nations have always cherished the right of free intercourse and trade in the world's markets, and in proportion as England champions the principle of the largest measure of general freedom of commerce, she undoubtedly strengthens her hold on the interested friendship of other nations, at least to the extent of making them feel less apprehensive of naval supremacy in the hands of a free trade England than they would in the face of a predominant protectionist Power. This is an aspect of the free trade question which is apt to be overlooked. It has been well said that every country, if it had the option, would, of course, prefer itself to hold the power of supremacy at sea, but that, this choice being excluded, it would rather see England hold that power than any other State.

History shows that the danger threatening the independence of this or that nation has generally arisen, at least in part, out of the momentary predominance of a neighbouring State at once militarily powerful, economically efficient, and ambitious to extend its frontiers or spread its influence, the danger being directly proportionate to the degree of its power and efficiency, and to the spontaneity or "inevitableness" of its ambitions. The only check on the abuse of political predominance derived from such a position has always consisted in the opposition of an equally formidable rival, or of a combination of several countries forming leagues of defence. The equilibrium established by such a grouping of forces is technically known as the balance of power, and it has become almost an historical truism to identify England's secular policy with the maintenance of this balance by throwing her weight now in this scale and now in that, but ever on the side opposed to the political dictatorship of the strongest single State or group at a given time.

If this view of British policy is correct, the opposition into which England must inevitably be driven to any country aspiring to such a dictatorship assumes almost the form of a law of nature, as has indeed been theoretically demonstrated, and illustrated historically, by an eminent writer on English national policy.

By applying this general law to a particular case, the attempt might be made to ascertain whether, at a given time, some powerful and ambitious State is or is not in a position of natural and necessary enmity towards

England; and the present position of Germany might, perhaps, be so
tested. Any such investigation must take the shape of an inquiry as to
whether Germany is, in fact, aiming at a political hegemony with the
object of promoting purely German schemes of expansion, and establishing a German primacy in the world of international politics at the cost
and to the detriment of other nations.

34. THE BALANCE OF POWER: PRESCRIPTION, CONCEPT OR PROPAGANDA?

Ernst B. Haas

CLASSIFICATION OF VERBAL MEANINGS

AMONG THE VARIOUS MEANINGS of the term "balance of power," one of
the more common is a mere factual description of the distribution of
political power in the international scene at any one time. But, in another
sense, the term is used to mean a theoretical principle acting as a guide to
foreign policy-making in any and all international situations, so that the
preponderance of any one state may be avoided. Expanding this notion
and assuming that almost all states guide their policies by this principle,
a general system of the balance of power is thought to come about, a
system in which each participating state has a certain role. Such a system
may take the form of two or more power blocs in mutual opposition to
each other and it may exist with or without the benefit of a balancer, i.e.,
a state willing and able to throw its weight on either scale of the balance,
to speak in terms of the classical metaphor, and thus presumably bring

From *World Politics,* V, No. 4 (July 1953), 446–477. Reprinted by permission of
the author and the publisher. Footnotes have been renumbered to appear in consecutive order.

ERNST B. HAAS (1924–   ) Professor of Political Science and Associate Director,
Institute for International Studies, University of California, Berkeley. Author of
Human Rights and International Action: The Case for Freedom of Association
(Stanford: Stanford University Press, 1970); *Web of Interdependence: The U.S.
and International Organizations* (Englewood Cliffs, N.J.: Prentice-Hall, 1970);
Tangle of Hopes (Englewood Cliffs, N.J.: Prentice-Hall, 1969); *Beyond the Nation
State: Functionalism and International Organization,* (Stanford: Stanford University
Press, 1964); *The Uniting of Europe,* (Stanford: Stanford University Press, 1957).

about the diplomatic or military victory of the bloc so supported, or possibly prevent any change in existing conditions. In addition to these various shades of theoretical meaning implying some sort of system, the term "balance of power" has frequently been used to describe the existence of a political equilibrium, i.e., such a distribution of power that each state (or each major state) is the approximate equal of every other. On the other hand, the term is commonly employed to connote the exact opposite of the equilibrium notion; it then comes to be identical with a notion of hegemony. Still other commentators insist on the presence of general historical laws of the balance of power, a notion to which the term "natural law" has been given by some. By this they mean that the search for hegemony by one state will inevitably be met by a coalition of all other states, thus forming a "counterweight" against political preponderance and tending to re-establish the *status quo ante*. And, finally, balance of power very frequently means power politics generally and the establishment of certain military and strategic conditions specifically. Some writers equate the term with peace, others with war. This general differentiation now remains to be supported with apposite illustrative citations.[1]

(1) *Balance meaning "Distribution of Power."* The simplest and most commonly found use of the term "balance of power" occurs in plain descriptive statements. Thus when Bolingbroke wrote that "Our Charles the First was no great politician, and yet he seemed to discern that the balance of power was turning in favor of France, some years before the treaty of Westphalia . . . ,"[2] he was merely saying that the Stuart ruler was noticing that the power of France was increasing as compared to that of Britain. Or, again, Henry Wallace once remarked that Japan's joining the Axis meant:

---

[1] It is of some signifiance that the terminological confusion is not confined to Western writing. Raymond L. Garthoff has shown that even though the Russian political vocabulary has separate expressions for most of the usages cited, in practice loose application creates exactly the same difficulty as in English so far as classification and analysis are concerned. Garthoff concludes that, from an examination of 250 citations using some form of balance of power expression, this summary can be made: 136 instances of balance meaning general "relation of forces," especially in the class struggle; 87 instances meaning a "general distribution" of power; 17 instances of balance meaning "equilibrium"; and 10 instances of balance meaning "preponderance" or hegemony. In discussions of international relations, the Soviet use of the term "balance of power" generally connotes an equilibrium of forces between the "imperialist" and "socialist" worlds, and is therefore associated with short-term polices of peaceful coexistence. "The Concept of the Balance of Power in Soviet Policy-Making," *World Politics*, IV (October 1951), pp. 89–90, 102–3, 108–9.

[2] Bolingbroke, *Works*, Philadelphia, 1841, II, p. 257.

that the old balance of power upon which the U.S. relied for safety is now gone. Only if we are speedy and efficient in our defense can we keep aggressor nations, or any combination of them, from coming to this country. . . . The old balance of power under which the Monroe Doctrine was easily defended is gone. We must look to our own defenses, relying on ourselves to repel any aggression.[3]

Balance of power, in usages such as these, means no more than distribution of power. It does not connote any "balancing" of weights at all. When a statesman says that the "balance of power has shifted," he wants to say that his opponent has grown more powerful than was the case previously.

(2) *Balance meaning "Equilibrium."* An imposing array of politicians and political scientists has urged that the term "balance of power" means what it seems to imply to the uninitiated layman: an exact equilibrium of power between two or more contending parties. Wrote Réal de Curban, for instance:

Speaking generally, the rulers regard Europe as a balance in which the heaviest side subdues the other side and believe that in order to retain Europe in a solid and peaceful condition it is necessary to maintain between the principal parties this point of equilibrium, which, preventing either side of the balance from sinking, proves that they are on an exactly equal level. . . . The House of France and the House of Austria have been regarded as the scales of the balance of Europe. One or the other of these scales have received their support from England and Holland, which acted as the balancers.[4]

His distinguished compatriots, Duplessis-Mornay and Rohan, agreed with this postulation in important seventeenth-century pamphlets on the nature of the balance of power, recommending, by the way, that the Bourbons subdue the Habsburgs in order to achieve this much-vaunted equilibrium.[5] In Germany Konstantin Frantz, in 1859, urged the same definition and denounced the Vienna settlement for not having permitted Prussia and Austria to gain equality of power with the other three major

---

[3] U.P. despatch in *Los Angeles Times*, September 1940, cited in Alfred Vagts, "The Balance of Power: Growth of an Idea," *World Politics*, I (October 1948), p. 86.

[4] Réal de Curban, *La science du gouvernement*, Paris, 1764, VI, pp. 443ff.

[5] Henri de Rohan, *De l'intérest des princes et estats de la Chréstienté;* Duplessis-Mornay, *Sur les moyens de diminuer l'Espanol;* both cited in A. de Stieglitz, *De l'équilibre politique, du légitimisme et du principe des nationalités*, Paris, 1893–1897, I, pp. 21ff. This work contains brief analyses of all the major pamphlets and treatises on the balance of power before 1800, and an analysis of the opinions of most writers on international law since Grotius.

states.[6] This juxtaposition of arguments gives considerable support to Professor Pollard's conclusion that the meaning of equilibrium should be taken with a great deal of reserve:

> One has a shrewd suspicion that those who believe in a balance of power, do so because they think it is like a balance at the bank, something better than mere equality, an advantage which they possess. Unconsciously they have both meanings in their minds when they use the phrase. The equality-meaning commends it as propaganda; the advantage is a mental reservation for private use. Statesmen and publicists have sometimes betrayed an uneasy consciousness of the ambiguity and incautiously talked about a just, good, or proper balance of power, admitting thereby that a mere balance was not good enough; and an eighteenth century biographer of Cardinal Wolsey lets the cat out of the bag when he refers to "that grand rule, whereby the counsels of England should always be guided, of preserving the balance of power *in her hands.*" [7]

These formulations of the balance of power as a purely external and international equilibrium between contending states or blocs of states take no account of the possible existence of a similar relationship between contending groups within the state. Such an addition to the theory, however, was furnished by Harold Lasswell.[8] Lasswell speaks of a balancing of power rather than a "balance," since the attempt toward equilibrium can never be a wholly successful one, owing to various non-objective factors which interfere with scientific balancing. Lasswell rounds out the conventional presentation of the search for equilibrium by pointing to the domestic political process as offering a parallel spectacle. Furthermore, he establishes a relationship between the domestic and international balancing processes by describing liaison and support between various societal groups in one state, working with or against certain other groups in the opposing state or in the "balancer" state.

(3) *Balance meaning "Hegemony."* This analysis leads easily to the meaning of balance of power equivalent to hegemony. Examples from the literature are numerous and only two will be given: one from the eighteenth century and one modern. Thus, the Count of Hauterive, a pamphleteer for Napoleon I, argued that the balance of power demanded Napoleon's breaking the Treaty of Campo Formio, to enable France to

---

[6] K. Krantz, *Untersuchungen über das Europäische Gleichgewicht,* cited in K. Jacob, "Die Chimäre des Gleichgewichts," *Archiv für Urkundenforschung,* VI (1918), pp. 359–60.

[7] A. F. Pollard, "The Balance of Power," *Journal of the British Institute on International Affairs,* II (1923), p. 59 (italics in original).

[8] H. D. Lasswell, *World Politics and Personal Insecurity,* New York, 1935, ch. III.

bring about a confederation of the continent against England and in this way reduce the hegemonial superiority of Britain on the seas and, incidentally, establish the hegemony of France.[9] And Napoleon himself, in December of 1813, expressed his desire for a peace "based on the balance of rights and interests"! [10]

Nicholas Spykman also understood the balance of power as implying a search for hegemony. His thesis—that all states seek a hegemonial position and therefore are in more or less continual conflict with each other—has for its natural corollary that this conflict, if it stops short of total war, has to result in some sort of equilibrium. This, however, can never be stable, because statesmen do not seek "balance" but hegemony:

> The truth of the matter is that states are interested only in a balance which is in their favor. Not an equilibrium, but a generous margin is their objective. There is no real security in being just as strong as a potential enemy; there is security only in being a little stronger. There is no possibility of action if one's strength is fully checked; there is a chance for a positive foreign policy only if there is a margin of force which can be freely used. Whatever the theory and the rationalization, the practical objective is the constant improvement of the state's own relative power position. The balance desired is the one which neutralizes other states, leaving the home state free to be the deciding force and the deciding voice.[11]

Should equilibrium be attained at one point, it would immediately be wiped out by the search for slight superiority.

(4) *Balance meaning "Stability" and "Peace."* A number of analysts have persisted in identifying what they have called the "balance of power" with the kind of idyllic world they desire to establish. They do not mean that the balance of power is a method for realizing peace and stability, but that peace and stability are identical with a balance of power. Typical of this approach is Francis Gould Leckie.[12] Leckie's tome is free from the usual recommendations of balancing the power of state A against state B, with states C and D holding the balance between them. He confines himself to recommending that feudal succession law be abolished and Europe go in for large-scale colonization in Africa and America, thus creating a "stable balance of power." At other times he does, however, lapse into more conventional meanings of the balance—an inconsistency unfortunately found all too frequently in these writings.

---

[9] Hauterive, *De l'état de la France à la fin de l'an VIII*, cited in Stern, *op. cit.*, p. 32.

[10] L. Donnadieu, *Essai sur la théorie d'équilibre*, Paris, 1900, p. 111.

[11] N. Spykman, *America's Strategy in World Politics*, New York, 1942, pp. 21–25.

[12] F. G. Leckie, *An Historical Research into the Nature of the Balance of Power in Europe*, London, 1817, pp. 4, 242ff., 292, 303, 350ff.

Similarly, Olof Höijer tends to use the term in this sense, arguing that whenever the powers decided peace was desirable and should be maintained on a given issue—e.g., the London Conference of 1830–1939—a true balance of power existed, though to some analysts it might appear as if here the term "concert" might be more appropriate.[13]

(5) *Balance meaning "Instability" and "War."* Occasionally, by contrast, we find writers using the term "balance of power" as being synonymous with the very kind of world conditions they abhor: war, intervention, competition, and instability. Thus the Abbé de Pradt argued that the balance of power means war, while peace is identical with the settling of all issues on their moral, economic, and ethnographic merits.[14] This approach is also typical of that extraordinary eighteenth-century writer, Johann Gottlob Justi, of Cobden and Bright, of the elder Mirabeau, and of Kant, who called the balance of power a *Hirngespinst*.[15] It is true of de Pradt, however, that he tends to identify "balance of power" with power politics generally, a very common identification indeed.

(6) *Balance meaning "Power Politics" generally.* Edmund Waller once exclaimed:

> Heav'n that has plac'd this island to give law,
> To balance Europe and her states to awe.

"Balance" in this jingle comes to mean the exertion of power pure and simple. And as the anonymous author of *The Present State of Europe* (ed. of 1757) stated, "The struggle for the balance of power, in effect, is the struggle for power."[16] Power, politics of pure power, *Realpolitik*, and the balance of power are here merged into one concept, the concept that state survival in a competitive international world demands the use of power uninhibited by moral considerations. Lord Bolingbroke, in his fascinating *Letters on the Study and Use of History*, expressed similar ideas. He argued, in effect, that the concept of the balance of power was simply an eminently practical contrivance by which the states of Europe could determine when to combine in defensive alliances against whichever state seemed to be working for hegemony, to "endanger their liberties," i.e., to absorb them. Since this desire was thought to be inherent in either France

---

[13] O. Höijer, *La théorie de l'équilibre et le droit des gens*, Paris, 1917, pp. 52–59.

[14] D. de Pradt, *Du Congrès de Vienne*, Paris, 1815, 1, pp. 67–69, 75ff., 84ff., 95, 104.

[15] A. Stern, "Das politische Gleichgewicht," *Archiv für Politik und Geschichte*, IV (1923), pp. 31–34.

[16] L. Bucher, "Uber politische Kunstausdrücke. II. Politisches Gleichgewicht," *Deutsch Revue*, XII (1887), pp. 336, 338.

or Austria at all times, the balance of power comes to mean any power combination to stop "aggression." [17]

This formulation of the term is commonly expanded to include all the factors making for state power, and especially military installations, military potentials, and strategic positions. State A's position in the balance of power is "good" after the construction of a given line of fortresses, or "bad" if that line is obliterated by boundary changes. The point need not be labored. Use of the term "balance of power" in this very commonly employed meaning signifies the over-all power position of states in an international scene dominated by power politics. States are pictured as fighting for power, and only for power—for whatever reasons —and the struggle in or for a balance of power is equivalent to the power political process as a whole. Balance of power here is not to be understood as a refinement of the general process of power politics, but as being identical with it.

(7) *Balance as implying a "Universal Law of History."* John Bassett Moore once wrote that

> What is called the balance of power is merely a manifestation of the primitive instinct of "self-defense," which tends to produce combinations in all human affairs, national as well as international, and which so often manifests itself in aggression. Not only was the Civil War in the United States the result of a contest over the balance of power but the fact is notorious that certain sections of the country have, during past generations, constantly found themselves in general relations of mutual support because of a continuing common interest in a single question.[18]

The point of departure of these usages is again the assumed inevitable and natural struggle among states for preponderance, and the equally natural resistance to such attempts. Given these two considerations, it follows that as long as they continue in force, there is bound to be a "balance" of states seeking aggrandizement and states opposing that search. In Frederick L. Schuman's version of the balance, there is a tendency for all revisionist states to line up against the ones anxious to conserve given treaties, and in Professor Morgenthau's analysis the "imperialistic" states tend to line up against those defending the status quo, producing a balance in the process.[19] It is often inherent in this

---

[17] Bolingbroke, *op. cit.,* pp. 249, 258, 266, 291; W. T. R. Fox, *The Super Powers,* New York, 1944, pp. 161ff.

[18] J. B. Moore, *International Law and Some Current Illusions,* New York, 1924, p. 310.

[19] H. J. Morgenthau, *Politics Among Nations,* New York, 1948, passim; also F. L. Schuman, *International Politics,* New York, 1941, pp. 281ff.

formulation to consider Europe as a great "confederation" unified by homogeneous morals and religion and tied together by international law. The balance of power struggle, equally, is part of that system and tends toward its preservation by avoiding the hegemony of a single member. And, of course, it is in this formulation that the analogy to the mechanical balance is most frequently found. As Rousseau put it:

> The nations of Europe form among themselves a tacit nation. . . . The actual system of Europe has precisely the degree of solidity which maintains it in a constant state of motion without upsetting it. The balance existing between the power of these diverse members of the European society is more the work of nature than of art. It maintains itself without effort, in such a manner that if it sinks on one side, it reestablishes itself very soon on the other. . . . This system of Europe is maintained by the constant vigilance which observes each disturbance of the balance of power.[20]

Ratzel gave this outlook a geographical orientation by arguing that during the "youth period" of states, a continuous process of expansion and contraction in a given *Raum* takes place, ending in a natural balance between the youthful contenders.[21] Whether in this version or without the benefit of geopolitical notions, the theory is a widely held one, corresponding roughly to what Professor Wright calls the "static balance of power." It was stated in detail by Donnadieu, who claimed that

> "Destiny takes along him who consents and draws along him who refuses!" said Rabelais. The balance of power is one of these necessary forces; in other words, it is the expression of a law in the life of nations.[22]

In the hands of Albert Sorel the universal law version of the balance of power underwent further sophistication. In the first place, Sorel made no claim for the "universality" of the principle, but confined its application to the Europe of the *ancien régime,* during which time politics among sovereign rulers was held to be entirely free from ideological determinants. Furthermore, while he treated balance of power policies as "natural" and largely instinctive, he admitted nevertheless that the practice of balancing was the result of reasoned decisions based on the principle of *raison d'état.* Political action is the result of the desire for "power after power," greed and covetousness. Aggrandizement is the policy motive

---

[20] J. J. Rousseau, *Extrait du project de paix perpetuelle de M. l'abbé de Saint-Pierre,* cited in Donnadieu, *op. cit.,* pp. 9–10.

[21] F. Ratzel, *Politische Geographie,* Munich, 1903, cited in Kaeber, *op. cit.,* p. 4.

[22] Donnadieu, *op. cit.,* p. xx. See also the description of Sir Eyre Crowe in the famous State Paper of 1907, in which the "universal law" approach predominates.

which holds the key to the understanding of international relations. And *raison d'état*

> rules in all situations in which one feels oneself strong enough to follow with impunity the policies suggested by it. It inspires the same thoughts in Vienna and in Berlin. Young rulers and future ministers are taught about it. I read in the *Institutions politiques* of Bielfeld: "In whatever situation a state may find itself, the fundamental principle of *raison d'état* remains unchanged. This principle, accepted by all ancient and modern nations, is that the welfare of the people should always be the supreme law." "The great powers," wrote an Austrian diplomat in 1791, "must only conduct themselves in accordance with *raison d'état*. . . . Interest must win all varieties of resentment, however just they may be."

Something that can be taught to young rulers clearly is not instinctive. Yet Sorel holds that the very excesses of unrestrained and aggressive *raison d'état* doctrines result in their antithesis: moderation, willingness to forego expansion when the prize is small, and a willingness to abide by treaties if no undue sacrifice seems implied. Sorel sums up these restraints in the term "understood interest" (*intérêt bien entendu*), and maintains that if practiced they result in a balance of power:

> The converging of ambitions is the limit to aggrandizement. Since there are no more unclaimed territories in Europe, one state can only enrich itself at the expense of its neighbors. But all the powers agreed in not permitting a single one among them to rise above the others. He who pretends to the role of the lion must see his rivals ally themselves against him. Thus there arises among the great states a sort of society, through common concern: they want to preserve what they possess, gain in proportion to their commitment and forbid each of the associated states to lay down the law to the others.[23]

Balance of power thus comes to mean the instinctive antithesis to the reasoned thesis of *raison d'état*. Unconscious moderation, temporarily, restrains deliberate greed. A general dialectic of power relationships is thus created in which balances of power play a definite part. However, no balance is permanent and is subject to change at a moment's notice. It guarantees neither peace nor law; in fact, it implies war and its own destruction whenever a former counterweight state acquires sufficient power to challenge the very balance which it was called upon to maintain.

(8) *Balance as a "System" and "Guide" to policy-making.* In the formulation of the balance of power as a universal law of history there was an element of instinctive, unconscious, and unplanned behavior

---

[23] A. Sorel, *L'Europe et la Révolution Française*, Paris, 1908, I, pp. 19–20, 30–35.

which would defy any analysis in terms of conscious human motivations. Statesmen were represented as acting in accordance with the prescriptions of the balance of power as if they were the unconscious pawns of some invisible hand, to borrow a phrase from Adam Smith. In the formulation of the balance of power as a system of political organization and guide to policy-making, emphasis is firmly thrown on conscious and deliberate behavior and decision-making.

What is the balance of power as a system and guide? A few short definitions might suggest tentative answers. Thus, Professor Fay says: "It means such a 'just equilibrium' in power among the members of the family of nations as will prevent any of them from becoming sufficiently strong to enforce its will upon the others." [24] Or, again, in the words of Professor Gooch, the balance of power is

> the determination, partly conscious and partly instinctive, to resist by diplomacy or arms the growth of any European state at once so formidable and so actually or so potentially hostile as to threaten our liberties, the security of our shores, the safety of our commerce, or the integrity of our foreign possessions. [25]

Needless to add, this is a particularly British understanding of the balance of power, underlining once more the difficulty—if not the impossibility—of stating the theory in such terms that all governments could subscribe to it at any one time. Both definitions, however, are in very close agreement with some of the classical statements of the nature of the balance of power, understood as a guide to statesmen on how to prevent any other state from acquiring enough power to threaten their state in any way. Thus Fénelon, a moralist with considerable experience in policy-making, said:

> To hinder one's neighbor from becoming too strong is not to do harm; it is to guarantee one's self and one's neighbor from subjection; in a word it is to work for liberty, tranquility, and public safety. Because the aggrandizement of one nation beyond a certain limit changes the general system of all nations connected with it . . . the excessive aggrandizement of one may mean the ruin and subjection of all the other neighbors. . . . This attention to the maintenance of a kind of equality and equilibrium between neighboring states is what assures peace for all. [26]

---

[24] S. B. Fay, *Encyclopedia of the Social Sciences*, article on the balance of power, I, pp. 395–99.

[25] G. P. Gooch. "European Diplomacy Before the War in the Light of the Archives," *International Affairs*, XVIII (1939), p. 78.

[26] Fay, *op. cit.*, p. 396. Stieglitz is to be counted among those in agreement with the guide-and-system theory.

Leagues to preserve the balance of power are then advocated by the learned bishop, but he is careful to specify that they may not be used for offensive purposes. Moreover, the balancing process was to assure that no state was eliminated from the map of Europe, no matter how much it might have to be "limited" to assure the security of its neighbors. No less a thinker than David Hume also understood the balance in this sense. He postulated, first, the existence of a multi-state system, dominated by competition and hostility among the members. Statesmen ever since Thucydides, said Hume, have made good policy when they checked in due time, through alliances and coalition wars, the growth of a state potentially able to absorb them all, and made bad policy when they ignored this guiding principle.[27] It is interesting to note in passing that Hume approved of the balance of power as a guide to "good" policy-making while opposing the mercantilist balance of trade theory, whereas most of the other opponents of mercantilism in his age—e.g., the elder Mirabeau —attacked the balance of power as well.[28] This, in essence, is the formulation given by the majority of publicists to the theory of the balance of power, considered only as a conscious guide to policy-making. It is stated succinctly and incisively by Dupuis:

> The simple instinct of prudence would suffice to suggest the idea of the balance of power; the meditations of statesmen and the lessons of experience have transformed the instinct into a rule of conduct and raised the idea to the dignity of a principle. And in the role of political principle, the balance of power does not only have the advantage of reminding councils of the prudence confirmed by the teachings of the past; it has the merit of opening, during periods of crisis, a field for negotiation and if it cannot dictate the solutions of the conflict, it can prepare the setting for an alliance.[29]

The guide, therefore, merely tells statesmen to prevent the growth of any state which, merely because of its power, is potentially able to absorb or limit their own states. There is a good deal of diplomatic evidence to support this contention, in that some leaders have actually made their decision to go to war on just these grounds. The policy of William III in going to war against France in 1701 is a case in point, as shown by the King's speech to Parliament. And the text of the treaty of peace with

---

27 D. Hume, "On the Balance of Power," *Essays Moral, Political and Literary,* London, 1889, I, pp. 352–53.

28 For a study of the relationship between balance of trade and balance of power theories, cf. K. Pribram, "Die Idee des Gleichgewichts in der älteren nationalökonomischen Theorie," *Zeitschrift für Volkswirtschaft, Sozialpolitik und Verwaltung,* XVII (1908), pp. 1–28; see also Felix Gilbert, "The 'New Diplomacy' of the Eighteenth Century," *World Politics,* IV (October 1951), pp. 1–38.

29 C. Dupuis, *Le principe d'équilibre et le concert européen,* Paris, 1909, pp. 104–5.

Spain, of July 18, 1713, gives expression to the same principle once more.[30] In the anonymous *Free Britain,* attributed to none other than Sir Robert Walpole himself, it is stated that

> Our liberty and our welfare depend on the greatest possible division and on a just balance of power among the princes of Europe: the British nation can and must maintain, and if need be, enclose the powers within the limits in which they find themselves today. She must make alliances with the princes who, for their own preservation, are interested in preventing the aggrandizement of others intending the eventual attack upon Great Britain.[31]

So much for the guide. How does the balance of power then become a system? It stands to reason that if all the states of Europe (or the world) were to base their policies on the prescription of the balance of power, a "system" would come about in the sense that the least movement toward hegemony by one would immediately result in the coalition of the other states into an opposing alliance. The ever-present readiness to do just that and the constant vigilance declared necessary to prevent any one state's hegemony would in themselves produce this system of the balance of power. It is at this point that the theory grows more fanciful. The earlier doctrines, based on the guide-and-system idea, contented themselves with the so-called simple balance. The analogy is that of a pair of scales, and the supposition was that there would be only two major states, with their satellites, in the "system." The idea of a strict physical equilibrium—or slight hegemony—would then apply. Later doctrines, however, introduced the notion of the complex balance, or the analogy of the chandelier. More than two states, plus satellites, were postulated, and the necessity for preserving the freedom of all from the lust for dominance by any one was thought to involve the setting into motion of various weights and counterweights on all sides of the chandelier. It is this system which is closely related to the idea of the "balancer," introduced into the theory by British writers during the seventeenth century and a commonplace in the eighteenth. It implied, of course, the existence of powers sufficiently unconcerned by the merits of whatever the issue of the crisis was to be willing to "add their weight" to whichever side was the weaker, and thus prevent the possible victory—and implied hegemony—of the stronger. The balance of power considered as a guide was the reasoning process at the base of the system.[32]

---

[30] The text of the speech and of the treaty are cited in E. Nys, "La théorie de l'équilibre européen," *Revue de droit international et de législation comparée,* XXV (1893), pp. 47–49.

[31] *Ibid.,* pp. 55–56.

[32] E. de Vattel, *Le doit des gens ou principes de la loi naturelle,* III, pt. 3, pars. 28, 33, 42, 43, 44, 47, 48, 49, 50; Sir R. Phillimore, *Commentaries upon International*

MEANINGS AND THE INTENTIONS OF USERS

The foregoing analysis of verbal applications of the term "balance of power" has resulted in the demonstration of eight more or less distinct meanings and connotations which the term may carry. Of more significance to the application of balance of power terminology in the discussion of international affairs, however, is the use to which these meanings may be put. For just as the emphasis on collective security and Wilsonian liberalism in international relations tends to exclude discussion of the balance of power—either as irrelevant or else as undesirable—for essentially ideological reasons, so can the application of the term by its proponents vary with their ideological, theoretical, and practical preoccupations. An attempt will therefore be made to correlate the application of various usages of the term with the intentions of its users, at least insofar as these intentions may be ascertained from the context of the writings and statements examined. Four areas of intention can thus be distinguished: a purely descriptive intent; a conscious or unconscious propagandistic intent; an intention of using the term as an analytical concept in the development of a theory of international relations; and an intention of using the term as a guide to foreign policy-making.

BALANCE OF POWER AS DESCRIPTION

Forswearing any theoretical or analytical purpose, writers commonly have recourse to the term "balance of power" in discussing international affairs. Current references to the balance of power by journalists and radio commentators most frequently fall into this category. And in most instances the meaning to be conveyed to the audience merely implies "distribution" of power, rather than "balance" in anything like the literal sense. The citations from Bolingbroke, . . . and the statement of Henry Wallace quoted above all meet these criteria. By using the term "balance of power" these writers were merely describing a particular distribution of power. Their intentions then did not carry them into any more ambitious realm.

On other occasions, however, the descriptive use of the term implies more than a mere distribution of power. It may then come to mean "equilibrium" or even "hegemony" or "preponderance" of power, still without implying more than a descriptive intent. It is quite possible that the political motivations of the particular user may make their entrance at this point. Thus Lisola, writing in the seventeenth century, saw in the balance of power the equilibrium between Habsburg and Bourbon inter-

---

Law, London, 1871, I, pp. 468–511. Examples of this usage are found most commonly in the writings of statesmen. They will be cited below.

ests. But he used his description to counsel war on France in order to maintain that very equilibrium. Austrian writers again invoked the balance of power principle during the wars of the Polish and Austrian Succession in order to secure allies against France and Prussia, represented as seeking hegemony. During the preceding century, French writers had used the equilibrium connotation of the term to demand war on Austria. And it might be pointed out parenthetically that during the Seven Years' War British officials frowned on the use of balance of power terms to justify British aid to Prussia, since it was Frederick II who had "disturbed the balance" with his attack on Austria.[33] In all these writings and statements the term "balance of power" is used and abused as a descriptive phrase, connoting the existence or non-existence of equilibrium and the actual or threatened hegemony of some state or alliance. The same easy transition in meaning from "distribution" to "equilibrium" and finally to "hegemony" can sometimes be detected in contemporary references to the balance of power. These usages are rarely kept in their separate compartments. And, when the users' intentions go beyond that of mere description, clarity of thought and purpose may be seriously jeopardized.

Balance of Power as Propaganda and "Ideology"

A precise understanding of the verbal meaning of the term "balance of power" becomes especially important when it is used as a propagandistic slogan or as an ideological phrase, in the Mannheimian sense. The meanings of "balance" as being identical with either "peace" or "war" fall into this category. Obviously, while it might be correct to speak of a state of balance or imbalance *implying* or *engendering* either war or peace, the balance as such cannot logically be equated with conditions which might arise as a consequence of the balance, i.e., war or peace. In the cases in which the authors employed it to mean "peace" or "war," "balance of power" then became no more than a convenient catchword to focus individual aspirations into a generally acceptable mold; and there can be no doubt that at certain times the concept of balance was an extremely popular one, whether it was used for policy-making or not. If used in a patently forced manner, the term becomes indistinguishable from plain propaganda. Of this particular usage some striking examples may be cited.

Thus, the anonymous author of the *Relative State of Great Britain in 1813* saw fit to make the phrase cover the total complex of his social, economic, moral, and political predilections:

---

[33] For examples, see E. Kaeber, *Die Idee des Europäischen Gleichgewichts in der publizistischen Literatur vom 16. bis zur Mitte des 18. Jahrhunderts*, Berlin, 1906, pp. 44–47.

The French revolution being founded in the principle of depraving and reversing the human heart and feeling (as the American Republic is built upon frigid indifference and calculation of gain), it is not difficult to perceive how everything which tended to preserve the bond of sacredness of national contracts, and the reciprocity of benefits and engagements—how history, and memory itself, became objects of hatred and jealousy, and organized assault and hostility—and how the balance of power, in particular, opposed and threatened the views of France, which were to ruin and destroy everything, and the views of America to make profit and percentage upon the ruin and destruction of everything. Nor is it easy to pronounce a juster or more happy panegyric upon that system, than what evidently and immediately results from the forced and unnatural coalition of such powers as these (the very worst extremes of democracy and despotism), and the common interest their leaders conceive themselves to have discovered in extinguishing it.

The depraved ideology of France and the United States seemed here to be identified with the upsetting of the balance of power. And the re-establishment of the balance would be the means to end this deplorable state of morality:

For my part, I shall never blush to confess, that I am able to form no conception of any security in any peace that shall have no guarantees—any effectual guarantee, without a distribution and partition of force, adjusted by political alliance and combination—of any defense or protection for that distribution without a permanent and recognized system of public law, and a real or reputed balance of power amongst the several states it embraces.[34]

This treatment, then, identifies the balance of power with the kind of world conditions, in their totality, which the author desires. The fact that domestic, moral, and ideological factors are haphazardly mixed up with considerations of pure power seems not to have made any difference.

This invocation of the balance of power was no more propagandistic, however, than the use made of it by Friedrich Wilhelm II in the Declaration of Pillnitz, June 25, 1792, which constituted the manifesto of the allied monarchs attacking France:

There was no power interested in maintaining the European balance which could be indifferent when the Kingdom of France, which formed such a considerable weight in that great balance, was delivered for long periods of time to internal agitation and to the

---

[34] Anon., *Considerations on the Relative State of Great Britain in 1813*, London, 1813, pp. 3–4.

horrors of disorder and anarchy, which, so to speak, have nullified its political existence.[35]

But the era of the Revolution and the Empire by no means provided the only examples of this type of application. It enjoyed a renaissance during World War I. Then F. J. Schmidt, for instance, asserted that "Germany has the historical call to realize the idea of the balance of power in all its territorial and maritime consequences."[36] And as detached a scholar as Friedrich Meinecke argued that the peace treaty should establish a "new balance of power" instead of depriving Germany of all her conquests.[37] Nor was the invocation of the balance by Louis XIV much different when he used it to justify the accession of his grandson to the throne of Spain, nor Fleury's use of it when he called upon its absolving force to explain France's attack on the Pragmatic Sanction in 1740.[38]

It is apparent that in all these cases the balance of power was invoked in such a way as to serve as the justification for policies not *ipso facto* related to balancing anything. In some instances it was used to cloak ideological conflicts, in others to sanctify the search for hegemony over Europe, and in still others to "justify" the continued strength and size of a defeated state. The significance of this invocation, then, lies not in any theoretical belief, but in the fact that the users of the term felt so convinced of its popularity as to make its conversion into a symbol of proper policy propagandistically profitable.

Propaganda assumes the dishonest use of facts and the distortion of concepts devised on intellectually sincere grounds. It implies conscious and deliberate falsification.[39] Ideology, as defined by Mannheim, how-

---

[35] Cited in Stieglitz, *op. cit.,* I p. 51. See also the facile use of the doctrine made by Bonald in (1) justifying Napoleonic expansion and (2) asking for a lenient peace in 1815 (Moulinié, *De Bonald,* Paris, 1915, pp. 390-97).

[36] F. J. Schmidt, in *Preussische Jahrbücher,* CLVIII (1914), pp. 1-15; also H. Oncken, *Das alte und das neue Mitteleuropa,* Gotha, 1917, passim.

[37] F. Meinecke, *Probleme des Weltkriegs,* Munich, 1917, p. 134. In his important *Die Idee der Staatsräson in der neueren Geschichte,* in which he claims to be analyzing the doctrine and philosophical meaning of the *raison d'état* idea completely dispassionately, the same argument shows up rather prominently in the last chapter, dressed up in terms of historical necessity.

[38] Jacob, *op. cit.,* pp. 349, 351, 354-55.

[39] My conception of propaganda may be expressed in Leonard W. Doob's definition: "Intentional propaganda is a systematic attempt by an interested individual (or individuals) to control the attitudes of groups of individuals through the use of suggestion and, consequently, to control their actions" (*Propaganda,* New York, 1935, p. 89). It is clear that this postulation does not assume that the propagandist himself accepts the material or shares the attitudes he attempts to disseminate. I cannot accept the definition of propaganda offered by Doob in *Public Opinion and Propa-*

ever, postulates belief in a set of symbols which, even though they may be "false" objectively, still characterize the total myth system of social groups and are essential to the spiritual cohesion of a ruling group which would lose its sense of control if it were conscious of the "real" state of affairs. It is therefore possible to raise the hypothesis that the balance of power may have served such "ideological" purposes. It may have been used to explain policies in terms of natural laws, in terms of moral rightness, or in terms of historical necessity if the symbol chosen to "put it over" was a sufficiently widely accepted one; indeed, if it was a symbol—even a metaphorical one—which the ruling groups themselves tended to accept. In this sense, the term "balance of power" would not serve a strictly propagandistic purpose, since the element of falsification yields to the element of self-deception.[40]

In a remarkable eighteenth-century essay the whole concept of the balance of power was criticized in these very terms. In his *Die Chimäre des Gleichgewichts von Europa,* Justi concluded that the balance of power theory is nothing but the ideological justification adopted by statesmen eager to hide their real motives, motives usually described by the term "aggression." As he put it:

> We regard the dependence of a free state upon another and more powerful state, the latter trying to prevent the former from adopting the proper measures for its happiness, as the greatest misfortune of a people, which should be avoided through the system of the balance of power. Yet such a course idea of universal monarchy which aims at reducing all states to provinces of its own state can scarcely ever be realized; however, the means proposed to avoid it are far more to be feared than the evil itself. If a balance of power were to exist in actuality then no slavery would be as hard, since each state would oppose every other state. Upon each new domestic arrangement, each internal improvement, the other states would be compelled to protest and interfere in order to prevent the first state from growing too powerful because of its domestic perfection. And the mutual dependence of such states would be far worse slavery than dependence upon one powerful neighbor. One state would object to one feature and the second to another feature of the internal improvement, and each state would concern itself more with the domestic business of its neighbors than with its own perfection.

---

ganda (New York, 1948, p. 240), since it seems almost indistinguishable from the more general concept of ideology.

[40] For a masterful analysis of this aspect of the balance of power, see Vagts, *op. cit.,* pp. 88-89, 100ff. I have explored the ideological significance of the concept with respect to European diplomacy in the 1830's in my doctoral dissertation, *Belgium and the Balance of Power,* Columbia University Library.

All this, Justi argues, means that the whole concept is impossible.[41] And again he urges what he considers the real *raison d'être* of the usage, thus, incidentally, coming perilously close to characterizing the balance of power as a purely propagandistic device:

> When a state which has grown more powerful internally is attacked
> . . . in order to weaken it, such action is motivated least of all by
> the balance of power. This would be a war which is waged by the
> several states against the strong state for specific interests, and the
> rules of the balance of power will only be camouflage under which
> these interests are hidden. . . . States, like private persons, are guided
> by nothing but their private interests, real or imaginary, and they are
> far from being guided by a chimerical balance of power. Name one
> state which has participated in a war contrary to its interests or
> without a specific interest, only to maintain the balance of power.[42]

The distinction between the propagandistic and ideological uses is thus a tenuous one. The "camouflage" is ideological only if the actors on the international stage are themselves convinced, to some extent, of the identity of "private interest" with a general need for balancing power *qua* power.

BALANCE OF POWER AS ANALYTICAL CONCEPT

At the opposite pole of the propaganda-oriented application of the term "balance of power" lies the user's intention to employ the term as a tool of analysis. It is in this area of intentions that the term rose to the status of a theory of international relations during the eighteenth and nineteenth centuries, no less than it has in our own era. It is also true, however, that in this area as well as in the other fields of intentions analyzed so far not one but several of the verbal meanings of the term find application. Even as a tool of scholarly analysis the term has been used to mean "power politics," "equilibrium," "hegemony" and, finally, a "universal law" of state conduct.

"The basic principle of the balance of power," wrote Réal de Curban, "is incontestable: the power of one ruler, in the last analysis, is nothing but the ruin and diminution of that of his neighbors, and his power is nothing but the weakness of the others."[43] And in a Hobbesian state of

---

[41] J. H. G. von Justi, *Die Chimäre des Gleichgewichts von Europa*, Altona, 1758, p. 60.

[42] *Ibid.*, p. 65. Albert Sorel's estimate of the invocation of balancing terminology by statesmen is a similar one. Since he denies that balancing policies are deliberately chosen by diplomats and since he urges that only the search for unilateral hegemony motivates policy, he argues in fact that the use of the term by statesmen implies a disguised hankering for superiority and no more (*op. cit.*, p. 34).

[43] Réal de Curban, *op. cit.*, VI, p. 442.

nature which was presupposed to exist among sovereign states no other
conclusion seemed possible. This reasoning has led numerous writers to
equate the balance of power with power politics or *Realpolitik* generally.
The struggle for self-preservation in the state of nature implies the
formation of alliances and mutually antagonistic blocs which in turn
make negotiations in "good faith" a contradiction in terms. Power politics
are the only discernible pattern in which balancing is an inherent process.
As such, it is not separate from but identical with competitive power
struggles. Consequently, in dispassionate analyses of international affairs
the "balance" of power carries no significance other than that usually
associated with "power politics," unrefined by any conception of equilibrium or deliberate balancing measures.[44]

Furthermore, the concept of evenly balanced power, or "equilibrium,"
finds frequent application as a tool of analysis. In the preceding discussion the equilibrium concept found application merely as a descriptive
phrase implying no generalized behavior pattern in international relations. In the present context the reverse is true. Lasswell, in speaking of
the "balancing process," for instance, assumes that under conditions of
expected future violence—domestic as well as international—any increase
in the coercion potential of one power unit will lead to a compensatory
increase in the competing unit or units. Further increases on the part of
one side will always bring corresponding increases on the part of its
competitors, so that in effect a rough equality of power potential will
always prevail, a factor which may make for either open conflict or
induce fear of refraining from hostilities, depending on circumstances, the
nature of the elites in question, and the accuracy of intelligence reports
concerning the degree of "balancing." The analytical application of the
equilibrium-meaning of the balance of power, in short, generalizes the
basic assumption of the absence of international consensus and the consequent inherent presence of conflict into a pattern of balancing.

Carrying the equilibrium-meaning one step further results in the application of the balance of power concept as implying the search for
hegemony. This application again finds its counterpart in the intentions
of detached analysts striving for a generalized understanding of phenomena rather than for description. Spykman, as demonstrated above,
clearly sets forth the assumptions of this approach. His argument is that
the search for power by sovereign states is an end in itself, since conflict—actual or potential—is the only consistent pattern in relations
between state units. While the search for power originally implied the

---

[44] See, e.g., H. N. Brailsford and G. Lowes Dickinson, as quoted in Georg Schwar-
zenberger, *Power Politics,* London, 1940, p. 123, and also the author's own comments,
which also tend to equate power politics with power balance.

desire for self-preservation, a generalized desire for power-seeking over a long period of time converts this process into an end in itself. On this level, the discussion of the balance of power is identical with power politics generally. As in the case of Lasswell's balancing process, however, the generalized process of competitive power-seeking must result in equilibrium if war is avoided—temporarily. But statesmen, as indicated above, seek a margin of safety in superiority of power and not in equality of power. Hence the search for equilibrium in effect is the search for hegemony, and the balance of power as an analytical concept becomes another term for the simultaneous search for preponderance of power by all the sovereign participants. No wonder Spykman exclaims that

> He who plays the balance of power can have no permanent friends. His devotion can be to no specific state but only to balanced power. The ally of today is the enemy of tomorrow. One of the charms of power politics is that it offers no opportunity to grow weary of one's friends. England's reputation as *perfide Albion* is the inevitable result of her preoccupation with the balance of power.[45]

In this refined analysis, the balance of power comes to be considered as a special case—either in its equilibrium or its hegemony connotation—in the general pattern of power politics, though Spykman in the passage just cited again tends to use the two terms interchangeably.

The supreme attempt to use the balance of power as an analytical concept arises in the case of those writers who make the balance the essence of a theory of international relations. It is here that the balance attains the quality of a "law of history," as indeed Rousseau and Donnadieu implied by their very choice of words, and many contemporary writers by their emphasis on the "naturalness" of state behavior in accordance with the dictates of balanced power. The universal law connotation of the balance of power presupposes state conduct in no way different from the assumptions of Spykman and Lasswell. But Professors Morgenthau and Schuman, for instance, in giving the balance of power this extended meaning, go beyond the characterization of equilibrium and hegemony. They develop the thesis that it is inherent in the nature of a multi-state system based on sovereignty to engage in mutually hostile policies, for whatever motives. In this process the search for balanced power, the need to form blocs and counterblocs to prevent the feared attainment of hegemony by one or the other of the participants in the conflict is a natural, if not instinctive, choice of policy. A group of revisionist states always lines up against a group of states devoted to the maintenance of the status quo in such a way that approximate balance results. So general is this pattern that it attains the quality of a historical

---

[45] Spykman, *op. cit.*, pp. 103–4, 121.

law. And the characteristic feature of this law is that it does not necessarily assume a conscious intention on the part of statesmen to "balance power with power" in a sense which would imply the official acceptance of a balance of power theory by governments. Statesmen, to be sure, may be consciously motivated by balancing notions. But, if they are not, the policies which they would most logically adopt would be those consistent with the balance of power. As Professor Morgenthau indicates, if they fail to do so, they do not make "logical" policy and thereby violate historically proven and generalized modes of conduct. The distinctive feature about the balance of power applied as a tool of analysis, then, is its possible separation from the motivations of governments.

BALANCE OF POWER AS PRESCRIPTION

While the analytical application of the term does not imply conscious acceptance of balancing rules by governments, there is a large body of thought—historical and contemporary—which does insist that the balance of power is—or should be—a guiding principle for decision-making on the part of governments. It is this application of the term which makes use of the meaning defined above as "guide-and-system." Once more international relations are pictured, in one version, as being in the Hobbesian state of nature, so that survival dictates the formation of alliances among those states committed to "preserving the balance" against the onslaught of the state(s) allegedly seeking world or regional domination or, as the eighteenth-century writers put it, "universal monarchy." In this sense, the balance is a conscious guide dictating the rules of survival. In another sense, however, the world (or Europe, in the earlier writing) is represented as a "system" of states tied together by mutual interdependence, common institutions, and a common system of law (the law of nations), and the search for hegemony of a single member of this "system" was then represented as an attack upon the whole organic unit.[46] The system was based on the continued independence of all members and their common will to resist the search for hegemony by any one of their number. The balance of power was inherent in the very system itself and also acted as a body of rules dictating the proper policies for preventing the attainment of hegemony, i.e., it acted as a "guide."

That Metternich subscribed in principle and in considerable detail to the theory of the balance of power as a guide to foreign policy-making is

---

[46] The extreme example of this body of thought is represented by Wolff with his concept of the *civitas maxima* and the role of the balance of power in preventing its destruction (*Ius Gentium Methoda Scientifica Pertractantum*, pars. 642–43, 646, 651, *Classics of International Law*, no. 13, 1934). Also Pufendorf, *Ius Naturae et Gentium*. Book VIII, ch. 6, *ibid.*, no. 17, 1934.

beyond any doubt. Consistent with his overall political philosophy of the
value of historically sanctioned social and political traditions, of the need
for preserving what the historical process had created and for protecting
it against the fanaticism and stupidity of misguided men, i.e., the liberals,
Metternich considered the balance of power as another of these time-
hallowed doctrines, and as an international institution vital to the preservation of the total institutional status quo which he so cherished. As he
wrote:

> Politics is the science of the life of the state, on its highest level.
> Since isolated states no longer exist . . . it is the society of states,
> this important condition of the contemporary world, which has to be
> watched carefully. Thus each state, in addition to its particular
> interests, has certain common interests, either with the totality of the
> other states or with certain groups among them. The great axioms of
> political science derive from the understanding of real political
> interests of all states; the guarantee for their existence rests in these
> general interests, whereas particular interests . . . only possess a
> relative and secondary value. History teaches that whenever the
> particular interests of one state are in contradiction with the general
> interest and whenever the latter is neglected or misunderstood, this
> condition . . . is to be regarded as exceptional and pathological.
> . . . The modern world is characterized, in distinction to the old
> world, by a tendency of states to approach one another and to enter
> into the bonds of society in some manner; so that the resulting bond
> rests on the same foundations as the great society which developed in
> the shadow of Christianity. This foundation consists of the command
> of the Book of Books: "Do not do unto others what you would not
> have others do unto you." Applying this basic rule of all human
> associations to the state, the result is reciprocity, politically speak-
> ing, and its effect is . . . : mutual respect and honest conduct. In
> the ancient world, politics sought pure isolation and practiced abso-
> lute egoism, without any control save common sense. . . . Modern
> history, however, shows us the application of the principle of soli-
> darity and the balance of power offers us the drama of the unified
> efforts of several states in restraining the hegemony of a single state
> and limiting the expansion of its influence, and thus forcing it to
> return to public law.[47]

This formulation of international relations in general as necessary and
close rapport between the states of Europe, which he regarded in the then
customary manner as so many atoms in a universe held together by
Christian moral rules and the dictates of international law, and of the

---

[47] Metternich, *Aus Metternichs Nachgelassenen Papieren*, Vienna, 1882, I, pp. 32ff.,
a section entitled, "Maxims on Which the Actions of My Political Career Have Been
Based."

balance of power as the *ad hoc* regulating mechanism of this system, is in almost all respects identical with the formulation of Ancillon, of Castlereagh, of Brougham, and of Gentz. Thus Ancillon, Prussian court chaplain in the 1820's, tutor to Frederick William IV, and State Secretary for Foreign Affairs from 1832 until 1835, argued:

> All forces are similar to the nature of expanding bodies; thus, in the society of large states in which law does not enjoy an external guarantee, we take as our point of departure the possible or even probable misuse of force. What will be the result? Mutual distrust, fear and restlessness, always recurring and always effective. Each state can have no other maxims in its external relations than these: whoever can do us damage through an excessive balance of power in his favor, or through his geographical position, is our natural enemy, but whoever in view of his position and forces is able to harm our enemy, is our natural friend. These simple maxims which the need for self-preservation has given to man, are and have been at all times the anchors on which all of politics rests.[48]

Nor was Castlereagh's understanding of the balance of power much different, even though he indicated that "my real and only object was to create a permanent counterpoise to the power of France in peace as well as in war." The Concert of Europe through its regular conferences was merely to be the consultative mechanism whereby the *ad hoc* balance could be maintained through timely negotiations.[49] However, the likelihood of the guide-and-system version of the balance implying different "rules" for different states is here betrayed.

Gentz's theory of the balance of power was stated in his *Fragmente aus der neusten Geschichte des politischen Gleichgewichts in Europa* (1806), the purpose of which was to give the Austrian and British governments an excuse for unleashing a new war on Napoleon without having been attacked first. Gentz, it might be added, was in the pay of the British cabinet to produce writings of this type. He rejected the arguments that an exact equilibrium is impossible and that power cannot be measured as irrelevant to the system, since all the system requires is eternal vigilance that no state acquires enough power to overawe all of Europe.[50] Also, he

---

[48] Paul Haake, *J. P. F. Ancillon and Kronprinz Friedrich Wilhelm IV. von Preussen*, Munich, 1920, p. 40. Of Ancillon's own works, see his *Ueber den Geist der Staatsverfassungen und dessen Einfluss auf die Gesetzgebung*, Berlin, 1825, pp. 16–19, 314–15, 317–31, and *Tableau des révolutions du système de l'Europe*, Paris, 1806, IV, pp. 5–19.

[49] Sir Charles Webster, *British Diplomacy, 1813–1815*, London, 1921, pp. 62, 218; and Castlereagh's memorandum of October 30, 1814, for Alexander I, cited in Angeberg, *Les traités de Vienne*, Paris, 1864, pp. 399–401.

[50] Gentz, *Fragmente aus der neusten Geschichte des politischen Gleichgewichts in Europa*, St. Petersburg, 1806, pp. 1–8.

thought that the certainty of a strong counterforce being mustered against the hegemony-seeker was a sufficient deterrent and that actual war would usually be unnecessary. And

> Only when one or the other state, with open violence, invented pretexts, or artificially concocted legal titles, undertakes enterprises which, directly or in their inevitable consequences, lead to the enslavement of its weaker neighbors, or to the constant endangering, gradual weakening and eventual demise of its stronger neighbors, only then there will come about a breach of the balance, according to the sound conceptions of the collective interest of a system of states; only then will the several states combine in order to prevent the hegemony of a single state, through a timely contrived counterweight.[51]

Yet Gentz opposed policies of partition and compensation as violating the true conservative character of the theory. Moreover, there could be no such thing as indifference to a given issue, since under the power rules all issues had to be of equal interest to all states in the system.[52] His comments on the right to intervene in the domestic affairs of other states are of the highest interest. Gentz urged that ideological distastes for internal changes elsewhere did not in themselves constitute a ground for balance of power intervention and war. But as soon as such changes had the necessary consequence of upsetting the balance of power, i.e., as soon as the new ideology seemed to suggest the search for hegemony, then the right to intervene existed, as in 1793.[53]

The case of Lord Brougham is a fascinating one for the study of the theory of the balance of power. In his essay on "The Balance of Power," written in 1803, he urged that the balance was the only tenable theory of international relations. He defined it in the same terms as Gentz and Ancillon and added:

> Had it not been for that wholesome jealousy of rival neighbors, which modern politicians have learned to cherish, how many conquests and changes of dominion would have taken place, instead of wars, in which some lives were lost, not perhaps the most valuable in the community, and some superfluous millions were squandered! How many fair portions of the globe might have been deluged in blood, instead of some hundreds of sailors fighting harmlessly on the barren plains of the ocean, and some thousands of soldiers carrying on a scientific and regular and quiet system of warfare in countries set apart for the purpose, and resorted to as the arena where the disputes of nations might be determined.

---

[51] *Ibid.*, pp. 10–14.
[52] *Ibid.*, ch. II.
[53] *Ibid.*, ch. IV.

The old argument of the tacit federation of Europe, the common system of law and morals, and the need for the regulating mechanism of the balance to keep one of the "federated" states from absorbing the others is restated in full.[54] The principle, as well as the detailed application of the theory in its guide-and-system form, were stated by the young Brougham in the classical manner, and with unsurpassed and brief lucidity:

> It is not then in the mere plan for forming offensive or defensive alliances; or in the principles of attacking a neighbor in order to weaken his power, before he has betrayed hostile views; or in the policy of defending a rival, in order to stay, in proper time, the progress of a common enemy; it is not in these simple maxims that the modern system consists. These are indeed the elements, the great and leading parts of the theory; they are the maxims dictated by the plainest and coarsest views of political expediency: but they do not form the whole system; nor does the knowledge of them . . . comprehend an acquaintance with the profounder and more subtle parts of modern policy. The grand and distinguishing feature of the balancing theory, is the systematic form to which it reduces those plain and obvious principles of national conduct; the perpetual attention to foreign affairs which it inculcates; the constant watchfulness which it prescribes over every movement in all parts of the system; the subjection in which it tends to place all national passions and antipathies to the views of remote expediency; the unceasing care which it dictates of national concerns most remotely situated, and apparently unconnected with ourselves; the general union, which it has effected, of all the European powers in one connecting system—obeying certain laws and actuated, for the most part, by a common principle; in fine, as a consequence of the whole, the right of mutual inspection, now universally recognized among civilized states, in the appointment of public envoys and residents [sic]. This is the balancing theory.[55]

Intervention in domestic developments of other states, of course, is legal if the balance of power is really and truly threatened by these changes. The superiority of the balance to all ideological considerations, so plainly stated here, is especially striking. This principle he repeated in his "General Principles of Foreign Policy" (1843) in most emphatic terms:

> But the mere circumstance of our preferring a democratic to an aristocratic or a monarchical to a republican scheme of government, can never afford any good ground for uniting with others who have the same preference, against a community or a league of states, whose views of national polity are of a contrary description.[56]

---

[54] Brougham, *Works*, London, 1872, viii, pp. 4–12.
[55] *Ibid.*, pp. 12–13, 33–38.
[56] *Ibid.*, pp. 70–71, 77, 79–80, 80–83.

Hence the Holy Alliance—or the Western bloc against it after 1832—was not consistent with the rules of the balance. Not only is ideological intervention condemned, but Brougham urged that

> it is the bounden duty of all rulers to discourage sentiments in their subjects leading to national enmities; and when a popular cry arises against any foreign people, a general clamor for war, there is no more sacred duty on the part of the government than to resist such a clamor and keep the peace in spite of it.[57]

In short, any manifestations of public opinion had to be rigorously excluded from policy-making under balancing rules, a sentiment heard more and more frequently in our present epoch.

Whether the balance of power is regarded merely as a set of rules to be applied to the preservation of the state or whether it is expanded into the defensive mechanism of some "system"—and by analogy the United Nations system might today be considered the successor to the European system postulated by the earlier writers—the rules laid down by Gentz and Brougham remain the same. The statesman who is anxious to preserve his state must have recourse to balancing principles in averting the hegemony of his rival. The perusal of the contemporary literature on this subject confirms this conclusion. George F. Kennan's *American Diplomacy* is merely the latest and best-known example of the continuing importance ascribed to balancing rules in international relations. And the fact that the examples cited concerned statesmen conscious of the balance as a motivating force underlines the possible importance of the concept as prescription.

INTENTIONS AND THEIR SIGNIFICANCE TO A THEORY OF INTERNATIONAL RELATIONS

The breakdown of the "balance of power" phrase into a series of eight distinct verbal meanings has now been categorized into four possible applications which these meanings have found in political literature, and perhaps in diplomacy as well. It is not to be inferred that in these classifications there is one which alone is of general value and applicability to the analysis of international relations. This problem is inherent in the inevitably somewhat arbitrary basis of distinction adopted in the foregoing analysis. It is not claimed, of course, that the term "balance of power," in any of its eight possible connotations, is used as propaganda or description in the intentions of any one writer to the exclusion of other possible intended applications. The four categories here established, in short, cannot be regarded as mutually exclusive even in the intentions of

---

[57] *Ibid.*, pp. 91–93, 100–2.

the same writer, analyst, commentator, or statesman.[58] A basic barrier
in communication is created by this apparently facile interchangeability of
meanings and intentions. A theoretical analysis, therefore, cannot proceed
on the basis of identifying one writer with one meaning or one category of
intentions. Each meaning and intention must be considered separately in
terms of the immediate context, even though meanings and intentions
may change as the context changes, either in compliance with the user's
overall scheme or in defiance of his thought. Nevertheless, it is clear that
not all of these categories are of equal relevance to the effort to construct
a theory of international relations. The effort to separate the theoretically
meaningful categories from those which, while important in the total
context of international relations, are based on inadequate logical or conceptual assumptions is one on which a few general observations must be
made.

Thus, the theoretical significance of the descriptive intention may be
open to several alternative interpretations. It may well be argued that as
long as the distribution of power, in general terms, in terms of equilibrium or lack of equilibrium, i.e., the implied hegomony of one camp, is
merely discussed with the intention of *describing* an objective state of
affairs, there can be no question of theoretical implications. A reference
to a "balance" of power in such a context would carry no more general
meaning than the application of such terminology to a summary of the
number of convention delegates pledged to a given presidential aspirant.
And, in fact, it is precisely in such situations that the term is finding a
new lease on life.

It can be argued, however, that even the meaning of "distribution" and
"equilibrium" in an ordinarily descriptive sense may carry with it theoretical implications. If it is desired to establish the general historical
conditions to which the rise of certain institutions can be attributed, for
instance, this meaning of "balance" may acquire a theoretical significance
beyond the scope indicated above. Thus, it may be suggested that modern
international law owes its growth to a "balance" of power—in the sense
of "distribution" avoiding "hegemony"—during its crucial decades and
that without such a "balance" it could not have developed at all, since
the strongest state(s) would have had no interest in its growth.[59] It is in
situations such as these that the user's context acquires tremendous significance, since it may well be that in applying the term in this sense

---

[58] This difficulty may be demonstrated by the perhaps unconscious ease with which
some modern writers present a balance of power picture as *description* and then
readily switch to a *prescriptive* continuation of their discussion, despite the semantic
and logical problems implied in this procedure.

[59] I am indebted for this suggestion to Professor Oliver J. Lissitzyn.

what was intended was not description, but analysis or a correlation between the balance as prescription and its historical consequences.

Applications of balance of power terminology for propagandistic or self-deceptive purposes similarly may be interpreted in several ways. *A priori,* such application could not carry with it a significance to a general theory of international relations, since it is used for intellectually dishonest purposes. It is intended for dissimulation, not clarification, and certainly not as a consistent guide to action. Furthermore, the meanings of "balance" subsumed in this category are in themselves open to considerable logical and conceptual doubts. The usage of the term as connoting peace and stability or war and instability, again, is largely descriptive, or else a pure value judgment of no theoretical significance whatever. The fact that some writers have indulged in this loose terminology merely indicates that the term "balance of power" had tended to become a catch-all to accommodate whatever policies writers wanted to recommend. The frankly propagandistic use of the term is thus merely an extreme species of the same genus.

To a general theory of politics based on Mannheimian concepts of ideology, however, even this category might prove to be of relevance. Should the theory be oriented toward the study of value systems—avowed and tacit—and toward the factors of manipulation of external and internal forces, this area of intentions might acquire some importance. What appears to the student of motivations as dishonesty and self-deception might assume far greater causative significance to a student of psychopathology in international relations.

In the area of concept, of course, the balance of power acquires immediate theoretical significance, deservedly or otherwise. It is deliberately chosen as the major support of a widely accepted method of analyzing intergroup relations. But even here some caution with respect to meanings is necessary. Thus, the usage which speaks of the balance of power in terms indistinguishable from power politics generally should not be given separate consideration, since the application of the phrase here is really misplaced in terms of logical consistency as well as of historical tradition. It would be absolutely correct to consider the balance of power as a refinement of a general system of power politics, should one be postulated, as indeed writers such as Dupuis, Donnadieu, Gentz, and Brougham did consider it. But the essential distinction between policies of power for the sake of power—unrefined by any thought of balancing some state's power with some other state's—and the balance of power as defined by Fay, Gooch, and Fénelon should still be maintained. History is full of examples of plain power policies, unqualified by balance notions.

It appears, however, that a theory of international relations which does not insist on the necessity of demonstrating general laws of conduct in terms of actual motivations leaves itself open to attack on grounds of lack of comprehensiveness. And it is this factor which has been responsible for a great deal of the skepticism with which the universal law version of the balance of power as an analytical concept has been treated ever since Justi. The treatment of the balance of power as prescription, in the sense of the guide-and-system connotation, therefore, acquires its theoretical significance in this context. The balancing of power is considered as the primary motivation of governments in this approach and, as Brougham clearly showed, the realization of this motivation assumes the subordination of all other possible policy motivations in international politics, at least insofar as they are inconsistent with the demands of balanced power. To a theory of international relations which relies on demonstrable motivations among policy-makers, therefore, the balance of power as prescription must be a fundamental point of departure.

SECTION THREE:

Alliances

35. THE NATURE OF ALLIANCES

Robert E. Osgood

1. WHY ALLIANCES?

ALLIANCES ARE an integral part of international politics. They are one of the primary means by which states seek the co-operation of other states in order to enhance their power to protect and advance their interests. This instrument of co-operation is so pervasive that every state must have an alliance policy, even if its purpose is only to avoid alliances.

The subject of this analysis, however, is broader than alliances. Alliances are only one kind of commitment by which states enhance their power. Moreover, there are many kinds of alliances, and alliances serve a variety of purposes. One cannot properly assess the value and the prospects of alliances without examining the alternatives to alliances and distinguishing between the various kinds of alliances.

In this study an alliance is defined as a formal agreement that pledges states to co-operate in using their military resources against a specific state or states and usually obligates one or more of the signatories to

From *Alliances and American Foreign Policy*, by Robert E. Osgood. Copyright © 1968 by The Johns Hopkins Press. Reprinted by permission of the publisher.

ROBERT E. OSGOOD (1921–   ) Professor, The School for Advanced International Studies, Johns Hopkins University; Director of the Washington Center of Foreign Policy Research. Author of *America and the World: From the Truman Doctrine to Vietnam* (Baltimore: Johns Hopkins Press, 1970); *Force, Order and Justice* (Baltimore: Johns Hopkins Press, 1967). Co-author, *NATO: The Entangling Alliance* (Chicago: University of Chicago Press, 1962); *Limited War: The Challenge to American Strategy* (Chicago: University of Chicago Press, 1957).

use force, or to consider (unilaterally or in consultation with allies) the use of force, in specified circumstances. It differs in principle from a "collective security" agreement. Strictly speaking, such an agreement obligates its members to abstain from recourse to violence against one another and to participate collectively in suppressing the unlawful use of force by any member. It may also obligate its members to resist aggression by a non-member against any of them, but what distinguishes it from a mere collective defense agreement is that it presupposes a general interest on the part of all its members in opposing aggression by any of them and entails procedures for the peaceful settlement of disputes among the members.

A defensive alliance presupposes only a common interest in opposing threats from specific states or groups outside the alliance and does not necessarily or usually entail provisions for settling disputes among its members. An offensive alliance aims at forcibly changing the international status quo, territorially or otherwise, to increase the assets of its members.

A defensive alliance may also be a local or regional collective security agreement. The OAS, for example, is both. Alliances, although ostensibly or actually directed against an external threat, may additionally or even primarily be intended to restrain a member, limit its options, support its government against an internal threat, or control its foreign policy in some fashion. In this respect, many alliances have actually been as much concerned as a collective security agreement would be with organizing relations between allies, although national sensitivities may have counseled against making such concern explicit or public. The internal concern of alliances tends to increase with their duration and with the diminished perception of an external threat.

Alliances commonly reflect more than a single, explicit, and identical interest between members. Allies may wish to support a variety of interests that include merely complementary or parallel interests and even divergent ones. Some of these interests may be specified in the agreement, but some are more prudently left unspecified, whether they are mutual or not. In any case, the full substance and significance of an alliance is seldom revealed in the formal contract or treaty for military co-operation, any more than the essence of marriage is revealed in the marriage certificate. The contract is simply an attempt to make more precise and binding a particular obligation or relationship between states, which is part of a continually changing network of interests and sentiments. An alliance, therefore, reflects a latent war community, based on general co-operation that goes beyond formal provisions and that the signatories must continually cultivate in order to preserve mutual confidence in each other's fidelity to specified obligations.

As a formal contract for military co-operation, however, an alliance may be difficult to distinguish from other kinds of military contracts such as military subsidies, military assistance agreements, or military base agreements. Most alliances specify (if only in a general phrase) the contingencies under which force will or will not be used by the members and against whom it will be used, but they may be worded so broadly that these particulars can only be inferred. Conversely, other kinds of military contracts may contain explicit political provisions concerning the use of weapons and facilities. In any case, like alliances, they are based on definite understandings and expectations (whether shared by both partners or not) about the purposes and circumstances of the specified military co-operation.

Even in the absence of formal contracts for military co-operation, unilateral declarations of intentions can go far to commit states to the use of force in behalf of other states. Such declarations are particularly important now that the communication of military intentions for the sake of deterrence plays such a prominent role in international politics. Their importance is indicated by their extensive use to reinforce and refine formal reciprocal commitments.

But military commitments need not depend even on unilateral declarations. They are often established and conveyed indirectly by countless official and unofficial words and actions, creating understandings and expectations that are no less significant for being implicit. These understandings and expectations are the substance of alignments of power and interest, and alliances and other explicit commitments would be useless without them.

Why, then, do states make alliances? Generally, because alliances are the most binding obligations they can make to stabilize the configurations of power that affect their vital interests. Alliances add precision and specificity to informal or tacit alignments.

More than that, the fact that alliances are *reciprocal* and *formal* agreements increases the obligation of signatories to carry out specified commitments and co-operation. The ceremony and solemnity accompanying the formation of an alliance signify that sovereign states have surrendered important aspects of their freedom of action and obligated themselves to an interdependent relationship.

Moreover, the obligation of alliance relates directly to the response of signatories to contingencies that call for a possible resort to war. Alliances impinge more fundamentally upon the vital interests of nations and more broadly upon the whole range of their foreign policies than agreements designed merely to provide for the use of goods and facilities. For this reason alliances are also more likely to provoke rivals and adversaries and lead to countervailing combinations, which may further limit the political options and enhance the interdependence of allies.

The political significance of alliances is all the greater in this era of popular (including undemocratic) governments because alliances generally presuppose national or ideological affinities that go beyond the matter-of-fact expediencies involved in more restricted contracts.

Thus, whatever its benefits, an alliance tends to cost more than other kinds of military commitments because it limits a member's political options and freedom of action more. For this reason the signatories of an alliance feel entitled to continual assurance of each other's fidelity and their own net benefit. Consequently, an alliance of some duration encourages further claims upon its members and tends to require repeated regeneration through adjustments of their liabilities and assets. Lacking recourse to supranational instrumentalities to enforce an obligation that could involve their very survival as nations, states must rely on diplomatic co-operation against an adversary and on other manifestations of good faith and common interest. These by-products of alliance may entangle states in each other's affairs to an extent that is not always easy to anticipate when an alliance is formed.

As an investment in future returns of national security and welfare, an alliance is apt to be more open-ended and consequential than other kinds of military contracts. Therefore, although alliances are a pervasive element of international politics, the capacity and incentive for states to engage in alliance are far from universal. Relatively few states have the resources, the internal cohesion, or the coherence of national interests to become effective allies. Some states that will freely seek and accept military assistance or base agreements may regard even the most limited alliance as an unwise political entanglement.

2. THE FUNCTIONS OF ALLIANCES

There are four principal functions of alliances, and they are not necessarily mutually exclusive: accretion of external power, internal security, restraint of allies, and international order.

The accretion of power entails increasing the military power of allies by combining resources and eliciting positive co-operation. This has been the basic and the most common function of alliances. The ultimate purpose of accretion is to enhance the relative power of one or more allies against another state or states for defensive or offensive ends (although some states, especially the smaller ones, may want power largely in the form of status).

Internal security is sometimes a more important function of alliance for a weak state than accretion of its external power. In recognition of the international significance of internal threats and developments, which are often supported covertly from outside, alliances may be intended principally to enhance the security or stability of an ally's government or regime, often by legitimizing material assistance or military intervention against internal opposition. This purpose is usually not made explicit, however, since intervention in the domestic affairs of another state, even at that state's invitation, has acquired a stigma in the age of popular national governments.

Next to accretion, the most prominent function of alliances has been to restrain and control allies, particularly in order to safeguard one ally against actions of another that might endanger its security or otherwise jeopardize its interests. This function may be accomplished directly by pledges of nonintervention or by other reassurances that one ally will not contravene the interests of another, or it may be the by-product of commitments that limit an ally's freedom of action and provide its partner with access to, and influence upon, its government.

International order is the broadest and the least attainable function of an alliance. An alliance may aim to preserve harmony among its members and establish an international order—that is, a stable, predictable, and safe pattern of international politics—within an area of common concern. In its ultimate form, this function of an alliance becomes collective security. In different ways, the Quadruple Alliance after the Napoleonic Wars and the OAS have exercised this function of maintaining order. Before the onset of the cold war, the United States expected the Big Three, as the core of the United Nations, to be guarantors of a new world order. Some people believe that NATO has served indirectly as a framework for a new Western European order or even an Atlantic Community.

3. THE DETERMINANTS OF ALLIANCES

Among the numerous factors that may affect the creation, continuation, or decline of alliances in various parts of the world, several "determinants" (in the nondeterministic sense) seem particularly important. These determinants also affect the characteristics of alliances and the nature of their functions, but they are principally relevant to the elementary questions of the existence or nonexistence, utility or disutility, and vitality or impotence of alliances. They are:

The pattern of conflicting and converging interests. If states have no interests that they need to support by military power against other states, they lack sufficient incentives to form alliances. If two or more states feel no need for each other's assistance in improving their military capacity to protect or advance their interests against other states, an alliance is not likely to be created, and an existing alliance is likely to erode.

Even if mutual military needs exist, the creation or maintenance of an alliance often requires a convergence of interests that goes beyond a common interest in security. Most notably, there must be sufficient affinity and harmony of policies. The importance of this convergence is directly proportionate to the comprehensiveness and mutuality of the alliance's obligations and to the duration of the alliance; it is inversely proportionate to the intensity of the security threat.

In the case of existing or prospective alliances in which interallied control or order is an important function, the urgency of a commonly felt threat to security may be less determinative, but then the pattern of conflicting as well as converging interests among allies becomes crucial.

The distribution of military power. The formation and preservation of an alliance depends on the military capacity of states as well as their political incentive to co-operate militarily (even though one state may only provide bases and facilities or promise to remain neutral). The capacity of states to help each other depends on the relationship of their concerted power to the power of potential adversaries.

The interaction of this distribution of power with the pattern of interests among states affects not only the desirability and feasibility of alliances but also the characteristics of alliances and the nature of alliance policies. For example, it establishes the polarity of power, or, more specifically, the number of states that are engaged in a dominant international political conflict, are projecting decisive military power, and are undertaking independent military commitments. Whether there are two, or many, "poles of power," has many implications for alliances, some of which we shall be considering.[1]

The changing distribution of power between an alliance and its opponents may affect the cohesion of an alliance. For example, adverse changes in the external distribution of power may create dissatisfaction with the distribution within an alliance. Such dissatisfaction and the effort to overcome it may change alliance policies and even alliance functions.

Alliance capability. Even if the preceding determinants should support the creation or maintenance of an alliance, the states that are concerned may lack certain minimum military and political prerequisites of alliance. Most important among these prerequisites are: (a) enough internal stability, executive authority, and economic strength, along with a sufficiently coherent and predictable foreign policy, to enable a state to be a reliable collaborator and (b) adequate capacity of a state to dispose its military power effectively for the benefit of an ally. (Again, the capacity of one state may be confined to a relatively passive role.)

Alliance-mindedness. Related to the preceding determinant, and also of special significance for the future of alliances among the small and newer states in the Third World, is the subjective attitude of governments toward alliances. For example, some small, recently independent states are averse to alliances with the chief protagonists of the cold war. The

---

[1] Reference to poles of power may involve an awkward geometrical analogy, but common use of the concepts of bipolarity and multipolarity in discussions of international politics has nevertheless established this analogy.

subjective inclination or disinclination to enter alliances may be closely related to considerations of expediency; yet it goes beyond sheer reasoned calculation of security requirements and reflects hopes, suspicions, and ideals that are deeply rooted in the national culture and experience. In America's period of physical invulnerability and political insulation, its high-principled denigration of alliances was as important as its glorification of them in the cold war.

These determinants should be considered as a whole because they reinforce, qualify, or offset each other. None of them is sufficient by itself to account for the past, present, or future of alliances. The first two determinants, however, are particularly important.

4. THE EVOLUTION OF ALLIANCES

All the functions and determinants of alliances that I have cited apply to contemporary alliances, but the context and methods of application have changed throughout modern history as basic changes occurred in the military and political environment. One way of comprehending these changes is to note the shifts of emphasis among several contrasting types of alliances: between offensive (or revisionist) and defensive (or status quo), wartime and peacetime, bilateral and multilateral, guarantee and mutual assistance, institutionalized and noninstitutionalized alliances. The distinctions among them should be apparent in the brief description of the evolution of alliances that follows.

In the eighteenth century, alliances were the primary means by which states tried to improve their military positions, since the strength of their armed forces was relatively fixed. The typical alliance was a bilateral agreement, or several interlocking bilateral agreements, made during a war or in anticipation of war, after which it was terminated or became inoperative. It usually involved one or several of the following kinds of commitments: a subsidy to support another state's troops; a guarantee to fight on the side of another state (often with a specific number of troops) under stated circumstances; a pledge of nonintervention or mutual abstention from war in the event that one or both of the signatories should become engaged in war with other states; or a division of the territorial and other spoils of war.

Before the last part of the nineteenth century, alliances entailed no extensive military preparations or co-ordination. The undeveloped state of technology, the limited economic capacity of states to carry on war, and the small scale of warfare made such arrangements infeasible and unnecessary. Moreover, states had few of the inhibitions against going to war that arose later when modern war revealed its awesome potential for civil destruction, and they lacked the need and the capacity to sustain alliances as peacetime instruments of military deterrence. War was not yet so terrifying as to create this need and capacity. It was a more or less normal recourse.

Consequently, although there were a few multilateral defensive alliances of long duration, there were scores of offensive alliances—chiefly bilateral —that were intended to acquire territory by means of war. Both offensive and defensive alliances aimed as often at restraining an ally by limiting his political options and deflecting him from an opposing alliance as they did at aggregating military power. The ideal was to keep alliances flexible and commitments limited. Toward this end secret alliances and secret clauses in published alliances were commonly arranged, not only to conceal aggressive designs, but also to increase diplomatic options by making deals with other states without giving offense to allies.

The eighteenth and the first half of the nineteenth centuries were notable for the large number of alliances that were formed and unformed; but a more significant feature of alliances at that time was their limited and flexible nature, which enabled them to adjust readily to shifting interests with little regard for the later constraints of sentiment and ideology or the imperatives of aggregating power in peacetime. The flexibility and secrecy of alliances created a good deal of diplomatic turmoil, but, because there was a fairly equal division of power among the several major states of Europe, these qualities helped to sustain a working equilibrium that restrained and moderated ambitions and acquisitions and kept any single state or coalition of states from dominating the others. The politics of alliances were punctuated by frequent wars, but the limited scale and destructiveness of warfare made it a tolerable instrument for maintaining an equilibrium.

The Napoleonic Wars revealed the new scope, intensity, and dynamism that war could attain when based on the mobilization of manpower and popular enthusiasm. This revelation compelled the European states to combine in a grand coalition to defeat Napoleon's bid for hegemony, just as they had combined against Louis XIV and earlier aspirants to hegemony. This time, however, a wartime alliance became a novel peacetime coalition. In 1815 the victors formed the Concept of Europe, which combined the eighteenth century conception of equilibrium (insofar as the territorial-political settlements and the Quadruple Alliance were aimed at checking France) with the new conception of a multilateral combination of states pledged to concert their power and to consult among themselves in order to preserve the international order against further liberal and nationalist revolutions as well as against divisions among themselves. Therefore the Concert might be called the first modern experiment to form an organization for international order—a forerunner of the League of Nations and the United Nations.

The Concert of Europe was undermined by differing national interests, especially by Britain's refusal to join in suppressing revolutions. After

1822, when the British left the Quadruple Alliance, nothing remained of the Concert except the habit of consultation during crises. International politics returned to flexible, limited, and mostly offensive alliances in a multipolar international system. Taking advantage of the fragmented structure of power, Bismarck acquired territory at the expense of Denmark and Austria, and he rounded out Germany's boundaries with a quick victory over France in 1871. He shored up his accomplishments with a complicated network of bilateral and trilateral alliances designed to keep power fragmented and to prevent combinations that could revise the status quo by setting up balanced antagonisms. Primarily his alliances were intended to limit the options of allies while keeping Germany's commitments to them equally limited.

Yet Bismarck actually helped to undermine his own system of alliances and to set the stage for a different kind of alliance system. The suddenness and decisiveness of Prussia's victories demonstrated the efficacy of its continuing peacetime military preparations, particularly the conscription system, the use of railroads, and the professional planning and direction of war under a general staff. To withstand such an assault, a state would have to be as well-prepared during peacetime as during wartime. Furthermore, military preparedness would require advance arrangements for the co-operation of other states and the co-ordination of military plans and operations. (The French defeat was partly due to France's mistaken calculation that she could acquire allies after war broke out.) The dramatic development in the last quarter of the nineteenth century of the technological and economic capacity of major states to advance their military positions by quantitative and qualititive arms increases indicated that the internal development of military capacity might replace shifting alliances as the dynamic element of power.

In these circumstances Bismarck's alliance system led to counteralliances that, under the growing pressure of military preparedness through arms races, tended to polarize international conflict between two opposing coalitions, the Triple Alliance and the Triple Entente. These two alliances were far from being tightly knit diplomatically, and they were only partially co-ordinated militarily by military conventions and staff conversations. Nevertheless, they provided the political frameworks within which military commitments were consolidated; and the consolidation of military commitments in turn tightened the alliances. Thus alliances evolved from a means of fragmenting military power to a means of aggregating it.

The consolidation of defensive alliances before World War I, combined with the build-up of military power, made states more susceptible to being triggered into war by an ally (as Austria's war against Serbia entangled Germany). This consolidation encouraged a chain reaction of involvement, once war began, and practically guaranteed that any war

involving one ally would become a general war. Nevertheless, if states
had been primarily concerned with military deterrence rather than simply
with preparing to fight, and if they had not permitted military plans
(especially those for total mobilization) to take precedence over diplomatic opportunities to accommodate disputes short of war, the polarization of alliances need not have been incompatible with the peace and
security of all. In fact these were not primarily deterrent alliances but
rather alliances formed in anticipation of war. Unfortunately, statesmen
deferred to their general staffs, who were absorbed in preparing maximum
offensive striking power for a war that they expected to be as short and
decisive as the Franco-Prussian War.

Contrary to prevailing expectations, World War I turned out to be a
devastating war of attrition, and modern firepower chewed up the manpower and resources of Europe. This grim surprise led to a widespread reaction in the victorious countries against alliances, which were regarded as
one of the principal causes of the war. Woodrow Wilson caught the popular
imagination by proposing an "association" of power, in opposition to the
discredited balance of power system. According to his conception of the
League of Nations, all states would be organized against aggression from
any quarter. He expected the chief deterrent to aggression to be the
power of world opinion rather than the threat of force. Other American
proponents of the League idea thought the United States should concert
its power with that of Britain and France to preserve a new postwar
order. However, it is doubtful that the nation as a whole was prepared
to participate in power politics to the extent required of a major ally, for
Americans still retained the sense of physical security that underlay their
isolationist tradition. Until they became convinced by America's involvement in World War II and the onset of the cold war that aggression
abroad impinged directly upon American security, they would not enter
a peacetime alliance.

The ascent of Hitler's Germany showed that a peacetime deterrent
coalition, whatever its effects in other circumstances might be, was essential to peace and order in the face of the most dangerous bid for hegemony since Napoleon. Unfortunately, the major democratic countries failed
to form such a coalition. Although Wilsonian collective security would
have been unworkable as a universal supranational order, even if the
United States had joined the League, this ideal served as an excuse for
avoiding an alliance, especially for Britain, which turned down France's
bid for a defensive alliance against Germany. Yet World War II led the
major democratic states to draw a lesson from this interwar experience
that became the psychological foundation of America's postwar system
of deterrent alliances. This system came to dominate the postwar history
of alliances.

In the cold war, alliances have been as important in international politics as in any other period of history. But among the advanced states several developments have reduced their flexibility (but, by the same token, enhanced their stability). Their primarily deterrent function, the inhibitions against major states going to war in the nuclear age, the increased importance of peacetime military forces, the sensitivity of governments to public sentiment and ideological positions, the persistence of a dominant international conflict and structure of power that have been essentially bipolar—all these developments have tended to restrict the number of alliances and the frequency of shifts of alliance among major states. At the same time, the emergence of many new states in previously colonial and politically inactive areas has meant that the great majority of states lack the basic external and internal prerequisites for engaging in alliances. One consequence of these new constraints on alliances is that other forms of military commitments have come to play a proportionately greater role in international politics. Another is that intra-alliance functions have assumed greater importance.

36.   NONALIGNMENT

Leo Mates

I

NONALIGNMENT emerged and developed in the years of the dominant bipolar pattern of great-power relations. It was a product of the rising tensions of the cold war and a reaction against the alignments formed at the end of the Second World War, when the split between East and West converted allies into rivals and then into enemies. It was the result of the desire to stay out of the developing conflict and have no part in the new alliances which later formalized the postwar division of

Reprinted by permission from *Foreign Affairs* (April 1970), 525–534. Copyright © by the Council on Foreign Relations.

LEO MATES (1911–   ) Director, Institute of International Politics and Economics, Belgrade, Yugoslavia; Former Yugoslav Ambassador to the United States and to the United Nations; Former Secretary General to the President of Yugoslavia and Undersecretary of State for Foreign Affairs. Co-editor of *Joint Business Ventures of Yugoslav Enterprises and Foreign Firms* (South Hackensack, N.J.: Fred B. Rothman and Company, 1968).

the world. This desire was prompted not only by lack of affinity for the causes of the split, but also by the determination to preserve as much freedom of behavior in international relations as possible.

This attitude (which came to be termed nonalignment much later) reflected aspirations toward the greatest possible measure of independence, not only in international relations but even more in internal developments. From the very beginning the postwar period was characterized everywhere by an intense urge toward accelerated economic development. This craving was particularly strong in countries which, when they reëmerged on the world scene as independent nations, had found themselves far behind those which were more industrially developed.

Unlike the first years of the past decade, the later sixties was a period in which coöperation among the nonaligned was at a low ebb even in matters connected with their own economic problems. In 1967 and 1968 a revival took place in connection with the second United Nations Conference on Trade and Development (UNCTAD) in New Delhi. Efforts were made, too, to plan for a third conference of the nonaligned as a sequel to the Bandung meeting in 1955 and the Cairo gathering in 1964.

Throughout the sixties the pattern of international relations changed profoundly. Its most significant aspects were the substantial lessening of tensions between the two superpowers and a loosening of ties within the two alliances. Though antagonism and rivalry between the two major powers remained, in practical matters they developed a better understanding of their problems. They recognized their mutual overkill capacity and on this recognition there developed a new modus vivendi. Indeed, they gradually became partners in a peculiar and quite unprecedented relationship. It appeared that their exalted position and the growth in their material strength, especially their military striking power, gave them an opportunity to preside over the affairs of mankind—provided they could work out an acceptable formula of coöperation.

But this trend, generally described as détente, did not bring about a general easing of tensions. Rather than opening an era of harmony and tranquility, it has been marked by a growth of disturbances, conflicts and upheavals, particularly in the third world. The major powers became entangled once again in conflicts and tense situations on all continents. But even when they faced each other as opponents, they never permitted themselves to be provoked into a degree of hostility comparable to the confrontation in the war in Korea in the early fifties. Moreover, they had to face new situations as they arose without the backing of their allies. In the war in Vietnam, the United States lacked the moral support and troop contributions from its allies which it had had in the war in Korea. The Soviet Union had to face China without the unwavering assistance of its allies in the Warsaw Pact.

The ability of the superpowers to influence the behavior of other and much less powerful states did not grow with the increasing superiority of their military power. Colonial empires crumbled at a time when the metropolitan powers had far greater material superiority than when they were establishing their empires through conquest. Moreover, a determination to strive for emancipation increased even among peoples who had not hitherto shown an inclination toward militancy.

It was in these general circumstances that a third power—China—started its ascent and began to seek recognition as a major world leader. China's challenge started with a split and confrontation within the Eastern bloc, in part due to the decline in cohesion in the bloc which accompanied the East-West détente, in part an escalation of a long-standing rivalry between Russia and China, and in part an expression of the ancient ambitions of a country which once considered itself the central power of the world. In any case, the strife has now intensified to the point where a reconciliation, in the sense of China's return to the fold under Soviet hegemony, appears impossible.

China's conflict with the U.S.S.R. was marked by acrimonious invective and hostility, yet at the same time it implied a recognition of affinity. The exaggerated accusation of collusion with "American imperialism" would have made no sense except on the assumption that the Soviet Union was ideologically related to Peking. Obviously the accusation was made in the hope it would create political and psychological difficulties for the U.S.S.R. in its pursuit of a rapprochement with the United States.

II

The emergence of China as an independent and undoubtedly major power made it even more difficult for the nonaligned countries to adjust to the great changes introduced by the détente and the ensuing local and regional disturbances. All earlier hopes of the third world proved greatly exaggerated if not altogether erroneous. The détente brought neither more stability and security for the less developed and militarily weak nonaligned countries nor economic aid in larger quantities. The position of these in the world market became still more unfavorable. Moreover, China, the major new power, had risen from the ranks of the less developed countries; she had been a partner in the first efforts to rally the underprivileged peoples in Bandung in 1955 under the banner of Afro-Asian coöperation, primarily with the aim of improving the lot of the new countries both politically and economically. Now China had, in a sense, defected from the group of nonaligned nations.

The conference of the leaders of the nonaligned countries in Cairo in 1964 demonstrated the internal differences provoked by these new circumstances. The divergencies at Cairo had a dramatic follow-up at the end of the year when Indonesia, one of the "radicals" at Cairo, temporarily abandoned nonalignment and left the United Nations. However, the consequences predicted in Djakarta and Peking, *i.e.* the breaking up of the nonaligned group and the collapse of the United Nations, did not occur; nor did the idea of a new international organization under the leadership of Peking and with headquarters in Indonesia prove more than a dream. This was, nevertheless, the most extreme crisis the nonaligned group had yet undergone.

It is important to establish whether or not this crisis, which was felt for years after the debates in Cairo, resulted from the disappearance of the raison d'être of nonalignment or because of difficulties of a temporary nature. As already stated, critics have always thought that nonalignment had no prospect because of its insistence on standing aloof from the general trend of alignment around the major powers. In fact, the alliances proved to be less attractive to outside states than was at first believed. There have been defections from the ranks of the nonaligned but not to either bloc. Moreover, the overwhelming majority of new states that attained independence in the sixties, like those in the fifties, supported the nonaligned group.

However, the East-West détente brought hesitation and discord into the camp of nonaligned countries exactly at a time when the cohesion among them should have increased. They themselves were as surprised as the rest of the world to observe signs of disintegration following the reduction in tensions between the two blocs. This unexpected result provoked a new definition of the alleged impracticability of nonalignment. It was stated that the end of the cold war would remove the need for any nation to be nonaligned since no rigid alignment would be possible after the loosening of ties within the two blocs.

But actually the détente did not develop along expected lines; it caused no general relaxation of tensions. Furthermore, the nonaligned did not abandon their sense of belonging to a distinct category of states; nonalignment remained alive as an article of faith, as the expression of identification with a separate and distinct position in international relations. This was best exemplified by the renewal of activity among the nonaligned countries in 1969. The crisis was not characterized by the loss of a sense of belonging. Rather it was a crisis of inactivity caused by frustration and by the search for a line of action which would promise results. It was not a decline in the will to coöperate.

The emphasis on staying out of cold-war alliances, the literal interpretation of the word "nonalignment," had led to the continued insistence that the nonaligned countries act as intermediaries between the two sides even when this was no longer necessary. It led to the insistence on the need to abolish the blocs at a time when the two alliances were neither the main cause of tension nor a threat to the independence and welfare of the less developed countries. Most of the statesmen of the nonaligned countries, however, did not pay enough attention to the shifts in the world situation to realize this.

The one attempt to explain the changes taking place had no decisive impact on the policies of the group as a whole. It was a statement made by President Tito of Yugoslavia before the plenary meeting of the General Assembly of the United Nations in New York in October 1963. The passage referring to these problems is rather general but still sufficiently clear to show an understanding of the changing circumstances. He emphasized that "nonalignment is thus changing, both in quantitative and in qualitative terms, and is transforming itself into a general movement for peace. . . ." Tito even went so far as to suggest that the very term "nonalignment" was being "overcome by new and positive developments in international relations." He was aware that "we stand at a historical crossroads." This did not mean abandoning nonalignment but rather adjusting the concept to the new conditions that prevailed.

For despite the changes in the world power structure, the nonaligned countries had good reason to continue to feel that they were a separate species among nations. They were no longer needed as the promoters of the détente; indeed they suffered from its becoming a reality, and were frequently the battleground of new clashes. India had a confrontation with China on the mountain ranges of the Himalayas and a second war over Kashmir; Egypt had two outbreaks of war with Israel; Ghana and Indonesia were shaken by coups d'état; and Sukarno and Nkrumah, two of the distinguished leaders of nonalignment, were deposed. The intervention in Vietnam, which continued over long years, as well as the interventions in the Dominican Republic and Czechoslovakia, were additional signs that the nonaligned could not assume the role of a third party but had to reorient their line of action. They could no longer blame the blocs or cold-war tensions for the insecurity of small nations.

Moreover, the appearance of China on the stage introduced another complicating factor. The comparatively simple pattern of the cold war made understanding and co-ördination among the nonaligned relatively easy. In the new situation there was no such certainty. For instance, when the nonaligned launched a campaign to stop the war in Vietnam, it gathered little momentum. Only 17 countries signed the letter of April 1965, sent to the governments of the United States, the Soviet Union, China, France, Britain and to all parties in Vietnam. The situation was no longer so clearly defined as it had been during the cold war. One of the disorienting elements was the divergent assessment of the role and position of China. Politically it was considered a potential ally of the third world by some of the nonaligned, while others saw in it another disturbing element for domination in the world.

China, of course, did not have the military capacity to threaten either of the two thermonuclear superpowers, but it could and did successfully defy both of them. The superpowers themselves, though for different reasons, were not able to use their tremendous striking forces in open military conflict. Thus, a new pattern came to replace the earlier bipolar pattern. And other nations, allies of the big powers, nonaligned countries, or those living in the shadow of power, formed a background of considerable significance to the new triangular constellation. The divergence in the ranks of the nonaligned grew substantially; and this was particularly felt at the time of the second nonaligned summit in the fall of 1964, when China tried to outmanœuvre the nonaligned by efforts to convene a second Afro-Asian conference in Algeria.

The influence of China in the third world has since dropped substantially. But the triangularity of the pattern of power politics has remained an important element—even during those years of the Cultural Revolution when China turned in upon itself. For the nonaligned, it became increasingly difficult to play the role of moderator or mediator; such a role in the triangular pattern proved beyond the diplomatic skills of the nonaligned and may well be altogether impossible.

The change also affected the position of the major powers. They experienced a significant decline in influence, even over minor allies who were thought to be utterly dependent. The United States could not prevent the defection of Cuba, and the Soviet Union was unable to control Albania. Moreover, the individual major powers proved to be unable to impress their less powerful friends and influence their policies even when serious efforts were made either individually or in concert with others. The latest example is the war in the Middle East. American and Soviet policies did occasionally arrive at certain agreed points; but it was impossible to carry them out in view of the opposition of the states in the Middle East directly involved.

The ability to resist outside pressure, the ability to survive against incomparably more powerful military forces, as in Vietnam or Algeria, has introduced new elements into the relations between states and peoples. We should therefore approach the problem of the possible influence and role of the nonaligned countries in the light of these observations.

III

The nonaligned countries have never influenced international developments by relying on their military or economic resources. Their military capability is mostly of a strictly defensive character. They can sustain heavy military pressure and survive, but they are not likely to be efficient in offensive actions. This is probably one of the explanations of why they have felt and continue to feel secure without seeking formal protection in military alliance or from either of the two major nuclear powers.

India has had no reason to abandon its nonalignment because of the military conflict with China. Although the Chinese pushed back the

Indian army from its positions at the border, they knew that this should not be confused with the bigger issue of the conquest of India. The cases of Algeria and Vietnam have had a profound effect upon a world already inclined to discount military reconquest of the lost colonial empires.

But the nonaligned counted on another factor even more. The major powers proved rather sensitive to repercussions of their behavior which occurred in the third world. One should not overestimate this factor, for no truly great power would jeopardize its vital interest because of loss in influence or prestige; nevertheless, the role of these imponderables should also not be underestimated. The Soviet Union may have been ready to sacrifice its prestige and influence in many places in the world when it decided to invade Czechoslovakia, but it made great efforts later to minimize the damage as much as possible.

Though public opinion has less influence within the U.S.S.R. than in the United States, some signs of dissatisfaction and protest were evident in Russia following the occupation of Czechoslovakia. But while the feelings of the Soviet masses could probably not be wholly ignored it is doubtful whether expressions of dissent did, or could in the future, influence the Soviet government's conduct of foreign affairs. However, the Soviets are not indifferent to the impact of public opinion in certain circles outside Russia. Of these, two are most important as areas where the Soviet government seeks approval and where dissent causes embarrassment. The first is, of course, the world communist movement. The second is among the nonaligned countries in the third world.

The limits of the Soviet Union's economic development and the exigencies of its internal needs have markedly reduced its economic impact on less developed countries. Furthermore, its restricted ability to deploy classical expeditionary forces in remote places of the world where it might like to back up one side or the other makes it imperative for it to strengthen its global role by cultivating ideological and political bonds with the leftist movements in the third world. This also helps to explain the extraordinary bitterness of the polemics between the Soviet Union and China. It has been caused not so much by the territorial dispute as by China's attempt to replace the Soviet Union as the center of the world communist movement and to take over the leadership of the third world.

Thus, the nonaligned countries can, at least to some extent, influence the attitude of one or possibly both of the major powers. The ability to influence the behavior of the United States is less significant, but should not be ruled out. China's emergence from its self-imposed isolation during the Cultural Revolution opens up new possibilities in this respect.

The nonaligned temporarily exercised some influence on the Soviet Union's attitude in economic relations during the first UNCTAD conference in Geneva in 1964, but after the second one in Delhi four years later the U.S.S.R. became less sensitive to third-world problems. This very likely resulted from China's disappearance from the scene after the outbreak of the Cultural Revolution and also was connected with the failure of the third world to exact concessions from the West at Delhi. Lacking the competition of China and in view of the loss of influence of the nonaligned countries, the Soviet Union could temporarily disregard their vital interests. Further, the cautious and rather general expressions of disapproval that came from the nonaligned countries concerning the Soviet action in Czechoslovakia only increased Moscow's conviction that this element in world public opinion could be almost completely disregarded.

Recent developments have once again changed the atmosphere. In the first place, the opening of talks between the United States and the Soviet Union on strategic arms limitation demonstrates that the two superpowers understand certain vital questions of common interest. The opening of this dialogue was postponed by the crisis over Czechoslovakia, but it now looks as though there is a good prospect for the continuation and progress of these talks. Thus, a growing rapprochement has developed between two of the triangular powers. It started with their experiences in connection with the war in the Middle East and the war in Vietnam, neither of which produced exaggerated tensions between them.

The reactivation of China's world role after the Cultural Revolution has brought a new dimension to the relations between Moscow and Washington. The Soviet Union seized the opportunity after the death of Ho Chi Minh to start a dialogue with China over border questions before the beginning of the talks in Helsinki on arms reductions with the United States. At the same time, there were signs of a lessening of tensions between the United States and China with the reopening of ambassadorial contacts and the easing of American trade restrictions. China, on her part, initiated efforts to expand diplomatic relations with Western countries; even the normalization of relations with Yugoslavia was announced.

This favorable climate is not likely to last. The détente within the Moscow-Washington-Peking triangle relies on the coincidence of a number of parallel developments. It would be wishful thinking to believe that it can remain a stable relationship among the three major powers. The same mechanics which have contributed to the détente could, at some future moment, produce the opposite effect.

There is and must be some interdependence in the behavior of the three pairs of partners. No one will permit too close a rapprochement between the other two. If such threatens, efforts will be made by the third power to drive them apart. When this is not possible, the one which feels threatened with isolation will obviously try to repair its relations with the one or the other in order to avoid being left out in the cold. In this respect, a certain tendency to preserve the symmetry of the triangle develops. A rapprochement or disruption along one of the connecting lines tends to cause a reaction along the two other lines. For antagonism still divides all three powers.

Thus, the transformation of the bipolar into a triangular pattern does more than add one more contender at the summit. In the new triangular pattern a total breakdown of world order and a catastrophic nuclear war appear less likely. There is more room for manœuvring. There are more possible combinations, more variables which could be manipulated, more uncertainties which impose caution and restraint. Consequently there are better chances for the restoration of an equilibrium, since the threat always exists that one party will be outnumbered in a bilateral quarrel with the third party standing by. Such a pattern is not likely to produce lasting peace and harmony, but neither could the bipolar pattern. The more likely prospect would be an oscillation of periods of higher and lower tension within the triangle.

This triangle is an ominous reminder of the Orwellian vision of a world divided among three major powers and constantly at war, with two changing partners temporarily united against the third. In the reality of the contemporary world, though, there is a difference because we have the rest of the world in addition to the three major powers. This other group is of considerable consequence. Finally, while it is most unlikely that this group could be divided and absorbed into clearly defined spheres of influence by the major powers, neither should it be assumed that it could be totally ignored by them. . . .

SECTION FOUR:

Arms Control and Disarmament

37. THE OBJECTIVES OF ARMS CONTROL

Hedley Bull

ARMS RACES are intense competitions between opposed powers or groups of powers, each trying to achieve an advantage in military power by increasing the quantity or improving the quality of its armaments or armed forces.[1] Arms races are not peculiar to the present time or the present century, but are a familiar form of international relationship. Arms races which are qualitative rather than quantitative, which proceed more by the improvement of weapons or forces than by the increase of them, have grown more important with the progress of technology: and what is peculiar to the present grand Soviet-Western arms race is the extent to which its qualitative predominates over its quantitative aspect. However, there have not always been arms races, and they are in no way

From *The Control of the Arms Race* by Hedley Bull (New York: Frederick A. Praeger, 1961), pp. 5–8; 25–27; 30–36. Reprinted by permission Frederick A. Praeger, Inc., and G. Weidenfeld & Nicholson, Ltd. Footnotes have been renumbered to appear in consecutive order.

HEDLEY BULL (1932–   ) Professor of International Relations, Australian National University; former Director of the Arms Control and Disarmament Research Unit, Her Majesty's Foreign Office, United Kingdom. Author of *Strategy and the Atlantic Alliance; A Critique of United States Doctrine* (Princeton: Center of International Studies, 1964); *The Control of the Arms Race* (New York: Praeger Publishers, 1965).

[1] For a pioneering study of arms races see the essay by Samuel P. Huntington: 'Arms Races: Prerequisites and Results', *Public Policy*, Yearbook of the Graduate School of Public Administration (Harvard University 1958).

inherent in international relations, nor even in situations of international political conflict. Where the political tensions between two powers are not acute; where each power can gain an advantage over the other without increasing or improving its armaments, but simply by recruiting allies or depriving its opponent of them; where the economic or demographic resources to increase armaments, or the technological resources to improve them, do not exist, we do not find arms races. The prominent place which the Soviet-Western arms race occupies in international relations at the present time arises from the circumstance that the opportunities available to each side for increasing its relative military power lie very much more in the exploitation and mobilization of its own military resources, than in the attempt to influence the direction in which the relatively meagre military resources of outside powers are thrown, by concluding favourable alliances or frustrating unfavourable ones. It arises from the circumstance that the balance of military power can at present be affected very much more by armaments policy than by diplomacy.

It is seldom that anything so crude is asserted as that all wars are caused by arms races, but the converse is often stated, that all arms races cause wars: that in the past they have always resulted in war; or even that they lead inevitably to war.

It is true that, within states, armaments tend to create or to shape the will to use them, as well as to give effect to it; and that, between states, arms races tend to sustain or to exacerbate conflicts of policy, as well as to express them. Within each state, the military establishment, called into being by the policy of competitive armament, develops its own momentum: it creates interests and diffuses an ideology favourable to the continuation of the arms race, and generates pressures which will tend to resist any policy of calling it off. In this respect, that they display a will to survive, the armed forces, the armaments industries, the military branches of science and technology and of government, the settled habits of mind of those who think about strategy and defence, are like any great institution involving vast, impersonal organizations and the ambitions and livelihood of masses of men. Apart from these internal pressures of armaments establishments upon policy, it is possible to see in the pressures which each state exerts upon the other, in the action and reaction that constitutes an arms race, a spiralling process in which the moving force is not, or not only, the political will or intention of governments, but their armaments and military capability. One nation's military security can be another's insecurity. One nation's military capability of launching an attack can be interpreted by its opponent as an intention to launch it, or as likely to create such an intention, whether that intention exists or not. Even where neither side has hostile intentions, nor very firmly believes the opponent to have them, military preparations may continue, since they must take into account a range of contingencies, which includes the worse cases. In so far as the competitors in an arms race are responsive to each other's military capabilities rather than to each other's intentions, in so far as they are led, by estimates of each other's capabilities, to make false estimates of each other's intentions, the arms race has a tendency to exacerbate a political conflict, or to preserve it where other circumstances are making towards its alleviation.

But the idea that arms races obey a logic of their own and can only result in war, is false; and perhaps also dangerous. It is false because it conceives the arms race as an autonomous process in which the military factor alone operates. The chief source of this error in recent years has been the belief in the importance of the various armaments competitions among the European powers, and especially the Anglo-German naval race, in contributing to the outbreak of the first world war. Even in this case, the importance of this factor is a matter of controversy. In the case of the origins of the second world war, the autonomous arms race cannot be regarded as having been important. On the contrary, we should say that the military factor which was most important in bringing it about was the failure of Britain, France and the Soviet Union to engage in the arms race with sufficient vigour, their insufficient response to the rearmament of Germany. In general, arms races arise as the result of political conflicts, are kept alive by them, and subside with them. We have only to reflect that there is not and has never been such a thing as a general or universal arms race, a war of all against all in military preparation. The context in which arms races occur is that of a conflict between particular powers or groups of powers, and of military, political, economic and technological circumstances in which an armaments competition is an appropriate form for this conflict to take.

Arms races have not always led to war, but have sometimes come to an end, like the Anglo-French naval races of the last century, and the Anglo-American naval race in this one, when, for one reason or another, the parties lost the will to pursue them. There is no more reason to believe that arms races must end in war than to believe that severe international rivalries, which are not accompanied by arms races, must do so. It is of course the case that wars are made possible by the existence of armaments. But the existence of armaments, and of sovereign powers commanding them and willing to use them, is a feature of international society, whether arms races are in progress or not. What is sometimes meant by those who assert that arms races cause wars is the quite different proposition that armaments cause wars. While armaments are among the conditions which enable wars to take place, they do not in themselves produce war, or provide in themselves a means of distinguishing the conditions of war from the conditions of peace. For all international experience has been accompanied by the existence of armaments, the experience of peace as much as the experience of war. To show why, in a context in which armaments are endemic, wars sometimes occur and sometimes do not; to show why, in this context, arms races sometimes arise, and either persist, subside or end in war, it is necessary to look beyond armaments themselves to the political factors which the doctrine of the autonomous arms race leaves out of account.

•   •   •

We began by asking what disarmament or arms control is for. We have considered the arguments that it promotes international security, that it promotes economic objectives and that it promotes moral objectives. It has been necessary to do this not only to discover what the claims of disarmament and arms control to contribute to such objectives as these are, to discover whether arms control should be pursued at all; but also in order to determine whether there is any conflict among these objectives, and if there is, what is the proper order of priority among them. For if we are indeed to attempt to increase the part played in international relations by disarmament and arms control, we must first of all know what it is we want of them, with regard to which of these objectives we must shape them. It is clearly possible to pursue each of these three objectives at the expense of one or both of the others. There are disarmament policies, for example, that will fill our pockets with gold, but increase the danger of war; and that would be, in consequence, morally wrong. There are disarmament policies shaped by certain moral objectives, such as that of preserving untainted our innocence of war or nuclear war, that might similarly undermine international security.

In my view it is chiefly in relation to the objective of international security that disarmament and arms control should be shaped and judged. By this I do not mean that situations do not arise in which moral or economic considerations override those of security: marginal increases in security may be pursued at exorbitant economical or moral cost. Moral judgments, indeed, should never be overridden or sacrificed: and the singling out of international security as what is most worthy of our attention is itself, in part, a moral judgment. The moral objective, if, as I have suggested, it is not a matter of rigid adherence to specific principles, should not be understood as something separate from, and opposed to, other objectives, but as a dimension in which we view all of them. In treating international security as of chief priority, I mean no more than that the chief relevance of arms control is to the preservation of peace and order, and that this is an objective generally regarded as morally desirable and worth paying for.

It is necessary to define international security more closely.

There is security of, and security from: that which we are concerned to secure, and that from which we are concerned to secure it. What we are concerned to secure is, on the one hand, our particular ways of life: our continued enjoyment of our own political, social, moral and economic habits and institutions; and, on the other hand, our physical survival, our continued existence as human communities of any kind. What we are concerned to secure these things from is, on the one hand, war, which threatens both of them; and, on the other hand, defeat, brought about by war or otherwise, which historically has also threatened both of them, but is more commonly regarded as threatening only the former.

I do not think of security as some future state or condition, some metaphysical plateau which we have not yet reached but towards which we are striving. International security is something we have and have had throughout the history of modern international society, in greater or lesser degree. The promotion of international security is a matter of preserving and extending something with which we are familiar, rather than of manufacturing, out of nothing, some novel device. At the present time it is a matter of restoring, or attempting to recapture, something, for much of it is beyond recapture, of the security of which modern weapons, and the continued existence alongside them of political conflicts bitter enough to promise the use of them, have deprived us; and, in the first instance, a matter of preserving such security as we have now, by arresting or stabilizing its tendency to rapid decline.

Absolute security from war and defeat has never been enjoyed by sovereign states living in a state of nature, and is foreign to all experience of international life. A great deal of public thinking about international relations is, however, absorbed in the pursuit of this fantasy. The solutions and recommendations produced by this kind of thinking are remote from the range of alternatives or spectrum of possible actions from which governments are able to choose. These solutions do not concern the problems with which the world is actually confronted, but concern the arbitrary dismantling or reconstruction of the world, in such a way that these problems would not arise: a reconstruction to be achieved by acts of will, constitutions for world government, declarations, the abolition of war, gestures, research, therapies and cures. They represent, in my view, a corruption of thinking about international relations, and a distraction from its proper concerns. The fact is that we are where we are, and it is from here that we have to begin. There can only be relative security.

The objective of security, as it has been defined, itself disguises awful choices which may have to be made between its different parts. It may be, for example, that certain nations will find themselves in the position of being able to secure their physical survival, their continued existence as organized communities, only by sacrificing their political, social and economic institutions: by the ancient expedient of surrender. The question whether the struggle to preserve political independence should be carried on in the face of the certainty of physical destruction is one which human communities have often faced in the past, and is not especially a product of modern military technology, though the latter does pose it in a peculiarly stark way. Some of the present support for unilateral nuclear disarmament in Great Britain derives from the view that this is the choice with which we are now confronted.[2] I do not believe that this is the position at present: but if it were the position, there is no doubt in my mind that surrender would be the better alternative. It is the view of a fanatic which prefers universal destruction to the acceptance of defeat.[3]

Another awful choice disguised within this objective of security is that between security from all kinds of war, and security from a particular kind of war: nuclear war. If we are specially concerned to increase security against nuclear war, we may find it necessary to maintain military forces and elaborate military doctrines that will diminish our security against other kinds of war. To illustrate: the doctrine that all military policy should be built around the idea of nuclear deterrence, that the only military act of which we should be capable is that of strategic nuclear bombardment, and the only military threat which we should employ is this one—this doctrine promises a world in which the likelihood of war may not be great, but in which any particular war is a catastrophe.

. . .

DISARMAMENT AND THE BALANCE OF POWER

i

The chief objective of arms control is international security. The contribution which arms control can make to international security is limited by the fact that it deals only with the military factor.

However, there is a military factor, and some military situations are more favourable to international security than others. The question with which this chapter is concerned is: if arms control is concerned to foster military situations favourable to international security, what are these? In particular, how far is *disarmament,* or the reduction of armaments, the proper object of arms control? And how far is it the proper object of arms control to promote a stable *balance of power?* The purpose of this analysis is not to provide final answers to these questions; and not, in particular, to demonstrate that the proper object of arms control is to perfect a stable balance or equilibrium of armaments rather than to secure a reduc-

---

[2] Only some, and perhaps not very much. Most of the supporters do not see any awful choices, but take the view that unilateral disarmament does not involve the surrender of our political independence: persuading themselves either that no one threatens it, or that we can defend ourselves against nuclear bombardment by conventional armaments or passive resistance.

[3] The policy of surrender is discussed in Chapter 4, "Arms Control and Unilateral Action" [of *The Control of the Arms Race* by Hedley Bull].

tion of armaments. Its purpose is to demonstrate the inadequacy of such prescriptions as 'reduce!' or 'abolish!', and the need to replace them with careful strategic analysis.[4] It is not to be assumed (though cases could conceivably arise in which it could be shown) that the answer to the question, 'what levels and kinds of armaments should arms control systems seek to perpetuate and make legitimate?' is the formula, 'the lowest levels and the most primitive kinds'. The conflict between this formula, and the doctrine of the balance of power, which is explored in this chapter, indicates only one of the many respects in which it is inadequate. When we consider—as we shall in later chapters in relation to particular arms control proposals—what should be the content of an arms control agreement or system, we must be guided not by any such formula as this, nor by an exclusive concern with the maintenance of the military balance, but by addressing ourselves with determination to the complicated strategic and political calculation demanded by the question: what kinds, levels, deployments or uses of armaments would best promote security?

ii

Disarmament is the reduction or abolition of armaments. The idea that the world is most secure when there is a *minimum* of armaments, the pursuit of the *maximum* disarmament, has been the central assumption of modern negotiations about arms control. The negotiations conducted under the auspices of the League of Nations between 1921 and 1934, and those under the auspices of the United Nations between 1946 and 1957 and in 1960, have had as their chief formal object the promotion of international security by a general reduction of armaments. Even in negotiations which have been concerned with limiting the further growth of armaments, rather than with reducing existing ones (as in the negotiations at the first Hague Conference in 1899, and in those which led to the Washington Naval Treaty of 1922), it was the idea of the desirability of the minimum armaments that provided the starting point. And where arms control negotiations have not been concerned with the quantity of armaments at all, but with regulating or controlling what should be done with them (like the negotiations leading to prohibition of the use of poison gas, those in the abortive East-West conference on surprise attack in November 1958, and the protracted negotiations at Geneva on the banning of nuclear test explosions, these negotiations are regarded as important partly because they may set off a train of events which might result in a general reduction of armaments.

---

[4] The spirit of these prescriptions is expressed in the title of a recent book: *Assault at Arms,* by Sir Ronald Adam and Charles Judd (Weidenfeld and Nicolson, 1960).

The idea that security is a matter of disarmament has seldom been held without qualification. Article VIII of the Covenant of the League of Nations, on the basis of which the inter-war negotiations were conducted, stated that: 'The members of the League recognize that the maintenance of peace requires the reduction of national armaments to the lowest point *consistent with national safety and the enforcement by common action of international obligations*' (my italics). This qualification provided the basis of the various French plans of the League period, which treated international security as a matter of the establishment of a strong international authority and centralized military force and disarmament as contributing to security only when linked with it. It was often held, moreover, even by nations which did not support plans for a centralized military force, that there were levels beneath which the reduction of armaments would not constitute a contribution to the maintenance of peace, levels determined by the need of members of the League to maintain forces adequate to enable them to contribute effectively to the system of collective security, or pooling of national military forces in defence of the Covenant, to which they were committed. Another qualification which received general assent in principle at the World Disarmament Conference in 1932, and which still has its adherents, is contained in the idea of qualitative disarmament: that 'specifically offensive' weapons undermine security in a way that defensive weapons do not: and that disarmament should not be indiscrimate, but should be especially concerned with reducing or abolishing the former.[5] Moreover, it has usually been recognized in disarmament negotiations that any reductions that are agreed upon should preserve an agreed balance or ratio of power: that the reductions should be so fashioned, and the phases by which they are carried out so ordered, that no nation should be set at what it considers a military disadvantage.

But, by and large, these qualifications have not been seen as detracting from the principle that it is in the reduction of armaments that the contribution of arms control to international security lies. They have rather been seen as qualifications which have to be made so as to bring about the international agreement that can alone set the process of reduction of armaments in motion. Sovereign powers, it has been considered, will not agree to disarm unless they can retain internal security forces, unless a central authority or collective security system will protect them from attack, and unless at all stages in their disarmament there is a balance between their own strength and that of their opponents.

But the idea that security lies in the minimum of armaments cannot be accepted uncritically. In considering this idea, we must examine sepa-

---

[5] See Philip Noel-Baker, *The Arms Race*, pp. 393–404 (Stevens and Sons, 1958).

rately two of the forms it takes: the stronger form, that the abolition of armaments makes war physically impossible; and the weaker form, that the reduction of armaments makes war less likely.

The stronger form is a doctrine which has great popular appeal, because it promises a form of security which is absolute and independent of the continuance of favourable political conditions. It suggests a world in which states cannot make war, even if they want to. It has played an important part in Soviet disarmament policy. Litvinov advocated total disarmament at a meeting of the preparatory commission of the League of Nations Disarmament Conference, on the occasion of the appearance of Soviet delegates at Geneva, in 1927. All armed forces were to be disbanded and all armaments destroyed; military expenditure, military service, war ministers and chiefs of staffs were to be abolished; military propaganda and military instruction were to be prohibited; and legislation was to be passed in each country making infringement of any of these provisions a crime against the state. Litvinov contrasted the Soviet objective of 'total disarmament' with the more modest objective of a 'reduction and limitation of armaments', which was the formula on which the League of Nations negotiations proceeded. He repeated his proposal at the World Disarmament Conference in February 1932. The speech he made on this occasion, and those which followed later in the conference, were directed towards exposing the hypocrisy of the capitalist powers in their treatment of the subject of disarmament: the gap between their professions of intention and their actions; the dilatoriness and humbug of disarmament proceedings; the passing of problems from committee to committee; the endless vista of 'preparation'; the adoption now of this 'method', now of that; the swathing of stark realities in a blanket of diplomatic nicety. His speeches are a brilliant critique of the diplomacy of disarmament and, indeed, of the most fundamental assumptions on which all diplomacy rests, and must rest. They contain a clarity of perception, a determination to call a spade a spade, to say what others only thought, that is extraordinary in the speeches of a foreign minister, and possible only because he himself was not taking part in diplomacy but in political warfare, and therefore saw the diplomatic process as an outsider. In defending his proposal for total disarmament, he advanced two main arguments. Total disarmament was 'the only way of putting an end to war',[6] something which the mere reduction and limitation of armaments could not do. And total disarmament was 'distinguished from all other plans by its simplicity and by the ease with which it could be carried out and with which its realization could be controlled'.[7] Total disarmament

---

[6] *League of Nations: Conference for the Reduction and Limitation of Armaments,* Verbatim Records of Plenary Meetings, Vol. I, p. 82 (Geneva, 1932).

[7] *Ibid.,* p. 85.

by-passed all those 'thorny questions' which prevented agreement on any lesser measure of disarmament: what armaments were to be abolished and what not, how far were reductions to be carried out, which would be reduced first, how was the treaty to provide equal security for all, and so on.

. . .

No system of disarmament can abolish the physical capacity to wage war, and the idea of an absolute security from war emerging from such a system is an illusion. However, it is at least logically and physically possible that the art of war might be rendered primitive: by the abolition of sophisticated weapons and the decay of sophisticated military organization and technique. There may be a great difference between an international society in which sovereign powers are bristling with modern weapons and organized military forces, and one in which they are not: just as there is a great difference between a society in which gentlemen carry swords, and one in which they do not. There is nothing contrary to logic, or nature either, in the idea of an international society not only without such weapons and forces, but with habits, institutions, codes or taboos which could impede the will to utilize the physical capacity for war inherent in it. We should have the imagination and the vision to contemplate the possibility of such a world, to recognize that the political and military structure of the world could be radically different from what it is now. But we should recognize that a world which was radically different from our own in respect of the primitiveness and extent of its national armaments would also be radically different in many other ways. If nations were defenceless, there could hardly be a political order worthy of the name unless there were an armed, central authority: the abolition of national military power appears to entail the concentration of military power in a universal authority. If a universal authority or world government were to be established in any other way than by conquest, and if, once established, it were to maintain itself in any other way than by the constant suppression of dissidence, the bitter political conflicts which now divide the world would have to have subsided. In a world fundamentally different from our own in all these respects, and in other respects, the reduction of national armaments to a primitive level might have a place. But the world in which we now find ourselves is not such as this: nor is it within the power of any political authority or combination of authorities to bring it about by *fiat*. The possession by sovereign powers of armaments and armed forces is not something extraneous to the structure of international society, something whose presence or absence does not affect other of its parts: it is, along with alliances, diplomacy and war, among its most central institutions. It is possible to conceive systems of world politics and political organization from which this institution is absent:

but they are systems from which some of the most familiar and persistent landmarks of international experience are also absent; and which, though they might occur, cannot be legislated.

In a world such as our own it seems doubtful whether the reduction of national armaments to a primitive level, even if it could be brought about in isolation from other fundamental changes, would contribute to international security. It would carry within itself no guarantee that arms races would not be resumed. The resumption of an arms race from a primitive level, with its attendant circumstances of unpredictability and surprise, would be likely to lead to extreme instability in the balance of power, and might well produce greater insecurity than that attending a higher quantitative and qualitative level of armaments.

38.   ARMS CONTROL IN THE 1970S

James E. Dougherty

I

. . .

EVER SINCE the onset of the atomic era, countless leaders and concerned citizens have warned that nuclear war is inevitable unless nations achieve complete nuclear disarmament. Yet more than twenty-five years after Hiroshima and Nagasaki, it is unthinkable that any one of the five existing nuclear states—not even China, perhaps especially not China—hopes to achieve any political purpose by initiating nuclear war. Paradoxically, despite the terrors of the thermonuclear age, not one of

From ORBIS, a quarterly journal of world affairs published by the Foreign Policy Research Institute, Spring 1971, 195–213. Reprinted by permission of the author and the Foreign Policy Research Institute. Footnotes have been renumbered to appear in consecutive order.

JAMES E. DOUGHERTY (1923–   ) Executive Vice President and Professor of Political Science, St. Joseph's College, Philadelphia. Coauthor of *Contending Theories of International Relations* (Philadelphia: J. B. Lippincott Company, 1971); *The Politics of the Atlantic Alliance* (New York: Frederick A. Praeger, 1964); *Building the Atlantic World* (New York: Harper and Row, 1963); and *Protracted Conflict* (New York: Harper and Brothers, 1959). Coeditor of *Arms Control for the Late Sixties* (Princeton, N.J.: D. Van Nostrand Company, 1967). Editor of *Prospects for Arms Control* (New York: Macfadden-Bartell, 1965).

the five—not even Britain—has acted consistently during the last decade as if she looks upon total nuclear disarmament as the only way, or necessarily the best way, of safeguarding her security. In all five countries we would find intellectuals, government officials, military leaders and others who, in moments of philosophical reflection, regard general disarmament as a desirable goal. But it would seem that in all five most political leaders conclude that the same advanced weapons technology that makes disarmament more ethically imperative than ever before also makes it more difficult than ever to attain technically, strategically and politically.

The United States and the Soviet Union never solved to their mutual satisfaction the technical problems inherent in implementing the 1961 McCloy-Zorin principle that the disarming process should place neither side at an unfair disadvantage. Given the different geostrategic requirements of the two superpowers and the different weapons systems at their disposal, it was impossible even to agree on where to begin the dismantling of arms. (Now, a decade later in the Helsinki-Vienna negotiations we are arguing the same question of where to start "freezing.") Back in the early 1960's U.S. analysts demonstrated their creative imagination by devising a remarkable variety of physical and non-physical inspection and control schemes to insure either compliance with the disarmament agreement or effective sanctions in case of violation. But that intellectual exercise remained rather theoretical. Virtually all the proposed schemes were vulnerable to serious criticism: they could be circumvented; they were politically obnoxious to the Soviets; or they were so bizarre that they would be unacceptable even in the more permissive framework of American politics.[1] One crucial inspection problem—that of "hidden stockpiles" sufficiently large to threaten a disarmed power's survival— was never overcome. Governments do not like to discuss those facts that inhibit their ability to engage in public rhetoric concerning persistent foreign policy themes.

The strategic obstacles to general disarmament can be simply put. Essentially they involve the issue of security and the propensity of governments in the nation-state system to seek that security through some form of power balancing and, when possible, deterring war by threatening to make it too costly. All five nuclear powers appear to assume, as John H. Herz has suggested in a revision of his earlier estimate concern-

---

[1] The author has dealt in detail with these technical problems in "The Disarmament Debate: A Review of Current Literature" (Parts One and Two), ORBIS, Fall 1961 and Winter 1962; "Nuclear Weapons Control," *Current History,* July 1964; "The Status of the Arms Negotiations," ORBIS, Spring 1965; and *Arms Control and Disarmament: The Critical Issues* (Washington: Center for Strategic Studies, Special Report Series, 1966), especially Chapters 6 and 7.

ing the "demise of the territorial state," that nuclear weapons for all practical purposes have become "unavailable" for any use except deterrence and that, despite lingering ambiguities, they now constitute a safeguard rather than a threat to national security.[2] The two superpowers cannot but wonder, both in their mutual strategic relations and with an eye to other powers, how fast and how far they could dare carry out reductions down the strategic scale before encountering the danger that mutual deterrence might give way to renascent incentives for surprise nuclear attack, based on the expectation of achieving a decisive advantage. This is the central strategic problem in all planning for nuclear disarmament.[3] It would be more accurate to say that we have forgotten it than that we have solved it.

II

The political obstacles to general disarmament were, and remain, insuperable. Essentially, Soviet opposition to Western proposals for inspection and control has been political. There are no signs that the Soviets are more ready today than a decade ago to permit international on-site inspection. (Whatever limited-risk arms control measures we and the Soviets agree upon—such as the Partial Nuclear Test Ban Treaty, the Outer Space Treaty, or the Seabed Treaty and the proposed Strategic Arms Limitation Agreement—require that the United States depend on its own national detection and verification capabilities.) Furthermore, there still exist serious political disagreements between the Western and the communist states over the development of an international peace-keeping organization (especially the United Nations) in lieu of national military establishments. Generally speaking, the nuclear powers appear unwilling to forsake an international environment in which the conditions of precarious stalemate have become relatively familiar for a radically transformed international system in which none of the great powers would be free to invoke either force or the threat of force to protect its interests and pursue its objectives. At present, each nuclear power attaches higher priority to policy objectives other than general

---

[2] John H. Herz, "The Territorial State Revisited: Reflections on the Future of the Nation-State," reprinted from *Polity*, I, 1, 1968 in James N. Rosenau, editor, *International Politics and Foreign Policy: A Reader in Research and Theory* (New York: The Free Press, 1969), pp. 76–89.

[3] See Thomas C. Schelling, "Surprise Attack and Disarmament," Chapter 10 of his *The Strategy of Conflict* (New York: Oxford University Press, 1963), especially pp. 235–236; Henry A. Kissinger, "Arms Control, Inspection and Surprise Attack," *Foreign Affairs*, July 1960, pp. 559–561; Hedley Bull, *The Control of the Arms Race* (New York: Praeger, 1961), pp. 168–169; Glenn H. Snyder, *Deterrence and Defense* (Princeton: Princeton University Press, 1961), pp. 97–103.

disarmament. None of them is ready to start talking seriously about disarmament—this for several reasons.

First of all, because among the five there are serious asymmetries of situation and power, two of the nuclear-weapon states, France and China, are unwilling to enter into serious negotiations at this time. Both have continued to conduct nuclear tests in the atmosphere. Neither power has signed the Nonproliferation Treaty, but neither indicates being motivated to encourage the diffusion of nuclear weapons to additional nations. France has given public assurances of an intention to "behave in this area exactly as do those States that decide to adhere to the nonproliferation treaty." [4] Now that the de Gaulle era is over, France may be able to return to the international conference table during the 1970's. But for China the strategic security situation is more difficult than it ever was for France. China's position vis-à-vis the superpowers is still quite weak, and she has a long way to go before she possesses the bargaining leverage that would make her feel comfortable about negotiating arms limitations, assuming that she will ever be willing to enter into such a process. Moreover, if China were to be invited some day to a world disarmament conference, in virtue of the fact that she is one of the nuclear *beati possedentes* [blessed possessors], and thereby have her international political prestige enhanced, India's incentive to acquire nuclear weapons would probably increase and the prospects for inhibiting the further proliferation of national deterrent forces would be correspondingly diminished. Thus even the timing and the form of international disarmament negotiations can be a tricky business. For now, "pentagonal" negotiations are untimely, and it is impossible to predict confidently whether circumstances would permit them to begin before the end of this decade. Perhaps they should appear no more remote than did such U.S.-USSR agreements as the test ban and the nonproliferation treaty at the height of the Cold War. . . .

The Soviets have been preoccupied for the last decade and more with the behavior of Germany and China—which causes them the greater worry, Western observers have been unable to decide. During the years of negotiating the Nonproliferation Treaty in the mid-1960's, it was sometimes suggested in the West that when Soviet propagandists inveighed against the militant revolutionism of the Chinese communists, this was really intended to disguise their deep-rooted fear of the Germans. It was also sometimes suggested that when Soviet diplomats at Geneva and elsewhere declaimed against the desire of the "West German revanchists" to acquire nuclear arms, they were only trying to tell us in Aesopian lan-

---

[4] *Documents on Disarmament 1969*, United States Arms Control and Disarmament Agency Publication 55, August 1970 (Washington: GPO, 1970), p. 579.

guage how worried they were about the Chinese nuclear capability. It is quite possible that Moscow is seriously afraid of both Peking and Bonn. It is also possible, and perhaps more likely, that the Soviet leaders are rational enough to perceive that both Germany and China are at present decidedly inferior in total military capabilities to the USSR; neither by itself can pose a serious threat to Soviet security. Possibly, too, they are more concerned about the one than the other at any given time, depending upon the circumstances—including, e.g., the political character of the government in West Germany and the degree of tension or conflict along the Sino-Soviet border.

III

. . .

Western observers have assumed that the dispute with China figured prominently in Soviet motivations for entering the SALT in late 1969. But we should not discount the possibility that Soviet apprehensions over China may have been exaggerated in the past by Soviet policymakers, or by Western observers, or by both. If the Soviets were mistaken, they might now be revising their assessment. The real threat from China, if there is to be one, probably lies in the future. The Peking leadership must certainly recognize its country's strategic vulnerability in this early nuclear phase of its history. There is no reason to believe that a generation nurtured on Maoist doctrine will risk everything by plunging into strategic adventurism.[5]

Once the SALT was under way, mutual hostility between China and the Soviet Union lessened considerably. By the end of 1970, one heard little of the Sino Soviet dispute, or of the earlier speculation that the superpowers were using the SALT to rationalize their acquisition of a missile defense capability against China. On the one hand, the U.S. move into Cambodia may have prompted Moscow and Peking to attenuate their animosity, lest the United States take advantage of it. On the other hand, recent developments, including the recognition of the Peking government by Canada and Italy, along with a perceptible softening of the U.S. position toward the Chinese People's Republic in respect to travel, trade and United Nations diplomacy, helped the CPR to inch toward international respectability, and also served to demonstrate that the triangular Washington-Moscow-Peking relationship is a highly complex phenomenon, comparable to the "three body" problem in physics.[6] It will

---

[5] For an analysis of Chinese attitudes toward arms control, see A. Doak Barnett, "A Nuclear China and U.S. Arms Policy," *Foreign Affairs*, April 1970.

[6] For a discussion of the complexities of this relationship, see Pierre Maillard, "The Effect of China on Soviet-American Relations," in *Soviet-American Relations*

complicate the arms control picture throughout the 1970's, and the three principals can be expected to try to make capital of it.

A French analyst, Michel Tatu, has recently suggested that it may be less appropriate to interpret the current détente in terms of the Soviets' desire to "safeguard their western rear" while coping with China than in terms of their interest in "safeguarding their eastern rear" while pursuing a more active diplomatic policy in Europe.[7] Such 1970 developments as the Bonn-Moscow treaty (whereby the USSR obtained much of what it sought to gain through a European security conference) should make us wary of any simplistic explanations of Soviet negotiating behavior vis-à-vis China and the West.

Nevertheless, in the future the Soviets will usually have reason, because of geographical factors, to be more worried than the United States about China's nuclear capability. Moreover, because of the population imbalance, the Soviets would not contemplate Sino-Soviet nuclear disarmament negotiations with much enthusiasm. As Peking's nuclear arsenal grows, it will become increasingly difficult for the Soviet political-military leadership to entertain the idea of a pre-emptive attack upon China. Historical-psychological factors rooted in the Russian character and culture, as well as the rationalist dictates of communist ideology, already militate in favor of caution and nonviolent conflict resolution. Perhaps the Soviets realize that, as a sheer matter of coldly calculated *Machtpolitik,* they have passed the point where they could deliberately opt for war with China, and that they must look forward to the inevitable development of conditions of mutual deterrence in Asia. But if so, they will probably strive to maintain a margin of strategic superiority over China as long as possible. There is no reason to think that the leaders in Moscow, in working out an arms limitation policy, would be willing to take the "down escalator" while the Chinese (still a few floors below) are on the "up escalator."

Why, then, are the Soviet Union and the United States involved in the Helsinki-Vienna negotiations? There is a variety of motives, not necessarily similar or of equal intensity on both sides. Both nations are beset by uncertainties. Decision-makers in each country cannot help wondering at times whether things are really going as well as they might, domestically and abroad. As a nation, the United States has become frustrated by the Viet Nam war and by her effort to establish some sort of equilibrium in Asia (despite a degree of success). She has ex-

---

and World Order: The Two and the Many (London: Institute for Strategic Studies, Adelphi Papers No. 66, March 1970).

[7] Michel Tatu, *The Great Power Triangle: Washington-Moscow-Peking* (Paris: The Atlantic Institute, Atlantic Papers No. 3, 1970).

perienced internal social disorders arising from urban crises, racial conflicts and campus unrest, as well as a pervading inflation which has contributed to general discontent with the existing institutional structure.
The intelligentsia and youth have fed on one another's alienation from
the nation's political, economic and technical culture. All of these factors
have generated a demand, led by youth and responded to by some politicians, for a reordering of national priorities from defense and outer space
to the environment and the inner city. . . .

The Soviets, too, have had their problems, quite apart from China.
Their counterpart of America's student rebels is the minority of scientists,
artists, writers and intellectuals—the Sakharovs and Solzhenitzyns—who
in a more restrained way embarrass the communist leaders with their
criticisms. Tens of thousands of Soviet Jews, unable to appreciate the
subtle distinction that Moscow tries to draw between anti-Zionism and
old-fashioned anti-Semitism, would like to depart from the socialist
fatherland, and if this were permitted it might lead to unflattering comparisons between the USSR and Nazi Germany. The Soviet leaders, when
they look toward Eastern Europe, are probably aware that the Common
Market exercises a powerful attraction upon East Europeans, and to an
extent even upon themselves. They must also realize that the sobering
effects of the invasion of Czechoslovakia may wear off in Eastern as well
as in Western Europe. Some East Europeans may still hope to exploit for
their own gains the tension on the Amur-Ussuri rivers. A series of repeated applications of the "Brezhnev Doctrine" (in Rumania, Poland
and elsewhere) is not something to be anticipated enthusiastically, although Moscow can be expected to apply the doctrine whenever necessary. In other words, the search for limited agreements with the West
may either reduce the necessity of further applications of the Brezhnev
Doctrine or increase the readiness of Western intellectuals and governments to excuse such "counterrevolutionary interventions" as may yet
occur.

IV

Neither the Soviet Union nor the United States appears seriously
worried today about a deliberately planned surprise attack by the other.
Neither side seems greatly concerned over mild disturbances in the prevailing equilibrium of mutual deterrence caused by fluctuating, marginal
differences in particular weapons sectors. Most policymakers in both
countries are probably convinced that, for all practical decision-making
purposes, there exists at least a temporary, crude parity based on com-
pensating offensive and defensive asymmetries. These asymmetries involve different numbers of bombers, land-based missiles and sea-based
missiles, all of differing ranges; different numbers of deliverable warheads
and total "throw-weight" (measured in megatons); differences in harden-

ing and dispersal (which affect vulnerability), firing reliability, guidance accuracy, re-entry speeds, penetration aids, detonation altitudes, and other weapons-design characteristics known only to the experts; and differences in warning systems, strategic intelligence, attack and defense strategies, offensive and defensive weapons mixes, and ability to over-come the unknowns of large-scale nuclear war (such as the operation of command and control systems under circumstances affecting electronic communications).

Given the present levels in numbers of strategic launchers (with growing numbers carrying multiple warheads), the case can be made that the uncertainties inherent in the calculus of a nuclear exchange are, on the whole, more stabilizing than destabilizing. Military strategists may continue to worry, as they must, about the numbers game, about the possibility of decisive technological breakthroughs, and about the "worst possible case" in which *our* systems fail to perform well while *theirs* work perfectly. But McGeorge Bundy was probably close to the mark when he said that the political leadership in Moscow and Washington cannot under existing circumstances conceive of any rational purpose to be served by a deliberately planned first strike, because the risks of retaliation are much too great.[8] This need not always be so, although it seems plausible now. The political leadership may be naïve in assessing the intentions of their counterparts in the opposite capital, or they may become so in the future, or they may at some time lose control over the first-strike decision to military leaders who have a different perception of the situation—but these are all possibilities political leaders are understandably reluctant to think about.

The widespread assumption of a U.S.-USSR crude parity of assured sufficiency is important because it is the first time in the twenty-five years of nuclear history that such a condition has been thought to exist. One might infer that American decision-makers have been virtually "marking time" for nearly a decade with respect to deploying strategic military capabilities, as if they were waiting for the Soviets to "catch up" to the point where serious negotiations for arms limitations could begin. But it is recognized that the USSR has been coming abreast at a disturbingly rapid rate within recent years.

There are apprehensions on both sides. The Soviets are not happy at the prospect of the Safeguard deployment around even a few sites, for they know that once ABM and radar technology has been produced on a small scale it could be extended rather quickly. They are probably also concerned over the U.S. ability to upgrade the quality of weapons by MIRV-ing them more rapidly than the Soviets can. Conversely, U.S. de-

---

[8] McGeorge Bundy, "To Cap the Volcano," *Foreign Affairs*, October 1969, p. 9.

fense and arms control planners wonder whether the Soviets will be content to level off at crude parity, or whether they might try to sustain and increase their recent momentum in an effort to achieve the kind of strategic superiority the United States has for all practical purposes renounced. The fear is that the Soviets will try to gain a substantial edge by deploying large numbers of SS-9's or other heavy-yield missile systems. During 1970, U.S. spokesmen speculated about the possible upgrading of low-performance Soviet anti-aircraft missiles into an effective ABM system; the possibility that the Soviets were developing a satellite-destroyer capability which could seriously hamper U.S. strategic reconnaissance efforts; and the significance of the buildup of the Soviet navy, including the submarine fleet.[9] All of these developments created suspicions that one side or the other was trying to take advantage of the SALT to gain a military margin over its rival, as well as misgivings that ongoing quantitative and qualitative developments in advanced military technology may quickly render obsolete or irrelevant any precisely formulated clauses of treaties on which the superpowers might reach agreement at Helsinki and Vienna.[10]

But beyond the uncertainties that make it so difficult for the superpowers to reach agreement, there are other uncertainties which motivate them to continue the negotiations. It is possible that both the United States and the Soviet Union see the SALT more in the framework of what may lie beyond 1975 than of presently projected deployments of familiar weapons systems during the next two or three years. The Soviets would probably like to use the SALT to inhibit the deployment of an operational ABM system in the United States (and under certain circumstances they might accomplish this objective). But even if they prove unable to

---

[9] See *New York Times,* January 11, February 5, October 4 and October 18, 1970 and April 29, 1971.

[10] Anyone interested in pursuing a highly sophisticated debate over the implications of quantitative and qualitative changes in U.S. and Soviet strategic forces for the continuation of mutual balanced deterrence and for arms limitation talks should refer to the following works: William C. Foster, "Prospects for Arms Control," Harold Brown, "Security through Limitations" and D. G. Brennan, "The Case for Missile Defense," all in *Foreign Affairs,* April 1969; George W. Rathjens, *The Future of the Strategic Arms Race: Options for the 1970's* (New York: Carnegie Endowment for International Peace, 1969); Matthew P. Gallagher, "The Uneasy Balance: Soviet Attitudes toward the Missile Talks," *Interplay,* December 1969/ January 1970; William R. Kintner, "The Uncertain Strategic Balance in the 1970's," *Arms Control and National Security,* I, 1969; Jeremy J. Stone, "When and How to Use SALT," *Foreign Affairs,* January 1970; J. I. Coffey, "The Soviet ABM and Arms Control," *Bulletin of the Atomic Scientists,* January 1970; Alexander De Volpi, "Expectations from SALT," *ibid.,* April 1970; Jerome B. Wiesner, "Arms Control: Current Prospects and Problems," *ibid.,* May 1970; and J. I. Coffey, "Strategic Superiority, Deterrence and Arms Control," ORBIS, Winter 1970.

obtain such a bonus, there are other reasons why they would not wish to withdraw from the effort to arrive at some limited-risk, limited-cost, mutual interest agreements. Some of these reasons also serve to explain, in varying degrees, U.S. motivations.

Both are aware that there might be technological breakthroughs in the future. If the SALT were to collapse, competition in military research, development and deployment could well be stepped up. The familiar action-reaction process, marked by occasional overreactions, might end the existing condition of crude parity, creating new military-technological imbalances, perhaps leading to imprudent decision-making in a future international crisis. Both sides share an interest in moderating the rate of competition between themselves as they watch China. (The term "arms race," insofar as it implies a hectic rush to pile up or to improve weapons as rapidly as possible, is not an apt one for describing the present situation. The United States is preparing to deploy a limited ABM system only after ten years of debate.) Both sides must ponder at times the "economics of futility," that is, indefinitely expanding their nuclear missile capabilities and investing in costly new weapons systems throughout the 1970's, only to find at the end of the decade that such programs have had a reciprocal canceling effect, and that neither side has thereby improved its security or its ability to deter, much less gain any meaningful superiority.

Curious contrasts can be drawn here. The Soviets have reason to be worried about the total productive capabilities of the American economic-technological system whether measured in time, quantitative or qualitative factors. In a prolonged and unbridled arms race, the U.S. system, theoretically speaking, should still perform better. Soviet planners may realize this. Moreover, Soviet leaders undoubtedly feel economic pressures to limit spending for strategic arms—pressures for increased investment in agriculture and consumer industries, for narrowing the "technological gap" with the West in nondefense sectors, and for a reallocation of defense resources to the army and navy.[11] But in actuality, the purely economic incentive to reach agreement in the SALT is probably stronger in the United States than in the Soviet Union, because domestic political pressures to reallocate national budgetary resources to nondefense purposes are considerably stronger on Washington than on Moscow. Soviet leaders are undoubtedly aware of such domestic U.S. constraints.

In the final analysis, the logic of the economist is not likely to be the ultimate determinant of defense choices in any country where the leaders

---

[11] An excellent analysis of conflicting economic, technological and strategic pressures upon Soviet decision-makers can be found in Thomas W. Wolfe, "Soviet Approaches to SALT," *Problems of Communism*, September/October 1970, pp. 1–10.

are worried about security. Both superpowers will do what they think they must do in the military sector. But economic rationality prompts the leadership groups in the two countries to carry out communications and negotiations designed to hold armaments competition to manageable rates, lower than they would be in a more suspicious, fearful climate.

Another important set of shared motives for negotiating strategic arms limitations arises out of the connection between the SALT and the Nonproliferation Treaty. The superpowers definitely prefer a world of five nuclear powers to a world of ten or fifteen, and hence they must consider the implications of SALT's outcome for the viability of the NPT. This is not the central issue, yet it is by no means negligible. Whether or not India or Israel or another country decides to go nuclear will probably not be determined solely by the success or failure of SALT. But if the SALT should collapse entirely or drag on without even producing what the Swedish neutrals call a "cosmetic" or face-saving agreement, it will become easier for several countries to justify decisions to move in directions that contravene the provisions of the Nonproliferation Treaty.

The diffusion of peaceful reactor technology during the last decade has considerably compounded the difficulty of halting the spread of nuclear weapons. "Atoms for peace" are not easily separated from "atoms for war." Despite a growing uneasiness about the dangers of environmental pollution from nuclear reactors, the fact that nuclear energy is becoming economically competitive ensures that it will become more common as a source of power throughout the globe.[12] Thus, the growth of reactor technology will render it easier in the decade ahead for several countries to divert fissionable materials into weapons production if they are determined to do so. The intimate relationship between military potential and the nuclear power industry makes it difficult to prevent the proliferation of weapons without at least seeming to jeopardize the freedom of such countries as West Germany, Japan, India and Brazil to exploit the atom's peaceful uses. The International Atomic Energy Agency will probably not be able to perform the desired control function for two or three more years.[13] By that time, the possibilities for manufacturing nu-

---

[12] See Lord Ritchie-Calder, "Mortgaging the Old Homestead," *Foreign Affairs*, January 1970, especially pp. 210–212; Sheldon Novick, *The Careless Atom* (Boston: Houghton Mifflin, 1969); Richard Curtis and Elizabeth Hogan, *The Perils of the Peaceful Atom* (New York: Doubleday, 1969); Philip F. Gustafson, "Nuclear Power and Thermal Pollution: Zion, Illinois," *Bulletin of the Atomic Scientists*, March 1970, pp. 17–23; Alvin M. Weinberg, "Nuclear Energy and the Environment," *ibid.*, June 1970, pp. 69–74.

[13] See the author's "The Treaty and the Nonnuclear States," ORBIS, Summer 1967 and Frank Barnaby, "Limits on the Nuclear Club," reprinted from *New Scientist*, 19 March 1970, in *Survival*, May 1970.

clear weapons through centrifuge technology and through the even more esoteric ruby laser or argon technologies may have further compounded the problem of thwarting proliferation through technical controls on international exports.

The superpowers acted out of a combination of self-interest and a sense of international responsibility in agreeing to a Nonproliferation Treaty at the height of the Viet Nam war. But it must be recognized that they can do no more than discourage proliferation, by providing disincentives and compensations; they cannot absolutely prevent it. Their shipment of conventional arms into regions of local conflict, such as between the Arabs and Israel or between India and Pakistan, may under some circumstances decrease incentives, and under other circumstances increase incentives, to acquire nuclear weapons for deterrence or defense. For several years the United States sought to persuade new aspirants to the nuclear club that the game is not worth the candle because small deterrents are costly, provocative, accident-prone, non-credible, subject to rapid obsolescence and highly dangerous because young nuclear powers are vulnerable to pre-emptive attack. But none of these arguments has proved overwhelmingly convincing and some have often seemed irrelevant to countries worried not about the superpowers but about their immediate neighbors. . . .

The Nonproliferation Treaty has been criticized on several different grounds. It is a device for "disarming the unarmed." Virtually all of its burdens fall on the nonnuclear weapons states; thus it fails to provide an acceptable balance of mutual responsibilities and obligations. It perpetuates the nuclear hegemony of the five. It prohibits peaceful nuclear explosions by nonweapon countries. It limits the rights of nonweapon countries to develop an export business in civilian reactor technology. It will facilitate industrial espionage. It could inhibit the movement toward European integration. It infringes upon the sovereign prerogatives of nonweapon states by requiring them to submit to international inspection and other forms of "intervention" or "bondage." It limits the choice of nations in respect to vital questions of defense without providing adequate compensations in the security field. Steady if undramatic progress has been made toward reducing some of the foregoing bases of objection to the Nonproliferation Treaty, but several misgivings remain in a number of countries—especially in regard to security—and these are sufficient to make governments reluctant to close off the nuclear weapons option.[14]

---

[14] See Elizabeth Young, *The Control of Proliferation: The 1968 Treaty in Hindsight and Forecast* (London: Institute for Strategic Studies, Adelphi Papers No. 56, April 1969); Ryukichi Imai, "The Non-Proliferation Treaty and Japan," *Bulletin of the Atomic Scientists,* May 1969, pp. 2–7; George Schwab, "Switzerland's Tactical Nuclear Weapons Policy," Orbis, Fall 1969, pp. 900–914; Shelton L. Williams, *The U.S., India and the Bomb* (Baltimore: The Johns Hopkins Press, 1969); George

The principal question concerning the danger of proliferation is whether the United States, Britain and the Soviet Union can offer credible security guarantees to nonweapon states which adhere to the treaty. At present the three "nuclear arms control powers" are committed to do no more than concert action through the United Nations Security Council in the event of a nuclear attack upon a nonnuclear signatory (and one can argue that the members of the Security Council always had such an obligation under the Charter). We must remember that a nonweapon state such as India is also concerned about the threat of conventional aggression. Indians have no reason to expect that, if their northeast frontier should again come under Chinese attack, they will receive help from the British (who have withdrawn irreversibly from "east of Suez"), from the Americans (who, according to the Nixon Doctrine, plan to reduce their Asian commitments in the post-Viet Nam era) or from the Soviets (who have to worry about their own troop commitments both in Eastern Europe and along the Chinese border).

Any nonnuclear weapon state confronted with either a serious conventional or nuclear threat will naturally fear that as the crisis mounts it will find itself under pressure from the superpowers to make substantial concessions in the interests of peace, so that they need not become involved in its defense. More than that, a nonnuclear weapon state has to worry about the possibility that, in a future defense crisis, the superpowers might be in an adversary rather than a détente relationship with each other. Thus it is understandable that a country in India's position should temporarily adopt the anomalous policy characterized as the "three negatives": No bomb, no treaty, no guarantees.[15] This enables India to defy the superpowers in their efforts to pressure her to sign, while moving steadily in the direction of reducing (perhaps to a matter of days) the leadtime problem between a decision to acquire nuclear weapons (if it should become vitally necessary) and their actual acquisition.

India's decision-making process is of crucial importance to international arms control efforts. Obviously, if she were to become a sixth nuclear power (whether for defense reasons or from a political desire to be guaranteed a place at the international negotiating table at least as early as China is seated there), pressures would quickly mount for several other states to pursue the nuclear weapons path. Indian officials may perceive

---

H. Quester, "India Contemplates the Bomb," *Bulletin of the Atomic Scientists,* January 1970, pp. 13–16; H. Jon Rosenbaum and Glenn M. Cooper, "Brazil and the Non-Proliferation Treaty," *International Affairs* (London), January 1970; George H. Quester, "Israel and the Non-Proliferation Treaty," *Bulletin of the Atomic Scientists,* June 1969, pp. 7–9, 44–45.

15 Hans R. Vohra, "India's Nuclear Policy of Three Negatives," *Bulletin of the Atomic Scientists,* April 1970, pp. 25–27.

that their country is not without political leverage vis-à-vis the delicate triangular relationship of the United States, the Soviet Union and China. During the years when the NPT was being negotiated, Indian spokesmen argued trenchantly that the treaty could be justified as equitable only if it eventually paved the way for nuclear disarmament, or at least a reduction of the symbolic importance of nuclear weapons in international politics. It was largely at the insistence of India that the superpowers agreed to insert Article VI into the treaty: "Each of the Parties to the Treaty undertakes to pursue negotiations in good faith on effective measures relating to cessation of the nuclear arms race at an early date and to nuclear disarmament, and on a Treaty on general and complete disarmament under strict and effective international control." Yet precisely because of India's dependence for security on the continued ability of the superpowers to deter Peking's aggressive behavior by maintaining a wide margin of strategic superiority over China, her leaders are forced to adopt an ambivalent attitude toward strategic arms limitation talks between the United States and the Soviet Union. At present, the New Delhi government is not berating the superpowers for talking about a "freeze" rather than about arms reductions. At the same time, Indian leaders probably take some comfort from the thought that international circumstances are scarcely propitious for a Chinese onslaught against India. Indeed, New Delhi's policy of abstention from nuclear weapons may depend as much upon China's prudent restraint as upon any hope that India could count on assistance from the superpowers *in extremis*.

V

We can see, then, that the prospects for significant progress toward arms control in the 1970's will depend on such a variety of factors as to render prediction difficult even if they do not make hope meaningless. Each of the major world powers suffers under its own unique set of problems, demands, supports, commitments, apprehensions, dilemmas, assets and liabilities. Certainly one of the imoprtant tasks of U.S. diplomacy in the Helsinki-Vienna talks is to find out whether the Soviets will be satisfied to accept the condition of crude strategic parity as a permanent part of the superpower relationship, or whether they seem determined to go beyond mild and temporary disturbances of the existing equilibrium (which need not cause panic) toward a more fundamental alteration of the strategic equation to the disadvantage of the United States. If the Soviets should opt for the second course, it will not augur well either for the superpowers or for the world. . . .

Part IX

World Community and the International System

B UILDING POLITICAL communities is one of the enduring problems
of politics. From ancient times to the present, students of
political science have attempted to comprehend the factors contributing to the cohesiveness of political communities, and those
leading to their disintegration. Nowhere has this quest been greater
than at the international level. Students of international relations,
especially in its utopian phase (See Selection 3), saw international
law and organization as the key to building a more cohesive and
peaceful world community. Other students, especially in the past
generation, have sought, by testing theories in historical examples
of integration, to understand more fully the essential conditions for
political community, particularly at the international level.

Karl Deutsch attempts to evoke an understanding of similarities
in the process of nation-building in order to develop a theory of
integration based upon historical data. He and his associates found
that the national units they studied were based on core areas of
superior economic growth and administrative capabilities, and that
peoples within integrating regions engaged in a wide range of mutual transactions and broadened social communication. In presenting these and other findings, the authors proposed tentative theories
about building nations, and thus contributed to our knowledge of
nationalism (see Part II). Their findings may perhaps be relevant
to conditions essential to the building of international political communities. To what extent, it is appropriate to ask, does the international system have characteristics similar to those of other kinds of

political systems, e.g. those described by Deutsch and his associates, or by Walker Connor in his discussion (Section 12) of the national self-determination movements which are diminishing the cohesiveness of existing nation-states in many parts of the world.

Legal norms are essential to the functioning of political systems. Without laws to govern human behavior, life would be intolerable, if not impossible. In discussing international law, a distinction is often made between enforcement mechanisms that exist within nation-states and which are relatively absent in the international system. If enforcement mechanisms are the essential prerequisite of law, one must conclude that there is little international law. If, however, one assumes that law exists because it embodies widely shared values in a society, then one has a quite different concept of law. According to William D. Coplin, international law functions as an "institutional device for communicating to the policymakers of various states a consensus on the nature of the international system." Even though there is no official voice of the states of the world as a community, international law "taken as a body of generally related norms is the closest thing to such a voice."

Implicit in this concept is the idea that laws are generally obeyed because they have widespread public support. If such support is absent, the problems of enforcement would be formidable, if not insurmountable, even in the most repressive political system. The character of law is determined by the character of the society within which it operates. The strength of a legal system is proportionate to the sentiment of shared responsibility expressed by the inhabitants of a political system.

If there is a high level of compliance to much of international law, the defects of the modern international legal system can be traced not only to the absence of enforcement mechanisms but also to the lack of widespread support for certain of its contemporary features. The emergence of states with widely differing national interests and goals will further weaken its position. Indeed, Coplin points out, international law no longer performs, as it once did, the function of communicating the assumptions of the international system to policymakers. This is the result of a gap between the structure of the law itself and the contemporary international practices of nation-states. Until the law is modernized to accommodate changes in the concept of statehood, the role of international organizations, the changed doctrines of war, and the changing relation of the individual to the international legal order, it cannot embody the assumptions of the international system, or reflect and reinforce the level of consensus among nation-states.

As envisaged by its founders, the United Nations was to play a role both in preventing conflict and in resolving international disputes. It was endowed with procedures and institutions for resolving such disputes. According to Article I of its Charter, the United Nations is "to take effective collective measures for the prevention and removal of threats to the peace, and for the suppression of acts of aggression or other breaches of the peace, and to bring about by lawful means, and in conformity with the principles of justice and international law, adjustment or settlement of international disputes or situations which might lead to a breach of the peace." A substantial portion of the Charter (Articles 33-51) contains methods for fulfilling these obligations.

Undoubtedly, in performing its peacekeeping functions, the United Nations has evolved in ways unforeseen by its founders. In contrast to the intention of those who drafted the Charter, the locus of decision-making has passed from the Security Council, where it was originally lodged, to the General Assembly, and more recently, after the financial crisis created by the United Nations Operation in the Congo in the early 1960s, back to the Security Council.

It has been argued that the gap between the international system that emerged after World War II was formidable. The world of the Charter was a "pluralistic yet controlled" order that never materialized. It was to be managed by a postwar version of the Concert of Europe, the five permanent members of the Security Council. The United Nations has influenced, and has been influenced by, the international system in which it has operated. The temporary transfer of decision-making in peacekeeping operations from the Security Council to the General Assembly caused by the Uniting for Peace Resolution of 1950, the expansion of U.N. membership, and the shaping of the peacekeeping function of the international organization have all reflected the international system of the past generation. The United Nations has influenced the international system in several ways.

By championing national independence, the United Nations has strengthened the principle of state sovereignty and has contributed to the balkanization of global regions once under European control, and even the emergence of new mini-states. The majoritarian principle based on one state, one vote, embodied in the General Assembly has magnified national sovereignty and given to small states a sense of power and a forum for international posturing far beyond that to which their material resources might entitle them. To the extent that the United Nations has reduced inequalities between superpowers and small states, the international organization has helped to transform the international system from bipolarity to multipolarity.

The question remains as to the prospects for international organization in the 1970s. According to Philip E. Jacob, the essential problem is to reconcile the powerful forces seeking political pluralism at the international level with the pressures of technological and social interdependence in the world arena. There exists a need, recognized by many, if not most, governments around the world for collaborative action on common needs in many fields: the mobilization of resources for economic and social development; the creation and administration of world law in outerspace; the exploitation for the benefit of mankind of the vast natural resources on the ocean floor; and the development of a capacity for peacekeeping. If the nation-state remains the dominant force in international politics, it is essential to develop international frameworks for common action based on consent. What is needed, Jacob contends, is "an approach to the use of the United Nations that will allow members to act when they share a common concern, even if they cannot persuade the entire organization to go along." A "consortium of the concerned" would assume the financial responsibility for its programs. Nations would remain free either to join, or to remain outside of, consortia and would have comparable access to the facilities of the United Nations. Within the framework of the international organization, multiple consortia having overlapping and sometimes separate membership for attaining a wide variety of objectives would be formed.

There is an abundance of literature on international relations in which authors argue for the creation of a world government. Similarly, there are many critiques of such proposals. In this literature many of the utopian or realist assumptions about international relations can be found (see Part I). In a survey, Inis Claude summarizes the arguments of proponents of world government: that the nation-state is no longer able to provide protection for its people, that modern man may doom himself to extinction unless he joins a new global organization, that through enforceable world law the prospects for the peaceful settlement of international disputes can be enhanced, that fear of nuclear annihilation may bridge differences in ideology and culture and thus provide a consensus upon which to build new international institutions.

In contrast, critics argue that governments, even if created by force, must rest at least upon some level of consensus. No national unit possesses the resources to impose political institutions upon the rest of mankind. Whatever their fear of annihilation, the peoples of the world have developed little, if any consensus about the form of institutions at the international level. Should they be based upon an American federalist model, or a Soviet model? Even if such agreement existed, would it be possible to achieve accord as to who would control such institutions? *Quis custodiet ipsos?* (Who watches the custodians?)

World government proponents, Claude suggests, place perhaps too much emphasis upon a positivist conception of law, namely, that law is obeyed because of the enforcement procedures available to the community. Instead, critics have contended that law is obeyed essentially because the community as a whole accepts it as corresponding to its conception of justice. Even in such political systems as the United States it becomes difficult, if not impossible, to enforce laws which do not have the consent of at least a majority of the population. In the international system a considerable body of international law is obeyed, even without elaborate enforcement procedures, because it rests upon a broadly based consensus. Thus Claude focuses on possible similarities between conditions in the international and national political systems. Even at the level of the national unit, conditions of civil conflict sometimes resemble conditions prevailing in the model of the international system described by many authors. Yet it is the differences between these systems which have contributed to the emergence of international relations as a field of study and rendered difficult, if not impossible, the development of more effective institutions and techniques for the management of power at the international level.

SECTION ONE:

The Integrative Process

39. SOME ESSENTIAL REQUIREMENTS FOR THE ESTABLISHMENT OF AMALGAMATED SECURITY-COMMUNITIES

Karl W. Deutsch, *et al.*

A NUMBER OF CONDITIONS appear to be essential, so far as our evidence goes, for the success of amalgamated security-communities—that is, for their becoming integrated. None of these conditions, of course, seems to be by itself sufficient for success; and all of them together may not be

From *Political Community and the North Atlantic Area* by Karl W. Deutsch, Sidney A. Burrell, Robert A. Kann, Maurice Lee, Jr., Martin Lichterman, Raymond E. Lindgren, Francis L. Loewenheim, Richard W. Van Wagenen. (Princeton, N.J.: Princeton University Press, 1957), pp. 46–58. Reprinted by permission of Princeton University Press, Copyright © 1957. Footnotes have been renumbered to appear in consecutive order.

KARL W. DEUTSCH (1912–   ) Professor of Government, Harvard University. Author of *Political Community at the International Level: Problems of Definition and Measurement* (Hamden, Conn.: Archon Books, 1970); *Nationalism and Its Alternatives* (New York: Alfred A. Knopf, 1969); *Analysis of International Relations* (Englewood Cliffs, N.J.: Prentice-Hall, 1968); *The Nerves of Government* (New York, Free Press of Glencoe, 1963). Co-author, *Arms Control and the Atlantic Alliance: Europe Faces Coming Policy Decisions* (New York: John Wiley and Sons, 1967); *France, Germany and the Western Alliance: A Study of Elite Attitudes on European Integration and World Politics* (New York: Charles Scribner's Sons, 1967).

sufficient either, for it is quite possible that we have overlooked some additional conditions that may also be essential. None the less, it does seem plausible to us that any group of states or territories which fulfilled all the essential conditions for an amalgamated security-community which we have been able to identify, should also be at least on a good part of the way to successful amalgamation.*

1. VALUES AND EXPECTATIONS

The first group of essential conditions deals with motivations for political behavior, and in particular with the values and expectations held in the politically relevant strata of the political units concerned. In regard to values, we found in all our cases a compatibility of the main values held by the politically relevant strata of all participating units. Sometimes this was supplemented by a tacit agreement to deprive of political significance any incompatible values that might remain. In this manner the gradual depoliticization of the continuing difference between Protestant and Catholic religious values in the course of the eighteenth century furnished an essential pre-condition for the successful amalgamation of Germany and Switzerland, respectively, in the course of the following century.[1] Examples of a partial depoliticization of conflicting values include the partial depoliticization of the slavery issue in the United States between 1775 and 1819, and of the race problem after 1876.[2] Similarly, Germany saw a reduction in the political relevance of the liberal-conservative cleavage after 1866 with the emergence of the National Liberal Party. A similar reduction of political relevance occurred in regard to the conflict of Scottish Presbyterianism with the Episcopal Church in England and Scotland after 1690, and in the further abatement of the Protestant–Catholic issue in Switzerland after the mid-eighteenth century, and further after 1848.

Whether values are "main" values can be determined from the internal

---

*Editor's Note: In an amalgamated security community, according to Deutsch and his collaborators, previously independent political units have formed a single unit with a common government.

[1] For the Swiss solution of the denominational problem, see Hermann Weilenmann, *Pax Helvetica oder die Demokratie der Kleinen Gruppen*, Zurich, Rentsch, 1951, pp. 300–311; Hans Kohn, *Der Schweizerische Nationalgedanke: Eine Studie Zum Thema "Nationalismus und Freiheit,"* Zurich, Verlag der "Neuen Zürcher Zeitung," 1955, pp. 77–78, 88–94; E. Bonjour, H. S. Offler, and G. R. Potter, *A Short History of Switzerland*, Oxford, Clarendon Press, 1952, pp. 272–273, 296–299, etc.

[2] Any survey of American history of the period up to about 1819 reveals how small a part the slavery issue played in politics in the early years of the republic. For the temporary depoliticization of the race problem after 1876 see Paul H. Buck, *The Road to Reunion*, Boston, 1947, pp. 283, 296–297; C. Vann Woodward, *Origins of the New South, 1877–1913*, Baton Rouge, 1951, p. 216.

politics of the participating units independently from the issue of union—although only, to be sure, within broad margins of error. How important is each value in the domestic politics of the participating units? Acceptance of slavery as a "positive good" had become an essential qualification of candidates for public office in many Southern states in the United States before 1861; this value, important in Southern internal politics, was then also important in the relations between South and North. Conversely, the importance of the distinction between Catholics and Protestants was declining in the domestic politics of nineteenth century Prussia and Bavaria, as well as—more slowly—in the relations between them.

Values were most effective politically when they were not held merely in abstract terms, but when they were incorporated in political institutions and in habits of political behavior which permitted these values to be acted on in such a way as to strengthen people's attachment to them. This connection between values, institutions, and habits we call a "way of life," and it turned out to be crucial. In all our cases of successful amalgamation we found such a distinctive way of life—that is, a set of socially accepted values and of institutional means for their pursuit and attainment, and a set of established or emerging habits of behavior corresponding to them. To be distinctive, such a way of life has to include at least some major social or political values and institutions which are different from those which existed in the area during the recent past, or from those prevailing among important neighbors. In either case, such a way of life usually involved a significant measure of social innovation as against the recent past.

Putting the matter somewhat differently, we noted in our cases that the partial shift of political habits required in transferring political loyalties from the old, smaller political units, at least in part, to a new and larger political community has only occurred under conditions when also a great number of other political and social habits were in a state of change. Thus we find that the perception of an American people and an American political community, as distinct from the individual thirteen colonies, emerged between 1750 and 1790. This occurred at the same time as the emergence of a distinct American way of life clearly different from that of most of the people of Great Britain or French Canada. This way of life had been developing since the beginnings of colonial settlement in the seventeenth century, but had undergone accelerated change and development in the course of the American Revolution and its aftermath. Another example of this process is the emergence of a distinct way of life of the Swiss people, in contrast to the way of life of the peasants and to a lesser extent of the town dwellers in most of the rest of Europe; here, too, the emergence of this distinctive way of life furnished the social and political background for the gradual emergence of Swiss political community.[3] Similarly, the unifications of Germany and of Italy occurred in the context of a much broader change in political values, institutions, and habits of behavior. These new values were implicit in the modern, liberal nineteenth-century way of life in contrast to the values and institutions of the "old regime" still represented by the policies of the Metternich era.

In regard to expectations, we found that in all our cases amalgamation was preceded by widespread expectations of joint rewards for the participating units, through strong economic ties or gains envisaged for the future. By economic ties, we mean primarily close relations of trade permitting large-scale division of labor and almost always giving rise to vested interests. It was not necessary, however, for such strong economic ties to exist prior to amalgamation. Expectations of rewards were conspicuous in the Anglo–Scottish union of 1707; [4] in the unification of Italy, where the South found itself to some extent disappointed; and in the unification of Germany, where such economic expectations were brilliantly fulfilled.

Only a part of such expectation had to be fulfilled. A "down payment" of tangible gains for a substantial part of the supporters of amalgamation soon after the event, if not earlier, seems almost necessary. This was accomplished by the land policies of Jefferson and the fiscal policies of Hamilton in the case of the United States, by Bismarck's "National Liberal" policies in the 1870's,[5] and by Cavour for at least Northern Italy. Somewhat different economic gains may result from the joint or parallel exploitation of some third resource, rather than from trade between one unit and another. Thus, exploitation of Western lands offered joint rewards to members of the American union, apart from the benefits of mutual trade; many Scotsmen, too, in 1707 were more impressed with the prospect of a Scottish share in English overseas markets than in direct trade with England.

---

[3] Cf. Leo Weisz, *Die Alten Eidgenossen,* Zurich, Niehaus, 1940, pp. 7–156. Wilhelm Oechsli, *History of Switzerland, 1499–1914,* Cambridge University Press, 1922, pp. 1–7, 17–21. Anton Castell, *Geschichte des Landes Schwyz,* Zurich, *Benziger* Verlag Einsiedelm, 1954, pp. 26–33. Wolfgang von Wartburg, *Geschichte der Schweiz,* Munich, Oldenbourg, 1951, pp. 31–56. Weilenmann, *Die vielsprachige Schweiz,* Basel-Leipzig, Rheim-Verlag, 1925, pp. 20–42, 50–51, 54–57, 60–63, 68; *Pax Helvetica,* pp. 221–284.

[4] One of the more important rewards from the Scottish point of view was participation in trade with England and England's colonies. P. Hume Brown, *History of Scotland,* Cambridge, Eng., 1911, III, 57–58; George S. Pryde, *The Treaty of Union of Scotland and England 1707,* Edinburgh, 1950, 13ff.

[5] Cf. Adalbert Wahl, *Deutsche Geschichte von der Reichsgründung bis zum Ausbruch des Weltkriegs (1871 bis 1914),* Stuttgart, 1926, I, 61–107; and Johannes Ziekursch, *Politische Geschichte des neuen deutschen Kaiserreiches,* Frankfurt, 1927, II, 279–308.

Some noneconomic expectations also turned out to be essential. In all our cases of successful amalgamation we found widespread expectations of greater social or political equality, or of greater social or political rights or liberties, among important groups of the politically relevant strata—and often among parts of the underlying populations—in the political units concerned.[6]

2. CAPABILITIES AND COMMUNICATION PROCESSES

Values and expectations not only motivate people to performance, but the results of this performance will in turn make tue original values and expectations weaker or stronger. Accordingly, we found a number of essential conditions for amalgamation which were related to the capabilities of the participating units or to the processes of communication occurring among them. The most important of these conditions was an increase in the political and administrative capabilities of the main political units to be amalgamated. Thus the amalgamation of Germany was preceded by a marked increase in the political and administrative capabilities of Prussia from 1806 onward, and by a lesser but still significant increase in the corresponding capabilities of Bavaria and of other German states. Similarly, there were important increases in the capabilities of Piedmont in the course of the last decades preceding Italian unification.[7] In the case of the American colonies, considerable increases in the capabilities of American state governments after 1776, and particularly the adoption of important and effective state constitutions by Pennsylvania, Virginia, Massachusetts, and other states, paved the way for the Articles of Confederation and later for federal union.[8]

Another essential condition for amalgamation, closely related to the increase in capabilities, is the presence of markedly superior economic growth, either as measured against the recent past of the territories to be amalgamated, or against neighboring areas. Such superior economic growth did not have to be present in all participating units prior to amalgamation, but it had to be present at least in the main partner or

---

[6] Hermann Oncken, *Lassalle, Eine politische Biographie*, 4th edn., Stuttgart and Berlin, 1923, pp. 236–237; Erich Eyck, *Der Vereinstag Deutscher Arbeitervereine 1863–1868*, Berlin, 1904; Gustav Mayer, *Johann Baptist von Schweitzer und die Sozialdemokratie*, Jena, 1909; and Eugene N. Anderson, *The Social and Political Conflict in Prussia 1858–1864*, Lincoln, Neb., 1954, pp. 119–175.

[7] The development of Piedmont is discussed in great detail by Giuseppe Prato in *Fatti e dottrine economiche alla vigilia del 1848: l'Associazione agraria subalpina e Camillo Cavour*, published in *Biblioteca di Storia Italiana recente (1800–1870)*, IX, Turin, 1921, pp. 133–484.

[8] Allan Nevins, *The American States During and After the Revolution, 1775–1789*, New York, 1924, 117ff., 621ff.

partners vis-à-vis the rest of the units to be included in the amalgamated security-community. The higher economic growth rates of England, Prussia, and Piedmont, both immediately before and during amalgamation, are conspicuous examples.

Another essential requirement for successful amalgamation was the presence of unbroken links of social communication between the political units concerned, and between the politically relevant strata within them. By such unbroken links we mean social groups and institutions which provide effective channels of communication, both horizontally among the main units of the amalgamated security-community and vertically among the politically relevant strata within them. Such links thus involve always persons and organizations.

Some of the links are horizontal or geographic between different participating units; others involve vertical communications, cutting across classes. An example of geographic links occurred during the course of the Industrial Revolution. The rapid growth of settlement and economic activity in Northern England and Southwestern Scotland deepened the integration of England and Scotland during the century after 1707.[9] Another example would be the rapid growth in population and economic activity in the Middle Atlantic states and in Kentucky, Tennessee, and Ohio which tended to strengthen the links between North and South in the United States during the first decades after 1776. A third example is the role of commerce and transport over St. Gotthard Pass, and of the institutions and organizations related to it, in the consolidation of Switzerland.[10]

An example of a vertical link within Scotland was that between the aristocracy and the middle classes and the people at large, made possible by the ministers and elders of the Scottish Presbyterian Church. In the course of the seventeenth century, the horizontal links of the Scottish Presbyterians to English Protestant sects facilitated Scottish participation in English theological disputes, and this in turn contributed to the acceptance of English (rather than lowland Scots) as the standard

---

[9] This, strictly speaking, cannot be documented, since the two areas are not fused industrially even today. They are, however, very close to one another, and there has been an extensive migration back and forth. The term "Geordie" as used to describe a Tyneside Scottish migrant is one indication, however, of the extent of population flow over the border. For evidence of the continuing distinctiveness of the two areas even so late as the early nineteenth century, see John Clapham, *Economic History of Modern Britain*, Cambridge, Eng., 1950, 2nd edn., I, pp. 50–51.

[10] See, eg., Hans Nabholz, *Geschichte der Schweiz*, Zurich, Schulthess, 1938, Vol. 1, pp. 105–106, 126, 150–152, 203, etc., Wolfgang von Wartburg, *op. cit.*, pp. 32–33, 43, 58, 82, etc., Weilenmann, *Pax Helvetica*, pp. 99–127, 177–181, 197–200, 205–207.

language of Scotland.[11] Another example would be the German financial and industrial community that came to link major interests in the Rhineland, Berlin, Darmstadt, Leipzig, and other German centers and states during the 1850's and 1860's.[12]

Another essential condition, related to the preceding one, is the broadening of the political, social, or economic elite, both in regard to its recruitment from broader social strata and to its continuing connections with them.[13] An example of such a broadening of the elite was the emergence of a new type of political leader among the landowners of Virginia, such as George Washington, who retained the respect of his peers and at the same time also knew, well before the American Revolution,[14] how to gain votes of poorer farmers and frontiersmen at the county elections in Virginia. Another example might be the shift in leadership in the Prussian elite, during the two decades before 1871, from a noble such as Edwin von Manteuffel, who was unwilling to work with the middle classes, to Bismarck, who retained the respect of his fellow aristocrats but knew how to attract and retain middle-class support.[15]

---

[11] For evidence of the growth of an Anglicized Scottish language during the early seventeenth century see Marjorie A. Bald, "The Anglicisation of Scottish Printing," *Scottish History Review*, XXIII, 1925–1926, pp. 107–115, and "The Pioneers of Anglicised Speech in Scotland," *Scottish History Review*, XXIV, 1926–1927, pp. 179–193.

[12] Cf. the great work of Pierre Benaerts, *Les Origines de la Grand Industrie Allemande*, Paris, 1933, which also indicates the extent to which Austria was increasingly excluded from German economic life. For basic statistical data on this subject see A. Bienengräber, *Statistik des Verkehrs und Verbrauchs im Zollverein für die Jahre 1842–1864*, Berlin, 1868.

[13] An exception must be made here for Germany. In Prussia, in particular, both before and after 1871 there was little, if any, broadening of the political "decision-making" elite; the top offices in the government, the foreign services, the bureaucracy, and the army, continued to be filled with aristocrats; and political considerations continued to govern individual appointments: no Social Democrat or Linksliberaler could hope for a government career, and members of the Catholic Center Party could only if their politics were known to be reliably conservative. Only in some of the South German states, notably Baden and Württemberg, was a somewhat greater political toleration to be found. Cf. Theodor Eschenburg, "Die improvisierte Demokratie der Weimarer Republik von 1919," in *Schweizer Beiträge zur Allgemeinen Geschichte,* IX, 1951, pp. 164–165.

For an important new comparative analysis of the Prussian and Austrian political and miliary elite in the nineteenth century, see Nikolaus von Preradovich, *Die Führungsschichten in Österreich und Preussen (1804–1918) mit einem Ausblick bis zum Jahre 1945*, Wiesbaden, 1955.

[14] Cf. Charles S. Sydnor, *Gentlemen Freeholders: Political Practices in Washington's Virginia*, Chapel Hill, 1952.

[15] Cf. Gordon A. Craig, *The Politics of the Prussian Army, 1640–1945*, Oxford, 1955, pp. 148–179.

3. MOBILITY OF PERSONS

Another condition present in all our cases of successful amalgamation was the mobility of persons among the main units, at least in the politically relevant strata. It is quite possible that this condition, too, may be essential for the success of amalgamation. In any event, our cases have persuaded us that the mobility of persons among the main political units of a prospective amalgamated security-community should be given far more serious consideration than has often been the case. Full-scale mobility of persons has followed every successful amalgamated security-community in modern times immediately upon its establishment. Examples of the inter-regional mobility of persons preceding amalgamation are the cases of the American colonies,[16] the German states, and the Anglo-Scottish union. Examples of personal mobility accompanying amalgamation are the unification of Italy, and the union of England and Wales. Taken together with our finding that the free mobility of commodities and money, like other economic ties, was not essential for political amalgamation, our finding of the importance of the mobility of persons suggests that in this field of politics persons may be more important than either goods or money.

4. MULTIPLICITY AND BALANCE OF TRANSACTIONS

We also found that it was not enough for a high level of communications and transactions to exist only on one or two topics, or in one or two respects, among two or more political units if their amalgamation was to be successful. Rather it appeared that successfully amalgamated security-communities require a fairly wide range of different common functions and services, together with different institutions and organizations to carry them out. Further, they apparently require a multiplicity of ranges of common communications and transactions and their institutional counterparts. Thus the unification of Germany on the political level in 1871 had been prepared by the setting up of common institutions in regard to customs policies, to postal matters, and to the standardization of commercial laws; and beyond the sphere of politics, amalgamation had been prepared by a multiplicity of common institutions in cultural, educational, literary, scientific, and professional affairs.[17] Similarly we find in

---

[16] See Michael Kraus, *Intercolonial Aspects of American Culture on the Eve of the American Revolution*, New York, 1928, pp. 42ff., 51, 53, 55, 75–89, 91–102, 146, 160–161, 208.

[17] On the German postal union see Josef Karl Mayr, "Der deutschöster-reichische Postverein," in *Gesamtdeutsche Vergangenheit. Festgabe für Heinrich Ritter von Srbik*, Munich, 1938, pp. 287–295; on the German commercial code, Rudolph von Delbrück, *Lebenserinnerungen*, Liepzig, 1905, ii, 90ff. and 161ff.; and Enno E.

the American colonies, in the period prior to the Articles of Confederation, a wide range of mutual communications and transactions, as well as of common institutions. The latter included intercolonial church organizations, universities training ministers and physicians, and a postal service, together with ties of travel, migration, friendship, and intermarriage among important elements of the colonial elites.

Two other conditions may well turn out to be essential for the success of amalgamation, but these will have to be investigated further. The first of them is concerned with the balance in the flow of communications and transactions between the political units that are to be amalgamated, and particularly with the balance of rewards between the different participating territories. It is also concerned with the balance of initiatives that originate in these territories or groups of population, and finally with the balance of respect—or of symbols standing for respect—between these partners. In the course of studying cases of successful amalgamation, we found that it was apparently important for each of the participating territories or populations to gain some valued services or opportunities. It also seemed important that each at least sometimes take the initiative in the process, or initiate some particular phase or contribution; and that some major symbol or representative of each territory or population should be accorded explicit respect by the others. Thus it seemed significant to us that in the unification of Wales and England, and of Scotland and England, it was a family of Welsh descent (the Tudors) and the Scottish Stuart dynasty who were elevated to the English throne during important stages of the process; and that in the reunion between North and South in the United States, the name of General Robert E. Lee became a symbol of respect even in the North,[18] and that of Abraham Lincoln even in the South. In the case of the Swiss Confederation the very name of the emerging political community was taken from the small rural canton of Schwyz rather than from the more populous and powerful cantons of Bern or Zurich. Likewise, in the unifications of Germany and Italy it was the strongest participating units, Prussia and Piedmont respectively, that had to accept some of the symbols of the larger unit with which they merged, rather than insist on first place for symbols of their own prestige.

The second condition follows from the preceding one. It was not essen-

---

Kraehe, "Practical Politics in the German Confederation, Bismarck and the Commerical Code," *Journal of Modern History*, xxv, March 1953, pp. 13–24; on the national significance of the new academic societies see R. Hinton Thomas, *Liberalism, Nationalism, and the German Intellectuals (1822–1847): An analysis of the academic and scientific conferences of the period,* Cambridge, Eng., 1951.

[18] Buck, *op. cit.,* pp. 251, 255. However, Lincoln never became as much a national hero to the South as Lee did in the North.

tial that the flow of rewards, of initiatives, or of respect should balance at any one moment, but it seems essential that they should balance over some period of time. Sometimes this was accomplished by alternating flows or by an interchange of group roles. Territories which received particular prestige, or material benefits, at one time might become sources of benefits for their partners at another; or initiatives might pass from one region to another; or territories whose political elites found them‑ selves ranged with a majority on one political issue might find themselves in a minority on another, without any one particular division between majorities and minorities becoming permanent. Where this was not the case, as in the instance of the permanent minority of Irish Catholics in Protestant Great Britain under the terms of the Anglo–Irish Union, amalgamation eventually failed.[19] In contrast, most political divisions in Switzerland since amalgamation in 1848 have showed every canton, Protestant as well as Catholic, alternating between majority and minority status in accordance with political divisions in terms of agricultural versus industrial cantons, liberal versus conservative, Alpine versus lowland, and the like. This frequent interchange of group roles seems to have aided in the consolidation of the Swiss political community, but further study would be required to say to what extent, if any, this condition was essential in all the other cases of successful amalgamation.

5. MUTUAL PREDICTABILITY OF BEHAVIOR

A final condition that may be essential for the success of amalgamation may be some minimum amount of mutual predictability of behavior. Members of an amalgamated security-community—and, to a lesser extent, of a pluralistic security-community—must be able to expect from one another some dependable interlocking, interchanging, or a least compatible behavior; and they must therefore be able, at least to that extent, to predict one another's actions. Such predictions may be based on mere familiarity. In this way, the Vermonters or English-speaking Canadians may know what to expect of their French-Canadian neighbors and to what extent to rely on them, even though they do not share their folkways and culture and do not know what it feels like to be a French-Canadian. Even so, familiarity may be sufficiently effective to permit the development of an attitude of confidence and trust. (The opposite of such successful predictions of behavior are the characteristic fears of the alleged treacherousness, secretiveness, or unpredictability of "foreigners." Such fear of unpredictable "treachery" seems to be more destructive, as

---

[19] Similarly, the Norwegian fears of a permanent minority status in an amalgamated Norwegian-Swedish union did much to prevent full amalgamation and to destroy eventually even the partial amalgamation that had existed.

far as the experiences from our cases go, than do any clearcut and realistic expectations of future disagreements. Thus Norwegians and Swedes in the nineteenth century often could predict fairly well the unfavorable response which a given political suggestion from one country would find in the other; but these two peoples, while they failed to maintain even limited amalgamation, did retain sufficient mutual confidence to establish later a successful pluralistic security-community.) While familiarity appears to have contributed successfully to the growth of mutual trust in some of our cases, such as that between Scottish Highlanders and Lowlanders, and later between Scots and Englishmen, or between German, French, and Italian Swiss during much of the eighteenth century, we found in a number of our cases that mutual predictability of behavior was eventually established upon a firmer basis.

This firmer basis was the acquisition of a certain amount of common culture or of common group character or "national character." In this manner, an increasing number of Germans in the German states, of Italians in the Italian principalities, and of Americans in the American colonies, came to feel that they could understand their countrymen in the neighboring political units by expecting them, by and large, to behave much as they themselves would behave in similar situations; that is to say, they came to predict the behavior of their countrymen in neighboring political units on the basis of introspection: by looking into their own minds they could make a fairly good guess as to what their neighbors would do, so they could trust them or at least understand them, to some extent much as they would trust or understand themselves. The extent of mutual predictability of behavior, however, seems to have varied from case to case, and it also seems to have varied with the particular political elites or relevant strata concerned. That some mutual predictability of political behavior is an essential condition for an amalgamated security-community seems clear from our cases; but the extent of such predictability must remain a matter for further research.

SECTION TWO:

International Law

40. LAW AND INTERNATIONAL POLITICS

William D. Coplin

M OST WRITERS ON international relations and international law still examine the relationship between international law and politics in terms of the assumption that law either should or does function only as a coercive restraint on political action. Textbook writers on general international politics like Morgenthau,[1] and Lerche and Said,[2] as well as those scholars who have specialized in international law like J. L. Brierly [3] and

Reprinted by permission of the author and *World Politics*, XVII (No. 4, 1964), 615–635.

WILLIAM D. COPLIN (1939–   ) Associate Professor of Political Science, Wayne State University. Author of *Introduction to International Politics: A Theoretical Overview* (Chicago: Markham Publishing Company, 1970); *The Functions of International Law* (Chicago: Rand McNally and Company, 1966). Editor, *Simulation in the Study of Politics* (Chicago: Markham Publishing Company, 1968). Co-editor, *A Multi-Method Introduction to International Politics: Observation, Explanation, and Prescription* (Chicago: Markham Publishing Company, 1970).

[1] Hans J. Morgenthau, *Politics Among Nations* (New York 1961), 275–311. The entire evaluation of the "main problems" of international law is focused on the question of what rules are violated and what rules are not.

[2] Charles O. Lerche, Jr., and Abdul A. Said, *Concepts of International Politics* (Englewood Cliffs, N.J., 1963), 167–87. That the authors have employed the assumption that international law functions as a system of restraint is evident from the title of their chapter which examines international law, "Limitations on State Actions."

[3] J. L. Brierly, *The Law of Nations* (New York 1963), 1. Briefly defines international law as "the body of rules and principles of action which are binding upon civilized states in their relations. . . ."

Charles De Visscher,[4] make the common assumption that international law should be examined as a system of coercive norms controlling the actions of states. Even two of the newer works, *The Political Foundations of International Law* by Morton A. Kaplan and Nicholas deB. Katzenbach [5] and *Law and Minimum World Public Order* by Myres S. McDougal and Florentino P. Feliciano,[6] in spite of an occasional reference to the non-coercive aspects of international law, are developed primarily from the model of international law as a system of restraint. Deriving their conception of the relationship between international law and political action from their ideas on the way law functions in domestic communities, most modern writers look at international law as an instrument of direct control. The assumption that international law is or should be a coercive restraint on state action structures almost every analysis, no matter what the school of thought or the degree of optimism or pessimism about the effectiveness of the international legal system.[7] With an intel-

---

[4] Charles De Visscher, *Theory and Reality in Public International Law* (Princeton 1957), 99–100.

[5] Morton A. Kaplan and Nicholas deB. Katzenbach, *The Political Foundations of International Law* (New York 1961), 5. In a discussion of how the student should observe international law and politics, the authors write: "To understand the substance and limits of such constraining rules (international law), it is necessary to examine the interests which support them in the international system, the means by which they are made effective, and the functions they perform. Only in this way is it possible to predict the areas in which rules operate, the limits of rules as effective constraints, and the factors which underlie normative change." Although the authors are asking an important question—"Why has international law been binding in some cases?"—they still assume that international law functions primarily as a direct restraint on state action. For an excellent review of this book, see Robert W. Tucker, "Resolution," *Journal of Conflict Resolution*, VII (March 1963), 69–75.

[6] Myres S. McDougal and Florentino P. Feliciano, *Law and Minimum World Public Order* (New Haven 1961), 10. The authors suggest that if any progress in conceptualizing the role of international law is to be made, it is necessary to distinguish between the "factual process of international coercion and the process of authoritative decision by which the public order of the world community endeavors to regulate such process of coercion." This suggestion is based on the assumption that international law promotes order primarily through the establishment of restraints on state actions.

[7] There are a few writers who have tried to approach international law from a different vantage point. For a survey of some of the other approaches to international law and politics, see Michael Barkun, "International Norms: An Interdisciplinary Approach," *Background*, VIII (August 1964), 121–29. The survey shows that few "new" approaches to international law have developed beyond the preliminary stages, save perhaps for the writings of F. S. C. Northrop. Northrop's works (e.g., *Philosophical Anthropology and Practical Politics* [New York 1960], 326–30) are particularly significant in their attempt to relate psychological, philosophical, and cultural approaches to the study of law in general, although he has not usually been concerned with the overall relationship of international law to international political

lectual framework that measures international law primarily in terms of constraint on political action, there is little wonder that skepticism about international law continues to increase while creative work on the level of theory seems to be diminishing.[8]

Therefore, it is desirable to approach the relationship between international law and politics at a different functional level, not because international law does not function at the level of coercive restraint, but because it also functions at another level. In order to illustrate a second functional level in the relationship between international law and politics, it is necessary to examine the operation of domestic law. In a domestic society, the legal system as a series of interrelated normative statements does more than direct or control the actions of its members through explicit rules backed by a promise of coercion. Systems of law also act on a more generic and pervasive level by serving as authoritative (i.e., accepted as such by the community) modes of communicating or reflecting the ideals and purposes, the acceptable roles and actions, as well as the very processes of the societies. The legal system functions on the level of the individual's perceptions and attitudes by presenting to him an image of the social system—an image which has both factual and normative aspects and which contributes to social order by building a consensus on procedural as well as on substantive matters. In this sense, law in the domestic situation is a primary tool in the "socialization"[9] of the individual.

International law functions in a similar manner: namely, as an insti-

---

action. Not mentioned in Barkun s survey but important in the discussion of international law and politics is Stanley Hoffmann, "International Systems and International Law," in Klaus Knorr and Sidney Verba, eds., *The International System* (Princeton 1961), 205–38. [See page 89.] However, Hoffmann's essay is closer in approach to the work by Kaplan and Katzenbach than to the approach developed in this article. Finally, it is also necessary to point to an article by Edward McWhinney, "Soviet and Western International Law and the Cold War in a Nuclear Age," *Canadian Yearbook of International Law*, I (1963), 40–81. Professor McWhinney discusses the relationship between American and Russian structures of action, on the one hand, and their interpretations of international law, on the other. While McWhinney's approach is basically similar to the one proposed in this article in its attempt to relate international law to politics on a conceptual level, his article is focused on a different set of problems, the role of national attitudes in the contemporary era on ideas of international law. Nevertheless, it is a significant contribution to the task of analyzing more clearly the relationship between international law and politics.

[8] See Richard A. Falk, "The Adequacy of Contemporary International Law: Gaps in Legal Thinking," *Virginia Law Review*, L (March 1964), 231–65, for a valuable but highly critical analysis of contemporary international legal theory.

[9] See Gabriel A. Almond and James S. Coleman, eds., *The Politics of the Developing Areas* (Princeton 1960), 26–31, for an explanation of the concept of socialization.

tutional device for communicating to the policy-makers of various states a consensus on the nature of the international system. The purpose of this article is to approach the relationship between international law and politics not as a system of direct restraints on state action, but rather as a system of quasi-authoritative communications to the policy-makers concerning the reasons for state actions and the requisites for international order. It is a "quasi-authoritative" device because the norms of international law represent only an imperfect consensus of the community of states, a consensus which rarely commands complete acceptance but which usually expresses generally held ideas. Given the decentralized nature of law-creation and law-application in the international community, there is no official voice of the states as a collectivity. However, international law taken as a body of generally related norms is the closest thing to such a voice. Therefore, in spite of the degree of uncertainty about the authority of international law, it may still be meaningful to examine international law as a means for expressing the commonly held assumptions about the state system.

The approach advocated in this article has its intellectual antecedents in the sociological school, since it seeks to study international law in relation to international politics. Furthermore, it is similar to that of the sociological school in its assumption that there is or should be a significant degree of symmetry between international law and politics on the level of intellectual constructs—that is, in the way in which international law has expressed and even shaped ideas about relations between states. It is hoped that this approach will contribute to a greater awareness of the interdependence of international law and conceptions of international politics.

Before analyzing the way in which international law has in the past and continues today to reflect common attitudes about the nature of the state system, let us discuss briefly the three basic assumptions which have generally structured those attitudes.[10] First, it has been assumed that the state is an absolute institutional value and 'that its security is

---

[10] The following discussion of the assumptions of the state system is brief, since students of international politics generally agree that the three assumptions listed' have structured most of the actions of states. This agreement is most complete concerning the nature of the "classical" state system. The author is also of the opinion that these assumptions continue to operate today in a somewhat mutated form. (See his unpublished manuscript "The Image of Power Politics: A Cognitive Approach to the Study of International Politics," chaps. 2, 4, 8.) Note also the agreement on the nature of classical ideas about international politics in the following: Ernst B. Haas, "The Balance of Power as a Guide to Policy-Making," *Journal of Politics,* XV (August 1953), 370–97; Morton A. Kaplan, *System and Process in International Politics* (New York 1957), 22–36; and Edward Vose Gulick, *Europe's Classical Balance of Power* (Ithaca, N.Y., 1955).

the one immutable imperative for state action. If there has been one thing of which policy-makers could always be certain, it is that their actions must be designed to preserve their state. Second, it has been assumed that international politics is a struggle for power, and that all states seek to increase their power. Although the forms of power have altered during the evolution of the state system, it has been generally thought that states are motivated by a drive for power, no matter what the stakes. The third basic assumption permeating ideas about the international system has to do with maintaining a minimal system of order among the states. This assumption, symbolized generally by the maxim "Preserve the balance of power," affirms the necessity of forming coalitions to counter any threat to hegemony and of moderating actions in order to avoid an excess of violence that could disrupt the system.

It is necessary at this point to note that an unavoidable tension has existed between the aim of maintaining the state and maximizing power, on the one hand, and of preserving the international system, on the other. The logical extension of either aim would threaten the other, since complete freedom of action by the state would not allow for the limitation imposed by requirements to maintain the system, and a strict regularization of state action inherent in the idea of the system would curtail the state's drive for power. However, the tension has remained constant, with neither norm precluding the other except when a given state was in immediate danger of destruction. At those times, the interests of the system have been subordinated to the drive for state survival, but with no apparent long-range effect on the acceptance by policy-makers of either set of interests, despite their possible incompatibility. The prescriptions that states should be moderate, flexible, and vigilant [11] have been a manifestation of the operation of the system. Together, the three basic assumptions about the state system have constituted the conceptual basis from which the policy-makers have planned the action of their state.

I. CLASSICAL INTERNATIONAL LAW AND THE IMAGE OF OF THE STATE SYSTEM

Almost every legal aspect of international relations from 1648 to 1914 reinforced and expressed the assumptions of the state system. State practices in regard to treaties, boundaries, neutrality, the occupation of new lands, freedom of the seas, and diplomacy, as well as classical legal doctrines, provide ample illustration of the extent to which the basic assumptions of the state were mirrored in international law.

---

[11] See Gulick, 34; and for a discussion of the principles of moderation, flexibility, and vigilance, *ibid.*, 11–16.

The essential role of treaties in international law reflected the three assumptions of the state system. First, treaty practices helped to define the nature of statehood. Emanating from the free and unfettered will of states, treaties were the expression of their sovereign prerogatives. Statehood itself was defined in part as the ability to make treaties, and that ability presupposed the equality and independence usually associated with the idea of the state. Moreover, certain definitive treaties, like those written at the Peace of Augsburg (1515) and the Peace of Westphalia (1648), actually made explicit the attributes of statehood. The former treaty affirmed the idea that the Prince had complete control over the internal affairs of the state, while the latter emphasized that states were legally free and equal in their international relationships.[12] Even the actual wording of treaties expressed the classical assumption about the sanctity of the state. Whether in the formal references to the "high contracting parties" or in the more vital statements about the agreement of sovereigns not to interfere with the actions of other sovereigns, treaties were clear expressions of the classical idea of the state.[13]

Treaty law also contributed to the evolution of the classical assumption regarding the maintenance of the international system. Both explicitly and implicitly, treaties affirmed the necessity of an international system. Whether or not they contained such phrases as "balance of power," "just equilibrium," "universal and perpetual peace," [14] common and public safety and tranquillity," [15] "public tranquillity on a lasting foundation," [16] or "safety and interest of Europe," [17] the most important treaties during the classical period affirmed the desirability of maintaining the international system.[18] Also, many treaties reaffirmed earlier treaty agreements, contributing to the idea that the international system was a continuing, operative unity.[19] Therefore, treaties usually reminded the policy-maker that the maintenance of the international system was a legitimate and necessary objective of state policy.

---

[12] For the effects of the two treaties, see Charles Petrie, *Diplomatic History, 1713–1939* (London 1949), 111; David Jayne Hill, *A History of Diplomacy in the International Development of Europe* (New York 1924), 603–6; and Arthur Nussbaum, *A Concise History of the Law of Nations* (New York 1961), 116.

[13] E.g., *The Treaty of Ryswick, 1697* in Andrew Browning, ed., *English History Documents*, VIII (New York 1963), 881–83.

[14] *Treaty of Ryswick*, Article I, in *ibid.*

[15] *Barrier Treaty of 1715*, Article I, in *ibid.*, Vol. X.

[16] *Treaty of Vienna, 1713*, in *ibid.*, Vol. VIII.

[17] *Treaty of Quadruple Alliance, 1815*, in *ibid.*, Vol. XI.

[18] Leo Gross, "The Peace of Westphalia, 1648–1948," *American Journal of International Law*, XLII (January 1948), 20–40. [See page 45.]

[19] For a treaty which expressed the necessity of keeping prior obligations, see *Treaty of Aix-la-Chapelle, 1748*, in Browning, ed., Vol. X.

Finally, treaties affirmed the necessity and, in part, the legality of the drive for power. The constant juggling of territory, alliances, and other aspects of capability was a frequent and rightful subject of treaty law. Treaties implicitly confirmed that power was the dynamic force in relations between states by defining the legal criteria of power and, more important, by providing an institutional means, subscribed to by most of the members of the system, which legalized certain political transactions, such as territorial acquisition and dynastic exchange.

A second state practice which contributed to the classical assumptions about the state system was the legal concept of boundaries. Inherent in the very idea of the boundary were all three assumptions of the classical system. First, the boundary marked off that most discernible of all criteria of a state's existence—territory.[20] A state was sovereign within its territory, and the boundary was essential to the demarcation and protection of that sovereignty. Freedom and equality necessitated the delineation of a certain area of complete control; the boundary as conceptualized in international law was the institutional means through which that necessity was fulfilled. Second, the boundary was essential for the preservation of the international system.[21] After every war the winning powers set up a new or revised set of boundaries which aided them in maintaining order by redistributing territory. More important, the boundary also provided a criterion by which to assess the intentions of other states. Change of certain essential boundaries signified a mortal threat to the whole system, and signaled the need for a collective response.[22] Finally, the legal concept of boundaries provided a means through which the expansion and contraction of power in the form of territory could be measured. Since the boundary was a legal means of measuring territorial changes, international law in effect reinforced the idea that the struggle for power was an essential and accepted part of international politics. All three assumptions of the state system, therefore, were mirrored in the classical legal concept of boundaries.

Another international legal concept which reflected the assumptions about the state system was the idea of neutrality. The primary importance of neutrality law lay in its relation to the classical emphasis on the preservation of the international system. The practice of neutrality was an essential element in the mitigation of international conflict because

---

[20] See John H. Herz, *International Politics in the Atomic Age* (New York 1962), 53, for a discussion of the role of territory in the classical state system and the international legal system.

[21] See Hoffmann, 212, 215, for a discussion of the way in which territorial settlements in treaties aided stability within the system. He calls this function part of the law of political framework.

[22] E.g., the English and French attitude toward Belgium.

it provided a legitimate means of lessening the degree of violence in any given war (by reducing the number of belligerents) and also made those involved in a war aware of the possibility of hostile actions from outside should the conflict weaken the participants too greatly. In short, the legal concept of neutrality implied that the actions of states must remain moderate and flexible in order to preserve the state system.[23]

There were other aspects of international legal practice which substantiated the assumptions of the state system. For instance, since the sixteenth century the law pertaining to the occupation of new lands and to freedom of the high seas constituted a vital aspect of international law, and provided "legitimate" areas in which the struggle for power could take place.

From the outset, most of the non-European areas of the world were considered by the great powers to be acceptable arenas for the struggle for power. International legal practice made it easy for states to gain control of land overseas by distinguishing between the laws of occupation and the laws of subjugation. This distinction made it easier for powers to extend control over non-European territorial expanses because it enabled states to "occupy" territory legally without actually controlling it.[24] Through the laws of occupation, international law confirmed the assumption that colonial expansion was part of the struggle for power.

The law of the high seas also contributed to the idea of the struggle for power. The expansion of trade, military power, and territorial domain was, throughout almost the entire history of the state system, greatly dependent upon the free use of the high seas. The laws of the sea were designed so that maximum use could be made of this relatively cheap mode of transportation. Like the laws of occupation of non-European territory, sea law helped to keep the distribution of power among European states in continuous flux.[25]

Therefore, both the laws of the seas and the laws governing the occupation of new lands were instrumental in "legalizing" areas for conflict. Given the assumption that states always maximize their power, a free sea and the easy acquisition of non-European lands provided the fluidity needed for the states to struggle for power. Moreover, both sets of laws removed the area of conflict from the home territory, thus enabling states

---

[23] For a discussion of the role of neutrality in the balance of power system, see McDougal and Feliciano, 391–413.

[24] L. Oppenheim, in H. Lauterpacht, ed., *International Law* (New York 1948), I, 507.

[25] The attempt to control a "closed sea" was sometimes a bid by a powerful state to freeze the status quo—e.g., Portugal's control of the Indian Ocean in the sixteenth and seventeenth centuries (Nussbaum, III).

to increase the scope of their struggle without proportionately increasing its intensity.[26]

A final category of international law which reinforced the assumptions about the state system was the law of diplomacy. The legal rationalization behind the rights and duties of diplomats (i.e., since diplomats represent sovereign states, they owe no allegiance to the receiving state) emphasized the inviolability of the state which was an essential aspect of the classical assumptions.[27] At the same time, the very fact that even semihostile states could exchange and maintain ambassadors emphasized that all states were part of a common international system.[28] Finally, the classical functions of a diplomat—to make sure that conditions are not changing to the disadvantage of his state and, if they are, to suggest and even implement policies to rectify the situation—exemplified the rule of constant vigilance necessary in a group of states struggling for power. Therefore, in their own way, the laws of diplomacy expressed all three of the assumptions of the state systems.

The assumptions of the state system were reinforced not only by the legal practices of states but also by the major international legal theories of the classical period. Three general schools of thought developed: the naturalists, the eclectics or Grotians, and the positivists.[29] In each school, there was a major emphasis on both the state and the state system as essential institutional values. Whether it was Pufendorf's insistence on the "natural equality of state," [30] the Grotians' concept of the sovereign power of state,[31] or Bynkershoek and the nineteenth-century positivists' point that treaties were the prime, if not the only, source of international law,[32] the state was considered by most classical theorists to be the essential institution protected by the legal system. At the same time, almost every classical writer on international law either assumed or argued for

---

[26] Analysts have argued over whether colonialism reduced or exacerbated international antagonism. Without settling the argument, it seems safe to say that the struggle for colonies was a more spectacular and relatively less dangerous system of conflict than was competition for European land.

[27] For the relationship of the assumption of statehood and the functioning of diplomatic immunities, see a discussion of the theoretical underpinnings of diplomatic immunities in Ernest L. Kelsey, "Some Aspects of the Vienna Conference on Diplomatic Intercourse and Immunities," American Journal of International Law, LXXXVIII (January 1962), 92–94.

[28] Morgenthau, 547.

[29] For a discussion of the precise meaning of these classifications, see Nussbaum.

[30] Ibid., 149.

[31] Hugo Grotius, The Rights of War and Peace, ed. with notes by A. C. Campbell (Washington 1901), 62.

[32] Cornelius Van Bynkershoek, De dominio maris dissertatio, trans. by Ralph Van Deman Mogoffin (New York 1923), 35.

the existence of an international system of some kind.[33] Along with Grotians, the naturalists maintained that a system of states existed, since man was a social animal. Vattel, probably the most famous international lawyer in the classical period, asserted that a balance of power and a state system existed.[34] Even the positivists of the nineteenth century assumed that there was an international system of some kind. This is apparent from their emphasis on the balance of power,[35] as well as from their assumption that relations between nations could be defined in terms of legal rights and duties.[36]

Therefore, there was a consensus among the classical theorists of international law that international politics had two structural elements: the state, with its rights of freedom and self-preservation; and the system, with its partial effectiveness in maintaining a minimal international order. That the theorists never solved the conflict between the idea of the unfettered sovereign state, on the one hand, and a regulating system of law, on the other, is indicative of a conflict within the assumptions of the state system,[37] but a conflict which neither prevented international lawyers from writing about an international legal order nor kept policy-makers from pursuing each state's objectives without destroying the state system.

Although the norms of classical international law sometimes went unheeded, the body of theory and of state practice which constituted "international law as an institution" nonetheless expressed in a quasi-authoritative manner the three assumptions about international politics. It legalized the existence of states and helped to define the actions neces-

---

[33] De Visscher, 88. For similar interpretations of classical and pre-twentieth-century theorists, see Walter Schiffer, *The Legal Community of Mankind* (New York 1951), chap. 1; or Percy E. Corbett, *Law and Society in the Relations of States* (New York 1951).

[34] Emeric de Vattel, *The Laws of Nations* (Philadelphia 1867), 412–14.

[35] G. F. Von Martens, *The Law of Nations: Being the Science of National Law, Covenants, Power & Founded upon the Treaties and Custom of Modern Nations in Europe,* trans. by William Cobbett (4th ed., London 1829), 123–24.

[36] Almost all of the nineteenth-century positivists assumed that relations between nations were systematized enough to allow for a system of rights and duties. E.g., William Edward Hall, *A Treatise on International Law* (Oxford 1904), 43–59; Henry Wheaton, *Elements of International Law* (Oxford 1936), 75. Wheaton does not discuss duties as such, but when he talks about legal rights he distinguishes between "absolute" and "conditional" rights. According to Wheaton, the "conditional" rights are those resulting from membership in the international legal system. This formulation implies the existence of corresponding duties.

[37] See Von Martens, 123–34, for the intellectual and legal problems growing out of the assumption that states may legally maximize power but that they also have a responsibility "to oppose by alliances and even by force of arms" a series of aggrandizements which threaten the community.

sary for the preservation of each state and of the system as a whole. It reinforced the ideas that vigilance, moderation, and flexibility are necessary for the protection of a system of competing states. And finally, international law established a legalized system of political payoffs by providing a means to register gains and losses without creating a static system. In fact, this last aspect was essential to the classical state system. With international law defining certain relationships (territorial expansion, empire-building, etc.) as legitimate areas for political competition, other areas seemed, at least generally in the classical period, to be removed from the center of the political struggle. By legitimizing the struggle as a form of political competition rather than as universal conflict, international law sanctioned a form of international system that was more than just an anarchic drive for survival.

II. CONTEMPORARY INTERNATIONAL LAW AND THE ASSUMPTIONS OF THE STATE SYSTEM

As a quasi-authoritative system of communicating the assumptions of the state system to policy-makers, contemporary international law no longer presents a clear idea of the nature of international politics. This is in part a result of the tension, within the structure of contemporary international law itself, between the traditional legal concepts and the current practices of states. International law today is in a state of arrested ambiguity—in a condition of unstable equilibrium between the old and the new. As a result, it no longer contributes as it once did to a consensus on the nature of the state system. In fact, it adds to the growing uncertainty and disagreement as to how the international political system itself is evolving. The following discussion will attempt to assess the current developments in international law in terms of the challenges those developments make to the three assumptions of the state system. It is realized that the three assumptions themselves have already undergone change, but our purpose is to show where contemporary international legal practice and theory stand in relation to that change.

THE CHALLENGE TO THE STATE AND THE SYSTEM

The current legal concept of the state is a perfect example of the arrested ambiguity of contemporary international law and of the threat that this condition represents to the assumptions of the state system. On the one hand, most of the traditional forms used to express the idea of statehood are still employed. Treaty-makers and statesmen still write about "respect for territorial integrity," the "right of domestic jurisdiction," and the "sovereign will of the high contracting parties." Moreover, most of the current substantive rights and duties, such as self-defense, legal equality, and territorial jurisdiction, that are based on the assumption that states as units of territory are the irreducible institutional values of the system continue to be central to international legal practice.[38] On the other hand, certain contemporary developments contrast sharply with the traditional territory-oriented conceptions of international law.[39] With the growth of international entities possessing supranational powers (e.g., ECSC), the legal idea of self-contained units based on territorial control lacks the clear basis in fact that it once enjoyed. Many of the traditional prerogatives of the sovereign state, such as control over fiscal policy,[40] have been transferred in some respects to transnational units. While the development of supranational powers is most pronounced in Europe, there is reason to believe, especially concerning international cooperation on technical matters, that organizations patterned on the European experience might occur elsewhere.

Another significant manifestation of ambiguity in the territorial basis of international law is found in the post-World War II practice of questioning the validity of the laws of other states. The "act of state doctrine" no longer serves as the guideline it once did in directing the national courts of one state to respect the acts promulgated in another.[41] Once

---

[38] E.g., Charles G. Fenwick, *International Law* (New York 1952), chap. II.

[39] For a survey of current challenges to traditional international law, see Wolfgang Friedmann, "The Changing Dimensions of International Law," *Columbia Law Review*, LXII (November 1962), 1147–65. Also, see Richard A. Falk, *The Role of the Domestic Courts in the International Legal Order* (Syracuse 1964), 14–19, for a discussion of the fact that while there is a growing "functional obsolescence" of the state system, the assumptions of the state system continue to operate for psychological and political reasons.

[40] E.g., Articles 3 and 4 of the *Treaty Establishing the European Coal and Steel Community* (April 18, 1951).

[41] For an excellent discussion of the legal and political problems related to the question of the "act of state doctrine" in particular, and of territorial supremacy as a concept in general, see Kenneth S. Carlston, *Law and Organization in World Society* (Urbana, Ill., 1962), 191–93, 266–69. Also, for a discussion of the problem in a larger framework, see Falk, *Role of the Domestic Courts*. Since World War II, states, especially on the European continent, have found increasingly broader bases to invalidate the effect of foreign laws. Traditionally, states have refused to give validity to the laws of other lands for a small number of narrowly constructed reasons (e.g., refusal to enforce penal or revenue laws). Today many states have declared foreign laws invalid for a variety of reasons, the most important being the formulation that the national court cannot give validity to a foreign law that is illegal in terms of international law (see *"The Rose Mary Case,"* *International Law Report* [1953]. 316ff.), and the most frequent being a broad interpretation of "sense of public order" (see Martin Domke, "Indonesian Nationalization Measures Before Foreign Courts," *American Journal of International Law*, LIV [April 1960], 305–23). The most recent case in American practice, the *Sabbatino* decision (Supplement, *International Legal Materials*, III, No. 2 [March 1964], 391), appears to reaffirm the traditional emphasis on the territorial supremacy of the national legal order in these matters, but is actually ambiguous. On the one hand, the Opinion of the Court applied the "act of state doctrine" in declaring the Cuban law valid, but on the other

based on the assumption of the "inviolability of the sovereign," the "act of state doctrine" today is the source of widespread controversy. The conflicting views of the doctrine are symptomatic of the now ambiguous role of territoriality in questions of jurisdictional and legal power. Although these developments in current legal practice are only now emerging, they nonetheless can be interpreted as a movement away from the strictly and clearly defined legal concept of the state that appeared in classical international law.

Other developments in contemporary international law represent, theoretically at least, a challenge to the assumption that the state and its freedom of action are an absolute necessity for the state system. Most noticeable has been the attempt to develop an international organization which would preserve a minimal degree of order. Prior to the League of Nations, there had been attempts to institutionalize certain aspects of international relations, but such attempts either did not apply to the political behavior of states (e.g., the Universal Postal Union) or did not challenge the basic assumptions of the state system (as the very loosely defined Concert of Europe failed to do). As it was formulated in the Covenant and defined by the intellectuals, the League represented a threat to the assumptions of the state system because it sought to settle once and for all the tension between the policy-maker's commitment to preserve his state and his desire to maintain the state system by subordinating his state to it through a formal institution.

Proponents of the League saw it as a means to formalize a system of maintaining international order by committing states in advance to a coalition against any state that resorted to war without fulfilling the requirements of the Covenant. If it had been operative, such a commitment would have represented a total revolution in the legal concept of the state as an independent entity, since it would have abolished the most essential of all sovereign prerogatives, the freedom to employ coercion. However, the ideal purpose of the League, on the one hand, and the aims of politicians and the actual constitutional and operational aspects of the League, on the other, proved to be quite different. Owing to certain legal formulations within the Covenant (Articles 10, 15, 21) and the subsequent application of the principles (e.g., in Manchuria and Ethiopia), the hoped-for subordination of the state to the system was not realized.[42]

---

hand, the Court stated that "international law does not require application of the doctrine."

[42] For a useful discussion of the relationship between the idea of collective security and the assumption of the balance of power system, see Inis L. Claude, *Swords into Plowshares* (New York 1962), 255–60; and Herz, chap. 5. It is necessary to make a distinction between the theory of collective security, which certainly would challenge the basic assumptions of the state system, and its operation, which would not.

Like the League, the United Nations was to replace the state as the paramount institutional value by establishing a constitutional concert of powers. However, it has succeeded only in underscoring the existing tension between the drive to maintain the state and the goal of maintaining the system. In the Charter itself, the tension between the state and the system remains unresolved.[43] Nor does the actual operation of the United Nations provide a very optimistic basis for the hope that tension will be lessened in the future.

In terms of international law, regional organizations constitute a mixed challenge to the traditional relationship between the state and the system. Although certain organizations represent an attempt to transcend the traditional bounds of their constituent members on functional grounds, this does not necessarily mean that those members have rejected the state as a political form. In reality, if regional organizations represent any transformation at all in the structural relationship between the state and the system, they constitute an attempt to create a bigger and better state, an attempt which is not contrary to the traditional assumptions of the state system. In spite of the fact that some organizations are given supranational power and present a challenge in that sense, most of the organizations are as protective of the sovereign rights of the state as is the United Nations Charter (e.g., the OAS Charter) or are not regional organizations at all, but military alliances.[44]

A more serious challenge, but one somewhat related to the challenge by regional organizations, is the changing relation of the individual to the international legal order. In the classical system, international law clearly relegated the individual to the position of an object of the law. Not the individual, but the state had the rights and duties of the international legal order.[45] This legal formulation was in keeping with the classical emphasis on the sanctity of the state. Today, however, the development of the concepts of human rights, international and regional organizations, and the personal responsibility of policy-makers to a higher law not only limit the scope of legally permissible international action

---

[43] Compare Articles 25–51, or paragraphs 2–7 in Article 2, for the contrast between system-oriented and state-oriented norms.

[44] This is not to say that regional organizations do not represent a challenge to the concept of the state on psychological or social grounds. Obviously, the type of allegiance to a United Europe would be different in kind and degree from the traditional allegiance to a European state. However, in terms of the challenge to the legal concept of the state, regional organizations still adhere to the idea that the constituent members are sovereign in their relationship with states outside the organization.

[45] See Corbett, 53–56, for a discussion of the place of the individual in classical international law.

but, more important, limit the traditional autonomy of the leaders of the state over internal matters.[46] The idea that the individual rather than the state is the unit of responsibility in the formulation of policy has a long intellectual tradition;[47] however, it is only recently that the norms associated with that idea have become a part of international law.

Although the role of the individual in international law is small and the chances for its rapid development in the near future slight, it represents a more vital challenge to traditional international law and to the assumptions of the state system than either international or regional organizations. Since the principle of collective responsibility (of the state) rather than individual responsibility has traditionally served as the infrastructure for the rights and duties of states,[48] the development of a place for the individual in the international legal system that would make him personally responsible would completely revolutionize international law. At the same time, by making the individual a higher point of policy reference than the state, the development of the role of the individual represents a challenge to the assumption once reflected in classical international law that the preservation and maximization of state power is an absolute guideline for policy-makers. The evolving place of the individual in the contemporary international legal system, then, is contrary to the traditional tendency of international law to reaffirm the absolute value of the state.

The Challenge to the Concept of Power

One of the most significant developments in international law today relates to the assumption that states do and should compete for power. In the classical period, international law, through the legal concepts of neutrality, rules of warfare, occupation of new lands, rules of the high seas, and laws of diplomacy, reinforced the idea that a struggle for power among states was normal and necessary. Today, many of these specific legal norms still apply, but the overall permissible range of the struggle for military power[49] has been limited by the concept of the just war.

---

[46] Most modern writers have noted that the individual no longer stands in relation to international law solely as the object (e.g., Corbett, 133–35, or Friedmann, 1160–62), though they are agreed that, to use Friedmann's words, "the rights of the individual in international law are as yet fragmentary and uncertain."

[47] According to Guido de Ruggiero, *The History of European Liberalism* (Boston 1959), 363–70, the liberal conception of the state has always assumed that the individual was the absolute value, though this idea has not always been operative.

[48] For an excellent discussion of the role of collective responsibility in international law, see Hans Kelsen, *Principles of International Law* (New York 1959), 9–13, 114–48.

[49] Although the military struggle today is considered to be only one aspect of the struggle for power, it is the one most closely related to the problem of order in

The idea of the just war is not new to international law. Most of the classical writers discussed it, but they refused to define the concept in strict legal terms and usually relegated it to the moral or ethical realm.[50] The nineteenth-century positivists completely abandoned the doctrine with the formulation that "wars between nations must be considered as just on both sides with respect to treatment of enemies, military arrangements, and peace."[51] However, with the increased capability of states to destroy each other, a movement has grown to regulate force by legal means.

This movement developed through the Hague Conventions and the League of Nations and, in some respects, culminated in the Kellogg-Briand Pact of 1928. Today, the just war is a more or less accepted concept in international law. Most authors write, and most policy-makers state, that aggression is illegal and must be met with the sanction of the international community. The portent of this formulation of the assumption regarding power is great since, theoretically at least, it deprives the states of the range of action which they once freely enjoyed in maximizing their power and in protecting themselves. If the only legal justification for war is self-defense, or authorization of action in accordance with the Charter of the United Nations,[52] then a war to preserve the balance of power or to expand in a limited fashion is outlawed. While the traditional formulation of international law provided a broad field upon which the game of power politics could be played, the new formulations concerning the legal use of force significantly limit and, one could argue, make illegal the military aspects of the game of power politics.[53] The freedom

---

both the classical and the contemporary system, and therefore the most crucial in the relationship between law and politics.

[50] See D. W. Bowett, *Self-Defense in International Law* (Manchester 1958), 156–57; and Nussbaum, 137, 153–55, 171.

[51] See Nussbaum, 182–83. Also see Ian Brownlie, *International Law and the Use of Force by States* (Oxford 1963), 15–18.

[52] Actually, the range of action provided by the contemporary formulation, especially regarding the authorization in accordance with the United Nations Charter, could be broad and could conceivably take in "balancing" action if the deadlock in the Security Council were broken. The reason for this is the very ambiguous mandate for Security Council action spelled out in the Charter. It is possible under this mandate to call the limited "balancing" action, typical of the eighteenth century, an action taken to counter a "threat to the peace." Nonetheless, given the current stalemate within the Security Council, and the nature of the General Assembly actions to date, it is safe to conclude that contemporary international law has greatly limited the wide-ranging legal capacity that states once had in deciding on the use of force.

[53] See Brownlie, 251–80, for a discussion of the contemporary legal restrictions on the use of force. Also see Kaplan and Katzenbach, 205, for a discussion of the just-war doctrine and its compatibility with the balance of power system.

to use military power, once an essential characteristic of sovereignty and an integral part of international law, is no longer an accepted international legal norm.

The concept of the just war directly challenges the assumptions of the state system, because it implies that the military struggle for power is no longer a normal process of international politics. No longer does international law legitimize the gains of war, and no longer do policy-makers look upon war as a rightful tool of national power.[54] This is not to say that states do not use force in their current struggles or that the doctrine of the just war would deter them in a particular case. However, the doctrine does operate on the conceptual level by expressing to the policy-makers the idea that the use of force is no longer an everyday tool of international power politics. In terms of the traditional assumption about the state's natural inclination to maximize power, the contemporary legal commitment to the just-war doctrine represents a profound and historic shift.

III. INTERNATIONAL LAW AND THE REALITY OF CONTEMPORARY INTERNATIONAL POLITICS

Contemporary international legal practice, then, is developing along lines which represent a threat not only to traditional concepts of international law but also to the assumptions of the state system. The sporadic developments in international and regional organizations, the evolving place of the individual in the international legal system, and the doctrine of the just war are manifestations of the transformation occurring today both in the structure of international law and in attitudes about the state system. Actually, of course, the traditional conceptions of international law and the classical assumptions about international politics are not extinct.[55] Rather, there is in both international law and politics a perplexing mixture of past ideas and current developments. The only thing one can be sure of is that behind the traditional legal and political symbols which exist today in a somewhat mutated form, a subtle transformation of some kind is taking place.

It is not possible to evaluate the line of future development of the

---

[54] Certainly, tehnological developments have been primarily responsible for the rejection of war as a typical tool of international power. In this case, as in most, international legal doctrine mirrors the existing attitudes and helps to reinforce them.

[55] As in the past, international lawyers are still concerned with definitions and applications of concepts of territorial integrity, self-defense, and domestic jurisdiction, and policy-makers are still motivated by the traditional ideas of state security and power. However, the traditional political and legal symbols have been "stretched" to apply to current conditions. For a development of this position see Coplin, chaps. 4 and 8.

assumptions about the state system or the international legal expression of those assumptions from the work of contemporary theorists of international law. The most apparent new expressions are those that propose increased formalizations of world legal and political processes.[56] On the other hand, much international legal theory today seems to be dedicated to an affirmation of the traditional assumptions of international politics. Political analysts like Hans Morgenthau,[57] E. H. Carr,[58] and George F. Kennan,[59] and legal theorists like Julius Stone,[60] P. E. Corbett, [61] and Charles De Visscher,[62] are predisposed to "bring international law back to reality."

This trend toward being "realistic" occupies the mainstream of current international legal theory,[63] and to identify its exact nature is therefore

---

[56] E.g., Arthur Larson, *When Nations Disagree* (Baton Rouge, La., 1961); or Grenville Clark and Louis B. Sohn, *World Peace Through World Law* (Cambridge, Mass., 1960). These theorists and others who fall under this classification are "radical" in the sense that what they suggest is antithetical to the assumptions of the state system as traditionally developed. These writers are not necessarily utopian in their radicalism. This is especially true since adherence today to the traditional assumptions might itself be considered a form of (reactionary) radicalism. However, the radical scholars, in the sense used here, are very scarce, especially among American students of international law. Today there is a very thin line separating the few radical scholars from the more numerous radical polemicists of world government.

[57] Morgenthau writes (277): "To recognize that international law exists is, however, not tantamount to assessing that . . . it is effective in regulating and restraining the struggle for power on the international scene."

[58] E. H. Carr, in *The Twenty Years' Crisis, 1919–1939* (London 1958), 170, writes: "We are exhorted to establish 'the rule of law' . . . and the assumption is made that, by so doing, we shall transfer our differences from the turbulent political atmosphere of self-interest to the purer, serener air of impartial justice." His subsequent analysis is designed to disprove this assumption.

[59] George F. Kennan, *Realities of American Foreign Policy* (Princeton 1954), 16.

[60] Julius Stone, *Legal Control of International Conflict* (New York 1954), introduction.

[61] Corbett, 68–79, 291–92.

[62] De Visscher writes (xiv): "International law cannot gather strength by isolating itself from the political realities with which international relations are everywhere impregnated. It can only do so by taking full account of the place that these realities occupy and measuring the obstacle which they present."

[63] The programs of the last two annual meetings of the American Society of International Law exemplify the way in which the concern for reality (as power) has come to dominate international legal theory. In the 1963 program, the relationship between international law and the use of force was not discussed by international legal theorists but by two well-known writers on the role of conflict in international politics. The 1964 program manifested the same tendency. It centered on the question of compliance with transnational law, a topic treated in a sociopolitical framework by most panelists. This point is not to be taken as a criticism of the two programs, both of which were excelllent and very relevant, but as proof of the assertion that

crucial. Many writers who express this viewpoint seem to fear being labeled as overly "idealistic." They utter frequent warnings that international law cannot restore international politics to order, but, on the contrary, can exist and flourish only after there is a political agreement among states to maintain order. In short, it is assumed that international law cannot shape international political reality, but can merely adjust to it. Although there are complaints of too much pessimism in current legal theory,[64] most writers, given the initial predisposition to avoid "idealism," do not heed them.

The desire of contemporary theorists to be "realistic" has been crucial to the relationship between contemporary international law and the assumptions of the state system. In their effort to achieve realism, current theorists have not examined their traditional assumptions about international politics. When they talk about adjusting international law to the realities of power, they usually have in mind the traditional reality of international politics. Today, a large share of the theoretical writing on international law that is designed to adapt law to political reality itself is rapidly becoming outmoded. Much contemporary international legal theory, then, has not contributed to the development of a new consensus on the nature of international politics but instead has reinforced many of the traditional ideas.

In order to understand more fully the relation of international law to world politics, it is necessary to do more than examine law merely as a direct constraint on political action. The changes in the conceptual basis of international law that are manifested in current practice and, to a lesser extent, in current legal theory are symptomatic of a series of social and institutional revolutions that are transforming all of international politics. To conclude that international law must adjust to political reality, therefore, is to miss the point, since international law is part of political reality and serves as an institutional means of de-

---

the mainstream of contemporary theory of international law is significantly oriented to the role of power.

[64] Many writers, even realists like Morgenthau (*op. cit.*, 275) and others like McDougal and Feliciano (*op. cit.*, 2–4), decry the modern tendency toward "cynical disenchantment with law," but it is obvious from their subsequent remarks that they are reacting more against the "utopianism" of the past than the cynicism of the present. There have been a few who have attacked the "realist" position on international law (e.g., A. H. Feller, "In Defense of International Law and Morality," *Annals of the Academy of Political and Social Science*, vol. 282 [July 1951], 77–84). However, these attacks have been infrequent and generally ineffective in starting a concerted action to develop more constructive theory. For another evaluation of the "realist" trend, see Covey T. Oliver, "Thoughts on Two Recent Events Affecting the Function of Law in the International Community," in George A. Lipsky, ed., *Law and Politics in the World Community* (Berkeley 1953).

veloping and reflecting a general consensus on the nature of international reality. In the contemporary period, where the international legal system is relatively decentralized, and international politics is subject to rapid and profound development, it is necessary to avoid a conceptual framework of international law which breeds undue pessimism because it demands too much. If international law does not contribute directly and effectively to world order by forcing states to be peaceful, it does prepare the conceptual ground on which that order could be built by shaping attitudes about the nature and promise of international political reality.

SECTION THREE:

International Organization and World Government

41. ORGANIZING NATIONS IN THE 1970s

Philip E. Jacob

INTERNATIONAL ORGANIZATIONS proliferated faster than nations in the the quarter-century after World War II, although the birth rate of new nations itself hit a record. They grew in numbers, in activities, in personnel at work for or with them, and in budgets. By 1970 there were over 200 full-fledged intergovernmental international agencies in operation, not counting any of the over 2,000 semi-official or private agencies organized across national boundaries.[1] On the basis of its reproductive capacity, this new breed of political institution would appear potent and destined for a decisive role in the conduct of international affairs.

However, there are those who argue that a high birth rate does not

From ORBIS, a quarterly journal of world affairs published by the Foreign Policy Research Institute, Spring 1971, 28–53. Reprinted by permission of the author and the Foreign Policy Research Institute.

PHILIP E. JACOB (1914–   ) Professor of Political Science, University of Hawaii. Author of *Changing Values in College* (New York: Harper and Brothers, 1957). Coauthor, *The Dynamics of International Organization: The Making of World Order* (Homewood, Ill.: Dorsey Press, 1965); *The Integration of Political Communities* (Philadelphia: J. B. Lippincott Company, 1964).

[1] *Yearbook of International Organizations* (12th edition; Brussels: Union International Associations, 1969).

assure a healthy population (in fact, it may mean that a lot of babies will die before maturity); and spending more money no more guarantees soundness of performance than an inflationary increase in GNP reflects a sound economy. Protagonists of international organizations of every variety are confronting a severe crisis of confidence in the 1970's; one would be tempted to forecast imminent bankruptcy were it not that alternatives of unilateral and bilateral action in coping with major world problems have already gone into receivership.

The truth is that we, the peoples and the governments of the 1970's, have yet to learn how to live in today's kind of world, or even to understand and admit what kind of a world it is. This being so, we are not effectively using the embryonic international institutions that in a strange and expediential manner have been devised to deal with crises in interstate relations. Because they were conceived piecemeal, with little relationship to each other, and as a kind of appendage to the existing state system, awareness of the truly innovative nature of these institutions has come slowly, to statesmen as well as the general public. They have often been seriously *mis*conceived—sometimes as supergovernments, but more often as alliances under a different name.

When used as supergovernments they have failed in most instances, because most of the world is not prepared to exchange life under a national government of whatever political system for life under the control of a regional or world regime, no matter how benign. We stand committed to a pluralistic, politically divided world, with decentralized authority. This is one of the inescapable realities.

Alliances have not worked either, even when camouflaged as international organizations. They have failed to recognize adequately the reality of global interdependence. In attempting to build cohesion around a common interest among countries within the alliance, they have underestimated the degree to which both the security and the welfare of their "in-group" has become intertwined with the destinies of peoples outside. When international organizations have been used as alliances, and their conduct manipulated to serve the national interests of only one segment of the world, they have exacerbated international conflict and rigidified political and social cleavages across the world. Paradoxically, they have usually been unable to achieve a sufficiently profound consciousness of interdependence among themselves to sustain long-continued and costly commitments to common action.

There are signs, however, that experience may be catching up with illusion, and that in the 1970's we shall openly face the problem of reconciling political pluralism with technological and social interdependence in the world arena. If this occurs, the role of international organizations will become critical, for they are of all available institutions the most peculiarly adapted to the task of engendering collaborative action on common needs among a multiplicity of governments, none of which is ready to give up final control over the people and resources in its territory. Assuming we all survive, these institutions should emerge as the great political innovation of our times, an instrument of political integration accomplishing what federalism set out to do two centuries ago, but by different processes, and much more extensive in scope.

WHAT INTERNATIONAL ORGANIZATIONS *CANNOT* DO

Experience suggests that international organizations are usually incapable of performing the customary functions of government. When they are pushed into doing so, they fail in the immediate task and are weakened for other assignments. They should not be expected to *legislate* in the sense of mandating rules binding on their constituent states or on persons under national jurisdictions. They should rarely be called upon to *adjudicate* conflicts in the sense of rendering a verdict that the parties are obligated to accept. Above all, they are basically unqualified for the *enforcement* function of the executive, whether in the traditional form of a well-armed professional police force or through the incongruous device of "collective security."

Let us face it. Governments are jealous of the prerogatives of governing. Leaving aside the exceptional adventure of the European Economic Community, the founders and members of international organizations have been unwilling to delegate real governing powers to these institutions, even though they often pretended to do so. This is what particularly confuses the uninitiated about actions in and toward international organizations: votes are taken, resolutions passed, demands made, and even armed forces deployed to be shot at and sometimes to shoot, as though these were the actions of a legitimate governing authority. They are at best the expression of a voluntary consensus reached by a group of autonomous decision-makers. Far more likely, they represent a perversion of the machinery of international organization to give the appearance of legitimacy to a power-play by one group of states seeking to impose its will on others.

For international organizations to fulfill the vital role required of them in the management of international relations in the 1970's, it is necessary first to strip away the delusion that they can govern, and to thwart any attempt to misuse them as though they were governments. Specifically, this means: (1) to declare invalid and without force any resolution that purports to order a state to do something it has not agreed to; (2) to declare invalid and without force any judicial-type decision (whether by a formal tribunal or a political body like the United Nations General Assembly) unless parties to a dispute have agreed they want it settled that way; (3) to declare inoperative all coercive provisions of international organization charters, where the object of coercion is a member-state of the organization.[2]

All this no doubt appears to many as a scandalous betrayal of international organizations to the jungle politics of contending nationalisms. But if the underbrush of misplaced expectations, compounded by hypocritical perjury on the part of official spokesmen who know better, cannot be cleared away, the capacity of these organizations to do the things for which they are really fitted will be stifled. The starting point for redirection toward the integrative tasks that should be their central mission is frank and full acknowledgment that they are not governments, are not likely soon to be transformed into governments, and should not be used as a smokescreen to hide the responsibility, or evasion of responsibility, of real governments. That path leads to total futility.

PIVOTAL MISSIONS OF MULTILATERALISM

The essential functions of intergovernmental multilateral institutions, for which they are uniquely qualified, are, first, *to harmonize the actions of states* in the attainment of common ends, as aptly expressed in the United Nations Charter; second, to develop and implement a special kind of *regulation appropriate to international interchange;* and third, to program and coordinate the *cross-national mobilization and utilization of resources* for human welfare, that is, to manage international development.

(1) The *harmonization function* implies the reconciliation of conflict by methods of what Secretary-General Dag Hammarskjöld called "preventive diplomacy." The objective of action is the accommodation of interests, rather than a finding of who is right or wrong. The diplomacy is problem-solving. It seeks alternatives to positions in impasse, and tries to persuade governments in dispute that such alternatives are more to their interest than a confrontation of force. In the process it injects the element of interdependence, making disputants aware that other countries feel their interests are also deeply at stake, and calling on each side to justify its position beyond its own borders. Sometimes, payoffs can be engineered as inducements to mutual agreement, outsiders undertaking to offset sacrifices by one or another disputant. If the situation is too tense, the presence of observers or a peacekeeping force as a physical demonstra-

---

[2] The latter step absolves so-called regional organizations from the ban on "security" operations against outsiders, but rips away the pretense that they are in any sense performing acts of "collective security" on behalf of the world community. They emerge in their true colors as straight-out power alliances—*unless* they are willing to abide strictly by the letter of Article 53 of the United Nations Charter and subject their actions to Security Council authorization except in repelling outright armed attack.

tion of "community interest" may successfully freeze the conflict and allow additional efforts to unravel it. The range of potential actions is great, and the flexibility of preventive diplomacy, in choice of practitioners as well as in form, has been a source of strength.

Two principles, however, appear fundamental. Compulsion must be eschewed, and third-party initiative must be persistent. Failure to observe either of these caveats has frustrated and sometimes wrecked the conciliation efforts of the United Nations and other organizations. The first principle recognizes the insistence of national states to be self-determining at whatever cost—the reality of the pluralistic international system. The second principle is the expression of organized interdependence, and a response to the fact that interdependence is *not* self-implementing. It takes an international institution to bring out and channel the convergent interests of states, and a skilled, impartial corps of preventive diplomats to focus the influence of interdependent interest effectively on interstate conflicts.

(2) The *regulatory function* of international institutions is different from the authoritarian restraint usually involved in typical governmental regulation. From the standpoint of *making* regulations, an intricate process of negotiation replaces legislation in the common sense of the term, leading to general agreement on "rules of the road" applicable to interstate communication and exchange. There are two kinds of input: on the one hand, a variety of proposals by or through national governments representing their initial preferences; on the other, a transnational technocratic initiative representing the results of study and forward planning by experts from different countries working jointly. The international "legislative process" bounces these ideas back and forth until consensus materializes among a large enough number of states to make the new set of rules practicable among themselves. Others may come to accept them later if they seem beneficial. What emerges is a growing body of *convenience law*, responsive to the problems created by increased interdependence. The process has become more continuous and systematized and there is every indication that it will be used much more regularly and extensively in the future.

Administration of this kind of law has followed three courses. It has frequently been left up to each state to apply the regulations, within its own jurisdiction, on a self-enforcing basis. The second approach has conferred general policing authority on one or more of the national governments that subscribe to a regulation. This practice, long since applied to combat piracy, is now customary in the execution of fisheries conservation agreements. The third method is to entrust regulation to an international agency with specific administrative powers—the International Civil Aviation Organization, the World Health Organization, the Universal Postal Union, the International Atomic Energy Agency, the Commission of the European Economic Community, to mention a few examples. The latter approach seems to be gathering momentum as these agencies acquire specialized competence, demonstrate impartiality, delicately finesse past the sensitive issue of sovereignty, and remain clearly accountable to organs representing the collectivity of states which established the regulations in the first place.

The absolute condition of effective international administration, that is, of the third method of implementing international regulations, is its separation from the rule-making power. Its ultimate potential lies precisely in the fact that it is the only one of the three patterns in which this separation is complete. There is no mixture of rule-making and rule-administration as when one or more states themselves undertake to administer an international regulation. The international administrator knows he is a civil servant employed by governments to do what *they* have decided they want to have done. He is no budding new sovereign, claiming to share in the powers of decision.[3]

(3) In the *mobilization of resources for economic and social development* international organizations have acquired their most direct and extensive impact upon human welfare.

We are now at the point where the balance of responsibility for programs of international assistance is shifting from individual donor countries to multilateral institutions. This is partly in response to growing disillusionment with the results of unilateral and bilateral management. The resource gap between givers and receivers has widened. So has a policy gap. Lines between have and have-not have hardened; positions have become more unreasonable and mutually incompatible. Bitterness has replaced cooperation, as givers perceive ingratitude and irresponsibility, and would-be receivers bridle at conditions they consider igno-

---

[3] Complaints are occasionally leveled against international officials for exceeding their proper powers; witness the famous Soviet challenge to Dag Hammarskjöld over the conduct of the United Nations operation in the Congo. While the limit of administrative competence can be variously interpreted, it is significant that in this and almost all similar cases, the complaining state has failed to win general support from the policymaking organs. The secretariat has in effect served as a lightning rod, attracting and also in part deflecting the anger of a frustrated government unable to bend the entire organization to its will.

The European Communities have built into their institutions procedural safeguards to prevent abuse of administrative power, the most significant being the Community Court to which decisions may be appealed by affected governments or enterprises. This has the secondary consequence of protecting the international administrators from the effects of head-on collision with one or more of their multiple masters. The issue is simply transferred to a special body empowered to interpret the treaty constituting the organization.

minious and an infringement of their national sovereignty. The reputation of unilateralism and bilateralism has also suffered because they have often mixed politics with welfare, allocating resources where they would shore up reliable allies or entice new ones, rather than where human need was greatest or development plans the best laid. Compound all this with the wastage that accompanies overlapping programs and with the day-to-day insensitivities of a huge bureaucracy operating largely in self-contained enclaves out of close touch with the people whose welfare is at stake, and one can understand the pall that has settled over national handling of the immense development effort.

Multilateral management, by contrast, has fared much better, granted that to date it has had less to manage. The World Bank group of lending agencies, the United Nations Development Program linking and integrating the efforts of specialized agencies with sections of the United Nations proper, the United Nations Children's Fund, have all channeled resources through national governments under conditions that assured efficient utilization, avoided political favoritism, and at the same time carefully respected each government's autonomy.

Multilateralism on a global scale has probably outclassed regional efforts in the effective mobilization and coordination of resources for development in the most impoverished areas of the world. It has been difficult for regional organizations to overcome the sense of dependence felt by the weak and the poor on one or two dominant rich and powerful members.

On the other hand, Western Europe has dramatically demonstrated how close integration of resources management among a group of well-endowed countries can make them boom into unprecedented prosperity. Whether their experience is transferable to other regions less advanced industrially and with fewer basic resources to start with appears doubtful, however, as first reports trickle in from attempts to follow suit. There is also the problem of forging a sufficiently unified political commitment to sustain the economic merger against the barrage of special interests in each country that are necessarily disadvantaged. After all, the Common Market itself almost foundered on the political power of French farmers, who in the end had to be bought off by subsidy out of the "equalization" tax and other levies paid by more loyal participants in the "community." Furthermore, the European Market has to date built its success at least in part on blatant protectionist discrimination against outsiders. It is a club of the privileged; so far it has insisted that any new member must itself be privileged, and bind itself to be equally discriminatory, no matter how close its ties to countries not in the club.

All this has made the global institutionalization of development management more and more appealing to the components of two-thirds of the noncommunist world that would like to find substance in the euphemism that they are "developing" countries. They see their main hope of assistance on tolerable terms coming through agencies in which they have a voice, preferably a voice whose strength is measured in numbers rather than capital. The lure of UNCTAD, the United Nations Conference on Trade and Development, was that for a brief moment of ecstatic delusion the have-nots thought they could transform voting power into resource commitments. (They fell into a trap of their own imagination that an international organization could *govern.*)

Actually, the discovery that the privileged have as yet no intention of turning over the management of their resources to the dispossessed, painful as it was, helped to set the stage for a major expansion of more meaningful multilateral operations, especially through the World Bank and its affiliates. Here the formula of decision calls for both the needy and the various custodians of capital to recognize a common interest in the most careful possible programming of the development process, with an emphasis on putting the resources at points of maximum human potential. Both planning and execution require the full cooperation of both sides, because the fact is they *are* interdependent. As Siamese twins, neither will survive if one dies.

Fortunately, confidence seems to be growing in the capacity of the Bank and other agencies of the United Nations to pull together resources and architect policies that will make the Second Development Decade as notable an achievement in man's material progress across the world as the First Decade was a false start.

EXTENDING THE FRONTIERS OF
INTERNATIONAL COMMUNITY

Technology is now opening two immense areas where no national jurisdiction exists, thus giving nations an opportunity to explore patterns of joint action and collective responsibility while they press forward the physical exploration of outer space and the deep floor of the oceans.

The nature of these new worlds is sufficiently strange that their utility is uncertain, and national governments have not yet asserted the old "territorial imperative" with customary vigor. To be sure, the United States has implanted its flags on the moon (but with an explicit disclaimer of American "occupation"). Space vehicles are carefully pedigreed by the countries which launch them. With reference to the seabed, the U.S. National Petroleum Council and other interests continue to lobby for policies that would place at least 20 per cent of the ocean floor under the jurisdiction of one national state or another. But the general mood is still one of restraint and caution on the part of the explorer's club of space and ocean powers, as well as of bystanders. In this atmosphere, tentative moves have been made toward establishing outer space and the seabed as preserves of the "international community." [4]

WORLD LAW IN OUTER SPACE

Though the exploration of space has been the monopoly so far of American and Soviet scientific acrobats, its repercussions were quickly seen to involve the fortunes of everyone. The potential for exciting developments in communication; the prediction and maybe even the control of weather; knowledge about the earth, the atmospheric cocoon in which it thrives, and about the physique of man himself and his adaptive capacities—these were of global import. So was the new dimension of destructive capacity that was opened up; the perils of the nuclear age, already so great as to threaten annihilation of a third of mankind by a moment of miscalculation or loss of cool, might now be brought through orbital weaponry to the point where all of life could be push-buttoned out of existence. The most spectacular of human achievements, it was recognized, put the entire race but one step from extinction.

The grandeur of the problem has not yet called forth a heroic solution. But painstakingly, working for once through UN machinery, national governments have laid a few building blocks. One of the first was the Outer Space Treaty providing for internationalization of the right of use and for demilitarization. The United States and the Soviet Union, joined by over 100 other states as of 1970, agreed that (1) outer space and celestial bodies would be free for exploration and use by all states on a basis of equality, and (2) all states would refrain from orbiting or stationing in space any objects carrying nuclear weapons or any other kinds of weapons of mass destruction, and from establishing military installations, testing weapons or conducting military maneuvers on celestial bodies. Coupled with these two basic principles was an explicit commitment that the exploration and use of outer space "shall be carried out for the benefit and in the interests of all countries . . . and shall be the province of all mankind"; and a rather more equivocal obligation to

---

[4] Groundwork for such a community approach was laid when, spurred by the cooperative scientific explorations achieved in the International Geophysical Year (1957), a treaty was negotiated that successfully bypassed conflicting national claims to the Antarctic continent and declared it open to all nations for scientific and other peaceful purposes. The arrangement falls short, however, of full-scale international regulation, a fact deplored by some leading authorities who feel that an opportunity was lost for a creative experiment in administration by international organization on behalf of the whole world community. See Howard J. Taubenfeld, "A Treaty for Antarctica," *International Conciliation*, January 1961; also, R. D. Hayton, "The Antarctic Settlement of 1959," *American Journal of International Law*, April 1960.

refrain from activities potentially harmful to other states at least until "appropriate international consultations" had been undertaken.

Internationalization was in several respects carried farther than in the Antarctic Treaty. Most obvious was a categorical ban on "national appropriation" of outer space, including the moon and other celestial bodies. This means no nations may claim sovereignty or in any other way assert unilateral control. But the treaty is silent on who does have the right to appropriate. It fails to designate the United Nations or any other international body as the proper custodian of space in the name and interests of all mankind.

For the moment, effective control clearly rests with those who have the technical capacity to send projectiles into space, although the treaty sets out the curious formula that *all* parties to it "bear *international* responsibility for national activities in outer space. . . ." While this might imply that each country is deputized to serve as policeman for the world community (as in the case of maritime piracy), the immediate intent was to place all space activity under some governmental authority and thereby make it possible to hold governments fully accountable for observing the terms of use set by the international community and for any damages that ensued from space exploits.[5] If activity should be undertaken by an international organization, both the organization and its individual member states are held responsible.

Compliance with the exceptionally specific demilitarization provisions, as well as the other principles of outer space use, is subject to verification by *reciprocal* inspection of all facilities stationed on the moon and other celestial bodies. Again, responsibility rests with national governments, not an international body; it is restricted to the active space powers willing to accept inspection on a basis of reciprocity. But this was as far as the Soviet Union was ready to commit itself in formal treaty to the unpredictable consequences of international policing of its prospective space colonies. Noticeably omitted from the scope of inspection are orbiting or other mobile space stations.

Much is said in the treaty about promoting international cooperation in the exploration and use of outer space; but there is no real commitment

---

[5] The likelihood of indiscriminate injury from the debris or misfire of space missions was sufficiently recognized to incorporate a specific provision making a state internationally liable for damage caused by objects launched from its territory, or component parts thereof. Drafting of a detailed convention on liability was urgently undertaken through the United Nations Outer Space Committee which encountered knotty problems as it tried to make explicit the basis of compensation to be paid, limitations of liability, the legal position of international organizations engaged in space activities and similar terms, all in advance of much practical experience. Prospects for the imminent conclusion of such a convention are promising, however.

to undertake the organization of multinational activity. Even the international sharing of information is dependent upon the space powers' discretion: they agree to inform the United Nations Secretary-General, the public and the international scientific community—"to the greatest extent feasible and practicable"—of the nature, conduct, locations and results of their activities. They will "consider on a basis of equality" requests to observe their space flights. While outer space "shall be the province of all mankind" according to Article I, the world community, at least for now, must be content to leave exploitation exclusively in the hands of the technologically equipped, and trust in their benevolent trusteeship.

On the other hand, the active involvement of many states in the legislative process for outer space, through the United Nations, has generated a mounting momentum of concern that augurs an expanding role for international organization as well as the further evolution of a world law of space.[6]

WORLD COMMUNITY ON THE OCEAN FLOOR

When Ambassador Arvid Pardo, from the seabound state of Malta, proposed to the United Nations in 1967 that it declare the deep bed of the sea, beyond the present limits of national jurisdiction, to be "the common heritage of mankind," he directly challenged the hallowed doctrine that states and states alone could be proprietors of the earth. Though the claim of common ownership on behalf of the entire world community was mainly to an ill-defined, lightless area where no human had ever set foot, spectacular advances in submarine technology had suddenly made the bottom of the oceans a potential source of riches—and of strategic dangers. Portents of a race by nations "to grab and to hold" were sufficiently grave to cause President Johnson, already in 1966, to warn against "a new form of colonial competition" and to associate his administration with the attempt to treat the lands under the high seas as "the legacy of all human beings."

The move toward world community for the bed of the sea, possibly with full international regulation under a United Nations Sea-Bed Authority and even the return of some revenue to be used internationally

---

[6] The gestation of United Nations involvement with the space problem is summarized by Lincoln P. Bloomfield, "Outer Space and International Cooperation," *International Organization,* Summer 1965. For an exhaustive and searching treatise on the regulation of space see Myres S. McDougal, Harold D. Lasswell and Ivan A. Vlasic, *Law and Public Order in Space* (New Haven: Yale University Press, 1964). See also an acute critique by the British scholar, C. W. Jenks, *Space Law* (New York: Praeger, 1965). The current scope of applicable law is reviewed by Gyula Gal, *Space Law* (New York: Oceana, 1969).

for economic and social development, has gathered momentum, official and private.[7] But it has also encountered strenuous opposition, official and private. The prospect of sequestering choice mineral deposits and living resources is tempting to governments and industries with the potential technical capacity to gain access to them.[8] Security fears, projected to the ocean floor along with new sets of weapons systems, have also pushed in the age-old direction of trying to maximize national control and have undercut the campaign for internationalization.[9]

On the issue of demilitarizing the seabed, debate polarized those that pressed for a complete ban on any military uses, as in the Outer Space Treaty, and a group led by the United States which argued that this would raise insuperable verification problems. The Soviet Union supported the broader position,[10] but a number of small coastal states joined the United States, wary of anything that would limit their various underwater defense facilities. They would accede only to a prohibition of nuclear weapons installations on the ocean floor. Canada suggested a compromise that would ban all "offensive" weapons from the seabed but allow coastal states to plant the continental shelf with submarine detec-

---

[7] Resolution 2574 of the Twenty-fourth General Assembly, December 15, 1969, specifically sought proposals for an international regime to regulate exploitation of the seabed. The 19th and 21st Reports of The Commission to Study the Organization of Peace, *The United Nations and the Bed of the Sea* (published by the Commission, New York, March 1969 and February 1970) present a strong case for comprehensive regulation by an international agency constituted for the purpose. The 21st Report includes a draft statute for a United Nations Sea-Bed Authority, and was submitted to the Secretary-General and the permanent UN Committee on the Sea-Bed, where it received intensive consideration.

[8] National rather than international regulation of economic exploitation is vigorously urged by American oil interests, among others, in advocating maximum extension of national jurisdiction over the seabed under the Continental Shelf Convention. See, for instance, Luke W. Finlay, "The Outer Limits of the Continental Shelf," *American Journal of International Law*, January 1970.

[9] The problems of developing anti-submarine defenses as well as protection for strategic missile installations have led military technologists generally to support a policy of unrestrained national supremacy over the continental shelf (with a broad interpretation of the limits of the shelf), and freewheeling exploitation of the ocean floor beyond by anyone with the technological capacity to do so. The rationale for this posture is defended by John P. Craven, "The Challenge of Ocean Technology to the Law of the Sea," *Judge Advocate General Journal*, September–October–November 1967. The position dovetails neatly with a concern to see that the private investor harvests the major return from exploitation of marine and sub-marine resources.

[10] The Soviet Union would accept inspection, however, only on a basis of reciprocity, as with the demilitarization of outer space. UN Doc. ENDC/240, March 18, 1969. The United States called for observation by all parties to the agreement. UN Doc. ENDC/249, May 22, 1969.

tion devices. But this too was rejected. The least common denominator finally prevailed: on February 11, 1971 the United States, the Soviet Union and Great Britain were among sixty-two nations which signed to bar the placement of weapons of mass destruction, and structures for such weapons, on the ocean floor or its subsoil. Each party may inspect for violations. Complaints go to the United Nations. Meanwhile submarines of all kinds, with or without nuclear projectiles, can roam the seas at will, and each country can arm its piece of seabed as it pleases in the hope of finding some "defense."

Progress toward the community of man on the seabed is at present more promising on the scientific than on the strategic-political front. The International Decade of Ocean Exploration is the culmination of an extraordinary outburst of cooperative international activity as oceanographers and ecologists have come to grips with the vital import of the oceans and what lies beneath them. This ambitious program, directed by UNESCO's Intergovernmental Oceanographic Commission, cuts across both national and disciplinary boundaries to knit together a coordinated attack on major problems of physical exploration, the development and conservation of resources, and determining the effects of how man exploits the seas. The ability of scientists from different countries to work and even live together, given tasks that they find demanding and challenging, has somewhat tempered the struggle for national advantage that has hamstrung creation of an adequate international regime.[11]

Of peculiar significance is the convincing demonstration by science that boundaries are an anachronism in the oceanic world. There is a geophysical and biological unity which defies efforts to carve jurisdictional lines between what is on the sea, in the sea, on the seabed or under it; equally nonsensical is cutting up laterally what belongs to a coastal state from what could be the "common heritage of mankind." What exists or happens in one sector intimately affects the others, whether in a sequence of nature or due to the intrusion of human engineering. The alarming discovery of recent scientific exploration is that men, working behind the shield of a political order which frustrates a community approach to the regulation of this activity in the oceans, can easily destroy the unity that maintains the balance of life. Pollution by oil, radioactivity or industrial waste, or the unrestrained scooping up of living resources whether from waters and bed considered territorial or open—these are obvious dangers calling for a global approach to human control which would match the integration inherent in the natural order of the seas.

---

[11] The experience and capacity of the Intergovernmental Oceanographic Commission is carefully appraised by Margaret Galey, *The Intergovernmental Oceanographic Commission* (Philadelphia: University of Pennsylvania, unpublished Ph.D. dissertation, 1970).

It is of some consolation that both experts and politicians are beginning to talk to this effect and even to pass relevant resolutions, within the United Nations and the appropriate specialized agencies. In 1968, the General Assembly established a permament Committee on the Peaceful Uses of the Sea-Bed and the Ocean Floor Beyond the Limits of National Jurisdiction. Carefully circumscribed though its assignment originally was, both in the area of concern (witness its title) and what it should do (mainly study), the committee moved vigorously to recommend action on pollution, conservation, exploration and indeed the whole question of setting up effective international machinery to deal with the exploitation of marine resources.

But technological, political and military events are moving so quickly that they may carry us beyond a point of no return, as the Commission to Study the Organization of Peace has warned in urging vigorous action "to avoid the evils of a new era of submarine imperialism and colonialism in the sea-bed beyond the limits of national jurisdiction and also to capitalize upon the great opportunities for international organization inherent in a regime for the sea-bed." [12] This point evidently struck home with the U.S. government, which became the first of the big oceanic powers to associate itself firmly with the proposal to have all coastal nations waive claims to the ocean floor beyond the continental shelf, and thereby preserve it as "the common heritage of mankind." President Nixon, in a comprehensive policy statement on May 23, 1970, called for an international regime, established by treaty, to authorize and regulate exploration and use of seabed resources beyond the continental shelf; and he went against the oil interests in specifying a definite and relatively restrained geophysical boundary separating shelf from the deep seabed—a depth of 660 feet (200 meters), whether or not a coastal state had the technical capacity to exploit beyond that depth. However, the "trustees" for the international community would be the coastal nations, rather than the UN, each receiving a share of the international revenues from the zone where it acted as trustee. This is thus a mixed regime, in which a few national governments are the operators, but subject to internationally agreed ground rules to insure the stake of others in the exploitation, including a part of any profit.

So, world community may be on the way, in one form or another, carried on the tip of the Glomar Challenger drill into the Sigsby Knolls 5,000 meters deep in the Gulf of Mexico, scrawled on a license by U.S. or similar international authority to tap some other ocean floor for a mineral deposit or a new oil dome, or in a set of marine laboratories

---

[12] 21st Report, *op. cit.*

studying the hazards of ecological changes precipitated by man's use and abuse of the seas.[13]

INSTITUTIONAL CAPACITY:
REGIONAL VS. GLOBAL POTENTIALS

Our prognosis is for a major swing toward multilateralism in the 1970's in all of the areas of international relations we have been discussing: harmonizing the actions of states, regulating interchange among them, managing resources for human development, and seeing to it that the conquest of new frontiers is turned to the benefit and not the destruction of all mankind. But there is a serious question of institutional capacity. Are international organizations, as presently structured and equipped, competent to handle these immense responsibilities?

INFIRMITIES OF GLOBALISM

Despite the note of optimism in some of the previous observations, we must admit that serious shortcomings have been revealed in the experiences of the UN "family" of global institutions. For one, they are paying the penalties of universalization. The policy of open-end membership, coupled with the epidemic proliferation of new states eager for visibility on the

---

[13] For further discussion of these issues, and the range of proposals under consideration for the regulation and development of the seas and seabed, see Edmund A. Gullion, editor, *Uses of the Seas: A Report to the American Assembly* (Englewood Cliffs, N.J.: Prentice-Hall, 1968). Note especially the chapters by Gullion, "New Horizons at Sea," and Henkin, "Changing Law for the Changing Seas." See also Louis Henkin, *Law for the Sea's Mineral Resources* (New York: Columbia University Institute for the Study of Science in Human Affairs, Monograph No. 1, 1968) and Lewis Alexander, editor, *Law of the Sea: Future of the Sea's Resources* (Kingston: University of Rhode Island, 1968).

U.S. policy was the object of a major study by the President's Commission on Marine Science, Engineering and Resources, the results of which were released in the Stratton Report, *Our Nation and the Sea* (Washington: GPO, 1969). The policy finally adopted follows closely recommendations of the American Assembly, especially the views of Professor Henkin, but seems to fall short of the full world regulatory authority envisaged by the Commission to Study the Organization of Peace, which would have the power to license, and probably to itself undertake considerable operational functions.

In process is a definitive study of the role of international organization in relation to the regulation and development of ocean resources by Professor Daniel Cheever, University of Pittsburgh. For a preliminary statement, see his article, "The Role of International Organization in Ocean Development," *International Organization*, Summer 1968.

For a systematic analysis of national positions on the major issues, as expressed in committee deliberations of the United Nations General Assembly, 1968–1969, see R. L. Friedheim and J. B. Kadane, "Quantitative Content Analysis of the United Nations Seabed Debate," *International Organization*, Summer 1970.

world stage, has flooded these agencies with bodies that occupy chairs, make speeches, clamor for appointments and cast votes. The principle of "sovereign equality" has so far defied attempts to introduce disciplined delegation of responsibilities to relieve the operational inefficiency that almost drags proceedings to a halt, even when issues are vital and urgent. (In fairness, one must not pin blame facilely on the smallness or newness of members for these troubles. Constructive leadership has come from tiny newcomers; big old-timers often cause the most serious obstruction.)

On the other hand, global agencies are not yet universal enough to function with full effectiveness. The isolation of Communist China severely limits their outreach. However difficult companionship with the Peking government might be, its continued ostracism contradicts the central reality of interdependence that underlies the whole rationale for global international organization. The problem is accentuated by exclusion of divided states, such as the two Koreas, the two Viet Nams and especially the two Germanys, from United Nations institutions. Another anachronism is the abstention of the Soviet bloc from the World Bank, the International Monetary Fund and the General Agreement on Tariffs and Trade, thus reducing these important organizations to subglobal status. This acknowledges the contemporary reality of two worlds rather than one in financial and trade relations, each part operating according to quite different principles. But the division appears increasingly artificial as economic relations become closer across the systemic divide. Technology presses constantly toward interchange, if not integration, especially among advanced industrial countries. Hence the need for fiscal and trading agencies of universal scope to negotiate and implement practicable arrangements for functional cooperation linking the differing systems and enabling them to do business with each other.

A third factor that obstructs the performance of global institutions is their fragmentation. Bloc politics impedes formation of a working consensus on critical issues, all the way from getting an item on the agenda to adopting a budget to pay for something to be done about it. Organizations are split not only along ideological lines, but by differences of wealth, region, color, religion, and pragmatic political ties. This encumbers the search for sound solutions to problems with extraneous considerations. Countries will oppose a proposal because it will benefit parties they do not like, or perhaps merely because another bloc is for it. An equally serious consequence is the division of appointments, from committee chairmen and rapporteurs to key jobs in the secretariats, according to "geographic" criteria (meaning, in fact, what bloc a man belongs to). Whether a person has the diplomatic, administrative and technical skills for the extraordinarily difficult tasks that face the organizations becomes secondary.

This is partly responsible for the weakness of leadership in the United

Nations and many of its affiliated agencies, weakness that afflicts both the international secretariats and national missions. Because political availability rather than statesmanship or craftsmanship in multilateralism is the primary qualification, governments have tended to put forward candidates who were dispensable, keeping top talent to staff their own cabinets and bureaucracies. Sometimes a UN assignment is a convenient honorific for a has-been, an also-ran or a financial angel in home politics. Caution amounting to timidity, concern for protocol that reaches the point of sycophantism, personal pride in office that overshadows disciplined commitment—these are earmarks of a sufficiently large number of those entrusted with major responsibilities in and for the UN family to induce institutional atrophy. In the secretariats, the problem is aggravated by tenure. The guarantee of job security was actually expected to stimulate independent, creative initiatives by protecting international civil servants against pressures to serve the interests of particular states. They could boldly put forward what they thought would advance the interest of the whole organization without laying their jobs on the line. Unfortunately, as observed by one who saw what went on from a position of major policy responsibility, "lifetime employment in an international bureaucracy produces the same Parkinsonian tendencies, and the same cautious time-serving, that are so evident in national career services."

The financial nightmare that has beset the United Nations, especially as an outgrowth of its peacekeeping activities, is a symptom, not so much of mutiny on the part of some members but of a profound misunderstanding by most members of the proper rules of behavior in international organizations. Neither those which refused to pay their "assessments" for activities they disapproved, nor those which voted the assessments and legitimized them by appeal to the International Court of Justice, really grasped the inescapably consensual basis of action through such an institution. If anything, the "mutineers" were closer to action consistent with the lessons Secretary-General Dag Hammarskjöld had derived from the peacekeeping experiences. *Consent at every point* was the condition of such operations—by the governments on whose territory the UN presence was established, by the countries contributing personnel, supplies and services, by the nations that agreed to stay out of the trouble zone, by the member-states which voted for the action by the authorizing organ, *and by the governments paying the money side of the bill.*

At several points in the confused and unpredictable unfolding of these totally unprecedented experiments in international conflict management, minorities and majorities in the UN forgot that they were not running a government. They went mandatory. A majority voted to do something and then sought to impose it on an unwilling minority, at least to the extent of paying a share. For its part, the minority, as well as declaring it would not be "taxed," tried in various other ways to frustrate the action approved by the majority. Even portions of the secretariat sometimes lapsed and became infatuated with the prospect of governing: witness Conor Cruise O'Brien leading the charge of "Blue Helmets" into Katanga (apparently without authorization from the Secretary-General or anybody else).

The point of all this is that global institutions suffer in performance and in reputation because the governments that control them persist in misusing them. It is not that they are weak because they are limited to consensual action. Consensual action is what they can and should be concerned with—*and nothing else.* Failure of member nations to understand this and act accordingly is the straitjacket that most constricts these agencies.

ILLUSIONS OF REGIONALISM

Regionalists urge that cutting back the membership spread of international institutions would bypass many of these problems. Smaller size would make them less cumbersome. Greater unity of purpose would forestall fragmentation. Catering more directly to some of the dominant national interests of members would enhance their prestige and attract higher-level leadership. At a certain point, the community of important interests might become so close that the members would readily let integration go the length of quasi-government, and adopt procedures which would enable the institution to act collectively for the participating nations. The European Economic Communities earn first prize in this, of course. NATO, the Warsaw Pact, COMECON, the Organization of American States, the Organization of African Unity have their advocates, varying in assurance from those who are convinced that these institutions have already amply proved their effectivenes and durability to those who cautiously see them as capable of limited but useful activities at the moment.

Frankly, this author holds a dim view of both past performance and potential future of most regional institutions in terms of the missions of multilateralism previously discussed.[14] Their segmental character tends

---

[14] These reservations are elaborated at some length with reference to both management of conflict and promotion of economic cooperation by various regional organizations in Philip E. Jacob and Alexine Atherton, *The Dynamics of International Organization* (Homewood, Ill.: Dorsey Press, 1965), especially Chapters 5, 6, 14 and 15.

A searching symposium has recently been published on *Regional Integration: Theory and Research,* edited by Leon Lindberg and Stuart A. Scheingold for *International Organization,* Autumn 1970. Some of the views expressed by contributors to this symposium appear to corroborate some of the basic conclusions on regionalism presented in this article.

to disqualify them from coping with interregional problems. The nature of regional perspectives, instead of facilitating the process of negotiation and consensus building across regions (as was anticipated in the United Nations Charter provisions for regional arrangements), has more often hardened irreconcilable positions. The firmer and more comprehensive their regional ties, the less likely are countries to be sensitive to interests of states outside the region. Experience has shown that a country will often yield to pressures from its regional partners, even when its own interest on a particular issue might be better served by agreeing to action more universally acceptable. The monolithic rigidity of the Soviet bloc is a case in point. Whether within the UN, or operating directly through the mechanisms of the Warsaw Pact and COMECON, these countries must toe the line of the "socialist commonwealth." Regionalism, at least in this form, has only served to obstruct the search for action that would be generally beneficial, for "mutuality" is conceived in exclusive rather than inclusive terms.

The result is similar even when the regional group is not united by ideological doctrine and so strictly disciplined by a dominant power. NATO, OECD and the European Communities all look inward rather than outward in devising their approaches to international problems. Hence they appear as competitors to other nations and generate hostility and resistance even if they genuinely believe they are only acting "defensively." NATO cannot avoid provoking counter-"deterrence" in its rivalry with the Warsaw Pact; OECD is inescapably tagged as the caucus of the wealthy when it consolidates common policies toward the have-nots among the capital surplus countries; EEC is envied and feared as the self-serving protectionist club it is.[15] Only the Commonwealth of

---

[15] For a strong indictment of EEC's exclusivist policies, charging that they tend to heighten tensions in Europe and elsewhere and foster a brand of regional patriotism, see David Mitrany, "The Prospect of Integration: Federal or Functional?," in Joseph S. Nye, Jr., editor, *International Regionalism* (Boston: Little, Brown, 1968). This view is largely substantiated by the study of Leon N. Lindberg and Stuart A. Scheingold, *Europe's Would-Be Polity: Patterns of Change in the European Community* (Englewood Cliffs, N.J.: Prentice-Hall, 1970). See also Scheingold's concluding article, "Domestic and International Consequences of Regional Integration," *International Organization*, Autumn 1970, especially pp. 987–998, in which he is particularly skeptical of the effects of the EEC on the progress of the less developed countries.

The Organization of American States seems to be moving toward expressing distinctive Latin Americanism, after a period when it served as a major instrument to devise and implement policies of mutual cooperation between the United States and the Latin republics. Indications are that this subregionalization of OAS is associated with a revival of the traditional antagonism of Latinos for the Yankee. But it is also symptomatic of the generally divisive influence of regionalism that the Latin American states are adopting much more inflexible stands on issues involving non-

Nations has been able to maintain fairly congenial cross-regional relations, largely as a result of the cross-ties of most of its members with
other regional groupings.

Other limitations impair the capacity of regional institutions to provide
adequate solutions for major problems of interdependence, unless their
efforts are closely coordinated with those of other countries through some
more universal facilities. Conditions of effective action vary from area
to area. For instance, the pattern of economic integration that grew up
in Western Europe may be region-specific, nontransferable to other parts
of the world. To assume that the success of the European Economic Communities proves the general utility of their institutional format may be
a ghastly mistake, as South and Central America and some of the African
states are apparently finding out in their experimentation with "Common
Markets." [16]

Regional organizations are also turning out to be function-specific,
contrary to early expectations that there would be a "spill-over effect." [17]
Even the European Six have not yet been able to match their degree of
economic integration with a parallel regionalization of defense systems
and political processes. The North Atlantic Treaty Organization is probably the stronger for having specialized in the military sphere; efforts to
broaden its functional base have been singularly unsuccessful. Multiple
functions within a regional framework seem to disperse rather than reinforce energies.

The Achilles heel of regional institutions is the very same commitment
of member-states to having final, independent say over their actions that
global agencies have encountered. They have to confront the same reality
of pluralism in international relations, even within the narrower confines
of a region. Few governments have gone on record as ready to merge their
sovereignty in a regional "community." Consensual cooperation instead
of centralized decision-making is just as much the practice in regional
organizations as in the United Nations, except possibly for the EEC.[18]

American states as well (laws of the sea and control of the seabed, for instance).
As they tie themselves closer together regionally, and the cross-regional associations
weaken, they become more ornery in their relations with the rest of the world.

[16] See Joseph S. Nye, Jr., "Comparing Common Markets: A Revised Neo-Func-
tionalist Model," *International Organization*, Autumn 1970; also, Ernst B. Haas, "The
Uniting of Europe and the Uniting of Latin America," *Journal of Common Market
Studies*, June 1967.

[17] The experience of the European Coal and Steel Community that fostered this
expectation was the subject of Ernst Haas' seminal work, *The Uniting of Europe*
(Stanford: Stanford University Press, 1958).

[18] Penetrating studies of the practice of the European Economic Communities indicate that there, also, consensual processes are the foundation of effective action,
even when the final format of the action appears authoritative. See Leon N. Lind-

Significantly, when such organizations have yielded to the temptation to "strengthen" themselves by moving even a little toward a hierarchical structure of control, they have provoked dissension that undermined their internal cohesion, leading sometimes to outright rejection of decisions reached and boycott of the decisional processes.

In short, regionalism has not replaced nationalism as the dominant force in the political organization of the world. The nation-state, not the region, remains the pivot of action. Meanwhile regionalism has done nothing to change the essentially global dimension of most of the problems that have to be solved. Interdependence operates within regions, to be sure; but it is just as powerful a reality across regions.

POWER BY CONSENT

This turns us back to the "globals" as the center of gravity for the organization of multilateral action to grapple with transnational problems. The immediate task is to find a strategy that will improve their capacity. Our contention is that this must rest on consent, and need involve little structural tampering.

Many current proposals for structural reform aim to streamline procedures of decision-making and gear them to power and other considerations in a way that would further "governmentalize" the operation of international organizations. This would only confuse the essentially consensual nature and tasks of these institutions. To the extent that such proposals require constitutional changes, they also run afoul of the difficult amending provisions of most international charters. Amendments to *reduce* the powers of individual states (even in the form of delegating partial responsibility) find few sponsors. The same is true of changes designed to formally increase the overall powers of the "Organization" or of its secretariat. What sometimes do get through are arrangements to give limelight to more states in the name of democratizing the institutions (for instance, increasing the size of the Security Council and the Economic and Social Council, and mandating a rigid formula for regionalizing the seats). Such an outcome runs directly counter to the desires of those advocating strength through streamlining.

---

berg, *The Political Dynamics of European Economic Integration* (Stanford: Stanford University Press, 1963); Lindberg's "Decision-Making and Integration in the European Community," in *International Political Communities: An Anthology* (Garden City, N.Y.: Doubleday Anchor, 1966); and Lindberg and Scheingold, *Europe's Would-Be Polity, op. cit.*, Chapters 1 and 2.

For a comprehensive evaluation of decision-making processes in regional organizations, see Joseph S. Nye, Jr., "Comparative Regional Integration: Concept and Measurement," *International Organization*, Autumn 1968; and his *International Regional Organizations* (Boston: Little, Brown, 1971).

But steps that will substantially improve the functioning of global institutions can be taken without jangling the nerves of national pride.[19] The World Bank and its affiliates have already vastly increased their funding of development efforts and overhauled their policies and administration under the leadership of Robert S. McNamara, following the bold lines laid out by the Commission on International Development headed by Lester Pearson.[20] Agencies associated in the United Nations Development Program are in process of implementing some of the far-reaching recommendations of Commander Jackson's *Study of the Capacity of the United Nations Development System.*[21]

No breakthrough of comparable proportions yet seems in sight to revivify the UN's unique peacekeeping potential and give new impetus to its mission of securing peaceful settlement of major international conflicts. However, the United Nations remains the principal vehicle of collective action by big states and small to tamp down the Arab-Israeli conflagration and find some basis of live-and-let-live in that hotbed of violence. Egypt at least has had second thoughts since 1967 about the utility of a UN peacekeeping force, as evidenced by President Sadat's call for its return (no doubt with Soviet concurrence).

On the score of universalization, it seems likely that within the year the General Assembly will move to find some formula for representation of the Chinese People's Republic.

With respect to leadership, much hinges on the quality of the new UN Secretary-General to be appointed this year, and of a whole series of replacements for the aging directorate of the Secretariat. This is an opportunity for strengthening that depends almost entirely on the priority given the tasks of the United Nations by its member governments. There are no structural hurdles to prevent their agreement on men and women of outstanding competence, vision and commitment to serve the international community in the decade ahead.

What is most needed is an approach to the use of the United Nations that will allow members to act when they share a common concern, even if they cannot persuade the entire organization to go along. Too often, action through the UN has been blocked by states simply because they saw no payoff in it for themselves, and objected to any undertaking carry-

---

[19] Richard N. Gardner, in "Can the United Nations be Revived?," *Foreign Affairs,* July 1970, proposes action in ten areas to make the UN more effective. Most of the steps could be undertaken within the present structure of the organization but would admittedly "require almost every member to modify one or more of its present positions."

[20] Commission on International Development, *Partners in Development* (New York: Praeger, 1969).

[21] UN Doc. DP/5 (Geneva: United Nations, 1969).

ing an implication that they would be held partly responsible. If it were clearly understood that a *"consortium of the concerned"* would voluntarily assume the full burden of a program, including its financing, while working through the United Nations and reporting to it, a great expansion of significant cooperative action could occur.

There are some precedents for such an approach: the voluntary funding of UNICEF, the Special Fund and now the UN Development Program; participation in the activities of the Geophysical Year and now the International Decade of Ocean Exploration; and to an extent the contributions of states that agreed to furnish contingents to UN peacekeeping forces (though regrettably their voluntary participation as concerned states got entangled with the attempt to treat these operations as obligations of the whole organization).

The genius of this strategy is that it is completely consensual, dedicated to multilateralism, functionally flexible, and, of vital importance, openended. Any government can opt into any "consortium," whenever and wherever it decides that the kind of cooperative action being undertaken is to its benefit. This would soften bloc lines, for it would encourage coalitions to form around many different interests, each state joining those promising it a useful payoff. A state might play an active role in one peacekeeping consortium and not another, take a hand in one kind of development program, but forgo other efforts.

One basic condition for successful evolution of the consortium strategy is that members agree to the coexistence of multiple consortia. In return for permission for one group to use the international organization's machinery to promote its particular concern, it must let others form consortia to forward their interests and have comparable access to the organization's facilities. Permissiveness is the watchword: I won't block you, if you don't try to harness me into something I don't want to do; I won't challenge the legitimacy of your proposal, if you're willing to pay for it, and will let me do my thing too. Vetoes are abandoned, unless some consortium forgets the rules and tries to make its program mandatory when others find it unacceptable.[22]

---

[22] The idea of developing a "consortium of the concerned" is forcefully urged by Harlan Cleveland, President of the University of Hawaii and formerly Assistant Secretary of State for International Organization Affairs, as a means of building up an international executive to keep the peace and mediate disputes of less than global magnitude. He envisages such a consortium working *outside* the established machinery of the UN, however, with its own arrangements for fact-finding, mediation, and quick mobilization of peacekeeping forces. See "Can We Revive the U.N.?," paper prepared for the Hoover Institution United Nations Conference, Stanford, California, January 12, 1971.

There might be a danger that such a consortium would be misinterpreted as a

There is an immense unexplored potential in multilateral cooperation. It remains unrealized in part because nations have deep and bitter conflicts and are in no mood to cooperate, even if rational consideration dictates that they should, in their basic long-term interests. Part of the problem, however, is the persistent "governing complex" that has misguided the development and use of international organizations. Government in the 1970's will surely be kept the prerogative of national governments. International organizations must be directed to the vital function of promoting *inter*government, that is, the process of enabling states to work together in pursuit of common interests—their interests in surviving in a world where they simply cannot live by themselves and by their own devices.

42.   APPRAISAL OF THE CASE FOR WORLD GOVERNMENT

Inis L. Claude, Jr.

M UCH OF THE LITERATURE pertaining to world government exhibits the qualities usually associated with impassioned advocacy. Typically, the major themes are as follows: The world is in a state of anarchy, which makes war inescapable; the elimination of war has become a dire necessity; this goal cannot be reliably achieved by any means other than world government; the establishment of this fundamentally new system is the necessary and probably sufficient means to world order. If the

From *Power and International Relations* by Inis L. Claude, Jr. (New York: Random House, 1962), pp. 210–223; 267–269; 271. © Copyright 1962 by Random House, Inc. Reprinted by permission. Footnotes have been renumbered to appear in consecutive order.

INIS L. CLAUDE, JR. (1922–   ) Edward R. Stettinius Professor of Government and Member, Center for Advanced Studies, University of Virginia. Author of *The Changing United Nations* (New York: Random House, 1967); *Swords into Plowshares: The Problems and Progress of International Organization* (New York: Random House, 1956); *National Minorities: An International Problem* (Cambridge: Harvard University Press, 1955).

form of alliance bypassing the U.N. Keeping the consortium *within* the UN framework would guard against its being so construed but might hamstring its freedom of action.

assurance of a peaceful order *with* world government is less than total, the hope for such an order *without* world government is virtually nil. Thus, world government is presented as a system—the uniquely promising system—for the management of power in international relations.

The theme of anarchy was flatly stated by Albert Einstein: "In relations among nations complete anarchy still prevails. I do not believe that we have made any real progress in this area during the last few thousand years." [1] The characterization of the present-day world as a congeries of fully sovereign states existing in wholly anarchical relationship with each other might be regarded as the product of minds that have not been exercised in any serious way in the study of international relations. In some instances, this is doubtless true. Einstein, for instance, was clearly operating outside his professional sphere when he commented on international relations, and it may well be that he was innocent of any familiarity with the history of international law and organization, or with the imperfect regulatory devices which figure in international politics, or with any of the other factors which would make a prudent scholar hesitant to proclaim that unmitigated anarchy prevails in the twentieth-century world. Only an uninformed man could take it to be a fact that states now claim, or are acknowledged to have, a theoretically complete sovereign right to behave as they please; only an unrealistic observer could take it to be true that any state—much less, every state—possesses sovereignty in the sense that it can determine its own course, unaffected by pressures and inhibitions, necessities and influences, deriving from the international environment. Although Einstein purported to regard anarchy as the cause of the world's precarious situation, it seems likely that he inferred anarchy from his awareness of that situation. He did not establish the fact of anarchy and demonstrate the derivation of the world's troubles from that fact, but he noted the troubles and assumed that their existence indicated a state of anarchy. There is a troublesome circularity in the process of arguing that anarchy causes a global mess while treating the fact of a global mess as the basis for the assertion that anarchy prevails, but it is a process which eliminates the burdensome necessity of examining the aspects of the international system which might be relevant to the question of whether it should be described as anarchic.

In general, however, the assertion that the present condition is one of world anarchy is not to be regarded as the reflection of basic unfamiliarity with the field of international relations. It is typically the product not

---

[1] Otto Nathan, and Heinz Norden, eds., *Einstein on Peace* (New York: Simon and Schuster, 1960), p. 494. Cf. Norman Cousins, *In Place of Folly* (New York: Harper and Brothers, 1961, pp. 56–57, 111.

of ignorance, but of strong conviction. Anarchy is a symbol of peril—the peril of uncontrollable disorder; the claim that the world is anarchic is a way of saying that the world situation is intolerably dangerous. Emphasis upon the theme of anarchy expresses the belief that all the devices which have been introduced into international relations for the purpose of the management of power are fundamentally inadequate to the task; they are mere palliatives, incapable of contributing meaningfully to the ordering of international relations. Thus, champions of world government who cry anarchy frequently do so not in ignorance of existing regulatory factors but in the conviction that those factors are, and are doomed to remain, inconsequential. Anarchy is also the symbol of an insistent denial of the relativity of order in international relations; the either-or proposition, anarchy or world government, is designed to convey a sense of the urgent necessity for discarding reliance on anything short of world government and accepting the prescription for drastic transformation of the international system. The conceptual opposition between anarchy and government suggests the distinctiveness of the world government solution and the exclusiveness of its claim to efficacy. As Einstein put it, "The only real step toward world government is world government itself"; [2] short of world government, one finds only varying forms of anarchy.

As we have noted, a major theme in the literature of advocacy is the proposition that no solution other than the establishment of world government can prevent war. Gilbert McAllister asserts that "War has never been banished from any part of the world except when warring nations have joined together under a common parliament and a common government," and quotes Prime Minister Nehru of India to the effect that "world government must and will come, for there is no other remedy for the world's sickness." [3] This conclusion may be reached by the process of reasoning that in the absence of government we have anarchy, and that anarchy, by definition, implies disorder—persistently in potentiality and recurrently in fact. Alternatively, it may be reached by taking a sweeping glance at history and observing that multistate systems, of either the modern or earlier varieties, have never been free from war and danger of war.

However reached, the conclusion that peace is impossible without world government is a generalization that is not wholly warranted by the available evidence. The international picture is not in fact marked by such a constant and universal "war of every state against every other state" as one might be led to expect by the colorful and extravagantly Hobbesian language employed by some commentators on world politics. The record

---

[2] Nathan and Norden, *Einstein on Peace*, p. 443.

[3] Gilbert McAllister, ed., *World Government: The Report of the First London Parliamentary Conference, Sept. 24–29, 1951* (London: The Parliamentary Group for World Government, 1952), pp. 7, 8.

of international relations is sorry enough, and the present situation dangerous enough, without the unrealistic embroidery of "realistic" analysis which take the image of an international "jungle" too literally. In sober fact, most states coexist in reasonable harmony with most other states, most of the time; the exceptions to this passable state of affairs are vitally important, but they are exceptions nonetheless. Most obviously, states which are widely separated, not involved in intimate interrelationships and not engaged competitively in the pursuit of interests far beyond their own territories, are unlikely to find themselves in strenuous conflict with each other in a world without government. The history of relations between Peru and Belgium, or Cuba and New Zealand, would presumably make rather dull reading; within such combinations as these, the incidence of war, not the maintenance of peace, would require special explanation. In such cases, it is not to be assumed that hostilities will occur unless prevented by the subjection of the states to a common government, but that peace will prevail in the absence of exceptional disruptive factors. More importantly, one should note that settled and highly reliable relationships of a peaceful nature exist in many instances between states that are not significantly isolated from each other. One might consider the relationships between Canada and the United States, or the United States and Britain, or Britain and Belgium. Within these pairs, we find situations of "peace without government," relationships marked by expectations of non-violence substantially higher than might be found within many national states.

As a British statesman described Anglo-American relations in 1935:

> War between us is, we hope, unthinkable. . . . I can say with confidence, after a Cabinet experience of more than a quarter of a century, that such a possibility has never entered into Great Britain's consideration of her requirements for defense and has never influenced the strength of the forces maintained by her, whether on land or sea.[4]

In the case of Norway and Sweden, Karl W. Deutsch has observed that peaceful relations between them have been more stable during the recent era of their sovereign separateness than in the earlier period of their linkage under a common government.[5] Moreover, Deutsch and his collaborators in an analysis of a number of historical *security-communities* —groupings within which dependable expectations of non-violence are to be found—concluded that the record of those characterized by the retention of political pluralism was generally more favorable than that of

---

[4] Sir Austen Chamberlain, "Great Britain," in *The Foreign Policy of the Powers*, p. 76.

[5] "Problems and Prospects of Federation," Publications in the Humanities, No. 26 (Cambridge: Massachusetts Institute of Technology, 1958), p. 242.

those which achieved amalgamation; in short, peace without government tended to be more secure in these cases than peace with government.[6]

These observations are not intended to suggest the general conclusion that anarchy is more productive of peace and order than is government. The fact that happy relationships sometimes develop between independent states does not overshadow the facts that the expectation of war somewhere within the system is endemic in the multistate pattern, that all members of the system are presently endangered by the possibilities of disorder inherent in the international situation, and that no reliable means of controlling or eliminating those possibilities has yet been devised. Proponents of the "no peace without government" line will properly point out that the instances of the formation of pluralistic security-communities are regrettably exceptional, and that we have no evidence that the process by which, say, Anglo-American relationships became dependably peaceful can be put into operation on a universal scale—or even on a Soviet-American scale. Quite so; but it might be retorted that the evidence for the peace-keeping efficacy of government is similarly limited. The point is simply that peace without government is a phenomenon which occurs with sufficient frequency to destroy the basis for the dogmatic assertion that human relationships cannot conceivably be ordered except by government. "Never" does not have to be invalidated by "Always"; "Sometimes" will suffice.

The assertion that peace cannot be maintained without world government is but an introduction to the theme that the latter can do the job. World government is necessary because all alternative schemes for producing order are inadequate; it is proper because it represents an adequate approach to the task. Jorge Castaneda puts the case for world government in these terms:

> Who could doubt the perfection of this ideal? History shows that when social units are broadened in order to include formerly uncontrolled and autonomous powers, and authority is centralized—as happened when the modern national state took shape, breaking with the feudal pattern—social relations are stabilized and finally order and domestic peace are achieved within the new social unit.[7]

The certainty that world government could transform chaos into order has never been more confidently expressed than in this passage from Emery Reves:

---

[6] Karl W. Deutsch *et al.*, *Political Community and the North Atlantic Area* (Princeton: Princeton University Press, 1957), pp. 29–31, 65–69, 163.

[7] *Mexico and the United Nations* (New York: Manhattan, for El Colegio de Mexico and the Carnegie Endowment for International Peace, 1958), p. 14.

We . . . know that, irrespective of the immediate and apparent causes of conflict among warring groups, these causes ceased producing wars and violent conflicts only through the establishment of a legal order, only when the social groups in conflict were subjected to a superior system of law, and that, *in all cases and at all times*, the effect of such a superior system of law has been the cessation of the use of violence among the previously warring groups.[8]

Many advocates of world government argue the case for its efficacy in less absolute, or at any rate more ambiguous, terms. Cousins, for instance, concedes that a world government could not guarantee peace, and describes world law as "not a hope but the *only* hope, the only chance" for the avoidance of war.[9] Einstein made occasional verbal concessions to the possibility of imperfection; at one point, he noted the risk of civil war within a unified global system, and he sometimes confined himself to the assertion that war would be *virtually* impossible.[10] More typically, however, he suggested that "the various parts of the federation could not make war on each other," and spoke of "a supranational solution which would make national preparations for war not only unnecessary but impossible." [11] Clearly, Einstein was not plagued by any substantial doubts; with reference to the question of the avoidability of war, he wrote confidently that "There is a very simple answer. If we ourselves have the courage to decide in favor of peace, we will *have* peace." [12]

Einstein's lack of serious concern for the possibility of the failure or inadequacy of world government is fairly typical of the champions of that system. Whether because of honest conviction or the dictates of good salesmanship, they tend to dismiss this possibility as inconsequential, and to concentrate on the positive assertion that world government is the obvious solution to the problem of international disorder. When a writer asserts that "the possibility of major destructive wars cannot be ruled out until the system of sovereign self-determining states has been replaced by some form of world government," [13] he obviously means to be understood as suggesting that this possibility *can* be ruled out when the system has been thus transformed, unless he qualifies his position with a cautious "and perhaps not even then." This brand of caution is seldom a prominent feature of world government thought.

Those who enjoy the blessed assurance that the establishment of a

---

[8] *The Anatomy of Peace* (New York: Harper, 1945), p. 254. Italics mine.

[9] *In Place of Folly*, pp. 90, 118. Italics in original.

[10] Nathan and Norden, *Einstein on Peace,* pp. 439, 487, 617.

[11] *Ibid.,* pp. 418, 487.

[12] *Ibid.,* p. 528. Italics in original.

[13] Geoffrey Sawer in Victor H. Wallace, ed., *Paths to Peace* (Melbourne, Australia: Melbourne University Press, 1959), p. 385.

world government would guarantee the elimination of war, or who estimate the possibility of failure as so negligible that prudent men can afford to disregard it, frequently appear to rely upon the dubious logic of a self-fulfilling definition. Government is defined as an institutional scheme characterized by authority to make rules prohibiting disorderly conduct and coercive competence to require conformity to those rules; if such a scheme were put into effect, it would, by definition, be able to prevent disorder. It is small wonder that Einstein could assert that "real security in the world can only come through the creation of a supranational body, a government of the world with powers adequate to preserve the peace." [14] Who can doubt that an institution capable of keeping the peace could keep the peace? In the same vein, a leader of the United World Federalists asserted in 1948 that "There can be no peace within or between nations unless there are both established laws, and the certain knowledge that these laws can be promptly and decisively enforced." [15] Reves declares that "Peace is law. It is order. It is government." [16] If government is defined as "that which produces peace," the creation of a world government is unchallengeably a promising method of preventing war.

Much contemporary thought on the problem of preventing war is characterized by this tendency to develop solutions-by-definition. If balance of power is defined as a system which produces equilibrium, and equilibrium is defined as a power configuration which effectively inhibits aggression, the problem seems to have been solved. If collective security is defined as a system which guarantees that a preponderance of power will confront any aggressor, and it is assumed that no state can prevail against such a massing of power, the effectiveness of the system can be regarded as self-evident. The world government school of thought tends to focus on disarmament, law, and enforcement of law, which can be taken to mean that states are rendered incapable of fighting, are forbidden to fight, and are compelled not to fight; if these things are effectively accomplished, there would seem to be little room for doubt that states will not fight.

Government, of course, is not a mere abstract concept, a hypothetical system the merits of which are to be determined by logical derivation from its definition. It is a social institution with which mankind has had considerable experience; it has a long and extensive record of performance, available for examination and evaluation. Advocates of world

---

[14] Nathan and Norden, *op. cit.*, p. 459.

[15] Cord Meyer, Jr., statement reproduced in Johnsen, *Federal World Government*, p. 91.

[16] *The Anatomy of Peace*, p. 150.

governments are, naturally, aware of this fact, and they do not by any means base their case entirely upon the demonstration that an institution which is by definition capable of keeping order must be judged suitable for that task. In many instances, the argument is explicitly grounded upon a favorable appraisal of the record of government as an order-keeping institution within national societies, followed by the assumption or reasoned contention that government would—or, more modestly, might —function equally well within a globally organized society. In some cases, reference is made to the record of government in general; thus, "An area of government is an area of peace. You are familiar with the keeping of peace in the areas of your city, your state and your nation. A world government is obviously the path to world peace—if government is somehow possible over so great an area." [17] Perhaps more frequently, attention is concentrated upon the federal type of governmental system, with the suggestion that the successes of small-scale federalism could be duplicated if it were applied on a larger scale: "The task of our genera-tion is to extend to a larger area the basic federal union principles that have already stood the test of time." [18] Not surprisingly, tributes to the efficacy of federalism are usually inspired by a favorable appraisal of the American experience. Everett Lee Millard, for instance, is explicit on this point:

> The formation of a federal union among the American colonies led to their subsequent freedom, peace and prosperity. Therefore, we may reason, a federal union among the world's nations, if it can be made possible, will permit all humanity to thrive in liberty and peace.[19]

Citation of the record of government within national societies as the basis for assurance that a world government could be relied upon to maintain global peace and order is a very dangerous expedient. Aside from the obvious point that macro-government would not necessarily function as effectively as micro-government, the hard fact is that the record does not support the generalization that the establishment of government, within a social unit of whatever dimensions, infallibly brings about a highly dependable state of peace and order.

The ominous phrase *civil war* serves as only the most dramatic symbol of the fallibility of government as an instrument of social order. The

---

[17] Stewart Boal, in the Preface to Everett Lee Millard, *Freedom in a Federal World*, 2nd ed. (New York: Oceana, 1961), p. 9. See also the quotations from Casta-neda and Reves, p. 216, above.

[18] "Publius II" (Owen J. Roberts, John F. Schmidt, and Clarence K. Streit), *The New Federalist* (New York: Harper, 1950), p. 3. This volume looks toward the crea-tion of an Atlantic Union, not a world federation.

[19] *Freedom in a Federal World*, p. 43.

student of history and contemporary world politics will discover numerous manifestations of the incapacity of government to guarantee peace; outcroppings of uncontrolled violence are a familiar phenomenon in human societies equipped with governmental mechanisms. Government, indeed, has a very mixed and spotty record in this respect. The glorification of government as a near-panacea for the ill of social disorder may come easily to Americans, whose civil war has faded into romantic historical memory and who are citizens of one of that small band of happy countries in which domestic order has become a normal and highly dependable expectation. It is likely to seem much less plausible to the unfortunately numerous "peoples whose country is the frequent scene of revolution and domestic violence or suffers the cruel terrors of tyranny; to them 'civil society,' or 'order under government,' if it is experienced at all, possesses most of the objectionable features we attribute to international anarchy." [20] The Latin American region is a notable example of an area in which government has worked badly as an orderkeeping institution: "In many Latin-American countries military rebellion is a recognized mode of carrying on political conflict." [21] In Bolivia, for instance, it has been estimated that 178 "revolutions or violent, illegal changes of regime" occurred between 1825 and 1952. [22]

Given the elementary facts about the record of government, historical and contemporary, it becomes impossible to conceive how Emery Reves could assert that the establishment of "a superior system of law" has produced, "in all cases and at all times," the elimination of the use of violence among previously discordant groups. [23] It becomes difficult, moreover, to understand the general tendency of champions of world government to minimize the significance of the civil war problem even when they concede its existence.

Henry Usborne states that, in principle, "War is eliminated by merging several states into one." He admits the possibility of civil war, but contends that "this does not affect the argument. Civil war is not inherent in the state; but war is inherent in interstate relations if those relations are based on national sovereignty." [24] Another commentator states the con-

---

[20] Arnold Wolfers and Lawrence W. Martin, eds., *The Anglo-American Tradition in Foreign Affairs* (New Haven: Yale University Press, 1956), Introduction, pp. xv-xvi.

[21] Raymond W. Mack and Richard C. Snyder, "The Analysis of Social Conflict—Toward an Overview and Synthesis," *Journal of Conflict Resolution*, June 1957, Vol. 1, p. 226.

[22] *The New York Times* editorial, Oct. 2, 1958.

[23] Cited above, fn. 8.

[24] "World Federal Government as a Means of Maintaining Peace," in Wallace, *Paths to Peace*, pp. 359, 360.

clusion that "only world government can prevent war in the future. Even this will not exclude the possibility of serious civil war, but civil wars are less probable than international wars." [25]

It must be retorted that while civil war is not inherent in an abstract definition of the governed state, or in an idealized image of the state, it is clearly inherent in the actual operating experience of real states. The historical slate cannot be wiped clear of civil wars by the simple device of asserting that, according to one's definition of the state, they should not have occurred. The judgment that civil wars are relatively improbable is subject to serious challenge. As Philip C. Jessup has observed, "Civil war, revolution, mob violence are more frequent manifestations of man's unruly and still savage will than are wars between states." [26] Moreover, such civil wars as those which have occurred in Spain and China certainly deserve a place in any list of the most significant events in world affairs of the last generation.

At the present time, the list of states that an informed student could describe as virtually immune from the threat of large-scale domestic violence is certainly shorter than the list of those in which such disorder must be ranked as an easily conceivable or highly probable occurrence. Moreover, a world government might have a relatively high susceptibility to organized revolt, since it would encompass previously independent states that would undoubtedly retain a considerable capacity to function as bases and organizing centers for dissident movements.[27]

This analysis should not be taken as inviting the conclusion that government is a device of negligible importance in the human quest for social order. Clearly, this is not the case. But, equally, the tactic of creating a government is not tantamount to the waving of a magic wand which dispels the problem of disorderliness. Peace without government is, despite dogmatic denials, sometimes possible; war with government is, despite doctrinaire assurances, always possible. Wars sometimes occur in the absence of government, in the exercise of the freedom from higher social discipline which prevails in that situation. Wars also occur in the presence of government, in protest against and defiance of the central control which is attempted.[28] In short, the concept of world government

---

[25] Excerpt from Harold C. Urey, in Julia E. Johnsen, *Federal World Government* (New York: Wilson, 1948), p. 96.

[26] *A Modern Law of Nations* (New York: Macmillan, 1950), p. 189. Cf. Hans J. Morgenthau, *Scientific Man vs. Power Politics* (Chicago: University of Chicago Press, 1946), p. 49.

[27] See Vernon Van Dyke, *International Politics* (New York: Appleton-Century-Crofts, 1957), p. 421.

[28] See the excerpt from I. Beverly Lake, in Johnsen, *Federal World Government*, p. 217.

deserves not to be seized upon as the one and only solution, the obviously effective solution, to the problem of the management of power in international relations, but to be treated as a theoretical approach promising enough to warrant careful consideration.

.   .   .

One of the lessons of governmental experience is that coercion can seldom be usefully invoked against significant collectivities which exhibit a determination to defend their interests, as they conceive them, against the public authority. The order-keeping function of government is not fulfilled by the winning of a civil war, but by its prevention. If groups cannot be coerced without the disruption of the order which government exists to maintain, it does not follow that the alternative tactic of coercing individuals should be adopted. What follows is rather that the difficult task of ordering group relationships by political means should be attempted.

Clearly, governments are not always able to carry out this task; the incidence of civil wars and analogous disorders testifies to this fact. The establishment of government does not automatically create a social situation in which group conflicts are subject to political accommodation, nor does it necessarily carry with it the development of the institutions and techniques best suited to the exploitation of such adjustment potential as the society may exhibit. But if government does not make order through political adjustment easy or certain, neither does it provide a substitute. Governments maintain social order by presiding over a successful political process, or not at all.

To some degree, this general conception of the operation of government may seem inapplicable to modern totalitarian governments. It is true that totalitarian regimes undertake to atomize their societies, breaking down the collectivities which are deemed likely to challenge the monolithic quality of the state, and to fasten a tyranny of coercion upon their peoples. In some instances, they have succeeded to a degree which is appalling to men who value human freedom, but the evidence suggests that they have never wholly succeeded in this infamous enterprise. Moreover, such regimes are not wholly reliant upon this technique; some trace of political methods of managing social forces always remains in their operations. In any case, advocates of world government are not motivated by the hope of reproducing the totalitarian pattern on a global scale. It would indeed be ironical if men passionately devoted to the rule of law should define their ideal pattern of order-keeping as one which is realized only, or best, in totalitarian systems. The sort of national government which champions of world government propose to emulate is best exemplified by liberal regimes which depend primarily upon processes of political adjustment for maintaining social order.

I would conclude that theorists of world government are not mistaken in their insistence that one should look to domestic governmental experience for clues as to the most promising means for achieving world order, but that they tend to misread the lessons of that experience. In some instances, they treat the domestic problem of crime prevention as comparable to the international problem of war, and draw from national experience the conclusion that the central function of a world government would be to maintain order by enforcing legal restrictions upon individual behavior. In other instances, they note the domestic problem of coping with dissident groups, acknowledge its compatibility to the problem of dealing with aggressive states, and suggest that the governmental pattern requires that a central authority be equipped with adequate military force to coerce any possible rebellion within the larger society.

In contrast, I would argue that the prevention of civil war is the function of national government most relevant to the problem of ordering international relations, that governments cannot and do not perform this function by relying primarily upon either police action against individuals or military action against significant segments of their societies, and that governments succeed in this vitally important task only when they are able to operate an effective system of political accommodation.

.   .   .

In the final analysis, it appears that the theory of world government does not *answer* the question of how the world can be saved from catastrophic international conflict. Rather, it helps us to *restate* the question: How can the world achieve the degree of assurance that inter-group conflicts will be resolved or contained by political rather than violent means that has been achieved in the most effectively governed states? This is a valuable and provocative restatement of the question—but it ought not to be mistaken for a definitive answer.

Index of Names

Index of Subjects